Three Complete Books

NORMAN VINCENT PEALE

Three Complete Books

NORMAN VINCENT PEALE

THE POWER OF POSITIVE THINKING

THE POSITIVE PRINCIPLE TODAY

ENTHUSIASM MAKES THE DIFFERENCE

WINGS BOOKS
New York

This edition contains the complete and unabridged texts of the original editions.
They have been completely reset for this volume.
This omnibus was originally published in separate volumes under the titles:

The Power of Positive Thinking, copyright © 1952 by Prentice-Hall, Inc.
The Positive Principle Today, copyright © 1976 by Dr. Norman Vincent Peale
Enthusiasm Makes the Difference, copyright © 1967 by Dr. Norman Vincent Peale

This 1994 edition is published by Wings Books, an imprint of Random House Value Publishing, a division of Random House, Inc., New York, by arrangement with Simon & Schuster, Inc.

Random House
New York • Toronto • London • Sydney • Auckland
www.randomhouse.com

Printed and bound in the United States of America

Library of Congress Cataloging-in-Publication Data
Peale, Norman Vincent, 1898–1993
[Selections. 1992]
Three complete books/Norman Vincent Peale.
p. cm.
First work originally published: Englewood, N.J.: Prentice-Hall, 1952.
2nd work originally published: Englewood, N.J.: Prentice-Hall, c1976.
3rd work originally published: Englewood, N.J.: Prentice-Hall, 1967.
Contents: The power of positive thinking—The positive principle today—Enthusiasm makes the difference.
ISBN 0-517-08472-4
1. Success—Religious aspects—Christianity. 2. Peace of mind—Religious aspects—Christianity. 3. Self esteem—Religious aspects—Christianity. I. Title.
BJ1611.2.P35425 1992
248.4—dc20 92-19453
CIP

30 29 28 27 26 25 24 23 22 21

Contents

THE POWER OF POSITIVE THINKING

Contents

Dedicated to my brothers
ROBERT CLIFFORD PEALE, M.D., F.I.C.S.
and
THE REVEREND LEONARD DELANEY PEALE

Effective Helpers of Mankind

Preface

to the 40th Anniversary Edition

At the time I wrote this book it never occurred to me that more than fifteen million copies would be sold in various hardcover editions and that it would one day attract a vast new readership through an anniversary edition such as this. Frankly, however, my gratitude for this event is not from the viewpoint of books sold, but in terms of the many persons to whom I have been privileged to suggest a simple, workable philosophy of living.

The dynamic laws which the book teaches were learned the hard way by trial and error in my personal search for a way of life. But I found in them an answer to my own problems and, believe me, I am the most difficult person with whom I have worked. The book is my effort to share my spiritual experience, for if it helped me, I felt it might also be of help to others.

In formulating this simple philosophy of life I found my own answers in the teachings of Jesus Christ. I have merely tried to describe those truths in the language and thought forms understandable to present day people. The way of life to which this book is a witness is very wonderful.

It is not easy. Indeed, it often is hard, but it is full of joy and hope and victory.

I well recall the day I sat down to begin writing the book. I knew that the best work required more ability than I possessed and therefore I needed help that only God could give. My wife and I have the policy of taking God into working partnership in all our problems and activities. So we had a very earnest session of prayer, asking for guidance, and we put the project into God's hands. When the manuscript was ready for the publisher Mrs. Peale and I again prayed, dedicating the manuscript. We asked only that it might help people to live more effective lives. When the first book of these millions of copies came from the press to us it was again a spiritual moment. We thanked God for His help and dedicated the book once more.

The book was written for the plain people of this world, of whom certainly I am one. I was born and reared in humble Midwestern circumstances in a dedicated Christian home. The everyday people of this land are my own kind whom I know and love and believe in with great faith. When anyone of them lets God have charge of his life the power and glory are amazingly demonstrated.

The book is written with deep concern for the pain, difficulty and struggle of human existence. It teaches the cultivation of peace of mind, not as an escape from life into protected quiescence, but as a power center out of which comes driving energy for constructive personal and social living. It teaches positive thinking, not as a means to fame, riches or power, but as the practical application of faith to overcome defeat and accomplish worthwhile creative values in life. It teaches a hard, disciplinary way of life, but one which offers great joy to the person who achieves victory over himself and the difficult circumstances of the world.

To all who have written me about the joyous victory they have had through practicing the spiritual techniques of this book and to those who will yet have such experience may I say how happy I am for all that is happening to them as they live by dynamic spiritual formulas.

I wish finally to express deep appreciation to my publishers for their never-failing support, cooperation and friendship. I have never worked with finer people than my cherished friends at Prentice-Hall. I look forward with great pleasure to my association with Fawcett Publications. May God continue to use this book in human helpfulness.

NORMAN VINCENT PEALE

Introduction

What This Book Can Do for You

This book is written to suggest techniques and to give examples which demonstrate that you do not need to be defeated by anything, that you can have peace of mind, improved health, and a never-ceasing flow of energy. In short, that your life can be full of joy and satisfaction. Of this I have no doubt at all for I have watched countless persons learn and apply a system of simple procedures that has brought about the foregoing benefits in their lives. These assertions, which may appear extravagant, are based on bona fide demonstrations in actual human experience.

Altogether too many people are defeated by the everyday problems of life. They go struggling, perhaps even whining, through their days with a sense of dull resentment at what they consider the "bad breaks" life has given them. In a sense there may be such a thing as "the breaks" in this life, but there is also a spirit and method by which we can control and even determine those breaks. It is a pity that people should let themselves be defeated by the problems, cares, and difficulties of human existence, and it is also quite unnecessary.

In saying this I certainly do not ignore or minimize the hardships and tragedies of the world, but neither do I allow them to dominate. You can permit obstacles to control your mind to the point where they are uppermost and thus become the dominating factors in your thought pattern. By learning how to cast them from the mind, by refusing to become mentally subservient to them, and by channeling spiritual power through your thoughts you can rise above obstacles which ordinarily might defeat you. By methods I shall outline, obstacles are simply not permitted to destroy your happiness and well-being. You need be defeated only if you are willing to be. This book teaches you how to "will" not to be.

The purpose of this book is a very direct and simple one. It makes no pretense to literary excellence nor does it seek to demonstrate any unusual scholarship on my part. This is simply a practical, direct-action, personal-improvement manual. It is written with the sole objective of helping the reader achieve a happy, satisfying, and worthwhile life. I thoroughly and enthusiastically believe in certain demonstrated and effective principles which, when practiced, produce a victorious life. My aim is to set them forth in this volume in a logical, simple, and understandable manner so that the reader, feeling a sense of need, may learn a practical method by which he can build for himself, with God's help, the kind of life he deeply desires.

If you read this book thoughtfully, carefully absorbing its teachings, and if you will sincerely and persistently practice the principles and formulas set forth herein, you can experience an amazing improvement within yourself. By using the techniques outlined here you can modify or change the circumstances in which you now live, assuming control over them rather than continuing to be directed by them. Your relations with other people will improve. You will become a more popular, esteemed, and well-liked individual. By mastering these principles, you will enjoy a delightful new sense of well-being. You may attain a degree of health not hitherto known by you and experience a new and keen pleasure in living. You will become a person of greater usefulness and will wield an expanded influence.

How can I be so certain that the practice of these principles will produce such results? The answer is simply that for many years in the Marble Collegiate Church of New York City we have taught a system of creative living based on spiritual techniques, carefully noting its operation in the lives of hundreds of people. It is no speculative series of extravagant assertions that I make, for these principles have worked so efficiently over so long a period of time that they are now firmly established as documented and demonstrable truth. The system outlined is a perfected and amazing method of successful living.

In my writings, including several books, in my regular weekly newspaper column in nearly one hundred dailies, in my national radio program over seventeen years, in our magazine, *Guideposts*, and in lectures in scores of cities, I have taught these same scientific yet simple principles of achievement, health, and happiness. Hundreds have read, listened, and practiced, and the results are invariably the same: new life, new power, increased efficiency, greater happiness.

Because so many have requested that these principles be put into book form, the better to be studied and practiced, I am publishing this new volume under the title, *The Power of Positive Thinking*. I need not point out that the powerful principles contained herein are not my invention but are given to us by the greatest Teacher who ever lived and who still lives. This book teaches applied Christianity; a simple yet scientific system of practical techniques of successful living that works.

NORMAN VINCENT PEALE

1

BELIEVE IN YOURSELF

Believe in yourself! Have faith in your abilities! Without a humble but reasonable confidence in your own powers you cannot be successful or happy. But with sound self-confidence you can succeed. A sense of inferiority and inadequacy interferes with the attainment of your hopes, but self-confidence leads to self-realization and successful achievement. Because of the importance of this mental attitude, this book will help you believe in yourself and release your inner powers.

It is appalling to realize the number of pathetic people who are hampered and made miserable by the malady popularly called the inferiority complex. But you need not suffer from this trouble. When proper steps are taken, it can be overcome. You can develop creative faith in yourself—faith that is justified.

After speaking to a convention of businessmen in a city auditorium, I was on the stage greeting people when a man approached me and with a peculiar intensity of manner asked, "May I talk with you about a matter of desperate importance to me?"

I asked him to remain until the others had gone, then we went backstage and sat down.

"I'm in this town to handle the most important business deal of my life," he explained. "If I succeed, it means everything to me. If I fail, I'm done for."

I suggested that he relax a little, that nothing was quite that final. If he succeeded, that was fine. If he didn't, well, tomorrow was another day.

"I have a terrible disbelief in myself," he said dejectedly. "I have no confidence. I just don't believe I can put it over. I am very discouraged and depressed. In fact," he lamented, "I'm just about sunk. Here I am, forty years old. Why is it that all my life I have been tormented by inferiority feelings, by lack of confidence, by self-doubt? I listened to your speech tonight in which you talked about the power of positive thinking, and I want to ask how I can get some faith in myself."

"There are two steps to take," I replied. "First, it is important to discover why you have these feelings of no power. That requires analysis and will take time. We must approach the maladies of our emotional life as a physician probes to find something wrong physically. This cannot be done immediately, certainly not in our brief interview tonight, and it may require treatment to reach a permanent solution. But to pull you through this immediate problem I shall give you a formula which will work if you use it.

"As you walk down the street tonight I suggest that you repeat certain words which I shall give you. Say them over several times after you get into bed. When you awaken tomorrow, repeat them three times before arising. On the way to your important appointment say them three additional times. Do this with an attitude of faith and you will receive sufficient strength and ability to deal with this problem. Later, if you wish, we can go into an analysis of your basic problem, but whatever we come up with following that study, the formula which I am now going to give you can be a large factor in the eventual cure."

Following is the affirmation which I gave him—"I can do all things through Christ which strengthen me." (Philippians 4:13) He was unfamiliar with these words so I wrote them on a card and had him read them over three times aloud.

"Now, follow that prescription, and I am sure things will come out all right."

He pulled himself up, stood quietly for a moment, then said with considerable feeling, "O.K., Doctor. O.K."

I watched him square his shoulders and walk out into the night. He seemed a pathetic figure, and yet the way he carried himself as he disappeared showed that faith was already at work in his mind.

Subsequently he reported that this simple formula "did wonders" for him and added, "It seems incredible that a few words from the Bible could do so much for a person."

This man later had a study made of the reasons for his inferiority attitudes. They were cleared away by scientific counseling and by the application of religious faith. He was taught how to have faith; was given certain specific instructions to follow (these are given later in this chapter). Gradually he attained a strong, steady, reasonable confidence. He never ceases to express amazement at the way in which things now flow toward rather than away from him. His personality has taken on a positive, not negative, character so that he no longer repels success, but, on the contrary, draws it to him. He now has an authentic confidence in his own powers.

There are various causes of inferiority feelings, and not a few stem from childhood.

An executive consulted me about a young man whom he wished to advance in his company. "But," he explained, "he cannot be trusted with important secret information and I'm sorry, for otherwise I would make him my administrative assistant. He has all the other necessary qualifications, but he talks too much, and without meaning to do so divulges matters of a private and important nature."

Upon analysis I found that he "talked too much" simply because of an inferiority feeling. To compensate for it he succumbed to the temptation of parading his knowledge.

He associated with men who were rather well-to-do, all of whom had attended college and belonged to a fraternity. But this boy was reared in poverty, had not been a college man or fraternity member. Thus he felt himself inferior to his associates in education and social background. To build himself up with his associates and to enhance his self-esteem, his subconscious mind, which always seeks to provide a compensatory mechanism, supplied him with a means for raising his ego.

He was on "the inside" in the industry, and accompanied his superior to conferences where he met outstanding men and listened to important private conversations. He reported just enough of his "inside information" to cause his associates to regard him with admiration and envy. This served to elevate his self-esteem and satisfy his desire for recognition.

When the employer became aware of the cause of this personality trait, being a kindly and understanding man, he pointed out to the young man the opportunities in business to which his abilities could lead him. He also described how his inferiority feelings caused his unreliability in confidential matters. This self-knowledge, together with a sincere practicing of the techniques of faith and prayer, made him a valuable asset to his company. His real powers were released.

I can perhaps illustrate the manner in which many youngsters acquire an inferiority complex through the use of a personal reference. As a small boy I was painfully thin. I had lots of energy, was on a track team, was healthy and hard as nails, but thin. And that bothered me because I didn't want to be thin. I wanted to be fat. I was called "skinny," but I didn't want to be called "skinny." I wanted to be called "fat." I longed to be hard-boiled and tough and fat. I did everything to get fat. I drank cod-liver oil, consumed vast numbers of milk shakes, ate thousands of chocolate sundaes with whipped cream and nuts, cakes and pies innumerable, but they did not affect me in the slightest. I stayed thin and lay awake nights thinking and agonizing about it. I kept on trying to get heavy until I was about thirty, when all of a sudden did I get heavy? I bulged at the seams. Then I became self-conscious because I was so fat, and finally had to take off forty pounds with equal agony to get myself down to respectable size.

In the second place (to conclude this personal analysis which I give only because it may help others by showing how this malady works), I was a minister's son and was constantly reminded of that fact. Everybody else could do everything, but if I did even the slightest little thing—"Ah, you are a preacher's son." So I didn't want to be a preacher's son, for preachers' sons are supposed to be nice and namby-pamby. I wanted to be known as a hard-boiled fellow. Perhaps that is why preachers' sons get their reputation for being a little difficult, because they rebel against having to carry the banner of the church all the time. I vowed there was one thing I would never do, and that was to become a preacher.

Also, I came of a family practically every member of which was a performer in public, a platform speaker, and that was the last thing I wanted to be. They used to make me get up in public to make speeches when it scared me to death, even filled me with terror. That was years ago, but the twinge of it comes to me every now and then when I walk onto a platform. I had to use every known device to develop confidence in what powers the good Lord gave me.

I found the solution of this problem in the simple techniques of faith taught in the Bible. These principles are scientific and sound and can heal any personality of the pain of inferiority feelings. Their use can enable the sufferer to find and release the powers which have been inhibited by a feeling of inadequacy.

Such are some of the sources of the inferiority complex which erect power barriers in our personalities. It is some emotional violence done to us in childhood, or the consequences of certain circumstances, or something we did to ourselves. This malady arises out of the misty past in the dim recesses of our personalities.

Perhaps you had an older brother who was a brilliant student. He got A's in school; you made only C's, and you never heard the last of it. So you believed that you could never succeed in life as he could. He got A's and you got C's, so you reasoned that you were consigned to getting C's all your life. Apparently you never realized that some of those who failed to get high grades in school have been the greatest successes outside of school. Just because somebody gets an A in college doesn't make him the greatest man in the United States, because maybe his A's will stop when he gets his diploma, and the fellow who got C's in school will go on later to get the real A's in life.

The greatest secret for eliminating the inferiority complex, which is another term for deep and profound self-doubt, is to fill your mind to overflowing with faith. Develop a tremendous faith in God and that will give you a humble yet soundly realistic faith in yourself.

The acquiring of dynamic faith is accomplished by prayer, lots of prayer, by reading and mentally absorbing the Bible and by practicing its faith techniques. In another chapter I deal with specific formulas of prayer, but I want to point out here that the type of prayer that produces the quality of faith required to eliminate inferiority is of a particular nature. Surface skimming, formalistic and perfunctory prayer is not sufficiently powerful.

A wonderful black woman, a cook in the home of friends of mine in Texas, was asked how she so completely mastered her troubles. She answered that ordinary problems could be met by ordinary prayers, but that "when a big trouble comes along, you have to pray deep prayers."

One of my most inspiring friends was the late Harlowe B. Andrews of Syracuse, New York, one of the best businessmen and competent spiritual experts I ever knew. He said the trouble with most prayers is that they aren't big enough. "To get anywhere with faith," said he, "learn to pray big prayers. God will rate you according to the size of your prayers." Doubtless he was right, for the Scriptures say, "According to your faith be it unto you." (Matthew 9:29) So the bigger your problems, the bigger your prayer should be.

Roland Hayes, the singer, quoted his grandfather to me, a man whose education was not equal to that of his grandson, but whose native wisdom was obviously sound. He said, "The trouble with lots of prayers is they ain't got no suction." Drive your prayers deep into your doubts, fears, inferiorities. Pray deep, big prayers that have plenty of suction and you will come up with powerful and vital faith.

Go to a competent spiritual adviser and let him teach you how to have faith. The ability to possess and utilize faith and gain the release of powers it provides are skills and, like any skills, must be studied and practiced to gain perfection.

At the conclusion of this chapter are listed ten suggestions for overcoming your inferiority pattern and for developing faith. Practice these rules diligently and they will aid you in developing confidence in yourself by dissipating your feelings of inferiority, however deeply imbedded.

At this point, however, I wish to indicate that to build up feelings of self-confidence the practice of suggesting confidence concepts to your mind is very effective. If your mind is obsessed by thoughts of insecurity and inadequacy it is, of course, due to the fact that such ideas have dominated your thinking over a long period of time. Another and more positive pattern of ideas must be given the mind, and that is accomplished by repetitive suggestion of confidence ideas. In the busy activities of daily existence thought disciplining is required if you are to re-educate the mind and make of it a power-producing plant. It is possible, even in the midst of your daily work, to drive confident thoughts into consciousness. Let me tell you about one man who did so by the use of a unique method.

One icy winter morning he called for me at a hotel in a Midwestern city to take me about thirty-five miles to another town to fill a lecture engagement. We got into his car and started off at a rather high rate of speed on the slippery road. He was going a little faster than I thought reasonable, and I reminded him that we had plenty of time and suggested that we take it easy.

"Don't let my driving worry you," he replied. "I used to be filled with all kinds of insecurities myself, but I got over them. I was afraid of everything. I feared an automobile trip or an airplane flight; and if any of my family went away I worried until they returned. I always went around with a feeling that something was going to happen, and it made my life miserable. I was saturated with inferiority and lacked confidence. This state of mind reflected itself in my business and I wasn't doing very well. But I hit upon a wonderful plan which knocked all these insecurity feelings out of my mind, and now I live with a feeling of confidence, not only in myself but in life generally."

This was the "wonderful plan." He pointed to two clips fastened on the instrument panel of the car just below the windshield and, reaching into the glove compartment, took out a pack of small cards. He selected one and slipped it beneath the clip. It read, "If ye have faith . . . nothing shall be impossible unto you." (Matthew 17:20) He removed that one, shuffled expertly through the cards with one hand, as he drove, selected another, and placed it under the clip. This one read, "If God be for us, who can be against us?" (Romans 8:31).

"I'm a traveling salesman," he explained, "and I drive around all day calling on my customers. I have discovered that while a man drives he thinks all kinds of thoughts. If his pattern of thought is negative, he will think many negative thoughts during the day and that, of course, is bad for him; but that is the way I used to be. I used to drive around all day between calls thinking fear and defeat thoughts, and incidentally that is one reason my sales were down. But since I have been using these cards as I drive and committing the words to memory, I have learned to think differently. The old insecurities that used to haunt me are just about all gone, and instead of thinking fear thoughts of defeat and ineffectiveness, I think thoughts of faith and courage. It is really wonderful the way this method has changed me. It has helped in my business, too, for how can one expect to make a sale if he drives up to a customer's place of business thinking he is not going to make a sale?"

This plan used by my friend is a very wise one. By filling his mind with affirmations of the presence, support, and help of God, he had actually changed his thought processes. He put an end to the domination of his long-held sense of insecurity. His potential powers were set free.

We build up the feeling of insecurity or security by how we think. If in our thoughts we constantly fix attention upon sinister expectations of dire events that might happen, the result will be constantly to feel insecure. And what is even more serious is the tendency to create, by the power of thought, the very condition we fear. This salesman actually created positive results by vital thoughts of courage and confidence through the process of placing the cards before him in his car. His powers, curiously inhibited by a defeat psychology, now flowed out of a personality in which creative attitudes had been stimulated.

Lack of self-confidence apparently is one of the great problems besetting people today. In a university a survey was made of six hundred students in psychology courses. The students were asked to state their most difficult personal problem. Seventy-five per cent listed lack of confidence. It can safely be assumed that the same large proportion is true of the population generally. Everywhere you encounter people who are inwardly afraid, who shrink from life, who suffer from a deep sense of inadequacy and insecurity, who doubt their own powers. Deep within themselves they mistrust their ability to meet responsibilities or to grasp opportunities. Always they are beset by the vague and sinister fear that something is not going to be quite right. They do not believe that they have it in them to be what they want to be, and so they try to make themselves content with something less than that of which they are capable. Thousands upon thousands go crawling through life on their hands and knees, defeated and afraid. And in most cases such frustration of power is unnecessary.

The blows of life, the accumulation of difficulties, the multiplications of problems tend to sap energy and leave you spent and discouraged. In such a condition the true status of your power is often obscured, and a person yields to a discouragement that is not justified by the facts. It is vitally essential to re-appraise your personality assets. When done in an attitude of reasonableness, this evaluation will convince you that you are less defeated than you think you are.

For example, a man fifty-two years of age consulted me. He was in great despondency. He revealed utter despair. He said he "was all through." He informed me that everything he had built up over his lifetime had been swept away.

"Everything?" I asked.

"Everything," he repeated. He was through, he reiterated. "I have nothing left at all. Everything is gone. There is no hope, and I am too old to start all over again. I have lost all faith."

Naturally I felt sympathetic toward him, but it was evident that his chief trouble was the fact that dark shadows of hopelessness had entered his mind and discolored his outlook, distorting it. Behind this twisted thinking his true powers had retreated, leaving him without force.

"So," I said, "suppose we take a piece of paper and write down the values you have left."

"There's no use," he sighed. "I haven't a single thing left. I thought I told you that."

I said, "Let's just see anyway." Then asked, "Is your wife still with you?"

"Why yes, of course, and she is wonderful. We have been married for thirty years. She would never leave me no matter how bad things are."

"All right, let us put that down—your wife is still with you and she will never leave you no matter what happens. How about your children? Got any children?"

"Yes," he replied, "I have three and they are certainly wonderful. I have been touched by the way they have come to me and said, 'Dad, we love you, and we'll stand by you.' "

"Well, then," I said, "that is number two—three children who love you and who will stand by you. Got any friends?" I asked.

"Yes," he said, "I really have some fine friends. I must admit they have been pretty decent. They have come around and said they would like to help me, but what can they do? They can't do anything."

"That is number three—you have some friends who would like to help you and who hold you in esteem. How about your integrity? Have you done anything wrong?"

"My integrity is all right," he replied. "I have always tried to do the right thing and my conscience is clear."

"All right," I said, "we will put that down as number four—integrity. How about your health?"

"My health is all right," he answered. "I have had very few sick days and I guess I am in pretty good shape physically."

"So let's put down as number five—good physical health. How about the United States? Do you think it's still doing business and is the land of opportunity?"

"Yes," he said. "It is the only country in the world I would want to live in."

"That is number six—you live in the United States, land of opportunity, and you are glad to be here." Then I asked, "How about your religious faith? Do you believe in God and that God will help you?"

"Yes," he said. "I do not think I could have gotten through this at all if I hadn't had some help from God."

"Now," I said, "let's list the assets we have figured out:

"1. A wonderful wife—married for thirty years.

"2. Three devoted children who will stand by you.

"3. Friends who will help you and who hold you in esteem.

"4. Integrity—nothing to be ashamed of.

"5. Good physical health.

"6. Live in the United States, the greatest country in the world.

"7. Have religious faith."

I shoved it across the table at him. "Take a look at that. I guess you have quite a total of assets. I thought you told me everything had been swept away."

He grinned ashamedly. "I guess I didn't think of those things. I never thought of it that way. Perhaps things aren't so bad at that," he said pensively. "Maybe I can start all over again if I can just get some confidence, if I can get the feel of some power within me."

Well, he got it, and he did start all over again. But he did so only when he changed his viewpoint, his mental attitude. Faith swept away his doubts, and more than enough power to overcome all his difficulties emerged from within him.

This incident illustrates a profound truth which is expressed in a very important statement made by the famous psychiatrist, Dr. Karl Menninger. He said, "Attitudes are more important than facts." That is worth repeating until its truth grips you. Any fact facing us, however difficult, even seemingly hopeless, is not so important as our attitude toward that fact. How you think about a fact may defeat you before you ever do anything about it. You may permit a fact to overwhelm you mentally before you start to deal with it actually. On the other hand, a confident and optimistic thought pattern can modify or overcome the fact altogether.

I know a man who is a tremendous asset to his organization, not because of any extraordinary ability, but because he invariably demonstrates a triumphant thought pattern. Perhaps his associates view a proposition pessimistically, so he employs what he calls "the vacuum-cleaner method." That is, by a series of questions he "sucks the dust" out of his associates' minds; he draws out their negative attitudes. Then quietly he suggests positive ideas concerning the proposition until a new set of attitudes gives them a new concept of the facts.

They often comment upon how different facts appear when this man "goes to work on them." It's the confidence attitude that makes the difference, nor does this rule out objectivity in an appraisal of facts. The inferiority complex victim sees all facts through discolored attitudes. The secret of correction is simply to gain a normal view, and that is always slanted on the positive side.

So if you feel that you are defeated and have lost confidence in your ability to win, sit down, take a piece of paper and make a list, not of the factors that are against you, but of those that are for you. If you or I or anybody thinks constantly of the forces that seem to be against us, we will build them up into a power far beyond that which is justified. They will assume a formidable strength which they do not actually possess. But if, on the contrary, you mentally visualize and affirm and reaffirm your assets and keep your thoughts on them, emphasizing them to the fullest extent, you will rise out of any difficulty regardless of what it may be. Your inner powers will reassert themselves and, with the help of God, lift you from defeat to victory.

One of the most powerful concepts, one which is a sure cure for lack of confidence, is the thought that God is actually with you and helping you. This is one of the simplest teachings in religion, namely, that Almighty God will be your companion, will stand by you, help you, and see you through. No other idea is so powerful in developing self-confidence as this simple belief when practiced. To practice it simply affirm "God is with me; God is helping me; God is guiding me." Spend several minutes each day visualizing His presence. Then practice believing that affirmation. Go about your business on the assumption that what you have affirmed and visualized is true. Affirm it, visualize it, believe it, and it will actualize itself. The release of power which this procedure stimulates will astonish you.

Feelings of confidence depend upon the type of thoughts that habitually occupy your mind. Think defeat and you are bound to feel defeated. But practice thinking confident thoughts, make it a dominating habit, and you will develop such a strong sense of capacity that regardless of what difficulties arise you will be able to overcome them. Feelings of confidence actually induce increased strength. Basil King once said, "Be bold, and mighty forces will come to your aid." Experience proves the truth of this. You will feel these mighty forces aiding you as your increasing faith reconditions your attitudes.

Emerson declared a tremendous truth, "They conquer who believe they can." And he added, "Do the thing you fear and the death of fear is certain." Practice confidence and faith and your fears and insecurities will soon have no power over you.

Once when Stonewall Jackson planned a daring attack, one of his generals fearfully objected, saying, "I am afraid of this" or "I fear that . . ." Putting his hand on his timorous subordinate's shoulder, Jackson said, "General, never take counsel of your fears."

The secret is to fill your mind with thoughts of faith, confidence, and security. This will force out or expel all thoughts of doubt, all lack of confidence. To one man who for a long time had been haunted by insecurities and fears I suggested that he read through the Bible underlining in red pencil every statement it contains relative to courage and confidence. He also committed them to memory, in effect cramming his mind full of the healthiest, happiest, most powerful thoughts in the world. These dynamic thoughts changed him from cringing hopelessness to a man of compelling force. The change in him in a few weeks was remarkable. From almost complete defeat he became a confident and inspiring personality. He now radiates courage and magnetism. He regained confidence in himself and his own powers by a simple process of thought conditioning.

To sum up—what can you do *now* to build up your self-confidence? Following are ten simple, workable rules for overcoming inadequacy attitudes and learning to practice faith. Thousands have used these rules, reporting successful results. Undertake this program and you, too, will build up confidence in your powers. You, too, will have a new feeling of power.

1. Formulate and stamp indelibly on your mind a mental picture of yourself as succeeding. Hold this picture tenaciously. Never permit it to fade. Your mind will seek to develop this picture. Never think of yourself as failing; never doubt the reality of the mental image. That is most dangerous, for the mind always tries to complete what it pictures. So *always* picture "success" no matter how badly things seem to be going at the moment.

2. Whenever a negative thought concerning your personal powers comes to mind, deliberately voice a positive thought to cancel it out.

3. Do not build up obstacles in your imagination. Depreciate every so-called obstacle. Minimize them. Difficulties must be studied and efficiently dealt with to be eliminated, but they must be seen for only what they are. They must not be inflated by fear thoughts.

4. Do not be awestruck by other people and try to copy them. Nobody can be you as efficiently as YOU can. Remember also that most people, despite their confident appearance and demeanor, are often as scared as you are and as doubtful of themselves.

5. Ten times a day repeat these dynamics words, "If God be *for* us, who can be *against* us?" (Romans 8:31) (Stop reading and repeat them NOW slowly and confidently.)

6. Get a competent counselor to help you understand why you do what you do. Learn the origin of your inferiority and self-doubt feelings which often begin in childhood. Self-knowledge leads to a cure.

7. Ten times each day practice the following affirmation, repeating it out loud if possible. "I can do all things through Christ which strength-

eneth me." (Philippians 4:13) Repeat those words NOW. That magic statement is the most powerful antidote on earth to inferiority thoughts.

8. Make a true estimate of your own ability, then raise it 10 per cent. Do not become egotistical, but develop a wholesome self-respect. Believe in your own God-released powers.

9. Put yourself in God's hands. To do that simply state, "I am in God's hands." Then believe you are NOW receiving all the power you need. "Feel" it flowing into you. Affirm that "the kingdom of God is within you" (Luke 17:21) in the form of adequate power to meet life's demands.

10. Remind yourself that God is with you and nothing can defeat you. Believe that you *now* RECEIVE power from Him.

2

A PEACEFUL MIND GENERATES POWER

At breakfast in a hotel dining room three of us fell to discussing how well we had slept the night before, a truly momentous topic. One man complained of a sleepless night. He had tossed and turned and was about as exhausted as when he retired. "Guess I'd better stop listening to the news before going to bed," he observed. "I tuned in last night and sure got an ear full of trouble."

That is quite a phrase, "an ear full of trouble." Little wonder he had a disturbed night. "Maybe the coffee I drank before retiring had something to do with it," he mused.

The other man spoke up, "As for me, I had a grand night. I got my news from the evening paper and from an early broadcast and had a chance to digest it before I went to sleep. Of course," he continued, "I used my go-to-sleep plan which never fails to work."

I prodded him for his plans, which he explained as follows: "When I was a boy, my father, a farmer, had the habit of gathering the family in the parlor at bedtime and he read to us out of the Bible. I can hear him yet. In fact, every time I hear those Bible verses I always seem to hear them in the tone of my father's voice. After prayers I would go up to my room and sleep like a top. But when I left home I got away from the Bible reading and prayer habit.

"I must admit that for years practically the only time I ever prayed was when I got into a jam. But some months ago my wife and I, having a number of difficult problems, decided we would try it again. We found it a very helpful practice, so now every night before going to bed she and I together read the Bible and have a little session of prayer. I don't know what there is about it, but I have been sleeping better and things have improved all down the line. In fact, I find it so helpful that even out on the road, as I am now, I still read the Bible and pray. Last night I got into bed and read the 23rd Psalm. I read it out loud and it did me a lot of good."

He turned to the other man and said, "I didn't go to bed with an ear full of trouble. I went to sleep with a mind full of peace."

Well, there are two cryptic phrases for you—"an ear full of trouble" and "a mind full of peace." Which do you choose?

The essence of the secret lies in a change of mental attitude. One must learn to live on a different thought basis, and even though thought change requires effort, it is much easier than to continue living as you are. The life of strain is difficult. The life of inner peace, being harmonious and without stress, is the easiest type of existence. The chief struggle then in gaining mental peace is the effort of revamping your thinking to the relaxed attitude of acceptance of God's gift of peace.

As an illustration of taking a relaxed attitude and therefore receiving peace, I always think of an experience in a certain city where I lectured one evening. Prior to going on the platform I was sitting backstage going over my speech when a man approached and wanted to discuss a personal problem.

I informed him that at the moment it was impossible to talk as I was just about to be introduced, and asked him to wait. While speaking I noticed him in the wings nervously pacing up and down, but afterward he was nowhere about. However, he had given me his card, which indicated that he was a man of considerable influence in that city.

Back at my hotel, although it was late, I was still troubled by this man so I telephoned him. He was surprised at my call and explained that he did not wait because obviously I was busy. "I just wanted you to pray with me," he said. "I thought if you would pray with me, perhaps I could get some peace."

"There is nothing to prevent us from praying together on the telephone right now," I said.

Somewhat in surprise, he replied, "I have never heard of praying on the telephone."

"Why not?" I asked. "A telephone is simply a gadget of communication. You are some blocks from me, but by means of the telephone we are together. Besides," I continued, "the Lord is with each of us. He is at both ends of this line and in between. He is with you and He is with me."

"All right," he conceded. "I'd like to have you pray for me."

So I closed my eyes and prayed for the man over the telephone, and I prayed just as though we were in the same room. He could hear and the Lord could hear. When I finished I suggested, "Won't you pray?" There was no response. Then at the other end of the line I heard sobbing and finally, "I can't talk," he said.

"Go on and cry for a minute or two and then pray," I suggested. "Simply tell the Lord everything that is bothering you. I assume this is a private line, but if not, and if anybody is listening, it won't matter. As far as anyone is concerned, we are just a couple of voices. Nobody would know it is you and I."

Thus encouraged, he started to pray, hesitantly at first, and then with great impetuosity he poured out his heart, and it was filled with hate, frustration, failure—a mass of it. Finally he prayed plaintively, "Dear Jesus, I have a lot of nerve to ask you to do anything for me, because I never did anything for you. I guess you know what a no-account I am, even though I put on a big front. I am sick of all this, dear Jesus. Please help me."

So I prayed again, and asked the Lord to answer his prayer, then said, "Lord, at the other end of the telephone wire, place your hand on my friend and give him peace. Help him now to yield himself and accept your gift of peace." Then I stopped, and there was a rather long pause, and I shall never forget the tone in his voice as I heard him say, "I shall always remember this experience, and I want you to know that for the first time in months I feel clean inside and happy and peaceful." This man employed a simple technique for having a peaceful mind. He emptied his mind and he received peace as a gift from God.

As a physician said, "Many of my patients have nothing wrong with them except their thoughts. So I have a favorite prescription that I write for some. But it is not a prescription that you can fill at a drugstore. The prescription I write is a verse from the Bible, 'Romans 12:2.' I do not write out that verse for my patients. I make them look it up and it reads: '. . . be ye transformed by the renewing of your mind . . .' To be happier and healthier they need a renewing of their minds, that is, a change in the pattern of their thoughts. When they 'take' this prescription, they actually achieve a mind full of peace. That helps to produce health and well-being."

A primary method for gaining a mind full of peace is to practice emptying the mind. This will be emphasized in another chapter, but I mention it here to underscore the importance of a frequent mental catharsis. I recommend a mind-emptying at least twice a day, more often if necessary. Definitely practice emptying your mind of fears, hates, insecurities, regrets, and guilt feelings. The mere fact that you consciously make this effort to empty your mind tends to give relief. Haven't you experienced a sense of release when you have been able to pour out to somebody whom you can trust worrisome matters that lay heavy upon the heart? As a pastor I have often observed how much it means to people to have someone to whom they can truly and in confidence tell everything troubling their minds.

I conducted a religious service on board the *S. S. Lurline* on a recent voyage to Honolulu. In the course of my talk I suggested that people who were carrying worries in their minds might go to the stern of the vessel and imaginatively take each anxious thought out of the mind, drop it overboard, and watch it disappear in the wake of the ship. It seems an almost childlike suggestion, but a man came to me later that day and said, "I did as you suggested and am amazed at the relief it has given me. During this voyage," he said, "every evening at sunset I am going to drop all my worries overboard until I develop the psychology of casting them entirely out of my consciousness. Every day I shall watch them disappear in the great ocean of time. Doesn't the Bible say something about 'forgetting those things that are behind'?"

The man to whom this suggestion appealed is not an impractical sentimentalist. On the contrary, he is a person of extraordinary mental stature, an outstanding leader in his field.

Of course, emptying the mind is not enough. When the mind is emptied, something is bound to enter. The mind cannot long remain a vacuum. You cannot go around permanently with an empty mind. I admit that some people seem to accomplish that feat, but by and large it is necessary to refill the emptied mind or the old, unhappy thoughts which you have cast out will come sneaking in again.

To prevent that happening, immediately start filling your mind with creative and healthy thoughts. Then when the old fears, hates, and worries that have haunted you for so long try to edge back in, they will in effect find a sign on the door of your mind reading "occupied." They may struggle for admission, for having lived in your mind for a long time, they feel at home there. But the new and healthy thoughts which you have taken in will now be stronger and better fortified, and therefore able to repulse them. Presently the old thoughts will give up altogether and leave you alone. You will permanently enjoy a mind full of peace.

At intervals during the day practice thinking a carefully selected series of peaceful thoughts. Let mental pictures of the most peaceful scenes you have ever witnessed pass across your mind, as, for example, some beautiful valley filled with the hush of evening time, as the shadows lengthen and the sun sinks to rest. Or recall the silvery light of the moon falling upon rippling waters, or remember the sea washing gently upon soft shores of sand. Such peaceful thought images will work upon your mind as a healing medicine. So now and then during every day allow motion pictures of peace slowly to cross your mind.

Practice the technique of suggestive articulation, that is, repeat audibly some peaceful words. Words have profound suggestive power, and there is healing in the very saying of them. Utter a series of panicky words and your mind will immediately go into a mild state of nervousness. You will perhaps feel a sinking in the pit of your stomach that will affect your entire physical mechanism. If, on the contrary, you speak peaceful, quieting words, your mind will react in a peaceful manner. Use such a word as "tranquillity." Repeat that word slowly several times. *Tranquillity* is one of the most beautiful and melodic of all English words, and the mere saying of it tends to induce a tranquil state.

Another healing word is "serenity." Picturize serenity as you say it. Repeat it slowly and in the mood of which the word is a symbol. Words such as these have a healing potency when used in this manner.

It is also helpful to use lines from poetry or passages from the Scriptures. A man of my acquaintance who achieved a remarkable peace of mind has the habit of writing on cards unusual quotations expressing peacefulness. He carries one of the cards in his wallet at all times, referring to it frequently until each quotation is committed to memory. He says that each such idea dropped into the subconscious "lubricates" his mind with peace. A peaceful concept is indeed oil on troubled thoughts. One of the quotations which he used is from a sixteenth-century mystic, "Let nothing disturb you. Let nothing frighten you. Everything passes away except God. God alone is sufficient."

The words of the Bible have a particularly strong therapeutic value. Drop them into your mind, allowing them to "dissolve" in consciousness, and they will spread a healing balm over your entire mental structure. This is one of the simplest processes to perform and also one of the most effective in attaining peace of mind.

A salesman told me of an incident that took place in a Midwestern hotel room. He was one of a group of businessmen having a conference. One man was very much on edge. He was snappy, argumentative, high-strung. Everyone present knew him quite well and realized he was under great nervous pressure. But finally his irritating attitudes began to get on everybody's nerves. Presently this nervous individual opened his traveling bag, took out a big bottle of brackish-looking medicine, and poured himself a large dose. Asked what this medicine was, he growled, "Oh, it's something for nerves. I feel like I'm going to break in pieces. The pressure I'm under makes me wonder if I am going to crack up. I try not to show it, but I suppose even you fellows have observed that I'm nervous. This medicine was recommended and I've swallowed several bottles of it, but I don't seem to get any better."

The other men laughed, then one said in a kindly manner, "Bill, I don't know anything about that medicine you are taking. Maybe it's all right. It probably is, but I can give you some medicine for those nerves that will do you more good than that. I know, because it cured me, and I was worse off than you are."

"What is this medicine?" snapped the other.

The other man reached into his bag and pulled out a book. "This book will do the job, and I really mean it. I suppose you think it strange that I carry a Bible around in my bag, but I don't care who knows it. I am not a bit ashamed of it. I have been carrying this Bible in my bag for the past two years, and I have marked places in it that help keep my mind at peace. It works for me, and I think it can do something for you too. Why not give it a trial?"

The others were listening with interest to this unusual speech. The nervous man had sunk low in his chair. Seeing that he was making an impression, the speaker continued, "I had a peculiar experience in a hotel one night which got me into the habit of reading the Bible. I was getting into a pretty tense state. I was out on a business trip and late one afternoon came up to my room terribly nervous. I tried to write some letters, but couldn't get my mind on them. I paced up and down the room, tried to read the paper, but that annoyed me, so I decided to go down and get a drink—anything to get away from myself.

"While standing by the dresser, my eye happened to fall upon a Bible lying there. I had seen many such Bibles in hotel rooms, but had never read any of them. However, something impelled me, and I opened the book to one of the Psalms and started to read it. I remember that I read that one standing up, then sat down and read another. I was interested but certainly surprised at myself—me reading the Bible! It was a laugh, but I kept on reading.

"Soon I came to the 23rd Psalm. I had learned that one as a boy in Sunday school and was surprised that I still knew most of it by heart. I tried saying it over, especially that line where it says, 'He leadeth me beside the still waters; he restoreth my soul.' I liked that line. It sort of got me. I sat there repeating it over and over—and the next thing I knew I woke up.

"Apparently I had dropped off to sleep and slept soundly. I slept only about fifteen minutes, but upon awakening was as refreshed and rested as if I'd had a good night's sleep. I can remember yet the wonderful feeling of complete refreshment. Then I realized that I felt peaceful, and said to myself, 'Isn't it strange? What is wrong with me that I have missed something as wonderful as this?'

"So after that experience," he said, "I bought a Bible, a little one I could put in my bag, and I've been carrying it ever since. I honestly like to read it, and I am not nearly so nervous as I used to be. So," he added, "try that, Bill, and see if it doesn't work."

Bill did try it, and he kept on trying it. He reported that it was a bit strange and difficult for him at first, and he read the Bible on the sly when nobody was around. He didn't want to be thought holy or pious. But now he says he brings it out on trains and planes or "any old place" and reads it, and it "does him a world of good."

"I no longer need to take nerve medicine," he declared.

This scheme must have worked in Bill's case, for he is easy to get along with now. His emotions are under control. These two men found that getting peace of mind isn't complicated. You merely feed your mind with thoughts that cause it to be peaceful. To have a mind full of peace merely fill it full of peace. It's as simple as that.

There are other practical ways by which you can develop serenity and quiet attitudes. One way is through your conversation. Depending upon the words we use and the tone in which we use them, we can talk ourselves into being nervous, high-strung, and upset. We can talk ourselves into either negative or positive results. By our speech we can also achieve quiet reactions. Talk peaceful to be peaceful.

In a group when the conversation takes a trend that is upsetting, try injecting peaceful ideas into the talk. Note how it counteracts the nervous tensions. Conversation filled with expressions of unhappy expectation, at breakfast, for example, often sets the tone of the day. Little wonder things turn out according to the unhappy specifications. Negative conversation adversely affects circumstances. Certainly talk of a tense and nervous nature enhances inner agitation.

On the contrary, start each day by affirming peaceful, contented, and happy attitudes and your days will tend to be pleasant and successful. Such attitudes are active and definite factors in creating satisfactory conditions. Watch your manner of speech then if you wish to develop a peaceful state of mind.

It is important to eliminate from conversation all negative ideas, for they tend to produce tension and annoyance inwardly. For example, when you are with a group of people at luncheon, do not comment that the "Communists will soon take over the country." In the first place, Communists are not going to take over the country, and by so asserting you create a depressing reaction in the minds of others. It undoubtedly affects digestion adversely. The depressing remark colors the attitude of all present, and everyone goes away with a perhaps slight but definite feeling of annoyance. They also carry away with them a mild but definite feeling that something is wrong with everything. There are times when we must face these harsh questions and deal with them objectively and vigorously, and no one has more contempt for Communism than I have, but as a general thing to have peace of mind, fill your personal and group conversations with positive, happy, optimistic, satisfying expressions.

The words we speak have a direct and definite effect upon our thoughts. Thoughts create words, for words are the vehicles of ideas. But words also affect thoughts and help to condition if not to create attitudes. In fact, what often passes for thinking starts with talk. Therefore if the average conversation is scrutinized and disciplined to be sure that it contains peaceful expressions, the result will be peaceful ideas and ultimately, therefore, a peaceful mind.

Another effective technique in developing a peaceful mind is the daily practice of silence. Everyone should insist upon not less than a quarter of an hour of absolute quiet every twenty-four hours. Go alone into the quietest place available to you and sit or lie down for fifteen minutes and practice the art of silence. Do not talk to anyone. Do not write. Do not read. Think as little as possible. Throw your mind into neutral. Conceive of your mind as quiescent, inactive. This will not be easy at first because thoughts are stirring up your mind, but practice will increase your efficiency. Conceive of your mind as the surface of a body of water and see how nearly quiet you can make it, so that there is not a ripple. When you have attained a quiescent state, then begin to listen for the deeper sounds of harmony and beauty and of God that are to be found in the essence of silence.

Americans unfortunately are not skilled in this practice, which is a pity, for as Thomas Carlyle said, "Silence is the element in which great things fashion themselves." This generation of Americans has missed something that our forefathers knew and which helped to condition their character—and that is the silence of the great forest or of the far-reaching plains.

Perhaps our lack of inner peace is due to some extent to the effect of noise upon the nervous system of modern people. Scientific experiments show that noise in the place where we work, live, or sleep reduces efficiency to a noticeable degree. Contrary to popular belief, it is doubtful if we ever completely adjust our physical, mental, or nervous mechanisms to noise. No matter how familiar a repeated sound becomes, it never passes unheard by the subconscious. Automobile horns, the roar of airplanes, and other strident noises actually result in physical activity during sleep. Impulses transmitted to and through the nerves by these sounds cause muscular movements which detract from real rest. If the reaction is sufficiently severe, it partakes of the nature of shock.

On the contrary, silence is a healing, soothing, healthy practice. Starr Daily says, "No man or woman of my acquaintance who knows how to practice silence and does it has ever been sick to my knowledge. I have noticed that my own afflictions come upon me when I do not balance expression with relaxation." Starr Daily closely associates silence with spiritual healing. The sense of rest that results from a practice of complete silence is a therapy of utmost value.

In the circumstances of modern life, with its acceleration of pace, the practice of silence is admittedly not so simple as it was in the days of our forefathers. A vast number of noise-producing gadgets exist that they did not know, and our daily program is more hectic. Space has been annihilated in the modern world, and apparently we are also attempting to annihilate the factor of time. It is only rarely possible for an individual to walk in deep woods or sit by the sea or meditate on a mountaintop or on the deck of a vessel in the midst of the ocean. But when we do have such experiences, we can print on the mind the picture of the silent place and the feel of the moment and return to it in memory to live it over and over again just as truly as when we were actually in that scene. In fact, when you return to it in memory the mind tends to remove any unpleasant factors present in the actual situation. The memory visit is often an improvement over the actual for the mind tends to reproduce only the beauty in the remembered scene.

For example, as I write these words, I am on a balcony of one of the most beautiful hotels in the world, the Royal Hawaiian on the famed and romantic Waikiki Beach in Honolulu, Hawaii. I am looking into a garden filled with graceful palm trees, swaying in the balmy breeze. The air is laden with the aroma of exotic flowers. Hibiscus, of which on these islands there are two thousand varieties, fill the garden. Outside my windows are papaya trees laden with ripening fruit. The brilliant color of the royal poinciana, the flame of the forest trees, add to the glamor of the scene; and the acacia trees are hung heavily with their exquisite white flowers.

The incredible blue ocean surrounding these islands stretches away to the horizon. The white waves are surging in, and the Hawaiians and my fellow visitors are riding gracefully on surfboards and outrigger canoes. Altogether it is a scene of entrancing beauty. It has an indescribably healing effect upon me as I sit here writing about the power generated in a peaceful mind. The insistent responsibilities under which I ordinarily live seem so far away. Though I am in Hawaii to give a series of lectures and to write this book, nevertheless the peace with which this place is filled envelops me. Yet I realize that when I have returned to my home in New York, five thousand miles away, I shall only then truly savor the exquisite joy of the beauty which I now behold. It will become enshrined in memory as a prized retreat to which my mind can go in the busy days that lie ahead. Often, when far from this idyllic place, I shall return in memory to find peace along the palm-lined, foam-washed beach at Waikiki.

Fill your mind with all peaceful experiences possible, then make planned and deliberate excursions to them in memory. You must learn that the easiest way to an easy mind is to create an easy mind. This is done by practice, by the application of some such simple principles as outlined here. The mind quickly responds to teaching and discipline. You can make the mind give you back anything you want, but remember the mind can give back only what it was first given. Saturate your thoughts with peaceful experiences, peaceful words and ideas, and ultimately you will have a storehouse of peace-producing experiences to which you may turn for refreshment and renewal of your spirit. It will be a vast source of power.

I spent a night with a friend who has a very lovely home. We had breakfast in a unique and interesting dining room. The four walls are painted in a beautiful mural picturing the countryside in which my host was reared as a boy. It is a panorama of rolling hills, gentle valleys, and singing streams, the latter clean and sun speckled, and babbling over rocks. Winding roads meander through pleasant meadows. Little houses dot the landscape. In a central position is a white church surmounted by a tall steeple.

As we breakfasted my host talked of this region of his youth, pointing out various points of interest in the painting around the wall. Then he said, "Often as I sit in this dining room I go from point to point in my memory and relive other days. I recall, for example, walking up that lane as a boy with bare feet, and I can remember yet how the clean dust felt between my toes. I remember fishing in that trout stream on many a summer afternoon and coasting down those hills in the wintertime.

"There is the church I attended as a boy." He grinned and said, "I sat through many a long sermon in that church but gratefully recall to mind the kindliness of the people and the sincerity of their lives. I can sit here and look at that church and think of the hymns I heard there with my mother and father as we sat together in the pew. They are long buried in that cemetery alongside the church, but in memory I go and stand by their graves and hear them speak to me as in days gone by. I get very tired and sometimes am nervous and tense. It helps to sit here and go back to the days when I had an untroubled mind, when life was new and fresh. It does something for me. It gives me peace."

Perhaps we all cannot have such murals on the dining-room walls, but you can put them around the wall of your mind: pictures of the most beautiful experiences of your life. Spend time among the thoughts which these pictures suggest. No matter how busy you may be or what responsibilities you carry, this simple, rather unique practice, having proved successful in many instances, may have a beneficial effect upon you. It is an easily practiced, easy way to a peaceful mind.

There is a factor in the matter of inner peace which must be stated because of its importance. Frequently I find that people who are lacking in inner peace are victims of a self-punishment mechanism. At some time in their experience they have committed a sin and the sense of guilt haunts them. They have sincerely sought Divine forgiveness, and the good Lord will always forgive anyone who asks Him and who means it. However, there is a curious quirk within the human mind whereby sometimes an individual will not forgive himself.

He feels that he deserves punishment and therefore is constantly anticipating that punishment. As a result he lives in a constant apprehension that something is going to happen. In order to find peace under these circumstances he must increase the intensity of his activity. He feels that hard work will give him some release from his sense of guilt. A physician told me that in his practice a number of cases of nervous breakdown were traceable to a sense of guilt for which the patient had unconsciously attempted to compensate by hectic overwork. The patient attributed his breakdown not to the sense of guilt, but to his overworked condition. "But," said the physician, "these men need not have broken down from overwork if first the sense of guilt had been fully released." Peace of mind under such circumstances is available by yielding the guilt as well as the tension it produces to the healing therapy of Christ.

At a resort hotel where I had gone for a few days of quiet writing I encountered a man from New York whom I knew slightly. He was a high-pressured, hard-driving, and exceedingly nervous business executive. He was sitting in the sun in a deck chair. At his invitation I sat down and chatted with him.

"I'm glad to see you relaxing in this beautiful spot," I commented.

He replied nervously, "I haven't any business being here. I've so much work to do at home. I'm under terrible pressure. Things have got me down. I'm nervous and can't sleep. I'm jumpy. My wife insisted that I come down here for a week. The doctors say there's nothing wrong with me if I just get to thinking right and relax. But how in the world do you do that?" he challenged. Then he gave me a piteous look. "Doctor," he said, "I would give anything if I could be peaceful and quiet. It's what I want more than anything in this world."

We talked a bit, and it came out in the conversation that he was always worrying that something sinister was going to happen. For years he had anticipated some dire event, living in constant apprehension about "something happening" to his wife or his children or his home.

It was not difficult to analyze his case. His insecurity arose from a double source—from childhood insecurities and from later guilty experiences. His mother had always felt that "something was going to happen," and he had absorbed her anxiety feelings. Later he committed some sins, and his subconscious mind insisted upon self-punishment. He became victim to the mechanism of self-punishment. As a result of this unhappy combination I found him this day in a highly inflamed state of nervous reaction.

Finishing our conversation, I stood beside his chair a moment. There was no one near, so I rather hesitantly suggested, "Would you by any chance like me to pray with you?" He nodded, and I put my hand on his shoulder and prayed, "Dear Jesus, as You healed people in the long ago and gave them peace, heal this man now. Give him fully of Thy forgiveness. Help him to forgive himself. Separate him from all his sins and let him know that You do not hold them against him. Set him free from them. Then let Thy peace flow into his mind, into his soul, and into his body."

He looked up at me with a strange look on his face and then turned away, for there were tears in his eyes and he didn't want me to see them. We were both a bit embarrassed, and I left him. Months later I met him, and he said, "Something happened to me down there that day when you prayed for me. I felt a strange sense of quietness and peace, and," he added, "healing."

He goes to church regularly now and he reads the Bible every day of his life. He follows the laws of God and he has lots of driving force. He is a healthy, happy man, for he has peace in his heart and mind.

3

HOW TO HAVE CONSTANT ENERGY

A major-league baseball pitcher once pitched a game when the temperature was over one hundred degrees. He lost several pounds as a result of the afternoon's exertion. At one stage of the game his energy sagged. His method for restoring his ebbing strength was unique. He simply repeated a passage from the Old Testament—"But they that wait upon the Lord shall renew their strength; they shall mount up with wings as eagles; they shall run, and not be weary, and they shall walk, and not faint." (Isaiah 40:31)

Frank Hiller, the pitcher who had this experience, told me that reciting this verse on the pitcher's mound actually gave him a renewal of strength so that he was able to complete the game with energy to spare. He explained the technique by saying, "I passed a powerful energy-producing thought through my mind."

How we think we feel has a definite effect on how we actually feel physically. If your mind tells you that you are tired, the body mechanism, the nerves, and the muscles accept the fact. If your mind is intensely interested, you can keep on at an activity indefinitely. Religion functions through our thoughts, in fact, it is a system of thought discipline. By supplying attitudes of faith to the mind it can increase energy. It helps you to accomplish prodigious activity by suggesting that you have ample support and resources of power.

A friend in Connecticut, an energetic man, full of vitality and vigor, says that he goes to church regularly to "get his batteries recharged." His concept is sound. God *is* the source of all energy—energy in the universe, atomic energy, electrical energy, and spiritual energy; indeed every form of energy derives from the Creator. The Bible emphasizes this point when it says, "He giveth power to the faint; and to them that have no might he increaseth strength." (Isaiah 40:29)

In another statement the Bible describes the energizing and re-energizing process: ". . . in Him we live (that is, have vitality), and move (have dynamic energy), and have our being (attain completeness)." (Acts 17:28)

Contact with God establishes within us a flow of the same type of energy that re-creates the world and that renews springtime every year. When in spiritual contact with God through our thought processes, the Divine energy flows through the personality, automatically renewing the original creative act. When contact with the Divine energy is broken, the personality gradually becomes depleted in body, mind, and spirit. An electric clock connected with an outlet does not run down and will continue indefinitely to keep accurate time. Unplug it, and the clock stops. It has lost contact with the power flowing through the universe. In general this process is operative in human experience though in a less mechanical manner.

A number of years ago I attended a lecture at which a speaker asserted before a large audience that he had not been tired in thirty years. He explained that thirty years before he had passed through a spiritual experience in which by self-surrender he had made contact with Divine power. From then on he possessed sufficient energy for all of his activities, and these were prodigious. He so obviously illustrated his teachings that everyone in that vast audience was profoundly impressed.

To me it was a revelation of the fact that in our consciousness we can tap a reservoir of boundless power as a result of which it is not necessary to suffer depletion of energy. For years I have studied and experimented with the ideas which this speaker outlined and which others have expounded and demonstrated, and it is my conviction that the principles of Christianity scientifically utilized can develop an uninterrupted and continuous flow of energy into the human mind and body.

These findings were corroborated by a prominent physician with whom

I was discussing a certain man whom we both know. This man, whose responsibilities are very heavy, works from morning until night without interruption, but always seems able to assume new obligations. He has the knack of handling his work easily and with efficiency.

I commented to the physician that I hoped this man was not setting a dangerous pace that might possibly lead to a breakdown. The physician shook his head. "No," he replied, "as his physician I do not think there is any danger of a crack-up, and the reason is that he is a thoroughly well-organized individual with no energy leaks in his make-up. He operates a well-regulated machine. He handles things with easy power and carries burdens without strain. He never wastes an ounce of energy, but every effort is applied with maximum force."

"How do you account for this efficiency, this seemingly boundless energy?" I asked.

The physician studied for a moment. "The answer is that he is a normal individual, emotionally well integrated, and, what is more important, he is a soundly religious person. From his religion he has learned how to avoid drainage of power. His religion is a workable and useful mechanism for preventing energy leaks. It is not hard work that drains off energy but emotional upheaval, and this man is entirely free from that."

Increasingly people are realizing that the maintenance of a sound spiritual life is important in enjoying energy and personality force.

The body is designed to produce all needed energy over an amazingly long period of time. If the individual takes reasonable care of his body from the standpoint of proper diet, exercise, sleep, no physical abuse, the body will produce and maintain astonishing energy and sustain itself in good health. If he gives similar attention to a well-balanced emotional life, energy will be conserved. But if he allows energy leaks caused by hereditary or self-imposed emotional reaction of a debilitating nature, he will be lacking in vital force. The natural state of the individual when body, mind, and spirit work harmoniously is that of a continuous replacement of necessary energy.

Mrs. Thomas A. Edison, with whom I often discussed the habits and characteristics of her famous husband, the world's greatest inventive wizard, told me that it was Mr. Edison's custom to come into the house from his laboratory after many hours of labor and lie down on his old couch. She said he would fall asleep as naturally as a child, in perfect relaxation, sinking into a deep and untroubled slumber. After three or four, or sometimes five hours he would become instantly wide awake, completely refreshed, and eager to return to his work.

Mrs. Edison, in answer to my request that she analyze her husband's ability to rest in a manner so natural and complete, said, "He was nature's man," by which she meant that he was completely in harmony with nature and with God. In him there were no obsessions, no disorganizations, no conflicts, no mental quirks, no emotional instability. He worked until he needed to sleep, then he slept soundly and arose and returned to his work. He lived for many years, and was in many respects the most creative mind ever to appear on the American continent. He drew his energy from emotional self-mastery, the ability to relax completely. His amazingly harmonious relationship with the universe caused nature to reveal to him its inscrutable secrets.

Every great personality I have ever known, and I have known many, who has demonstrated the capacity for prodigious work has been a person in tune with the Infinite. Every such person seems in harmony with nature and in contact with the Divine energy. They have not necessarily been pious people, but invariably they have been extraordinarily well organized from an emotional and psychological point of view. It is fear, resentment, the projection of parental faults upon people when they are children, inner conflicts and obsessions that throw off balance the finely equated nature, thus causing undue expenditure of natural force.

The longer I live the more I am convinced that neither age nor circumstance needs to deprive us of energy and vitality. We are at last awakening to the close relationship between religion and health. We are beginning to comprehend a basic truth hitherto neglected, that our physical condition is determined very largely by our emotional condition, and our emotional life is profoundly regulated by our thought life.

All through its pages, the Bible talks about vitality and force and life. The supreme over-all word of the Bible is life, and life means vitality—to be filled with energy. Jesus stated the key expression, ". . . I am come that they might have life, and that they might have it more abundantly." (John 10:10) This does not rule out pain or suffering or difficulty, but the clear implication is that if a person practices the creative and re-creative principles of Christianity he can live with power and energy.

The practice of the above-mentioned principles will serve to bring a person into the proper tempo of living. Our energies are destroyed because of the high tempo, the abnormal pace at which we go. The conservation of energy depends upon getting your personality speed synchronized with the rate of God's movement. God is in you. If you are going at one rate and God at another, you are tearing yourself apart. "Though the mills of God grind slowly, yet they grind exceeding small."

The mills of most of us grind very rapidly, and so they grind poorly. When we become attuned to God's rhythm we develop a normal tempo within ourselves and energy flows freely.

The hectic habits of this age have many disastrous effects. A friend of mine commented upon an observation made by her aged father. He said that in early days when a young man came courting in the evening he sat with his intended in the parlor. Time in those days was measured by the deliberate, ponderous strokes of the grandfather clock, which has a very long pendulum. It seemed to say, "There—is—plenty—of—time. There—is—plenty—of—time. There—is—plenty—of—time." But modern clocks, having a shorter pendulum with a swifter stroke, seem to say, "Time to get busy! Time to get busy! Time to get Busy! Time to get Busy!"

Everything is speeded up, and for that reason many people are tired. The solution is to get into the time synchronization of Almighty God. One way to do this is by going out some warm day and lying down on the earth. Get your ear close down to the ground and listen. You will hear all manner of sounds. You will hear the sound of the wind in the trees and the murmur of insects, and you will discover presently that there is in all these sounds a well-regulated tempo. You cannot get that tempo by listening to traffic in the city streets, for it is lost in the confusion of sound. You can get it in church where you hear the word of God and the great hymns. Truth vibrates to God's tempo in a church. But you can also find it in a factory if you have a mind to.

A friend of mine, an industrialist in a large plant in Ohio, told me that the best workmen in his plant are those who get into harmony with the rhythm of the machine on which they are working. He declares that if a worker will work in harmony with the rhythm of his machine he will not be tired at the end of the day. He points out that the machine is an assembling of parts according to the law of God. When you love a machine and get to know it, you will be aware that it has a rhythm. It is one with the rhythm of the body, of the nerves, of the soul. It is in God's rhythm, and you can work with that machine and not get tired if you are in harmony with it. There is a rhythm of the stove, a rhythm of the typewriter, a rhythm of the office, a rhythm of an automobile, a rhythm of your job. So to avoid tiredness and to have energy, feel your way into the essential rhythm of Almighty God and all His works.

To accomplish this, relax physically. Then conceive of your mind as likewise relaxing. Follow this mentally by visualizing the soul as becoming quiescent, then pray as follows: "Dear God, You are the source of all energy. You are the source of the energy in the sun, in the atom, in all flesh, in the bloodstream, in the mind. I hereby draw energy from You as from an illimitable source." Then practice believing that you receive energy. Keep in tune with the Infinite.

Of course many people are tired simply because they are not interested in anything. Nothing ever moves them deeply. To some people it makes no difference what's going on or how things go. Their personal concerns are superior even to all crises in human history. Nothing makes any real difference to them except their own little worries, their desires, and their hates. They wear themselves out stewing around about a lot of inconsequential things that amount to nothing. So they become tired. They even become sick. The surest way not to become tired is to lose yourself in something in which you have a profound conviction.

A famous statesman who made seven speeches in one day was still boundless in energy.

"Why are you not tired after making seven speeches?" I asked.

"Because," he said, "I believe absolutely in everything I said in those speeches. I am enthusiastic about my convictions."

That's the secret. He was on fire for something. He was pouring himself out, and you never lose energy and vitality in so doing. You only lose energy when life becomes dull in your mind. Your mind gets bored and therefore tired doing nothing. You don't have to be tired. Get interested in something. Get absolutely enthralled in something. Throw yourself into it with abandon. Get out of yourself. Be somebody. Do something. Don't sit around moaning about things, reading the papers, and saying, "Why don't they do something?" The man who is out doing something isn't tired. If you're not getting into good causes, no wonder you're tired. You're disintegrating. You're deteriorating. You're dying on the vine. The more you lose yourself in something bigger than yourself, the more energy you will have. You won't have time to think about yourself and get bogged down in your emotional difficulties.

To live with constant energy it is important to get your emotional faults corrected. You will never have full energy until you do.

The late Knute Rockne, one of the greatest football coaches this country ever produced, said that a football player cannot have sufficient energy unless his emotions are under spiritual control. In fact, he went so far as to say that he would not have a man on his team who did not have a genuinely friendly feeling for every fellow player. "I have to get the most energy out of a man," he said, "and have discovered that it cannot be done if he hates another man. Hate blocks his energy and he isn't up to par until he eliminates it and develops a friendly feeling." People who lack energy are disorganized to one degree or another by their deep, fundamental emotional and psychological conflicts. Sometimes the results of this disorganization are extreme, but healing is ever possible.

In a Midwestern city I was asked to talk with a man, formerly a very active citizen of that community, who had suffered an acute decline in vitality. It was thought by his associates that he had had a stroke. This impression was given by the shuffling manner in which he moved, by an extraordinary lethargic attitude, and by his complete detachment of himself from the activities to which he had formerly given a large portion of his time. He sat despondently in his chair hour after hour, and often he would weep. He exhibited many of the symptoms of a nervous breakdown.

I arranged to see him in my hotel room at a certain hour. My door was open and through it I could see the elevator. I chanced to be looking in that direction when the elevator door opened and this man came shuffling down the hall. It seemed that at any moment he would topple over, and he gave every evidence of scarcely being able to negotiate the distance. I asked him to be seated and engaged him in conversation, which conversation was rather fruitless, for it revealed little enlightenment because of his tendency to complain about his condition and his inability to give thoughtful consideration to my questions. This was apparently due to his enormous self-pity.

When I asked him if he would like to be well, he looked up at me in the most intense and pathetic manner. His desperation was revealed by his answer which was that he would give anything in the world if he could regain the energy and the interest in life which he formerly enjoyed.

I began to draw out of him certain facts regarding his life and experience. These were all of a very intimate nature and many of them so deeply imbedded in his consciousness that it was with the utmost difficulty that his personality yielded them up. They had to do with old infantile attitudes, fears that stemmed from earliest days, most of them deriving from the mother-child relationship. Not a few guilt situations appeared. It seemed that over the course of the years these factors had accumulated like drifting sand across the channel of a river. The flow of power was gradually decreased so that an insufficient amount of energy was passing through. The man's mind was in such a complete state of retreating that a process of reasoning and enlightenment seemed quite impossible.

I sought for guidance and found myself, quite to my surprise, standing beside him and placing my hand upon his head. I prayed, asking God to heal the man. I suddenly became aware of what seemed to be the passing of power through my hand which rested upon his head. I hasten to add that there is no healing power in my hand, but now and then a human being is used as a channel, and it was evidently so in this instance, for presently the man looked up with an expression of the utmost happiness and peace and he said simply, "He was here. He touched me. I feel entirely different."

From this time on his improvement was pronounced, and at the present time he is practically his old self again, except for the fact that he now possesses a quiet and serene confidence which was not present previously. Apparently the clogged channel in his personality through which the passage of power had been impeded was opened by an act of faith and the free flow of energy was renewed.

The facts suggested by this incident are that such healings do take place and that a gradual accumulation of psychological factors can cut off the flow of energy. The further fact is stressed that these same factors are susceptible to the power of faith to disintegrate them and thus reopen the channel of Divine human energy within an individual.

The effect of guilt and fear feelings on energy is widely recognized by all authorities having to do with the problems of human nature. The quantity of vital force required to give the personality relief from either guilt or fear or a combination of each is so great that often only a fraction of energy remains for the discharge of the functions of living. Energy drainage occasioned by fear and guilt is of such an amount as to leave little power to be applied to a person's job. The result is that he tires quickly. Not being able to meet the full requirements of his responsibility, he retreats into an apathetic, dull, listless condition and is indeed even ready to give up and fall back sleepily in a state of enervation.

A businessman was referred to me by a psychiatrist whom the patient had been consulting. It appeared that the patient, generally regarded as quite morally strict and upright, had become involved with a married woman. He had attempted to break off this relationship but was encountering resistance from his partner in infidelity, although he had earnestly besought her to abandon their practice and allow him to return to his former state of respectability.

She had threatened him with the possibility that she might enlighten her husband concerning these escapades if he insisted in his desire to cease the relationship. The patient recognized the fact that if the husband became apprised of the situation, it would result in disgrace for him in his community. He happened to be a prominent citizen and prized his high standing.

As a result of his fear of exposure and a sense of guilt he had been unable to sleep or rest. And since this had gone on for two or three months he was in a very serious slump in energy and did not possess the vitality to perform his job efficiently. Inasmuch as some important matters were pending, the situation was serious.

When the psychiatrist suggested that he see me, a clergyman, because of his inability to sleep, he remonstrated by saying there was no way in which a clergyman could correct the condition which caused his sleeplessness, but, on the contrary, he felt that a medical doctor might supply effective medication.

When he stated his attitude to me I simply asked him how he expected to sleep when he had two very annoying and unpleasant bedfellows with whom he was attempting to sleep.

"Bedfellows?' he asked in surprise. "I have no bedfellows."

"Oh, yes, you have," I said, "and there is nobody in this world who can sleep with those two, one on either side."

"What do you mean?" he asked.

I said, "You are trying to sleep every night between fear on one side and guilt on the other, and you are attempting an impossible feat. It makes no difference how many sleeping pills you take, and you admit you have taken many such pills, but they have had no effect upon you. The reason they do not affect you is that they cannot reach the deeper levels of your mind where this sleeplessness originates and which is siphoning off your energy. You must eradicate fear and guilt before you will ever be able to sleep and regain your strength."

We dealt with the fear which was of exposure by the simple expedient of getting him ready in mind to face whatever might ensue as a result of doing the right thing, which was of course to break off the relationship regardless of consequences. I assured him that whatever he did that was right would turn out right. One never does wrong by doing right. I urged him to put the matter in God's hands and simply do the right thing, leaving the outcome to God.

He did that, not without trepidation, but with considerable sincerity just the same. The woman, either through shrewdness or some expression of her own better nature or through the more doubtful expedient of transferring her affections elsewhere, released him.

The guilt was handled by seeking God's forgiveness. When this is sincerely sought it is never denied, and our patient found surcease and relief. It was astonishing how when this double weight was lifted from his mind his personality once again began to function normally. He was able to sleep. He found peace and renewal of strength. Energy quickly returned. A wiser and thankful man, he became able to carry on his normal activities.

A not infrequent case of diminishing energy is staleness. The pressure, monotony, and unceasing continuity of responsibilities dull the freshness of mind which a person must have to approach his work successfully. As an athlete goes stale so does the individual, whatever his occupation, tend to come upon dry and arid periods. During such a condition of mind the expenditure of greater energy is required to do with difficulty what one formerly did with comparative ease. As a result the vital powers are hard put to it to supply the force required, and the individual often loses his grip and power.

A solution for this state of mind was employed by a prominent business leader, president of the board of trustees of a certain university. A professor who had formerly been outstanding and extraordinarily popular had begun to slip in teaching ability and in the power to interest students. It was the verdict of the students as well as the private opinion of the trustees that this teacher must either recover his former capacity to teach with interest and enthusiasm or it would be necessary to replace him. This latter expedient was entertained with hesitancy for the reason that there still remained a normal expectancy of several active years before he reached the age of retirement.

The businessman above referred to asked the professor to come to his office and announced to him that the board of trustees was giving him a six months' leave of absence with all expenses paid and with full salary. There was only one stipulation, and that was that he go away to a place of rest and give himself over to gaining a complete renewal of strength and energy.

The businessman invited him to use a cabin which he himself owned in a wilderness setting and made the curious suggestion that he take no books except one book, the Bible. He suggested that the professor's daily program be walking, fishing, and some manual work in the garden; that he read the Bible every day for such a period as would enable him to read the Book through three times in the six months. He further suggested that he memorize as many passages as possible for the purpose of saturating his mind with the great words and ideas which the Book contains.

The businessman said, "I believe that if you spend six months outdoors chopping wood, digging in the soil, reading the Bible, and fishing in the deep lakes you will become a new man."

The professor agreed to this unique proposal. His adjustment to this radically different mode of life was an easier one than he or anyone who knew him expected. In fact, he was surprised to find that he actually liked it. After he became conditioned to active outdoor living he discovered that it had an immense appeal for him. He missed his intellectual associates and his reading for a while, but forced back upon the Bible, his only book, he became immersed in it, and to his amazement found, as he put it, "a library within itself." In its pages he found faith and peace and power. In six months he was a new man.

The businessman now tells me that this professor has become, as he puts it, "a person of compelling power." Staleness passed away, the old-time energy returned, power surged back, zest for living was renewed.

4

TRY PRAYER POWER

In a business office high above the city streets two men were having a serious conversation. One, heavily troubled by a business and personal crisis, paced the floor restlessly, then sat dejectedly, head in hand, a picture of despair. He had come to the other for advice, since he was considered a man of great understanding. Together they had explored the problem from every angle but seemingly without result, which only served to deepen the troubled man's discouragement. "I guess no power on earth can save me," he sighed.

The other reflected for a moment, then spoke rather diffidently. "I wouldn't look at it that way. I believe you are wrong in saying there is no power that can save you. Personally, I have found that there is an answer to every problem. There is a power that can help you." Then slowly he asked, "Why not try prayer power?"

Somewhat surprised, the discouraged man said, "Of course I believe in prayer, but perhaps I do not know how to pray. You speak of it as something practical that fits a business problem. I never thought of it that way but I'm willing to try prayer if you will show me how."

He did apply practical prayer techniques and in due course got his answer. Matters ultimately turned out satisfactorily. That is not to say he did not have difficulties. In fact, he had rather a hard time of it but ultimately he worked out of this trouble. Now he believes in prayer power so enthusiastically that I recently heard him say, "Every problem can be solved and solved right if you pray."

Experts in physical health and well-being often utilize prayer in their therapy. Disability, tension, and kindred troubles may result from a lack of inner harmony. It is remarkable how prayer restores the harmonious functioning of body and soul. A friend of mine, a physiotherapist, told a nervous man to whom he was giving a massage, "God works through my fingers as I seek to relax your physical body, which is the temple of your soul. While I work on your outward being, I want you to pray for God's relaxation inwardly." It was a new idea to the patient, but he happened to be in a receptive mood and he tried passing some peace thoughts through his mind. He was amazed at the relaxing effect this had on him.

Jack Smith, operator of a health club, which is patronized by many outstanding people, believes in the therapy of prayer and uses it. He was at one time a prize fighter, then a truck driver, later a taxi driver, and finally opened his health club. He says that while he probes his patrons for physical flabbiness he also probes for spiritual flabbiness because, he declares, "You can't get a man physically healthy until you get him spiritually healthy."

One day Walter Huston, the actor, sat by Jack Smith's desk. He noted a big sign on the wall on which were penciled the following letters: A P R P B W P R A A. In surprise Huston asked, "What do those letters mean?"

Smith laughed and said, "They stand for 'Affirmative Prayers Release Powers By Which Positive Results Are Accomplished.' "

Huston's jaw dropped in astonishment. "Well, I never expected to hear anything like that in a health club."

"I use methods like that," said Smith, "to make people curious so they will ask what those letters mean. That gives me an opportunity to tell them that I believe affirmative prayers always get results."

Jack Smith, who helps men to keep physically fit, believes that prayer is an important, if not more important, than exercise, steam baths, and a rubdown. It is a vital part of the power-releasing process.

People are doing more praying today than formerly because they find that it adds to personal efficiency. Prayer helps them to tap forces and to utilize strength not otherwise available.

A famous psychologist says, "Prayer is the greatest power available to the individual in solving his personal problems. Its power astonishes me."

Prayer power is a manifestation of energy. Just as there exist scientific techniques for the release of atomic energy, so are there scientific procedures for the release of spiritual energy through the mechanism of prayer. Exciting demonstrations of this energizing force are evident.

Prayer power seems able even to normalize the aging process, obviating or limiting infirmity and deterioration. You need not lose your basic energy or vital power or become weak and listless merely as a result of accumulating years. It is not necessary to allow your spirit to sag or grow stale or dull. Prayer can freshen you up every evening and send you out renewed each morning. You can receive guidance in problems if prayer is allowed to permeate your subconscious, the seat of the forces which determines whether you take right or wrong actions. Prayer has the power to keep your reactions correct and sound. Prayer driven deeply into your subconscious can remake you. It releases and keeps power flowing freely.

If you have not experienced this power, perhaps you need to learn new techniques of prayer. It is well to study prayer from an efficiency point of view. Usually the emphasis is entirely religious though no cleavage exists between the two concepts. Scientific spiritual practice rules out stereotyped procedure even as it does in general science. If you have been praying in a certain manner, even if it has brought you blessings, which it doubtless has, perhaps you can pray even more profitably by varying the pattern and by experimenting with fresh prayer formulas. Get new insights; practice new skills to attain greatest results.

It is important to realize that you are dealing with the most tremendous power in thc world when you pray. You would not use an old-fashioned kerosene lamp for illumination. You want the most up-to-date lighting devices. New and frcsh spiritual techniques are being constantly discovered by men and women of spiritual genius. It is advisable to experiment with prayer power according to such methods as prove sound and effective. If this sounds new and strangely scientific, bear in mind that the secret of prayer is to find the process that will most effectively open your mind humbly to God. Any method through which you can stimulate the power of God to flow into your mind is legitimate and usable.

An illustration of a scientific use of prayer is the experience of two famous industrialists, whose names would be known to many readers were I permitted to mention them, who had a conference about a business and technical matter. One might think that these men would approach such a problem on a purely technical basis, and they did that and more; they also prayed about it. But they did not get a successful result.

Therefore, they called in a country preacher, an old friend of one of them, because, as they explained, the Bible prayer formula is, "Where two or three are gathered together in my name, there am I in the midst of them." (Matthew 18:20) They also pointed to a further formula, namely, "If two of you shall agree on earth as touching any thing that they shall ask, it shall be done for them of my Father which is in heaven." (Matthew 18:19)

Being schooled in scientific practice, they believe that in dealing with prayer as a phenomenon they should scrupulously follow the formulas outlined in the Bible which they described as the textbook of spiritual science. The proper method for employing a science is to use the accepted formulas outlined in the textbook of that science. They reasoned that if the Bible provides that two or three should be gathered together, perhaps the reason they were not succeeding was that they needed a third party.

Therefore the three men prayed, and to guard against error in the process they also brought to bear on the problem various other Biblical techniques such as those suggested in the statements: "According to your faith be it unto you." (Matthew 9:29) "What things soever ye desire, when ye pray, believe that ye receive them, and ye shall have them." (Mark 11:24)

After several thoroughgoing sessions of prayer the three men together affirmed that they had received the answer. The outcome was entirely satisfactory. Subsequent results indicated that Divine guidance was actually obtained.

These men are great enough scientists not to require precise explanation of the operation of these spiritual laws any more than in the case of naturalistic laws but are content with the fact that the law does operate when "proper" techniques are employed.

"While we cannot explain it," they said, "the fact remains that we were baffled by our problem and we tried prayer according to the formulas in the New Testament. That method worked and we got a beautiful result." They did add that it seemed to them that faith and harmony are important factors in the prayer process.

A man opened a small business in New York City a number of years ago, his first establishment being, as he characterized it, "a little hole in the wall." He had one employee. In a few years they moved into a larger room and then into extensive quarters. It became a very successful operation.

This man's method of business as he described it was "to fill the little hole in the wall with optimistic prayers and thoughts." He declared that hard work, positive thinking, fair dealing, right treatment of people, and the proper kind of praying always get results. This man, who has a creative and unique mind, worked out his own simple formula for solving his problems and overcoming his difficulties through prayer power. It is a curious formula but I have practiced it and personally know that it works. I have suggested it to many people who also found real value in its use. It is recommended to you.

The formula is (1) PRAYERIZE, (2) PICTURIZE, (3) ACTUALIZE.

By "prayerize" my friend meant a daily system of creative prayer. When a problem arose he talked it over with God very simply and directly in prayer. Moreover, he did not talk with God as to some vast and far-off shadowy being but conceived of God as being with him in his office, in his home, on the street, in his automobile, always nearby as a partner, as a close associate. He took seriously the Biblical injunction to "pray without ceasing." He interpreted it as meaning that he should go about every day discussing with God in a natural, normal manner the questions that had to be decided and dealt with. The Presence came finally to dominate his conscious and ultimately his unconscious thinking. He "prayerized" his daily life. He prayed as he walked or drove his car or performed other everyday activities. He filled his daily life full of prayer—that is, he lived by prayer. He did not often kneel to offer his prayers but would, for example, say to God as to a close associate, "What will I do about this, Lord?" or "Give me a fresh insight on this, Lord." He prayerized his mind and so prayerized his activities.

The second point in his formula of creative prayer is to "picturize." The basic factor in physics is force. The basic factor in psychology is the realizable wish. The man who assumes success tends already to have success. People who assume failure tend to have failure. When either failure or success is picturized it strongly tends to actualize in terms equivalent to the mental image pictured.

To assure something worthwhile happening, first pray about it and test it according to God's will; then print a picture of it on your mind as happening, holding the picture firmly in consciousness. Continue to surrender the picture to God's will—that is to say, put the matter in God's hands—and follow God's guidance. Work hard and intelligently, thus doing your part to achieve success in the matter. Practice believing and continue to hold the picturization firmly in your thoughts. Do this and you will be astonished at the strange ways in which the picturization comes to pass. In this manner the picture "actualizes." That which you have "prayerized" and "picturized" "actualizes" according to the pattern of your basic realizable wish when conditioned by invoking God's power upon it, and if, moreover, you give fully of yourself to its realization.

I have personally practiced this three-point prayer method and find great power in it. It has been suggested to others who have likewise reported that it released creative power into their experience.

For example, a woman discovered that her husband was drifting from her. Theirs had been a happy marriage, but the wife had become preoccupied in social affairs and the husband had gotten busy in his work. Before they knew it, the close, old-time companionship was lost. One day she discovered his interest in another woman. She lost her head and became hysterical. She consulted her minister, who adroitly turned the conversation to herself. She admitted being a careless homemaker and that she had also become self-centered, sharp-tongued, and nagging.

She then confessed that she had never felt herself the equal of her husband. She had a profound sense of inferiority regarding him, feeling unable to maintain equality with him socially and intellectually. So she retreated into an antagonistic attitude that manifested itself in petulance and criticism.

The minister saw that the woman had more talent, ability, and charm than she was revealing. He suggested that she create an image or picture of herself as capable and attractive. He whimsically told her that "God runs a beauty parlor" and that faith techniques could put beauty on a person's face and charm and ease in her manner. He gave her instruction in how to pray and how spiritually to "picturize." He also advised her to hold a mental image of the restoration of the old-time companionship, to visualize the goodness in her husband, and to picture a restored harmony between the two of them. She was to hold this picture with faith. In this manner he prepared her for a most interesting personal victory.

About this time her husband informed her that he wanted a divorce. She had conquered herself to the extent of being able to receive this request with calmness. She simply replied that she was willing if he wanted it, but suggested a deferral of the decision for ninety days on the ground that divorce is so final. "If at the end of ninety days you still feel that you want a divorce, I will cooperate with you." She said this calmly. He gave her a quizzical look, for he had expected an outburst.

Night after night he went out, and night after night she sat at home, but she pictured him as seated in his old chair. He was not in the chair, but she painted an image of him there comfortably reading as in the old days. She visualized him puttering around the house, painting and fixing things as he had formerly done. She even pictured him drying the dishes as he did when they were first married. She visualized the two of them playing golf together and taking hikes as they once did.

She maintained this picture with steady faith, and one night there he actually sat in his old chair. She looked twice to be sure that it was the reality rather than the picturization, but perhaps a picturization is a reality, for at any rate the actual man was there. Occasionally he would be gone but more and more nights he sat in his chair. Then he began to read to her as in the old days. Then one sunny Saturday afternoon he asked, "What do you say to a game of golf?"

The days went by pleasantly until she realized that the ninetieth day had arrived, so that evening she said quietly, "Bill, this is the ninetieth day."

"What do you mean?" he asked, puzzled, "the ninetieth day?"

"Why, don't you remember? We agreed to wait ninety days to settle that divorce matter and this is the day."

He looked at her for a moment, then hidden behind his paper turned a page, saying, "Don't be silly. I couldn't possibly get along without you. Where did you ever get the idea I was going to leave you?"

The formula proved a powerful mechanism. She prayerized, she picturized, and the sought-for result was actualized. Prayer power solved her problem and his as well.

I have known many people who have successfully applied this technique not only to personal affairs but to business matters as well. When sincerely and intelligently brought into situations, the results have been so excellent that this must be regarded as an extraordinarily efficient method of prayer. People who take this method seriously and actually use it get astonishing results.

At an industrial convention banquet I was seated at the speaker's table next to a man who, though a bit on the rough side, was very likable. He may have felt a bit cramped by his proximity to a preacher, which obviously wasn't his usual company. During the dinner he used a number of theological words, but they were not put together in a theological manner. After each outburst he apologized, but I advised him that I had heard all those words before.

He told me he had been a church attendant as a boy but "had gotten away from it." He gave me that old story which I have heard all my life and which even now people will get off as something entirely new, viz., "When I was a boy my father made me go to Sunday school and church and crammed religion down my throat. So when I got away from home I couldn't take it any more and have seldom been to church since."

This man then observed that "perhaps he should start going to church since he was getting old." I commented that he would be lucky to find a seat. This surprised him for he "did not think anybody went to church anymore." I told him that more people attend church each week than frequent any other institution in the country. This rather bowled him over.

He was head of a medium-sized business and he fell to telling me how much money his firm took in last year. I told him I knew quite a few churches whose take exceeded that. This really hit him in the solar plexus, and I noted his respect for the church mounting by leaps and bounds. I told him about the thousands of religious books that are sold, more than any other type of book. "Maybe you fellows in the church are on the ball at that," he slangily remarked.

At this moment another man came up to our table and enthusiastically told me that "something wonderful" had happened to him. He said he had been very depressed, for things hadn't been going well with him. He decided to get away for a week or so and on this vacation read one of my books* in which practical faith techniques are outlined. He said this brought him the first satisfaction and peace he had felt. It encouraged him as to his own possibilities. He began to believe that the answer to his trouble was practical religion.

"So," he said, "I began to practice the spiritual principles presented in your book. I began to believe and affirm that with God's help the objectives I was endeavoring to accomplish could be achieved. A feeling came over me that everything was going to be all right, and from then on nothing could upset me. I absolutely knew it was going to be O.K. So I began to sleep better and feel better. I felt as if I had taken a tonic. My new understanding and practice of spiritual techniques were the turning point."

When he left us, my table companion, who had listened in on this recital, said, "I never heard anything like that before. That fellow talks about religion as happy and workable. It was never presented to me that way. He also gives the impression that religion is almost a science, that you can use it to improve your health and do better in your job. I never thought of religion in that connection."

* A *Guide to Confident Living*. Prentice-Hall, Inc., Englewood Cliffs, N.J., 1948.

Then he added, "But do you know what struck me? It was the look on that guy's face."

Now the curious fact is that when my table companion made that statement a semblance of the same look was on his own face. For the first time he was getting the idea that religious faith is not something piously stuffy but is a scientific procedure for successful living. He was observing at firsthand the practical working of prayer power in personal experience.

Personally, I believe that prayer is a sending out of vibrations from one person to another and to God. All of the universe is in vibration. There are vibrations in the molecules of a table. The air is filled with vibrations. The reaction between human beings is also in vibration. When you send out a prayer for another person, you employ the force inherent in a spiritual universe. You transport from yourself to the other person a sense of love, helpfulness, support—a sympathetic, powerful understanding—and in this process you awaken vibrations in the universe through which God brings to pass the good objectives prayed for. Experiment with this principle and you will know its amazing results.

For example, I have a habit, which I often use, of praying for people as I pass them. I remember being on a train traveling through West Virginia when I had a curious thought. I saw a man standing on a station platform, then the train moved on and he passed from sight. It occurred to me that I was seeing him for the first and last time. His life and mine touched lightly for just a fraction of an instant. He went his way and I went mine. I wondered how his life would turn out.

Then I prayed for that man, sending out an affirmative prayer that his life would be filled with blessings. Then I began praying for other people I saw as the train passed. I prayed for a man plowing in the field and asked the Lord to help him and give him a good crop. I saw a mother hanging up clothes, and that line of freshly washed garments told me she had a large family. A glimpse of her face and the way in which she handled the clothes of the children told me she was a happy woman. I prayed for her, that she would have a happy life, that her husband would always be true to her and that she would be true to him. I prayed that they might be a religious family and that the children would grow up strong, honorable young people.

In one station I saw a man leaning half asleep against a wall, and I prayed that he would wake up and get off relief and amount to something.

Then we stopped at a station, and there was a lovable little kid, one pants leg longer than the other, shirt open at the neck, wearing a too-big sweater, hair tousled, face dirty. He was sucking a lollipop and working hard on it. I prayed for him, and as the train started to move he looked up at me and gave me the most wonderful smile. I knew my prayer had caught him, and I waved to him, and he waved back at me. I shall never see that boy again in all likelihood, but our lives touched. It had been a cloudy day up to that point, but suddenly the sun came out and I think there was a light in the boy's heart, for it was revealed on his face. I know that my heart felt happy. I am sure it was because the power of God was moving in a circuit through me, to the boy and back to God; and we were all under the spell of prayer power.

One of the important functions of prayer is as a stimulus to creative ideas. Within the mind are all of the resources needed for successful living. Ideas are present in consciousness which, when released and given scope together with proper implementation, can lead to the successful operation of any project or undertaking. When the New Testament says, "The kingdom of God is within you," (Luke 17:21) it is informing us that God our Creator has laid up within our minds and personalities all the potential powers and ability we need for constructive living. It remains for us to tap and develop these powers.

For example, a man of my acquaintance is connected with a business where he is the chief of four executives. At regular intervals these men have what they call an "idea session," the purpose of which is to tap all the creative ideas lurking in the minds of any of the four. For this session they use a room without telephones, buzzers, or other usual office equipment. The double window is fully insulated so that street noises are for the most part eliminated.

Before starting the session the group spends ten minutes in silent prayer and meditation. They conceive of God as creatively working in their minds. Each in his own way silently prays, affirming that God is about to release from his mind the proper ideas needed in the business.

Following the quiet period all start talking, pouring out ideas that have come to their minds. Memos of the ideas are written upon cards and thrown on the table. No one is permitted to criticize any idea at this particular juncture for argument might stop the flow of creative thought. The cards are gathered up and each one is evaluated at a later session; but this is the idea-tapping session, stimulated by prayer power.

When this practice was inaugurated a high percentage of the ideas suggested proved to be without particular value, but as the sessions continued the percentage of good ideas increased. Now many of the best suggestions which have later demonstrated their practical value were evolved in the "idea session."

As one of the executives explained, "We have come up with insights that not only show on our balance sheet but we have also gained a new feeling of confidence. Moreover, there is a deeper feeling of fellowship among the four of us and this has spread to others in the organization."

Where is the old-fashioned businessman who says that religion is theoretical and has no place in business? Today any successful and competent businessman will employ the latest and best-tested methods in production, distribution, and administration, and many are discovering that one of the greatest of all efficiency methods is prayer power.

Alert people everywhere are finding that by trying prayer power they feel better, work better, do better, sleep better, are better.

My friend Grove Patterson, editor of the Toledo *Blade*, is a man of remarkable vigor. He says that his energy results, in part at least from his methods of prayer. For example, he likes to fall asleep while praying, for he believes that his subconscious is most relaxed at that time. It is in the subconscious that our life is largely governed. If you drop a prayer into the subconscious at the moment of its greatest relaxation, the prayer has a powerful effect. Mr. Patterson chuckled as he said, "Once it worried me because I would fall asleep while praying. Now I actually try to have it so."

Many unique methods of prayer have come to my attention, but one of the most effective is that advocated by Frank Laubach in his excellent book, *Prayer, the Mightiest Power in the World*. I regard this as one of the most practical books on prayer, for it outlines fresh prayer techniques that work. Dr. Laubach believes that actual power is generated by prayer. One of his methods is to walk down the street and "shoot" prayers at people. He calls this type of praying, "flash prayers." He bombards passers-by with prayers, sending out thoughts of good will, and love. He says that people passing him on the street as he "shoots" prayers at them often turn around and look at him and smile. They feel the emanation of a power like electrical energy.

In a bus he "shoots" prayers at his fellow passengers. Once he was sitting behind a man who seemed to be very gloomy. He had noticed when he entered the bus that the man had a scowl on his face. He began to send out toward him prayers of good will and faith, conceiving of these prayers as surrounding him and driving into his mind. Suddenly the man began to stroke the back of his head, and when he left the bus the scowl was gone and a smile had replaced it. Dr. Laubach believes that he has often changed the entire atmosphere of a car or bus full of people by the process of "swishing love and prayers all around the place."

In a Pullman club car a half-intoxicated man was quite boorish and rude, talking in an overbearing manner and generally making himself obnoxious. I felt that everyone in the car took a dislike to him. Halfway down the car from him I determined to try Frank Laubach's method. So I started to pray for him, meanwhile visualizing his better self and sending out thoughts of good will toward him. Presently, for no seemingly apparent reason, the man turned in my direction, gave me a most disarming smile, and raised his hand in the gesture of salute. His attitude changed and he became quiet. I have every reason to believe that the prayer thoughts effectively reached out toward him.

It is my practice before making a speech to any audience to pray for the people present and to send out thoughts of love and good will toward them. Sometimes I select out of the audience one or two people who seem to be either depressed or even antagonistic and send my prayer thoughts and good-will attitude specifically toward them. Recently addressing a Chamber of Commerce annual dinner in a southwestern city, I noted a man in the audience who seemed to be scowling at me. It was altogether possible that his facial expression was not in any way related to me, but he seemed antagonistic. Before starting to speak I prayed for him and "shot" a series of prayers and good-will thoughts in his direction. As I spoke, I continued to do this.

When the meeting was over, while shaking hands with those around me, suddenly my hand was caught in a tremendous clasp and I was looking into the face of this man. He was smiling broadly. "Frankly I did not like you when I came to this meeting," he said. "I do not like preachers and saw no reason for having you, a minister, as speaker at our Chamber of Commerce dinner. I was hoping that your speech would not be successful. However, as you spoke something seemed to touch me. I feel like a new person. I had a strange sense of peace—and doggone it, I like you!"

It was not my speech that had this effect. It was the emanation of prayer power. In our brains we have about two billion little storage batteries. The human brain can send off power by thoughts and prayers. The human body's magnetic power has actually been tested. We have thousands of little sending stations, and when these are tuned up by prayer it is possible for a tremendous power to flow through a person and to pass between human beings. We can send off power by prayer which acts as both a sending and receiving station.

There was a man, an alcoholic, with whom I had been working. He had been "dry" (as the Alcoholics Anonymous term it) for about six months. He was on a business trip, and one Tuesday afternoon about four o'clock I had a strong impression that he was in trouble. This man dominated my thoughts. I felt something drawing me so I dropped everything and started praying for him. I prayed for about a half-hour, then the impression seemed to let up and I discontinued my prayers.

A few days later he telephoned me. "I have been in Boston all week," he said, "and I want you to know I'm still 'dry,' but early in the week I had a very hard time."

"Was it on Tuesday at four o'clock?" I asked.

Astonished, he replied, "Why, yes, how did you know? Who told you?"

"Nobody told me," I replied. "That is, no human told me." I described my feelings concerning him on Tuesday at four o'clock and told about praying for him for half an hour.

He was astounded, and explained, "I was at the hotel and stopped in front of the bar. I had a terrible struggle with myself. I thought of you, for I needed help badly right then, and I started to pray."

Those prayers starting out from him reached me, and I began to pray for him. Both of us joining in prayer completed the circuit and reached God, and the man got his answer in the form of strength to meet the crisis. And what did he do?

He went to a drugstore, bought a box of candy, and ate all of it without stopping. That pulled him through, he declared—"prayer and candy."

A young married woman admitted she was filled with hates, jealousy, and resentment toward neighbors and friends. She was also very apprehensive, always worrying about her children, whether they would be sick or get into an accident or fail in school. Her life was a pathetic mixture of dissatisfaction, fear, hate, and unhappiness. I asked her if she ever prayed. She said, "Only when I get so up against it that I am just desperate; but I must admit that prayer doesn't mean anything to me, so I don't pray very often."

I suggested that the practice of real prayer could change her life and gave her some instructions in sending out love thoughts instead of hate thoughts and confidence thoughts instead of fear thoughts. I suggested that every day at the time for the children to come home from school she pray, and make her prayers an affirmation of God's protective goodness. Doubtful at first, she became one of the most enthusiastic advocates and practicers of prayer I have ever known. She avidly reads books and pamphlets and practices every effective prayer-power technique. This procedure revamped her life as is illustrated by the following letter which she wrote me recently:

"I feel that my husband and I have both made wonderful progress in the last few weeks. My greatest progress dates from the night you told me that 'every day is a good day if you pray.' I began to put into practice the idea of affirming that this would be a good day the minute I woke up in the morning, and *I can positively say that I have not had a bad or upsetting day since that time.* The amazing thing is that my days actually haven't been any smoother or any more free from petty annoyances than they ever were, but they just don't seem to have the power to upset me any more. Every night I begin my prayers by listing all the things for which I am grateful, little things that happened during the day which added to the happiness of my day. I know that this habit has geared my mind to pick out the nice things and forget the unpleasant ones. The fact that for six weeks I have not had a single bad day and have refused to get downhearted with anyone is really marvelous to me."

She discovered amazing power in trying prayer power.

You can do the same. Following are ten rules for getting effective results from prayer:

1. Set aside a few minutes every day. Do not say anything. Simply practice thinking about God. This will make your mind spiritually receptive.

2. Then pray orally, using simple, natural words. Tell God anything that is on your mind. Do not think you must use stereotyped pious phrases. Talk to God in your own language. He understands it.

3. Pray as you go about the business of the day, on the subway or bus or at your desk. Utilize minute prayers by closing your eyes to shut out the world and concentrating briefly on God's presence. The more you do this every day the nearer you will feel God's presence.

4. Do not always ask when you pray, but instead affirm that God's blessings are being given, and spend most of your prayers giving thanks.

5. Pray with the belief that sincere prayers can reach out and surround your loved ones with God's love and protection.

6. Never use a negative thought in prayer. Only positive thoughts get results.

7. Always express willingness to accept God's will. Ask for what you want, but be willing to take what God gives you. It may be better than what you ask for.

8. Practice the attitude of putting everything in God's hands. Ask for the ability to do your best and to leave the results confidently to God.

9. Pray for people you do not like or who have mistreated you. Resentment is blockade number one of spiritual power.

10. Make a list of people for whom to pray. The more you pray for other people, especially those not connected with you, the more prayer results will come back to you.

5

HOW TO CREATE YOUR OWN HAPPINESS

Who decides whether you shall be happy or unhappy? The answer—you do!

A television celebrity had as a guest on his program an aged man. And he was a very rare old man indeed. His remarks were entirely unpremeditated and of course absolutely unrehearsed. They simply bubbled up out of a personality that was radiant and happy. And whenever he said anything, it was so naïve, so apt, that the audience roared with laughter. They loved him. The celebrity was impressed, and enjoyed it with the others.

Finally he asked the old man why he was so happy. "You must have a wonderful secret of happiness," he suggested.

"No," replied the old man, "I haven't any great secret. It's just as plain as the nose on your face. When I get up in the morning," he explained, "I have two choices—either to be happy or to be unhappy, and what do you think I do? I just choose to be happy, and that's all there is to it."

That may seem an oversimplification, and it may appear that the old man was superficial, but I recall that Abraham Lincoln, whom nobody could accuse of being superficial, said that people were just about as happy as they made up their minds to be. You can be unhappy if you want to be. It is the easiest thing in the world to accomplish. Just choose unhappiness. Go around telling yourself that things aren't going well, that nothing is satisfactory, and you can be quite sure of being unhappy. But say to yourself, "Things are going nicely. Life is good. I choose happiness," and you can be quite certain of having your choice.

Children are more expert in happiness than adults. The adult who can carry the spirit of a child into middle and old age is a genius, for he will preserve the truly happy spirit with which God endowed the young. The subtlety of Jesus Christ is remarkable, for He tells us that the way to live in this world is to have the childlike heart and mind. In other words, never get old or dull or jaded in spirit. Don't become super-sophisticated.

My little daughter Elizabeth, aged nine, has the answer to happiness. One day I asked her, "Are you happy, honey?"

"Sure I'm happy," she replied.

"Are you always happy?" I asked.

"Sure," she answered, "I'm always happy."

"What makes you happy?" I asked her.

"Why, I don't know," she said, "I'm just happy."

"There must be something that makes you happy," I urged.

"Well," she said, "I'll tell you what it is. My playmates, they make me happy. I like them. My school makes me happy. I like to go to school. (I didn't say anything, but she never got that from me.) I like my teachers. And I like to go to church. I like Sunday school and my Sunday-school teacher. I love my sister Margaret and my brother John. I love my mother and father. They take care of me when I'm sick, and they love me and are good to me."

That is Elizabeth's formula for happiness, and it seems to me that it's all there—her playmates (that's her associates), her school (the place where she works), her church and Sunday school (where she worships), her sister, brother, mother, and father (that means the home circle where love is found). There you have happiness in a nutshell, and the happiest time of your life is in relation to those factors.

A group of boys and girls were asked to list the things that made them happiest. Their answers were rather touching. Here is the boys' list: "A swallow flying; looking into deep, clear water; water being cut at the bow of a boat; a fast train rushing; a builder's crane lifting something heavy; my dog's eyes."

And here is what the girls said made them happy: "Street lights on the river; red roofs in the trees; smoke rising from a chimney; red velvet;

the moon in the clouds." There is something in the beautiful essence of the universe that is expressed, though only half-articulated, by these things. To become a happy person have a clean soul, eyes that see romance in the commonplace, a child's heart, and spiritual simplicity.

Many of us manufacture our own unhappiness. Of course not all unhappiness is self-created, for social conditions are responsible for not a few of our woes. Yet it is a fact that to a large extent by our thoughts and attitudes we distill out of the ingredients of life either happiness or unhappiness for ourselves.

"Four people out of five are not so happy as they can be," declares an eminent authority, and he adds, "Unhappiness is the most common state of mind." Whether human happiness strikes as low a level as this, I would hesitate to say, but I do find more people living unhappy lives than I would care to compute. Since a fundamental desire of every human being is for that state of existence called happiness, something should be done about it. Happiness is achievable and the process for obtaining it is not complicated. Anyone who desires it, who wills it, and who learns and applies the right formula may become a happy person.

In a railroad dining car I sat across from a husband and wife, strangers to me. The lady was expensively dressed, as the furs, diamonds, and costume which she wore indicated. But she was having a most unpleasant time with herself. Rather loudly she proclaimed that the car was dingy and drafty, the service abominable, and the food most unpalatable. She complained and fretted about everything.

Her husband, on the contrary, was a genial, affable, easygoing man who obviously had the capacity to take things as they came. I thought he seemed a bit embarrassed by his wife's critical attitude and somewhat disappointed, too, as he was taking her on this trip for pleasure.

To change the conversation he asked what business I was in, and then said that he was a lawyer. Then he made a big mistake, for with a grin he added, "My wife is in the manufacturing business."

This was surprising, for she did not seem to be the industrial or executive type, so I asked, "What does she manufacture?"

"Unhappiness," he replied. "She manufactures her own unhappiness."

Despite the icy coolness that settled upon the table following this ill-advised observation, I was grateful for his remark, for it describes exactly what so many people do—"They manufacture their own unhappiness."

It is a pity, too, for there are so many problems created by life itself that dilute our happiness that it is indeed most foolish to distill further unhappiness within your own mind. How foolish to manufacture personal unhappiness to add to all the other difficulties over which you have little or no control!

Rather than to emphasize the manner in which people manufacture their own unhappiness, let us proceed to the formula for putting an end to this misery-producing process. Suffice it to say that we manufacture our unhappiness by thinking unhappy thoughts, by the attitudes which we habitually take, such as the negative feeling that everything is going to turn out badly, or that other people are getting what they do not deserve and we are failing to get what we do deserve.

Our unhappiness is further distilled by saturating the consciousness with feelings of resentment, ill will, and hate. The unhappiness-producing process always makes important use of the ingredients of fear and worry. Each of these matters is dealt with elsewhere in this book. We merely want to make the point at the present time and stress it forcefully that a very large proportion of the unhappiness of the average individual is self-manufactured. How, then, may we proceed to produce not unhappiness but happiness?

An incident from one of my railroad journeys may suggest an answer. One morning in an old-style Pullman car approximately a half-dozen of us were shaving in the men's lounge. As always in such close and crowded quarters after a night on the train, this group of strangers was not disposed to be gay, and there was little conversation and that little was mostly mumbled.

Then a man came in wearing on his face a broad smile. He greeted us all with a cheery good morning, but received rather unenthusiastic grunts in return. As he went about his shaving he was humming, probably quite unconsciously, a gay little tune. It got a bit on the nerves of some of the men. Finally one said rather sarcastically, "You certainly seem to be happy this morning! Why all the cheer?"

"Yes," the man answered, "as a matter of fact, I am happy. I do feel cheerful." Then he added, "I make it a habit to be happy."

That is all that was said, but I am sure that each man in that lounge left the train with those interesting words in mind, "I make it a habit to be happy."

The statement is really very profound, for our happiness or unhappiness depends to an important degree upon the habit of mind we cultivate. That collection of wise sayings, the book of Proverbs, tells us that ". . . he that is of a merry heart hath a continual feast." (Proverbs 15:15) In other words, cultivate the merry heart; that is, develop the happiness habit, and life will become a continual feast, which is to say you can enjoy life every day. Out of the happiness habit comes a happy life. And because we can cultivate a habit, we therefore have the power to create our own happiness.

The happiness habit is developed by simply practicing happy thinking. Make a mental list of happy thoughts and pass them through your mind several times every day. If an unhappiness thought should enter your mind, immediately stop, consciously eject it, and substitute a happiness thought. Every morning before arising, lie relaxed in bed and deliberately drop happy thoughts into your conscious mind. Let a series of pictures pass across your mind of each happy experience you expect to have during the day. Savor their joy. Such thoughts will help cause events to turn out that way. Do not affirm that things will not go well that day. By merely saying that, you can actually help to make it so. You will draw to yourself every factor, large and small, that will contribute to unhappy conditions. As a result, you will find yourself asking, "Why does everything go badly for me? What is the matter with everything?"

The reason can be directly traced to the manner in which you began the day in your thoughts.

Tomorrow try this plan instead. When you arise, say out loud three times this one sentence, "This is the day which the Lord hath made; we will rejoice and be glad in it." (Psalm 118:24) Only personalize it and say, "I will rejoice and be glad in it." Repeat it in a strong, clear voice and with positive tone and emphasis. The statement, of course, is from the Bible and it is a good cure for unhappiness. If you repeat that one sentence three times before breakfast and meditate on the meaning of the words you will change the character of the day by starting off with a happiness psychology.

While dressing or shaving or getting breakfast, say aloud a few such remarks as the following, "I believe this is going to be a wonderful day. I believe I can successfully handle all problems that will arise today. I feel good physically, mentally, emotionally. It is wonderful to be alive. I am grateful for all that I have had, for all that I now have, and for all that I shall have. Things aren't going to fall apart. God is here and He is with me and He will see me through. I thank God for every good thing."

I once knew an unhappy sort of fellow who always said to his wife at breakfast, "This is going to be another tough day." He didn't really think so, but he had a mental quirk whereby if he said it was going to be a tough day, it might turn out pretty well. But things really started going badly with him, which was not surprising, for if you visualize and affirm an unhappy outcome, you tend thereby to create just that type of condition. So affirm happy outcomes at the start of every day, and you will be surprised at how often things will turn out so.

But it is not sufficient to apply to the mind even such an important affirmation therapy as I have just suggested unless throughout the day you also base your actions and attitudes upon fundamental principles of happy living.

One of the most simple and basic of such principles is that of human love and good will. It is amazing what happiness a sincere expression of compassion and tenderness will induce.

My friend Dr. Samuel Shoemaker once wrote a moving story about a mutual friend, Ralston Young, famous as Redcap No. 42 in the Grand Central Station in New York. He carries bags for a living, but his real job is living the spirit of Christ as a redcap in one of the world's greatest railway stations. As he carries a man's suitcase, he tries to share a little Christian fellowship with him. He carefully watches a customer to see if there is any way in which he can give him more courage and hope. He is very skillful in the way he goes about it too.

One day, for example, he was asked to take a little old lady to her train. She was in a wheel chair, so he took her down on the elevator. As he wheeled her into the elevator he noticed that there were tears in her eyes. Ralston Young stood there as the elevator descended, closed his eyes, and asked the Lord how he could help her, and the Lord gave him an idea. As he wheeled her off the elevator, he said with a smile, "Ma'am, if you don't mind my saying so, that is a mighty pretty hat you are wearing."

She looked up at him and said, "Thank you."

"And I might add," he said, "that sure is a pretty dress you have on. I like it so much."

Being a woman, this appealed to her, and despite the fact that she was not feeling well, she brightened up and asked, "Why in the world did you say those nice things to me? It is very thoughtful of you."

"Well," he said, "I saw how unhappy you were. I saw that you were crying, and I just asked the Lord how I could help you. The Lord said, 'Speak to her about her hat.' The mention of the dress," he added, "was my own idea." Ralston Young and the Lord together knew how to get a woman's mind off her troubles.

"Don't you feel well?" he then asked.

"No," she replied. "I am constantly in pain. I am never free from it.

Sometimes I think I can't stand it. Do you, by any chance, know what it means to be in pain all the time?"

Ralston had an answer. "Yes, ma'am, I do, for I lost an eye, and it hurt like a hot iron day and night."

"But," she said, "you seem to be happy now. How did you accomplish it?"

By this time he had her in her seat in the train, and he said, "Just by prayer, ma'am, just by prayer."

Softly she asked, "Does prayer, just prayer, take your pain away?"

"Well," answered Ralston, "perhaps it doesn't always take it away. I can't say that it does, but it always helps to overcome it so it doesn't seem like it hurts so much. Just keep on prayin', ma'am, and I'll pray for you too."

Her tears were dried now, and she looked up at him with a lovely smile, took him by the hand, and said, "You've done me so much good."

A year passed, and one night in Grand Central Station Ralston Young was paged to come to the Information booth. A young woman was there who said, "I bring you a message from the dead. Before she died my mother told me to find you and to tell you how much you helped her last year when you took her to the train in her wheelchair. She will always remember you, even in eternity. She will remember you, for you were so kind and loving and understanding." Then the young woman burst into tears and sobbed in her grief.

Ralston stood quietly watching her. Then he said, "Don't cry, missy, don't cry. You shouldn't cry. Give a prayer of thanksgiving."

Surprised, the girl said, "Why should I give a prayer of thanksgiving?"

"Because," said Ralston, "many people have become orphans much younger than you. You had your mother for a long, long time, and besides you still have her. You will see her again. She is near to you now and she always will be near to you. Maybe," he said, "she is right with us now—the two of us, as we talk."

The sobs ended and the tears dried. Ralston's kindness had the same effect on the daughter as it had had on the mother. In this huge station, with thousands of people passing by, the two of them felt the presence of one who inspired this wonderful redcap to go around this way spreading love.

"Where love is," said Tolstoy, "God is," and, we might add, where God and love are, there is happiness. So a practical principle in creating happiness is to practice love.

A genuinely happy man is a friend of mine, H. C. Mattern, who, with his equally happy wife, Mary, travels throughout the country in the course of his work. Mr. Mattern carries a unique business card on the reverse side of which is stated the philosophy which has brought happiness to him and his wife and to hundreds of others who have been so fortunate as to feel the impact of their personalities.

The card reads as follows: "The way to happiness: keep your heart free from hate, your mind from worry. Live simply, expect little, give much. Fill your life with love. Scatter sunshine. Forget self, think of others. Do as you would be done by. Try this for a week and you will be surprised."

As you read these words you may say, "There is nothing new in that." Indeed, there is something new in it if you have never tried it. When you start to practice it you will find it the newest, freshest, most astonishing method of happy and successful living you have ever used. What is the value of having known these principles all your life if you have never made use of them? Such inefficiency in living is tragic. For a man to have lived in poverty when all the time right on his doorstep is gold indicates an unintelligent approach to life. This simple philosophy is the way to happiness. Practice these principles for just one week, as Mr. Mattern suggests, and if it has not brought you the beginnings of real happiness, then your unhappiness is very deep seated indeed.

Of course in order to give power to these principles of happiness and make them work it is necessary to support them with a dynamic quality of mind. You are not likely to secure effective results even with spiritual principles without spiritual power. When one experiences a dynamic spiritual change inwardly, success with happiness-producing ideas becomes extraordinarily easy. If you begin to use spiritual principles, however awkwardly, you will gradually experience spiritual power inwardly. I can assure you that this will give you the greatest surge of happiness you have ever known. It will stay with you, too, as long as you live a God-centered life.

In my travels about the country I have been encountering an increasing number of genuinely happy individuals. These are persons who have been practicing the techniques described in this book and which I have presented in other volumes and in other writings and talks and which other writers and speakers have likewise been giving to receptive people. It is astonishing how people can become inoculated with happiness through an inner experience of spiritual change. People of all types everywhere are having this experience today. In fact, it has become one of the most popular phenomena of our times, and if it continues to develop and expand, the person who has not had a spiritual experience will soon be considered old-fashioned and behind the times. Nowadays it is smart to be spiritually alive. It is old-fogyism to be ignorant of that happiness-producing transformation which people everywhere are enjoying at this time.

Recently, after finishing a lecture in a certain city, a big, strapping, fine-looking man came up to me. He slapped me on the shoulder with such force that it almost bowled me over.

"Doctor," he said in a booming voice, "how about coming out with the gang? We are having a big party at the Smiths' house, and we would like you to come along. It's going to be a whale of a shindig and you ought to get in on it." So ran his racy invitation.

Well, obviously this didn't sound like a proper party for a preacher, and I was hesitant. I was afraid I might cramp everyone's style, so I began to make excuses.

"Oh, forget it," my friend told me. "Don't worry, this is your kind of party. You will be surprised. Come on along. You will get the kick of your life out of it."

So I yielded and went along with my buoyant and racy friend and he was certainly one of the most infectious personalities I had encountered in quite a while. Soon we came to a big house set back among trees with a wide, sweeping driveway up to the front door. From the noise issuing from the open windows there was no question but that quite a party was in progress, and I wondered what I was getting myself into. My host, with a great shout, dragged me into the room, and we had quite a handshaking time, and he introduced me to a large group of gay and exuberant people. They were a happy, joyous lot of folk.

I looked around for a bar, but there wasn't any. All that was being served was coffee, fruit juice, ginger ale, sandwiches, and ice cream, but there was lots of those.

"These people must have stopped somewhere before coming here," I remarked to my friend.

He was shocked, and said, "Stopped somewhere? Why, you don't understand. These people have got the spirit all right, but not the kind of 'spirit' you are thinking about. I am surprised at you," he said. "Don't you realize what makes this crowd so happy? They have been renewed spiritually. They have got something. They have been set free from themselves. They have found God as a living, vital, honest-to-goodness reality. Yes," he said, "they have got spirit all right, but it isn't the kind that you get out of a bottle. They have got spirit in their hearts."

Then I saw what he meant. This wasn't a crowd of sad-faced, stodgy people. They were the leaders of that town—businessmen, lawyers, doctors, teachers, society people, and a lot of simpler folk besides, and they were having a wonderful time at this party—talking about God, and they were doing it in the most natural manner imaginable. They were telling one another about the changes that had occurred in their lives through revitalized spiritual power.

Those who have the naïve notion that you can't laugh and be gay when you are religious should have been in on that party.

Well, I went away from that party with a Bible verse running through my mind, "In him was life; and the life was the light of men." (John 1:4) That was the light I saw on the faces of those happy people. An inner light was reflected outwardly on their faces, and it came from an effervescent spiritual something that they had taken into themselves. Life means vitality, and these people obviously were getting their vitality from God. They had found the power that creates happiness.

This is no isolated incident. I venture the assertion that in your own community, if you will look around for them, you will find lots of people just like those described above. If you don't find them in your own home town, come to the Marble Collegiate Church in New York City and you will find them by the score. But you can get the same spirit by reading this book if you practice the simple principles set forth.

As you read this book believe what you read, because it is true; then start working on the practical suggestions the book contains and you, too, will have the spiritual experience that produces this quality of happiness. I know this is so, because many of those to whom I have referred and shall refer in later chapters got their vital new life in the same way. Then, having been changed inwardly, you will begin to create out of yourself not unhappiness, but a happiness of such quality and character that you will wonder if you are living in the same world. As a matter of fact it won't be the same world because you are not the same, and what you are determines the world in which you live, so as you change, your world changes also.

If happiness is determined by our thoughts it is necessary to drive off the thoughts which make for depression and discouragement. This can be done first by simply determining to do it; second, by utilizing an easily employed technique which I suggested to a businessman. I met him at a luncheon and have seldom heard such gloom as he got off. His conversation would have been ultra-depressing had I permitted it to affect me. It reeked with pessimism. To hear him talk you would think everything was headed for ruin. Of course the man was tired. Accumulated problems had swamped his mind which was seeking release in retreat from a world which was too much for his depleted energy. His principal trouble was in his depressed thought pattern. He needed an infusion of light and faith.

So rather boldly I said, "If you want to feel better and stop being miserable, I can give you something that will fix you up."

"What can you do?" he snorted. "Are you a miracle worker?"

"No," I replied, "but I can put you in touch with a miracle worker who will drain off that unhappiness of yours and give you a new slant on life. I mean that," I concluded, as we separated.

Apparently he became curious, for he got in touch with me later and I gave him a little book of mine called *Thought Conditioners.** It contains forty health and happiness producing thoughts. Inasmuch as it is a pocket-sized booklet, I suggested that he carry it for easy consultation and that he drop one of the suggested thoughts in his mind every day for forty days. I further suggested that he commit each thought to memory, thus allowing it to dissolve in consciousness, and that he visualize this healthy thought sending a quieting and healing influence through his mind. I assured him that if he would follow this plan, these healthy thoughts would drive off the diseased thoughts that were sapping his joy, energy, and creative ability.

The idea at first impressed him as being a bit queer and he had his doubts, but he followed directions. After about three weeks he called me on the telephone and shouted, "Boy, this sure works! It is wonderful. I have snapped out of it, and I wouldn't have believed it possible."

He remains "snapped out of it" and is a genuinely happy person. This pleasant condition resulted because he became skilled in the power to create his own happiness. He later commented that his first mental hurdle was honestly to face the fact that while his unhappiness made him miserable, yet he was at home in self-pity and self-punishment thoughts. He knew that these sick thoughts were the cause of his trouble, but he shrank from the effort required to desire change sufficiently to actually go about changing. But when he began systematically to insert healthy spiritual thoughts into his mind as directed, he began first to want new life, then to realize the thrilling fact that he could have it, then the even more

* *Thought Conditioners*, published by Sermon Publications, Inc., Distribution Office, Pawling, New York.

amazing fact that he was getting it. The result was that after some three weeks of a self-improvement process new happiness "burst" upon him.

Everywhere in this country today are groups of people who have found the happy way. If we can have even one such group in every city, town, and hamlet in America, we can change the life of this country within a very short time. And what kind of group do we mean? Let me explain.

I was speaking in a Western city and returned to my hotel room rather late. I wanted to get a little sleep, for I was to be up at five-thirty next morning to catch a plane. As I was preparing for bed, the telephone rang, and a lady said, "There are about fifty of us at my house waiting for you."

I explained that I could not come due to the early hour of my departure in the morning.

"Oh," she said, "two men are on their way to get you. We have been praying for you, and we want you to come and pray with us before you leave the city."

I am glad I went, though I had very little sleep that night.

The men who came for me were a couple of alcoholics who had been healed by the power of faith. They were two of the happiest, most lovable fellows you can imagine.

The home to which they took me was packed. People were sitting on the stairways, on the tables, on the floor. One man was even perched on the grand piano. And what were they doing? They were having a prayer meeting. They told me that sixty such prayer groups were going on in that city all the time.

I was never in such a meeting. They were anything but a stuffy group. They were a released, happy crowd of real people. I found myself strangely moved. The spirit in that room was tremendous in its lifting force. The group would burst into song, and I never heard such singing. The room was filled with a wonderful spirit of laughter.

Then a woman stood up. I saw that she had braces on her legs, and she said, "They told me I would never walk again. Do you want to see me walk?" And she walked up and down the room.

"What did it?" I asked.

"Jesus," she replied simply.

Then another fine-looking girl said, "Did you ever see a victim of the narcotics habit? Well, I was one and I was healed." There she sat, a beautiful, modest, charming young woman and she, too, said, "Jesus did it."

Then a couple who had drifted apart told me that they had been brought together and they were happier than ever before.

"How did it come about?" I asked. And their reply was, "Jesus did it."

A man said he had been a victim of alcohol, that he had dragged his family down until they were living in abject poverty and he was a complete failure. And now as he stood before me he was a strong, healthy personality. I started to ask how, but he nodded and said, "Jesus did it."

Then they burst into another song, and then someone dimmed the lights and we all held hands around in a great circle. I had a feeling as though I had hold of an electric wire. Power was flowing around that room. Without any question I was the least spiritually developed person in that group. I knew in that moment that Jesus Christ was right there in that house and those people had found Him. They had been touched by His power. He had given them new life. This life bubbled up in an irrepressible effervescence.

This is the secret of happiness. All else is secondary. Get this experience and you've got real, unalloyed happiness, the best the world offers. Don't miss it whatever you do in this life, for this is it.

6

STOP FUMING AND FRETTING

Many people make life unnecessarily difficult for themselves by dissipating power and energy through fuming and fretting.

Do you ever "fume" and "fret"? Here is a picture of yourself if you do. The word "fume" means to boil up, to blow off, to emit vapor, to be agitated, to be distraught, to seethe. The word "fret" is equally descriptive. It is reminiscent of a sick child in the night, a petulant half-cry, half-whine. It ceases, only to begin again. It has an irritating, annoying, penetrating quality. To fret is a childish term, but it describes the emotional reaction of many adults.

The Bible advises us to "Fret not thyself . . ." (Psalm 37:1) This is sound advice for the people of our time. We need to stop fuming and fretting and get peaceful if we are to have power to live effectively. And how do we go about doing so?

A first step is to reduce your pace or at least the tempo of your pace. We do not realize how accelerated the rate of our lives has become, or the speed at which we are driving ourselves. Many people are destroying their physical bodies by this pace, but what is even more tragic, they are tearing their minds and souls to shreds as well. It is possible for a person to live a quiet existence physically and yet maintain a high tempo emotionally. Even an invalid can live at too high a pace from that standpoint. The character of our thoughts determines pace. When the mind goes rushing on pell-mell from one feverish attitude to another it becomes feverish and the result is a state bordering on petulance. The pace of modern life must be reduced if we are not to suffer profoundly from its debilitating over-stimulation and super-excitement. This over-stimulation produces toxic poisons in the body and creates emotional illness. It produces fatigue and a sense of frustration so that we fume and fret about everything from our personal troubles to the state of the nation and the world. If the effect of this emotional disquiet is so pronounced physically, what must its effect be on that deep inner essence of the personality known as the soul?

It is impossible to have peace of soul if the pace is so feverishly accelerated. God won't go that fast. He will not endeavor to keep up with you. He says in effect, "Go ahead if you must with this foolish pace and when you are worn out I will offer my healing. But I can make your life so rich if you will slow down now and live and move and have your being in me." God moves imperturbably, slowly, and with perfect organization. The only wise rate at which to live is God's rate. God gets things done and they are done right and He does them without hurry. He neither fumes nor frets. He is peaceful and therefore efficient. This same peace is offered to us—"Peace I leave with you, my peace I give unto you . . ." (John 14:27)

In a sense this is a pathetic generation, especially in the great cities because of the effect of nervous tension, synthetic excitement, and noise; but the malady extends into the country districts also, for the air waves transmit tension.

I was amused by an old lady who, in talking about this matter, said, "Life is so daily." That remark certainly spoke volumes about the pressure, responsibilities, and tension of daily life. Its persistent, insistent demand upon us is provocative of pressure.

One wonders whether this generation of Americans is not so accustomed to tension that many are in the unhappy state of not being comfortable without it. The deep quietness of woods and valleys so well known to our forefathers is an unaccustomed state to them. The tempo of their lives is such that in many instances they have an incapacity to draw upon the sources of peace and quietness which the physical world offers.

One summer afternoon my wife and I went for a long walk in the woods. We were stopping at the beautiful Lake Mohonk Mountain House which is set in one of the finest natural parks in America, 7,500 acres of virgin mountainside in the middle of which is a lake lying like a gem in the forest. The word *mohonk* means "lake in the sky." Aeons ago some giant upheaval of the earth cast up these sheer cliffs. You come out of the deep woods onto some noble promontory and rest your eyes on great valleys set among hills, rock-ribbed and ancient as the sun. These woods, mountains, and valleys constitute what ought to be a sure retreat from every confusion of this world.

On this afternoon as we walked there was a mixture of summer showers and sunlit hours. We were drenched and started to fret about it a bit because it took the press out of our clothes. Then we told each other that it doesn't hurt a human being to get drenched with clean rain water, that the rain feels cool and fresh on one's face, and that you can always sit in the sun and dry yourself out. We walked under the trees and talked and then fell silent.

We were listening, listening deeply to the quietness. In a strict sense, the woods are never still. There is tremendous activity always in process, but nature makes no strident noises regardless of the vastness of its operation. Nature's sounds are quiet, harmonious.

On this beautiful afternoon, nature was laying its hand of healing quietness upon us, and we could actually feel the tension being drawn off.

Just as we were falling under this spell, the faint sounds of what passes for music came to us. It was nervous, high-strung music of the jitterbug variety. Presently through the woods came three young people, two young women and a young man, and the latter was lugging a portable radio.

They were three young city people out for a walk in the woods and tragically enough were bringing their noise along with them. They were nice young folk, too, for they stopped and we had a pleasant talk with them. It occurred to me to ask them to turn that thing off and listen to the music of the woods, but I didn't feel it was my business to instruct them, and finally they went on their way.

We commented on the loss they were incurring, that they could pass through this peacefulness and not give ear to the music that is as old as the world, harmony and melody the like of which man has never equaled: the song of the wind through the trees, the sweet notes of birds singing their hearts out, the whole background of the music of the spheres.

This is still to be found in America in our woods and great plains, in our valleys, in our mountain majesties, and where the ocean foams on soft shores of sand. We should avail ourselves of its healing. Remember the words of Jesus, "Come ye yourselves apart into a desert place, and rest awhile." (Mark 6:31) Even as I write these words and give you this good advice, I recall instances where it has been necessary to remind myself to practice the same truth, which emphasizes that we must everlastingly discipline ourselves to quietness if we expect its benefits in our lives.

One autumn day Mrs. Peale and I took a trip into Massachusetts to see our son John at Deerfield Academy. We told him we would arrive at 11 A.M., and we pride ourselves on the good old American custom of promptness. Therefore, being a bit behind schedule, we were driving at breakneck speed through the autumnal landscape. My wife said, "Norman, did you see that radiant hillside?"

"What hillside?" I asked.

"It just went by on the other side," she explained. "Look at that beautiful tree."

"What tree?" I was already a mile past it.

"This is one of the most glorious days I have ever seen," my wife said. "How could you possibly imagine such amazing colors as these New England hillsides in October? In fact," she said, "it makes me happy inside."

That remark of hers so impressed me that I stopped the car and went back a quarter of a mile to a lake backed by towering hills dressed in autumn colors. We sat and looked and meditated. God with His genius and skill had painted that scene in the varied colors which He alone can mix. In the still waters of the lake lay a reflected vision of His glory, for the hillside was unforgettably pictured in that mirrorlike pond.

For quite a while we sat without a word until finally my wife broke the silence by the only appropriate statement that one could make, "He leadeth me beside the still waters." (Psalm 23:2) We arrived at Deerfield at eleven, but we were not tired. In fact, we were deeply refreshed.

To help reduce this tension which seems to dominate our people everywhere, you can start by reducing your own pace. To do that you will need to slow down, quiet down. Do not fume. Do not fret. Practice being peaceful. Practice "the peace of God which passeth all understanding." (Philippians 4:7) Then note the quiet power sense that wells up within you.

A friend of mine who was compelled to take an enforced rest as a result of "pressure" wrote me, "Many lessons have been learned during this enforced retreat. Now I know better than before that in the quiet we become aware of His presence. Life can get muddled. But 'muddied water,' says Lao-tse, 'let stand, will become clear.' "

A physician gave some rather whimsical advice to a patient, an aggressive, go-getter type of businessman. Excitedly he told the doctor what an enormous amount of work he had to do and that he had to get it done right away quick or else.

"I take my brief case home every night and it's packed with work," he said with nervous inflection.

"Why do you take work home with you at night?" the doctor asked quietly.

"I have to get it done," he fumed.

"Cannot someone else do it, or help you with it?" asked the doctor.

"No," the man snapped. "I am the only one who can do it. It must be done just right, and I alone can do it as it must be done, and it has to be done quickly. Everything depends upon me."

"If I write you a prescription, will you follow it?" asked the doctor.

This, believe it or not, was the prescription. His patient was to take off two hours every working day and go for a long walk. Then he was to take off a half-day a week and spend that half-day in a cemetery.

In astonishment the patient demanded, "Why should I spend a half-day in a cemetery?"

"Because," answered the doctor, "I want you to wander around and look at the gravestones of men who are there permanently. I want you to meditate on the fact that many of them are there because they thought even as you do, that the whole world rested on their shoulders. Meditate on the solemn fact that when you get there permanently the world will go on just the same and, as important as you are, others will be able to do the work you are now doing. I suggest that you sit on one of those tombstones and repeat this statement, '. . . a thousand years in Thy sight are but as yesterday when it is past, and as a watch in the night.' " (Psalm 90:4)

The patient got the idea. He slowed his pace. He learned to delegate authority. He achieved a proper sense of his own importance. He stopped fuming and fretting. He got peaceful. And, it might be added, he does better work. He is developing a more competent organization and he admits that his business is in better condition.

A prominent manufacturer was afflicted with tension, in fact, he was in a very high-strung frame of mind. As he himself described it, "he leapt out of bed every morning and immediately got himself into high gear. He was in such a rush and dither that he 'made his breakfast on soft-boiled eggs because they slid down fast.' " This hectic pace left him fagged and worn at about midday. He sank into bed every night exhausted.

It so happens that his home is situated in a grove of trees. Very early one morning, unable to sleep, he arose and sat by the window. He became interested in watching a bird emerge from his night's sleep. He noticed that a bird sleeps with his head under his wing, the feathers pulled all around himself. When he awakened, he pulled his bill out from under his feathers, took a sleepy look around, stretched one leg to its full length, meanwhile stretching the wing over the leg until it spread out like a fan. He pulled the leg and wing back and then repeated the same process with the other leg and wing, whereupon he put his head down in his feathers again for a delicious little cat nap (only in this case a bird nap), then the head came out again. This time the bird looked around eagerly, threw his head back, gave his wings and legs two more big stretches, then he sent up a song, a thrilling, melodic song of praise to the day, wherewith he hopped down off the limb, got himself a drink of cold water, and started looking for food.

My high-strung friend said to himself, "If that's the way the birds get up, sort of slow and easy like, why wouldn't it be a good method for me to start the day that way?" He actually went through the same performance, even to singing, and noticed that the song was an especially beneficial factor, that it was a releasing mechanism.

"I can't sing," he chuckled, "but I practiced sitting quietly in a chair and singing. Mostly I sang hymns and happy songs. Imagine, me singing, but I did. My wife thought I was bereft of my senses. The only thing I had on the bird was that I did a little praying, too, then, like the bird, I felt like some food, and I wanted a good breakfast—bacon and eggs. And I took my time eating it. After that I went to work in a released frame of mind. It surely did start me off for the day minus the tension, and it helped me go through the day in a peaceful and relaxed manner."

A former member of a championship university crew told me that their shrewd crew coach often reminded them, "To win this or any race, row slowly." He pointed out that rapid rowing tends to break the stroke and when the stroke is broken it is with the greatest difficulty that a crew recovers the rhythm necessary to win. Meanwhile other crews pass the disorganized group. It is indeed wise advice—"To go fast, row slowly."

In order to row slowly or to work slowly and maintain the steady pace that wins, the victim of high tempo will do well to get the coordinating peace of God into his mind, his soul, and, it might be added, into his nerves and muscles also.

Have you ever considered the importance of having the peace of God in your muscles, in your joints? Perhaps your joints will not pain so much when they have the peace of God in them. Your muscles will work with correlation when the peace of God who created them governs their action. Speak to your muscles every day and to your joints and to your nerves, saying, "Fret not thyself." (Psalm 37:1) Relax on a couch or bed, think of each important muscle from head to feet, and say to each, "The peace of God is touching you." Then practice "feeling" that peace throughout your entire body. In due course your muscles and joints will take heed.

Slow down, for whatever you really want will be there when you get there if you work toward it without stress, without pressing. If, proceeding under God's guidance and in His smooth and unhurried tempo, it is not there, then it was not supposed to be there. If you miss it, perhaps you should have missed it. So definitely seek to develop a normal, natural, God-ordered pace. Practice and preserve mental quiet. Learn the art of letting go all nervous excitement. To do this, stop at intervals and affirm, "I now relinquish nervous excitement—it is flowing from me. I am at peace." Do not fume. Do not fret. Practice being peaceful.

To attain this efficient state of living, I recommend the practice of thinking peaceful thoughts. Every day we perform a series of acts designed to care for the body properly. We bathe, brush the teeth, take exercise. In similar fashion we should give time and planned effort to keeping the mind in a healthy state. One way to do this is to sit quietly and pass a series of peaceful thoughts through the mind. For example, pass through the thoughts the memory of a lofty mountain, a misty valley, a sun-speckled trout stream, silver moonlight on water.

At least once in every twenty-four hours, preferably in the busiest part of the day, deliberately stop whatever you are doing for ten or fifteen minutes and practice serenity.

There are times when it is essential resolutely to check our headlong pace, and it must be emphasized that the only way to stop is to stop.

I went to a certain city on a lecture date and was met at the train by a committee. I was rushed to a bookstore where I had an autographing party and then to another bookstore where another autographing party was held. Then they rushed me to a luncheon. After rushing through the luncheon I was rushed to a meeting. After the meeting I was rushed back to the hotel where I changed my clothes and was rushed to a reception where I met several hundred people and drank three glasses of fruit punch. Then I was rushed back to the hotel and told I had twenty minutes to dress for dinner. When I was getting dressed the telephone rang and somebody said, "Hurry, hurry, we must rush down to dinner."

Excitedly I chattered, "I will rush right down."

I rushed from the room and was so excited that I could scarcely get the key into the lock. Hastily I felt myself, to be sure that I was completely dressed, and rushed toward the elevator. All of a sudden I stopped. I was out of breath. I asked myself, "What is this all about? What is the meaning of this ceaseless rush? This is ridiculous!"

Then I declared independence, and said, "I do not care if I go to dinner. I do not care whether I make a talk. I do not have to go to this dinner and I do not have to make a speech." So deliberately and slowly I walked back to my room and took my time about unlocking the door. I telephoned the man downstairs and said, "If you want to eat, go ahead. If you want to save a place for me, I will be down after a while, but I am not going to rush any more."

So I removed my coat, sat down, took off my shoes, put my feet up on the table, and just sat. Then I opened the Bible and very slowly read aloud the 121st Psalm, "I will lift up mine eyes unto the hills from whence cometh my help." I closed the book and had a little talk with myself, saying, "Come on now, start living a slower and more relaxed life," and then I affirmed, "God is here and His peace is touching me.

"I do not need anything to eat," I reasoned. "I eat too much anyway. Besides, the dinner will probably not be very good, and if I am quiet now I will give a better speech at eight o'clock."

So I sat there resting and praying for fifteen minutes. I shall never forget the sense of peace and personal mastery I had when I walked out of that room. I had the glorious feeling of having overcome something, of having taken control of myself emotionally, and when I reached the dining room the others had just finished the first course. All I missed was the soup, which by general consent was no great loss.

This incident was an amazing experience of the healing presence of God. I gained these values by simply stopping, by quietly reading the Bible, by sincerely praying, and by thinking some peaceful thoughts for a few moments.

Physicians generally seem to feel that much physical trouble could be avoided or overcome by practicing the philosophy and methodology of not fuming or fretting.

A prominent citizen of New York told me that his doctor suggested that he come to our clinic at the church "because," said his physician, "you need to develop a calm philosophy of living. Your power resources are played out."

"My doctor says I am pushing myself to the limit. He tells me I'm too tense, too high-strung, that I fume and fret too much, and," he concluded, "my doctor declares the only sure cure is for me to develop what he calls a calm philosophy of living."

My visitor arose and paced the floor, then demanded, "But how in the world can I do that? It's a lot easier said than done."

Then this excited gentleman went on to say that his doctor had given him certain suggestions for developing this calm philosophy of living. The suggestions as outlined were indeed wise. "But then," he explained, "the doctor suggested that I see you people here at the church, for he feels that if I learn to use religious faith in a practical manner it will give me peace of mind and bring down my blood pressure. Then I will feel better physically. While I realize the doctor's prescription is sensible," he complained, "how can a man fifty years old, of a high-strung nature such as mine, suddenly change the habits of a lifetime and develop this so-called calm philosophy of living?"

That did indeed seem to be a problem, for he was a bundle of excitable and explosive nerves. He paced the floor, he thumped the table, his voice was high-pitched. He gave the impression of a thoroughly disturbed and baffled man. Obviously he was showing up at his worst, but he was clearly revealing the inner state of his personality, and the insight thus gained gave us a chance to help him through understanding him better.

As I listened to his words and observed his attitude, I again understood why Jesus Christ retains his remarkable hold on men. It is because He has the answer to such problems as this, and I proved that fact by suddenly changing the line of the conversation. Without any introductory words I began to recite certain Bible texts such as, "Come unto me, all ye that labor and are heavy laden, and I will give you rest." (Matthew 11:28) And again, "Peace I leave with you, my peace I give unto you: not as the world giveth, give I unto you. Let not your heart be troubled, neither let it be afraid." (John 14:27) And still again, "Thou wilt keep him in perfect peace, whose mind is stayed on thee." (Isaiah 26:3)

I recited these words slowly, deliberately, reflectively. As this reciting went on, I noticed that my visitor stopped being agitated. Quietness came over him and then we both sat in silence. It seemed that we sat so for several minutes. Perhaps it wasn't that long, but finally he took a deep breath.

"Why, that's funny," he said. "I feel a lot better. Isn't that queer? I guess it was those words that did it."

"No, not the words alone," I answered, "though they do have a remarkable effect upon the mind, but something deeper happened just then. He touched you a minute ago—the Physician with the healing touch. He was present in this room."

My visitor evidenced no surprise at this assertion, but eagerly and impetuously agreed—and conviction was written on his face. "That's right, He sure was. I felt Him. I see what you mean. Now I understand—Jesus Christ will help me develop a calm philosophy of living."

This man found what increasing thousands are presently discovering, that a simple faith in and practice of the principles and techniques of Christianity bring peace and quietness and therefore new power to body, mind, and spirit. It is the perfect antidote to fuming and to fretting. It helps a person to become peaceful and thus to tap new resources of strength.

Of course it was necessary to teach this man a new pattern of thinking and acting. This was done in part by suggesting literature written by experts in the field of spiritual culture. For example, we gave him lessons in the skill of church going. We showed him how to make church worship a therapy. He was instructed in the scientific use of prayer and relaxation. And as a result of this practice eventually he became a healthy man. Anyone willing to follow this program and sincerely put these principle into day-by-day practice can, I believe, develop inner peace and power. Many of these techniques are outlined in this book.

In attaining emotional control the daily practice of healing techniques is of first importance. Emotional control cannot be gained in any magical or easy way. You cannot develop it by merely reading a book, although that is often helpful. The only sure method is by working at it regularly, persistently, scientifically, and by developing creative faith.

I suggest that you begin with such a primary procedure as simply the practice of keeping physically still. Don't pace the floor. Don't wring your hands. Don't pound or shout or argue or walk up and down. Don't let yourself get worked up into a dither. In excitement one's physical movements become accentuated. Therefore begin at the simplest place, that is by ceasing physical movement. Stand still, sit down, lie down. Certainly keep the voice down to a low pitch.

In developing a calm control it is necessary to think calmness, for the body responds sensitively to the type of thoughts that pass through the mind. It is also true that the mind can be quieted by first making the body quiet. That is to say, a physical attitude can induce desired mental attitudes.

In a speech I related the following incident which occurred in a committee meeting I attended. A gentleman who heard me tell this story was greatly impressed by it and took its truth to heart. He tried the technique suggested and reports that it has been very effective in controlling his fuming and fretting.

I was in a meeting where a discussion was going on which finally became rather bitter. Tempers were becoming frayed and some of the participants were decidedly on edge. Sharp remarks were passed. Suddenly one man arose, deliberately took off his coat, opened his collar, and lay down upon a couch. All were astonished, and someone asked if he felt ill.

"No," he said, "I feel fine, but I am beginning to get mad, and I have learned that it is difficult to get mad lying down."

We all laughed, and the tension was broken. Then our whimsical friend went on to explain that he had "tried a little trick" with himself. He had a quick temper, and when he felt himself getting mad he found that he was clenching his fist and raising his voice, so he deliberately extended his fingers not allowing them to form into a fist. In proportion to the rising of his tension or anger, he depressed his voice and talked in exaggerated low tones. "You cannot carry on an argument in a whisper," he said with a grin.

This principle can be effective in controlling emotional excitements, fretting, and tension, as many have discovered by experimentation. A beginning step, therefore, in achieving calmness is to discipline your physical reactions. You will be surprised at how quickly this can reduce the heat of your emotions, and when emotional heat is driven off, fuming and fretting subside. You will be amazed at the energy and power you will save. You will be much less tired.

It is, moreover, a good procedure to practice being phlegmatic or apathetic, even indifferent. To a certain extent even practice being sluggish. People thus constituted are less likely to emotional breaks. Highly organized individuals may do well to cultivate these reactions to a degree at least.

Naturally one does not want to lose the keen, sensitive responsiveness characteristic of the highly organized individual. But the practice of being phlegmatic tends to bring such a keyed-up personality to a balanced emotional position.

Following is a technique consisting of six points which I have personally found of great helpfulness in reducing the tendency to fume and fret. I have suggested its use to countless people who practice it and find it of great value:

1. Sit relaxed in a chair. Completely yield yourself to the chair. Starting with your toes and proceeding to the top of your head, conceive of every portion of the body as relaxing. Affirm relaxation by saying, "My toes are relaxed—my fingers—my facial muscles."

2. Think of your mind as the surface of a lake in a storm, tossed by waves and in tumult. But now the waves subside, and the surface of the lake is placid and unruffled.

3. Spend two or three minutes thinking of the most beautiful and peaceful scenes you have ever beheld, as, for example, a mountain at sunset, or a deep valley filled with the hush of early morning, or a woods at noonday, or moonlight upon rippling waters. In memory relive these scenes.

4. Repeat slowly, quietly, bringing out the melody in each, a series of words which express quietness and peace, as, for example, (a) tranquillity (say it very deliberately and in a tranquil manner); (b) serenity; (c) quietness. Think of other such words and repeat them.

5. Make a mental list of times in your life when you have been conscious of God's watchful care and recall how, when you were worried and anxious, He brought things out right and took care of you. Then recite aloud this line from an old hymn, "So long Thy power hath kept me, sure it STILL will lead me on."

6. Repeat the following, which has an amazing power to relax and quiet the mind: "Thou wilt keep him in perfect peace, whose mind is stayed on thee." (Isaiah 26:3) Repeat this several times during the day, whenever you have a fraction of a moment. Repeat it aloud if possible, so that by the end of the day you will have said it many times. Conceive of these words as active, vital substances permeating your mind, sending into every area of your thinking a healing balm. This is the best-known medicine for taking tension from the mind.

As you work with the techniques suggested in this chapter, the tendency to fume and fret will gradually be modified. In direct proportion to your progress the power heretofore drawn off by this unhappy habit will be felt in your increased ability to meet life's responsibilities.

7

EXPECT THE BEST AND GET IT

"Why does my boy fail in every job he gets?" asked a puzzled father about his thirty-year-old son.

It was indeed difficult to understand the failure of this young man, for seemingly he had everything. Of good family, his educational and business opportunities were beyond the average. Nevertheless, he had a tragic flair for failure. Everything he touched went wrong. He tried hard enough, yet somehow he missed success. Presently he found an answer, a curiously simple but potent answer. After practicing this new-found secret for a while he lost the flair for failure and acquired the touch of success. His personality began to focus, his powers to fuse.

Not long ago at luncheon I could not help admiring this dynamic man at the height of his power. "You amaze me," I commented. "A few years ago you were failing at everything. Now you have worked up an original idea into a fine business. You are a leader in your community. Please explain this remarkable change in you."

"Really it was quite simple," he replied. "I merely learned the magic of believing. I discovered that if you expect the worst you will get the worst, and if you expect the best you will get the best. It all happened through actually practicing a verse from the Bible."

"And what is that verse?"

" 'If you canst believe, all things are possible to him that believeth.' (Mark 9:23) I was brought up in a religious home," he explained, "and heard that verse many times, but it never had any effect upon me. One day in your church I heard you emphasize those words in a talk. In a flash of insight I realized that the key I had missed was that my mind was not trained to believe, to think positively, to have faith in either God or myself. I followed your suggestion of putting myself in God's hands and practiced your outlined techniques of faith. I trained myself to think positively about everything. Along with that I try to live right." He smiled and said, "God and I struck up a partnership. When I adopted that policy, things began to change almost at once for me. I got into the habit of expecting the best, not the worst, and that is the way my affairs have turned out lately. I guess it's a kind of miracle, isn't it?" he asked as he concluded his fascinating story.

But it wasn't miraculous at all. Actually what had happened was that he had learned to use one of the most powerful laws in this world, a law recognized alike by psychology and religion, namely, change your mental habits to belief instead of disbelief. Learn to expect, not to doubt. In so doing you bring everything into the realm of possibility.

This does not mean that by believing you are necessarily going to get everything you want or think you want. Perhaps that would not be good for you. When you put your trust in God, He guides your mind so that you do not want things that are not good for you or that are inharmonious with God's will. But it does definitely mean that when you learn to believe, then that which has seemingly been impossible moves into the area of the possible. Every great thing at last becomes for you a possibility.

William James, the famous psychologist, said, "Our belief at the beginning of a doubtful undertaking is the one thing (now get that—*is the one thing*) that insures the successful outcome of your venture." To learn to believe is of primary importance. It is the basic factor of succeeding in any undertaking. When you expect the best, you release a magnetic force in your mind which by a law of attraction tends to bring the best to you. But if you expect the worst, you release from your mind the power of repulsion which tends to force the best from you. It is amazing how a sustained expectation of the best sets in motion forces which cause the best to materialize.

An interesting illustration of this fact was described some years ago by Hugh Fullerton, a famous sports writer of a bygone era. As a boy, Hugh Fullerton was my favorite writer of sports stories. One story which I have never forgotten concerned Josh O'Reilly, one-time manager of the San Antonio Club of the Texas league. O'Reilly had a roster of great players, seven of whom had been hitting over three hundred, and everybody thought his team would easily take the championship. But the club fell into a slump and lost seventeen of the first twenty games. The players simply couldn't hit anything, and each began to accuse the other of being a "jinx" to the team.

Playing the Dallas Club, a rather poor team that year, only one San Antonio player got a hit, and that, strangely enough, was the pitcher. O'Reilly's team was badly beaten that day. In the clubhouse after the game the players were a disconsolate lot. Josh O'Reilly knew that he had an aggregation of stars and he realized that their trouble was simply that they were thinking wrong. They didn't expect to get a hit. They didn't expect to win. They expected to be defeated. They were thinking not victory but defeat. Their mental pattern was not one of expectation but of doubt. This negative mental process inhibited them, froze their muscles, threw them off their timing, and there was no free flow of easy power through the team.

It so happened that a preacher named Schlater was popular in that neighborhood at that time. He claimed to be a faith healer and apparently was getting some astounding results. Throngs crowded to hear him and most everybody had confidence in him. Perhaps the fact that they did believe in his power enabled Schlater to achieve results.

O'Reilly asked each player to lend him his two best bats. Then he asked the members of the team to stay in the clubhouse until he returned. He put the bats in a wheelbarrow and went off with them. He was gone for an hour. He returned jubilantly to tell the players that Schlater, the preacher, had blessed the bats and that these bats now contained a power that could not be overcome. The players were astounded and delighted.

The next day they overwhelmed Dallas, getting 37 base hits and 20 runs. They hammered their way through the league to a championship, and Hugh Fullerton said that for years in the Southwest a player would pay a large sum for a "Schlater bat."

Regardless of Schlater's personal power, the fact remains that something tremendous happened in the minds of those ballplayers. Their thought pattern was changed. They began thinking in terms of expectation, not doubt. They expected not the worst, but the best. They expected hits, runs, victories, and they got them. They had the power to get what they wanted. There was no difference in the bats themselves, I am quite sure of that, but there was certainly a difference in the minds of the men who used them. Now they knew they could make hits. Now they knew they could get runs. Now they knew they could win. A new thought pattern changed the minds of those men so that the creative power of faith could operate.

Perhaps you have not been doing so well in the game of life. Perhaps you stand up to bat and cannot make a hit. You strike out time and again and your batting average is lamentably low. Let me give you a suggestion. I guarantee that it will work. The basis for my assurance is the fact that thousands of people have been trying it with very great results. Things will be very different for you if you give this method a real trial.

Start reading the New Testament and notice the number of times it refers to faith. Select a dozen of the strongest statements about faith, the ones that you like the best. Then memorize each one. Let these faith concepts drop into your conscious mind. Say them over and over again, especially just before going to sleep at night. By a process of spiritual osmosis they will sink from your conscious into your subconscious mind and in time will modify and reslant your basic thought pattern. This process will change you into a believer, into an expecter, and when you become such, you will in due course become an achiever. You will have new power to get what God and you decide you really want from life.

The most powerful force in human nature is the spiritual-power technique taught in the Bible. Very astutely the Bible emphasizes the method by which a person can make something of himself. Faith, belief, positive thinking, faith in God, faith in other people, faith in yourself, faith in life. This is the essence of the technique that it teaches. "If thou canst believe" it says, "all things are possible to him that believeth." (Mark 9:23) "If ye have faith . . . nothing shall be impossible unto you." (Matthew 17:20) "According to your faith be it unto you." (Matthew 9:29) Believe—believe—so it drives home the truth that faith moves mountains.

Some skeptical person who has never learned this powerful law of the effect of right thinking may doubt my assertions regarding the amazing results which happen when this technique is employed.

Things become better when you expect the best instead of the worst, for the reason that being freed from self-doubt, you can put your whole self into your endeavor, and nothing can stand in the way of the man who focuses his entire self on a problem. When you approach a difficulty as a personal unity, the difficulty, which itself is a demonstration of disunity, tends to deteriorate.

When the entire concentration of all your force—physical, emotional, and spiritual—is brought to bear, the consolidation of these powers properly employed is quite irresistible.

Expecting the best means that you put your whole heart (i.e., the central essence of your personality) into what you want to accomplish. People are defeated in life not because of lack of ability, but for lack of wholeheartedness. They do not wholeheartedly expect to succeed. Their heart isn't in it, which is to say they themselves are not fully given. Results do not yield themselves to the person who refuses to give himself to the desired results.

A major key to success in this life, to attaining that which you deeply desire, is to be completely released and throw all there is of yourself into your job or any project in which you are engaged. In other words, whatever you are doing, give it all you've got. Give every bit of yourself. Hold nothing back. Life cannot deny itself to the person who gives life his all. But most people, unfortunately, don't do that. In fact, very few people do, and this is a tragic cause of failure, or, if not failure, it is the reason we only half attain.

A famous Canadian athletic coach, Ace Percival, says that most people, athletes as well as non-athletes, are "holdouts," that is to say, they are always keeping something in reserve. They do not invest themselves 100 per cent in competition. Because of that fact they never achieve the highest of which they are capable.

Red Barber, famous baseball announcer, told me that he had known few athletes who completely give themselves.

Don't be a "holdout." Go all out. Do this, and life will not hold out on you.

A famous trapeze artist was instructing his students how to perform on the high trapeze bar. Finally, having given full explanations and instruction in this skill, he told them to demonstrate their ability.

One student, looking up at the insecure perch upon which he must perform, was suddenly filled with fear. He froze completely. He had a terrifying vision of himself falling to the ground. He couldn't move a muscle, so deep was his fright. "I can't do it! I can't do it!" he gasped.

The instructor put his arm around the boy's shoulder and said, "Son, you can do it, and I will tell you how." Then he made a statement which is of inestimable importance. It is one of the wisest remarks I have ever heard. He said, "Throw your heart over the bar and your body will follow."

Copy that one sentence. Write it on a card and put it in your pocket. Place it under the glass on your desk top. Tack it up on your wall. Stick it in your shaving mirror. Better still, write it on your mind, you who really want to do something with life. It's packed with power, that sentence. "Throw your heart over the bar and your body will follow."

Heart is the symbol of creative activity. Fire the heart with where you want to go and what you want to be. Get it so deeply fixed in your unconscious that you will not take no for an answer, then your entire personality will follow where your heart leads. "Throw your heart over the bar" means to throw your faith over your difficulty, throw your affirmation over every barrier, throw your visualization over your obstacles. In other words, throw the spiritual essence of you over the bar and your material self will follow in the victory groove thus pioneered by your faith-inspired mind. Expect the best, not the worst, and you will attain your heart's desire. It is what is in the heart of you, either good or bad, strong or weak, that finally comes to you. Emerson said, "Beware of what you want for you will get it."

That this philosophy is of practical value is illustrated by the experience of a young woman whom I interviewed a number of years ago. She made an appointment to see me in my office at two o'clock on a certain afternoon. Being quite busy that day, I had gotten a little behind schedule, and it was about five minutes after two when I walked into the conference room where she was waiting. It was obvious that she was displeased for her lips were pressed firmly together.

"It's five minutes after two, and we had an appointment at 2 P.M.," she said. "I always admire promptness."

"So do I. I always believe in being prompt, and I hope you will forgive me for my unavoidable delay," I said with a smile.

But she was not in a smiling mood, for she said crisply, "I have a very important problem to present to you and I want an answer, and I expect an answer." Then she shot out at me: "I might as well put it to you bluntly. I want to get married."

"Well," I replied, "that is a perfectly normal desire and I should like to help you."

"I want to know why I can't get married," she continued. "Every time I form a friendship with a man, the next thing I know he fades out of the picture and another chance is gone by, and," she added, speaking frankly,

"I am not getting any younger. You conduct a personal-problem clinic to study people and you have had some experience, and I am putting my problem right up to you. Tell me, why can't I get married?"

I studied her to see if she was the kind of person to whom one could speak frankly, for certain things had to be said if she really meant business. Finally I decided that she was of big enough caliber to take the medicine that would be required if she was to correct her personality difficulties, so I said, "Well, now, let's analyze the situation. Obviously you have a good mind and a fine personality, and, if I may say so, you are a very handsome lady."

All of these things were true. I congratulated her in every way that I honestly could, but then I said, "I think that I see your difficulty and it is this. You took me to task because I was five minutes late for our appointment. You were really quite severe with me. Has it ever occurred to you that your attitude represents a pretty serious fault? I think a husband would have a very difficult time if you checked him up that closely all the time. In fact, you would so dominate him that, even if you did marry, your marital life would be unsatisfactory. Love cannot live under domination."

Then I said, "You have a very firm way of pressing your lips together which indicates a domineering attitude. The average male, I might as well tell you, does not like to be dominated, at least so that he knows it." Then I added, "I think you would be a very attractive person if you got those too-firm lines out of your face. You must have a little softness, a little tenderness, and those lines are too firm to be soft." Then I observed her dress, which was obviously quite expensive, but she didn't wear it very well, and so I said, "This may be a bit out of line, and I hope you won't mind, but perhaps you could get that dress to hang a little better." I know my description was awkward, but she was a good sport about it and laughed right out loud.

She said, "You certainly don't use style phraseology, but I get the idea."

Then I suggested, "Perhaps it might help to get your hair fixed up a little. It's a little—floaty. Then you might also add a little sweet-smelling perfume—just a whiff of it. But the really important thing is to get a new attitude that will change the lines on your face and give you that indefinable quality known as spiritual joy. This I am certain will release charm and loveliness in you."

"Well," she burst out, "never did I expect to get this combination of advice in a minister's office."

"No," I chuckled, "I suppose not, but nowadays we have to cover the whole field in a human problem."

Then I told her about an old professor of mine at Ohio Wesleyan University, "Rolly" Walker, who said, "God runs a beauty parlor." He explained that some girls when they came to college were very pretty, but when they came back to visit the campus thirty years later their beauty had faded. The moonlight-and-roses loveliness of their youth did not last. On the other hand, other girls came to college who were very plain, but when they returned thirty years later they were beautiful women. "What made the difference?" he asked. "The latter had the beauty of an inner spiritual life written on their faces," and then he added, "God runs a beauty parlor."

Well, this young lady thought about what I told her for a few minutes and then she said, "There's a lot of truth in what you say. I'll try it."

Here is where her strong personality proved effective, for she did try it.

A number of years went by and I had forgotten her. Then in a certain city, after making a speech, a very lovely-looking lady with a fine-looking man and a little boy about ten years of age came up to me. The lady asked smilingly, "Well, how do you think it hangs?"

"How do I think what hangs?" I asked, puzzled.

"My dress," she said. "Do you think it hangs right?"

Bewildered, I said, "Yes, I think it hangs all right, but just why do you ask?"

"Don't you know me?" she asked.

"I see a great many people in my life," I said. "Frankly, no, I don't think I have ever seen you before."

Then she reminded me of our talk of years ago which I have described.

"Meet my husband and my little boy. What you told me was absolutely true," she said very earnestly. "I was the most frustrated, unhappy individual imaginable when I came to see you, but I put into practice the principles you suggested. I really did, and they worked."

Her husband then spoke up and said, "There was never a sweeter person in the world than Mary here," and I must say that she looked the part. She had evidently visited "God's beauty parlor."

Not only did she experience a softening and mellowing of her inner spirit, but she properly used a great quality which she possessed, namely, the driving force to get what she wanted. This led her to the point where she was willing to change herself so that her dreams could be realized. She had that quality of mind whereby she took herself in hand, she applied the spiritual techniques, and she had a profound and yet simple faith that what her heart told her she wanted could be obtained by the proper creative and positive procedures.

So the formula is to know what you want, test it to see if it is a right thing, change yourself in such a manner that it will naturally come to you, and always have faith. With the creative force of belief you stimulate that particular gathering together of circumstances which brings your cherished wish to pass.

Students of modern dynamic thought are realizing more and more the practical value of the ideas and teachings of Jesus, especially such truths as the dictum, "According to your faith, be it unto you." (Matthew 9:29) According to your faith in yourself, according to your faith in your job, according to your faith in God, this far will you get and no further. If you believe in your job and in yourself and in the opportunities of your country, and if you believe in God and will work hard and study and put yourself into it—in other words, if you "throw your heart over the bar," you can swing up to any high place to which you want to take your life and your service and your achievement. Whenever you have a bar, that is to say a barrier, in front of you, stop, close your eyes, visualize everything that is above the bar and nothing that is below it, then imaginatively throw "your heart" over that bar and see yourself as being given lifting power to rise above it. Believe that you are experiencing this upthrust of force. You will be amazed at the lifting force you will receive. If in the depth of your mind you visualize the best and employ the powers of faith and energy, you will get the best.

Naturally in this process of achieving the best it is important to know where you want to go in life. You can reach your goal, your best dreams can come true, you can get where you want to go only if you know what your goal is. Your expectation must have a clearly defined objective. Lots of people get nowhere simply because they do not know where they want to go. They have no clear-cut, precisely defined purpose. You cannot expect the best if you think aimlessly.

A young man of twenty-six consulted me because he was dissatisfied with his job. He was ambitious to fill a bigger niche in life and wanted to know how to improve his circumstances. His motive seemed unselfish and entirely worth while.

"Well, where do you want to go?" I asked.

"I just don't know exactly," he said hesitantly. "I have never given it any thought. I only know I want to go somewhere other than where I am."

"What can you do best?" I then asked. "What are your strong points?"

"I don't know," he responded. "I never thought that over either."

"But what would you like to do if you had your choice? What do you really want to do?" I insisted.

"I just can't say," he replied dully. "I don't really know what I would like to do. I never thought it over. Guess I ought to figure that one out too."

"Now, look here," I said, "you want to go somewhere from where you are, but you don't know where you want to go. You don't know what you can do or what you would like to do. You will have to get your ideas organized before you can expect to start getting anywhere."

That is the failure point with many people. They never get anywhere because they have only a hazy idea where they want to go, what they want to do. No objective leads to no end.

We made a thorough analysis, testing this young man's capabilities, and found some assets of personality he did not know he possessed. But it was necessary to supply a dynamic to move him forward, so we taught him the techniques of practical faith. Today he is on the way to achievement.

Now he knows where he wants to go and how to get there. He knows what the best is and he expects to attain it and he will—nothing can stop him.

I asked an outstanding newspaper editor, an inspiring personality, "How did you get to be the editor of this important paper?"

"I wanted to be," he replied simply.

"Is that all there is to it?" I asked. "You wanted to be and so there you are."

"Well, that may not be all of it, but that was a large part of the process," he explained. "I believe that if you want to get somewhere, you must decide definitely where you want to be or what you want to accomplish. Be sure it is a right objective, then photograph this objective on your mind and hold it there. Work hard, believe in it, and the thought will become so powerful that it will tend to assure success. There is a deep tendency," he declared, "to become what your mind pictures, provided you hold the mental picture strongly enough and if the objective is sound."

So saying, the editor pulled a well-worn card from his wallet and said, "I repeat this quotation every day of my life. It has become my dominating thought."

I copied it and am giving it to you: "A man who is self-reliant, positive, optimistic, and undertakes his work with the assurance of success magnetizes his condition. He draws to himself the creative powers of the universe."

It is indeed a fact that the person who thinks with positive self-reliance and optimism does magnetize his condition and releases power to attain his goal. So expect the best at all times. Never think of the worst. Drop it out of your thought, relegate it. Let there be no thought in your mind that the worst will happen. Avoid entertaining the concept of the worst, for whatever you take into your mind can grow there. Therefore take the best into your mind and only that. Nurture it, concentrate on it, emphasize it, visualize it, prayerize it, surround it with faith. Make it your obsession. Expect the best, and spiritually creative mind power aided by God power will produce the best.

It may be that as you read this book you are down to what you think is the worst and you may remark that no amount of thinking will affect your situation. The answer to that objection is that it simply isn't so. Even if you may be down to the worst, the best is potentially within you. You have only to find it, release it, and rise up with it. This requires courage and character, to be sure, but the main requirement is faith. Cultivate faith and you will have the necessary courage and character.

A woman was compelled by adversity to go into sales work, a type of activity for which she had no training. She undertook to demonstrate vacuum cleaners from house to house. She took a negative attitude toward herself and her work. She "just didn't believe she could do this job." She "knew" she was going to fail. She feared to approach a house even though she came for a requested demonstration. She believed that she could not make the sale. As a result, as is not surprising, she failed in a high percentage of her interviews.

One day she chanced to call upon a woman who evidenced consideration beyond the average. To this customer the saleswoman poured out her tale of defeat and powerlessness. The other woman listened patiently, then said quietly, "If you expect failure, you will get failure, but if you expect to succeed, I am sure you will succeed." And she added, "I will give you a formula which I believe will help you. It will restyle your thinking, give you new confidence, and help you to accomplish your goals. Repeat this formula before every call. Believe in it and then marvel at what it will do for you. This is it. 'If God be for us, who can be against us?' (Romans 8:31) But change it by personalizing it so that you say, 'If God be for *me*, who can be against *me?*' If God be for me, then I know that with God's help I can sell vacuum cleaners. God realizes that you want security and support for your little children and yourself, and by practicing the method I suggest you will be given power to get what you want."

She learned to utilize this formula. She approached each house expecting to make a sale, affirming and picturizing postitive, not negative, results. As the saleswoman employed this principle she presently acquired new courage, new faith, and deeper confidence in her own ability. Now she declares, "God helps me sell vacuum cleaners," and who can dispute it?

It is a well-defined and authentic principle that what the mind profoundly expects it tends to receive. Perhaps this is true because what you really expect is what you actually want. Unless you really want something sufficiently to create an atmosphere of positive factors by your dynamic desire, it is likely to elude you. "If with all your heart"—that is the secret. "If with all your heart," that is to say, if with the full complement of your personality, you reach out creatively toward your heart's desire, your reach will not be in vain.

Let me give you four words as a formulation of a great law—*faith power works wonders*. Those four words are packed with dynamic and creative force. Hold them in your conscious mind. Let them sink into the unconscious and they can help you to overcome any difficulty. Hold them in your thoughts, say them over and over again. Say them until your mind accepts them, until you believe them—*faith power works wonders*.

I have no doubt about the effectiveness of this concept, for I have seen it work so often that my enthusiasm for faith power is absolutely boundless.

You can overcome any obstacle. You can achieve the most tremendous things by faith power. And how do you develop faith power? The answer is: to saturate your mind with the great words of the Bible. If you will spend one hour a day reading the Bible and committing its great passages to memory, thus allowing them to recondition your personality, the change in you and in your experience will be little short of miraculous.

Just one section of the Bible will accomplish this for you. The eleventh chapter of Mark is enough. You will find the secret in the following words, and this is one of the greatest formulas the Book contains: "Have faith in God (that's positive, isn't it?) for verily I say unto you, that whosoever shall say unto *this* mountain (that's specific) be thou removed (that is, stand aside) and be thou cast into the sea (that means out of sight—anything you threw into the sea is gone for good. The *Titanic* lies at the bottom of the sea. And the sea bottom is lined with ships. Cast your opposition called a "mountain" into the sea) and shall not doubt in his heart (Why does this statement use the word heart: Because it means you are not to doubt in your subconscious, in the inner essence of you. It isn't so superficial as a doubt in the conscious mind. That is a normal, intelligent questioning. It's a deep fundamental doubt that is to be avoided) but shall believe that those things which he saith shall come to pass, he shall have whatsoever he saith." (Mark 11:22–23)

This is not some theory that I have thought up. It is taught by the most reliable book known to man. Generation after generation, no matter what develops in the way of knowledge and science, the Bible is read by more people than any other book. Humanity rightly has more confidence in it than any other document ever written, and the Bible tells us that faith power works wonders.

The reason, however, that great things do not happen to some people is that they are not specific in their application of faith power. We are told, "Ye shall say to *this* mountain." That is to say, do not address your efforts to the entire mountain range of all your difficulties, but attack one thing that may be defeating you at the moment. Be specific. Take them one by one.

If there is something you want, how do you go about getting it? In the first place, ask yourself, "Should I want it?" Test that question very honestly in prayer to be sure you should want it and whether you should have it. If you can answer that question in the affirmative, then ask God for it and don't be backward in asking Him. And if God, having more insight, believes that you shouldn't have it, you needn't worry—He won't give it to you. But if it is a right thing, ask Him for it, and when you ask, do not doubt in your heart. Be specific.

The validity of this law was impressed upon me by something that a friend of mine, a Midwestern businessman, told me. This man is a big, extrovertish, outgoing, lovable gentleman, a truly great Christian. He teaches the largest Bible class in his state. In the town where he lives he is Mr. "Town" himself. He is head of a plant employing forty thousand people.

His office desk is full of religious literature. He even has some of my sermons and pamphlets there. In his plant, one of the biggest in the United States, he manufactures refrigerators.

He is one of those whole-souled, rugged individuals who has the capacity to have faith. He believes that God is right there in his office with him.

My friend said, "Preach a big faith—not any little old watered-down faith. Don't be afraid that faith isn't scientific enough. I am a scientist," he said. "I use science in my business every day, and I use the Bible every day. The Bible will work. Everything in the Bible works if you believe in it."

When he was made general manager of this plant it was whispered around town, "Now that Mr. ——— is a general manager, we'll have to bring our Bibles to work with us." After a few days he called into his office some of the men who were making this remark. He uses language they understand, and he said, "I hear you guys are going around town saying that now I am general manager, you will have to bring your Bibles to work with you."

"Oh, we didn't mean that," they said in embarrassment.

He said, "Well, you know, that's a good idea, but I don't want you to come lugging them under your arms. Bring them here in your hearts and in your minds. If you come with a spirit of good will and faith in your hearts and minds, believe me, we'll do business.

"So," he said, "the kind of faith to have is the specific kind, the kind that moves this particular mountain."

Suddenly he said to me, "Did you ever have a toe bother you?"

I was rather astonished by that, but before I could answer he said, "I had a toe that bothered me and I took it to the doctors here in town, and they are wonderful doctors, and they said there wasn't anything wrong with the toe that they could see. But they were wrong, because it hurt. So I went out and got a book on anatomy and read up on toes. It is really a simple construction. There's nothing but a few muscles and ligaments and a bony structure. It seemed that anybody who knows anything about a toe could fix it, but I couldn't get anybody to fix that toe, and it hurt me all the time. So I sat down one day and took a look at that toe. Then I said, 'Lord, I'm sending this toe right back to the plant. You made that toe. I make refrigerators and I know all there is to know about a refrigerator. When we sell a refrigerator, we guarantee the customer service. If his refrigerator doesn't work right and if our service agents can't fix it, he brings it back to the plant and we fix it, because we know how.' So I said, 'Lord, you made this toe. You manufactured it, and your service agents, the doctors, don't seem to know how to get it working right, and if you don't mind, Lord, I would like to have it fixed up as soon as possible, because it's bothering me.' "

"How is the toe now?" I asked.

"Perfect," he replied.

Perhaps this is a foolish kind of story, and I laughed when he told it, but I almost cried, too, for I saw a wonderful look on that man's face as he related that incident of a specific prayer.

Be specific. Ask God for any right thing, but as a little child, don't doubt. Doubt closes the power flow. Faith opens it. The power of faith is so tremendous that there is nothing that Almighty God cannot do for us, with us, or through us if we let Him channel His power through our minds.

So roll those words around on your tongue. Say them over and over again until they lodge deeply in your mind, until they get down into your heart, until they take possession of the essence of you: ". . . whosoever shall say unto this mountain, be thou removed, and be thou cast into the sea, and shall not doubt in his heart, but shall believe that those things which he saith shall come to pass, he shall have whatsoever he saith." (Mark 11:23)

I suggested these principles some months ago to an old friend of mine, a man who perpetually expects the worst. Up to the time of our discussion, never did I hear him say anything other than that things would not turn out right. He took this negative attitude toward every project or problem. He expressed vigorous disbelief in the principles outlined in this chapter and offered to make a test to prove that I am wrong in my conclusions. He is an honest man, and he faithfully tried these principles in connection with several matters and actually kept a score card. He did this for six months. He volunteered the information at the end of that period that 85 per cent of the matters under investigation had turned out satisfactorily.

"I am now convinced," he said, "although I wouldn't have believed it possible, but it is evidently a fact, that if you expect the best, you are given some strange kind of power to create conditions that produce the desired results. From now on I am changing my mental attitude and shall expect the best, not the worst. My test indicates that this is not theory, but a scientific way to meet life's situations."

I might add that even the high percentage he attained can be raised with practice, and of course practice in the art of expectation is as essential as practice on a musical instruction or with a golf club. Nobody ever mastered any skill except through intensive, persistent, and intelligent practice. Also it should be noted that my friend approached this experiment at first in a spirit of doubt which would tend adversely to affect his earlier results.

Every day as you confront the problems of life, I suggest that you affirm as follows: "I believe God gives me power to attain what I really want."

Never mention the worst. Never think of it. Drop it out of your consciousness. At least ten times every day affirm, "I expect the best and with God's help will attain the best."

In so doing your thoughts will turn toward the best and become conditioned to its realization. This practice will bring all of your powers to focus upon the attainment of the best. It will bring the best to you.

8

I DON'T BELIEVE IN DEFEAT

If you are thinking thoughts of defeat, I urge you to rid yourself of such thoughts, for as you think defeat you tend to get it. Adopt the "I don't believe in defeat" attitude.

I want to tell you about some people who have put this philosophy into effect with excellent results and shall explain the techniques and formulas which they used so successfully. If you read these incidents carefully and thoughtfully and believe as they did and think positively and put these techniques into operation, you, too, can overcome defeats which at the present moment may seem inevitable.

I hope you are not like an "obstacle man" of whom I was told. He was called an obstacle man because, regardless of whatever suggestion was advanced, his mind instantly went to all possible obstacles in connection with it, but he met his match and learned a lesson which helped to change his negative attitude. It came about in the following manner.

The directors of his firm had a project under consideration which involved considerable expense and some definite hazards as well as success possibilities. In the discussions regarding this venture the obstacle man would invariably say, and always with a scholarly air (invariably this type acts wise, probably a cover-up for inner doubt feelings), "Now just a moment. Let's consider the obstacles involved."

Another man, who said very little but who was respected by his associates for his ability and achievements and for a certain indomitable quality which characterized him, presently spoke up and asked, "Why do you constantly emphasize the obstacles in this proposition instead of the possibilities?"

"Because," replied the obstacle man, "to be intelligent one must always be realistic, and it is a fact that there are certain definite obstacles in connection with this project. What attitude would you take toward these obstacles, may I ask?"

The other man unhesitatingly replied, "What attitude would I take toward these obstacles? Why, I would just remove them, that's all, and then I would forget them."

"But," said the obstacle man, "that is easier said than done. You say you would remove them and then you would forget them. May I ask if you have any technique for removing obstacles and for forgetting them that the rest of us have never discovered?"

A slow smile came over the face of the other man as he said, "Son, I have spent my entire life removing obstacles and I never yet saw one that could not be removed provided you had enough faith and guts and were willing to work. Since you want to know how it's done, I will show you."

He then reached into his pocket and took out his wallet. Under the isinglass window was a card on which were written some words. He shoved the wallet across the table and said, "There, son, read that. That is my formula, and don't give me the song and dance that it won't work either. I know better from experience."

The obstacle man picked up the wallet and with a strange look on his face read the words to himself.

"Read them out loud," urged the owner of the wallet.

This is what he read in a slow, dubious voice, "I can do all things through Christ which strengtheneth me." (Philippians 4:13)

The owner of the wallet put it back in his pocket and said, "I have lived a long time and have faced a lot of difficulties in my time, but there is power in those words—actual power—and with them you can remove any obstacle."

He said this with confidence and everybody knew he meant it. This positiveness, together with the facts of his experience which were known to all, for he was a remarkable man who had overcome many odds, and because of the further fact that he was not in any sense "holier than thou," made his words convincing to the men around the table. At any rate, there was no more negative talk. The project was put into operation and, despite difficulties and risks, turned out successfully.

The technique used by this man is based on the primary fact about an obstacle which is—don't be afraid of it. Practice believing that God is with you and that in combination with Him you have the power to handle it.

So the first thing to do about an obstacle is simply to stand up to it and not complain about it or whine under it but forthrightly attack it. Don't go crawling through life on your hands and knees half-defeated. Stand up to your obstacles and do something about them. You will find that they haven't half the strength you think they have.

A friend in England sent me a book by Winston Churchill entitled *Maxims and Reflections*. In this book Churchill tells of the British General Tudor, who commanded a division of the British Fifth Army which faced the great German assault in March 1918. The odds were heavily against him, but General Tudor knew how to meet an apparently immovable and undefeatable obstacle. His method was simple. He merely stood and let the obstacle break on him and he, in turn, broke the obstacle.

Here is what Churchill said about General Tudor. This is a very great sentence and it is filled with power: "The impression I had of Tudor was of an iron peg, hammered into the frozen ground, immovable."

General Tudor knew how to stand up to an obstacle. Just stand up to it, that's all, and don't give way under it, and it will finally break. You will break it. Something has to break, and it won't be you, it will be the obstacle.

You can do this when you have faith, faith in God and faith in yourself. Faith is the chief quality you need. It is enough. In fact, it is more than enough.

Use the formula which the businessman suggested and you will develop this brand of powerful faith in God and in yourself. You will learn to know yourself, your own ability, your power to do things. To the degree to which your attitude shifts from negative to positive the mastery touch will come to you. Then, with assurance, you can say to yourself under any and all circumstances and mean it, "I don't believe in defeat."

Take the story of Gonzales, who won the national tennis championship a few years ago in a grueling battle. He had been practically unknown, and because of wet weather he had not been able to perfect his game prior to the tournament. The sports writer of a metropolitan newspaper in analyzing Gonzales said that there were certain defects in his techniques, and gave it as his opinion that probably greater champions had played on the courts, however, he credited Gonzales with a marvelous serve and a skillful volley. But the factor that won the championship, said the writer, was his staying power and the further fact that "he was never defeated by the discouraging vicissitudes of the game."

That is one of the most subtle lines I have ever read in any sports story—"He was never defeated by the discouraging vicissitudes of the game."

It means, does it not, that when the game seemed to go against him he did not let discouragement creep in nor negative thoughts dominate and thus lose the power needed to win. This mental and spiritual quality made that man a champion. He was able to face obstacles, to stand up to them and overcome them.

Faith supplies staying power. It contains the dynamic to keep one going when the going is hard. Anybody can keep going when the going is good, but some extra ingredient is needed to enable you to keep fighting when it seems that everything is against you. It is a great secret, that of never being "defeated by the discouraging vicissitudes of the game."

You may counter, "But you don't know my circumstances. I am in a different situation than anybody else and I am as far down as a human being can get."

In that case you are fortunate, for if you are as far down as you can get there is no further down you can go. There is only one direction you can take from this position, and that is up. So your situation is quite encouraging. However, I caution you not to take the attitude that you are in a situation in which nobody has ever been before. There is no such situation.

Practically speaking, there are only a few human stories and they have all been enacted previously. This is a fact that you must never forget—there are people who have overcome every conceivable difficult situation, even the one in which you now find yourself and which to you seems utterly hopeless. So did it seem to some others, but they found an out, a way up, a path over, a pass through.

One of the most inspiring illustrations of this fact is the story of Amos Parrish who twice every year brings together hundreds of leading department-store executives and style experts in two huge clinics held in the Grand Ballroom of the Waldorf-Astoria Hotel in New York City. At these clinics Mr. Parrish gives advice to the merchants and their associates on business trends, on merchandise, on selling methods, and other matters important to the conduct of their business. Having attended a number of the clinics, however, I am convinced that the greatest values Mr. Parrish transmits to his customers are courage and positive thinking, a deep belief in themselves, and the confidence that they can overcome all difficulties.

He seems a living example of the philosophy which he teaches. As a boy he was sickly. Moreover, he stuttered. He was sensitive and a victim of an inferiority complex. It was thought that he would not live because of his weakened physical condition, but one day Amos Parrish had a spiritual experience. Faith dawned in his mind, and from then on he knew that with the help of God and the utilization of his own powers he could achieve.

He developed a unique idea of service to businessmen, and so highly do they rate it that they are willing to pay large fees to attend a two-day session twice a year under the business wisdom and inspiration of Amos Parrish. To me it is a moving experience to sit with that big crowd in a hotel ballroom and listen to "A. P.," as he is affectionately called, talk positive thinking to those important businessmen and women.

Sometimes he has the greatest difficulty with his stuttering, but he is never discouraged. He refers to it frankly and with a sense of humor. One day, for example, he was trying to say the word Cadillac. He tried several times and was unable to get it out, and finally did so with a powerful effort. Then he commented, "I can't even say C-C-C-Cadillac, let alone buy one." The audience roared with laughter, but I noted that they looked up at him with affection written on their faces. Everyone leaves a meeting at which he speaks with the conviction that they, too, can turn their obstacles into assets.

Again I repeat, there is no difficulty you cannot overcome. A wise and philosophical man once said to me, when asked how he overcame his difficulties, "How do I get through a trouble? Well, first I try to go around it, and if I can't go around it, I try to get under it, and if I can't get under it, I try to go over it, and if I can't get over it, I just plow right through it." Then he added, "God and I plow right through it."

Take seriously that formula of a businessman given earlier in this chapter. Stop reading for a moment and repeat it over to yourself five times, and each time you say it conclude with this affirmation, "I believe that." Here is the formula again, "I can do all things through Christ which strengtheneth me." (Philippians 4:13) Say that five times every day and it will release indomitable power in your mind.

Your subconscious, which always resents any change, may say to you, "You don't believe any such thing." But remember that your subconscious mind in a sense is one of the greatest liars in existence. It concurs in and sends back to you your own errors about your abilities. You have created the negative attitude in your subconscious and it gives this error back to you. So just turn on your subconscious and say to it, "Now look here, I do believe that. I insist upon believing it." If you talk to your subconscious mind with that positiveness, in due course it will be convinced. One reason is because you are now feeding it positive thoughts. In other words, you are at last telling the truth to your subconscious. After a while your subconscious mind will begin to send back the truth to you, the truth being that with the help of Jesus Christ there isn't any obstacle you cannot overcome.

An effective method for making your subconscious positive in character is to eliminate certain expressions of thought and speech which we may call the "little negatives." These so-called "little negatives" clutter up the average person's conversation, and while each one is seemingly unimportant in itself, the total effect of these attitudes is to condition the mind negatively. When this thought of "little negatives" first occurred to me, I began to analyze my own conversational habits and was shocked by what I found. I discovered that I was making such statements as, "I'm afraid I'll be late," or "I wonder if I'll have a flat tire," or "I don't think I can do that," or "I'll never get through this job. There's so much to do." If something turned out badly, I might say, "Oh, that's just what I expected." Or, again, I might observe a few clouds in the sky and would gloomily state, "I knew it was going to rain."

These are "little negatives" to be sure, and a big thought is of course more powerful than a little one, but it must never be forgotten that "mighty oaks from little acorns grow," and if a mass of "little negatives" clutter up your conversation, they are bound to seep into your mind. It is surprising how they accumulate in force, and presently, before you know it, they will grow into "big negatives." So I determined to go to work on the "little negatives" and root them out of my conversation. I found that the best way to eliminate them was deliberately to say a positive word about everything. When you keep asserting that things are going to work out well, that you can do the job, that you will not have a flat tire, that you will get there on time, by talking up good results you invoke the law of positive effects and good results occur. Things do turn out well.

On a roadside billboard I saw an advertisement of a certain brand of motor oil. The slogan read, "A clean engine always delivers power." So will a mind free of negatives produce positives, that is to say, a clean mind will deliver power. Therefore flush out your thoughts, give yourself a clean mental engine, remembering that a clean mind, even as a clean engine, always delivers power.

So to overcome your obstacles and live the "I don't believe in defeat" philosophy, cultivate a positive-idea pattern deeply in your consciousness. What we do with obstacles is directly determined by our mental attitude. Most of our obstacles, as a matter of fact, are mental in character.

"Ah," you may object, "mine are not mental, mine are real."

Perhaps so, but your attitude toward them is mental. The only possible way you can have an attitude is by the mental process, and what you think about your obstacles largely determines what you do about them. Form the mental attitude that you cannot remove an obstacle and you will not remove it, not if you think you can't. But get the idea firmly fixed that the obstacle is not so great as you previously considered it to be. Hold the idea that it is removable, and however faintly you entertain this positive thought, from the very moment you begin to think in this manner, the process is inaugurated which will lead to its ultimate removal.

If you have been long defeated by a difficulty, it is probably because you have told yourself for weeks, months, and even for years that there is nothing you can do about it. You have so emphasized your inability to yourself that your mind gradually accepted the conclusion upon which you have insisted, and when your mind is convinced, you are convinced, for as you think so are you.

But, on the contrary, when you employ this new and creative concept, "I can do all things through Christ," then you develop a new mental slant. Emphasize and reemphasize that positive attitude and you will finally convince your own consciousness that you can do something about difficulties. When at last your mind becomes convinced, astonishing results will begin to happen. Of a sudden you discover that you have the power you would never acknowledge.

I played golf with a man who was not only an excellent golfer but a philosopher as well. As we went around the golf course the game itself drew out of him certain gems of wisdom for one of which I shall ever be grateful.

I hit a ball into the rough, into some high grass. When we came up to my ball I said in some dismay, "Now just look at that. I certainly am in the rough. I have a bad lie. It is going to be tough getting out of here."

My friend grinned and said, "Didn't I read something about positive thinking in your books?"

Sheepishly I acknowledged that such was the case.

"I wouldn't think negatively about that lie of yours," he said. "Do you think you could get a good hit if this ball were lying out on the fairway on the short grass?"

I said I thought so.

"Well," he continued, "why do you think you could do better out there than here?"

"Because," I replied, "the grass is cut short on the fairway and the ball can get away better."

Then he did a curious thing. "Let's get down on our hands and knees," he suggested, "and examine the situation. Let's see how this ball does lie."

So we got down on our hands and knees, and he said, "Observe that the relative height of the ball here is about the same as it would be on the fairway, the only difference being that you have about five or six inches of grass above the ball."

Then he did an even more whimsical thing. "Notice the quality and character of this grass," he said. He pulled off a blade and handed it to me. "Chew it," he said.

I chewed, and he asked, "Isn't that tender?"

"Why, yes," I replied. "It certainly does seem to be tender grass."

"Well," he continued, "an easy swing of your number-five iron will cut through that grass almost like a knife." And then he gave me this sentence which I am going to remember as long as I live, and I hope you will also.

"The rough is only mental. In other words," he continued, "it is rough because you think it is. In your mind you have decided that here is an obstacle which will cause you difficulty. The power to overcome this obstacle is in your mind. If you visualize yourself lifting that ball out of the rough, believing you can do it, your mind will transfer flexibility, rhythm, and power to your muscles and you will handle that club in such a manner that the ball will rise right out of there in a beautiful shot. All you need to do is to keep your eye on that ball and tell yourself that you are going to lift it out of that grass with a lovely stroke. Let the stiffness and tension go out of you. Hit it with exhilaration and power. Remember, the rough is only mental."

To this day I remember the thrill, the sense of power and delight I had in the clean shot that dropped the ball to the edge of the green.

That is a very great fact to remember in connection with difficult problems—"the rough is only mental."

Your obstacles are present all right. They are not fanciful, but they are not actually so difficult as they seem. Your mental attitude is the most important factor. Believe that Almighty God has put in you the power to lift yourself out of the rough by keeping your eye firmly fixed on the source of your power. Affirm to yourself that through this power you can do anything you have to do. Believe that this power is taking the tension out of you, that this power is flowing through you. Believe this, and a sense of victory will come.

Now take another look at that obstacle that has been bothering you. You will find that it isn't so formidable as you thought. Say to yourself, "The rough is only mental. I think victory—I get victory." Remember that formula. Write it on a piece of paper, put it in your wallet, stick it up on your mirror where you shave each morning, put it over the kitchen sink, put it on your dressing table and on your desk—keep looking at it until its truth drives into the depths of your consciousness, until it permeates your whole mental attitude, until it becomes a positive obsession—"I can do all things through Christ which strengtheneth me."

What may seem to be a difficult proposition is, as I have pointed out, hard or easy in proportion to how we think about it. It may be said that three men vitally affected the thought processes of Americans—Emerson, Thoreau, and William James. Analyze the American mind even to this late date and it is evident that the teachings of these three philosophers combined to create that particular genius of the American who is not defeated by obstacles and who accomplishes "impossibles" with amazing efficiency.

A fundamental doctrine of Emerson is that the human personality can be touched with Divine power and thus greatness can be released from it. William James pointed out that the greatest factor in any undertaking is one's belief about it. Thoreau told us that the secret of achievement is to hold a picture of a successful outcome in mind.

Still another wise American was Thomas Jefferson, who, like Franklin, set for his guidance a series of rules. Franklin had thirteen daily rules; Jefferson only ten. One of Jefferson's rules was this, and I think it is priceless. "Always take hold of things by the smooth handle." That is, go at a job or at your difficulty by the use of a method that will encounter the least resistance. Resistance causes friction in mechanics, therefore it is necessary in mechanics to overcome or reduce friction. The negative attitude is a friction approach. That is why negativism develops such great resistance. The positive approach is the "smooth handle" technique. It is in harmony with the flow of the universe. It not only encounters less resistance, but actually stimulates assistance forces. It is remarkable how from early life until the end of your earthly existence the application of this philosophy will enable you to attain successful results in areas where otherwise you would be defeated.

For example, a woman sent her fifteen-year-old son to us. She said she wanted him "straightened out." It annoyed her no end that her boy could never get over 70 in any of his studies. "This boy has a great mind potentially," she declared proudly.

"How do you know he has a great mind?" I asked.

"Because he is my son," she said. "I graduated from college *magna cum laude.*"

The boy came in very glumly, so I asked, "What's the matter, son?"

"I don't know. My mother sent me to see you."

"Well," I commented, "you don't seem to be burning with enthusiasm. Your mother says you get only 70's."

"Yes," he said, "that's all I get, and," he added, "that isn't the worst of it. I've even received less than that."

"Do you think you have a good mind, son?" I asked.

"My mother says I have. I don't know—I think I'm awful dumb, Dr. Peale," he said earnestly, "I study the stuff. At home I read it over once and then close the book and try to remember it. I repeat this process about three times, and then I think that if three times doesn't get it into my head how am I ever going to get it into my head? And then I got to school thinking maybe I have it, and the teacher calls on me to say something, and I stand up and can't remember a thing. Then," he said, "examinations come along and I sit there and just get hot and cold all over and I can't think of the answers. I don't know why," he continued. "I know that my mother was a great scholar. I guess I just haven't got it in me."

This negative thought pattern combined with the inferiority feeling stimulated by his mother's attitude was of course overwhelming him. He froze up in his mind. His mother had never told him to go to school and study for the wonder and glory of learning knowledge. She was not wise enough to encourage him to compete with himself rather than with others. And she was constantly insisting that he duplicate her success in scholarship. Little wonder that under this pressure he froze mentally.

I gave him some suggestions that proved helpful. "Before you read your lessons, pause a moment and pray in this manner, 'Lord, I know I have a good mind and that I can get my work.' Then get yourself relaxed and read the book without strain. Imagine you are reading a story. Do not read it twice unless you wish. Simply believe that you got it on the first reading. Visualize the material as soaking in and germinating. Then next morning, as you go to school, say to yourself, 'I have a wonderful mother. She is very pretty and sweet, but she must have been an old bookworm to get those high marks. And who wants to be an old bookworm anyway? I don't want to become magna cum nothing. I only want to get through school creditably.'

"In class, when the teacher calls on you, quickly pray before answering. Then believe the Lord will at that moment help your mind to deliver. When an examination is given, affirm in prayer that God is releasing your mind and that the right answers are given you."

The boy followed these ideas, and what marks do you think he got the following semester? Ninety! I am sure that this boy, having discovered the amazing workability of the "I don't believe in defeat philosophy," will employ the amazing power of positive thinking in all the affairs of his life.

I could use so many illustrations of the manner in which men's lives have been revamped by these procedures that this book would grow to unwieldy size. Moreover, these are incidents and experiences out of everyday life that are in no way theoretical, but are entirely practical. My mail is literally filled with testimonials sent by people who, having heard or read accounts I have told of victorious life experiences, have felt moved to relate similar occurrences in their own lives.

Such a letter came from a gentleman who tells about his father as follows. I know several people who have used the plan in this letter with amazing results.

"My father was a traveling salesman. One time he sold furniture, another time hardware, sometimes it was leather goods. He changed his line every year.

"I would hear him telling Mother that this was his last trip in stationery or in bed lamps or whatever it was he was selling at the moment. Next year everything would be different; we would be on Easy Street. He had a chance to go with a firm that had a product that sold itself. It was always the same. My father never had a product that sold. He was always tense, always afraid of himself, always whistling in the dark.

"Then one day a fellow salesman gave Father a copy of a little three-sentence prayer. He was told to repeat it just before calling on a customer. Father tried it, and the results were almost miraculous. He sold 85 percent of all calls made during the first week, and every week thereafter the results were wonderful. Some weeks the percentage ran as high as 95, and

Father had sixteen weeks in which he sold every customer called on.

"Father gave this prayer to several other salesmen, and in each case it brought astounding results.

"The prayer my father used is as follows:

'I believe I am always divinely guided.

I believe I will always take the right turn of the road.

I believe God will always make a way where there is no way.' "

The head of a small firm who had a great many difficulties in establishing his business told me that he was immeasurably helped by a technique which he invented. He had trouble, he said, with the tendency to "blow up" a small difficulty into a seemingly insurmountable obstacle. He knew that he was approaching his problems in a defeatist attitude, and had common sense enough to realize that these obstacles were not so difficult as he made them appear to be. As he told the story, I wondered if he did not have that curious psychological difficulty known as the will to fail.

He employed a device which reconditioned his mental attitude and after a time had a noticeable effect on his business. He simply placed a large wire basket on his office desk. The following words were printed on a card and wired to this basket, "With God all things are possible." Whenever a problem came up which the old mechanism of defeat began to develop into a big difficulty, he threw the paper pertaining to it into the basket marked "With God all things are possible" and let it rest there for a day or two. "It is queer how each matter when I took it out of that basket again didn't seem difficult at all," he reported.

In this act he dramatized the mental attitude of putting the problem in God's hands. As a result he received power to handle the problem normally and therefore successfully.

As you finish this chapter please say the following line aloud: "I don't believe in defeat." Continue to affirm that until the idea dominates your subconscious attitudes.

9

HOW TO BREAK THE WORRY HABIT

You do not need to be a victim of worry. Reduced to its simplest form, what is worry? It is simply an unhealthy and destructive mental habit. You were not born with the worry habit. You acquired it. And because you can change any habit and any acquired attitude, you can cast worry from your mind. Since aggressive, direct action is essential in the elimination process, there is just one proper time to begin an effective attack on worry, and that is now. So let us start breaking your worry habit at once.

Why should we take the worry problem this seriously? The reason is clearly stated by Dr. Smiley Blanton, eminent psychiatrist, "Anxiety is the great modern plague."

A famous psychologist asserts that "fear is the most disintegrating enemy of human personality," and a prominent physician declares that "worry is the most subtle and destructive of all human diseases." Another physician tells us that thousands of people are ill because of "dammed-up anxiety." These sufferers have been unable to expel their anxieties which have turned inward on the personality, causing many forms of ill health. The destructive quality of worry is indicated by the fact that the word itself is derived from an old Anglo-Saxon word meaning "to choke." If someone were to put his fingers around your throat and press hard, cutting off the flow of vital power, it would be a dramatic demonstration of what you do to yourself by long-held and habitual worry.

We are told that worry is not infrequently a factor in arthritis. Physicians who have analyzed the causes of this prevalent disease assert that the following factors, at least some of them, are nearly always present in arthritic cases: financial disaster, frustration, tension, apprehension, loneliness, grief, long-held ill will, and habitual worry.

A clinic staff is said to have made a study of one hundred seventy-six American executives of the average age of forty-four years and discovered that one half had high blood pressure, heart disease, or ulcers. It was notable in every case of those thus afflicted that worry was a prominent factor.

The worrier, so it seems, is not likely to live as long as the person who learns to overcome his worries. The *Rotarian* magazine carried an article entitled "How Long Can You Live?" The author says that the waistline is the measure of your life line. The article also declares that if you want to live long, observe the following rules: (1) Keep calm. (2) Go to church. (3) Eliminate worry.

A survey shows that church members live longer than non-church members (better join the church if you don't want to die young). Married people, according to the article, live longer than single people. Perhaps this is because a married couple can divide the worry. When you are single, you have to do it all alone.

A scientific expert on length of life made a study of some 450 people who lived to be one hundred years of age. He found that these people lived long and contented lives for the following reasons: (1) They kept busy. (2) They used moderation in all things. (3) They ate lightly and simply. (4) They got a great deal of fun out of life. (5) They were early to bed and early up. (6) They were free from worry and fear, especially fear of death. (7) They had serene minds and faith in God.

Haven't you often heard a person say, "I am almost sick with worry," and then add with a laugh, "But I guess worry never really makes you ill." But that is where he is wrong. Worry can make you ill.

Dr. George W. Crile, famous American surgeon, said, "We fear not only in our minds but in our hearts, brains, and viscera, that whatever the cause of fear and worry, the effect can always be noted in the cells, tissues, and organs of the body."

Dr. Stanley Cobb, neurologist, says that worry is intimately connected with the symptoms of rheumatoid arthritis.

A doctor recently stated that there is an epidemic of fear and worry in this country. "All doctors," he declared, "are having cases of illness which are brought on directly by fear, and aggravated by worry and a feeling of insecurity."

But do not be discouraged, for you can overcome your worries. There is a remedy that will bring you sure relief. It can help you break the worry habit. And the first step to take in breaking it is simply to believe that you can. Whatever you believe you can do, you can do, with God's help.

Here, then, is a practical procedure which will help to eliminate abnormal worry from your experience.

Practice emptying the mind daily. This should be done preferably before retiring at night to avoid the retention by the consciousness of worries while you sleep. During sleep, thoughts tend to sink more deeply into the subconscious. The last five minutes before going to sleep are of extraordinary importance, for in that brief period the mind is most receptive to suggestion. It tends to absorb the last ideas that are entertained in waking consciousness.

This process of mind drainage is important in overcoming worry, for fear thoughts, unless drained off, can clog the mind and impede the flow of mental and spiritual power. But such thoughts can be emptied from the mind and will not accumulate if they are eliminated daily. To drain them, utilize a process of creative imagination. Conceive of yourself as actually emptying your mind of all anxiety and fear. Picture all worry thoughts as flowing out as you would let water flow from a basin by removing the stopper. Repeat the following affirmation during this visualization: "With God's help I am now emptying my mind of all anxiety, all fear, all sense of insecurity." Repeat this slowly five times, then add, "I believe that my mind is now emptied of all anxiety, all fear, all sense of insecurity." Repeat that statement five times, meanwhile holding a mental picture of your mind as being emptied of these concepts. Then thank God for thus freeing you from fear. Then go to sleep.

In starting the curative process the foregoing method should be utilized in midmorning and midafternoon as well as at bedtime. Go into some quiet place for five minutes for this purpose. Faithfully perform this process and you will soon note beneficial results.

The procedure may be further strengthened by imaginatively thinking of yourself as reaching into your mind and one by one removing your worries. A small child possesses an imaginative skill superior to that of adults. A child responds to the game of kissing away a hurt or throwing away a fear. This simple process works for the child because in his mind he believes that that is actually the end of it. The dramatic act is a fact for him and so it proves to be the end of the matter. Visualize your fears as being drained out of your mind and the visualization will in due course be actualized.

Imagination is a source of fear, but imagination may also be the cure of fear. "Imagineering" is the use of mental images to build factual results, and it is an astonishingly effective procedure. Imagination is not simply the use of fancy. The word imagination derives from the idea of imaging. That is to say, you form an image either of fear or of release from fear. What you "image" (imagine) may ultimately become a fact if held mentally with sufficient faith.

Therefore hold an image of yourself as delivered from worry and the drainage process will in time eliminate abnormal fear from your thoughts. However, it is not enough to empty the mind, for the mind will not long remain empty. It must be occupied by something. It cannot continue in a state of vacuum. Therefore, upon emptying the mind, practice refilling it. Fill it with thoughts of faith, hope, courage, expectancy. Say aloud such affirmations as the following: "God is now filling my mind with courage, with peace, with calm assurance. God is now protecting me from all harm. God is now protecting my loved ones from all harm. God is now guiding me to right decisions. God will see me through this situation."

A half-dozen times each day crowd your mind with such thoughts as these until the mind is overflowing with them. In due course these thoughts of faith will crowd out worry. Fear is the most powerful of all thoughts with one exception, and that one exception is faith. Faith can always overcome fear. Day by day, as you fill your mind with faith, there will ultimately be no room left for fear. This is the one great fact that no one should forget. Master faith and you will automatically master fear.

So the process is—empty the mind and cauterize it with God's grace, then practice filling your mind with faith and you will break the worry habit.

Fill your mind with faith and in due course the accumulation of faith will crowd out fear. It will not be of much value merely to read this suggestion unless you practice it. And the time to begin practicing it is now while you think of it and while you are convinced that the number-one procedure in breaking the worry habit is to drain the mind daily of fear and fill the mind daily with faith. It is just as simple as that. Learn to be a practicer of faith until you become an expert in faith. Then fear cannot live in you.

The importance of freeing your mind of fear cannot be overemphasized. Fear something over a long period of time and there is a real possibility that by fearing you may actually help bring it to pass. The Bible contains a line which is one of the most terrible statements ever made—terrible in its truth: "For the thing which I greatly feared is come upon me . . ." (Job 3:25) Of course it will, for if you fear something continuously you tend to create conditions in your mind propitious to the development of that which you fear. An atmosphere is encouraged in which it can take root and grow. You tend to draw it to yourself.

But do not be alarmed. The Bible also constantly reiterates another great truth, "That which I have greatly believed has come upon me." It does not make that statement in so many words, and yet again and again and still again the Bible tells us that if we have faith "nothing is impossible" unto us, and "according to your faith be it done unto you." So if you shift your mind from fear to faith you will stop creating the object of your fear and will, instead, actualize the object of your faith. Surround your mind with healthy thoughts, thoughts of faith, and not fear, and you will produce faith results instead of fear results.

Strategy must be used in the campaign against the worry habit. A frontal attack on the main body of worry with the expectation of conquering it may prove difficult. Perhaps a more adroit plan is to conquer the outer fortifications one by one, gradually closing in on the main position.

To change the figure, it might be well to snip off the little worries on the farthest branches of your fear. Then work back and finally destroy the main trunk of worry.

At my farm it was necessary to take down a large tree, much to my regret. Cutting down a great old tree is fraught with sadness. Men came with a motor-driven saw and I expected them to start by cutting through the main trunk near the ground. Instead, they put up ladders and began snipping off the small branches, then the larger ones, and finally the top of the tree. Then all that remained was the huge central trunk, and in a few moments my tree lay neatly stacked as though it had not spent fifty years in growing.

"If we had cut the tree at the ground before trimming off the branches, it would have broken nearby trees in falling. It is easier to handle a tree the smaller you can make it," so explained the tree man.

The vast tree of worry which over long years has grown up in your personality can best be handled by making it as small as possible. Thus it is advisable to snip off the little worries and expressions of worry. For example, reduce the number of worry words in your conversation. Words may be the result of worry, but they also create worry. When a worry thought comes to mind, immediately remove it with a faith thought and expression. For example: "I'm worried that I will miss the train." Then start early enough to be sure you get there on time. The less worrying you do, the more likely you are to start promptly, for the uncluttered mind is systematic and is able to regulate time.

As you snip off these small worries you will gradually cut back to the main trunk of worry. Then with your developed greater power you will be able to eliminate basic worry, i.e., the worry habit, from your life.

My friend Dr. Daniel A. Poling gives a valuable suggestion. He says that every morning before he arises he repeats these two words, "I believe" three times. Thus at the day's beginning he conditions his mind to faith, and it never leaves him. His mind accepts the conviction that by faith he is going to overcome his problems and difficulties during the day. He starts the day with creative positive thoughts in his mind. He "believes," and it is very difficult to hold back the man who believes.

I related Dr. Poling's "I believe" technique in a radio talk and had a letter from a woman who told me that she had not been very faithful to her religion which happened to be the Jewish faith. She said their home was filled with contention, bickering, worry, and unhappiness. Her husband, she declared, "drank far too much for his own good" and sat around all day doing no work. He weakly complained that he couldn't find a job. This woman's mother-in-law lived with her and the latter "whined and complained of her aches and pains all the while."

This woman said that Dr. Poling's method impressed her and she decided to try it herself. So the next morning upon awakening she affirmed, "I believe, I believe, I believe." In her letter she excitedly reported, "It has been only ten days since I started this plan and my husband came home last night and told me he had a job paying $80 a week. And he also says that he is going to quit drinking. I believe he means it. What is even more wonderful, my mother-in-law has practically stopped complaining of her aches and pains. It is almost as if a miracle has happened in this house. My worries seem to have just about disappeared."

That does indeed seem almost magical, and yet that miracle happens every day to people who shift over from negative fear thoughts to positive faith thoughts and attitudes.

My good friend, the late Howard Chandler Christy, the artist, had many a sound anti-worry technique. Scarcely ever have I known a man so filled with the joy and delight of life. He had an indomitable quality, and his happiness was infectious.

My church has a policy of having the minister's portrait painted sometime during his pastorate. This portrait hangs in the minister's home until his death, when it reverts to the church and is placed in a gallery along with pictures of his predecessors. It is usually the policy of the Board of Elders and Deacons to have a portrait painted when in their wise judgment the minister is at the height of his good looks (mine was painted several years ago).

While sitting for Mr. Christy, I asked, "Howard, don't you ever worry?"

He laughed. "No, not on your life. I don't believe in it."

"Well," I commented, "that is quite a simple reason for not worrying. In fact, it seems to me too simple—you just don't believe in it, therefore you don't do it. Haven't you ever worried?" I asked.

He replied, "Well, yes, I tried it once. I noticed that everybody else seemed to worry and I figured I must be missing something, so one day I made up my mind to try it. I set aside a day and said, 'That is to be my worry day.' I decided I would investigate this worry business and do some worrying just to see what it was like.

"The night before the day came I went to bed early to get a good night's sleep to be rested up to do a good job of worrying the next day. In the morning I got up, ate a good breakfast—for you can't worry successfully on an empty stomach—and then decided to get to my worrying. Well, I tried my best to worry until along about noon, but I just couldn't make heads nor tails of it. It didn't make sense to me, so I just gave it up."

He laughed one of those infectious laughs of his.

"But," I said, "you must have some other method overcoming worry." He did indeed, and it is perhaps the best method of all.

"Every morning I spend fifteen minutes filling my mind full of God," he said. "When your mind is full of God, there is no room for worry. I fill my mind full of God every day and I have the time of my life all day long."

Howard Christy was a great artist with a brush, but he was an equally great artist with life because he was able to take a great truth and simplify it down to its basic fact, namely, that only that comes out of the mind which originally you put into the mind. Fill the mind with thoughts of God rather than with thoughts of fear, and you will get back thoughts of faith and courage.

Worry is a destructive process of occupying the mind with thoughts contrary to God's love and care. Basically that is all worry is. The cure is to fill the mind with thoughts of God's power, His protection, and His goodness. So spend fifteen minutes daily filling your mind full of God. Cram your mind full of the "I believe philosophy, " and you will have no mental room left to accommodate thoughts of worry and lack of faith.

Many people fail to overcome such troubles as worry because, unlike Howard Christy, they allow the problem to seem complicated and do not attack it with some simple technique. It is surprising how our most difficult personal problems often yield to an uncomplicated methodology. This is due to the fact that it is not enough to know what to do about difficulties. We must also know how to do that which should be done.

The secret is to work out a method of attack and keep working at it. There is value in doing something that dramatizes to our own minds that an effective counterattack is in process. In so doing we bring spiritual forces to bear upon the problem in a manner both understandable and usable.

One of the best illustrations of this technique strategy against worry was a scheme developed by a businessman. He was a tremendous worrier. In fact he was fast getting himself into a bad state of nerves and ill-health. His particular form of worry was that he was always doubtful as to whether he had done or said the right thing. He was always rehashing his decisions and getting himself unnerved about them. He was a post-mortem expert. He is an exceptionally intelligent man, in fact a graduate of two universities, in both instances with honors. I suggested that he ought to work out some simple method that would help him to drop the day when it was over and go ahead into the future and forget it. I explained the gripping effectiveness of simple, dramatized spiritual truth.

It is always true that the greatest minds have the best ability to be simple, that is, they have the capacity to work out some simple plans for putting profound truths into operation, and this man did that in connection with his worries. I noticed that he was improving and commented on it.

"Oh, yes," he said, "I finally got the secret and it has worked amazingly well." He said that if I would drop into his office sometime toward the close of the day he would show me how he had broken the worry habit. He telephoned me one day and asked me to have dinner that evening. I met him at his office at closing time. He explained that he had broken his worry habit by working out "a little ritual" that he performed every night before leaving his office. And it was very unique. It made a lasting impression upon me.

We picked up our hats and coats and started toward the door. By the door of his office stood a wastebasket and above it on the wall was a calendar. It was not one of those calendars where you see a week or a month, or three months, it was a one-day calendar. You could see only one date at a time, and that date was in large print. He said, "Now I will perform my evening ritual, the one that has helped me break the worry habit."

He reached up and tore off the calendar page for that particular day. He rolled it into a small ball and I watched with fascination as his fingers slowly opened and he dropped the "day" into the wastebasket. Then he closed his eyes and his lips moved, and I knew that he was praying, so was respectfully silent. Upon finishing his prayer he said aloud, "Amen. O.K., the day is over. Come on, let's go out and enjoy ourselves."

As we walked down the street I asked, "Would you mind telling me what you said in that prayer?"

He laughed and said, "I don't think it is your kind of prayer." But I persisted, and he said, "Well, I pray something like this: 'Lord, you gave me this day. I didn't ask for it, but I was glad to have it. I did the best I could with it and you helped me, and I thank you. I made some mistakes. That was when I didn't follow your advice, and I am sorry about that. Forgive me. But I had some victories and some successes, too, and I am grateful for your guidance. But now, Lord, mistakes or successes, victories or defeats, the day is over and I'm through with it, so I'm giving it back to you. Amen.' "

Perhaps that isn't an orthodox prayer, but it certainly proved to be an effective one. He dramatized the finishing of the day and he set his face to the future, expecting to do better the next day. He cooperated with God's method. When the day is over, God blacks it out by bringing down the curtain of night. By this method this man's past mistakes and failures, his sins of omission and commission gradually lost their hold on him. He was released from the worries that accumulated from his yesterdays. In this technique this man was practicing one of the most effective antiworry formulas, which is described in these words, ". . . but this one thing I do, forgetting those things which are behind, and reaching forth unto those things which are before, I press toward the mark for the prize of the high calling of God in Christ Jesus." (Philippians 3:13–14)

Other practical anti-worry techniques may suggest themselves to you, and I should like to hear of those which after careful use prove effective. I believe that all of us who are interested in self-improvement are fellow students in God's great spiritual laboratory. Together we work out practical methods of successful living. People from everywhere are kind enough to write me about their methods and the results attained. I try to be helpful in making tested methods available to others through books, sermons, newspaper columns, radio, television, and other media. In this manner there can be developed a great many people who have the know-how for overcoming not only worry but other personal problems as well.

To conclude this chapter in a manner designed to help you go to work *now* to break the worry habit, I list a ten-point worry-breaking formula.

1. Say to yourself, "Worry is just a very bad mental habit. And I can change any habit with God's help."

2. You became a worrier by practicing worry. You can become free of worry by practicing the opposite and stronger habit of faith. With all the strength and perseverance you can command, start practicing faith.

3. How do you practice faith? First thing every morning before you arise say out loud, "I believe," three times.

4. Pray, using the formula, "I place this day, my life, my loved ones, my work in the Lord's hands. There is no harm in the Lord's hands, only good. Whatever happens, whatever results, if I am in the Lord's hands it is the Lord's will and it is good."

5. Practice saying something positive concerning everything about which you have been talking negatively. Talk positively. For example, don't say, "This is going to be a terrible day." Instead, affirm, "This is going to be a glorious day." Don't say, "I'll never be able to do that." Instead, affirm, "With God's help I will do that."

6. Never participate in a worry conversation. Shoot an injection of faith into all your conversations. A group of people talking pessimistically can infect every person in the group with negativism. But by talking things up rather than down you can drive off that depressing atmosphere and make everyone feel hopeful and happy.

7. One reason you are a worrier is that your mind is literally saturated with apprehension thoughts, defeat thoughts, gloomy thoughts. To counteract, mark every passage in the Bible that speaks of faith, hope, happiness, glory, radiance. Commit each to memory. Say them over and over again until these creative thoughts saturate your subconscious mind. Then the subconscious will return to you what you have given it, namely, optimism, not worry.

8. Cultivate friendships with hopeful people. Surround yourself with friends who think positive, faith-producing thoughts and who contribute to a creative atmosphere. This will keep you restimulated with faith attitudes.

9. See how many people you can help to cure their own worry habit. In helping another to overcome worry you get greater power over it within yourself.

10. Every day of your life conceive of yourself as living in partnership and companionship with Jesus Christ. If He actually walked by your side, would you be worried or afraid? Well, then, say to yourself, "He is with me." Affirm aloud, "I am with you always." Then change it to say, "He is with me now." Repeat that affirmation three times every day.

10

POWER TO SOLVE PERSONAL PROBLEMS

I want to tell you about some fortunate people who found the right solution to their problems.

They followed a simple but highly practical plan and in each case the outcome was a happy and successful one. These people are in no sense different than you. They had the same problems and difficulties that you have, but they found a formula which helped them to get the right answers to the difficult questions facing them. This same formula applied by you can get similar results.

First, let me tell you the story of a husband and wife, long-time friends of mine. For years Bill, the husband, worked hard until he finally reached the ring next to the top of the ladder in his company. He was in line for the presidency of the firm and felt certain that upon retirement of the president he would be advanced to that position. There was no apparent reason why his ambition should be not realized, for by ability, training, and experience he was qualified. Besides, he had been led to believe he was to be chosen.

However, when the appointment was made he was by-passed. A man was brought in from the outside to fill the post.

I arrived in his city just after the blow had fallen. The wife, Mary, was in an especially vindictive state of mind. At dinner she bitterly outlined all that she would "like to tell them." The intense disappointment, humiliation, frustration, focused in a burning anger which she poured out to her husband and me.

Bill, on the contrary, was quiet. Obviously hurt, disappointed, and bewildered, he took it courageously. Being essentially a gentle person, it was not surprising that he failed to become angry or violent in his reaction. Mary wanted him to resign immediately. She urged him to "tell them off and tell them plenty, then quit."

He seemed disinclined to take this action, saying perhaps it was for the best and he would go along with the new man and help him in any way that he could.

That attitude admittedly might be difficult, but he had worked for the company for so long that he would not be happy elsewhere, and, besides, he felt that in the secondary position the company could continue to use him.

The wife then turned to me and asked what I would do. I told her that I would, like herself, undoubtedly feel disappointed and hurt, but that I would try not to allow hate to creep in, for animosity not only corrodes the soul, but disorganizes thought processes as well.

I suggested that what we needed was Divine guidance, a wisdom beyond ourselves in this situation. There was such an emotional content in the problem that we might possibly be incapable of thinking the matter through objectively and rationally.

I suggested, therefore, that we have a few minutes of quietness, no one saying anything, that we sit quietly in an attitude of fellowship and prayer, turning our thoughts to the One who said, "Where two or three are gathered together in my name, there am I in the midst of them." (Matthew 18:20) I pointed out that there were three of us, and if we sought to achieve the spirit of being gathered in "His" name, He would also be present to quiet us and show us what to do.

It was not easy for the wife to accommodate herself to the mood suggested, but basically she was an intelligent, high-type person, and she joined in the plan.

Presently, after a few quiet minutes, I suggested that we join hands, and even though we were in a public restaurant I would quietly offer a prayer. In the prayer I asked for guidance. I requested peace of mind for Bill and Mary, and I went a step further and even asked God's blessing upon the new appointee. I also prayed that Bill would be able to fit in with the new administration and give more effective service than before.

After the prayer we sat silent for a time, then with a sigh the wife said, "Yes, I guess that is the way to do it. When I knew you were coming to dinner with us I feared that you would tell us to take a Christian position on this. Frankly, I didn't feel like doing that. I was boiling inwardly, but of course I realize that the right answer to this problem is to be found through that approach, I will try it faithfully, as difficult as it may be." She smiled wanly, but the animus was gone.

From time to time I checked with my friends, and found that while everything was not entirely as they desired, they gradually became contented under the new arrangement. They were able to overcome their disappointment and ill will.

Bill even confided to me that he liked the new man and in a way enjoyed working with him. He told me that the new president often called him in for consultation and seemed to lean on him.

Mary was nice to the president's wife, and in fact they went to the fullest extent to be cooperative.

Two years passed. One day I arrived in their city and telephoned them.

"Oh, I am so excited I can hardly speak," Mary said.

I commented that anything that could put her in that state must be of unusual importance.

Ignoring this remark, she cried, "Oh, the most wonderful thing has happened. Mr. So-and-So," naming the president, "has been selected by another company at a big promotion for a special job which will take him out of our organization into a much better position and"—she posed the question—"guess what? Bill has just been notified that he is now president of this company. Come over right away and let the three of us give thanks together."

Later, as we sat together, Bill said, "Do you know, I am beginning to realize that Christianity isn't theoretical after all. We have solved a problem according to well-defined spiritually scientific principles. I shudder to think," he said, "of the terrible mistake we would have made had we not gone at this problem according to the formula contained in the teachings of Jesus.

"Who in the world," he asked, "is responsible for the silly idea that Christianity is impractical? Never again will I let a problem come up without attacking it in just the way the three of us solved this one."

Well, several years have passed, and Mary and Bill have had other problems, and to each of them they have applied this same technique, invariably with good results. By the "put it in God's hands" method they have learned to solve their problems right.

Another effective technique in problem solving is the simple device of conceiving of God as a partner. One of the basic truths taught by the Bible is that God is with us. In fact, Christianity begins with that concept, for when Jesus Christ was born He was called Immanuel, meaning "God with us."

Christianity teaches that in all the difficulties, problems, and circumstances of this life God is close by. We can talk to Him, lean upon Him, get help from Him, and have the inestimable benefit of His interest, support and help. Practically everybody believes in a general way that this is true, and many have experienced the reality of this faith.

In getting correct solutions to your problems, however, it is necessary to go a step further than believing this, for one must actually practice the idea of presence. Practice believing that God is as real and actual as your wife, or your business partner, or your closest friend. Practice talking matters over with Him; believe that He hears and gives thought to your problem. Assume that He impresses upon your mind through consciousness the proper ideas and insights necessary to solve your problems. Definitely believe that in these solutions there will be no error, but that you will be guided according to truth which results in right outcomes.

A businessman stopped me one day following a Rotary Club meeting in a Western city at which I had made a speech. He told me that something he had read in one of my newspaper columns had, as he put it, "completely revolutionized his attitude and saved his business."

Naturally I was interested and pleased that any little thing I had said would bring about such a splendid result.

"I had been having quite a difficult time in my business," he said. "In fact, it was beginning to be a very serious question as to whether I could save my business. A series of unfortunate circumstances together with market conditions, regulatory procedures, and dislocations to the economy of the country generally affected my line profoundly. I read this article of yours in which you advanced the idea of taking God in as a partner. I think you used the phrase, 'effect a merger with God.'

"When I first read that it seemed to me a rather 'cracked-brain idea.' How could a man on earth, a human being, take God as a partner? Besides, I had always thought of God as a vast being, so much bigger than man that I was like an insect in His sight, and yet you were saying that

I should take Him as a partner. The idea seemed preposterous. Then a friend gave me one of your books and I found similar ideas scattered all through it. You told actual life stories about people who followed this advice. They all seemed to be sensible people, but still I was unconvinced. I always had the idea that ministers are idealistic theorists, that they know nothing about business and practical affairs. So I sort of 'wrote you off,' " he said with a smile.

"However, a funny thing happened one day. I went to my office so depressed that I actually thought perhaps the best thing for me to do would be to blow my brains out and get away from all these problems which seemed completely to floor me. Then into my mind came this idea of taking God as a partner. I shut the door, sat in my chair, and put my head on my arms on the desk. I might as well confess to you that I hadn't prayed more than a dozen times in as many years. However, I certainly did pray on this occasion. I told the Lord that I had heard this idea about taking Him in as a partner, that I wasn't actually sure what it meant, or how one did it. I told Him I was sunk, that I couldn't get any ideas except panicky ones, that I was baffled, bewildered, and very discouraged. I said, 'Lord, I can't offer You much in the way of a partnership, but please join with me and help me. I don't know how You can help me, but I want to be helped. So I now put my business, myself, my family, and my future in Your hands. Whatever You say goes. I don't even know how You are going to tell me what to do, but I am ready to hear and will follow Your advice if You will make it clear.'

"Well," he continued, "that was the prayer. After I finished praying I sat at my desk. I guess I expected something miraculous to happen, but nothing did. However, I did suddenly feel quiet and rested. I actually had a feeling of peacefulness. Nothing out of the ordinary occurred that day nor that night, but next day when I went to my office I had a brighter and happier feeling than usual. I began to feel confident that things would turn out right. It was hard to explain why I felt that way. Nothing was any different. In fact, you might even say things were a shade worse, but I was different, at least a little different.

"This feeling of peacefulness stayed with me and I began to feel better. I kept praying each day and talked to God as I would to a partner. They were not churchy prayers—just plain man-to-man talk. Then one day in my office, all of a sudden an idea popped up in my mind. It was like toast popping up in a toaster. I said to myself, 'Well, what do you know about that?' for it was something that had never occurred to me, but I knew instantly that it was just the method to follow. Why I had never thought of it before I haven't the slightest idea. My mind was too tied up, I guess. I hadn't been functioning mentally.

"I immediately followed the hunch." Then he stopped. "No, it was no hunch, it was my partner talking to me. I immediately put this idea into operation and things began to roll. New ideas began to flow out of my mind, and despite conditions I began to get the business back on an even keel. Now the general situation has improved considerably, and I'm out of the woods."

Then he said, "I don't know anything about preaching or about writing the kind of books you write, or any books for that matter, but let me tell you this—whenever you get a chance to talk to businessmen tell them that if they will take God as a partner in their business they will get more good ideas than they can ever use, and they can turn those ideas into assets. I don't merely mean money," he said, "although a way to get a good return on your investment, I believe, is to get God-guided ideas. But tell them that the God-partnership method is the way to get their problems solved right."

This incident is just one of many similar demonstrations of the law of Divine-human relationship working itself out in practical affairs. I cannot emphasize too strongly the effectiveness of this technique of problem solving. It has produced amazing results in the many cases coming under my observation.

In the very necessary business of solving personal problems, it is important, first of all, to realize that the power to solve them correctly is inherent within you. Second, it is necessary to work out and actualize a plan. Spiritual and emotional planlessness is a definite reason for the failure of many people to meet their personal problems successfully.

A business executive told me that he puts his dependence upon the "emergency powers of the human brain." It is his theory, and a sound one, that a human being possesses extra powers that may be tapped and utilized under emergency situations. In the ordinary conduct of day-by-day living, these emergency powers lie dormant, but under extraordinary circumstances the personality is able, when called upon, to deliver extra power if needed.

A person who develops a working faith does not allow these powers to lie dormant, but in proportion to his faith brings many of them into play in connection with normal activity. This explains why some people demonstrate greater force than others in daily requirements and in a crisis.

They have made it a habit normally to draw upon powers that would otherwise be ignored except in some dramatic necessity.

When a difficult situation arises, do you know how to meet it? Have you any clearly defined plan for solving unusually difficult problems as they develop? Many people proceed on a hit-or-miss method, and, sadly, enough, most frequently they miss. I cannot urge too strongly the importance of a planned use of your greater powers in meeting problems.

In addition to the method of two or three praying together in the "surrender of God" technique and that of establishing a partnership with God and the importance of a plan to tap and utilize emergency inner powers, there is still another tremendous technique—that of practicing faith attitudes. I read the Bible for years before it ever dawned on me that it was trying to tell me that if I would have faith—and really have it—that I could overcome all of my difficulties, meet every situation, rise above every defeat, and solve all of the perplexing problems of my life. The day that realization dawned on me was one of the greatest, if not the greatest, of my life. Undoubtedly many people will read this book who have never gotten the faith idea of living. But I hope you will get it now, for the faith technique is without question one of the most powerful truths in the world having to do with the successful conduct of human life.

Throughout the Bible the truth is emphasized again and again that "If ye have faith as a grain of mustard seed . . . nothing shall be impossible unto you." (Matthew 17:20) The Bible means this absolutely, factually, completely, and literally. It isn't an illusion, it isn't a fantasy. It is not an illustration, nor a symbol, nor a metaphor, but the absolute fact—"Faith, even as a grain of mustard seed," will solve your problems, any of your problems, all of your problems, if you believe it and practice it. "According to your faith, be it unto you." (Matthew 9:29) The requirement is faith, and directly in proportion to the faith that you have and use will you get results. Little faith gives you little results, medium faith gives you medium results, great faith gives you great results. But in the generosity of Almighty God, if you have only the faith symbolized by a grain of mustard seed, it will do amazing things in solving your problems.

For example, let me tell you the thrilling story of my friends Maurice and Mary Alice Flint. I became acquainted with them when a previous book of mine, *A Guide to Confident Living*, was condensed in *Liberty* magazine. Maurice Flint at that time was failing, and failing badly. Not only was he failing in his job, but as a person as well. He was filled with fear and resentment and was one of the most negative persons I have ever encountered. He was endowed with a nice personality and at heart was a wonderful fellow, but he had simply messed life up as he himself admitted.

He read the condensation of the book in which is emphasized the idea of "mustard-seed faith." At this time he was living in Philadelphia with his family, a wife and two sons. He telephoned my church in New York, but for some reason did not make contact with my secretary. I mention this to show his already changing mental attitude for normally he would never have called the second time, because it was his pathetic habit to give up everything after a feeble effort, but in this instance he persevered until he got through and secured the information relative to the time of church services. The next Sunday he drove from Philadelphia to New York with his family to attend church, which he continued to do even in the most inclement weather.

In an interview later he told me his life story in full detail and asked if I thought he could ever make anything of himself. The problems of money, of situations, of debts, of the future, and primarily of himself were so complicated and he was so overwhelmed with difficulty that he regarded the situation as completely hopeless.

I assured him that if he would get himself personally straightened out and get his mental attitudes attuned to God's pattern of thought, and if he would learn and utilize the technique of faith, all of his problems could be solved.

One attitude that both he and his wife had to clear out of their minds was that of resentment. They were dully mad at everybody and acutely so at some. They were in their present unhappy condition, so they reasoned in their diseased thoughts, not because of any failure on their part but because of "dirty deals" other people had given them. They actually used to lie in bed at night telling each other what they would like to say to other people by way of insult. In this unhealthy atmosphere they tried to find sleep and rest, but with no successful result.

Maurice Flint really took to the faith idea. It gripped him as nothing ever had. His reactions were weak, of course, for his will power was disorganized. At first he was unable to think with any power or force due to his long habit of negativism, but he held on tenaciously, even desperately, to the idea that if you have "faith as a grain of mustard seed, nothing is impossible." With what force he did have he absorbed faith. Of course, his capacity to have faith gradually increased as he practiced it.

One night he went into the kitchen where his wife was washing dishes. He said, "The faith idea is comparatively easy on Sunday in church, but

I can't hold it. It fades. I was thinking that if I could carry a mustard seed in my pocket, I could feel it when I began to weaken and that would help me to have faith." He then asked his wife, "Do we have any of those mustard seeds, or are they just something mentioned in the Bible? Are there mustard seeds today?"

She laughed and said, "I have some right here in a pickle jar."

She fished one out and gave it to him. "Don't you know, Maurice," Mary Alice said, "that you don't need an actual mustard seed. That is only the symbol of an idea."

"I don't know about that," he replied. "It says mustard seed in the Bible and that's what I want. Maybe I need the symbol to get faith."

He looked at it in the palm of his hand and said wonderingly, "Is that all the faith I need—just a small amount like this tiny grain of mustard seed?" He held it for a while and then put it in his pocket, saying, "If I can just get my fingers on that during the day, it will keep me working on this faith idea." But the seed was so small he lost it, and he would go back to the pickle jar for another one, only to lose it also. One day when another seed became lost in his pocket, the idea came to him. Why couldn't he put the grain of mustard seed in a plastic ball? He could carry this ball in his pocket or put it on his watch chain always to remind him that if he had "faith as a grain of mustard seed, nothing would be impossible unto him."

He consulted a supposed expert in plastics and asked how to insert a mustard seed in a plastic ball so there would be no bubble. The "expert" said it could not be done for the reason that it had never been done, which of course was no reason at all.

Flint had enough faith by this time to believe that if he had faith "even as a grain of mustard seed" he could put a mustard seed in a plastic sphere. He went to work, and kept at it for weeks, and finally succeeded. He made up several pieces of costume jewelry: necklace, bow pin, key chain, bracelet, and sent them to me. They were beautiful, and on each gleamed the translucent sphere with the mustard seed within. With each one was a card which bore the title, "Mustard Seed Remembrancer." The card also told how this piece of jewelry could be used; how the mustard seed would remind the wearer that "if he had faith, nothing was impossible."

He asked me if I thought these articles could be merchandised. I was no expert in such matters so I showed them to Grace Oursler, consulting editor of *Guideposts* magazine. She took the jewelry to our mutual friend, Mr. Walter Hoving, president of Bonwit Teller Department Store, one of the greatest executives in the country. He at once saw the possibilities in this project. Imagine my astonishment and delight when in the New York papers a few days later was a two-column advertisement reading, "Symbol of faith—a genuine mustard seed enclosed in sparkling glass makes a bracelet with real meaning." And in the advertisement was the Scripture passage, "If ye have faith as a grain of mustard seed . . . nothing shall be impossible unto you." (Matthew 17:20) These articles sold like hot cakes. Now hundreds of great department stores and shops throughout the country find difficulty keeping them in stock.

Mr. and Mrs. Flint have a factory in a Midwestern city producing Mustard Seed Remembrancers. Curious, isn't it—a failure goes to church and hears a text out of the Bible and creates a great business. Perhaps you had better listen more intently to the reading of the Bible and the sermon the next time you go to church. Perhaps you, too, will get an idea that will rebuild not only your life but your business as well.

Faith in this instance created a business for manufacturing and distributing a product that has helped and will help thousands upon thousands of people. So popular and effective is it that others have copied it, but the Flint Mustard Seed Remembrancer is the original. The story of the lives that have been changed by this little device is one of the most romantic spiritual stories of this generation. But the effect on Maurice and Mary Alice Flint—the transformation of their lives, the remaking of their characters, the releasing of their personalities—this is a thrilling demonstration of faith power. No longer are they negative—they are positive. No more are they defeated—they are victorious. They no longer hate. They have overcome resentment and their hearts are filled with love. They are new people with a new outlook and a new sense of power. They are two of the most inspiring people I ever knew.

Ask Maurice and Mary Alice Flint how to get a problem solved right. They will tell you—"Have faith—really have faith." And believe me, they know.

If as you read this story you have said to yourself negatively (and that is being negative), "The Flints were never so bad off as I am," let me tell you that I have scarcely ever seen anybody as badly off as were the Flints. And let me say further that regardless of however desperate your situation may be, if you will use the four techniques outlined in this chapter, as did the Flints, you, too, can get your problem solved right.

In this chapter I have tried to show various methods for solving a problem. Now I wish to give ten simple suggestions as a concrete technique to use generally in solving your problems:

1. Believe that for every problem there is a solution.

2. Keep calm. Tension blocks the flow of thought power. Your brain cannot operate efficiently under stress. Go at your problem easy-like.

3. Don't try to force an answer. Keep your mind relaxed so that the solution will open up and become clear.

4. Assemble all the facts impartially, impersonally, and judicially.

5. List these facts on paper. This clarifies your thinking, bringing the various elements into orderly system. You see as well as think. The problem becomes objective, not subjective.

6. Pray about your problem, affirming that God will flash illumination into your mind.

7. Believe in and seek God's guidance on the promise of the 73rd Psalm, "Thou wilt guide me by thy counsel."

8. Trust in the faculty of insight and intuition.

9. Go to church and let your subconscious work on the problem as you attune to the mood of worship. Creative spiritual thinking has amazing power to give "right" answers.

10. If you follow these steps faithfully, then the answer that develops in your mind, or comes to pass, is the right answer to your problem.

11

HOW TO USE FAITH IN HEALING

Is religious faith a factor in healing? Important evidence indicates that it is. There was a time in my own experience when I was not convinced of this, but now I am, and that very definitely. I have seen too many evidences to believe otherwise.

We are learning that faith properly understood and applied is a powerful factor in overcoming disease and establishing health.

My conviction regarding this important question is shared by many medical men. Newspapers carried an account of the visit to this country of the famous Viennese surgeon, Dr. Hans Finsterer. I quote the newspaper story which was headed "Honor Surgeon 'Guided by God.' "

"A Viennese doctor, Dr. Hans Finsterer, who believes 'the unseen hand of God' helps make an operation successful, was selected by the International College of Surgeons for its highest honor, 'master of surgery.' He was cited for his work in abdominal surgery with the use of local anesthesia only.

"Finsterer, seventy-two-year-old professor at the University of Vienna, has performed more than 20,000 major operations, among them 8,000 gastric resections (removal of part or all of the stomach) using only local anesthesia. Finsterer said that although considerable progress has been made in medicine and surgery in the past few years 'all advances are not sufficient in themselves to insure a happy outcome in every operation. In many instances,' he said, 'in what appeared to be simple surgical procedures the patients died, and in some cases where the surgeon despaired of a patient there was recovery.

" 'Some of our colleagues attribute these things to unpredictable chance, while others are convinced that in those difficult cases their work has been aided by the unseen hand of God. Of late years, unfortunately, many patients and doctors have lost their conviction that all things depend on the providence of God.

" 'When we are once again convinced of the importance of God's help in our activities, and especially in the treatment of our patients, then true progress will have been accomplished in restoring the sick to health.' "

So concludes the account of a great surgeon who combines his science with faith.

I spoke at the national convention of an important industry. It was a large gathering of the leaders in an amazingly creative merchandising enterprise that has established this particular industry as a vital factor in American business life.

I was somewhat surprised when one of the leaders of this organization at the convention luncheon where the discussion centered around taxation, rising costs, and business problems, turned to me and asked, "Do you believe that faith can heal?"

"There are a good many well-authenticated examples on record of people who have been healed by faith," I answered. "Of course, I do not think we should depend on faith alone to heal a physical ailment. I believe in the combination of God and the doctor. This viewpoint takes advantage of medical science and the science of faith, and both are elements in the healing process."

"Let me tell you my story," the man continued. "A number of years ago I had a malady that was diagnosed as osteoma of the jaw, that is, a bone tumor on my jaw. The doctors told me it was practically incurable. You can imagine how that disturbed me. Desperately I sought for help. Although I had attended church with fair regularity, still I was not a particularly religious man. I scarcely ever read the Bible. One day, however, as I lay in my bed it occurred to me that I would like to read the Bible, and I asked my wife to bring one to me. She was very surprised, for I have never before made such a request.

"I began to read, and found consolation and comfort. I also became a bit more hopeful and less discouraged. I continued to read for extended periods every day. But that wasn't the chief result. I began to notice that the condition which had troubled me was growing less noticeable. At first I thought I imagined this, then I became convinced that some change was taking place in me.

"One day while reading the Bible I had a curious inward feeling of warmth and great happiness. It is difficult to describe, and long ago I got over trying to explain the feeling. From that time on my improvement was more rapid. I went back to the doctors who had first diagnosed my case. They examined me carefully. They were obviously surprised and agreed that my condition had improved, but warned me that this was only a temporary respite. Later, however, upon further examination, it was determined that the symptoms of osteoma had disappeared entirely. Still the doctors told me it would probably start all over again. This did not disturb me, for in my heart I knew that I was healed."

"How long has it been since your healing?" I asked.

"Fourteen years," was the answer.

I studied this man. Strong, sturdy, healthy, he is one of the outstanding men in his industry. The incident was told to me in the factual way that a businessman would recount it. There was not the slightest indication of doubt in this man's mind. Indeed how could there be, for whereas he had been condemned to death, here he was alive and vigorous.

What did it? The skillful work of the physician plus! And what was the plus? Obviously the faith that heals.

The healing described by this gentleman is but one of many similar accounts, and so many of them are attested by competent medical evidence that it seems we must encourage people to make greater use of the amazing power of faith in healing. Sadly the healing element in faith has suffered neglect. I am certain that faith can and does work what we call "miracles" but which are, in truth, the operation of spiritually scientific laws.

There is a growing emphasis in present-day religious practice which is designed to help people find healing from the sicknesses of mind, heart, soul, and body. This is a return to the original practice of Christianity. Only in recent times have we tended to overlook the fact that for centuries religion carried on healing activities. The very word "pastor" derives from a word meaning "the cure of souls." In modern times, however, man made the false assumption that it is impossible to harmonize the teachings of the Bible with what is called "science" and so the healing emphasis of religion was abandoned almost entirely to materialistic science.

Today, however, the close association of religion and health is increasingly recognized.

It is significant that the word "holiness" derives from a word meaning "wholeness" and the word "meditation," usually used in a religious sense, closely resembles the root meaning of the word "medication." The affinity of the two words is startlingly evident when we realize that sincere and practical meditation upon God and His truth acts as a medication for the soul and body.

Present-day medicine emphasizes psychosomatic factors in healing, thus recognizing the relationship of mental states to bodily health. Modern medical practice realizes and takes into consideration the close connection between how a man thinks and how he feels. Since religion deals with thought and feeling and basic attitudes, it is only natural that the science of faith should be important in the healing process.

Harold Sherman, author and playwright, was asked to revise an important radio presentation with the promise that he would be contracted as the permanent writer. After some months of work, he was dismissed and his material used without credit. This resulted in financial difficulty and humiliation. The injustice rankling in his mind developed into a growing bitterness against the radio executive who had broken faith with him. Mr. Sherman declares that this is the one time in his life when he had murder in his heart. His hatred made him subject to a physical affliction in the form of a mycosis, a fungus growth which attacked the membranes of his throat. The best medical attention was secured, but something in addition was required. When he gave up his hate and developed a feeling of forgiveness and understanding, the condition gradually corrected itself. With the aid of medical science and a new mental attitude, he was healed of his affliction.

A sensible and effective pattern for health and happiness is to utilize the skills and methods of medical science to the fullest possible extent and at the same time apply the wisdom, the experience, and the techniques of spiritual science. There is impressive evidence to support the belief that God works through both the practitioner of science, the doctor, and the practitioner of faith, the minister. Many physicians join in this point of view.

At a Rotary Club luncheon I sat at a table with nine other men, one of them a physician who had recently been discharged from military service and had resumed his civilian practice. He said, "Upon my return from the Army, I noticed a change in my patients' troubles. I found that a high percentage do not need medicine but better thought patterns.

They are not sick in their bodies so much as they are sick in their thoughts and emotions. They are all mixed up with fear thoughts, inferiority feelings, guilt, and resentment. I found that in treating them I needed to be about as much a psychiatrist as a physician, and then I discovered that not even those therapies helped me fully to do my job. I became aware that in many cases the basic trouble with people was spiritual. So I found myself frequently quoting the Bible to them. Then I fell into the habit of 'prescribing' religious and inspirational books, especially those that give guidance in how to live."

Directing his statements to me, he said, "It's about time you ministers began to realize that in the healing of many people you, too, have a function to perform. Of course you are not going to overlap on the work of the physician any more than we shall intrude on your function, but we doctors need the cooperation of ministers in helping people find health and well-being."

I received a letter from a physician in an upstate New York town who said, "Sixty per cent of the people in this town are sick because they are maladjusted in their minds and in their souls. It is hard to realize that the modern soul is sick to such an extent that the physical organs pain. I suppose in time," continues the doctor, "that ministers, priests, and rabbis will understand this relationship."

This physician was kind enough to say that he prescribes my book, *A Guide to Confident Living*, and other similar books to his patients and that noteworthy results have been achieved thereby.

The manager of a Birmingham, Alabama, bookstore sent me a prescription form made out by a physician of that city to be filled not at a drugstore, but at her bookstore. He prescribes specific books for specific troubles.

Dr. Carl R. Ferris, formerly president of the Jackson County Medical Society of Kansas City, Missouri, with whom I had the pleasure of appearing on a joint health-and-happiness radio program, declared that in treating human ills the physical and spiritual are often so deeply interrelated that there is often no clearly defined dividing line between the two.

Years ago my friend, Dr. Clarence W. Lieb, pointed out to me the effect on health of spiritual and psychiatric problems, and through his wise guidance I began to see that fear and guilt, hate and resentment, problems with which I was dealing, were often closely connected with problems of health and physical well-being. So profoundly does Dr. Lieb believe in this therapy that he with Dr. Smiley Blanton inaugurated the religio-psychiatric clinic which for years has ministered to hundreds at the Marble Collegiate Church in New York.

The late Dr. William Seaman Bainbridge and I worked closely together in the relationship of religion and surgery, and we were able to bring health and new life to many.

Two of my medical friends in New York, Dr. Z. Taylor Bercovitz and Dr. Howard Westcott, have been of inestimable help in my pastoral work through their wisely scientific and yet deeply spiritual understanding of the ills of the body, mind, and soul as related to faith.

"We have discovered the psychosomatic cause of high blood pressure as some form of subtle, repressed fear—a fear of things that might happen, not of things that are," says Dr. Rebecca Beard. "They are largely fears of things in the future. In that sense, therefore, they are imaginary, for they may never happen at all. In the case of diabetes, it is grief or disappointment which we found uses up more energy than any other emotion, thereby exhausting the insulin which is manufactured by the pancreas cells until they are worn out.

"Here we find the emotions involved in the past—reliving the past and not being able to go forward into life. The medical world can give relief in disorders like these. They can give something that can lower the blood pressure when it is high, or raise it when it is low, but not permanently. They can give insulin which will burn up more sugar into energy and give the diabetic relief. These are definite aids, but they do not offer complete cure. No drug or vaccine has been discovered to protect us from our own emotional conflicts. A better understanding of our own emotional selves and a return to religious faith seem to form the combination that holds the greatest promise of permanent help to any of us.

"The answer," Dr. Beard concludes, "is in the healing teachings of Jesus."

Another efficient woman physician wrote me of her own development in combining the therapy of medicine and faith. "I became interested in your straightforward religious philosophy. I had been working at top speed and getting tense, irritable, and at times beset with old fears and guilts, in fact in need of a release from morbid tension. At a low moment early one morning I picked up your book and began to read it. This was the prescription that I needed. Here was God, the great Physician, with faith in Him as an antibiotic to kill the germs of fear and render useless the virus of guilt.

"I began to practice the good Christian principles outlined in your book. Gradually there came a release of tension and I felt relaxed and happier and I slept well. I quit taking vitamin and pep pills. Then," she adds, and this is what I want to emphasize, "I began to feel that I wanted to share this new experience with my patients, those who came to me with neuroses. I was surprised to find how many had read your book and others. The patient and I seemed to have a common ground to work on. It has been an enriching experience. To talk about a faith in God has become a natural and easy thing to do.

"As a doctor," she adds, "I have seen a number of miraculous recoveries due to Divine aid being given. In the past few weeks I have had an additional experience. My sister had to undergo a serious operation about three weeks go. Following the operation she developed an intestinal obstruction. On her fifth day she was very critically ill, and as I left the hospital at noon I realized that she must take a turn for the better very soon or her hope of recovery would be slim. I was very worried, so I drove slowly around for about twenty minutes praying for a relief of this obstruction. (Everything that could be done medically was being taken care of.) I had not been home more than ten minutes when the phone rang and her nurse told me that the obstruction had relieved itself and that she had taken a definite turn for the better, and since that time she has recovered completely. Could I feel otherwise than that God's intervention had saved her life?"

So runs the letter of a successful practicing physician.

In the light of this viewpoint based on a strictly common-sense scientific attitude we may approach the phenomenon of healing through faith with credibility. If I did not believe sincerely that the faith factor in healing is sound I would certainly not develop the point of view contained in this chapter.

Over a period of time I have received from many readers and radio listeners as well as from my own parishioners accounts of healings in which the element of faith has been present. I have meticulously investigated many of these to satisfy my own mind as to their truthfulness. Also I wanted to be able to declare to the most cynical that here is a way of health, happiness, and successful living which is so buttressed by evidence that only the person who wants to remain ill because of some subconscious will-to-fail attitude will ignore his possibilities for health implied in these experiences.

The formula which these many incidents together present is briefly stated—the employment of all the resources of medical and psychological science combined with the resources of spiritual science. This is a combination of therapies that can surely bring health and well-being if it is the plan of God for the patient to live. Obviously for each of us there comes a time for this mortal life to end (life itself never ends, only the earthly phase of it).

We in the so-called old-line churches have, in my humble judgment, missed one of our greatest possible contributions by failing to point out with positiveness that there is a sound message of health in Christianity. Failing to find this emphasis in the church, groups, organizations, and other spiritual bodies have been created to supply this deficiency in Christian teaching. But there is no longer any valid reason why all the churches should not recognize that which is authenticated, namely, that there is healing in faith and more generally offer sound healing techniques to our people. Fortunately everywhere today throughout our religious organizations thoughtful, scientifically minded spiritual leaders are taking that extra step of faith based on the facts (and the Scripture) and are making available to the people as never before the formulas of the marvelous healing grace of Jesus Christ.

In all of the investigations I have made into successful cases of healing, there seem to be certain factors present. First, a complete willingness to surrender oneself into the hands of God. Second, a complete letting go of all error such as sin in any form and a desire to be cleansed in the soul. Third, belief and faith in the combined therapy of medical science in harmony with the healing power of God. Fourth, a sincere willingness to accept God's answer, whatever it may be, and no irritation or bitterness against His will. Fifth, a substantial, unquestioning faith that God can heal.

In all these healings there seems to be an emphasis upon warmth and light and a feeling of assurance that power has passed through. In practically every case that I have examined, in one form or another, the patient talks about a moment when there was warmth, heat, beauty, peace, joy, and a sense of release. Sometimes it has been a sudden experience; other times a more gradual unfolding of the conviction that the healing has occurred.

Always in my investigation of these matters I have waited for elapsed time to prove that the healing is permanent and those cases which I report are not based on any temporary improvement which might conceivably be the result of a momentary resurgence of strength.

For example, may I relate a healing experience written for me by a woman whose reliability and judgment I profoundly respect. Documentation in this case is thorough-going and scientifically impressive. This woman was told that an immediate operation was necessary to remove a growth which had been diagnosed as malignant.

I quote her exact words: "All precautionary treatments were taken, but the manifestations returned. As may be expected, I was terrified; I knew further hospital treatments were futile. There was no hope, so I turned to God for help. A very consecrated and spiritual child of God helped me by prayer to realize that the right knowledge of God and His healing Christ would help me too. I was most receptive to this kind of thinking, and placed myself in God's hands.

"I had asked for this help one morning, as usual, and spent the day going about my household duties, which were many at that time. I was preparing the evening meal, all alone in the kitchen. I was aware of an unusually bright light in the room and felt a pressure against my whole left side, as though a person were standing very close beside me. I had heard of healings; I knew prayers were being offered in my behalf, so I decided this must be the healing Christ who was with me.

"I decided to wait until morning, to be sure; if the symptoms of the trouble were gone, then I would know. By morning, the improvement was so noticeable, and I was so free in my mind, that I was certain, and reported to my friend that the healing had taken place.

"The memory of that healing and the presence of Christ are as fresh in my mind today as then. That was fifteen years ago, and my health steadily improved until I am in excellent condition now."

In many heart cases the therapy of faith (a quiet, serene faith in Jesus Christ) undoubtedly stimulates healing. People who experience "a heart attack" who thereupon thoroughly and completely practice faith in Christ's healing grace, observing at the same time the rules prescribed by their physicians, report remarkable recovery histories. Perhaps such a person may even gain a greater degree of health than previously for having learned his limitations and, realizing the excess strains he has been placing upon himself, now conserves his strength.

But more than that he has learned one of the greatest techniques of human well-being, that of surrendering himself to the recuperative power of God. This is done by consciously attaching himself to the creative process through mentally conceiving of re-creative forces as operating within himself. The patient opens his consciousness to the tides of vitality and re-creative energy inherent in the universe which have been barred from his life through tension, high pressure, and other departures from the laws of well-being.

An outstanding man suffered a heart attack about thirty-five years ago. He was told that he would never be able to work again. The orders were that he must spend much of his time in bed. He would likely be an invalid the remainder of his days, which days would be relatively few in number, so he was informed. It is doubtful whether such statements would be made to him in present-day medical practice. At any rate he listened to these dire prophecies about his future and considered them carefully.

One morning he awakened early and picked up his Bible and by chance (or was it chance?) opened it to the account of one of the healings of Jesus. He also read the statement, "Jesus Christ the same yesterday, and today and forever." (Hebrews 13:8) It occurred to him that if Jesus could and did heal people long ago, and that if He is the same as He was then, why couldn't He heal today? "Why cannot Jesus heal me?" he asked. Then faith welled up within him.

Therefore, with simple confidence, he asked the Lord to heal him. He seemed to hear Jesus say, "Believest thou that I can do this?" And his answer was, "Yes, Lord, I believe that You can."

He closed his eyes and "seemed to feel the touch of the healing Christ upon his heart." All that day he had a strange sense of rest. As the days passed he became convinced that there was a rising tide of strength within him. Finally one day he prayed, "Lord, if it is Your will, tomorrow morning I am going to get dressed, go outside, and within a few days I am going back to work. I put myself completely in Your care. If I should die tomorrow as a result of the increased activity, I want to thank You for all the wonderful days I have had. With You to help me, I shall start out tomorrow and You will be with me all day long. I believe I will have sufficient strength, but if I should die as a result of this effort, I will be with You in eternity, and all will be well in either case."

In this calm faith he increased his activities as the days passed. He followed this formula every day for the entire period of his active career, which numbered thirty years from the date of his heart attack. He retired at seventy-five. Few men I have known have been more vigorous in their undertakings or have made a greater contribution to human welfare. Always, however, he conserved his physical and nervous strength. It was invariably his habit to lie down and rest after lunch, and he never allowed himself to get under stress. He was early to bed and early up, always employing rigorous and disciplinary rules of living.

In all his activities there was an absence of worry, resentment, and tension. He worked hard but easily.

The doctors were right. Had he continued according to the debilitating habits of his earlier life he would probably have long since been dead or at least an invalid. The advice of the physicians brought him to the point where the healing work of Christ could be accomplished. Without the heart attack he would not have been mentally or spiritually ready for healing.

Another friend of mine, a prominent businessman, suffered a heart attack. For weeks he was confined to his bed, but presently returned to his important responsibilities where he now accomplishes all that he ever did previously, but with much less tension. He seems to possess a new power that he did not enjoy before. His recovery proceeded from a definite and scientific spiritual approach to his health problem. He had competent physicians and followed their directions explicitly, which is an important factor in such situations.

In addition to the program of medication and treatment, however, he worked out a spiritual healing formula. He outlined it as follows, writing from the hospital, "An intimate friend of mine, only twenty-five years old, was brought into the hospital with an attack similar to mine and died within four hours. Two acquaintances of mine have suffered a similar fate in rooms nearby. It must be that I have work yet to do. So I shall return and apply myself to the tasks before me with the expectation of living longer and more abundantly than I might have done without this experience. The doctors were wonderful, the nurses grand, the hospital ideal."

He then proceeds to outline the technique of spiritual convalescence which he employed. The formula consists of three parts. "(1) During the first stages, when absolute rest was demanded, I heeded the admonition of the Psalmist, 'Be still and know that I am God.' " (Psalm 46:10) That is to say, he completely relaxed and rested in the hands of God. "(2) As the days grew brighter, I used the affirmation, 'Wait on the Lord: be of good courage, and he shall strengthen thine heart.' " (Psalm 27:14) The patient put his heart under the care of God and God placed His hand of healing upon his heart and renewed it. "(3) Finally with the return of strength came a new assurance and confidence to which I gave expression in the affirmation, 'I can do all things through Christ which strengtheneth me.' " (Philippians 4:13) In this he affirmed positively that strength was being conferred upon him and in so doing he received new power.

In this three-point formula this man found healing. The able ministrations of his physicians conserved and stimulated the healing forces of his physical being. The equally wise application of faith completed his recovery by stimulating the spiritual powers within his nature. The two therapies together draw upon the two great renewal forces within our life, one the recuperative power of the human body and the other the restorative forces resident within the mind. One responds to medical treatment, the other to faith treatment, and God presides in both areas. He made both body and mind and He established the processes of health and well-being governing both. ". . . In Him we live and move and have our being." (Acts 17:28)

In the prevention of sickness and in healing mind and body, do not fail to draw upon one of the greatest resources available to you—the faith that heals.

In the light of the principles outlined in this chapter, what can you do of a constructive nature when a loved one or you are ill? Following are eight practical suggestions:

1. Follow the advice of a prominent medical school head who said, "In sickness, send for your minister even as you send for your doctor." In other words, believe that spiritual forces as well as medical technique are important in healing.

2. Pray for the doctor. Realize that God uses trained human instrumentality to aid His healing powers. As one doctor has put it, "We treat the patient and God heals him." Pray, therefore, that the doctor may be an open channel of God's healing grace.

3. Whatever you do, do not become panicky or filled with fear, for if you do, you will send out negative thoughts and therefore destructive thoughts in the direction of your loved one when he requires positive and healing thoughts to assist him.

4. Remember that God does nothing except by law. Also remember that our little materialistic laws are only fragmentary revelations of the great power flowing through the universe. Spiritual law also governs illness. God has arranged two remedies for all illness. One is healing through natural laws applicable by science, and the other brings healing by spiritual law applicable through faith.

5. Completely surrender your loved one into the hands of God. By your faith you can place him in the flow of Divine power. There is healing there, but in order for it to be effective the patient must be completely released to the operation of God's will. This is difficult to understand and equally difficult to perform, but it is a fact that if the great desire for the loved one to live is matched with an equally great willingness to relinquish him to God, healing powers are amazingly set in motion.

6. It is also important that harmony prevail in the family, that is, a spiritual harmony. Remember the emphasis in the scripture, Matthew 18:19: "If two of you shall agree on earth as touching anything that they shall ask, it shall be done for them of my Father which is in heaven." Apparently disharmony and disease are akin.

7. Form a picture in your mind of the loved one as being well. Visualize him in perfect health. Picture him as radiant with the love and goodness of God. The conscious mind may suggest sickness, even death, but nine-tenths of your mind is in the subconscious. Let the picture of health sink into the subconscious and this powerful part of your mind will send forth radiant health energy. What we believe in the subconscious we usually get. Unless your faith controls the subconscious, you will never get any good thing, for the subconscious gives back only that which your real thought is. If the real thought is negative, the results will also be negative. If the real thought is positive, you will get positive and healing results.

8. Be perfectly natural. Ask God to heal your loved one. That is what you want with all your heart, so ask Him please to do it, but we suggest that you say PLEASE just once. Thereafter in your prayer, thank Him for His goodness. This affirmative faith will help to release deep spiritual power and also joy through reassurance of God's loving care. This joy will sustain you, and remember that joy itself possesses healing power.

12

WHEN VITALITY SAGS, TRY THIS HEALTH FORMULA

A woman, so I have heard, went into a drugstore and asked for a bottle of psychosomatic medicine.

Such medicine, of course, is not found on drugstore shelves for it does not come in pills or bottles. But there is a psychosomatic medicine just the same and many of us need it. It is a prescription compounded of prayer, faith, and dynamic spiritual thinking.

It has been variously computed that from 50 to 75 per cent of present-day people are ill because of the influence of improper mental states on their emotional and physical make-up. Therefore such a medicine is of great importance. Many people who are below par will find that there is a health formula which, in addition to the services of their physicians, can be of great value to them.

The manner in which spiritual and emotional treatment can restore declining vitality is illustrated by the sales manager referred to us by the head of a large company. This sales executive, formerly a man of outstanding efficiency and energetic driving power, experienced a serious decline both in ability and energy. He lost his creative skill. Previously his sales ideas had been unique and outstanding. It soon became noticeable to his associates that this sales manager was slipping badly. He was urged to consult a doctor, and the company sent him to Atlantic City for a rest and later to Florida for a second attempt at recovery. Neither of these vacations seemed to be productive of any definite improvement.

His physician, who knew about our religio-psychiatric clinic, recommended to the company president that his sales manager come to us for an interview. The president asked him to come, which he did, but he was rather indignant at being sent to a church.

"This is a pretty pass," he fumed, "when they send a businessman to a preacher. I suppose you are going to pray with me and read the Bible," he said irritably.

"I wouldn't be surprised," I answered, "for sometimes our trouble lies in an area where prayer and the therapy of the Bible can have an important effect."

He proved most sullen and uncooperative until finally I was forced to say to him, "I want to tell you bluntly that you had better cooperate with us or you're going to be fired."

"Who told you that?" he demanded.

"Your boss," I replied. "In fact, he says that unless we can straighten you out, as much as he regrets it, you are going to be through."

You never saw such a stunned expression on anybody's face. "What do you think I ought to do?" he stammered.

"Often," I replied, "a person gets into the state in which you find yourself because the mind is filled with fear, anxiety, tension, resentment, guilt, or a combination of all of them. When these emotional impediments accumulate to a certain weight, the personality cannot support them any longer and gives way. Normal sources of emotional, spiritual, and intellectual power becomes clogged up. So a person becomes bogged down by resentment, by fear, or by guilt. I do not know your trouble, but I would suggest that you think of me as a sympathetic friend with whom you can be absolutely confident, and that you tell me about yourself." I emphasized that it was important he conceal nothing and that he completely empty himself of whatever fears, resentments, or guilt feelings might be in his mind. "I assure you that our interview will be held in strictest confidence. All your company wants is to have you back, the same highly efficient person you were."

In due course the trouble came out. He had committed a series of sins and these had involved him in a complicated maze of lies. He was living in fear of exposure, and all in all it was a most pathetic mass of inner confusion. It came little short of mental filth.

It was rather difficult to get him to talk, for he was essentially a decent person and had a strong sense of shame. I told him that I understood his reticence, but that this operation had to be performed and that it could not be accomplished without a thorough mind-emptying.

When it was all over, I shall never forget the manner in which he reacted. Standing on his feet he began to stretch. He stood on tiptoes, reaching his fingers toward the ceiling, and then took a deep breath. "My," he said, "I feel good." It was a dramatic expression of release and relief. Then I suggested that he pray and ask God to forgive him and to fill him with peace and cleanness.

"Do you mean for me to pray aloud?" he asked dubiously. "I never did that in my life."

"Yes," I said, "it is a good practice and will strengthen you."

It was a simple prayer, and as best as I can recall it, this is what he said, "Dear Lord, I have been an unclean man and I am sorry for the wrong I have done. I have poured it all out to my friend here. I now ask You to forgive me and to fill me with peace. Also make me strong so that I will never repeat these actions. Help me to be clean again and better—lots better."

He went back to his office that very day. Nothing was ever said to him, and it did not need to be, for soon he got back into stride and is one of the best sales managers in his city today.

Later I met his president, who said, "I don't know what you did to Bill, but he is certainly a ball of fire."

"I did nothing. God did it," I replied.

"Yes," he said. "I understand. Anyway, he is the old-time Bill."

When this man's vitality sagged, he tried a health formula that restored him to normal efficiency. He "took" some psychosomatic medicine which cured him of an unhealthy spiritual and mental condition.

Dr. Franklin Ebaugh of the University of Colorado Medical School maintains that one third of all cases of illness in general hospitals are clearly organic in nature and onset, one third are a combination of emotional and organic, and one third are clearly emotional.

Dr. Flanders Dunbar, author of *Mind and Body*, says, "It is not a question of whether an illness is physical or emotional, but how much of each."

Every thoughtful person who has ever considered the matter realizes that the doctors are right when they tell us that resentment, hate, grudge, ill will, jealousy, vindictiveness, are attitudes which produce ill health. Have a fit of anger and experience for yourself that sinking feeling in the pit of your stomach, that sense of stomach sickness. Chemical reactions in the body are set up by emotional outbursts that result in feelings of ill health. Should these be continued either violently or in a simmering state over a period of time, the general condition of the body will deteriorate.

In speaking of a certain man whom we both knew a physician told me that the patient died of "grudgitis." The physician actually felt that the deceased passed away because of a long-held hatred. "He did his body such damage that his resistance was lowered," the doctor explained, "so that when a physical malady attacked him he did not possess the stamina or renewing force to overcome it. He had undermined himself physically by the malignancy of his ill will."

Dr. Charles Miner Cooper, San Francisco physician, in an article entitled, "Heart-to-Heart Advice About Heart Trouble," says, "You must curb your emotional reactions. When I tell you that I have known a patient's blood pressure to jump sixty points almost instantaneously in response to an outburst of anger, you can understand what strain such reactions can throw upon the heart." One who is "quick on the trigger," he wrote, is likely to blame someone else, impulsively, for a fault or mistake, when it would be wiser simply to avoid being so much disturbed by what is done and is therefore unavoidable. He quoted the great Scottish surgeon, John Hunter. Dr. Hunter had a heart condition himself, and a thorough understanding of the effect of strong emotion on his heart. He said that his life was at the mercy of anyone who could annoy him. And, in fact, his death resulted from a heart attack caused by a fit of anger when he forgot to discipline himself.

Dr. Cooper concludes, "Whenever a business problem starts to vex you or you begin to get angry, let yourself go limp all over. This will dissipate your mounting inner turmoil. Your heart asks that it be permanently housed in a lean, cheerful, placid man who will intelligently curb his physical, mental, and emotional activities."

So if you are under par I suggest that you do a very scrupulous job of self-analysis. Honestly ask yourself if you are harboring any ill will or resentment or grudges, and if so cast them out. Get rid of them without delay. They do not hurt anybody else. They do no harm to the person against whom you hold these feelings, but every day and every night of your life they are eating at you. Many people suffer poor health not because of what they eat but from what is eating them. Emotional ills turn in upon yourself, sapping your energy, reducing your efficiency, causing deterioration in your health. And of course they siphon off your happiness.

So we realize today the effect of thought patterns upon physical states. We realize that a person can make himself ill by resentment. We know he can develop various kinds of physiological symptoms because of a sense of guilt. Also one may show definite physical symptoms as a result of fear and anxiety. We know that healing has been accomplished when the thoughts are changed.

Recently a diagnostician told me of a young woman who was admitted to the hospital with a temperature of one hundred and two degrees. She had a definite case of rheumatoid arthritis; her joints were badly swollen.

In order to study the case thoroughly the doctor gave her no medication except a slight sedative to relieve the pain. After two days the young woman asked the doctor, "How long will I be in this condition, and how long must I remain in the hospital?"

"I think I must tell you," replied the physician, "that you will probably be in the hospital for about six months."

"You mean it will be six months before I can get married?" she demanded.

"I am sorry," he said, "but I cannot promise you anything better than that."

This conversation took place in the evening. The next morning the patient's temperature was normal and the swelling was gone from her joints. Unable to account for the change, the doctor observed her for a few days, then sent her home.

In a month she was back in the hospital in the same condition as before: temperature one hundred and two, joints swollen. Counseling disclosed that her father insisted that she marry a certain man who would be an asset to him in his business connections. The girl loved her father, wanted to do as he wished, but did not want to marry a man whom she did not love. So her subconscious mind came to her assistance and in effect gave her rheumatoid arthritis and a temperature.

The doctor explained to the father that if he forced this marriage his daughter could become an invalid. When told that she need not go through with the marriage, the girl's recovery was quick and permanent.

Do not get the idea that if you have arthritis you are married to the wrong person! This incident merely illustrates the profound effect of mental pain on physical conditions.

I was interested to read a statement by a psychologist that infants can "catch" fear and hatred from people around them more quickly than they can catch measles or other infectious diseases. The virus of fear may burrow deeply into their subconsciousness and remain there for a lifetime. "But," adds the psychologist, "fortunately infants can also catch love and goodness and faith and so grow up to become normal, healthy children and adults."

In an article in the *Ladies' Home Journal*, Constance J. Foster quotes Dr. Edward Weiss of Temple University Medical School in a speech to the American College of Physicians in which Dr. Weiss stated that chronic victims of pains and aches in the muscles and joints may be suffering from nursing a smoldering grudge against someone close to them. He added that such persons usually are totally unaware that they bear a chronic resentment.

"To clear up any possible misunderstanding," the author continues, "it is necessary to state emphatically that emotions and feelings are quite as real as germs and no less respectable. The resultant pain and suffering of diseases caused primarily by the emotions are no more imaginary than those caused by bacteria. In no case is the patient consciously to blame for developing the disease. Such persons are not suffering from any disease of the mind, but rather from a disorder of their feelings, often linked to a marital or parent-child problem."

In this same magazine article the story is told of a certain Mrs. X who came to the doctor's office complaining of a breaking out on her hands which was diagnosed as eczema. The doctor encouraged Mrs. X to talk about herself. It developed that she was a very rigid person. Her lips were thin and unyielding. She was also rheumatoid. The doctor sent Mrs. X to a psychiatrist who saw at once that there was some irritating situation in her life which she was translating outwardly in the form of a skin rash, thus taking out on her own person the urge to scratch some thing or person.

The doctor finally put it to her bluntly. "What is eating you?" he asked. "You're peeved at something, aren't you?"

"She stiffened up like a ramrod and marched right out of the office, so I knew I'd hit the target too closely for comfort. A few days later she came back. Due to the agony of the eczema, she was ready to let me help her even if it meant she had to give up a hate.

"It turned out to be a family row over a will with Mrs. X feeling she had been treated unfairly by a younger brother. When she got rid of the hostility, she got well, and when she made up the quarrel with her brother, within twenty-four hours the eczema vanished."

That there is even a relationship between emotional disturbance and the common cold is indicated by Dr. L. J. Saul of the University of Pennsylvania Medical School, who has made a study of this subject.

"Emotional disturbances are believed to affect the blood circulation in the linings of the nose and throat. They also affect glandular secretions. These factors make the mucous membranes more susceptible to attack by cold viruses or germ infection."

Dr. Edmund P. Fowler, Jr., of Columbia University's College of Physicians and Surgeons, stated, "There are colds which develop in medical students at the time of their examinations and colds which develop in many persons before or after a trip. Colds develop in housewives when they must care for a large family. And one often sees a cold develop in a patient when his mother-in-law comes to live in the house, and it often disappears when she leaves." (Dr. Fowler does not specify the effects on the mother-in-law of a daughter-in-law or son-in-law. Perhaps she has a cold also.)

One of the cases Dr. Fowler reports concerned a twenty-five-year-old salesgirl. When she visited his office her nose was stuffy, the lining was red and congested, and she suffered from a headache and a mild temperature. These symptoms had persisted for nearly two weeks. Questioning disclosed that they had started a few hours after a violent quarrel with her fiancé.

Local treatments cleared up the cold but the young woman was back in a few weeks with another attack. This time the trouble had started after an argument with the butcher. Again local treatments brought relief. But the girl continued to have recurring colds, and each time they were traced to a fit of anger. Finally Dr. Fowler was able to persuade the girl that her bad temper was at the root of her chronic cold symptoms. When she learned to lead a calmer existence, her sneezes and sniffles disappeared.

And yet people still think that when the Bible tells you not to hate or to get angry that it is "theoretical advice." The Bible is not theoretical. It is our greatest book of wisdom. It is filled with practical advice on living and on health. Anger, resentment, and guilt make you sick, modern physicians tell us, which proves once again that the most up-to-date book on personal well-being is the Holy Bible, neglected by so many or regarded by them as purely a religious book and certainly as one that is not practical. No wonder more copies are read than all other books. That is because in this book we discover not only what is wrong with us but how to correct it as well.

Dr. Fowler calls attention to the "emotional colds" suffered by children who feel insecure. He reports that many cases of chronic colds occur in children who come from broken homes. An older child often has recurring respiratory infection when a new baby is born because he feels neglected and jealous. A nine-year-old boy had an extremely dictatorial father and an indulgent mother. The conflict between the strictness of one parent and the lenience of the other obviously was disturbing to the child. He particularly feared punishment by his father. This boy suffered for several years from continuous coughs and sniffles. It was noted that the colds disappeared when he went to camp—away from his parents.

Since irritation, anger, hate, and resentment have such a powerful effect in producing ill health, what is the antidote? Obviously it is to fill the mind with attitudes of good will, forgiveness, faith, love, and the spirit of imperturbability. And how is that accomplished? Following are some practical suggestions. They have been used successfully by many in counterattacking especially the emotion of anger. A consistent application of these suggestions can produce feelings of well-being:

1. Remember that anger is an emotion, and an emotion is always warm, even hot. Therefore to reduce an emotion, cool it. And how do you cool it? When a person gets angry, the fists tend to clench, the voice rises in stridency, muscles tense, the body becomes rigid. (Psychologically you are poised for fight, adrenalin shoots through the body.) This is the old caveman hangover in the nervous system. So deliberately oppose the heat of this emotion with coolness—freeze it out. Deliberately, by an act of will, keep your hands from clenching. Hold your fingers out straight. Deliberately reduce your tone; bring it down to a whisper. Remember that it is difficult to argue in a whisper. Slump in a chair, or even lie down if possible. It is very difficult to get mad lying down.

2. Say aloud to yourself, "Don't be a fool. This won't get me anywhere, so skip it." At that moment it may be a bit hard to pray, but try it anyway; at least conjure up a picture of Jesus Christ in your mind and try to think of Him mad just as you are. You can't do it, and the effort will serve to puncture your angry emotions.

3. One of the best techniques for cooling off anger was suggested by Mrs. Grace Oursler. She formerly employed the usual "count to ten" technique but happened to notice that the first ten words of the Lord's Prayer worked better. "Our Father who art in Heaven, hallowed be Thy name." When angry, say that ten times and your anger will lose its power over you.

4. Anger is a great term expressing the accumulated vehemence of a multitude of minor irritations. These irritations, each rather small in itself, having gathered force by reason of the one being added to the other, finally blaze forth in a fury that often leaves us abashed at ourselves. Therefore, make a list of everything that irritates you. No matter how inconsequential it may be or how silly each is, list it just the same. The purpose in doing this is to dry up the tiny rivulets that feed the great river of anger.

5. Make each separate irritation a special object of prayer. Get a victory over each, one at a time. Instead of attempting to destroy all of your anger, which as we have pointed out is a consolidated force, snip away by prayer each annoyance that feeds your anger. In this way you will weaken your anger to the point where presently you will gain control over it.

6. Train yourself so that every time you feel the surge of anger you say, "Is this really worth what it is doing to me emotionally? I will make a fool of myself. I will lose friends." In order to get the full effect of this technique, practice saying to yourself a few times every day, "It is never worth it to get worked up or mad about anything." Also affirm: "It isn't worth it to spend $1000 worth of emotion on a five-cent irritation."

7. When a hurt-feeling situation arises, get it straightened out as quickly as possible. Don't brood over it for a minute longer than you can help. Do something about it. Do not allow yourself to sulk or indulge in self-pity. Don't mope around with resentful thoughts. The minute your feelings are hurt, do just as when you hurt your finger. Immediately apply the cure. Unless you do so the situation can become distorted out of all proportion. So put some spiritual iodine on the hurt at once by saying a prayer of love and forgiveness.

8. Apply grievance drainage to your mind. That is, open your mind and let the grievance flow out. Go to someone you trust and pour it out to him until not a vestige of it remains within you. Then forget it.

9. Simply start praying for the person who has hurt your feelings. Continue this until you feel the malice fading away. Sometimes you may have to pray for quite a while to get that result. A man who tried this method told me that he kept account of the number of times he needed to pray until the grievance left and peace came. It was exactly sixty-four times. He literally prayed it out of his system. This is positively guaranteed to work.

10. Say this little prayer: "May the love of Christ fill my heart." Then add this line: "May the love of Christ for——(insert the other's

name) flood my soul." Pray this, mean it (or ask to mean it), and you will get relief.

11. Actually take the advice of Jesus to forgive seventy times seven. To be literal, that means four hundred ninety times. Before you have forgiven a person that many times you will be free of resentment.

12. Finally, this wild, undisciplined, primitive urge in you which flames to the surface can be tamed only by allowing Jesus Christ to take control. Therefore, complete this lesson by saying to Jesus Christ, "Even as You can convert a person's morals, so now I ask You to convert my nerves. As You give power over the sins of the flesh, so give me power over the sins of the disposition. Bring my temper under Your control. Give me Thy healing peace in my nervous system as well as in my soul." If you are beset by temper, repeat the above prayer three times every day. It might be advisable to print it on a card and put it on your desk, or above the kitchen sink, or in your pocketbook.

13

INFLOW OF NEW THOUGHTS CAN REMAKE YOU

One of the most important and powerful facts about you is expressed in the following statement by William James, who was one of the wisest men America has produced. William James said, "The greatest discovery of my generation *is that human beings can alter their lives by altering their attitudes of mind.*" As you think, so shall you be. So flush out all old, tired, worn-out thoughts. Fill your mind with fresh, new creative thoughts of faith, love, and goodness. By this process you can actually remake your life.

And where do you find such personality remaking thoughts?

I know a business executive, a modest man, but the type of individual who is never defeated. No problem, no setback, no opposition ever gets him down. He simply attacks each difficulty with an optimistic attitude and a sure confidence that it will work out right, and, in some strange way, it always does for him. He seems to have a magic touch on life—a touch that never fails.

Because of that impressive characteristic this man always interested me. I knew there was a definite explanation of his being this way and of course wanted to hear his story, but in view of his modesty and reticence it was not easy to persuade him to talk about himself.

One day when he was in the mood he told me his secret, an amazingly simple but effective secret. I was visiting his plant, a modern, up-to-date structure, much of it air-conditioned. Latest-type machinery and methods of production make it a factory of outstanding efficiency. Labor-management relations seem as nearly perfect as is possible among imperfect human beings. A spirit of good will pervades the entire organization.

His office is ultra-modernistically decorated and furnished with handsome desks, rugs, and paneled with exotic woods. The decorating scheme is five startling colors blended together pleasingly. All in all it is the last word, and then some.

Imagine, then, my surprise to see on his highly polished white mahogany desk an old battered copy of the Bible. It was the only old object in those ultra-modern rooms. I commented upon this seemingly strange inconsistency.

"That book," he replied, pointing to the Bible, "is the most up-to-date thing in this plant. Equipment wears out and furnishing styles change, but that book is so far ahead of us that it never gets out of date.

"When I went to college, my good Christian mother gave me that Bible with the suggestion that if I would read and practice its teachings, I would learn how to get through life successfully. But I thought she was just a nice old lady"—he chuckled—"at my age she seemed old—she wasn't really, and to humor her, I took the Bible, but for years practically never looked at it. I thought I didn't need it. Well," he continued slangily, "I was a dope. I was stupid. And I got my life in a terrific mess.

"Everything went wrong primarily because I was wrong. I was thinking wrong, acting wrong, doing wrong. I succeeded at nothing, failed at everything. Now I realize that my principle trouble was wrong thinking. I was negative, resentful, cocky, opinionated. Nobody could tell me anything. I thought I knew everything. I was filled with gripes at everybody. Little wonder nobody liked me. I certainly was a 'washout.' "

So ran his dismal story. "One night in going through some papers," he continued, "I came across the long-forgotten Bible. It brought up old memories and I started aimlessly to read it. Do you know it is strange how things happen; how in just a flashing moment of time everything becomes different. Well, as I read, a sentence leaped up at me, a sentence that changed my life—and when I say changed, I mean changed. From the minute I read that sentence everything has been different, tremendously different."

"What is this wonderful sentence?" I wanted to know, and he quoted it slowly. " 'The Lord is the strength of my life . . . in this I will be confident.' (Psalm 27:1, 3)

"I don't know why that one line affected me so," he went on, "but it did. I know now that I was weak and a failure because I had no faith, no confidence. I was very negative, a defeatist. Something happened inside my mind. I guess I had what they call a spiritual experience. My thought pattern shifted from negative to positive. I decided to put my faith in God and sincerely do my best, trying to follow the principles outlined in the Bible. As I did so I began to get hold of a new set of thoughts. I began to think differently. In time my old failure thoughts were flushed out by this new spiritual experience and an inflow of new thoughts gradually but actually remade me."

So concluded the story of this businessman. He altered his thinking, and the new thoughts which flowed in displaced the old thoughts which had been defeating him and his life was changed.

This incident illustrates an important fact about human nature: you can think your way to failure and unhappiness, but you can also think your way to success and happiness. The world in which you live is not primarily determined by outward conditions and circumstances but by thoughts that habitually occupy your mind. Remember the wise words of Marcus Aurelius, one of the great thinkers of antiquity, who said, "A man's life is what his thoughts make of it."

It has been said that the wisest man who ever lived in America was Ralph Waldo Emerson, the Sage of Concord. Emerson declared, "A man is what he thinks about all day long."

A famous psychologist says, "There is a deep tendency in human nature to become precisely like that which you habitually imagine yourself to be."

It has been said that thoughts are things, that they actually possess dynamic power. Judged by the power they exercise one can readily accept such an appraisal. You can actually think yourself into or out of situations. You can make yourself ill with your thoughts and by the same token you can make yourself well by the use of a different and healing type of thought. Think one way and you attract the conditions which that type of thinking indicates. Think another way and you can create an entirely different set of conditions. Conditions are created by thoughts far more powerfully than conditions create thoughts.

Think positively, for example, and you set in motion positive forces which bring positive results to pass. Positive thoughts create around yourself an atmosphere propitious to the development of positive outcomes. On the contrary, think negative thoughts and you create around yourself an atmosphere propitious to the development of negative results.

To change your circumstances, first start thinking differently. Do not passively accept unsatisfactory circumstances, but form a picture in your mind of circumstances as they should be. Hold that picture, develop it firmly in all details, believe in it, pray about it, work at it, and you can actualize it according to that mental image emphasized in your positive thinking.

This is one of the greatest laws in the universe. Fervently do I wish I had discovered it as a very young man. It dawned upon me much later in life and I have found it to be one of the greatest if not my greatest discovery, outside of my relationship to God. And in a deep sense this law is a factor in one's relationship with God because it channels God's power into personality.

This great law briefly and simply stated is that if you think in negative terms you will get negative results. If you think in positive terms you will achieve positive results. That is the simple fact which is at the basis of an astonishing law of prosperity and success. In three words: Believe and succeed.

I learned this law in a very interesting manner. Some years ago a group of us consisting of Lowell Thomas, Captain Eddie Rickenbacker, Branch Rickey, Raymond Thornburg, and others established an inspirational self-help magazine called *Guideposts*. This magazine has a double function: first, by relating stories of people who through their faith have overcome difficulties, it teaches techniques of victorious living, victory over fear, over circumstances, over obstacles, over resentment. It teaches faith over all manner of negativism.

Second, as a non-profit, non-sectarian, inter-faith publication it teaches the great fact that God is in the stream of history and that this nation was founded on belief in God and His laws.

The magazine reminds its readers that America is the first great nation in history to be established on a definitely religious premise and that unless we keep it so our freedoms will deteriorate.

Mr. Raymond Thornburg as publisher and I as editor in starting the magazine had no financial backing to underwrite it. It was begun on faith. In fact, its first offices were in rooms above a grocery store in the little village of Pawling, New York. There was a borrowed typewriter, a few rickety chairs, and that was all; all except a great idea and great faith. Slowly a subscription list of 25,000 developed. The future seemed promising. Suddenly one night a fire broke out, and within an hour the publishing house was destroyed and with it the total list of subscribers. Foolishly no duplicate list had been made.

Lowell Thomas, loyal and efficient patron of *Guideposts* from the very start, mentioned this sad circumstance on his radio broadcast and as a result we soon had 30,000 subscribers, practically all the old ones and many new ones.

The subscription list rose to approximately 40,000, but costs increased even more rapidly. The magazine, which has always been sold for less than cost in order widely to disseminate the message, was more expensive than anticipated and we were faced with difficult financial problems. In fact, at one time it seemed almost impossible to keep it going.

At this juncture we called a meeting, and I'm sure you never attended a more pessimistic, negative, discouraging meeting. It dripped with pessimism. Where were we going to get the money to pay our bills? We figured out ways of robbing Peter to pay Paul. Complete discouragement filled our minds.

A woman had been invited to this meeting whom we all regarded most highly. But one reason she was included in this meeting was because, on a previous occasion, she had contributed $2,000 to help inaugurate *Guideposts* magazine. It was hoped that lightning might strike twice in the same place. But this time she gave us something of more value than money.

As this dismal meeting progressed she remained silent for a long time, but finally said, "I suppose you gentlemen would like me to make another financial contribution. I might as well put you out of your misery. I am not going to give you another cent."

This did not put us out of our misery. On the contrary, it put us deeper into our misery. "But," she continued, "I will give you something far more valuable than money."

This astonished us, for we could not possibly imagine anything of more value than money in the circumstances.

"I am going to give you an idea," she continued, "a creative idea."

"Well," we thought to ourselves unenthusiastically, "how can we pay our bills with an idea?"

Ah, but an idea is just what will help you pay bills. Every achievement in this world is first projected as a creative idea. First the idea, then faith in it, then the means of implementing the idea. That is the way success proceeds.

"Now," she said, "here is the idea. What is your present trouble? It is that you *lack* everything. You *lack* money. You *lack* subscribers. You *lack* equipment. You *lack* ideas. You *lack* courage. Why do you *lack* all these requirements? Simply because you are thinking *lack*. If you think *lack* you create the conditions that produce a state of *lack*. By this constant mental emphasis upon what you *lack* you have frustrated the creative forces that can give impetus to the development of *Guideposts*. You have been working hard from the standpoint of doing many things, but you have failed to do the one all-important thing that will lend power to all your other efforts: you have not employed positive thinking. Instead, you have thought in terms of *lack*.

"To correct that situation—reverse the mental process and begin to think prosperity, achievement, success. This will require practice but it can be done quickly if you will demonstrate faith. The process is to visualize; that is, to see *Guideposts* in terms of successful achievement. Create a mental picture of *Guideposts* as a great magazine, sweeping the country. Visualize large numbers of subscribers, all eagerly reading this inspirational material and profiting thereby. Create a mental image of lives being changed by the philosophy of achievement which *Guideposts* teaches monthly in its issues.

"Do not hold mental pictures of difficulties and failures, but lift your mind above them and visualize powers and achievements. When you elevate your thoughts into the area of visualized attainment you look down on your problems rather than from below up at them and thus you get a much more encouraging view of them. Always come up over your problems. Never approach a problem from below.

"Now let me continue further," she said. "How many subscribers do you need at the moment to keep it going?"

We thought quickly and said, "100,000." We had 40,000.

"All right," she said confidently, "that is not hard. That is easy. Visualize 100,000 people being creatively helped by this magazine and you will have them. In fact, the minute you can see them in your mind, you already have them."

She turned to me and said, "Norman, can you see 100,000 subscribers at this minute? Look out here, look ahead of you. In your mind's eye can you see them?"

I wasn't convinced yet, and I said rather doubtfully, "Well, maybe so, but they seem pretty dim to me."

She was a little disappointed in me, I thought, as she asked. "Can't you imaginatively visualize 100,000 subscribers?"

I guess my imagination wasn't working very well because all I could see was the insufficient but actual 40,000.

Then she turned to my old friend Raymond Thornburg who has been blessed with a gloriously victorious personality, and she said, calling him by his nickname, "Pinky, can you visualize 100,000 subscribers?"

I rather doubted that Pinky would see them. He is a rubber manufacturer who gives his time freely from his own business to help advance this inspirational, non-profit magazine, and you would not ordinarily think that a rubber manufacturer would respond to this type of thinking. But he has the faculty of creative imagination. I noticed by the fascinated look on his face that she had him. He was gazing straight ahead with rather a look of wonder when she asked, "Do you see 100,000 subscribers?"

"Yes," he cried with eagerness, "yes, I do see them."

Electrified, I demanded, "Where? Point them out to me."

Then I, too, began to visualize them.

"Now," continued our friend, "let us bow our heads and together thank God for giving us 100,000 subscribers."

Frankly I thought that was pushing the Lord rather hard, but it was justified by a verse in the Scriptures where it says, "And all things, whatsoever ye shall ask in prayer, believing, ye shall receive them." (Matthew 21:22) That means when you pray for something, at the same time visualize what you pray for. Believe that if it is God's will and is worth-while, not selfishly sought after, but for human good, that it is at that moment given you.

If you have difficulty in following this reasoning, let me tell you that from that moment until the present writing *Guideposts* never lacked for anything. It has found wonderful friends and has had fine support. It has been able always to meet its bills, purchase needed equipment, finance itself and as I write these words *Guideposts* is nearing the half million mark and more subscriptions are coming in regularly, sometimes as many as three or four thousand per day.

I recite this instance not for the purpose of advertising *Guideposts*, although I strongly recommend this magazine to all my readers, and if you would like to be a subscriber, write to *Guideposts*, Pawling, New York, for information. But I tell the story because I was awed by this experience, realizing that I had stumbled upon a law, a tremendous law of personal victory. I decided to apply it thereafter to my own problems and wherever I have done so can report a marvelous result. Wherever I have failed to do so, I have missed great results.

It is as simple as this—put your problem in God's hands. In your thoughts rise above the problem so that you look down upon it, not up at it. Test it according to God's will. That is, do not try to get success from something that is wrong. Be sure it is right morally, spiritually, and ethically. You can never get a right result from an error. If your thinking is wrong, it is wrong and not right and can never be right so long as it is wrong. If it is wrong in the essence it is bound to be wrong in the result.

Therefore be sure it is right, then hold it up in God's name and visualize a great result. Keep the idea of prosperity, of achievement, and of attainment firmly fixed in your mind. Never entertain a failure thought. Should a negative thought of defeat come into your mind, expel it by increasing the positive affirmation. Affirm aloud, "God is now giving me success. He is now giving me attainment." The mental vision which you create and firmly hold in consciousness will be actualized if you continually affirm it in your thoughts and if you work diligently and effectively. This creative process simply stated is: visualize, prayerize, and finally actualize.

People in all walks of life who accomplish notable achievements know the value of this law in their experience.

Henry J. Kaiser told me that at one time he was building a levee along a riverbank, and there came a great storm and flood which buried all his earth-moving machinery and destroyed the work that had been done. Upon going out to observe the damage after the water receded, he found his workers standing around glumly looking at the mud and the buried machinery.

He came among them and said with a smile, "Why are you so glum?"

"Don't you see what happened?" they asked. "Our machinery is covered with mud."

"What mud?" he asked brightly.

"What mud!" they repeated in astonishment."Look around you. It is a sea of mud."

"Oh," he laughed, "I don't see any mud."

"But how can you say that?" they asked him.

"Because," said Mr. Kaiser, "I am looking up at a clear blue sky, and there is no mud up there. There is only sunshine, and I never saw any mud that could stand against sunshine. Soon it will be dried up, and then you will be able to move your machinery and start all over again."

How right he is. If your eyes are looking down in the mud and you feel a sense of failure, you will create defeat for yourself. Optimistic visualization combined with prayer and faith will inevitably actualize achievement.

Another friend of mine who started from the lowliest beginnings has performed some outstanding achievements. I remember him in his schooldays as an awkward, unprepossessing, very shy country boy. But he had character and one of the keenest brains I have ever encountered. Today he is an outstanding man in his line. I asked him, "What is the secret of your success?"

"The people who have worked with me across the years and the unlimited opportunity given any boy in the United States of America," he replied.

"Yes, I know that is true, but I am sure you must have some personal technique, and I would be interested in having it," I said.

"It all lies in how you think about problems," he replied. "I attack a problem and shake it to pieces with my mind. I put all the mental power I have upon it. Second, I pray about it most sincerely. Third, I paint a mental picture of success. Fourth, I always ask myself, 'What is the right thing to do?' for," he said, "nothing will be right if it is wrong. Nothing that is wrong will ever come out right. Fifth, I give it all I've got. But let me emphasize again," he concluded, "If you're thinking defeat, change your thoughts at once. Get new and positive thoughts. That is primary and basic in overcoming difficulties and in achieving."

At this very minute, as you read this book, potential ideas are in your mind. By releasing and developing these ideas you can solve your financial problem, your business situation, and you can care for yourself and your family, and attain success in your ventures. A steady inflow and practical use of these creative thoughts can remake your life and you along with it.

There was a time when I acquiesced in the silly idea that there is no relationship between faith and prosperity; that when one talked about religion he should never relate it to achievement, that it dealt only with ethics and morals or social values. But now I realize that such a viewpoint limits the power of God and the development of the individual. Religion teaches that there is a tremendous power in the universe and that this power can dwell in personality. It is a power that can blast out and defeat and lift a person above all difficult situations.

We have seen the demonstration of atomic energy. We know that astonishing and enormous energy exists in the universe. This same force of energy is resident in the human mind. Nothing on earth is greater than the human mind in potential power. The average individual is capable of much greater achievement than he has ever realized.

This is true regardless of who is reading this statement. When you actually learn to release yourself you will discover that your mind contains ideas of such creative value that you need not lack anything. By the full and proper use of your power stimulated by God power, you can make your life successful.

You can make just about anything of your life—anything you will believe or will visualize, anything you will pray for and work for. Look deeply into your mind. Amazing wonders are there.

Whatever your situation may be, you can improve it. First, quiet your mind so that inspirations may rise from its depths. Believe that God is now helping you. Visualize achievement. Organize your life on a spiritual basis so that God's principles work within you. Hold firmly in your mind a picture not of failure but of success. Do these things and creative thoughts will flow freely from your mind. This is an amazing law, one that can change anybody's life including your own. An inflow of new thoughts can remake you regardless of every difficulty you may now face, and I repeat—*every difficulty*.

In the last analysis the basic reason a person fails to live a creative and successful life is because of error within himself. He thinks wrong. He needs to correct the error in his thoughts. He needs to practice right thinking. When the 23rd Psalm says, "He leadeth me in the paths of righteousness," it not only means the paths of goodness, but the paths of right-mindedness as well. When Isaiah says, "Let the wicked forsake his way and the unrighteous man his thoughts," (Isaiah 55:7) it not only means that a person is to depart from evil and do good, but that he is to change his thinking from wrong to right, from error to truth. The great secret of successful living is to reduce the amount of error in oneself and increase the amount of truth. An inflow of new, right, health-laden thoughts through the mind creatively affects the circumstances of life, for truth always produces right procedures and therefore right results.

Years ago I knew a young man who for a while was one of the most complete personality failures in my entire experience. He had a delightful personality, but he failed at everything. A person would employ him and be enthusiastic about him, but soon his enthusiasm would cool and it was not long until he was out of that position. This failure pattern was repeated many times. He was a failure as a person as well as an employee. He missed connections with everything. He just couldn't do anything right, and he used to ask me, "What is wrong with me that everything goes wrong?"

Still he had a lot of conceit. He was cocky and smug, and had the irritating habit of blaming everybody but himself. Something was wrong with every office with which he was connected or every organization that employed him. He blamed everybody else for his failures—never himself. He would never look inside himself. It never occurred to him that anything could be wrong with him.

One night, however, he wanted to talk with me, and as I had to make a drive of about a hundred miles to deliver a speech he drove there and back with me. On our return we stopped along about midnight at a roadside stand for a hamburger and a cup of coffee. I don't know what was in that hamburger sandwich, but since this incident I have had a new respect for hamburgers, for of a sudden he shouted, "I've got it! I've got it!"

"You've got what?" I asked in astonishment.

"I've got the answer. Now I know what's the trouble with me. It's that everything goes wrong with me because I myself am wrong."

I clapped my hand on his back and said, "Boy, at last you are on your way."

"Why, it's as clear as a crystal," he said. "I have been thinking wrong, and as a result I have created wrong outcomes."

By this time we were out in the moonlight standing alongside my car, and I said to him, "Harry, you must go one step further and ask God to make you right inwardly." I quoted this passage from the Bible, " 'Ye shall know the truth, and the truth shall make you free.' " (John 8:32) Get the truth into your mind and you will be free of your failures.

He became an enthusiastic practicing follower of Jesus Christ. Through real faith and a complete change of thoughts and personal habits, wrong thinking and wrong acting were removed from his nature. He straightened out by developing a right (or righteousness) pattern instead of an error pattern. When he was made right, then everything began to go right for him.

Following are seven practical steps for changing your mental attitudes from negative to positive, for releasing creative new thoughts, and for shifting from error patterns to truth patterns. Try them—keep on trying them. They will work.

1. For the next twenty-four hours, deliberately speak hopefully about everything, about your job, about your health, about your future. Go out of your way to talk optimistically about everything. This will be difficult, for possibly it is your habit to talk pessimistically. From this negative habit you must restrain yourself even if it requires an act of will.

2. After speaking hopefully for twenty-four hours, continue the practice for one week, then you can be permitted to be "realistic" for a

day or two. You will discover that what you meant by "realistic" a week ago was actually pessimistic, but what you now mean by "realistic" is something entirely different; it is the dawning of the positive outlook. When most people say they are being "realistic" they delude themselves: they are simply being negative.

3. You must feed your mind even as you feed your body, and to make your mind healthy you must feed it nourishing, wholesome thoughts. Therefore, today start to shift your mind from negative to positive thinking. Start at the beginning of the New Testament and underscore every sentence about *Faith*. Continue doing this until you have marked every such passage in the four books, Matthew, Mark, Luke, and John. Particularly note Mark 11, verses 22, 23, 24. They will serve as samples of the verses you are to underscore and fix deeply in your consciousness.

4. Then commit the underscored passages to memory. Commit one each day until you can recite the entire list from memory. This will take time, but remember you have consumed much more time becoming a negative thinker than this will require. Effort and time will be needed to unlearn your negative pattern.

5. Make a list of your friends to determine who is the most positive thinker among them and deliberately cultivate his society. Do not abandon your negative friends, but get closer to those with a positive point of view for a while, until you have absorbed their spirit, then you can go back among your negative friends and give them your newly acquired thought pattern without taking on their negativism.

6. Avoid argument, but whenever a negative attitude is expressed, counter with a positive and optimistic opinion.

7. Pray a great deal and always let your prayer take the form of thanksgiving on the assumption that God is giving you great and wonderful things; for if you think He is, He surely is. God will not give you any greater blessing than you can believe in. He wants to give you great things, but even He cannot make you take anything greater than you are equipped by faith to receive. "According to your faith (that is, in proportion to) be it unto you." (Matthew 9:29)

The secret of a better and more successful life is to cast out those old dead, unhealthy thoughts. Substitute for them new vital, dynamic faith thoughts. You can depend upon it—an inflow of new thoughts will remake you and your life.

14

RELAX FOR EASY POWER

"Every night in these United States more than six million sleeping tablets are required to put the American people to sleep."

This startling statement was made to me several years ago by a drug manufacturer at a convention of that industry where I was giving a speech. Though his assertion seemed incredible, I have been told by others who are in a position to know that the above estimate is now an understatement.

In fact, I heard another good authority assert that the American people are using about twelve million doses of sleeping tablets per day. That is enough to put every twelfth American to sleep tonight. Statistics show that the use of sleeping tablets has risen 1000 per cent in recent years. But a more recent statement is ever more startling. According to the vice-president of a large drug manufacturing concern approximately seven billion one-half-grain tablets are consumed yearly, which works out at about nineteen million tablets per night.

What a pathetic situation. Sleep is a natural restorative process. One would think that any person after a day's work would be able to sleep peacefully, but apparently Americans have even lost the art of sleeping. In fact, so keyed up are they that I, a minister with ample opportunity to test the matter, must report that the American people are so nervous and high-strung that now it is almost next to impossible to put them to sleep with a sermon. It has been years since I have seen anyone sleep in church. And that is a sad situation.

A Washington official who loves to juggle figures, especially astronomical figures, told me that last year in the United States there was a total of seven and a half billion headaches. This works itself out at approximately fifty headaches per head per annum. Have you had your quota yet this year? Just how this official arrived at these figures he did not say, but shortly after our conversation I noticed a report that in a recent year the drug industry sold eleven million pounds of aspirin. Perhaps this era might appropriately be termed "The Aspirin Age," as one author has called it.

An authoritative source declares that every other hospital bed in the United States is occupied by a patient who was put there not because he encountered a germ or had an accident or developed an organic malady, but because of his inability to organize and discipline his emotions.

In a clinic five hundred patients were examined hand running and 386, or 77 per cent, were found to be ill of psychosomatic difficulties—physical illness caused largely by unhealthy mental states. Another clinic made a study of a large number of ulcer cases and reported that nearly half were made ill, not as a result of physical troubles, but because the patients worried too much or hated too much, had too much guilt, or were tension victims.

A doctor from still another clinic made the observation that in his opinion medical men, despite all extraordinary scientific developments, are now able to heal by the means of science alone less than half the maladies brought them. He declares that in many cases patients are sending back into their bodies the diseased thoughts of their minds. Prominent among these diseased thoughts are anxiety and tension.

This unhappy situation has become so serious that in our own Marble Collegiate Church, Fifth Avenue at 29th Street, New York City, we now have twelve psychiatrists on the staff under the supervision of Dr. Smiley Blanton. Why psychiatrists on the staff of a church? The answer is that psychiatry is a science. Its function is the analysis, diagnosis, and treatment of human nature according to certain well-authenticated laws and procedures.

Christianity may also be thought of as a science. It is a philosophy, a system of theology, a system of metaphysics, and a system of worship. It also works itself out in moral and ethical codes. But Christianity also has the characteristics of a science in that it is based upon a book which contains a system of techniques and formulas designed for the understanding and treatment of human nature. The laws are so precise and have been so often demonstrated when proper conditions of understanding, belief, and practice are applied that religion may be said to form an exact science.

When a person comes to our clinic the first counselor is perhaps a psychiatrist who in a kindly and careful manner studies the problem and tells the patient "why he does what he does." This is a most important fact to learn. Why, for example, have you had an inferiority complex all your life long, or why have you been haunted by fear, or, again, why do you nurse resentment? Why have you always been shy and reticent, or why do you do stupid things or make inept statements? These phenomena of your human nature do not just happen. There is a reason why you do what you do and it is an important day in your life experience when at last you discover the reason. Self-knowledge is the beginning of self-correction.

Following the self-knowledge process the psychiatrist turns the patient over to the pastor who tells him how to do what he ought to do. The pastor applies to the case, in scientific and systematic form, the therapies of prayer, faith, and love. The psychiatrist and the minister pool their knowledge and combine their therapies with the result that many people have found new life and happiness. The minister does not attempt to be a psychiatrist nor the psychiatrist a pastor. Each performs his own function but always in cooperation.

The Christianity utilized in this procedure is the undiluted teachings of Jesus Christ, Lord and Saviour of man's life. We believe in the practical, absolute workability of the teachings of Jesus. We believe that we can indeed "do all things through Christ." (Philippians 4:13) The Gospel as we work with it proves to be a literal fulfillment of the astonishing promise, "Eye hath not seen, nor ear heard, neither have entered into the heart of man, the things which God hath prepared for them that love Him." (I Corinthians 2:9) Believe (in Christ); believe in His system of thought and practice; believe and you will overcome all fear, hate, inferiority, guilt, and every form and manner of defeat. In other words, no good thing is too good to be true. You have never seen, never heard, never even imagined the things God will give to those who love Him.

In the work of the clinic one frequent problem is that of tension. This, to a very large degree, may be called the prevailing malady of the American people. But not only the American people seem to suffer from tension. The Royal Bank of Canada some time ago devoted its monthly letter to this problem under the title, "Let's Slow Down," and says in part: "This monthly letter does not set itself up as a counselor of mental and physical health, but it is attempting to break down a problem that bedevils every adult person in Canada," and, I might add, in the United States as well.

The bank letter goes on to say: "We are victims of a mounting tension; we have difficulty in relaxing. Our high-strung nervous systems are on a perpetual binge. Caught up as we are in the rush all day, every day, and far into the night, we are not living fully. We must remember what Carlyle called 'the calm supremacy of the spirit over its circumstances.' "

When a prominent banking institution calls to the attention of its customers the fact that they are failing to derive from life what they really want from it because they have become victims of tension, it is certainly time something was done about the situation.

In St. Petersburg, Florida, I actually saw a machine on the street equipped with a sign, "What is your blood pressure?" You could put a coin in a slot and get the bad news. When you can buy a reading on blood pressure like you buy gum out of a slot machine, it indicates that many people have this problem.

One of the simplest methods for reducing tension is to practice the easy-does-it attitude. Do everything more slowly, less hectically, and without pressure. My friend Branch Rickey, famous baseball man, told me that he would not use a player no matter how well he hits, fields, or runs if he is guilty of "overpressing." To be a successful big-league baseball player there must be a flow of easy power through every action and of course through the mind. The most effective way to hit a ball is by the easy method, where all the muscles are flexible and operating in correlated power. Try to kill the ball and you will slice it or maybe miss it altogether. This is true in golf, in baseball, in every sport.

From 1907 through 1919, except for one year, 1916, Ty Cobb's batting average led the American League, a record so far as I know that has never been surpassed. Ty Cobb presented the bat with which he performed his extraordinary feats to a friend of mine. I was permitted to take this bat in my hand, which I did with considerable awe. In the spirit of the game I struck a pose, as if to bat. Doubtless my batting stance was not in any sense reminiscent of the immortal slugger. In fact, my friend, who was himself at one time a minor league baseball player, chuckled and said, "Ty Cobb would never do it that way. You are too rigid, too tense. You are obviously overtrying. You would probably strike out."

It was beautiful to watch Ty Cobb. The man and the bat were one. It was a study in rhythm, and one marveled at the ease with which he got into the swing. He was a master of easy power. It is the same in all success. Analyze people who are really efficient and they always seem to do things easily, with a minimum of effort. In so doing they release maximum power.

One of my friends, a famous businessman who handles important affairs and varied interests, always seems to be at ease. He does everything efficiently and quickly but is never in a dither. He never has that anxious, frazzled look on his face which marks people who cannot handle either their time or their work. I inquired the secret of his obviously easy power.

He smiled and replied, "Oh, it isn't much of a secret. I just try to keep myself in tune with God. That's all. Every morning after breakfast," he explained, "my wife and I go into the living room for a period of quietness. One of us reads aloud some inspirational piece to get us into the mood of meditation. It may be a poem or a few paragraphs of a book. Following that we sit quietly, each praying or meditating according to his own mood and manner, then together we affirm the thought that God is filling us with strength and quiet energy. This is a definite fifteen-minute ritual and we never miss it. We couldn't get along without it. We would crack up. As a result I always seem to feel that I have more energy than I need and more power than is required." So said this efficient man who demonstrates easy power.

I know a number of men and women who practice this or similar techniques for reducing tension. It is becoming a quite general and popular procedure nowadays.

One February morning I was rushing down the long veranda of a Florida hotel with a handful of mail just in from my office in New York. I had come to Florida for a midwinter vacation, but hadn't seemed to get out of the routine of dealing with my mail the first thing in the morning. As I hurried by, headed for a couple hours' work with that mail, a friend from Georgia who was sitting in a rocking chair with his hat partially over his eyes stopped me in my headlong rush and said in his slow and pleasant Southern drawl, "Where are you rushing for, Doctor? That's no way to do down here in the Florida sunshine. Come over here and 'set' in one of these rocking chairs and help me practice one of the greatest of the arts."

Mystified, I said, "Help you practice one of the greatest of the arts!"

"Yes," he replied, "an art that is passing out. Not many people know how to do it any more."

"Well," I asked, "please tell me what it is. I don't see you practicing any art."

"Oh, yes, I am," he said. "I am practicing the art of just sittin' in the sun. Sit here and let the sun fall on your face. It is warm-like and it smells good. It makes you feel peaceful inside. Did you ever think about the sun?" he asked. "It never hurries, never gets excited, it just works slowly and makes no noise—doesn't push any buzzers, doesn't answer any telephones, doesn't ring any bells, just goes on a-shining, and the sun does more work in the fraction of an instant than you and I could ever do in a lifetime. Think of what it does. It causes the flowers to bloom, keeps the trees growing, warms the earth, causes the fruit and vegetables to grow and the crops to ripen, lifts water to send back on the earth, and it makes you feel 'peaceful like.'

"I find that when I sit in the sun and let the sun work on me it puts some rays into me that give me energy; that is, when I take the time to sit in the sun.

"So throw that mail over in the corner," he said, "and sit down here with me."

I did so, and when finally I went to my room and got at my mail I finished it in no time at all. And there was a good part of the day left for vacation activities and for more "sittin' in the sun."

Of course I know a lot of lazy people who have been sittin' in the sun all their lives and never amounted to anything. There is a difference between sittin' and relaxing, and just sittin'. But if you sit and relax and think about God and get yourself in tune with Him and open yourself to the flow of His power, then sittin' is not laziness; in fact, it is about the best way to renew power. It produces driving energy, the kind of energy *you* drive, not the kind that drives you.

The secret is to keep the mind quiet, avoiding all hectic reactions of haste, and to practice peaceful thinking. The essence of the art is to keep the tempo down; to perform your responsibilities on the basis of the most efficient conservation of energy. It is advisable to adopt one or two workable plans through the use of which you can become expert in the practice of relaxed and easy power.

One of the best such plans was suggested to me by Captain Eddie Rickenbacker. A very busy man, he manages to handle his responsibilities in a manner indicating reserves of power. I found one element of his secret quite by accident.

I was filming a program for television with him. We had been assured that the work could be done quickly, leaving him free to go to the many other matters on his daily agenda.

However, the filming was long delayed beyond the time anticipated. I noted, however, that the Captain showed no signs of agitation. He did not become nervous or anxious. He did not pace up and down, putting in frantic calls to his office. Instead, he accepted the situation gracefully. There were a couple of old rocking chairs at the studio, apparently intended for use in a set other than ours. He sat in one rocker in a very relaxed manner.

I have always been a great admirer of Eddie Rickenbacker and I commented on his lack of tension. "I know how busy you are," I said, "and I marvel at the way you sit quiet, composed, and peaceful like."

For myself, I was a bit disturbed largely because I regretted to take so much of Captain Rickenbacker's time."How can you be so imperturbable?" I asked.

He laughingly replied, "Oh, I just practice what you preach. Come on, easy does it. Sit down here beside me."

I pulled up the other rocking chair and did a little relaxing on my own. Then I said, "Eddie, I know you have some technique to attain this impressive serenity. Tell me about it, please."

He is a modest man, but because of my persistence he gave me a formula which he says he uses frequently. I now use it myself and it is very effective. It may be described as follows:

First, collapse physically. Practice this several times a day. Let go every muscle in the body. Conceive of yourself as a jellyfish, getting your body into complete looseness. Form a mental picture of a huge burlap bag of potatoes. Then mentally cut the bag, allowing the potatoes to roll out. Think of yourself as the bag.

What is more relaxed than an empty burlap bag?

The second element in the formula is to "drain the mind." Several times each day drain the mind of irritation, all resentment, disappointment, frustration, and annoyance. Unless you drain the mind frequently and regularly, these unhappy thoughts will accumulate until a major blasting-out process will be necessary. Keep the mind drained of all factors which would impede the flow of relaxed power.

Third, think spiritually. To think spiritually means to turn the mind at regular intervals to God. At least three times a day "lift up your eyes unto the hills." This keeps you in tune with God's harmony. It refills you with peace.

This three-point program greatly impressed me, and I have been practicing it for some months. It is an excellent method for relaxing and living on the basis of easy does it.

From my friend Dr. Z. Taylor Bercovitz, of New York City, I have learned much of the art of working relaxed. Often when under pressure, with an office full of patients and telephone calls coming in, he will suddenly stop, lean against his desk, and talk to the Lord in a manner both natural and respectful. I like the style of his prayer. He tells me that it runs something like this: "Look, Lord, I am pushing myself too hard. I am getting jittery. Here I am counseling people to practice quietness, now I must practice it. Touch me with your healing grace. Give me composure, quietness, strength, and conserve my nervous energy so that I can help these people who come to me."

He stands quietly for a minute or two. Then he thanks the Lord and proceeds with full but easy power to do his work.

Often in making sick calls about the city he finds himself in a traffic jam. He has a most interesting method of using these potentially irritating delays as opportunities to relax. Shutting off his engine, he slumps in his seat, putting his head back, closing his eyes, and has even been known to go to sleep. He says there is no reason to be concerned about going to sleep because the strident honking of horns will awaken him when traffic begins to move.

These interludes of complete relaxation in the midst of traffic last only for a minute or two, but they have energy-renewal value. It is surprising how many minutes or fractions of minutes during the day you can use to rest where you are. If even in such fractional periods you deliberately draw on God's power, you can maintain adequate relaxation. It isn't length of relaxation time that produces power; it is the quality of the experience.

I am told that Roger Babson, the famous statistician, frequently goes into an empty church and sits quietly. Perhaps he reads one or two hymns and in so doing finds rest and renewal. Dale Carnegie, under tension, goes to a church near his New York City office to spend a quarter-hour in prayerful meditation. He says he leaves his office for this purpose when busiest. This demonstrates control of time rather than being controlled by it. It also indicates watchfulness lest tension develop beyond a controllable degree.

I encountered a friend on a train from Washington to New York one night. This man is a member of Congress and he explained that he was on his way to his district to speak at a meeting of his constituents. The particular group he was about to address was hostile to him, he said, and would probably try to make things very difficult for him. Although they represented a minority in his district, he was going to face them just the same.

"They are American citizens and I am their representative. They have a right to meet with me if they want to."

"You do not seem to be much worried about it," I commented.

"No," he answered, "if I get worried about it, then I will be upset and will not handle the situation well."

"Do you have any particular method for handling such a tense situation?" I asked.

"Oh, yes," he replied, "they will be a noisy crowd. But I have my own way of meeting such situations without tension. I will breathe deeply, talk quietly, speak sincerely, be friendly and respectful, hold my temper, and trust in God to see me through.

"I have learned one important fact," the Congressman continued, "and that is in any situation be relaxed, keep calm, take a friendly attitude, have faith, do your best. Do this, and usually you can make things come out all right."

I have no doubt about the ability of this Congressman to live and work without tension, and, what is more, successfully to attain his objectives.

When we were doing some construction work at my farm in Pawling, New York, I watched a workman swinging a shovel. He was shoveling a pile of sand. It was a beautiful sight. Stripped to the waist, his lean and muscular body worked with precision and correlation. The shovel rose and fell in perfect rhythm. He would push the shovel into the pile, lean his body against it, and drive it deep into the sand. Then, in a clear, free swing it came up and the sand was deposited without a break in the motion. Again the shovel went back into the sand, again his body leaned against it, again the shovel lifted easily in a perfect arc. One almost had a feeling that he could sing in rhythm to the motion of this workman. Indeed the man did sing as he worked.

I was not surprised when the foreman told me that he is considered one of his best workmen. The foreman also spoke of him as good-humored, happy, and a pleasant person with whom to work. Here was a relaxed man who lived with joyous power, master of the art of easy does it.

Relaxation results from re-creation, and the process of re-creation should be continuous. The human being is meant to be attached to a continual flow of force that proceeds from God through the individual and back to God for renewal. When one lives in tune with this constantly re-creative process he learns the indispensable quality to relax and work on the basis of easy does it.

Now, how to master this skill. Here are ten rules for taking the hard way out of your job. Try these proven methods for working hard easily. They will help you to relax and have easy power.

1. Don't get the idea that you are Atlas carrying the world on your shoulders. Don't strain so hard. Don't take yourself so seriously.

2. Determine to like your work. Then it will become a pleasure, not drudgery. Perhaps you do not need to change your job. Change yourself and your work will seem different.

3. Plan your work—work your plan. Lack of system produces that "I'm swamped" feeling.

4. Don't try to do everything at once. That is why time is spread out. Heed that wise advice from the Bible, "This one thing I do."

5. Get a correct mental attitude, remembering that ease or difficulty in your work depends upon how you think about it. Think it's hard and you make it hard. Think it's easy and it tends to become easy.

6. Become efficient in your work. "Knowledge is power" (over your job). It is always easier to do a thing right.

7. Practice being relaxed. Easy does it. Don't press or tug. Take it in your stride.

8. Discipline yourself not to put off until tomorrow what you can do today. Accumulation of undone jobs makes your work harder. Keep your work on schedule.

9. Pray about your work. You will get relaxed efficiency by so doing.

10. Take on the "unseen partner." It is surprising the load He will take off you. God is as much at home in offices, factories, stores, kitchens, as in churches. He know more about your job than you do. His help will make your work easy.

15

HOW TO GET PEOPLE TO LIKE YOU

We might as well admit it, we want people to like us.

You may hear someone say, "I don't care whether people like me or not." But whenever you hear anyone say that, just put it down as a fact that he is not really telling the truth.

The psychologist, William James, said, "One of the deepest drives of human nature is the desire to be appreciated." The longing to be liked, to be held in esteem, to be a sought-after person, is fundamental in us.

A poll was taken among some high-school students on the question, "What do you most desire?" By overwhelming majority the students voted that they wanted to be popular. The same urge is in older people as well. Indeed it is doubtful if anybody ever outlives the desire to be well thought of, to be highly regarded, or to have the affection of his associates.

To be master of the art of popularity, be artless. Strive deliberately after popularity and the chances are you will never attain it. But become one of those rare personalities about whom people say, "He certainly has something," and you can be certain you are on the way to having people like you.

I must warn you, however, that despite your attainments in popularity you will never get everybody to like you. There is a curious quirk in human nature whereby some people just naturally don't like you. A quatrain inscribed on a wall at Oxford says:

> *"I do not love thee, Dr. Fell,*
> *The reason why I cannot tell;*
> *But this alone I know full well,*
> *I do not love thee, Dr. Fell."*

That verse is very subtle. The author did not like Dr. Fell. He didn't know why but he just didn't like him. It was most likely an unreasonable dislike, for undoubtedly Dr. Fell was a very nice person. Perhaps if the author had known him better he would have liked him, but poor Dr. Fell never did become popular with the author of those lines. It may have been due simply to a lack of *rapprochement*, that baffling mechanism by which we either do or do not "click" with certain people.

Even the Bible recognizes this unhappy fact about human nature, for it says, "If it be possible, as much as lieth in you, live peaceably with all men." (Romans 12:18) The Bible is a very realistic book and it knows people, their infinite possibilities as well as their imperfections. The Bible advised the disciples that if they went into a village and after trying their best to get along with people still couldn't do so, they were to shake off the very dust of the village from their feet—"And whosoever will not receive you, when ye go out of that city, shake off the very dust from your feet for a testimony against them." (Luke 9:5) This is all by way of saying that you will be wise if you do not let it too seriously affect you if you do not achieve perfect popularity with everyone.

However, there are certain formulas and procedures which, if followed faithfully, can make you a person whom other people like. You can enjoy satisfactory personal relationships even if you are a "difficult" person or by nature shy and retiring, even unsocial. You can make of yourself one who enjoys easy, normal, natural, and pleasing relationships with others.

I cannot urge you too strongly to consider the importance of this subject and to give time and attention to its mastery, for you will never be fully happy or successful until you do. Failure in this capacity will adversely affect you psychologically. To be liked is of profounder importance than mere ego satisfaction. As necessary as that is to your success in life, normal and satisfactory personal relations are even more important.

The feeling of not being wanted or needed is one of the most devastating of all human reactions. To the degree to which you are sought after or needed by other people will you become a fully-released person. The "lone wolf," the isolated personality, the retiring individual, these people suffer a misery which is difficult to describe. In self-defense they retire ever further within themselves. Their ingrowing, introverted nature is denied the normal development which the outgoing, self-giving person experiences. Unless the personality is drawn out of itself and can be of value to someone, it may sicken and die. The feeling of not being wanted or needed produces frustration, aging, illness. If you have a feeling of uselessness, if nobody needs or wants you, you really ought to do something about it. It is not only a pathetic way to live but is serious psychologically. Those who deal with the problems of human nature constantly encounter this problem and its unfortunate results.

For example, at a Rotary Club luncheon in a certain city two physicians were at my table: one an elderly man who had been retired for several years, the other the most popular young doctor in town. The young doctor, looking frazzled, dashed in late and slumped down with a weary sigh. "If only the telephone would stop ringing," he complained. "I can't get anywhere because people call me all the time. I wish I could put a silencer on that telephone."

The old doctor spoke up quietly, "I know how you feel, Jim," he said. "I used to feel that way myself, but be thankful the telephone does ring. Be glad people want and need you." Then he added pathetically, "Nobody ever calls me any more. I would like to hear the telephone ring again. Nobody wants me and nobody needs me. I'm a has-been."

All of us at the table who sometimes feel a bit worn by numerous activities did a lot of thinking as we listened to the old doctor.

A middle-aged woman complained to me that she didn't feel well. She was dissatisfied and unhappy. "My husband is dead, the children are grown, and there is no place for me anymore. People treat me kindly, but they are indifferent. Everyone has its own interest and nobody needs me—nobody wants me. I wonder, could that be a reason I do not feel well?" she asked. Indeed that could very likely be an important reason.

In a business office the founder of the firm just past seventy was walking restlessly and aimlessly around. He talked with me while his son, present head of the business, whom I had come to see, was on the telephone. The older man said gloomily, "Why don't you write a book on how to retire? That is what I need to know. I thought it was going to be wonderful to give up the burdens of the job," he continued, "but now I find that nobody is interested in anything I say. I used to think I was a popular fellow, but now when I come down here and sit around the office everyone says hello, then they forget me. I might as well stay away altogether for all they care. My son is running the business and he is doing a good job of it, but," he concluded pathetically, "I'd like to think they needed me a little bit."

These people are suffering one of the most pathetic and unhappy experiences in this life. Their basic desire is to be sought after and this desire is not being satisfied. They want people to appreciate them. The personality longs for esteem. But it isn't only in retirement that this situation develops.

A girl of twenty-one told me that she had been unwanted ever since birth. Someone had given her the notion she was an unwanted child. This serious idea had sunk into her subconscious, giving her a profound sense of inferiority and self-depreciation. It made her shy and backward, causing her to retreat into herself. She became lonely and unhappy and was, in fact, an underdeveloped personality. The cure for her condition was to revamp her life spiritually, especially her thinking, which process in time made her a well-liked person by setting her personality free of herself.

Countless other people, not particularly victims of deep, unconscious psychological conflicts, have never mastered the knack of being popular. They try hard enough. They even go to extremes, often acting in a manner they do not really enjoy, but which they employ only because of their intense desire to have people like them. Everywhere today we see people putting on an act because of their inordinate desire for popularity in the superficial sense in which the word is often used in modern society.

The fact is that popularity can be attained by a few simple, natural, normal, and easily mastered techniques. Practice them diligently and you can become a well-liked person.

First, become a comfortable person, that is, one with whom people can associate without a sense of strain. Of some persons it is said, "You can never quite get next to him." There is always a barrier that you can't get over. A comfortable person is easy-going and natural. He has a pleasant, kindly, genial way about him. Being with him is not unlike wearing an old hat or an old pair of shoes, or an easy old coat. A stiff, reserved, unresponsive individual never meshes into the group. He is always just a bit out of it. You never quite know how to take him or how he will react. You just aren't easy-like with him.

Some young people were talking about a seventeen-year-old boy whom they liked very much. Of him they said, "He is good company. He is a good sport. He is easy to be with." It is very important to cultivate the quality of being natural. Usually that sort of individual is large-souled. Little people who are much concerned about how you treat them, who are jealous of their place or position, who meticulously stand on their prerogatives, are stiff and easily offended.

A man who is an outstanding example of these truths is James A. Farley, former Postmaster General of the United States.

I met Mr. Farley for the first time a number of years ago. Months later I met him in a large crowd of people and he called me by name. Being human, I never forgot that, and it is one reason I have always liked Mr. Farley.

An interesting incident illustrates the secret of this man who is an expert in how to get people to like him. I was to speak in Philadelphia at a book-and-author luncheon along with Mr. Farley and two other authors. I did not actually witness the scene I am about to describe, as I was late in arriving, but my publisher did. The speakers at this luncheon were walking along the hotel corridor together when they passed a maid standing by a cart loaded with sheets, towels, and other equipment with which she was servicing the rooms. She was paying no attention to this group of people as they turned aside to avoid her cart. Mr. Farley walked up to her, put out his hand, and said, "Hello, there. How are you? I'm Jim Farley. What's your name? Glad to see you."

My publisher looked back at her as the group passed down the hall. The girl's mouth was wide with astonishment and her face broke into a beautiful smile. It was an excellent example of how an unegotistical, comfortable, outgoing person is successful in personal relationships.

A university psychology department conducted an analysis of the personality traits by which people are liked or disliked. One hundred traits were scientifically analyzed and it was reported that one must have forty-six favorable traits in order to be liked. It is rather discouraging to realize that you must have so large a number of characteristics to be popular.

Christianity, however, teaches that one basic trait will go far toward getting people to like you. That trait is a sincere and forthright interest and love for people. Perhaps if you cultivate this basic trait, other traits will naturally develop.

If you are not the comfortable type of person, I suggest that you make a study of your personality with a view toward eliminating conscious and unconscious elements of strain which may exist. Do not assume that the reason other people do not like you is because of something wrong with them. Assume, instead, that the trouble is within yourself and determine to find and eliminate it. This will require scrupulous honesty and it may also involve the assistance of personality experts. The so-called "scratchy" elements in your personality may be qualities which you have taken on through the years. Perhaps they have been assumed defensively, or they may be the result of attitudes developed in your younger days. Regardless of origin they can be eliminated by a scientific study of yourself and by your recognition of the necessity for change followed by a process of personality rehabilitation.

A man came to our clinic at the church seeking help in the problem of personal relationships. About thirty-five years of age, he was the type of person whom you would certainly look at twice if not three times. He was splendidly proportioned and impressive. Superficially regarding him it was surprising that people should not like him. But he proceeded to outline an unhappy and continuous set of circumstances and instances to illustrate his dismal failure in human relations.

"I do my best," he explained. "I have tried to put into practice the rules I have been taught about getting along with people, but get nowhere with the effort. People just don't like me and what is more I am aware of it."

After talking with him it was not difficult to understand the trouble. There was in his manner of speech a persistently critical attitude thinly veiled but nonetheless apparent. He had an unattractive manner of pursing his lips which indicated a kind of primness or reproof for everybody, as if he felt just a bit superior and disdainful toward other people. In fact there was about him a noticeable attitude of superiority. He was very right, with no flexibility of personality.

"Isn't there some way to change myself so that people will like me?" he demanded. "Isn't there some way I can stop unconsciously rubbing people the wrong way?"

The young man was decidedly self-centered and egotistical. The person he really liked was himself. Every statement, every attitude was unconsciously measured in terms of how it reacted on himself. We had to teach him to love other people and to forget himself, which was of course a complete reversal of his development. It was vital, however, to the solution of his problem. I found that this young man was irritable with people and he picked on them in his own mind, though no outward conflicts with other persons developed. Inwardly he was trying to make everybody over to suit himself. Unconsciously people realized this, though perhaps they did not define the trouble. Barriers were erected in their minds toward him.

Since he was being unpleasant to people in his thoughts, it followed that he was less than warm in his personal attitudes. He was polite enough and managed not to be boorish and unpleasant, but people unconsciously felt coolness in him, so gave him the "brush-off" of which he complained. The reason they did so was because in his mind he had "brushed them off." He liked himself too well, and to build up his self-esteem he disliked others. He was suffering from self-love, a chief cure for which is the practice of love for others.

He was bewildered and baffled when we outlined his difficulty. But he was sincere and meant business. He practiced the suggested techniques for developing love of others in place of self-love. It required some fundamental changes to accomplish this, but he succeeded in doing so.

One method suggested was that at night before retiring he make a list of persons he had met during the day, as, for example, the bus driver or the newsboy. He was to picture mentally each person whose name appeared on the list, and as he brought each face up before him he was to think a kindly thought about that person. Then he was to pray for each one. He was to pray around his little world. Each of us has his own world, people with whom we do business or are associated in one way or another.

For example, the first person outside the family whom this young man saw in the morning was the elevator man in his apartment house. He had not been in the habit of saying anything to him beyond a perfunctory and growled good morning. Now he took the time to have a little chat with the elevator man. He asked him about his family and about his interests. He found that the elevator operator had an interesting point of view and some experiences which were quite fascinating. He began to see new values in a person who to him previously had been a mechanical robot, who ran the elevator up and down between floors. He actually began to like the elevator operator and in turn the elevator man, who had formed a pretty accurate opinion of the young man, began to revise his views. They established a friendly relationship. So the process went from person to person.

One day the young man said to me, "I have found that the world is filled with interesting people and I never realized it before."

When he made that observation he proved that he was losing himself, and when he did that, as the Bible so wisely tells us, he found himself. In losing himself he found himself and lots of new friends besides. People learned to like him.

Learning to pray for people was important in his rehabilitation, for when you pray for anyone you tend to modify your personal attitude toward him. You lift the relationship thereby to a higher level. The best in the other person begins to flow out toward you as your best flows toward him. In the meeting of the best in each a higher unity of understanding is established.

Essentially, getting people to like you is merely the other side of liking them. One of the most popular men who lived in the United States within the lifetime of most of us was the late Will Rogers. One of the most characteristic statements he ever made was, "I never met a man I didn't like." That may have been a slight exaggeration, but I am sure Will Rogers did not regard it as such. That is the way he felt about people, and as a result people opened up to him like flowers to the sun.

Sometimes the weak objection is offered that it is difficult to like some people. Granted, some people are by nature more likable than others, nevertheless a serious attempt to know any individual will reveal qualities within him that are admirable, even lovable.

A man had the problem of conquering feelings of irritation toward persons with whom he was associated. For some people he had a very profound dislike. They irritated him intensely, but he conquered these feelings simply by making an exhaustive list of everything he could possibly admire about each person who annoyed him. Daily he attempted to add to this list. He was surprised to discover that people whom he thought he did not like at all proved to have many pleasing qualities. In fact, he was at a loss to understand how he ever disliked them after becoming conscious of their attractive qualities. Of course, while he was making these discoveries about them, they, in turn, were finding new and likable qualities in him.

If you have gone through life up to this point without having established satisfactory human relationships, do not assume that you cannot change, but it will be necessary to take very definite steps toward solving the problem. You can change and become a popular person, well liked and esteemed, if you are willing to make the effort. May I remind you as I remind myself that one of the greatest tragedies of the average person is the tendency to spend our whole lives perfecting our faults? We develop a fault and we nurse it and cultivate it, and never change it. Like a needle caught in the groove of a defective record on a victrola, it plays the same old tune over and over again. You must lift the needle out of the groove, then you will have disharmony no longer, but harmony. Don't spend more of your life perfecting faults in human relations. Spend the rest of your life perfecting your great capacities for friendliness, for personal relations are vitally important to successful living.

Still another important factor in getting people to like you is to practice building up the ego of other persons. The ego, being the essence of our personalities, is sacred to us. There is in every person a normal desire for a feeling of self-importance. If I deflate your ego and therefore your self-importance, though you may laugh it off, I have deeply wounded you. In fact, I have shown disrespect for you, and while you may exercise charity toward me, even so, unless you are finely developed spiritually, you are not going to like me very well.

On the other hand, if I elevate your self-respect and contribute to your feeling of personal worth, I am showing high esteem for your ego. I have helped you to be your best self and therefore you appreciate what I have done. You are grateful to me. You like me for it.

The deflation of another person's ego may be mildly done perhaps, but one can never evaluate how deep the depreciation goes from even a remark or an attitude that is not meant to be unkind. Here is the way in which ego is often deflated.

The next time you are in a group and someone tells a joke and everybody laughs with appreciation and pleasure except yourself, when the laughter has died down say patronizingly, "Well, that is a pretty good joke all right. I saw it in a magazine last month."

Of course it will make you feel quite important to let others know of your superior knowledge, but how does it make the man feel who told the joke? You have robbed him of the satisfaction of having told a good story. You have crowded him out of his brief moment in the limelight and usurped attention to yourself. In fact you have taken the wind out of his sails and left him flat and deflated. He enjoyed his momentary little prominence, but you took it away from him. Nobody in that group is going to like you for what you did, and certainly not the man whose story you spoiled. Whether you like the joke or not, let the storyteller and the others enjoy it. Remember he may be a little bit embarrassed and shy. It would have done him good to have received a response. Don't deflate people. Build them up and they will love you for it.

While writing this chapter I enjoyed a visit with an old and dear friend, Dr. John W. Hoffman, one-time president of Ohio Wesleyan University. As I sat with him in Pasadena, I realized once again how much this great personality has always meant to me. Many years ago, on the night before my graduation from college, we had a banquet at our fraternity house at which he was present and made a talk. After dinner he asked me to walk with him to the president's house.

It was a beautiful moonlight night in June. All the way up the hill he talked to me about life and its opportunities and told me what a thrill awaited me as I entered the outside world. As we stood in front of his house he put his hand on my shoulder and said, "Norman, I have always liked you. I believe in you. You have great possibilities. I shall always be proud of you. You have got it in you." Of course he overestimated me, but that is infinitely better than to depreciate a person.

It being June and the night before graduation and excitement being in my heart, my sentiments were pretty close to the surface, and I said good night to him through a mist of tears which I tried to conceal. It has been many years since then, but I never forgot what he said nor how he said it on that June night long ago. I have loved him all across the years.

I discovered that he made similar statements to many other boys and girls long since become men and women and they, too, love him because he respected their personalities and was constantly building them up. Through the years he would write to me and to others congratulating us on some little thing that we had done, and a world of approval from him meant much. Little wonder this honored guide of youth has the affection and devotion of thousands of people whose lives he touched.

Whomever you help to build up and become a better, stronger, finer person will give you his undying devotion. Build up as many people as you can. Do it unselfishly. Do it because you like them and because you see possibilities in them. Do this and you will never lack for friends. You will always be well thought of. Build people up and love them genuinely. Do them good and their esteem and affection will flow back toward you.

The basic principles of getting people to like you need no prolonged and labored emphasis, for they are very simple and easily illustrate their own truth. However, I list ten practical rules for getting the esteem of others. The soundness of these principles has been demonstrated innumerable times. Practice them until you become expert at them and people will like you.

1. Learn to remember names. Inefficiency at this point may indicate that your interest is not sufficiently outgoing. A man's name is very important to him.

2. Be a comfortable person so there is no strain in being with you—be an old-shoe, old-hat kind of individual. Be homey.

3. Acquire the quality of relaxed easy-goingness so that things do not ruffle you.

4. Don't be egotistical. Guard against giving the impression that you know it all. Be natural and normally humble.

5. Cultivate the quality of being interesting so that people will want to be with you and get something of stimulating value from their association with you.

6. Study to get the "scratchy" elements out of your personality, even those of which you may be unconscious.

7. Sincerely attempt to heal, on an honest Christian basis, every misunderstanding you have had or now have. Drain off your grievances.

8. Practice liking people until you learn to do so genuinely. Remember what Will Rogers said, "I never met a man I didn't like." Try to be that way.

9. Never miss an opportunity to say a word of congratulation upon anyone's achievement, or express sympathy in sorrow or disappointment.

10. Get a deep spiritual experience so that you have something to give people that will help them to be stronger and meet life more effectively. Give strength to people and they will give affection to you.

16

PRESCRIPTION FOR HEARTACHE

"Please give me a prescription for heartache."

This curious and rather pathetic request was made by a man who had been informed by his doctor that the feelings of disability of which he complained were not of a physical nature. His trouble lay in an inability to rise above sorrow. He was suffering from "an ache in his personality" as a result of grief.

His doctor advised him to secure spiritual consultation and treatment. So continuing to use the terminology of medicine, he repeated his question, "Is there a spiritual prescription which will reduce my constant inner suffering? I realize that sorrow comes to everyone and I should be able to meet it the same as others. I have tried my best but find no peace." Again he asked with a sad, slow smile, "Give me a prescription for heartache."

There is indeed a "prescription" for heartache. One element in the prescription is physical activity. The sufferer must avoid the temptation to sit and brood. A sensible program which substitutes physical activity for such fruitless brooding reduces the strain on the area of the mind where we reflect, philosophize, and suffer mental pain. Muscular activity utilizes another part of the brain and therefore shifts the strain and gives relief.

An old country lawyer who had a sound philosophy and much wisdom told a sorrowing woman that the best medicine for a broken heart is "to take a scrubbing brush and get down on your knees and go to work. The best medicine for a man," he declared, "is to get an ax and chop wood until physically tired." While this is not guaranteed to be a complete cure for heartache, yet it does tend to mitigate such suffering.

Whatever the character of your heartache, one of the first steps is to resolve to escape from any defeatist situation which may have been created around yourself, even though it is difficult to do so, and return once again to the normal course of your life. Get back into the main stream of life's activities. Take up your old associations. Form new ones. Get busy walking, riding, swimming, playing—get the blood to coursing through your system. Lose yourself in some worth-while project. Fill your days with creative activity and emphasize the physical aspect of activity. Employ healthy mind-relieving busyness, but be sure that it is of a worth-while and constructive nature. Superficial escapism through feverish activity merely deadens pain temporarily and does not heal, as, for example, parties and drinking.

An excellent and normal release from heartache is to give way to grief. There is a foolish point of view current today that one should not show grief, that it is not proper to cry or express oneself through the natural mechanism of tears and sobbing. This is a denial of the law of nature. It is natural to cry when pain or sorrow comes. It is a relief mechanism provided in the body of Almighty God and should be used.

To restrain grief, to inhibit it, to bottle it up, is to fail to use one of God's means for eliminating the pressure of sorrow. Like every other function of the human body and nervous system, this must be controlled, but it should not be denied altogether. A good cry by either a man or a woman is a release from heartache. I should warn you, however, that this mechanism should not be used unduly nor allowed to become a habitual process. Should that happen, it partakes of the nature of abnormal grief and could become a psychosis. Unrestraint of any kind should not be allowed.

I receive many letters from people whose loved ones have died. They tell me that it is very difficult for them to go to the same places they were in the habit of frequenting together or to be with the same people with whom they associated with as a couple or as a family. Therefore they avoid the old-time places and friends.

I regard this as a serious mistake. A secret of curing heartache is to be as normal and natural as possible. This does not imply disloyalty or indifference. This policy is important in avoiding a state of abnormal grief. Normal sorrow is a natural process and its normality is evidenced by the ability of the individual to return to his usual pursuits and responsibilities and continue therein as formerly.

The deeper remedy for heartache, of course, is the curative comfort supplied by trust in God. Inevitably the basic prescription for heartache is to turn to God in an attitude of faith and empty the mind and heart to Him. Perseverance in the act of spiritual self-emptying will finally bring healing to the broken heart. This generation, which has suffered fully as much if not more heartache than people in preceding eras, needs to relearn that which the wisest men of all time have known, namely, that there is no healing of the pain suffered by humanity except through the benign ministrations of faith.

One of the greatest souls of the ages was Brother Lawrence, who said, "If in this life we would know the serene peace of Paradise, we must school ourselves in familiar, humble, and loving converse with God." It is not advisable to attempt to carry the burden of sorrow and mental pain without Divine help, for its weight is more than the personality can bear. The simplest and most effective of all prescriptions for heartache then is to practice the presence of God. This will soothe the ache in your heart and ultimately heal the wound. Men and women who have experienced great tragedy tell us that this prescription is effective.

Another profoundly curative element in the prescription for heartache is to gain a sound and satisfying philosophy of life and death and deathlessness. For my part, when I gained the unshakable belief that there is no death, that all life is indivisible, that the here and hereafter are one, that time and eternity are inseparable, that this is one unobstructed universe, then I found the most satisfying and convincing philosophy of my entire life.

These convictions are based upon sound foundations, the Bible for one. I believe that the Bible gives us a very subtle, and as will be proved ultimately, a scientific series of insights into the great question, "What happens when a man leaves this world?" Also the Bible very wisely tells us that we know these truths by faith. Henri Bergson, the philosopher, says that the surest way into truth is by perception, by intuition, by reasoning to a certain point, then by taking a "mortal leap," and by intuition attaining the truth. You come to some glorious moment where you simply "know." That is the way it happened to me.

I am absolutely, wholeheartedly, and thoroughly convinced of the truth of which I write and have no doubt of it, even to an infinitestimal degree. I arrived at this positive faith gradually, yet there came one moment when I knew.

This philosophy will not ward off the sorrow which comes when a loved one dies and physical, earthly separation ensues. But it will lift and dissipate grief. It will fill your mind with a deep understanding of the meaning of this inevitable circumstance. And it will give you a deep assurance that you have not lost your loved one. Live on this faith and you will be at peace and the ache will leave your heart.

Take into your mind and heart one of the most marvelous texts in the Holy Bible—"Eye hath not seen, nor ear heard, neither have entered into the heart of man, the things which God hath prepared for them that love Him." (I Corinthians 2:9)

This means that you have never seen, no matter what you have seen, however wonderful it is, you have never seen anything to compare with the marvelous things that God has prepared for those who love Him and who put their trust in Him. Moreover, it says that you have never heard anything to compare with the astonishing marvels that God has laid up for those who follow His teachings and live according to His spirit. Not only have you never seen nor ever heard but you have never even dimly imagined what He is going to do for you. This sentence goes all out in promising comfort and immortality and reunion and every good thing to those who center their lives in God.

After many years of reading the Bible and being intimately connected with all the phases of the lives of hundreds of people, I wish to state unequivocally that I have found this Biblical promise to be absolutely true. It applies even to this world. People who really practice living on a Christlike basis have the most incredible things happen to them.

This passage also relates to the state of existence of those now living on the other side and our relationship, while we live, to those who have preceded us across that barrier which we call death. I use the word "barrier" somewhat apologetically. We have always thought of death as a barrier with a concept of a separatist nature.

Scientists working today in the field of parapsychology and extrasensory perception and experimenting in precognition, telepathy, clairvoyance (all of which were formerly considered paraphernalia of the cranks, but which are now of sound, scientific usage in the laboratories), are expressing themselves as believing that the soul survives the barrier of time and space. In effect, we are on the edge of one of the greatest scientific discoveries in history which will substantiate, on a laboratory-exploratory basis, the existence of the soul and its deathlessness.

For many years I have been accumulating a series of incidents, the validity of which I accept and which bear out the conviction that we live in a dynamic universe where life, not death, is the basic principle. I have confidence in the people who have described the following experiences and am convinced that they indicate a world impinged upon or intertwined with our own through the meshes of which human spirits, on both sides of death, live in unbroken fellowship. The conditions of life on the other side, as we know them in mortality, are modified. Undoubtedly those who have crossed to the other side dwell in a higher medium than we do and their understanding is amplified beyond ours, yet all the facts point to the continued existence of our loved ones and the further fact that they are not far away, and still another fact implied, but no less real, that we shall be reunited with them. Meanwhile, we continue in fellowship with those who dwell in the spirit world.

William James, one of America's greatest scholars, after a lifetime of study said he was satisfied that the human brain is only a medium for the soul's existence and that the mind as now constituted will be exchanged at last for a brain that will allow the owner to reach out into untapped areas of understanding. As our spiritual being is amplified here on earth and as we grow in age and experience we become more conscious of this vaster world all around us, and when we die it is only to enter into an enlarged capacity.

Euripides, one of the greatest thinkers of antiquity, was convinced that the next life would be of infinitely greater magnitude. Socrates shared the same concept. One of the most comforting statements ever made was his remark, "No evil can befall a good man in this life or in the next."

Natalie Kalmus, scientific expert in technicolor, tells about the death of her sister. The following account given by this scientifically trained woman appeared in the inspirational magazine *Guideposts*.

Natalie Kalmus quotes her dying sister as saying, " 'Natalie, promise me that you won't let them give me any drugs. I realize that they are trying to help relieve my pain, but I want to be fully aware of every sensation. I am convinced that death will be a beautiful experience.'

"I promised. Alone, later, I wept, thinking of her courage. Then as I tossed in bed on through the night, I realized that what I thought to be a calamity my sister intended to be a triumph.

"Ten days later the final hour drew near. I had been at her bedside for hours. We had talked about many things, and always I marveled at her quiet, sincere confidence in eternal life. Not once did the physical torture overcome her spiritual strength. This was something that the doctors simply hadn't taken into account.

" 'Dear kind God, keep my mind clear and give me peace,' she had murmured over and over again during those last days.

"We had talked so long that I noticed she was drifting off to sleep. I left her quietly with the nurse and retired to get some rest. A few minutes later I heard my sister's voice calling for me. Quickly I returned to her room. She was dying.

"I sat on her bed and took her hand. It was on fire. Then she seemed to rise up in bed almost to a sitting position.

" 'Natalie,' she said, 'there are so many of them. There's Fred . . . and Ruth . . . what's she doing here? Oh, I know!'

"An electric shock went through me. She had said Ruth. Ruth was her cousin who had died suddenly the week before. But Eleanor had not been told of Ruth's sudden death.

"Chill after chill shot up and down my spine. I felt on the verge of some powerful, almost frightening knowledge. She had murmured Ruth's name.

"Her voice was surprisingly clear. 'It's so confusing. So many of them!' Suddenly her arms stretched out as happily as when she had welcomed me! 'I'm going up,' she said.

"Then she dropped her arms around my neck—and relaxed in my arms. The will of her spirit had turned final agony into rapture.

"As I laid her head back on the pillow, there was a warm, peaceful smile on her face. Her golden-brown hair lay carelessly on the pillow. I took a white flower from the vase and placed it in her hair. With her petite, trim figure, her wavy hair, the white flower, and the soft smile, she looked once more—and permanently—just like a schoolgirl."

The mention of her cousin Ruth by the dying girl and the evident fact that she saw her clearly is a phenomenon that recurs again and again in the incidents which have come to my attention. So repetitive is this phenomenon and so similar are the characteristics of this experience as described by many that it amounts to a substantial evidence that the people whose names are called, whose faces are seen, are actually present.

Where are they? What is their condition? What sort of body have they? These are questions that are difficult. The idea of a different dimension is probably the most tenable, or it may be more accurate to believe that they live in a different frequency cycle.

It is impossible to see through the blades of an electric fan when it is in a stationary position. At high speed, however, the blades appear to be transparent. In the higher frequency or the state in which our loved ones dwell, the impenetrable qualities of the universe may open to the gaze of one passing into the mysteries. In deep moments of our own lives it is entirely possible that we enter to a degree at least into that higher frequency. In one of the most beautiful lines in English literature, Robert Ingersoll suggests this great truth, "In the night of death, hope sees a star and listening love can hear the rustle of a wing."

A famous neurologist tells of a man who was at death's door. The dying man looked up at the physician sitting beside his bed and began to call off names which the physician wrote down. The doctor was personally unfamiliar with any name mentioned. Later the physician asked the man's daughter, "Who are these people? Your father spoke of them as if he saw them."

"They are all relatives," she said, "who have been dead a long time."

The physician said he believes his patient did see them.

Friends of mine, Mr. and Mrs. William Sage, lived in New Jersey and I was often in their home. Mr. Sage, whom his wife called Will, died first. A few years later, when Mrs. Sage was on her deathbed, the most surprised look passed across her face, and it lighted up in a wonderful smile as she said, "Why, it is Will." That she saw him those about her bed had no doubt whatsoever.

Arthur Godfrey, famous radio personality, tells of being asleep in his bunk on a destroyer in World War I. Suddenly his father stood beside him. He put out his hand, smiled, and said, "So long, son," and Godfrey answered, "So long, Dad."

Later he was awakened and given a cablegram telling him of the death of his father. The time of his passing was given, and it was the precise period during which Godfrey in his sleep "saw" his father.

Mary Margaret McBride, also a famous radio personality, was overwhelmed with grief upon the death of her mother. They had been very close to each other. She awakened one night and sat on the edge of her bed. Suddenly she had the feeling, to use her own words, that "Mama was with me." She did not see her mother nor hear her speak, but from that time on, "I knew that my mother isn't dead—that she is nearby."

The late Rufus Jones, one of the most famous spiritual leaders of our time, tells about his son Lowell who died at twelve years of age. He was the apple of his father's eye. The boy took sick when Dr. Jones was on the ocean bound for Europe. The night before entering Liverpool, while lying in his bunk, he experienced an indefinable, inexplainable feeling of sadness. Then he said that he seemed to be enveloped in the arms of God. A great feeling of peace and a sense of a profound possession of his son came to him.

Upon landing in Liverpool he was advised that his son had died, his death occurring at the precise hour when Dr. Jones had felt a sense of God's presence and the everlasting nearness of his son.

A member of my church, Mrs. Bryson Kalt, tells of an aunt whose husband and three children were burned to death when their house was destroyed by fire. The aunt was badly burned but lived for three years. When finally she lay dying a radiance suddenly came over her face. "It is all so beautiful," she said. "They are coming to meet me. Fluff up my pillows and let me go to sleep."

Mr. H. B. Clarke, an old friend of mine, was for many years a construction engineer, his work taking him into all parts of the world. He was of a scientific turn of mind, a quite restrained, factual, unemotional type of man. I was called one night by his physician, who said that he did not expect him to live but a few hours. His heart action was slow and the blood pressure was extraordinarily low. There was no reflex action at all. The doctor gave no hope.

I began to pray for him, as did others. The nextday his eyes opened and after a few days he recovered his speech. His heart action and blood pressure returned to normal. After he recovered strength he said, "At some time during my illness something very peculiar happened to me. I cannot explain it. It seemed that I was a long distance away. I was in the most beautiful and attractive place I have ever seen. There were lights all about me, beautiful lights. I saw faces dimly revealed, kind faces they were, and I felt very peaceful and happy. In fact, I have never felt happier in my life.

"Then the thought came to me, 'I must be dying.' Then it occurred to me, 'Perhaps I have died.' Then I almost laughed out loud, and asked myself, 'Why have I been afraid of death all my life? There is nothing to be afraid of in this.' "

"How did you feel about it?" I asked. "Did you want to come back to life? Did you want to live, for you were not dead, although the doctor felt that you were very close to death. Did you want to live?"

He smiled and said, "It did not make the slightest difference. If anything, I think I would have preferred to stay in that beautiful place."

Hallucination, a dream, a vision—I do not believe so. I have spent too many years talking to people who have come to the edge of "something" and had a look across, who unanimously have reported beauty, light, and peace, to have any doubt in my own mind.

The New Testament teaches the indestructibility of life in a most interesting and simple manner. It describes Jesus after His crucifixion in a series of appearances, disappearances, and reappearances. Some saw Him and then He vanished out of their sight. Then others saw Him and again He vanished. It is as if to say, "You see me and then you do not see me." This indicates that He is trying to tell us that when we do not see Him, it does not mean He is not there. Out of sight does not mean out of life. Occasional mystical appearances which some experience indicate the same truth, that He is nearby. Did He not say, ". . . because I live, ye shall live also." (John 14:19) In other words, our loved ones who have died in his faith are also nearby and occasionally draw near to comfort us.

A boy serving in Korea wrote to his mother, saying, "The strangest things happen to me. Once in a while at night, when I am afraid, Daddy seems to be with me." Daddy had been dead for ten years. Then the boy wistfully asks his mother, "Do you think Daddy can actually be with me here on these Korean battlefields?" The answer is, "Why not?" How can we be citizens of a scientific generation and not believe that this could be true? Again and again proofs are offered that this is a dynamic universe, surcharged with mystic, electric, electronic, atomic forces, and all are so wonderful that we have never yet comprehended them. This universe is a great spiritual sounding house, alive and vital.

Albert E. Cliff, well-known Canadian writer, tells of the death of his father. The dying man had sunk into a coma and it was thought he was gone. Then a momentary resurgence of life occurred. His eyes flickered open. On the wall was one of those old time mottoes which said, "I Know That My Redeemer Liveth." The dying man opened his eyes, looked at that motto, and said, "I *do know* that my Redeemer liveth, for they are all here around me—mother, father, brothers and sisters." Long gone from this earth were they all, but evidently he saw them. Who is to gainsay?

The late Mrs. Thomas A. Edison told me that when her famous husband was dying he whispered to his physician, "It is very beautiful over there." Edison was the world's greatest scientist. All his life he had worked with phenomena. He was of a factual cast of mind. He never reported anything as a fact until he saw it work. He would never have reported, "It is very beautiful over there" unless, having seen, he knew it to be true.

Many years ago a missionary went to the South Sea Islands to work among a cannibal tribe. After many months he converted the chief to

Christianity. One day this old chief said to the missionary, "Remember the time you first came among us?"

"Indeed I do," replied the missionary. "As I went through the forest I became aware of hostile forces around me."

"They did indeed surround you," said the chief, "for we were following you to kill you, but something prevented us from doing it."

"And what was that?" asked the missionary.

"Now that we are friends, tell me," coaxed the chief, "who were those two shining ones walking on either side of you?"

My friend, Geoffrey O'Hara, famous song writer, author of the popular World War I song, "Katy," also "There Is No Death," "Give a Man a Horse He Can Ride," and other songs, tells of a colonel in World War I whose regiment was wiped out in a bloody engagement. As he paced up and down the trench he says he could feel their hands and sense their presence. He said to Geoffrey O'Hara, "I tell you, there is no death." Mr. O'Hara wrote one of his greatest songs using that title, "there is no death."

Of these deep and tender matters I personally have no doubt whatsoever. I firmly believe in the continuation of life after that which we call death takes place. I believe there are two sides to the phenomenon known as death—this side where we now live and the other side where we shall continue to live. Eternity does not start with death. We are in eternity now. We are citizens of eternity. We merely change the form of the experience called life, and that change, I am persuaded, is for the better.

My mother was a great soul, and her influence on me will ever stand out in my life as an experience that cannot be surpassed. She was a wonderful conversationalist. Her mind was keen and alert. She traveled the world over and enjoyed wide contacts as a Christian leader in missionary causes. Her life was full and rich. She had a marvelous sense of humor. She was good company, and I always loved to be with her. She was considered by all who knew her an unusually fascinating and stimulating personality.

During my adult years whenever I had the opportunity I would go home to see her. I always anticipated the arrival at the family home, for it was an exciting experience in which everyone talked at once as we sat around the breakfast table. What happy reunions—what glorious meetings. Then came her death, and we tenderly laid her body in the beautiful little cemetery at Lynchburg in southern Ohio, a town where she had lived as a girl. I was very sad the day we left her there, and went away heavy-hearted. It was in the fullness of summertime when we took her home to her last resting place.

It came autumn, and I felt that I wanted to be with my mother again. I was lonely without her, therefore I decided to go to Lynchburg. All night long on the train I thought sadly of the happy days now gone and how things were utterly changed and would never be the same again.

So I came to the little town. The weather was cold and the sky overcast as I walked to the cemetery. I pushed through the old iron gates and my feet rustled in the leaves as I walked to her grave where I sat sad and lonely. Of a sudden the clouds parted and the sun came through. It lighted up the Ohio hills in gorgeous autumn colors, the hills where I grew up as a boy, which I have always loved so well, where she herself had played as a girl in the long ago.

Then all of a sudden I seemed to hear her voice. Now I didn't actually hear her voice, but I seemed to. I am sure I heard it by the inward ear. The message was clear and distinct. It was stated in her beloved old-time tone, and this is what she said, "Why seek ye the living among the dead? I am not here. Do you think that I would stay in this dark and dismal place? I am with you and my loved ones always." In a burst of inner light I became wondrously happy. I knew that what I had heard was the truth. The message came to me with all the force of actuality. I could have shouted, and I stood up and put my hand on the tombstone and saw it for what it was, only a place where mortal remains lay. The body was there, to be sure, but it was only a coat that had been laid off because the wearer needed it no longer. But she, that glorious lovely spirit, she was not there.

I walked out of that place and only rarely since have I returned. I like to go back there and think of her and the old days of my youth, but no longer is it a place of gloom. It is merely a symbol, for she is not there. She is with us her loved ones. "Why seek ye the living among the dead?" (Luke 24:5)

Read and believe the Bible as it tells about the goodness of God and the immortality of the soul. Pray sincerely and with faith. Make prayer and faith the habit of your life. Learn to have real fellowship with God and with Jesus Christ. As you do this you will find a deep conviction welling up in your mind that these wonderful things are true indeed.

". . . if it were not so, I would have told you." (John 14:2) You can depend upon the reliability of Christ. He would not let you believe and hold convictions so sacred in nature unless they are absolutely true.

So in this faith, which is a sound, substantial, and rational view of life and eternity, you have the prescription for heartache.

17

HOW TO DRAW UPON THAT HIGHER POWER

Four men were sitting in the locker room of a country club after a game. Talk about golf scores drifted into a discussion of personal difficulties and problems. One man was especially despondent. The others, his friends, realizing his unhappy state of mind, had arranged this game to get his mind off his difficult situation. They hoped a few hours on the golf course might afford him some relief.

Now, as they sat around after the game, various suggestions were offered him. Finally one of the men arose to go. He knew about the difficulties, for he'd had plenty himself, but he had found some vital answers to *his* problems. He stood hesitantly, then laid his hand on his friend's shoulder. "George," he said, "I hope you won't think I am preaching at you. Really, I'm not, but I would like to suggest something. It's the way I got through my difficulties. It really works if you work at it, and it's this. 'Why not draw upon that Higher Power?' "

He slapped his friend affectionately on the back and left the group. The other men sat mulling this over. Finally the discouraged man said slowly, "I know what he means and I know where the Higher Power is. I only wish I knew how to draw upon it. It's what I need all right."

Well, in due course he discovered how to draw upon that Higher Power, and it changed everything for him. Now he is a healthy, happy man.

The advice given at the golf club is really very wise. There are many people today who are unhappy and depressed and just not getting anywhere with themselves or with conditions. And they do not need to be that way. Really they don't. The secret is to draw upon that Higher Power. And how is that done?

Let me tell you about a personal experience. When quite young I was called to a large church in a university community and many of my congregation were professors in the university as well as leading citizens of the city. I wanted to justify the confidence of those who gave me such an outstanding opportunity and accordingly worked very hard. As a result I began to experience overstrain. Everyone should work hard, but there is no virtue in overtrying or overpressing to such an extent that you do not work efficiently. It is somewhat like making a golf shot. Try to "kill" the ball and you execute the shot poorly. You can do likewise in your job. I began to get rather tired and nervous and had no feeling of normal power.

One day I decided to call on one of the professors, the late Hugh M. Tilroe, a great friend of mine. He was a wonderful teacher, and he was also a great fisherman and hunter. He was a man's man, an outdoor personality. I knew that if I did not find him at the university he would be out on the lake fishing, and sure enough there he was. He came ashore at my hail. "The fish are biting—come on," he said. I climbed in his boat and we fished awhile.

"What's the matter, son?" he asked with understanding. I told him how hard I was trying and that it was getting me down nervously. "I have no feeling of lift or power," I said.

He chuckled. "Maybe you're trying too hard."

As the boat scraped the shore he said, "Come in the house with me." As we entered his cabin he ordered, "Lie down there on that couch. I want to read you something. Shut your eyes and relax while I find the quotation."

I did as directed, and thought he was going to read me some philosophical or perhaps diverting piece, but instead he said, "Here it is. Listen quietly while I read it to you. And let these words sink in. 'Hast thou not known? Hast thou not heard, that the everlasting God, the Lord, the Creator of the ends of the earth, fainteth not, neither is weary? There is no searching of his understanding. He giveth power to the faint; and to them that have no might he increaseth strength. Even the youths shall faint and be weary, and the young men shall utterly fall. But they that wait upon the Lord shall renew their strength; they shall mount up with wings as eagles; they shall run, and not be weary; and they shall walk, and not faint.' " (Isaiah 40:28–31) Then he asked, "Do you know from what I am reading?"

"Yes, the fortieth chapter of Isaiah," I answered.

"I'm glad you know your Bible," he commented. "Why don't you practice it? Now relax. Take three deep breaths—in and out slowly. Practice resting yourself in God. Practice depending upon Him for His support and power. Believe He is giving it to you now and don't get out of touch with that power. Yield yourself to it—let it flow through you.

"Give your job all you've got. Of course you must do that. But do it in a relaxed and easy manner like a batter in a big-league ball game. He swings the bat easy-like, and doesn't try to knock the ball out of the park. He just does the best he can and believes in himself because he knows that he has lots of reserve power." Then he repeated the passage again. " 'They that wait upon the Lord shall renew their strength.' "

That was a long time ago, but I never forgot that lesson. He taught me how to draw upon that Higher Power, and believe me, his suggestions worked. I continue to follow my friend's advice, and it has never failed me in the more than twenty years that have passed since then. My life is crowded with activity but that power formula gives me all the strength I need.

A second method for drawing upon that Higher Power is to learn to take a positive, optimistic attitude toward every problem. In direct proportion to the intensity of the faith which you muster will you receive power to meet your situations. "According to your faith be it unto you," (Matthew 9:29) is a basic law of successful living.

There is a Higher Power, and that Power can do everything for you. Draw upon it and experience its great helpfulness. Why be defeated when you are free to draw upon that Higher Power? State your problem. Ask for a specific answer. Believe that you are getting that answer. Believe that now, through God's help, you are gaining power over your difficulty.

A man and his wife who were in real trouble came to see me. This gentleman, a former magazine editor, was a distinguished figure in music and artistic circles. Everyone liked him for his geniality and friendliness. His wife was held in similar high regard. She was in poor health and as a result they had retired to the country where they were living in semi-seclusion.

This man told me he had experienced two heart attacks, one quite severe. His wife was in a steady decline and he was deeply concerned about her. The question he put was this: "Can I get hold of some power that can help us recover ourselves physically and give us new hope and courage and strength?" The situation as he described it was a series of discouragements and defeats.

Frankly I felt that he was a bit too sophisticated to permit himself to adopt and utilize the simple trust that would be necessary if faith were to rehabilitate him. I told him I rather doubted he had the capacity to practice simple faith enough to open the sources of power according to the techniques of Christianity.

But he assured me he was in earnest and was open-minded and would follow any directions given. I saw his honesty and the real quality of his soul and have had a great affection for him ever since. I gave him a simple prescription. He was to read the New Testament and the Psalms until his mind was saturated with them. I gave him the usual suggestion of committing passages to memory. Principally I urged him to utilize the formula of putting his life in the hands of God, at the same time believing that God was filling him with power, and his wife also, and that the two of them were to believe unfalteringly that they were being guided in even the most commonplace details of their lives.

They were also to believe that in cooperation with their physician, whom I happened to know and admire, that the healing grace of Jesus Christ was being given them. I suggested that they picturize the healing power of the Great Physician as already working within them.

Seldom have I seen two people who became more gloriously childlike in their faith and whose trust was more complete. They became enthusiastic about the Bible and would often telephone me about "some wonderful passage" they had just found. They gave me fresh insights into the truths of the Bible. It was a truly creative process working with this man and his wife.

The next spring Helen (that is the wife's name) said, "I have never experienced a more wonderful springtime. The flowers this year are the loveliest I have ever seen, and have you noticed the sky with its extraordinary cloud formations and the delicate colors at dawn and sunset? The leaves seem greener this year, and I have never heard the birds sing with such ecstasy and melody." When she said this there was an ecstatic light on her face and I knew she had been reborn in the spirit. And she began to improve physically, regaining a large share of her old-time strength. Her native creative power began to flow forth once again and life took on new meaning.

As for Horace, there has been no more heart trouble, and physical, mental, and spiritual vigor mark him as extraordinarily vital. They have moved into a new community and have become a center of its life. Wherever they go they touch people with a strange uplifting force.

What is the secret which they discovered? Simply that they learned to draw upon that Higher Power.

This Higher Power is one of the most amazing facts in human existence. I am awestruck, no matter how many times I have seen the phenomenon, by the thoroughgoing, tremendous, overwhelming changes for good that it accomplishes in the lives of people. Personally, I am so enthusiastic about all that the Higher Power can do for people that I am loath to bring this book to a close. I could recite story after story, incident after incident of those who by laying hold of this power have had a new birth of life.

This power is constantly available. If you open to it, it will rush in like a mighty tide. It is there for anybody under any circumstances or in any condition. This tremendous inflow of power is of such force that in its inrush it drives everything before it, casting out fear, hate, sickness, weakness, moral defeat, scattering them as though they had never touched you, refreshing and restrengthening your life with health, happiness, and goodness.

For many years I have been interested in the problem of the alcoholic and in the organization known as Alcoholics Anonymous. One of their basic principles is that before a person can be helped he must recognize that he is an alcoholic and that of himself he can do nothing; that he has no power within himself; that he is defeated. When he accepts this point of view he is in a position to receive help from other alcoholics and from the Higher Power—God.

Another principle is the willingness to depend upon the Higher Power from whom he derives a strength which he does not himself possess. The working of this power in men's lives is the most moving and thrilling fact in this world. No other manifestation of power of any kind is equal to it. Materialistic power achievement is a romantic story. Men discover laws and formulas and harness power to do remarkable things. Spiritual power also follows laws. Mastery of these laws works wonders in an area more complicated than any form of mechanics, namely, human nature. It is one thing to make a machine work right. To make human nature work right is something else. It requires greater skill, but it can be done.

I sat one day under swaying palm trees in Florida listening to the story of a demonstration of Higher Power activity in the life of a man who narrowly escaped tragedy. He told me that he started drinking at the age of sixteen, "as it was the so-called smart thing to do." After twenty-three years, beginning as a social drinker, he "came to the end of the road on April 24, 1947." A growing hatred and bitterness toward his wife who had deserted him and toward his mother-in-law and sister-in-law culminated in his decision to kill these three women. I relate the story as he told it to me, in his own language.

"To strengthen myself for this gory task I went into the bar. A few more drinks would give me the courage to commit this triple murder. As I entered the bar I saw a young man by the name of Carl drinking coffee. Although I had hated Carl from boyhood I was utterly astounded to note his immaculate appearance, and I was also astonished to see him drinking coffee in a bar where he had spent on an average of $400 a month for drinks alone. Also I was mystified by what seemed a strange light on his face. Being fascinated by his appearance, I approached Carl and asked, 'What happened to you that you are drinking coffee?'

" 'I have not had a drink for a year,' Carl replied.

"I was utterly amazed, because Carl and I had been on many drinking bouts together. A strange incident in this affair is that even though I hated Carl I was strangely moved. I could not help but listen when he asked, 'Ed, did you ever want to quit drinking?'

" 'Yes, I have quit a thousand times,' I replied.

"Carl smiled and said, 'If you really want to do something about your problem, get sober and attend a meeting at the Presbyterian Church at nine on Saturday. It is a meeting of Alcoholics Anonymous.'

"I told him I had no interest in religion, but that maybe I would come. I was unimpressed, but still I could not get that light in his eyes out of my mind.

"Carl did not insist that I attend the meeting, but repeated that if I wanted to do something for myself he and his associates had an answer to my problem. After making that statement Carl left and I stood up to the bar to order a drink, but somehow it had lost its appeal. So, instead, I went home, the only home I had remaining, my mother's home.

"May I explain that I had been married for seventeen years to a very fine girl, but being an impatient person and having no faith in me due to my drinking, she finally decided upon getting a divorce, so not only my job and all my material assets but my home also were completely lost.

"Upon getting to my mother's home I wrestled with a bottle until 6 A.M., but still could not take the drink. I kept thinking of Carl's appearance. So on Saturday morning I went to Carl and asked him what I could do to keep from taking a drink until nine o'clock that night when the meeting would be held.

"Carl said, 'Every time you come to a bar or whiskey sign or beer garden, just say one little prayer—"Please, God, get me past this place," ' and then he added, 'Run like hell. That will be cooperating with God. He will hear your prayer and the running will be your part.'

"I did exactly as Carl told me to do. For many hours, anxious and shaky, accompanied by my sister, I walked around the streets of the town. Finally at eight o'clock my sister said, 'Ed, there are seven drinking joints between here and the place where you are to attend the meeting. You go by yourself, and if you don't make it and come home drunk we will still love you and hope for the best, but somehow I feel that this meeting will be different than any you ever attended.' With God's help I got by those seven places.

"At the church entrance I happened to look around and the sign over one of my favorite drinking places glared me straight in the eyes. The battle to decide whether to go into that bar or into the Alcoholics Anonymous meeting is one I shall never forget, but a Power greater than myself pulled me to the meeting.

"Upon entering the meeting room I was utterly astounded to receive the firm handshake of my ex-hated friend, Carl. My resentment toward him was disappearing. A round of introductions began to many men in all walks of life—doctors, lawyers, bricklayers, millwrights, coal miners, construction workers, plasterers, laborers—all types were there. I had been drinking with some of these men for the last ten to twenty-five years and here they were all sober on a Saturday night, and, above all, they were happy.

"What happened at that meeting is rather vague. All I know is that a rebirth had taken place. I felt different deep within.

"Happily leaving the meeting room at midnight, I went home with a glorious air-lifting feeling and slept peaceably for the first time in more than five years. Upon awakening the next morning, I recall something clearly saying to me, 'There is a Power greater than yourself. If you will turn your will and your life over to the care of God as you understand Him, He will give you strength.'

"It was Sunday morning, and I decided to go to church. I attended a service where the preacher was a man whom I had hated from childhood. (The author wishes to comment at this point how inevitably hate is associated with emotional and spiritual sickness. When the mind is emptied of hate, a long step has been taken toward recovery. Love is a tremendous curative force.) This preacher was one of those sedate, swallowtailed-coat-wearing Presbyterian ministers. I had no use for him, but that was my fault. He was all right really. I sat nervously through the singing and the collection taking. Then the preacher read his Scripture, and his sermon was based upon the theme, 'Never belittle anyone's experience—he had it.' I shall never forget that sermon as long as I live. It taught me a valuable lesson—never to belittle an experience because someone had it, for he and God know the depth and sincerity of that experience.

"Later I came to love this minister as one of the greatest, most sincere men I have ever known.

"Just where my new life began is a matter that is difficult to determine. Whether it was when I met Carl in the bar, or wrestling past the drinking places, or at the Alcoholics Anonymous meeting or at the church, I do not know. But I, who had been a hopeless alcoholic for twenty-five years, suddenly became a sober man. I could never have done this alone, for I had tried it a thousand times and failed. But I drew upon a Higher Power and the Higher Power, which is God, did it."

I have known the narrator of the foregoing story for several years. Since becoming "dry" he has had to face some difficult financial and other problems. But never once has he weakened. In talking with him I find myself strangely moved. It isn't what he says or even the way he says it, but one is conscious of a power emanating from this man. He is not a famous person. He is an everyday, hard-working salesman, but the Higher Power is in him, flowing through him, operating within his experience, and it transmits itself to others. It transmitted itself to me.

This chapter is not intended as a dissertation on alcoholism, although I will use still another reference in connection with this problem. I cite these experiences to show conclusively that if there is a Power able to deliver a person from alcoholism, this same Power can help any other person to overcome any other form of defeat he may face. There is nothing more difficult to overcome than the problem of alcoholism. The Power that can accomplish that difficult feat can, I assure you, help you to overcome your difficulties whatever they may be.

Let me give still another experience. I narrate this incident for the same purpose, namely, to emphasize that there is a Power which can be applied, drawn upon, and used that mysteriously but surely gives to people who demonstrate faith the most remarkable victories.

In the Hotel Roanoke at Roanoke, Virginia, one night a man who has since become a good friend told me the following story. Two years before he had read my book, *A Guide to Confident Living*. At that time he was considered by himself and by others to be an utterly hopeless alcoholic. He is a businessman in a Virginia town and is of such ability that despite his drinking problem he was able to keep going with fair success. He had absolutely no control over his drinking, however, and evident deterioration was taking place.

Upon reading the book above mentioned, the idea was lodged in his mind that if he could only get to New York he could be cured of his difficulty. He came to New York but was dead drunk when he arrived. A friend took him to a hotel and left him. He recovered sufficient consciousness to call a bellboy and told him he wanted to go to the Townes Hospital, a famous institution for alcoholics, presided over by the late Dr. Silkworth, one of the greatest men in the field of alcoholism—now deceased but never to be forgotten.

After robbing him of one hundred or more dollars which he had in his pocket, the bellboy delivered him to the hospital. After several days of treatment, Dr. Silkworth came in to see him and said, "Charles, I think we have done for you all that we can do. I have a feeling that you are well."

This was not Dr. Silkworth's usual practice, and the fact that he handled this case in this manner causes one to sense the guiding hand of a Higher Power.

Still somewhat shaky, Charles made his way downtown until he found himself outside the office door of the Marble Collegiate Church, 1 West 29th Street, New York City. It happened to be a legal holiday and the church was closed. (Other than such holidays the church is always open.) He stood there hesitantly. He had hoped that he might go into the church and pray. Not being able to gain entrance, he did a strange thing. He took from his wallet one of his business cards and dropped it through the mail slot in the door.

The instant he did that a tremendous wave of peace came over him. He had an amazing sense of release. He put his head against the door and sobbed like a baby, but he knew that he was free, that some tremendous change had happened to him the validity of which is attested by the fact that from that minute on there has been no turning back. He has lived in complete sobriety from that moment.

There are several features about this incident which mark it as impressive. For one, Dr. Silkworth seemed to have released him from the hospital at the proper psychological, spiritual, and shall we say supernatural moment, indicating that the doctor himself was the subject of Divine guidance.

When Charles told me this story in the Hotel Roanoke two years after it happened, I had a feeling as he related it that I had heard it before in precise detail. But he had never told me this story. In fact, I had never previously talked to him. It occurred to me that perhaps he had written the story to me and I had read it, but he said he had never written me. I then asked him if he had told the story to one of my secretaries, associates, or any other person who could have related it to me, but he said he had never told the story to any other individual save his wife and I had not met her until that night. Apparently this incident had been transmitted to my subconscious at the time it happened for now I "remembered" it.

Why did he drop the card in the mail slot? Perhaps he was symbolically reporting to his spiritual home, reporting to God. It was a dramatic and symbolic separation of himself from his defeat and the turning to a Higher Power which immediately took him out of himself and healed him.

The incident indicates that if there is deep desire, intensity of longing, and a sincere reaching out after the Power that it will be given.

In this chapter I have related victory stories out of human experience, each in its own way indicating the continual presence and availability of a life-renewing Power, beyond but resident within ourselves. Your problem may not be alcoholism, but the fact that the Higher Power can heal a person of this most difficult malady emphasizes the tremendous truth related in this chapter and throughout the entire book that there is no problem, difficulty, or defeat that you cannot solve or overcome by faith, positive thinking, and prayer to God. The techniques are simple and workable. And God will help you always, just as the writer of the following letter was helped.

> "Dear Dr. Peale: When we think of all the wonderful things that have happened to us since we first met you and started coming to the Marble Church, it seems nothing short of a miracle. When you realize that just six years ago this month I was totally broke—in fact thousands of dollars in debt—a complete physical washout—and had hardly a friend in the world because of my excess drinking—you can see why we have to pinch ourselves every now and then to realize that our good fortune isn't all a dream.
>
> "As you well know, alcohol wasn't the only problem I had six years ago. It has been said that I was one of the most negative people you ever saw.

That's only a half truth. For I was filled with gripes, all sorts of irritation, and was one of the most supercritical, impatient, cocky individuals that you could have possibly met even in your travels.

"Now, please don't think I feel I have overcome all these obsessions. I haven't. I am one of those people that have to do a day-to-day job on myself. But gradually, by trying to follow your teachings, I am learning to control myself and be less critical of my fellow man. And it is like being released from a prison. I just never dreamed that life could be so full and wonderful. Sincerely (Signed) Dick."

Why not draw upon that Higher Power?

Epilogue

You have finished this book. What have you read?

Simply a series of practical and workable techniques for living a successful life. You have read a formula of belief and practice which should help you win victory over every defeat.

Examples have been given of people who have believed and who have applied the suggested techniques. These stories have been told to demonstrate that through the same methods you can obtain the same results as they did. But reading is not enough. Now please go back and persistently practice each technique given in this book. Keep at it until you obtain the desired results.

I wrote this book out of a sincere desire to help you. It will give me great happiness to know that the book has helped you. I have absolute confidence and belief in the principles and methods outlined in this volume. They have been tested in the laboratory of spiritual experience and practical demonstration. They work when worked.

We may never meet in person, but in this book we have met. We are spiritual friends. I pray for you. God will help you—so believe and live successfully.

NORMAN VINCENT PEALE

THE POSITIVE PRINCIPLE TODAY

How to Renew and Sustain the Power of Positive Thinking

Contents

To five friends and associates with gratitude for their special helpfulness over the years

MYRON L. BOARDMAN
ARTHUR CALIANDRO
GERALD DICKLER
ARTHUR GORDON
MILTON D. KETCHUM

Foreword

This book, of course, has a purpose, a definite objective. Let me explain it in the hope that what follows may be meaningful and helpful to you.

For a long time I have caught myself saying to people who are doing well, reaching goals and accomplishing desirable objectives—"Keep it going." To those who were obviously on the right track, I am likely to say in a friendly way—"Keep it going." And to people who seem to be dragging along with only a fragment of the enthusiasm they once had, I find myself encouraging them to remember the positive principle and—"Keep it going."

Then among the hundreds of letters received was a rather special one, as it turned out, for the question it posed led me to an in-depth study and research of the positive principle, and how to keep it going.

The letter reads as follows:

> Dear Mr. Peale:
>
> I read as many inspirational and motivational books as I can find, yours among them. They lift me to a higher mental level, and I'm fired with zest and enthusiasm for everything.

As a result I do much better in my job and certainly I'm a great deal happier. But somehow I cannot hold the inspiration all that long, especially if I run into problems and setbacks. They act as a drain on my high spirits and presently I find myself feeling like a deflated balloon—really down.

I know you will think I'm flighty and superficial, and perhaps that's true. Yet at the same time I'm genuinely responsive to motivational and inspirational suggestions and teaching. What I want to know is how to keep the positive principle going in the tough experiences which everyone has to face.

You and other writers have the power to activate my mind. Please tell me how to be consistently reactivated; how to have a constant renewal of inspiration sufficient to withstand situations and depressing moments. What I want to know is how to keep motivation going—always to keep it going! And I'll thank you a lot if you will tell me.

The foregoing letter rather clearly expresses a perennial human problem—that of maintaining inspirational attitudes over the long pull, in dark days as well as in sunny and fortuitous times. The tendency of the mental level to sag or droop is a common problem. How to sustain the positive principle and keep an upbeat mental attitude is a concern to which an inspirational writer should, I believe, address himself.

That is what we mean to do. It is the author's hope that this book will not only inspire and motivate you to think, act and live victoriously, but will also help you always and under whatever circumstances to keep it going, ever stronger and more vitally.

NORMAN VINCENT PEALE

Introduction

What Is the Positive Principle?

There is a deep tendency in human nature to become precisely what we imagine or picture ourselves to be. We tend to equate with our own self-appraisal of either depreciation or appreciation. We ourselves determine either self-limitation or unlimited growth potential.

The negative thinker engages ultimately in a self-destroying process. As he constantly sends out negative thoughts, he activates the world around him negatively. There is a law of attraction, in which like attracts like. Birds of a feather flock together. Thoughts of a kind have a natural affinity. The negative thinker, projecting negative thoughts, tends thereby to draw back to himself negative results. This is a definite and immutable law of mind.

The positive thinker, on the contrary, constantly sends out positive thoughts, together with vital mental images of hope, optimism and creativity. He therefore activates the world around him positively and strongly tends to draw back to himself positive results. This, too, is a basic law of mind action.

But the negative thinker can dramatically improve his outcomes by a thorough revamping of the negative type of thinking hitherto employed.

As William James, the noted philosopher-psychologist, suggested, "The greatest discovery of my generation is that human beings can alter their lives by altering their attitudes of mind."

The positive principle is the vital process of mental and spiritual alteration whereby the individual shifts from a concept of self-limitation to that of self-improvement, from deterioration to growth, from failure to accomplishment.

The positive principle is a totality of sound thinking, dealing forthrightly and creatively with the realistic facts of human existence. The positive thinker sees every difficulty and sees them straight. Nor is he abashed by them, nor does he seek an escapist "out" from them. He knows that every problem contains the seeds of its own solution, as the well-known expert Stanley Arnold said. He also knows that by the help of God and the release of his own inherent powers, he has what it takes to deal with, handle and solve any problem. Therefore, as a healthy-minded individual, he or she stands up to difficulty fearlessly and confidently. The positive thinker does not react emotionally when in difficulty, recognizing the fact that the human mind cannot function at its best when it is hot or emotionally conditioned. The positive thinker is aware that only when the mind is cool, even cold, and under strong mental control, will it produce those dispassionate, rational and intellectual concepts that lead to sound and viable solutions.

The positive principle is based on the fact that there is always an answer, a right answer, and that positive thinking through a sound intellectual process can always produce that answer.

It is, of course, true that the negative is important in preserving balance. Opposites are involved in the structure of nature. And in the realm of thought the negative has an important function in the consideration of alternatives. But when the negative takes over as the controlling element in the thinking process, the balance swings away from the positive, and negative aspects become dominant.

The negative principle negates. The positive principle creates. The negative principle doubts. The positive principle believes. The negative principle accepts defeat. The positive principle goes for victory.

The positive principle is solidly based on spiritual truth, resting firmly upon those dynamic words "This is the victory that overcometh the world, even our faith."*

* I John 5:4.

FIRST WAY TO KEEP THE POSITIVE PRINCIPLE GOING

Organize Your Personality Forces Into Action

Mastering the positive principle and developing the ability to keep it going are basic to successful performance in life. With them you can keep your motivation, your enthusiasm, your inspiration, sustained and replenished—every day, all the way! That is the central message of this book. And supportive of that message, specific techniques are presented, techniques that many persons have found to be highly effective. This book presents a methodology for maintaining the keep-it-going dynamic at high level.

To keep the positive principle going, it is vitally important to maintain an enthusiastic spirit at all times and under whatever conditions. The blows and vicissitudes of personal and business life can, if allowed to do so, draw off enthusiasm and weaken positive attitudes. And since such erosion of spirit is a process of deterioration that every creative person wishes to avoid, it is essential to have a program of reinspiration constantly going for you. Systematic and consistent replenishment of vital spirit is required to keep enthusiasm and motivation at top level.

People can learn to become positive thinkers, and as a result their lives take on new meaning. They are more successful in their jobs. Enthusiasm lifts them to higher levels. Things flow toward them rather than away from them. Even so, unforeseen difficulties may arise, troubles emerge, setbacks occur and the going becomes hard and difficult. It is then that the positive viewpoint must be shored up by a revitalization of inspiration, a renewal of enthusiasm. In this book we mean to lay out simple and workable principles for keeping vital motivation operative regardless of adverse circumstances. It will show how, under varying conditions and situations, personality forces may be organized to produce effective action.

An outstanding positive thinker who stresses the need for "renewable" positive attitudes is Dr. Jan S. Marais of Cape Town, South Africa, Chairman of The Trust Bank. Dr. Marais founded this important banking organization in a modest office on one floor of a business building only a very few years ago. By sound banking principles and innovative procedures he has developed The Trust Bank into one of the great financial institutions of the world. He has employed positive thinking, enthusiasm and top administrative skill in the outstanding success he and his associates have achieved. In a recent letter he says:

> My personal experience and that of my colleagues is that inspiration and motivation are exactly like nutrition. You have to keep on taking it daily, in healthy doses. Otherwise depletion, fatigue, depression and lack of ambition and achievement will very soon manifest themselves. Your books, Norman, are mandatory companions of the leadership echelon of The Trust Bank.

This influential business leader, being a wise and understanding man, is aware that the extremely important qualities of inspiration and enthusiasm are not to be taken for granted; they can and often do decline in force and must therefore be replenished daily by a new intake of motivational thinking. It is necessary to activate and reactivate personality forces constantly, and even impel them into action, in order to keep them going, always going. The positive principle must ever be nourished and renourished.

UNLIMITED POWER IN PERSONALITY

A listener to our radio broadcasts wrote me about an article he had read in a scientific journal which he thought quite fascinating. It stated, so he reports, that an ordinary piece of quartz, electrically stimulated, will vibrate 4,194,302 times a second. That causes one to wonder! If an ordinary piece of quartz responds to stimulus in such extraordinary fashion, what may be expected from the mind and spirit of a human being when personality forces are really activated? The potential, obviously, is unlimited.

For a long time now we have been reading appraisals by various psychologists and scientists in human behavior that the average person uses perhaps only 20 percent of his mental power; even geniuses use but a fraction more. Some even rate the average use of creative power as low as 10 percent. It seems incredible, does it not, that human beings endowed by nature with high potential should employ only about one fifth of it in meeting their problems and in building careers in this world? Why is it, one asks, that a piece of quartz, actually a stone, when stimulated can react so incredibly, and at the same time men and women are content to go along acquiescing in a limited human reaction to the opportunities all about them and to the potential within themselves?

The truth is that there is much more strength and power in the individual than he has ever known or even visualized as a possibility. Remember the insight of the great thinker of antiquity Marcus Aurelius, who said, "Dig within. There lies the well-spring of good: ever dig and it will ever flow."* The motivational writer Kermit W. Lueck tells of an unconscious truck driver pinned in the burning cab of an overturned gasoline truck. Even strong men in the gathered crowd were unable to open the cab door which had been warped in the crash. Then suddenly an average-sized man appeared, threw off his jacket, grabbed hold of the door handle and with a powerful jerk wrenched it open. Climbing into the cab around which flames raged, he kicked the pedals to free the unconscious driver's feet, arched his slight back against the crushed roof of the cab, and pulled the driver out to safety. Asked later how a man of his build could perform such a feat, he explained that his two children had been burned to death, and that as a result he hated fire with an intense passion.

When he saw this helpless man pinned in a high-octane gasoline truck that could go up in flaming explosion at any moment, his antipathy toward fire brought out of him a strength he did not know he possessed. He only knew that he was going to get that man away from that hated fire. Crisis summoned forth a strength that we call superhuman; but would it not be

* *Meditations*, Bk. 7, No. 59.

more accurate to think of it as normal human force hitherto unused? If such strength can emerge under crisis, the fact is that it is present, but untapped, at all times. "Dig within. . . . ever dig and it will ever flow."

GIs PICK UP JEEP IN CRISIS

Lueck also gives us an account of four GIs who were ambushed on a very narrow road in Vietnam. They leaped into a ditch. Fully aware of their exposed position, suddenly, with common mind, they jumped back to the road and rushed to the jeep, which could not be turned around for lack of space to maneuver. Each man took a wheel and together they lifted the jeep, turned it around quickly, jumped in, and at full speed, through cross fire, headed back to safety. Back at camp, the four men together could not lift one wheel of the jeep off the ground. From what source came the enormous strength of the men at the place of ambush? From within themselves, of course, is the answer.

The question therefore is why, in the problems and difficulties of regular daily existence, do we fail to tap and utilize the amazing powers that are usually produced only under intense crisis? The answer may lie in the fact that we are not sufficiently intense in belief, in faith and in thought. When we develop such intensity, may we not expect that we shall be able to stimulate immense personality forces into action? It seems not too much to believe that we shall release from ourselves capacities we have never actually even dreamed of bringing into play.

RETIREE GETS REACTIVATED

The following incident, which I wrote about in *Senior Power*, a magazine edited and published by Dr. Kenneth P. Berg, happened some years ago in the stock room of Krock's and Brentano's bookstore in Chicago, where I was autographing copies of my book *The Power of Positive Thinking*. To my surprise Adolph Krock, the founder and then recently retired president of the company, came in and began helping me. "Haven't anything else to do," he grumbled. He told me that he tried to stay away from the store, but decades of habit drew him back. Everyone treated him fine, he explained, and his son, Carl, now president, always acted glad to see him. But he was sensitively aware that he was "out of it," didn't really belong anymore. "Guess I'm useless," he declared sadly, "so I'm glad to serve you like a stockroom boy."

Then suddenly he asked, "About this positive thinking—why don't you write a book on retirement?"

"Oh, that is not my field. I really am not adequately informed on the subject," I replied. Then I turned the question back on him. "Why don't you write such a book, now that you are retired?"

"Not me," he answered quickly. "I don't write books. I sell them."

We went on for a few minutes in a silence broken only by the stacking up of volumes and the scratching of my pen. "Okay," he said, "perhaps you can take a detached attitude toward the trauma of retirement and express an objective point of view. Give me some advice. If you were in my position, what would you do? What should I do? My health is good and I'm not short on energy and I like to do things that count for something. But here I am on a plateau in my life from which I see no excitement or even usefulness."

"Well, now, look," I replied, "anything I say is bound to be off the cuff, and remember that I'm no expert on the subject of retirement. Yet I do have some knowledge of what others in like position have done, and we can perhaps learn from their experience." I told him that in my opinion it is wise to play down the word "retirement" and to emphasize instead the word and concept "readjustment." Retirement somewhat suggests a drop-out status, a finished state. Readjustment, on the other hand, indicates continuity of activity, though in different capacity and perhaps in entirely new form.

An old Korean man once told me that in his country people think of beginning a new and different life at sixty years; they assume a new birth, gearing themselves for new activity. "I became a resurrected person at sixty," my Korean friend declared, "and have been living as a new man ever since."

Thus there is no reason why anyone in health and strength need acquiesce to the idea so generally and supinely accepted today that an arbitrary set retirement age must necessarily mean an ipso facto disqualification from new and fresh forms of useful activity. No person, at any age, needs to remain on an uninspiring level of accomplishment.

Therefore I suggested to this unhappy retired executive that he practice the principle of adaptability—say good-bye to his old business, sell his home and move to a different section of the country. See himself once again as he was at the start, an immigrant boy arriving in a new land and looking for opportunities.

"As soon as you get settled in your new home, join a church and tell the minister you want to help him; get in there and get involved. Then hunt up a political club and say you want to be an active worker. Get into a service club and work on its committees. Join the Chamber of Commerce and become a leader. Go all out and you'll get outside yourself. And," I added, "forget all about this bookstore except for your pension check. Practice the spiritual principle suggested in the words 'forgetting those things which are behind, and reaching forth unto those things which are before. . . .' "*

There was, of course, nothing unique about this advice, but the result was unique in that the erstwhile book dealer took the advice seriously and acted upon it. And how!

In the small West Coast city where he settled, he became a real estate dealer, a banker, a service club leader, chairman of the local hospital board and head of the Chamber of Commerce. As one local man put it, "Whence came this young-old Lochinvar—this revitalized ball of fire?" And he was still going strong twenty years later. Practically the only time he returned to the old home city was for the funeral of some contemporary who acquiesced in retirement and became a dropout: mentally, physically and spiritually. Mr. Krock practiced positive thinking in retirement, with positive results. He discovered that he was not through, far from it. He tapped some inner resource never before discovered and brought forth extra capacities he did not know he possessed. By stimulating the forces of his personality into revitalized action he created a new and exciting life. The enthusiasms and motivations which had made him a leader in business and community were reemployed in the retired situation. He became an inspiring example of how to keep the positive principle going, and vigorously.

HANDLING THE IFs IN LIFE

It is very important to be on top of life's circumstances, always in control, for human existence can and often does follow an uncertain and variable pattern. It can turn on you, trip you up, hit you hard, throw the book at you—unless it is managed and controlled. Nevertheless, existence on earth is, I believe, intended to be *for* us rather than against us. If everyone followed the purposes of the Creator, the general thrust of life would be in our favor, though not without some hard going at times, for the Great

* Philippians 3:13.

Architect of the Universe did not eliminate pain and struggle and difficulty. He knew these to be for our good in the development of a strong person, and that objective just has to be basic to His purpose in creating man and woman in the first place. No person can become strong without struggle, without the effort of pitting himself against trouble and hardship. And to meet and deal with life creatively we will always need to be alert and thoughtful and to think in a positive manner, constantly rallying personality forces into effective and desirable action. We must be aware of and prepared for life's variable, unpredictable and uncertain nature, caused basically by that same mix of qualities in ourselves.

I happened to notice one day that the word "life"—*l-i-f-e*—significantly has an *if* at its center. The central two letters of the four-letter word representing existence form a concept of uncertainty which is designated by *if*. And the potency of *if* is every day underscored in the language of many persons. "If I do this," "If I do that," "If this happens," "If that happens," "If only I had not said [or done] that." So it goes, on and on and still on, the repetitive *if* element. Can it be a fact that half of life is an *if* even as it constitutes half of the word which stands for existence on earth? If so, or whatever proportion the *if* factor represents, it is all the more reason why we must assume a firmer control of those uncertainties, the *ifs*, and make them into certainties, thereby contributing to, rather than detracting from, our best potential.

STRANGE THING HAPPENS

On a speaking trip in the West I met Jeff, a thirty-five-year-old man who had been, as he put it, "in the grip of a failure pattern for some time." It appeared that hardly anything was going right, and that fact was getting him to such an extent that he was admitting defeat and failure. He had developed into a negative "if only" man, constantly bemoaning, "If only I had not done that stupid thing." "If that guy had only given me a break"; one dismal *if* after another. His career, he had come to admit, had become dependent upon whims and variables, and he had practically no sense of control over the circumstances, to his mind all negative, which seemed to gang up on him.

Some time before our meeting Jeff was sitting, glum and desultory, in his motel room, listening to a late-night television show originating in New York and on which I happened to appear as a guest. The interviewer took as the subject of our discussion the question of how people who are not making it on their jobs can get a new grip on themselves and start strong motivations going. I developed the concept that one can impel his personality powers into action by intense desire, intense belief and intense prayer, using the word "intense" to differentiate these factors from the usual bland attitudes of so many. I recall quoting from James Russell Lowell:

I, that still pray at morning and at eve, . . .
Thrice in my life perhaps have truly prayed,
Thrice, stirred below my conscious self, have felt
That perfect disenthralment which is God. . . .

We had a stimulating give-and-take on the TV show about the meaning of that concept and agreed that by thrusting beneath the surface of the mind and into the area of faith by intense and in-depth desire, a person could reorganize personality forces that had been floundering and reducing him to ineffectiveness.

Two thousand miles away, Jeff told me, he was listening to this TV show, which certainly had no reputation of being dedicated generally to God- or prayer-talk. Suddenly he had a remarkable experience of deep insight. In a flash he became aware that in this intense prayer-faith formula lay the correction of his failure pattern. Acting at once upon the suggestions which were made on the air, he began a prayer-faith program. Continuing it daily, he found God like never before—like he never thought possible. One result was that his negative *if* emphasis began to give way to the positive *how* principle. Rather than futilely mumbling *ifs*, he began to stress "How can it be done?" "How can I do it better?" "How can I really get going?" Result—a dramatic reorganization of his personality forces. Moreover, along with this personality reconstruction, Jeff became infused with such strong motivation that discouragements gradually lessened and over a period of time he developed a new sense of control over difficulties. This man definitely learned the secret of keeping it going. He got aboard the positive principle and went on successfully from there.

AMAZING PERSONALITY FORCES

No doubt there are those who, for one reason or another, either doubt or resist the assertion that as persons they possess forces that are beyond the average abilities they have been able to develop. "There just isn't all that in me despite your flattering appraisal of my worth. I'm just a normal, average person." To that I must answer, "Maybe average, but hardly normal, for the word 'normal' refers to 'norm,' and that in turn stands for a level of attainment that is open to our determination. It is hardly normal to be less than your best, for if less than best is normal, or the norm of achievement, we would scarcely ever be activated by a discontent with ourselves as we are. And thus progress would be stymied."

To settle for self-limitation is to lock yourself up within yourself and therefore to deny to yourself the God-given opportunity for growth. So I urge you to avoid that "I'm an average person" expression of self-depreciation. Instead, get a new view of your personality, which presupposes greater abilities than you have ever before visualized. Move your idea of your norm up to higher levels, as the bar is moved from one level to another in a track meet for high jumpers or pole vaulters. Always you can go higher, for within yourself you are greater than you think. Believe that, for it is a fact—a great, big, truthful, wonderful fact. It is the positive principle in action.

The famous Olympic champion Bob Richards, who is also a popular and highly respected motivational speaker and writer, has pointed out* that all Olympic champions are people who believe in themselves and therefore in that extra power built into personality. Some have even specified to the split second how they are going to do in a race. Mark Spitz said he would win seven gold medals. On the first try he won only two, but in his last competition he did win the visualized seven. He knew he was capable of seven if he used his potential. Such champions prove the fact that there is a greater personality force that can, under appropriate circumstances, be summoned into magnificent action.

Richards tells of teaching a Sunday School class and telling the students about the qualities that go into making champion athletes. He was interrupted by a very fat little girl with thick bifocals who kept jumping up and down and saying she was going to be the greatest woman tennis player in the world. This little girl was Billie Jean Moffitt, later Billie Jean King, perhaps the greatest woman tennis player in the world, and perhaps we would not be amiss to drop the qualifying word "woman." She responded with powerful motivation and belief to the idea of super-faculties within that could be mustered into action.

Bob Richards declares in this article that if you write on a card what

* "How to Get What You Deserve—The Best," *Success*, New York, N.Y.

you intend to be in life, making it specific, and keep that card for constant reference and embed that goal deeply in your mind for a period of two years, you will become what you said you would achieve. He asserts that he can demonstrate this faith from athletic history. Bill Vandervoort, prominent sportswriter, supports the positive concept of being the best you can be in quoting the football coach Woody Hayes, of Ohio State University, famous for great teams:

> Ohio State's Woody Hayes sounded like Norman Vincent Peale Saturday following the Buckeyes' 32–7 romp over North Carolina. Peale, the noted theologian, has no better exponent of his "power of positive thinking" than Bill Buck. A Chicago writer asked Hayes in the locker-room afterwards how he continued to attract top players.
>
> "It's very simple," replied Woody. "We recruit and coach on a positive basis. We seek quality, the best kids. I couldn't get along with any other kind. Then we set high standards, we challenge them to be better than they think they can be.
>
> "Once they find out how they can be better, they respond to you, respect you. I get sick and tired of the way our society talks down to everyone. I believe in reaching the best in the boy."*

Someone sent me a newspaper clipping in which a woman tells of her remarkable experience with the visualization or mental image principle in making the best things happen:

> Twelve years ago, Helen Hadsell's husband wanted an outboard motor that was the top prize in a contest.
>
> She concentrated, wrote a 25-word entry, and won it.
>
> Her daughter wanted a bicycle. A little concentration on mother's part and the daughter had her bike.
>
> The family wanted to go to Europe. Mom found a contest offering a European vacation prize, concentrated, and off they went. They returned to Europe two more times the same way.
>
> Thirty-three times Mrs. Hadsell concentrated on winning contest prizes, and 33 times she won, including the $50,000 house that was top prize in a contest at the New York World's Fair in 1964.
>
> "There were 2 million entries in the house contest," said Mrs. Hadsell. "I did what I had done in every other contest: I simply pictured myself owning that house.

* Dayton *Daily News*.

> "I have won everything by applying the principle of Dr. Norman Vincent Peale's book, 'The Power of Positive Thinking.' I picked up the book at a newsstand 12 years ago and read it.
>
> "What he was saying is if you *know* what you want, and you hang in there long enough and strong enough, you'll get what you want. It is simply constructive thinking. I got from Dr. Peale's book the endless possibilities that are available from positive thinking. I applied that to contests, and I won.
>
> "The secret," she said, "is always stressing the end result, knowing you have what it is you want. If I was vying for a prize, I visualized a check, right there in my hand."*

We may comment that Mrs. Hadsell made a valid principle operationally effective, but obviously she added the force of a facile and innovative mind. The point of the matter is that creative attitudes can create wonders. That which we intensely image can and often does actualize in fact.

THE MAGIC OF BELIEVING

In my opinion, one of the few greatest inspirational and motivational books ever written in the United States is *The Magic of Believing*, by Claude Bristol. I knew Mr. Bristol personally and through the years was profoundly affected by the dynamic spirit of this man's mind and writings. He truly believed in the spiritual principle "If thou canst believe, all things are possible to him that believeth."†

Claude Bristol in his book deals with the immense powers of the mind when activated by strong belief freed of stultifying doubt. In compelling illustration after illustration he documents the magic of believing in the varied lives of the failures turned into successes who march triumphantly across the pages of his book. He, too, knew the astonishing power of the mind when committed to the realization of a specified goal. One of the techniques for realization which he often suggested is to take five 3″ by 5″ cards, and on one of them write succinctly but in explicit detail what you want, deeply want with all your mind and heart. Duplicate this on the

* Indianapolis *News*.

† Mark 9:23.

other four cards. Then put one in your wallet or purse, another over the kitchen sink, one on your car's instrument panel and the fifth on your desk. Look intently at the card every day, meanwhile printing the mental image firmly in consciousness. Visualize your objective or goal, which is now in the process of being actualized. That this method works can be attested to by the thousands of grateful readers and practitioners of *The Magic of Believing*. This book is one of the great expositions of the positive principle.

SAW HIMSELF AS GREAT EDITOR

A highly successful friend of mine always credited the success he achieved as one of America's greatest newspaper publishers to Orison Swett Marden, a much earlier but profoundly influential motivational writer. This friend and close associate for many years was the late Roger Ferger, publisher and editor of the Cincinnati *Enquirer*, onc of the outstanding newspapers in the nation. Mr. Ferger was a notably strong and capable leader in community affairs and was greatly respected for his high order of intelligence.

One day as Mr. Ferger and I were returning to the *Enquirer* office after a luncheon together at the Queen City Club, of which he was president, we stopped in front of the newspaper building. I asked him, "Roger, tell me, just how did you become editor and publisher of the Cincinnati *Enquirer*?"

He said, "Many years ago as a young boy I stood on this very spot and, looking into that window, saw a man sitting at a desk. He was the editor and publisher of this paper. Right then and there I had a vision of myself sitting in his place, bearing his title and carrying forward his work. I suddenly wanted to be editor and publisher. I visualized myself as in that position and from that moment forward worked diligently to attain that goal. I believed, I believed, I believed, and became a practitioner of the power of positive thinking which you have so long been advocating and teaching."

He then took from his wallet a yellowed and somewhat tattered clipping from the writings of Orison Swett Marden, and standing on the sidewalk, traffic roaring by, he read it to me. I think I shall always remember the look of enthusiastic faith which was reflected on his countenance as he spoke words which had motivated him as a young boy and had continued to stir his personality forces into action throughout a notably successful life. And these are the dynamic words which started him and which helped him always to keep it going: "A man who is self-reliant, positive, optimistic, and undertakes his work with the assurance of success magnetizes his condition. He draws to himself the creative powers of the universe."

I related this story in less detail some years ago when I wrote *The Power of Positive Thinking*, and re-emphasize it here for the reason that in the thousands of letters received since publication of that book, many have referred gratefully to the activation of their own personality force by Mr. Ferger's experience.

Maybe the objection will be made that this was an unusually gifted man, that he would have attained successful outcomes without recourse to such believing and reactivating principles. May I then give you, in concluding this chapter, the experience of another man mentioned in that same book whose story has been the spark that lifted countless others out of failure and set them on the road to making something extra good of their lives?

I reprint a letter received a few years ago from a man telling how the positive principle dramatically changed his father's business experience, and his life in general. He wrote as follows:

> My father was a traveling salesman. One time he sold furniture, another time hardware, sometimes it was leather goods. He changed his line every year.
>
> I would hear him telling Mother that this was his last trip in stationery or in bed lamps or whatever he was selling at the moment. Next year everything would be different; we would be on Easy Street; he had a chance to go with a firm that had a product that sold itself. It was always the same. My father never had a product that sold. He was always tense, always afraid of himself, always whistling in the dark.
>
> Then one day a fellow-salesman gave Father a copy of a little three-sentence prayer. He was told to repeat it just before calling on a customer. Father tried it and the results were almost miraculous. He sold 85 percent of all calls during the first week, and every week thereafter the results were wonderful. Some weeks the percentage ran as high as 95 percent, and Father had 16 weeks in which he sold every customer called on.
>
> Father gave this prayer to several other salesmen, and in each case it brought astounding results. The prayer Father used is as follows:

"I believe I am always divinely guided.
I believe I will always take the right turn
of the road.
I believe God will always make a way where
there is no way."

A simple prayer, I grant you, but as a thought and action stimulator it is invested with rare power. Unconsciously this hitherto desultory salesman had employed the amazing resources of faith in God, the belief in guidance, and the power of visualization and affirmation. As a result his personality underwent dramatic change. The power within him, so long held in abeyance, surged forth in an incredible stream of effective action. He became literally a new man, remade and vital. His personality forces, so long dormant, were released into action, and not merely on a temporary basis. So great were the newly activated powers that they constantly replenished themselves. Hence, as Dr. Marais said at the opening of this chapter, "Inspiration and motivation are exactly like nutrition. You have to keep on keep on taking it daily, in healthy doses. Otherwise depletion, fatigue, depression and lack of ambition and achievement will very soon manifest themselves."

This salesman, by use of that simple but powerful affirmative and visualized spiritual principle, took in vitalized thought food and his entire life was changed. He thereafter possessed a new and vigorous power to keep it going.

And now here is the way personality forces are released into action:

1. Motivation is like nutrition. It must be taken daily and in healthy doses to keep it going.
2. There is much more power in personality than has ever been used; release it.
3. Life has an *if* at the center of the word and of our existence as well. Assume control of those variable and uncertain *ifs*.
4. Believe in and accept and affirm the powerful personality force inherent within you.
5. Practice the amazingly creative magic of believing.
6. "See" yourself, "image" yourself as what you want to be; then be just that.
7. Believe that the miracle of change is always possible—for you. Indeed, believe it is even *now* taking place.
8. Make a new and total commitment to the positive principle and master the skill of keeping it going.

SECOND WAY TO KEEP THE POSITIVE PRINCIPLE GOING

Take a New Look at That Word "Impossible"

The positive principle will help you get out of trouble and stay out thereafter. Let me tell you a story about Fred and Jennifer, who were in trouble—real trouble. They were heavily in debt and the small clothing shop they operated showed every ominous sign of failing.

It was a time of acute financial depression and their city had been hit hard. Indeed, businesses were closing all around them. It appeared as if their turn to fold would not be long in coming. The number of unpaid accounts on their books totaled a dangerously high figure. So little money was coming in that the bills from their suppliers could not be paid unless something happened, and quickly.

One morning Fred and Jennifer were sitting glumly in their little office going over their bills and unpaid accounts. It all seemed completely futile. No patrons at all were in the shop, which had been allowed to run down into shabby appearance.

Then something quite unexpected but very exciting happened. A scientist, prominent in chemical research and a friend of the couple, was walking along a street not far away. Some impulse told him to go around to see Fred and Jennifer. He could not shake off the impression that it was urgently important for him to make this call.

HOW THE IMPOSSIBLE TURNED INTO POSSIBLES

The scientist friend found the young couple in a state of mind bordering on despair mixed with panic. To his quite unnecessary question, "How's business?" Fred took a sheet of paper and printed on it in large letters the word IMPOSSIBLE and shoved it in front of their friend, a great human being named Dr. Alfred E. Cliffe. He studied the graphic word, then said thoughtfully, "Let's take a look at that word, 'impossible.' Just see what can be done with it if you don't let it overwhelm you." So saying, he took a big black pencil and drew two lines, one through the I, the other through the M, so that now it looked like this: ~~IM~~POSSIBLE. The word POSSIBLE, freed of the IM, stood out strong and clear. "Nothing," he said, "nothing is impossible if you do not think impossible. So what do you say? Let's start seeing only possibles. Let's apply the positive principle to your situation."

Al Cliffe picked up the top invoice from the stack of bills ready to be sent to their accounts. "John Abbott," he read. "What do you know about Mr. Abbott? Has he a wife and children? Wonder how he is getting along in his own business?"

"How should I know?" growled Fred. "He's just a customer and a slow-paying one at that."

"Tell you what," said Al, "look him up in the telephone directory. Give him a call and just ask in a friendly sort of way how things are. And do it now."

Grudgingly Fred did as directed and had a conversation that must have been pleasing judging by the first smile he had come up with. "He seemed pleased," he reported, "and quite surprised at my interest. He asked how we were doing and when I told him we were having a time collecting and paying bills he said he was in the same fix and added that he hadn't forgotten us, though I assured him that was not the reason for my call."

Then Al Cliffe did a strange thing. He asked Fred and Jennifer to join him in placing their right hands on that stack of outgoing bills. He prayed aloud for all the persons represented in that pile of bills, not for them to pay up, but that each of them would be blessed according to his own particular problems.

"Now, let's have an idea session," he suggested. "Got enough money for a can of paint?"

"Yeah, we're not all that low," grumbled Fred.

"Okay, get busy and paint the interior of the store shiny white. Then wash those showcases and windows until they glisten. Get some new light bulbs in those overhead fixtures. Most of all, get a smile on your faces and stay in the shop expecting business. When people start coming, greet them with real friendliness. Keep thinking in terms of the possibles. Skip that *impossible* concept for good. It's not going to be easy sailing, but do as I say and you will keep on sailing—you will keep it going."

Within a month the young couple had taken in enough money to keep their heads above water. And gradually they began making a little profit. They survived the depression, and all because they heeded the wise counsel of a friend and took a new look at the word "impossible."

This man Al Cliffe was one of the most intuitively wise men I have ever known. As a truth teacher he was superb in his insights and inspiration. He was a practical genius in the uses of the positive principle.

He himself learned creative and positive truth when desperately ill, so much so that he had been practically given up to die. In that moment of ultimate extremity Cliffe turned everything over to God, saying, "Thy will be done. Take me if you wish. But if it is Your will that I live, I will spend my years in teaching the amazing power of spiritual truth to overcome sickness, failure and all manner of difficulty." Always thereafter Dr. Cliffe taught a most basic truth, one that enormously benefited me personally and, similarly, thousands of others; and he expressed it in an unforgettable and felicitous phrase: "Let go and let God." This means essentially to do the best, the very best you possibly can do. Then, to quote St. Paul, ". . . having done all, to stand.* When you have done all you can do, what more can you do? That is the time to let it go and let God take over. With this methodology of the positive principle you need never be discouraged or defeated. Nothing is any longer impossible. On the basis of this philosophy you can always and forever keep it going.

KEEP INSPIRATION GOING BY CHECK ON WORDS

A sure way to keep inspiration going, strongly going, is to do a check on the words you commonly use. A word, or word combination, forms a thought symbol, so that one tends to reveal in his words the basic concept

* Ephesians 6:13.

in his mind. Thoughts invariably show through in habitual word use. If you wish to know what a person is really thinking, simply listen to his usual word pattern. And to know why your own mental upbeat level declines, study carefully the downbeat words you are habitually using in daily conversation. Emerson has been quoted as saying, "Cut a vital word and it will bleed," which is to say that words are alive and have the power to create or to destroy.

Of all destructive words in common use, surely one of the most powerful is the word *impossible*. More people may have failed by using that one word than almost any other in the English language.

"It's impossible" is the recurring depressant that puts the damper on enthusiasm and throws cold water on many a project that could otherwise be a success. It is therefore of first importance to eliminate the word *impossible* from daily speech, for such elimination will in time lessen its influence on your determinative thought process. Then when you are motivated to reach some goal or to make something better of yourself and your situation, the concept of the impossible will no longer have sufficient force to interfere with the operation of the positive principle. You will be able to keep inspiration going with power. You will constantly be supplied and resupplied with a motivational force that will not decline but, indeed, will grow ever stronger and more vital.

Appraising yourself on the basis of past demonstrations of weakly held inspiration, you may react to these assertions with doubt, if not disbelief. The word *impossible* at once flashes up in your mind. You may complain, "It is impossible for me to maintain at steady level an upbeat, positive attitude. It is impossible for inspiration to so grab me that it can constantly govern my reactions and keep me going in the face of the difficulties that are always ganging up." If your expressions are of this type, it indicates that a frontal attack needs to be made on that word *impossible* and the failure-generating concept for which it stands.

HE TOSSES OUT THE WORD "IMPOSSIBLE"

At the conclusion of a talk which I gave to a large sales meeting in Toronto's Massey Hall, a man came rushing backstage. His face was positively glowing. No other word could adequately describe his expression of wonderment and happiness. Obviously thrilled and excited, he insisted upon telling his story. And when I heard it, I, too, was excited. It is always a tremendous experience to meet a person to whom something significant has happened which has totally captured his personality.

"I owe everything to a story on pages 112 and 113 in your book *You Can If You Think You Can,*" he declared. "It's the story about Napoleon Hill, the widely read inspirational writer, whose younger life was adversely conditioned by the word *impossible*. And this caused him to live in failure and unhappiness. He wanted to be a writer, so he bought a dictionary to become a master of words. One day it occurred to him that he must, once and for all, get rid of that hated word 'impossible." His method was simple; with a pair of scissors he clipped it from the dictionary, crumpled it and vigorously threw it into the fire. So what do you know? I did exactly the same, and it is amazing how some really great possibles have taken the place of those miserable impossibles."

"Did you actually cut that word out of your dictionary?" I asked in amazement. My purpose was not to encourage mutilation of dictionaries but, rather, to motivate impossibility-type thinkers to cut the concept from their mentalities.

"I needed something dramatic," he replied. "Always before, I would get fired up to some new goal or get going on some exciting project. Then the fear that I could not do it would creep in to chill my enthusiasm, and the concept 'impossible' would take over. Result—I was washed up, licked, defeated. But I've tossed out that word *impossible* for good. And now when I get inspired I've got what it takes to keep it going. I've bought the positive principle and I don't mean maybe."

I was not surprised to discover that the change in this man's attitudes had a spiritual source, for he took from his pocket a copy of our regular monthly publication *PLUS: The Magazine of Positive Thinking*. In this periodical are published my talks given every Sunday at Marble Collegiate Church on Fifth Avenue in New York City and mailed to hundreds of thousands of recipients in every state and 110 foreign countries.* This particular issue contained a message entitled "Take a New Look at the Impossible," and he had underscored a passage which read:

> What are the most pathetic, the saddest, most sinister words in the English language? John Greenleaf Whittier's answer:
>
> *For of all words of tongue or pen,*
> *The saddest are these:*
> *It might have been!*

* To receive *Plus* regularly, send your name and address (with ZIP code) to *Plus*, P.O. Box 8000, Pawling, N.Y. 12564-8000. There is no required payment; your gift and those of others help to defray the cost of our worldwide, nonprofit ministry (approximately $10 per person per year).

That does indeed rate high as a sad expression. And there may be other nominations as well. But actually the word "impossible" is perhaps the most pathetic word in the English language. And it is unfortunate that this word is engraved so vividly on the consciousness of hundreds of thousands of people, reminding them constantly that they cannot do it; they can't make it; they haven't got it. And so they are defeated by blown-up, impressive, so-called impossibles.

What shall one do about those big obstacles, those huge, dreamed-up impossibles? When did you last speak the word "impossible"? Are you going to acquiesce supinely with the false notion that your situation is impossible? Are you about to let it throw you? Is it a very important decision; what to do about those so-called impossibles that have harassed and defeated you for so long.

Take a new look at your present "impossible." Consider positive ways to handle it. Start by studying the New Testament, which is packed full of ideas about dealing with the impossible, and which should be thought of as a textbook of the positive principle. It presents the workable formula for turning the "impossible" into great possibles. For example, think about this terrific truth: "The things which are impossible with men are possible with God."* That is to say, if a person gets going with faith in God, with belief in tapping Divine power, then his situation becomes at once no longer impossible, because "the things which are impossible with men are possible with God." It is just that simple.

And consider that other amazing statement: "If ye have faith as a grain of mustard seed . . ."† Did you ever see a grain of mustard seed? Put it in your hand and the wind will blow it away. It is very small. So even if you have only a little faith like a grain of mustard seed, if it is real, "nothing"—and we mean *nothing*—"shall be impossible unto you."

There are many negative thinkers today who will eagerly tell you dogmatically that this sort of thing just isn't so, and they marshal argument after argument to bolster the negative, since it is their nature always to decry the positives. And why? Perhaps because they do not want success or victory. Strange, but some people are happier being defeated; they have the will to fail—a sick mental attitude. Nor do they want anyone else to succeed. Could be they actually want things to go badly so that they may further complain and criticize, or because it equates with

* Luke 18:17.

† Matthew 17:20.

their own failure pattern. But an intelligent, straight thinker will go for a big structured concept of spiritual truth when convinced that it has worked miracles in the experience of many previously defeated persons.

So take a new look at that impossible. Rise above it mentally so that you attain the position of looking down on your problem. All generals who have won important victories have maneuvered to higher ground. Any person wanting to overcome a problem must get above the problem in his thought processes. Then it does not appear nearly so formidable; and he has greater confidence in his ability to deal with it.

I have spent many years endeavoring to persuade people of the fact that they possess a built-in inner power to withstand and overcome all the blows that circumstances can bring to bear upon them. There are thousands, perhaps hundreds of thousands, who have heard this message and responded exultantly to the power of positive thinking. Inspired and filled with dynamic spirit, life for them has taken on new and joyous meaning. They have discovered the power—the wonderful power to keep motivation going.

When, as is common in the experience of every person on earth, challenges to inspiration come, positive confidence may undergo acute stress. Sickness, sorrow, frustration, financial problems, personal hardship and many other vicissitudes draw so heavily upon personal resources that the erosion, perhaps even collapse, of built-up inspiration can and often does result.

Letters by the hundreds come from readers, saying, in effect: "I have followed your positive teachings and it gave me courage, strength and real happiness. But now this terrible thing has occurred and my faith is shaken. How can I keep from giving up? How can I keep the positive principle going?"

DOWN TO $1.76

Take, for example, the woman, a regular reader of our publication, *Creative Help for Daily Living*, who in a period of severe recession wrote me of her struggle to maintain a positive faith. She told me she had that day exactly $1.76 in the bank. In addition, the firm employing her husband had been able to give only a moderate cost of living increase to employees, and with inflationary prices it was very hard to keep going. "But," she said, "I hold the sure faith that God will take care of us if we keep our spiritual and mental attitudes at high level. My husband and I have decided not to panic, to think positively and to keep our faith going strong."

Some weeks later, in answer to our letter of reassurance and caring concern, she wrote again describing the most "surprising occurrences" in which a new source of additional income came about, a modest amount but helpful. By refusing to panic, by keeping her courage up, her faith strong, her thinking sound, the impossibility concept which might have frustrated such a good outcome had no negative influence in this human and rather common domestic situation.

PHYSICAL TROUBLE COULDN'T BUILD UP IMPOSSIBLES

How can you keep your upbeat mind level going on a sustained basis when a physical problem develops? By what method may inspirational attitudes be maintained when some devastating blow strikes and undermines your health, your strength and your well-being? These are questions asked by uncounted thousands every day, everywhere.

Take, for example, the experience of Chet Craig, a friend of mine, a dedicated positive thinker, who was always working at building up his body, sometimes jogging as much as a hundred miles a week. Suddenly one day a severe pain, and next, an operation for cancer of the prostate. But he kept his spirit going, even so. "I have to work with my mind so that diseased thoughts do not grow, as diseased tissue has grown in my body. I'm keeping on top of it all," he declared positively. "I'm going to come out on top." And latest reports indicate that he is indeed doing just that. The positive principle sustains him.

Again, there was a man whom I always think of as one of the inspiring persons I have encountered over the years. I was on a program to speak to a couple of thousand salespeople in Omaha, and before coming on for my talk this famous industrial psychologist preceded me. He could not stand, being paralyzed in both legs. But for sure he was not paralyzed in his head, for he made a brilliant speech, sitting in his wheelchair. As the members of the large audience listened, it was only for a moment that anyone was interested out of pity. He was caustic, abrasive persuasive, kindly, humorous. He had everything a man needs to be an effective communicator, a powerful public speaker.

Later when I commented on his magnificent performance, expressing admiration by saying that I found it rough going to hold a crowd while standing on two feet, he replied, "Brains aren't in the legs. They are in the head. My legs are paralyzed, but so far my head is in working order. I've found that I can live my life minus workable legs because I still possess a workable brain."

Obviously, both of these men had an inner inspiration, a built-in motivation that enabled them to keep going against a physical adversity. Both of them scoffed at the word "impossible." "What do you mean, impossible?" they each told me. "Forget it. I think in terms of the possible." They had taken a look at that word "impossible" and obviously were not impressed.

HE DREW UPON A DEEP SOURCE IN TRAGEDY

But there are greater stresses than financial stringency or even problems of health, notably those tragic events that now and then occur in human experience, such as the sudden and violent death of dear ones. Such times try the spirit to the utmost breaking point to such an extent that the word "impossible" exerts a menacing power that requires deep and extraordinary resources to meet and deal effectively with it.

My wife, Ruth, recently spoke to a conference of eleven thousand Baptist pastors in the huge auditorium at Miami Beach at a meeting presided over by my friend. Dr. James L. Pleitz, of Pensacola. The only woman to address this large and important gathering, Ruth showed me the program of the event and I noted that it contained the words of the songs to be used in the convention. One of them was by the late Luther H. Bridgers, another friend of many years and a masterful leader of gospel singing; it was called "He Keeps Me Singing."

This reminded me of the time Luther Bridgers invited me to his home for breakfast, and we had a happy time of friendship together with his family. I discovered that this was his second family group. He told of an earlier tragedy when as young pastor he went to another city to participate in a series of meetings.One night late he was awakened by the telephone. Hesitantly over the wire came the voice of a friend telling him the almost incredible news that fire had swept through his home while his wife and two children were sleeping. Every effort was made to save them, but the flames were too far advanced and the three members of his family perished in the holocaust that ravaged the house.

Stunned, Luther dropped the receiver and sat in agony of spirit. It couldn't be true! It couldn't be truc! It just could not be true! Anguished, he paced the floor. Then he bolted from the room and out of the hotel into the early-morning emptiness of the streets. For a long time he walked up and down, desperately fighting for self-control.

Then in his search for peace he came to the river which flowed wide and deep through the town. He regarded it with fascination. In its cool depths lay forgetfulness. It would require only a moment of struggle for his spirit to leave his body and be reunited with his wife and little children. Life was so utterly impossible now. Impossible! Impossible! The word hammered at his brain. It was impossible to go on. He must die now in that swift-moving stream.

But deep within his mind was a long-established faith and a love of God as his Father. The struggle was intense. He dropped finally to his knees, and the tears that had not yet come from dry eyes now poured out in a flood. Along with thc tears was a prayer in depth asking for understanding and strength to handle this tragedy with the power vouchsafed to a true believer. The struggle was long and hard, but he found his way back. Later he married again and raised a second family in whose home I had breakfasted that morning.

Completing his story, Luther sat at the piano and played movingly and with deep meaning some of the famous compositions of the great composers. Then finally hc went into one of his own well-known songs. I shall never cease to be moved in memory of this strong man singing words known to thousands:

Jesus, Jesus, Jesus,
Sweetest name I know,
Fills my ev'ry longing,
*Keeps me singing as I go.**

Golden sunlight streamed into the room, lighting up the face of the singer. As he sang, a canary in a cage above the piano also began to sing. And I am sure it was not in imagination that man and bird seemed in perfect attunement as together they poured forth praise to the Lord who gives victory of such magnitude to human beings. And who knows? Perhaps to birds also. At any rate, the sum and substance of the matter is

* He Keeps Me Singing" by Luther B. Bridgers.

that even in such ultimate tragedy as he experienced, Luther Bridgers knew how to keep the positive principle going. Faith of this caliber never recognizes the word or concept "impossible."

One of the chief lessons or truths to be learned by thoughtful people is that the so-called impossible is indeed possible to those who have the will, the courage and the faith. Built into the fabric of human existence is the fact that whatever is proper for man to attain or accomplish is possible for him to achieve. Marcus Aurelius phrased it potently: "Do not think that what is hard for thee to master is impossible for man; but if a thing is possible and proper to man, deem it attainable by thee."* Those things that an individual can conceive in the mind may be achieved by the use of the mind. Samuel Johnson declared that "few things are impossible to diligence and skill."† Berton Braley summed it up in a swinging sort of verse:

Got any river they say isn't crossable?
Got any mountains that can't be cut through?
We specialize in the wholly impossible.
Doing things "nobody ever could do."‡

So take a new look, shall we say a masterful new look, at that word "impossible." Rebuild your motivation. Become a specialist in doing the wholly impossible. And keep the positive principle going.

Now a sum-up of the basic points made in this chapter:

1. Cut the "im" out of impossible, leaving that dynamic word standing out free and clear—*possible*.
2. Do all you can about a tough situation; then let go and let God.
3. Never use the word "impossible" seriously again. Toss it into the verbal wastebasket.
4. Practice the positive principle—the principle of the possible. "If ye have faith . . . nothing shall be impossible unto you."**
5. Store up a body of indomitable faith sufficient to draw upon in crisis to sustain you.

* *Meditations* VI, 19.

† *Rasselas*, Chap. 1.

‡ At Your Service: The Panama Gang."

** Matthew 17:20.

6. Whatever is proper to a human being may be considered to be attainable by him.
7. Become a specialist in doing the "wholly impossible," the things that "can't " be done.
8. A new, straight look at that word "impossible" will make it possible always to keep your motivation going.

THIRD WAY TO KEEP THE POSITIVE PRINCIPLE GOING

Hold the Thought That Nothing Can Get You Down

It is surprising how many things get so many people down. And usually they are not the big things, the great tragedies, but rather the smaller, pesky frustrations and irritations. These seem to be the real depressants of spirit, for human beings possess deep within themselves an amazing power to meet the big issues.

For example, consider the case of Major H. P. S. Ahluwalia, of India, who climbed Everest, the highest mountain on earth. With incredible exhilaration he stood finally on that great and colossal peak. But now Major Ahluwalia cannot even climb from the garden to his door. He was shot in the neck by a Pakistani sniper in Kashmir, ironically after the cease-fire between the two countries was declared and hostilities had ceased. His only locomotion now is by wheelchair—this man whose powerful legs and sturdy heart carried him to the summit of the world's highest eminence.

But did this super tragedy get him down? Well, hardly. He was able to overcome a profound depression and, to use his own felicitous phrase, he "climbed the Everest within." And, explained the major, to stand on the peak of himself after struggling with his own spirit was every bit as exhilarating as the thrill of standing on the summit of the vast mountain.

He dramatically demonstrated that nothing can really get a person down provided he has learned the skill, the ability, the power to keep it going.

Perhaps few readers of this book will ever face a challenge to the spirit even remotely comparable to that of Major Ahluwalia. But nearly everyone has to deal with daily irritations, monotony and those annoyances that take a toll of inspiration and motivational vitality. To keep it going in the presence of cumulative frustrations certainly isn't easy.

Common frustration sometimes takes quite uncommon forms and expressions. As, for example, the housewife who got completely fed up with the constant and unending annoyances to which she felt desperately subjected. In a moment of feeling quite unable to cope with them anymore, she simply set fire to the house and walked away without looking back! I read this little human tempest and furor story in a newspaper somewhere.

Then there was the case of the quiet and submissive husband who had meekly and supinely given in for years to his irritable and nagging wife. But the pent-up frustration within the husbandly breast finally broke through. Still true to his uncombative nature, the harassed man left home one morning without a word and was gone for twenty-five years. Then he returned home and the wife reported that he was much easier to get along with than before. As to his own reactions, no report was forthcoming, but this time he stayed. This story I also read in some forgotten daily sheet in which were recounted the foibles of human nature.

In another book* I told about a curious incident of frustration and irritation and their power to get one down. It concerned the businessman who had turned home and office into a hell because of his temper tantrums, his acute lack of self-control. He was, as his wife and office associates described it, always "hitting the ceiling." It appears that his asperity and annoyance were so sharp and continuous that the ceiling was his usual habitat.

THE WORM TURNS

But one day "the worm turned." He had been storming about the house violently declaiming that he could no longer take it and that everything was getting him down. The tirade was laced with salty and sulfurous words.

About the worm turning. His wife had endured all that she could take. With eyes blazing, she shoved him into a chair and stood before him in

* *Positive Thinking for a Time Like This.*

unabashed fury. "Now you just listen to me and don't you say a word. I've let you shout and fume and swear until I am completely sick of it. It's my turn, and you sit there and listen until I get through with you." Whereupon she proceeded to lay him out with a sharp, clear picture of the mean, irritable, self-centered person he had become.

It wasn't only things that were getting him down, she declared. He was getting himself down, victimized by his raw, nervous state in which frustration compounded irritation until she and everyone else found it impossible to deal with him or, indeed, to endure him.

While his wife belabored him, suddenly she seemed to fade from his sight. He was no longer aware of her, or of the room in which this dialogue was proceeding. Instead, he seemed to be standing on a strange riverbank along which flowed a slow-moving current, and there in midstream was a dark, even repulsive object bobbing sluggishly. Suddenly he was sharply aware that he was seeing within himself the stream of his own selfhood. And that dark and ugly thing floating sluggishly he now realized was the error and evil in his nature. This was the source of his uptight tension that would finally destroy him unless quickly contained. This he saw clearly and without doubt.

The vision passed gradually to reveal the highly exercised wife still vehemently excoriating her husband, but now she regarded him quizzically. Startled, she fell into bewildered silence. "I see myself clearly," he said, rather awed. "Never before have I had a sharp insight into my own self. I now know that I must break up that inner failure center. Because out of it seem to rise the irritants that goad me into unreasonableness."

This story represents a curious demonstration of the cumulative effect of frustrations built up and up. The man involved, due to his acute and extraordinary revelation of self-knowledge, recovered his shattered sense of balance. He operated thereafter on an organized motivational basis. His personality normalized. A new control over frustrating and irritating factors enabled him to hold firmly to the conviction that nothing could get him down. He relearned the ability to keep the positive principle going effectively by authoritatively containing hitherto uncontrolled emotional reaction.

FRUSTRATED CANADIAN FINDS ANSWER

The struggle with the irritations and exasperations which plague so many and the possible solutions to overcoming them were illustrated in the experience of a man from Canada. "I just could not go on with it," he declared. He therefore left home without any explanation to anyone and took off in his car for New York. He had only one objective in mind—to sign on as a deckhand on a slow freighter bound for some distant port, he did not care where. Anywhere that would put distance between his home and himself was all that he wanted.

He arrived in New York on a Saturday to find that port activities were shut down until Monday. He wandered aimlessly about the city, trying for forgetfulness in movie houses, but they all left him cold. On Sunday morning, still aimlessly walking, he found himself on Fifth Avenue. There he was surprised to see crowds of people lined up to go into a church. Never before having seen a crowd queued up for church, he joined the line more in curiosity than in a desire to go to church, and he was lucky to get the last seat in the last row.

Five years later this man wrote me to tell of his experience that Sunday morning. Looking about him, he noticed that the people were both black and white, indeed persons of various races and of all ages, lots of young people, the congregation seeming to consist of perhaps more than 50 percent men. Everyone appeared friendly, and a strange feeling that he finally decided to call love plus excitement seemed to pervade the atmosphere.

As he listened to the outstanding choir and the reading of verses from the Scriptures and the prayers, and hesitantly participated in the enthusiastic singing of old familiar hymns, he began to have a warm feeling of belonging. Memories of "the good days of my youth stirred within my mind. A profound sense of peace filled my heart. Tears came to my eyes as I sat within your great stone refuge."

The service came to a close and the big congregation began to leave the church. Everybody seemed uplifted, renewed, happy. Then the lady he had been sitting beside offered her hand in greeting and all she said was, "God loves you." That was enough. It broke him up. Out on the avenue he walked for blocks, and it was like walking on air. He knew that he could cope—cope with anything. He now believed with deepening certainty that he could rise above all frustration. This new motivational inspiration that he strongly felt was surely the real thing, and he had no doubt that it would keep him going and that he could keep it going. Which is precisely what he did. He immediately drove home to Canada and was still going strong when five years later he wrote of the experience which taught him the dynamic truth that nothing need keep you down.

LIFE CAN BE TOUGH, VERY TOUGH

That life on earth has a powerful crushing quality can hardly be denied. Circumstances relating to health, job, money, hostility, misunderstanding, and numerous other adversaries of well-being are constantly making it difficult, if not downright painful, for multitudes of people every day. Little wonder that the psychoanalyst Freud is reported to have said, "The chief duty of a human being is to endure life." And life can indeed be tough, very tough.

In a profound sense it is true that a chief, if not *the* chief, duty of any of us is simply to endure what life brings. There are certain inevitables with which one must live. Learning to live with some painful disability, because no release formula has been found, is in itself an achievement.

My father was a very happy and creative man. In middle life he developed a painful arthritic condition which bothered him no end. "Almost got me down," he admitted. "But I outsmarted it. I finally learned that it could not be cured, only palliated. So I accepted that fact and learned to live with it." He never talked much about it in later years and lived to celebrate his eighty-fifth birthday. One thing is sure: It never got him down—not at all. He even declared that it seemed less painful when he accepted it as an inevitable with which he must get along. He applied the positive principle to that physical problem.

With due respect to the "endure it" principle, which often makes the difficulties of human existence pretty grim, there is another attitude that is upbeat, called the "master it" principle. Basically, nothing can get you down if you use that quality deep within your human nature that resists defeat, the upthrusting force designed to meet and overcome any crushing element in your experience. One potent sentence may describe it: "This is the victory that overcometh the world, even our faith."* Faith is the most powerful of all forces operating in humanity, and when you have it in depth, nothing can get you down. *Nothing*. This is the positive principle, and it is full of healing power.

DWARF BECOMES A GIANT

If you consider yourself weak and inadequate and lacking in power to stand up to life's challenges and rigorous difficulties, you are taking an

* I John 5:4.

erroneous view of yourself. You simply are not so inadequate and lacking in strength as you assume yourself to be. Indeed, such assumption is dangerous, for it tends to create the fact. You are likely to build a case against yourself if you continue such thoughts. This process of self-limitation and self-depreciation is seldom expressed outwardly where you put on a front. But it does work in consciousness. And upon emphasis and re-emphasis, it can and often does pass, by mental osmosis, into the unconscious, where it may become determinative.

This results in an individual's attempts to put down the giant that the Creator has placed at the center of every personality. For there is a giant in every person, and nothing can get this giant down unless that giant is kept down by himself.

Ernie Belz had a frozen personality when he first arrived in America from Europe. He was so abnormally short of stature (only a little over four feet) that he had developed a deep-seated inferiority feeling. A thirty-year-old Swiss, who had come to the United States hoping to find himself, Ernie discovered it hard going at first.

His broken English usually brought a smile, and his minuscule size was always a handicap. Mounting a bus, he could not negotiate the step but had to swing himself up. When he went into a store for clothing, he was referred to the boys' department.

One day Ernie Belz was lunching alone in a restaurant when a young man from Marble Collegiate Church invited him to our Young Adults Group. He accepted and received friendship and understanding instead of the curious looks to which he was accustomed. But the thawing of a frozen personality does not happen in a day—or a month.

A big turning point came one night at a Young Adults meeting when a member spoke convincingly on the theme "God Has a Plan for My Life." Ernie had some questions about this idea. "Do I understand that you really believe God has a plan for my life, a little fellow like me?" Ernie asked doubtfully.

"Sure—God has a plan for every one of us, and this means you, too, Ernie. The problem is you must be willing to do whatever He wants you to do."

In other meetings with these spiritually alive and with-it young people, he was shown that size or color or handicap had nothing to do with how much or how effective one could become.

As a result of this encouragement, Ernie began to think more creatively. He learned the positive principle. He stopped trying to lose himself in crowds and began to take an interest in others as individuals. He volunteered for church work projects. He also developed the art of discovering other persons' interests and bringing out the best in each individual's personality.

Good things began happening to Ernie Belz. One was that he escaped from his shell of inferiority and became a released individual. Several years later he secured an administrative job with an educational institution in Africa.

Ernie must have grown and grown big in this job, for an executive under whom he worked wrote: "How much better this world would be if we had more people like Ernie Belz. He may be small in physical stature, but actually he is a giant when it comes to helping other people find themselves."

All the time there was an undetected giant in Ernie Belz. And that giant finally emerged to disclose a man with dynamic motivation and power to keep the positive principle going and influence everyone he met. By the same line of factual reasoning, there is a giant in you, too. When that giant takes charge, nothing can get you down, ever.

YOU CAN DO INCREDIBLE THINGS

When that inner giant is alive and vital, you are no longer hampered by negative and inferiority thoughts. When you are packed full of faith in God and in yourself, you can do just about anything you firmly and authoritatively decide to do. When you wholeheartedly adopt a "with all your heart" attitude and go all out with the positive principle, you can do incredible things. Strange, the tendency of some skeptics to disparage such an assertion as "You can do just about anything you decide to do." Actually, I am minded to drop those two qualifying words "just about," especially when I recall the amazing story of Legson Kayira, a teen-ager living in a tiny African village who walked a distance of 2,500 miles across the continent and then made his way to the American West Coast—but let him tell the story in his own words. "Barefoot to America," he calls his incredible tale.*

> My mother did not know where America was. I said to her, "Mother, I want to go to America to go to college. Will you give me your permission?"

* *Guideposts* magazine.

"Very well," she said. "You may go. When will you leave?"

I did not want to give her time to discover how far away America was, for fear that she would change her mind. "Tomorrow," I said.

"I will prepare some maize for you to eat along the way," she said.

Next day I left my home in northern Nyasaland, East Africa. I had only the clothes I wore, a khaki shirt and shorts. I carried the two treasures I owned; a Bible and a copy of *Pilgrim's Progress*. I carried, too, the maize my mother had given me, wrapped in banana leaves.

My goal was a continent and an ocean away, but I did not doubt that I would reach it. I had no idea how old I was. Such things mean little in a land where time is always the same. I suppose I was 16 or 18. My father died when I was very young. My mother listened to the words of the missionaries, with the result that our family became Christian.

From the missionaries I learned I was not the victim of circumstances but the master of them. I learned that I had an obligation to use whatever talents I had to make life better for others. And to do that I would need education. I learned about America. I read the life of Abraham Lincoln and grew to love this man who suffered so much to help the enslaved in his country. I read, too, the autobiography of Booker T. Washington, himself born in slavery in America, and who had risen in dignity and honor to become a benefactor of his people and his country.

I gradually realized that in America I could receive the training and opportunities to prepare myself to emulate these men in my own land, to be, like them, a leader, perhaps even the president of my country.

My intention was to make my way to Cairo, where I hoped to get passage on a ship to America. Cairo was over 3,000 miles away, a distance I could not comprehend, and I foolishly thought I could walk it in four or five days. But in four or five days I was about 25 miles from home, my food was gone, I had no money, and I did not know what to do, except that I must keep going.

I developed a pattern of travel that became my life for more than a year. Villages were usually five or six miles apart, on forest paths. I would arrive at one in the afternoon and ask if I could work to earn food, water and a place to sleep. When this was possible, I would spend the night there, then move on to the next village in the morning. I was actually defenseless against the forest animals I dreaded, but although I heard them at night none of them approached me. Malaria mosquitoes, however, were constant companions, and I often was sick.

By the end of a year I had walked 1,000 miles and had arrived in Uganda, where a family took me in and I found a job making bricks. I remained there six months and sent most of my earnings to my mother.

In Kampala, I unexpectedly came upon a directory of American colleges. Opening it at random, I saw the name of Skagit Valley College,

Mount Vernon, Washington. I had heard that American colleges sometimes give scholarships to deserving young people, so I wrote and applied for one. I realized that I might be refused but was not discouraged: I would write to one school after another in the directory until I found one that would help me.

Three weeks later I was granted a scholarship and assured that the school would help me find a job. Overjoyed, I went to the United States authorities, only to be told that this was not enough. I would need a passport and the round-trip fair in order to obtain a visa.

I wrote to my government for a passport but it was refused because I could not tell them when I was born. I then wrote to the missionaries who had taught me in my childhood, and through their efforts was granted a passport. But I still could not get the visa because I did not have the fare.

Still determined, I resumed my journey. So strong was my faith that I used my last money to buy my first pair of shoes: I knew I could not walk into college in my bare feet. I carried the shoes to save them.

Across Uganda and into the Sudan I walked. The villages were farther apart and the people were less friendly. Sometimes I had to walk 20 or 30 miles in a day to find a place to sleep or to work to earn some food. At last I reached Khartoum, where I learned that there was a United States consulate.

Once again I heard about the U.S. entrance requirements, but this time the Consul was interested enough to write the college about my plight. Back came a cable.

The students, hearing about me and my problems, had raised the fare of $1,700 through benefit parties. I was thrilled and deeply grateful; overjoyed that I had judged Americans correctly for their friendship and brotherhood.

News that I had walked for over two years and 2,500 miles circulated in Khartoum. The Communists came to me and offered to send me to school in Yugoslavia, all expenses paid, including travel, and a subsistence during my studies. "I am a Christian," I told them, "and I could not be educated into the kind of man I want to be in your godless schools." They warned me that, as a black boy, I would have racial difficulties in the United States, but I had read enough to feel this was a diminishing factor.

After many, many months, carrying my two books and wearing my first suit, I arrived at Skagit Valley College. In my speech of gratitude to the student body I disclosed my desire to become prime minister or president of my country, and I noticed some smiles. I wondered if I had said something naïve. I do not think so.

When God has put an impossible dream in your heart, He means to help you fulfill it. I believed this to be true when, as an African bush boy, I felt compelled to become an American college graduate. And my dream of becoming president of Nyasaland can also become true.

STORY UPDATE

To update the story, Mr. Kayira is still walking up and forward with his inner giant, and walking strong. He never fails to live by the positive principle. He became professor of political science at Cambridge University in England. He has authored a novel, *The Looming Shadow*, and a nonfiction book based on African life.

What do you mean, you can't do anything? What do you mean, things can get you down? Not when you have the urge, the impulse, the motivation, to keep it going, to everlastingly keep it going. Hold that thought and hold it strong and sturdy—that nothing can ever get you down. If you think you are down, tell you what . . . do not stay down. Get right up; shake off defeat. Reactivate the giant within you and get going—and keep it going. Live always by the amazing positive principle. That is the realistic and proven philosophy that succeeds and keeps on succeeding.

HOW TO HIT IT AGAIN AND KEEP GOING

But suppose you have already been knocked down before you started reading this book and have accepted the negative thought that you are down and guess you are down for good. What then? Change your attitude, really change it. Simply start affirming: "I do not mean to stay down. What an advantage to have hit bottom. I will never minimize the value of the bottom, for it is a very advantageous place to be. The bottom is as far down as I can go. The only direction from here is up. And up I am going."

So, then, start looking up. Start thinking up. Begin acting in an up manner. And keep going in an up direction, no matter how steep or how long the climb. If you keep thinking positively, affirming positively, acting positively, always practicing the positive principle, the way will clear and you will reach that greatly-to-be-desired top away up there. With this spirit, that top is not all that far off, and this time you will stay there, having learned how always to keep it going.

EXECUTIVE, FIFTY-TWO, LOSES JOB, BUT—

A friend, at fifty-two, was operating vice-president of an apparently strong manufacturing company. He was an engineer by profession, with outstanding managerial ability. Then two adverse conditions arose: a recessionary period and some innovative inventions by a competitor which rendered his firm's line practically obsolete. The company failed at a time when jobs were scarce, especially for men over fifty. Finally the unhappy situation got to where he would have to take whatever kind of employment he could get. He wasn't proud; he simply wanted to work. Indeed, he had to work. He knocked on lots of doors. "Sorry, but nothing now. Leave your name." So it went, day after day.

Finally one employment manager, looking over his résumé, hesitantly said, "You have good engineering experience. We don't need anyone right now, but there may be a vacancy later in a small, and I'm sure for you uninteresting, job with us. You see, the trouble is that you are overqualified."

"Overqualified, nothing. As an engineer, I can handle a broom. I'll prove to be the best sweeper-outer you ever had in this place." He was actually hired as a janitor's assistant, a clean-up man.

But to his menial job he applied his organizational know-how, so much so that he finished every job in record time and was back for more assignments. Each minor job was done not only quickly but in an innovative way that saved time and effort.

Later he became divisional manager of that organization and last I heard he was headed for that place that may be called the antithesis of the bottom—namely, the top.

You do not need to let anything get you down, but if you are down you certainly need not let anything keep you down.

ART FLEMING'S METHOD FOR KEEPING IT GOING

I like the way Art Fleming, famous host-star of the longtime television show *Jeopardy*, handled the matter of not letting anything get him down. Art knows how to keep it going. He lives by the positive principle.

You see, Art is a deacon in my church and knows how to handle a tough matter spiritually. And that, of course, is the only sound basis on which to deal with anything of importance.

Here is how Art reacted to the news that his long-running and popular quiz program was being dropped, according to Steve Tinney of the *National Enquirer:*

> "I'm not the least bit upset about it," the famous emcee said. "In fact, I can't wait to see what God has in store for me. It may sound strange, but I really believe every time one door closes, another, even better one, opens. My life," he continued, "has always been in the hands of God and knowing that gives me a positive mental attitude. I can accept whatever He has in store for me and whatever it is, it'll be better than *Jeopardy*—I just know it.
>
> "I don't claim to be holier than thou," Fleming said. "But the way I see it, if God is for me, who can be against me? My inspiration and guidance come from my everyday conversations with God. I thank Him for each and every day—regardless of what happens."

Fleming then told how, saddened by the death of his father some years ago, he was so hard hit that he took off for the wilds of Canada where there was no telephone, no contact with the outside world. While there, a prominent manufacturer tried to reach him with an attractive offer to promote his merchandise on television, but, unable to reach him, signed someone else to the lucrative contract. Art admits to disappointment when he returned, but then he got the *Jeopardy* offer, which he held for eleven years, and which he would have missed had he been around to accept the first offer.

"God watches out for all of us," Fleming concluded. "When things go wrong, He's strengthening you for even better things to come."

So firmly hold the thought that nothing can get you down and keep the positive principle going—always keep it going.

Remember:

1. Don't be concerned about your ability to handle the big disasters; shore yourself up against the little irritations and frustrations.
2. Always remember when frustrated that it isn't all that bad—and that God loves you.
3. Know for sure that there is a giant within you. And then release the giant YOU.
4. Remember and never doubt it—with God's help you can do incredible things.
5. Never think down—always think up.
6. Put problems into God's hands and leave them there. He will take care of you and bring things out right.

FOURTH WAY TO KEEP THE POSITIVE PRINCIPLE GOING

Get Turned On with Self-Repeating Enthusiasm

It happened on a Fifth Avenue bus in New York. A friend of mine came aboard and sank with a sigh into the seat alongside of me. "Hello, Mr. Positive Thinking, you're just the guy I need. Fancy meeting you here."

"How come?" I asked. "Please elucidate." We were old friends and banter was the usual procedure.

"Boy, am I out of enthusiasm! And listen, don't start giving me any of that positive stuff. Look, I've had about a dozen bad breaks and everything has gone wrong lately. Not a thing has gone right, not a thing."

So saying, he started reeling off the dozen bad breaks, but I noticed that after about four of them he slowed down and with an effort could not get beyond six. "You sure are a poor counter, or else you have an overdeveloped imagination," I remarked. "You said you had a dozen bad breaks and yet you can only come up with six. Why the exaggeration?"

"Well," he hesitated, "it seems like a dozen, even more like a hundred. Anyway, all that old enthusiasm you got me started with the last time I heard you make a speech has gone down the drain."

"Pretty thin enthusiasm, if you ask me, to go down the drain that fast just because you've had a couple of bad breaks which anybody with any stuff on the ball could handle without all this dramatization. In my opinion you're overplaying it. Anyway, what you need is not a vacuous enthusiasm that runs out of you at the first sign of a little difficulty. Here's my suggestion: get turned on—really turned on—with a self-repeating enthusiasm. And to do that, think, pray and act with enthusiasm until it takes over in you."

"Okay, okay, thanks for the sermon. I'll try it," he said as we left the bus and separated at the corner of Fifty-seventh Street. I'm glad to report that he made the grade all right. And he did so by a buildup of enthusiasm that lent enhanced power to all of his activities. In fact, he was doing all right when I rode the bus with him, but he was just talking wrong. That in itself is dangerous, for wrong talking can lead to wrong thinking, and then you can get into real trouble.

Funny thing, how some people get turned on with a self-repeating enthusiasm and remain turned on regardless of a lot of things that might turn it off . . . and as a matter of fact do turn it off in a great many desultory-reacting individuals.

But there are others, more than might be imagined, who have learned the skill of an enthusiasm that is self-renewing. They really know how to keep the positive principle going. Like the lady of ninety years whom I saw in Ontario. I was about to describe her as an old lady, but since she really isn't that except chronologically, I will bypass the word "old" as inexact in her case. At any rate, she is a shining example of the positive principlc in action.

HER SOURCE OF SELF-REPEATING ENTHUSIASM

The woman was in a wheelchair. One leg had been amputated, but enthusiastically she described how, though she lived alone, she did all her own housework from that wheelchair, even to running a vacuum cleaner, cooking meals and making the bed. "Must be tough going," I commented.

"Not if you know the tricks, and I know 'em. Have to. Nobody else around, and I can't get help. Couldn't pay for a girl if one could be found. But don't worry; I'm not complaining, I enjoy it," she concluded vigorously.

"How long have you been without that leg?" I asked.

"Oh, about five years. Sure could use it. And if I had it I'd be on the go a lot more."

"You get out even with that wheelchair?"

"Of course. Do you expect me to stay cooped up in this house all the time?"

"This dynamic ninety-year-old runs the rest of us ragged," said her twenty-seven-year-old granddaughter, who added, "I drop in every other day just to get a new shot of enthusiasm from Grandma. Mine runs down so easily."

"But don't you ever get discouraged?" I asked this elderly female ball of fire.

"Discouraged? Of course I do."

"And what do you do when you get discouraged?" I prodded.

"Why, I just get over it. What else is there to do?"

"Okay. That's the best answer I ever heard. And what about all this enthusiasm you exhibit—how did you come by it? And, more important still, how do you keep it going, what with one leg and this wheelchair and being ninety and all that?"

"Listen, son," she said, pointing a finger at me (and believe me, I went for that "son" business), "here's the way it is. I read the Bible and I believe what it says, and one thing I keep repeating is this: 'I am come that they might have life, and that they might have it more abundantly.'* And do you know something? The Bible doesn't qualify that promise by saying except if you are in a wheelchair minus a leg and if you are ninety years old, or what. It just promises abundant life—period. And so I repeat this promise to myself and take abundant life and I'm happy and I have a ball."

Quite a contrast to the "old man" who told me in a half-quavering voice that he was sixty-nine and said, "Don't let anyone kid you. It's hell getting old. It's day-by-day deterioration and just plain misery. And I'd just about as soon get the whole thing over with, and fast. And," he continued, "I was full of enthusiasm once, same as you are."

"What happened to your enthusiasm?" I asked.

"I'm getting old, I tell you, and you can't be old and have enthusiasm."

Which is, of course, a dogmatic and erroneous assertion based on highly personalized, negative opinion. The fact that a ninety-year-old one-legged woman could be perpetually enthusiastic and a sixty-nine-year-old two-legged man felt otherwise does not prove his didactic assertion that one cannot be of senior status and enthusiastic simultaneously.

* John 10:10.

HOW ONE MAN GOT TURNED ON

It was a hot day in the convention hall of a Florida east coast hotel. I was the speaker at the morning session of a national convention, and could look from the platform directly out at the beach where the rolling sea was breaking in surf on the shore. That sight of the cool seawater looked good, for the air conditioning was not working too well that day. Everyone had removed his coat except me, and I was anything but comfortable. I determined to finish my talk and get out into that ocean as soon as possible.

Diving into the waves, I came up beside another swimmer. We passed the usual greetings, then, apparently not recognizing me, the man asked, "Were you in the convention meeting this morning?"

"Yes, I was there," I replied.

"Then you heard that talk by Peale."

"Yes, I heard it."

"Well," he continued, "What did you think of it?"

I hesitated to comment upon my own speech, so I countered with, "What did you think of it?" He started to give me his opinion and, not being sure what his appraisal might be, I plunged into a convenient wave as he started talking and came up as he was finishing his comments. I said to him, "Look, my friend, I'd better level with you and tell you that I am Peale." Whereupon he plunged into a wave! I never did know his opinion. We both laughed, and after a good swim we sat on the beach and chatted for a while.

"You were talking about enthusiasm at the convention," he said, "and that is a very important quality for anyone to have. Trouble is, I get steamed up about a new project but after a while that enthusiasm starts cooling off. I just can't seem to hang in there and keep motivated. Really, I believe I could move up in our company if I didn't goof off so often. What do you suppose is wrong with a guy who has the know-how and experience but just plain runs out of gas?" The question indicated a rather common problem, and he continued, "If you've got a moment, how about giving me some practical suggestions for getting turned on and keeping it going that way?" The man seemed genuinely concerned, so I suggested the following thoughts for his consideration:

1. The secret of changing one's personality, regardless of the problem, is to think in new categories. This might mean a re-education of the thought pattern so that enthusiasm is put into the top-

priority category. To change the routine of being enthused only to have it begin to reduce, one needs to think in terms of renewal, replenishment and reinvigoration. The mind will, in time, accept the concept of undiminished supply, and this use of the positive principle will lead to perpetuity of enthusiasm.

2. Begin at once the mental practice of seeing yourself as a completely different person, an altogether new individual. This new person would be one who was never variable or mercurial but constantly the same, always vital, vigorous, excited. That which we constantly image will emerge as fact.
3. Employ creative word therapy. This means to change a personality defect by the use of corrective words. For example, a person afflicted by tension, let us say, might articulate such words as "serenity," "imperturbability," "quietness." The repetitive saying of the word tends to induce the concept for which words are symbols. So, to upgrade enthusiasm, set aside a few minutes every day to say aloud such words as "exciting," "dynamic," "marvelous," "fabulous," "terrific." I admitted that the idea might seem a bit corny, but nevertheless it is a fact that the unconscious mind will ultimately accept repetitive suggestions strongly affirmed.
4. Finally I described how helpful in maintaining my own enthusiasm at high level was the daily morning practice of a particular affirmation of enthusiasm. This one sentence has changed not a few persons from being desultory to being continually powered with enthusiasm: "This is the day that the Lord has made; I will rejoice and be glad in it."*

My swimming companion apparently found these suggestions of practical value, for later he reported that he had "really put this enthusiasm formula into operation, with incredible results." What the results were he did not say, but that they proved effective was evidenced by the enthusiasm with which he reported.

OLD AGE AND ENTHUSIASM

This book may be read by people who have accumulated some years, and for them, as for all of us, enthusiasm is important. I want to touch on the

* Psalm 118:24 (paraphrased).

positive principles operational in this area (and will have more to say about this subject in Chapter 12). I like the position of Russell A. Kemp, who in his book *Live Youthfully Now** says, "Time has no power to age me. We do not live by time," he points out, "but by God's creative and re-creative life force within. And that life force is not regulated by a human time system, which is an arbitrary, man-made chronology measurement. With God, 'a thousand years in thy sight are but as yesterday when it is past, and as a watch in the night.' "†

It is true that all our lives we are conditioned to assume that mental and physical vigor is supposed to decline after we have made, say, sixty or seventy or eighty trips around the sun on a whirling sphere called earth. I heard a man say one evening as we sat by the fireplace in his home and listened to the romantic ticking of an old Seth Thomas clock, "This clock is ticking my life away." But no instrument manufactured a hundred years or so ago can determine the quality of anyone's life. No mechanism for time measurement should cause a person one day to say, "Now I'm old; the end is near."

Old age may perhaps more properly be thought of as a state of mind in which certain mental attitudes, built by customary and traditional thinking into the conscious and unconscious mind, convince us that the life force is declining and we are therefore expected to think aged, act aged and, in fact, be aged. That fascinating description of aging in the Bible says nothing about time measurements such as minutes, days, weeks or years but refers, rather, to deteriorating mental attitudes. "When they shall be afraid of that which is high [i.e., when they shall have lost enthusiasm, or when the positive principle has sagged], and fears shall be in the way . . ."‡

It is altogether likely that people of all ages—so-called old age as well as those of fewer or younger years—can live better, healthier, happier lives by getting turned on to self-repeating enthusiasm. The real fountain of youth is not to be discovered by a Ponce de León hunting in some magic isle, but, rather, in revitalized attitudes of mind. And certainly it is present in the dynamic thought that we can live youthfully now and always. I have never forgotten something that was said to me by former Postmaster General James A. Farley. I asked how he accounted for the

* Published by Unity Books, Unity Village, MO 64063.

† Psalm 90:4.

‡ Ecclesiastes 12:5.

seemingly slight effect the passing years had on him. His reply was classic: "I never think any old thoughts."

LIVE YOUTHFULLY NOW

"If most of us surrender to the passing of years," says Mr. Kemp,* "and let them make us old, but certain others defy the passage of an even greater number of years and retain the vigor and enjoyment of life associated with youth, can it be possible that aging is really our own fault? Is the effect that passing years have on our body really an individual matter? Here is what some modern medical scientists have to say upon this point.

"After a conference of medical and surgical specialists at the Decourcy Clinic in Cincinnati some years ago, the following report was issued: 'Time is not toxic. All of those who develop a time-neurosis subscribe to the prevalent superstition that time is in some way a poison exerting a mysterious cumulative action . . . time has no effect on human tissues under any conditions . . . vigor does not necessarily vary inversely with the age of an adult. Belief in the effects of time by those who subscribe to such a belief is the thing that acts as a poison.'

"To put it another way, there is no scientific basis for believing, as most of us do, that the passage of years automatically causes our body to age. [And, presumably, that would go for spirit and mind as well.] 'It is ignorance of the truth about the passage of time,' the report continues, 'that causes us to cringe in fear before the accumulation of years. We need not surrender to age, if our mind is sufficiently enlightened.' "

Mr. Kemp continues by telling us that a Michigan doctor, Frederick C. Swartz, debunked the so-called infirmities of age. " 'The forgetful mind, the doddering gait, the shaky hand—these are caused by the lack of physical and mental exertion, and not by the passage of time. There are no diseases caused by the mere passage of time. Our present conception of the aging process must be shattered, and our already brainwashed oldsters made to see the nature of their ailments. Daily mental and physical exercise practiced with some degree of self-discipline should raise the life-expectancy figure ten years in one generation.'

"Dr. Swartz spoke of the fatal concept that debilities come with age, and that at sixty-five one is 'over the hill.' If accepted, this condemns one

* *Live Youthfully Now*, p. 19.

to a period of ever-narrowing horizons, until the final sparks of living are the psychoneurotic concerns with the workings of his own body."

ENTHUSIASM KEY TO CONTINUOUS YOUTH

One wonders if an enthusiastic young person who kept it going all his life could not restrain and slow up the aging process. A philosopher may have spoken a wise insight when he said, "The secret of genius is to carry the spirit of the child into old age." Children are by nature enthusiastic, and the effective person retains that spirit throughout his entire life. As Wordsworth has it, "Trailing clouds of glory . . . we come from God, who is our home."* The child remains dynamic, excited, interested, eager—until a negative time concept gets in its deadly work; and the jaded so-called sophistication of our time takes its toll; until it may be said, as the poet expressed so graphically:

The youth, who daily farther from the east
Must travel, still is Nature's priest,
And by the vision splendid
Is on his way attended;
At length the man perceives it die away,
And fade into the light of common day.†

Indeed, it could be that the saddest phenomenon in the developing life of any individual is the decay of enthusiasm. But this sad process need not take place if creative and positive thought is made a consistent practice. And, if the mind has not been disciplined to those practices that are propitious to the maintenance of enthusiasm, it is always possible to begin a program of cultivation at any time. And inevitably, with such revamping will come a powerful rebirth or rejuvenation of personality force and, who knows, perhaps of physical force as well!

The methods of developing a self-repeating enthusiasm that will not run down may not be easy, but still they are not all that difficult, either.

A case in point is that of the professional copywriter who complained that he had gone stale in his job. Fresh ideas would no longer come. His

* *Ode* "Intimations of Immortality," lines 64–65.

† *Ibid.*, lines 71–76.

copy ran too long and had no flow of thought or expression. It was stilted and lacked the power to communicate. "And communication is my business," he concluded glumly. The reason he gave for all this was that his enthusiasm had leaked out. Nothing seemed to motivate or activate him any longer. The bottom had dropped out of his spirit. "It's too bad," he remarked wryly, "that you cannot go to the corner drugstore and buy a bottle of enthusiasm elixir."

MEDICINE NOT IN A BOTTLE

"But there is a cure," I reminded him. "The medicine for it is not contained in a bottle but is a concept in your mind. And it isn't a complex procedure to get enthusiasm going again. All you need is to start acting enthusiastic and continue to so act until in time you become enthusiastic." I then called his attention to the famous principle announced by Professor William James, who was considered by some to be the father of psychological science, which he described as the "as if" principle. This means simply that by acting as you wish yourself to be, in due course you will become as you act. If you are fearful, act as if you had courage. Continue to act courageously and ultimately your fear will diminish as courage increases. If you are inclined to criticize, start acting generously, placing the best connotation on everyone and everything, and you will become less critical and more compassionate.

The principle operates similarly in the matter of increasing enthusiasm. Begin to act enthusiastically. At first the effort may appear ineffective and even phony or insincere, inasmuch as you do not feel enthusiastic. But persevere, and, surprisingly, you will become increasingly enthusiastic. It is a law of behavior described as the "as if" principle.

But I only half persuaded the glum and unenthusiastic writer, for he apparently thought the idea too simple. Being insecure, he felt that he could shore up his basic negativism only with an intellectual system of complexities. Later he attended a meeting where I was addressing a large audience of sales people on the subject "Why Positive Thinkers Get Positive Results," and made the points that successful achievement is based on these premises: 1. Cool, rational thinking, not heated emotional reaction, leads to the solution of problems. 2. Never think negatively, for the negative thinker does a very dangerous thing. He pumps out negative thoughts into the world around him and thus activates that world negatively. On the basis of the law of attraction—like attracts like—he tends to draw back to himself negative results. 3. There is value in thinking and acting enthusiastically.

As an illustration of this third point, I suggested that every man in the audience could make the next day the best in his life. The method for so doing was not to lie in bed moaning, groaning and grumbling as usual, pouring into the ears of his patient and long-suffering wife his aches, pains and negativisms. Instead, when he awoke he was to throw back the bedcovers with a gesture of masterful self-assertion and leap out of bed, exclaiming to his startled wife, "Honey, I feel wonderful."

Of course, she might very well have a heart attack and expire on the spot! But she would die happy. Then, this man was to sing in the shower, thereby washing out of mind all the old, tired, dead thoughts of yesterday while washing the body with soap and water. After this, feeling alive to the fingertips, he was to get dressed and descend to the dining room and sit down to the breakfast his wife had so thoughtfully and lovingly prepared for him. He was to take a long, respectful look at that breakfast and say, "Honey, this is by all odds the most magnificent breakfast I ever sat down to." That assuredly would inspire her so that the next day he would not need to lie about it!

START THE DAY WITH ENTHUSIASTIC ATTITUDES

Then, having put under his belt a good, man-sized breakfast, he was to go out into the crisp morning air and stand tall, reaching for the sky with the crown of his head. He was to kiss his wife good-bye with enthusiasm, and I suggested that he go so far as to pick her up and swing her around. I admitted that for some that would be quite a tussle, but it would transmit enthusiasm to her.

Then, standing in the brisk morning air, he was to say, "Honey, do you know something? I'm going to go downtown today and deal in goods and services [or sell, or write, or manage] with enthusiasm, and I'm going to have the time of my life all day long." Finally, he was to gather his little family about him and offer a prayer. "How," I asked, "do you expect to get anywhere without recourse to the Great Power?" But if he did not know a prayer, I suggested a very short one in affirmative form, one that I personally use every day and without which I just could not get along. "This is the day that the Lord has made; I will rejoice and be glad in it."

Well, as I say, my unenthusiastic writer friend listened to this whimsical sort of suggestion made to the audience in my talk. Afterward he confessed that at first it seemed a bit farfetched and a kind of put-on. But as he thought it over he realized that the decision to be negative or positive, glum or enthusiastic, was to be made in one's own thinking and action. "Believe it or not," he said a bit defensively, "I tried that crazy morning technique of yours and what do you know? It has already begun to work. Even my wife gets a big kick out of it. Says I'm different and a lot of fun. So I buy that 'as if' principle. I'm convinced that as I act out enthusiasm, enthusiasm does indeed return to me."

"MUCH TOO MUCH" AND ENTHUSIASM DRAIN-OFF

Some people who get into a hectic, "much-too-much" sort of living pattern complain that it's all so hard and demanding that enthusiasm is knocked right out of them. For example, I'm told that some wives seem to resent the term "housewife" as being in some way derogatory. They complain that housework—cooking, washing, cleaning—is drudgery and indeed a form of slavery imposed on them by male chauvinists. Of course such daily tasks can become tiresome, and with that we are sympathetic. But even the maternal instinct, the love and joy of caring for children, seems boring, not to the majority, of course, but still apparently to a fair number, judging from what I hear. And I've heard not a few husbands gripe about working around the house after coming home from a hard day at the office and having to "fix this" and "fix that." Many husbands work enthusiastically all day long, then come home and revert into gloomy negativists, making life miserable for hardworking wives.

Well, I know two couples who represent the opposite ends of the enthusiasm spectrum, and both shall be nameless, for they wouldn't like this form of publicity. Strangely enough, each couple is approximately the same age and each has four boys, the last one just a baby. Of one complaining couple I asked, "How come you had these four boys if they annoy you so? What do you want—to be out dancing and partying every night? How about responsibility and maturity? Why all this playboy stuff?" I knew this young couple had quality of character; it just was not coming through at the time.

"Oh, it's all so lousy dull" was the reply. "It's just nothing but work, work, work, and noise and more noise. Haven't we got a right to our own lives?"

"Where is your enthusiasm for the wonderful and exciting opportunity to be parents and have a terrific family life with four growing boys? Just think of it—four of the most interesting characters in the world, four alive, healthy and vigorous boys."

"Okay, play it up as you will, but we have had just more than we can take." So ended an expression of futility at its insipid ultimate.

The second couple? Well, I met them in a restaurant recently. Daddy, it seemed, had taken Mommy out for dinner and they were both enjoying it, but obviously could hardly wait to get home to those four terrific kids.

"Bill and I have such an exciting time with our four boys. They are each different and so terribly interesting as personalities. Hasn't the Lord been good to us?"

"Come on, Jane, hurry with that chocolate mousse and let's get home. I promised to tell the boys that story about the magic airplane."

Let us hope the first couple gets turned on with enthusiasm for home and family before it's too late and the boys have left home emotionally marred. And let us hope the second couple will never lose that top skill of successful living—to keep enthusiasm going.

TIREDNESS AND ENTHUSIASM

Let's face it. Getting tired and worn out with unremitting demands exerts a strong draw against enthusiasm for all of us. The solution is to mingle interests into a creative life pattern. In the case of the second couple, they are both active in church work. The husband is a member of the board of deacons, the wife is superintendent of the beginner's department. She also takes leadership in a woman's club once a month, and he bowls every other week. They get out together for an occasional golf game. They are part of a couples group that meets around at homes with people who also have children. "Someday," said Jane, "I'm going to have a second career, but meanwhile my kids are my first career. And just in case you are wondering—yes, I feel liberated and very creative."

The other couple, the two people for whom enthusiasm had seemingly leaked away, had apparently been thus far unable to cope with the continuous demands of family life due to their value pattern, which gave precedence to social engagements. Theirs, it might seem, was primarily a priority problem and, not having worked out a balanced activity system, one that gave the parental function its due relationship to other aspects of life, they tended to react resentfully.

A new turn-on of enthusiasm could help give a more comprehensive mingling of interesting activities, which most well-organized and with-it people can effect. Indeed, organization itself contributes to the development of enthusiasm, and lack of it can produce the worn-out attitude that siphons off enthusiasm. It's not all that simple to get run down with weariness and at the same time stay up strong with enthusiasm. But as one seeks to do just that, hard or not, the result is greatly to diminish the weariness. Enthusiasm, in a deep sense and a solid one, is an energy-producer and, instead of reducing vitality, it tends to accentuate vitality due to its mental and emotional stimulation.

Tough blows coming one after another may understandably reduce the quality of living enthusiastically, at least temporarily, and if a person reacts in this manner, he is entitled to sympathetic appreciation of his problem. But still, the application of a solid and normal enthusiasm, despite a series of difficult experiences, can do much to nullify harsh effects and, indeed, to help the individual to rise above the blows he has suffered.

The ability to meet adversity and failure, sorrow and misfortune, with a smile and never to lose enthusiasm but to keep going at a high level is one of the most exciting demonstrations of the positive principle. But the persons who do this successfully and come through to new achievements are those who have something inside, something called faith and confidence and belief. They learn how to meet trouble with high heart. They never panic, but always keep thinking and probing for answers and for solutions. For them, a failure is but an incident in a success-motivated life; an incident from which they draw know-how and experience and added strength. Because always when you suffer a setback and overcome it, you emerge stronger than before. The following may be a bit grim as an illustration, but it makes a point: The American Indians once believed that when a brave scalped an enemy, the strength of that warrior passed into him. Many scalps of enemies meant more strength to the victor. It could be that the more big hardships you overcome, the stronger you are thereby.

People with enthusiasm of the self-repeating variety have an incalculable asset going for them, one that compensates for other deficiencies that they may possess. Some, for example, may be lacking in education, but if they have a vital and constantly revitalized enthusiasm, they ignore drawbacks and just go out and do a superior job. Like the story of "The New Salesman," which someone gave me not long ago:

> A new salesman wrote his first report to the home office and it stunned the brass to learn that obviously the "new hope" was a blithering illiterate. He

wrote: "I seen this outfit which they ain't never bought a dime's worth of nothing from us and sole them a couple thousand dollars worth of guds. I am now going to Chicago." Before the illiterate could be given the heave-ho by his manager, another report came in: "I cum here and sole them a half-millyun." Fearful if he did and fearful if he didn't fire the peddler, the sales manager dumped the problem into the lap of the company's president. The following morning, members of the Ivory Tower were flabbergasted to see the two letters on the bulletin board and this letter from the president tacked above them. "We ben spending to much time trying to spel instead of trying to sel. Let's watch them sails! I want everybody should read them letters from Cooch who is on the rode and doing a grate job for us and should go out and do like he dun!"

"THINGS ARE TERRIFIC—TERRIFIC"

W. Clement Stone, Chicago industrialist and philanthropist, began his life career at age six by selling newspapers on the South Side. By strong determination and positive thinking he became one of the top salesmen in this country. The more money he made (and he made plenty), the more he gave away to help poor boys and girls, to rehabilitate prisoners, to advance mental health, to strengthen religion, the arts and sciences. Indeed, the late Dr. Arnaud C. Marts, one of the greatest American fund-raisers for benevolent purposes, said, "Clem Stone is the most generous man I have ever known."

Mr. Stone sometimes overextends himself by giving so much that it threatens to impair his resources, and he, like all businessmen, suffers the ups and downs of the economy. But always he comes back, because he is a comeback sort of man.

Never in all the vicissitudes of his personal and business life have I ever known him to show one moment of depreciated enthusiasm. Whenever I have picked up the telephone and asked him how he is and how things are going, always in strong voice and strong spirit I have received the very alive answer, "Terrific, absolutely terrific!" Is this bravado or a superficial denial of trouble? Not at all. For this man knows the score. He is aware of difficulty, realistically aware. But the difference between Mr. Stone and some others is an interesting one. Mr. Stone likes success for the pleasure of succeeding, of overcoming difficulty. To him the resulting money is regarded as a tool by which to do good, raise the level of life, and motivate others to the potentials inherent within themselves. His enthusiasm is based on a burning desire to stimulate others to move up, always to move up.

As a result, in dark days as well as in sunny days, his reactions are always the same—terrific, terrific. He was turned on to enthusiasm as a ragged street urchin selling papers, and in a career of meeting roadblock after roadblock he has kept it going ever since. His method for doing this, as I have studied him, is never to react emotionally to what happens but always to look for and find in every circumstance the good that is surely present there. He believes that to every disadvantage there is a corresponding advantage. With this dispassionate attitude of cool, factual thinking, his batting average of successes over failures is remarkable. And the ability never to allow a setback to reduce enthusiasm has kept this man going, always going, through rough seas as well as calm waters. He is an outstanding example of the positive principle in action.

"HE TURNED ME ON"

On an airplane I sat by a young man, an outgoing, interesting fellow. He told me that he had been a hostile kid on drugs and had always been dodging the police. Then he was induced to read a book by Mr. Stone.* For the first time in his mixed-up life this boy had a flicker of hope that he might become, as he put it, "a somebody." "That book turned me on, and I mean turned me on," he said in a voice that shook just enough to betray emotion. "I think I've got the enthusiasm to keep going no matter what tough breaks I may meet up with."

PERSONAL EXPERIENCE OF ENTHUSIASM

I have my own method for getting turned on with self-repeating enthusiasm, and the procedure has worked well in my experience. Actually I'm sure that I have a greater enthusiasm now than at any previous time, and indeed it seems to increase in depth and quality. As a boy I was terrifically enthusiastic, but personal inner conflicts sometimes took the bloom off. Fortunately, that seems no longer a problem, for, having solved those

* *The Success System That Never Fails.*

conflicts, there remains little to interfere with a free flow of enthusiastic motivation.

This is not to say that there are no problems. Indeed, there are plenty of them, but finally I learned to tackle these difficulties with a positive assurance of dealing with them successfully. Naturally I have my "down" moments but not so many as formerly, nor do they last so long as they once did. This, of course, represents no perfection on my part. All it says, and believe me it is a lot, is that by the grace of God I finally found the answer to living a happy, exciting, and victorious life; and as a result learned how to get turned on with a self-repeating enthusiasm. So let me tell you how it came about for what it may be worth to you.

Back in 1932 I became minister of the Marble Collegiate Church on Fifth Avenue in New York City. For five years I had led a successful church in Syracuse where everything was going smoothly, indeed very well, and I myself was charged up with boundless enthusiasm. Then I received a call to this famous church. But things are not always the way they appear and I soon became aware that this church had problems. In fact, the congregation had dwindled to about two hundred persons. Sundays the big church was almost empty. It was the time of the Great Depression of the early thirties, and dollars were scarce. In Syracuse I'd had it good, something that certainly could not be said of this new responsibility.

Naturally I gave the job all I had of thought, energy, prayer, and indeed everything it takes to make things go, but they just did not go at all, or at the best, slowly. Every Sunday I looked out at rows of empty seats and big vacant balconies and from Monday to Saturday wondered where I was going to get the money to pay the bills.

After some months my energy began to run out. Mentally I became really discouraged and the natural enthusiasm which before had carried me over many a hurdle went down the drain. Finally I had to admit I'd about had it. I never quite came to the point of quitting, but still couldn't get much lower and really hit bottom. Then I learned a fabulous truth, a factor basic to the positive principle, that the bottom is really a great place. For when you hit bottom you've gone down as far as you can go. The only direction from there is up.

To get away for a vacation and hopefully a new perspective, my wife and I went to the Lake District in northern England. There I moped about daily pouring a lot of negativism into my poor wife's ears until finally she became fed up with it. She led me to a bench in a far corner of the beautiful garden of the hotel. She proceeded to imply that I was considerably less than a man to let my problems throw me, and how come I had the audacity to advocate a victorious way of life and at the same time be so defeated myself?

She then informed me, and gentle lady that she is she can be pretty tough, that I was going to remain on that bench until I had "turned my life with all of its problems over to God." While officially I was her pastor as well as her husband, she was taking over as my pastor. And believe me she knew how to handle a case like me. She told me what to do and how to do it.

Finally I prayed, at her direction, a simple prayer. It went something like this: "Dear Lord, I can't handle my life. My problems have me licked. I need help. So I turn my life over to You here and now."

This produced a strange and remarkable effect. It seemed that all dark thoughts immediately left my mind. A remarkable feeling of peace came over me. I now knew for sure that God and I together could handle that church. I found myself sort of walking on air. And the old enthusiasm and excitement came surging back! Plans and ideas and innovations bombarded my mind and I could hardly wait to get home to implement them.

I can honestly say that from that experience on a bench in that English garden until the present I have been turned on with self-repeating enthusiasm. Ruth and I have returned several times to sit on that bench. But a revisit hasn't been necessary really. It is only a sort of pilgrimage to a spot where something unforgettable happened. Find your own bench somewhere . . . but get turned on.

And that is a vital secret of successful living—to get turned on with self-repeating enthusiasm, in-depth enthusiasm, and to keep the positive principle going.

Let us recapitulate the methods for keeping enthusiasm operating at high levels suggested in this chapter:

1. Study the source of enthusiasm of the ninety-year-old one-legged woman who accepted as fact the promise of abundant life.
2. Don't see yourself as old and getting older, as one who has just about had it because time has passed, even lots of time.
3. Live youthfully now—and always.
4. Never forget that all the enthusiasm you need is in your mind. Let it out—let it live—let it motivate you.
5. Practice thinking enthusiasm—practice turning your thoughts on to enthusiasm.

6. Act as if you had enthusiasm. Believe that you have it and you will be enthusiastic.
7. Never let the swamped feeling dampen enthusiasm. Keep the positive principle going with enthusiasm and nothing will ever be too much for you.
8. Cushion the painful effects of hard blows by keeping enthusiasm going strong, even if doing so requires struggle.
9. Always take the attitude that you can make things *terrific—terrific*—no matter the hazards. Indeed, the "terrific—terrific" attitude can nullify hazards.
10. Affirm enthusiasm—affirm, affirm, affirm.

FIFTH WAY TO KEEP THE POSITIVE PRINCIPLE GOING

Drop Old, Tired, Gloomy Thoughts and Come Alive

New Year's Eve in Rome! It was really something and totally unlike anything we had previously experienced. As longtime residents of New York City, which can notably celebrate any event, nothing my wife and I ever witnessed at home could remotely compare with the turn-of-the-year observance in the Eternal City.

It all started about noon on December 31 with the booming of guns, a mounting crescendo of noisemakers; everywhere great reverberations. As night came on, tracer flashes cut the sky until finally at the stroke of midnight bedlam broke forth with cannonading from every quarter, underscoring the enormous concert of sound magnified and magnified. As we looked from the window toward the dome of St. Peter's with tracers leaping all about it, the effect was as if some huge army were attacking the city. (And the hotel manager told us that he had given us a quiet room!)

But this was not all. The Romans seem to have an idea that New Year's Eve is the appropriate time to rid themselves of the old and take on the new, not symbolically but practically, by throwing out of the window any old thing, such as a dress, a suit, cracked dishes, a dilapidated chair. Our Roman friends warned us to stay in our hotel to avoid the possibility of an old television set or something equally devastating bouncing off our heads.

The idea is a sound one not only for New Year's Eve but also every day, and the throwaway of the old might properly go far beyond unwanted objects to the disposal of all old, tired, gloomy thoughts. Every night before retiring, the ritual of mental thought-emptying will get the mind into good working order for the succeeding day. So every night deliberately drop those old, tired, gloomy thoughts and come alive.

LESSON FROM A TAILOR

Years ago in Brooklyn I had a good friend who was also my tailor. When Mr. S. Pearson made a suit he also gave instructions for keeping it in good shape. "Every night at bedtime," he said, "remove everything from every pocket to prevent sagging of the garment." He then showed how to hang trousers with the lower part of one leg folded over the other on the hanger so that the trousers hung suspended, thus tending to eliminate wrinkles.

Like most men, I carry a wallet, a credit card case, keys, pencils and pens. I also carry with me miniature scissors for clipping out interesting articles. My pockets constitute a filing system for all sorts of notations and memos accumulated during the day and even some from days past. My pocket-emptying program stimulated the process of consolidating and laying those memos in one place. And what a pleasure to check off the ones that had been attended to, then to toss them one by one into the wastebasket. I put out on the dresser, along with keys, et cetera, notes to be handled tomorrow. The mass of reminders was in this fashion kept to a well-organized and manageable number and helped send me to bed with a mind at peace and a minimal feeling of guilt about things undone.

After performing this suit-emptying ritual for some weeks and experiencing the relief of dealing efficiently with notes and memos, the idea got through to me of employing the same procedure on the thoughts one accumulates, the worn-out attitudes, the gloomy impressions, regrets, discouragements with which the mind becomes cluttered. Accordingly, I began to bring up and do something about all the old, tired, dead, gloomy thoughts and consciously visualize them as passing out of consciousness, somewhat like watching them flow down a drain. I affirmed, "These thoughts are now flowing out of my mind—out of my mind. They are passing from me—passing, passing, now this very moment passing away."

Following this affirmation I employed the suggestion made by M. R. Kopmeyer in one of his books* relative to a quick falling asleep by "seeing" a dense fog swirling and spreading across consciousness, blotting everything out completely. I found that sleep was induced much more quickly by this procedure; thoughts that otherwise might have agitated the mind were lost in the heavy padded vagueness of that impenetrable fog which established an effective barrier between mind and the active world. The result was sound and restful sleep from which I awoke feeling a boundless sense of new life. This program helped reactivate the energy and vitality needed for each succeeding day. It became for me one viable method by which to keep inspiration going.

HE DID A JOB ON HIS THOUGHTS

A man told me he was having a lot of trouble with himself. "You are not the only one," I reflected, thinking of the many letters I receive from people who ask for help with problems. And also thinking of myself; for I must admit that the person who has caused me the most trouble over the years has been Norman Vincent Peale. And most people will admit to the same, I believe, if they tell the full truth about themselves. If we are our own chief problem, the basic reason may be found in the type of thoughts which habitually occupy and direct our minds.

At least this was the conclusion reached by the man mentioned above. He was a person who genuinely desired to do a constructive job and he studied to perfect his work performance by attending professional seminars and sales motivational meetings. Also he was an avid reader of inspirational and self-help books. I came to know him when he wrote me after reading *The Power of Positive Thinking*. He was a sincere student who definitely worked at putting the book's principles into practice.

By such exposure he would in each instance become inspired and take on a strong, fresh motivation. But seemingly he could not hold his inspiration beyond a certain time frame. There would come a gradual reversal. Inspiration would start declining, excitement die down, energy lessen, motivation slow up. This process of motivational buildup and decline was repeated a number of times. He just could not seem to keep a positive mental attitude going without a reversal pattern taking place.

* *Here's Help!* P.O. Box 6302, Louisville, Ky. 40207.

When enthusiastically motivated he could sell very effectively and would move up into a higher echelon of opportunity in his organization. But when a decline in spirit attacked him, the decline in sales performance was in direct proportion to the falling off of his mental and spirit vibrancy.

This up-and-down reaction was naturally disturbing and he wrote at some length describing the mercurial nature of his responses. I suggested that he enter upon a course of psychological counseling. My personal opinion was that the problem lay somewhere in his intellectual-emotional balance system. But he lived some two thousand miles away, so I suggested that he get help locally, which he did to good effect.

In replying to his letter, apparently I unconsciously contributed a thought which may have turned the tide of his career. Somewhere a long time ago I read a quotation, for which I have never known the source, to the effect that "history turns on small hinges." Similarly, it may be assumed that the history of a personal life can turn on an offhand suggestion. In my message to him I quoted a line from the Bible: "Be renewed in the spirit of your mind."* This suggestion was made because of the fact that "running down" often originates in attitudes before it becomes evidenced in performance.

HE GETS A NEW SPIRIT GOING

Months later when I waited my turn to speak at a sales convention in the Rocky Mountain area, this man introduced himself, reminding me of his letter and my reply. He said that the statement from the Scriptures had done more to bring about a change in him than even the counseling sessions he had undertaken, which had been very helpful.

Just what does "renewed in the spirit of your mind" really mean? It puzzled our friend at first, but the idea really "grabbed" his thinking. He knew what was meant by team spirit, school spirit, company spirit—a kind of esprit de corps, a deep feeling interfused with loyalty and a carry-on-no-matter-what attitude. The process of thinking, he reasoned, was perhaps more than an intellectual exercise. There had to be such a thing as a spirit in the mind, which must surely mean an emotionally tinged attitude of commitment, dedication, renewal—in a word, inspiration—which he now saw clearly meant to be inspirited or filled full of

* Ephesians 4:23.

spirit. In other words, a liveliness that cannot be depressed but continues with vigor, whatever the circumstances.

"As a result of thinking along this line," he said, "I came up with four principles which enabled me not only to be motivated, but to keep that spirit of motivation going, unaffected by setbacks or resistances.

"1. At all times I had to maintain the 'keep-it-going' attitude.

"2. I had to cultivate my spirit quality to assure that I could sustain the 'keep-it-going' attitude in good days or bad.

"3. I had to renew myself on a spiritual basis if I expected to be renewed constantly in the spirit of my mind.

"4. I had to believe and affirm that nothing could anymore take the bloom off my spirit."

That these four principles had worked effectively in the personality and, consequently, in the career of this man was evident not only in attitude but also factually in his achievement record. "If you use this story," he cautioned, "I ask that my name not be mentioned, for I believe that my taking any credit for changing a spiritual basis of life can break the power flow, and the flow of spirit power is of first importance to me. Some amazing things started happening in my life and to me personally. Then changes came in my family and in my business when I really got down to it and did a job on my thoughts. But in the last analysis it was the revamping of the spirit that effected the greatest change in me and in everything with which I am connected," he concluded.

LOVE CANCELS OUT GLOOMY THOUGHTS

In dropping old, tired, dead thoughts and coming alive I discovered early in my own personal experience that the simple practice of outgoing love toward people is almost magically effective. Whenever I detect that my thoughts are going stale, I deliberately search for some opportunity to express love by a thoughtful and kindly act, and if I do enough of this, a new vigor, even fervor, shows in my mental state. And along with it, a revitalized feeling of aliveness and sensitivity becomes evident. To me this practice is of tremendous importance.

Moreover, even a return in memory to personal experiences of proffered goodwill and compassion has the effect of washing out of mind the accumulation of old, tired, gloomy thoughts which constantly recur unless arrested by some stronger mental force. A powerful curative process of mental and spiritual attitudes is brought to bear by the infusion of caring thoughts followed by caring action.

I would like to relate three stories, all of them strangely enough, associated with Christmases of other years. But each has lingered in mind, and while of course I try to do kindly deeds currently, the memory of the following very human incidents still possesses the power to help me drop the old, tired, listless or gloomy thoughts that, in all of us, are always endeavoring to take over our consciousness.

IT HAPPENED ON A CINCINNATI STREET

Some of my most impressionable boyhood years were spent in Cincinnati, Ohio. I still remember the huge Christmas tree in Fountain Square—the gleaming decorations, the frosty streets ringing with the sound of carols. Up on East Liberty Street where we lived, our mother and father always had a Christmas tree with real candles on it, magical candles which, combined with the fir tree, gave off a foresty aroma, unique and unforgettable.

One Christmas Eve when I was twelve, I was out with my minister father doing some late Christmas shopping. We were both loaded down with packages and I was getting tired of it and a bit cross. I was thinking how good it would be to get home, when a beggar—a bleary-eyed, unshaven, dirty old man—came up to me, touched my arm with a hand like a claw, and asked for money. He was so repulsive that instinctively I recoiled. Softly my father said, "Norman, it's Christmas Eve. You shouldn't treat a man that way."

I was unrepentant. "Dad," I complained, "he's nothing but a bum."

My father spoke strongly. "Maybe he hasn't made much of himself, but he's still a child of God." He then handed me a dollar—a lot of money for those days and certainly for a preacher's income. "I want you to take this and give it to that man," he said. "Speak to him respectfully. Tell him you are giving it to him in Christ's name."

"Oh, Dad," I protested, "I can't do anything like that."

My father's voice was firm. "Go and do as I tell you."

So, reluctant and resisting. I ran after the old man and said, "Excuse me, sir. I give you this money in the name of Christ."

He stared at the dollar bill, then looked at me in utter amazement. A wonderful smile came to his face, a smile so full of life and beauty that

I forgot that he was dirty and unshaven. I forgot that he was ragged and old. With a gesture that was almost courtly, he took off his hat. Graciously he said, "And I thank you, young sir, in the name of Christ."

All my irritation, all my annoyance faded away. The street, the houses, everything around me suddenly seemed beautiful because I had been part of a miracle that I have seen many times since—the transformation that comes over people when you think of them as children of God, when you offer them love in the name of a Baby born two thousand years ago in a stable in Bethlehem, a Person who still lives and walks with us and makes His presence known.

That was my Christmas discovery that year—the gold of human dignity that lies hidden in every living soul, waiting to shine through if only we'll give it a chance. Early in life I began to understand that the positive principle is deeply part of loving human relationships, and for that insight I am very grateful.

DRAMA AT LIFE'S END

The telephone call to my father came late at night, and from a most unlikely place—a house in what was called in those days the red-light district of the city. The woman who operated the house said that one of the girls was very ill, perhaps even dying. And the girl in her illness kept calling for a minister. Somehow the woman had heard of my father, pastor of a well-known church. Would he come?

My father never failed to respond to any human appeal. Quietly he explained to my mother where he was going. Then his eyes fell upon me. "Get your coat, Norman," he said, "I want you to come too."

My mother was aghast. "You don't mean you'd take a fifteen-year-old boy into a place like that!"

My father said, "There's a lot of sin and sadness and despair in human life. Norman can't be shielded from it forever."

We walked through the snowy streets and I remember how the Christmas trees glowed and winked in the darkness. We came to the place, a big old frame house. A woman opened the door and led us to an upstairs room. There, lying in a big brass bed, was a pathetic, almost doll-like young girl, so white and frail that she seemed like a child, scarcely older than I was.

Before he became a minister, my father had been a physician and he knew the girl was gravely ill. When he sat by her bed, the girl reached for his hand. She whispered that she had come from a good Christian home and was sorry for the things she had done and the life she had led. She said she knew she was dying and that she was afraid. "I've been so bad," she said. "So bad."

I stood by my father's side listening. I didn't know what anybody could do to help her. But my father knew. He put both his big strong hands around her small one. He said, "There is no such thing as a bad girl. There are girls who act badly sometimes, but there are no bad girls—or bad boys either—because God made them and He makes all things good. Do you believe in Jesus?" The girl nodded. He continued, "Then let me hear you say, 'Dear Jesus, forgive me for my sins.' " She repeated those words. "Now," he said, "God loves you, His child, and He has forgiven you, and no matter when the time comes, He will take you to your heavenly home."

If I live to be a hundred, I will never forget the feeling of power and glory that came into that room as my father prayed for that dying girl. There were tears on the faces of the other women standing there, and on my own, too. And everything sordid, everything corrupt, was simply swept away. Actually there was beauty in that place of evil. The love born in Bethlehem was revealing itself again in a dark and dismal house in Cincinnati, Ohio, and nothing could withstand it. It seemed to wash all evil from human hearts.

So that was the gift I received that Christmas, the frankincense-knowledge that there is good in all people, even the sad and the forlorn, and that no one need be forsaken because of past mistakes.

UNFORGETTABLE CHRISTMAS EVE

It was still another Christmas Eve, this time in Brooklyn, New York. I was feeling happy because things were going well with my church. As a young bachelor minister I had just had a fine visit with some friends and was saying good-bye to them on their front steps.

All around us up and down the street houses were decorated in honor of Christ's birthday. Suddenly a pair of wreaths on the house across the street caught my eye. One had the traditional red bow, bright and gay. But the ribbon on the other was a somber black—the symbol of a death in the family, a funeral wreath. It was the custom at that time and place to hang such wreaths outside a house of mourning.

Something about that unexpected juxtaposition of joy and sorrow made a strange and moving impression on me. I asked my host about it. He said that a young couple with small children lived in the house but he did not know them. They were new in the neighborhood.

I said good night and walked down the street. But before I had gone far, something made me turn back. I did not know those people either. But it was Christmas Eve, and if there was joy or suffering to be shared, my calling was to share it.

Hesitantly I went up to the door and rang the bell. A tall young man opened it and spoke pleasantly to me. I told him that I was a minister whose church was in the neighborhood. I had seen the wreaths and wanted to offer my sympathy.

"Come in," he said quietly. "It's very kind of you to come."

The house seemed very still. In the living room a wood fire was burning. In the center of the room was a small casket. In it reposed the body of a little girl about six years old. Over the years in memory I can see her yet, lying there in a pretty white dress, ironed fresh and dainty. Nearby was an empty chair where the young man had been sitting, keeping watch beside the body of his child.

I was so moved that I could barely speak. *What a Christmas Eve*, I thought. Alone in a new neighborhood, no friends or relatives, a crushing loss. The young man seemed to read my thoughts. "It's all right," he said, as if he were reassuring me. "She's with the Lord, you know." His wife, he said, was upstairs with their two smaller children. He took me to meet her.

The young mother was reading to two small boys. She had a lovely face, sad yet serene. And suddenly I knew why this little family had been able to hang two wreaths on the door, one signifying life, the other death. They had been able to do it because they knew it was all one process, all part of God's wonderful and merciful and perfect plan for all of us. They had heard the great promise: "Because I live, ye shall live also."* They had heard it and they believed it. That was why they could move forward together with love and dignity, courage and acceptance.

The young couple asked if they could join my church. They did. We became good friends. Many years have passed since then, but not one has gone by without a Christmas card from some member of that family expressing love and gratitude.

* John 14:19.

But I am the one who is grateful.*

And one chief reason that I am grateful is that these three experiences of expressed love did something unforgettable for me. They showed me one important method for constantly flushing from the mind the old, tired, gloomy thoughts that will surely accumulate there unless love and compassion displace them. This aspect of the positive principle has been of incalculable benefit.

Unhealthy thought patterns can block the flow of creative inspiration and inhabit the ability to function at maximum effectiveness. And there is perhaps nothing in life that may subject an individual to more intense torment than thoughts rooted in fear or hate or depressiveness. People in Bible times who were thus afflicted were said to be possessed of devils; demoniac possession, it was called. As mankind became more sophisticated, such notions came to be rather smiled at in amusement. But as people have become more educated, some scientists in human problems are persuaded that an individual can be possessed by what might be termed mental spirits that are so evil in the consequences they effect that perhaps the demon concept is not all that wide of the mark.

SHE KILLED A DEVIL

That the positive principle working in the mind has a powerful effect in eliminating the devil of fear, one of the most devastating enemies of personal happiness and well-being, we see in the following letter:

> Dr. Norman Peale:
>
> I found your book "The Power of Positive Thinking" in a large box of books from a friend. It has changed my life!
>
> We live in a remote logging camp 35 minutes by air from a small town.
>
> The being afraid pressures were terrible. With four very lively children under 9 years old, I was sometimes *very* scared and most of the time fearful. So much so that I was on tranquilizers. Without them I couldn't function, with them I could *just* get along. I *knew* the plane wouldn't get our food or medicine in to us. Or the children would get hurt or ill. Or the snows would come early and the men would be off work too soon.
>
> When I started reading your book I hadn't done anything to my house for over a week. So you can well imagine what it looked like. All I could do was pace the floor.

* "I Remember Three Christmases," *Guideposts*, Carmel, N.Y. 10512.

I could lose myself in a book if it was interesting enough, and then I wouldn't worry. Your book was the last one left in the box, as it looked far from interesting; or strong enough to tame the savage beast that was running rampant inside me.

It took me 3 days to read it. Which was a record, as I usually finished a book an afternoon. I would try the methods of all the people you wrote about. I was frantic; none of them would work.

So I would read and try again. I felt my mind running in circles, tighter and tighter ones too.

One morning I got up, took my pills (out of habit), and realized I had slept through the night without waking up. I had a terrific amount of hope. But I knew I couldn't work up any Faith. By the end of the day it dawned on me that hope was the underside of faith, peace and joy the outside of it.

That night I didn't take any sleeping pills. Not because of faith or hope, but because I forgot.

I had been hoping for an instant miracle. Now I realize there has been a miracle. The miracle of creation took seven days and the miracle of life takes 9 months. So even though it took longer than an instant, it is no less a mighty work of God.

I'm now not taking anything in the way of pills. Praise God!

For the first time in 6 months my house is clean, my hair is fixed, my nails manicured.

My husband is very proud of me and was teasing one night. He asked me if I had got a boyfriend. I told him I had. His name was Jesus.

MAN IN HELL

May I tell you another incident about one of America's most prominent writers, a longtime friend, who telephoned my office in the village of Pawling, New York, and abruptly began the conversation by saying, "I'm in hell."

"Where are you speaking from?" I asked, not quite convinced of the seriousness of the approach.

"Danbury, Connecticut," he replied.

"Now, look; Danbury [a city near to us] is not to be described in such a manner," I said. "It's a very nice town."

Somewhat exasperated, my caller declared, "The hell is not in Danbury; it's in me, right smack in my mind, and I'm sick and tired of it. May I come and see you?"

Such a request was not to be denied. Besides, I had great admiration for this man as a writing genius and affection for him as a friend.

He paced the floor of my office. "I can no longer write," he stormed. "I've lost the hang of it; no inspiration, no ideas, and no ability to express them even if I did have them. I feel dead. That's it—completely dead." I allowed him fully to ventilate his feelings, then reminded him that he had a superior mind and outstanding skill as a craftsman with ideas and the words to express them brilliantly. "But I can't think straight anymore because my mind is full of a mass of miserable thoughts that so plague me that creative thinking is just not possible."

"Okay," I said, "let's get it out. Let's have a real catharsis and mind-emptying and then a mind-cleaning. Come clean in our confidential relationship as a poor, mixed-up guy with a pastor. And don't fool around, for I will know if you are telling a phony story. The therapy will not work unless, with complete honesty, you unload all those sick thoughts that have taken over your mind and are destroying your happiness and, perhaps, you yourself in the process."

As he talked, a mass of fear and anxiety thoughts, interspersed with strong guilt reactions, spilled out in so continuous a stream that it evidenced a deep psychosis rooted, no doubt, in the unconscious area of personality. That this process brought temporary relief was obvious. But I suggested a course of in-depth counseling which he followed scrupulously over a period of time with the result that he was finally able to drop those old, dead, gloomy thoughts and come into a quality of aliveness that he had not known for many months. In fact, he exulted that he had never felt so alive. Moreover, he was able to keep his newly released mental powers going. "I killed that devil," he declared, "and got out of that hell, or maybe I should say that I got hell out of me. And am I happy! It was amazing how those old unhealthy thoughts had blocked off inspiration and brought motivation to a halt. I wouldn't have believed it possible."

But of course such complete renewal is possible. In fact, it is certain that the dropping or removal of old, tired, depressive or fear thoughts releases a strong flow of power through the mind. And when that exorcism happens, inspirational and motivational forces again operate unhindered. Such treatment, moreover, gives an individual a new grasp upon his control potential so that he is better able to keep the positive principle going regardless of whatever adverse circumstances may develop.

So when you have the problem of old, negative and gloomy thoughts, what steps may you take to overcome and correct the situation?

1. Vigorously cleanse out the old unhealthy thought pattern and dispose of it. And for good.
2. Take charge of your thoughts instead of allowing them to control you.
3. Every night empty your mind of unhappy thoughts as you empty your pockets.
4. "Be renewed in the *spirit* of your mind."
5. Do kindly things for people, for nothing can so completely erase gloom as the practice of caring and goodwill.
6. Kill your devil of fear, or inferiority, or whatever. Endure it no longer. Now—today—get rid of it for good and always. Admit it, face it, and with God's help act against it. You will win.

SIXTH WAY TO KEEP THE POSITIVE PRINCIPLE GOING

Let Seven Magic Words Change Your Life

Amazing indeed is the power of words or of word combinations to affect persons and situations. William Lyon Phelps, famed writer and professor of English, said that the ten greatest words in the English language are found in a familiar statement from *Hamlet*, "To be or not to be, that is the question." It can hardly be denied that those words do contain a solemn and far-reaching thought about personal destiny.

A well-known Shakespearean actor once declared that the greatest sentence is an eight-word line from an old spiritual: "Nobody knows the trouble I've seen, glory hallelujah!" That a victory over trouble, however gigantic, can be accomplished is certainly worthy of an alleluia!

I once spoke on the same program at a convention with a man who delivered a compelling talk in which he asserted that the success of any business or enterprise may be explained by a six-word formula. He traced the history of a number of businesses and showed how they owed their success to having carried out the creative idea in this six-word expression: "Find a need and fill it."

But there is a seven-word combination which has perhaps affected more people than any other statement ever made. It has demonstrated power to erase failure, increase strength, eliminate fear and overcome self-doubt. It will help any individual become a more successful human being in the top meaning of that term. Indeed, these seven words have the incredible power to make you everything you ever wanted to be when they are applied in depth. And that seven-word formula is this: "I can do all things through Christ. . . ."* If you are of other than the Christian heritage, simply change the words to read: "I can do all things through God." In those seven magic words is your formula for inspiration, power, motivation and the ability to keep it going—always to keep it going. Here is the positive principle in super-operative force.

HOW THE SEVEN MAGIC WORDS CHANGED ONE LIFE

If you feel we are overstating the facts, or if you doubt the power of these seven words to change lives and motivate careers, read carefully the dramatic true story which follows. Then ponder the fact that whatever can happen to one person can happen to another.

One night a speech I was delivering in Danville, Virginia, was carried live on radio to a wide area in Virginia and North Carolina. In the latter state a young man, George Shinn, driving his car in the vicinity of Raleigh, tuned to the broadcast. It seemed to interest him and later he asked that our representative come to see him. Following that interview his executive assistant, C. L. Jenkins, inspected our Foundation for Christian Living, the headquarters of which is located at Pawling, New York. Mr. Jenkins gave a favorable report on the objectives and activities of this nonprofit religious enterprise which distributes some 30 million items of Christian and inspirational literature yearly.

This was my introduction to George Shinn, an attractive young man, whose life story is a dramatic illustration of the manner in which religious commitment, strong motivation and innovative thinking can indeed make something remarkable of a human being.

A few years earlier Mr. Shinn and his mother were hard put to make ends meet. The father had died and the family was in debt. His mother, obviously a remarkable woman, pumped gasoline, was a check-out clerk

* Philippians 4:13.

in a supermarket, and worked as a telephone operator. George washed cars, worked in a bakery, later in a cotton mill. At one period he had to wear clothes other people handed down. These facts are stated here to indicate the degree of success later attained.

George graduated from high school, but his grades were "pretty low," he modestly remembers. It was necessary to attend summer school to secure his diploma. He realized, financially poor as he was, that he would need education, so he entered a business college, serving as janitor in lieu of paying tuition charges.

JANITOR MOVES UP

Then occurred one of those seemingly small happenings out of which big things grow, and because he knew how to handle this small matter he set the pace for greater things to follow. On a Saturday while engaged in his cleaning duties, two young women from out of town came in to inquire about the school, and George dealt with these prospective students. Unlike so many employees in business, he did not churlishly remark, "Don't you see the office is closed? This isn't my job. Come around on Monday. Don't bother me." That kind of reaction, the bench mark of the unsuccessful, never entered George's mind. He was proud of the school and showed the girls the classrooms, library and all the facilities and ended by signing them up as students, receiving their deposits. On Monday morning the boss changed his job from that of janitor to recruiter of students.

George became so successful in this activity that after his own graduation he continued in that capacity. The owner of the business college purchased other schools and in time offered George a partnership. Now he was on his way to success in business—a partner in six business colleges.

DISASTER STRIKES

The partnership perhaps expanded too rapidly and financial problems developed. The schools verged toward bankruptcy. George consulted a law firm, expert business advisers, and laid his papers before the heads of the firm and a certified public accountant. For several hours they studied his accounts and finally said, "We've got to give it to you straight. You'll have to give up. You haven't a prayer."

"No, no," George cried, "it can't be, it must not be."

Numbed, he headed along Interstate 85 driving almost unseeingly, eyes blurred with tears. The tar strips in the road seemed to thump out the dismal refrain, "Failure! Failure! Failure!" Overwhelmed by these thoughts of failure, he pulled off the road and sat slumped over the wheel. "You haven't a prayer—you haven't a prayer." The words of the lawyer hammered into his brain. And when a brain gets hammered, it often opens up some new and powerful insight, which is precisely what happened in this instance.

Suddenly a terrific thought flashed up. "Why, I *do* have a prayer! Of course I have a prayer, but not like the lawyer meant it. Prayer is my hope, prayer is my answer." So he prayed a simple prayer but a powerful one, powerful because he meant it completely, and it activated amazing results. "Dear Lord," he said humbly, "I never was very bright but I do so much want to be a creative person. I want to be somebody and do things to help people. I give my life into Your hands to guide and direct me." Then he added this pertinent promise, which was to change him from a failure to a success: "Dear Lord, if You will do the thinking, I will do the work. Amen."

Every day affirming the seven magic words, George went at his problems with new confidence and increasingly constructive thinking. He began reorganizing his schools and expanding the curriculum. People came to his aid with refinancing when they saw that he was sincerely trying to render a constructive service. And besides that he had unquestioned ability.

DRAMATIC RECOVERY

Now he had developed a strange new capacity of mind and spirit. He became an inspiring and effective leader in the industry. Enrollment grew, new schools were added to his chain of educational institutions. As expertise increased, other schools throughout the country started coming to him for consulting services. Today the once nearly bankrupt organization has over five thousand students, with a staff of six hundred, and serves as management consultants to over forty other business and junior colleges. While the schools are profitable, their earnings are relatively modest compared with the profits created by other businesses operated by George Shinn & Associates—a consulting agency, an automobile leasing firm, an insurance business, a dealership in furniture and equipment, and so on.

Shinn, a confirmed tither, gives more than 10 percent of his income to religious work. He and his wife and children live modestly. He is himself a down-to-earth person, taking his rapid success at age thirty-four with simplicity and humility. Recently a recipient of the distinguished Horatio Alger Award given to persons who have attained outstanding success from lowly beginnings, he sincerely gave the credit, in his case, to "God working in my life." He speaks frequently in churches and to various types of organizations, in each speech telling of "the miracles God performed" in his experience, a partnership in which "the Lord does the thinking and I do the work." His foundation gives generously to the education of pastors through scholarship aid, and to other religious enterprises, including the Foundation for Christian Living.

Some may possibly regard such outgoing religious commitment as admirable but still a bit odd for a successful businessman. But Shinn is far from being odd. He is a normal American boy who grew up in difficult circumstances but who had the motivation to build a creative life. That dynamic motivation came through intense prayer in a time of looming failure. As a result he "committed everything to the Lord" and put his faith in the seven magic words. Mr. Shinn's experience demonstrates that anyone who fully embarks on such a program can indeed accomplish outstanding achievements.

We do not have to be failures. We were not born to fail; we were born to succeed. The secret of so doing is to drop the negatives and the excuses. Get going with a God-directed program, adopt a policy of giving, believe in hard work plus consistent application of the positive principle, and any person can become what he wants to be. He will reach his goal if he wants to badly enough.

TRUST YOURSELF

"Self-trust is the first secret of success" is an oft-quoted remark attributed to Ralph Waldo Emerson. By the in-depth practice of the seven magic words one finds that he can, indeed, "do all things." Then that person is on the way to developing the most important of all success qualities—self-trust and self-belief. One thing is sure: The road to success is never via a supine self-doubt or a weasel inferiority complex. Success requires a humble yet real sense of adequacy, a normal self-respect, and with it the conviction that you can accomplish what you want to do.

Virgil, wise man of antiquity, said, "They can because they think they can."* And Goethe agreed with this vital principle by saying, "As soon as you trust yourself you will know how to live."† The practice of the seven magic words leads to a normal and sound trust in oneself and to a belief in the quality and integrity of one's own personality.

An Australian newspaper carried a fascinating story about a friend of mine, Sir John Walton, of Sydney.‡ The article stressed the place of positive thinking and faith in the remarkable career of Sir John, who once told me that in his early life he was plagued by insecurity feelings and suffered from a failure pattern. The newspaper, describing the career of this illustrious retail business leader, made reference to an effective sixteen-word spiritual formula in developing attitudes that helped him to keep motivation going to a high level of successful achievement:

> The 71-year-old retail tycoon this week announced his retirement after 45 years of "working flat out."
>
> The man who started on a shilling a week as a shop boy in a factory believes there is still room at the top for the self-made man.
>
> "I can't see anything to stop a man from pulling himself up by his bootstraps if he's prepared to pay the price," Sir John said.
>
> "I think there are always opportunities to make it, but I believe the vast majority of people are not really trying their hardest; they give up when the going gets tough.
>
> "You have to work long hours, strive hard and apply yourself to the limit before you achieve your goal," he said.
>
> "I once read a book called *The Power of Positive Thinking,* by Dr. Norman Vincent Peale.
>
> "I was so impressed I attended his church in New York to hear him lecture.
>
> "He was talking about faith, using the Biblical text, 'If ye have faith, as a grain of mustard seed, nothing shall be impossible unto you' [Sir John's sixteen-word formula].
>
> "That's been my philosophy ever since—you can do anything if you have faith in yourself.
>
> "That's why I carry a mustard seed token to remind me that I can do anything I want to," he said.

* *The Aeneid,* Bk. 5.

† *Faust,* Pt. 1, Apprentice Scene.

‡ *Sun-Herald,* Sydney.

But things have not always been easy for Sir John.

In his soft spoken voice he recalled how he did badly at school, found it hard to keep a job and concentrated on enjoying himself.

"Until I was 26 I just drifted along with the tide," he said.

"I had a succession of jobs but couldn't keep them for long.

"Then I took stock of myself, gave up drinking and smoking, and joined the National Cash Register Company as a salesman."

He went on to become manager for New South Wales and, later, Australian managing director.

"This is going to sound terribly pompous but my success didn't surprise me," he said.

In 1951, with the help of two former NCR directors, Sir John bought Murdoch's—the rundown menswear store that was to become the first link of one of the biggest retail chains in Australia.

The mammoth American retailer, Sears Roebuck, was impressed by the rapid growth of the company and invested in its future.

In 1970 John Walton was knighted by Queen Elizabeth II.

BELIEVE IN YOURSELF

Sir John Walton had to learn, as a faltering and stumbling young man weighed down by a hindering inferiority complex, that he must believe in himself and trust himself if he expected to realize his hopes and dreams. He did find himself through the philosophy and faith contained in positive Scriptural teachings. His career illustrates the truth that as a person learns to believe in God and to trust Him in everything, fully and completely, he also learns to believe in and trust himself. And this is a logical sequence, for every individual created by God has something of God-quality within him which positive faith can release.

Some people falsely, I believe, argue that believing in God and then believing in one's self is somehow "using God" to advance one's own interests. But as I view the matter, an urge, impulse or motivation has been built into an individual by the Creator to do the best possible with himself in this world. This does not mean, of course, that he should attempt to achieve his goals at the expense of others. It means simply that a basic force operating in human nature is the Divine Nature, which in turn means that we are designed to possess the self-confidence necessary for meeting tests and responsibilities.

Since a book is to some extent a documentary on the author's experience, I must confess that one of the chief problems I had to deal with was developing self-confidence. I have often declared that mine was the most enormous inferiority complex ever born in the state of Ohio, my native state. I was shy, reticent, scared, retiring and bashful. The word "bashful" is seldom used in current speech but is a highly descriptive term meaning, literally, to be abashed. Just about everything floored me.

Curiously, despite these pathetic inferiority feelings, I always wanted to become a public speaker. I was impressed when I heard some of the great speakers of that day, political figures like Theodore Roosevelt and William Jennings Bryan, and outstanding preachers—all great masters of public assemblage. I wanted to be like them. In that era there were many notable orators in the pulpit and on the platform. Perhaps it was the golden age of great public speaking. This was a period in American history when there was a galaxy of men who had a genius, hardly seen since, to sway vast audiences by their eloquence. It was thrilling to hear them, and to a small, scared boy with an inferiority complex they were heroes worshipped from afar.

Once in Greenville, Ohio, Williams Jennings Bryan, one of the greatest public speakers this country ever produced, three times a candidate for president, came to town. He spoke from an improvised platform set up on the high school grounds and surrounded by a huge crowd from all the countryside around. Another kid, as shy as I, joined me in an effort to be tough and swaggering, a common form of compensation for inferiority. We got a big cigar, cut it in two, and crawled under the speaker's platform for a clandestine and first smoke. After a few puffs I became sick, and I mean sick, so much so that it finished me on smoking. To this day I can recall lying on the ground under that platform while the great man stomped and thundered above me. My bravado faded and back I went to that shy state of being like a scared rabbit.

LEARNED THE SELF-CONFIDENCE SECRET

My father was an outstanding speaker widely sought after in Ohio for all kinds of events. Once he offered a prayer at the State Republican Convention in Columbus and waxed so eloquent as he described the stirring events of American history and the great leaders (all Republicans) which it produced that when he said, "Amen," the audience burst into thunderous applause. The chairman of the meeting said it was "the greatest speech ever delivered to a political convention in Ohio." But my father humbly reminded him that the speech was delivered to God as a prayer.

At any rate, my father understood my dream of becoming a public speaker and strongly empathized with my nervousness and shyness, for he had experienced the same feelings in his younger days. He taught me first that a speaker must have a message in which he thoroughly believes; and he must be completely sincere, for if there is anything phony his insincerity will come through loud and clear. He also taught me that a truly great speaker must love people and want to help them. To be effective, he must talk to people in their own thought and language forms, using illustrations with which they can identify. He used the figure that even as a mountain gathers up moisture and sends it back upon the countryside as rain, so the great speaker gathers up the hopes, dreams and needs of the people and sends back upon them inspiration to help them realize those values which they seek.

My father realized that he had a problem in the acute inferiority attitudes of his son and that it would do little good to suggest that the boy take himself in hand, start believing in himself and stand up like a man instead of crawling like a worm. Having been a physician before he became a preacher, and having learned from both disciplines a subtle understanding of the effect of subconscious attitudes in determining personality reactions, my father was aware that only an in-depth revision could give me self-confidence. He handled the self-defeating attitudes of his young son carefully and with skill. Over months he spelled out the fact that only a basic change in the boy's nature could bring about release from the hold upon him of inferiority and inadequacy feelings. Never did he employ such superficial methods as to say, "Buck up, be a man. Don't crawl through life cringing like a coward." No, my father was too smart for that. He simply encouraged me to hope that there was an answer, a way to change, and gradually he led me to it.

HE TAUGHT THE SEVEN MAGIC WORDS

One beautiful summer Sunday after church my father took me for a long walk in the country near Greenville, where we lived. We tramped for several miles over meadows, along a peaceful country road and through the woods. I recall with fond memory that we stopped at a farmhouse to say hello to a family, members of his church. They brought out cold glasses of milk, cookies and some of the most delicious homemade ice cream I ever put in my mouth. So wonderful was it that this moment remains forever unforgettable.

It was twilight as we turned toward home, having some five or six miles to walk. As the sun was sinking lower in the west and the sky lighted up in sunset glory, we sat to rest on two stumps, looking out over the fields of Darke County, one of the richest agricultural lands in America. Dad said, "Norman, may I say that only Jesus Christ can change your life. If you will put yourself in His hands, He will take from you all fear, all self-doubt, all of those miserable inferiority feelings. He will make you confident and strong. If you want to be a public speaker, able to touch and move the minds and hearts of men and women, let Jesus take charge of your own mind and heart. And the time to do that is now, here with your father who loves and believes in you." So saying, he, in the old-fashioned way, knelt by the stump on which he had been seated; and I, too, knelt, and he committed me to Christ.

"Now," he said as he walked down the lane toward our little house, "always remember this truth—with Christ as your Helper you can be confident and strong and live a great life. Remember and never forget that the seven magic words will change your life: 'I can do all things through Christ. . . .' "

Father was a wonderful man, a man's man, a great and unusual personality. He has been gone a good many years from this world, but actually he lives and always shall live for me, for he taught me that summer afternoon the meaning of strong and loving fatherhood and then he led me to the Source of confidence.

The years have been many since that Sunday afternoon walk, but even now when the old self-doubt tends to grab me again, I hear over the mists of time my father's voice in the dear old familiar accents saying, "Don't be afraid; remember the seven magic words." Today my schedule has me speaking to some large audience on an average of three or four times weekly in every section of the United States and Canada and even overseas. But every now and then, there is a moment just as I am being introduced when the old fear crops up, the fear that I cannot do it; the old self-doubt tries to take over. Then I remember my father, who still guides his son, saying, "You can do all things through Christ." So I put my faith in Him and do the best I can. I owe an enormous personal debt of gratitude for the seven magic words which changed my life and which guide my life every day.

SEVEN MAGIC WORDS IN TIME OF CRISIS

People are called upon to face crises and difficult situations and here again the seven magic words supply the strength required under such circumstances. The promise that "I can do all things through Christ . . ." has probably pulled more persons through more difficulties than almost any other ever made. Like the man I met on a street with whom I talked for perhaps five minutes. He stopped me to say that he had been "passing through deep, dark waters," to use his own dramatic phrase. Standing alongside the flow of traffic, both motor and pedestrian, he recounted the mass of difficulties pressing upon him. His wife was in the hospital for an operation. He had just received a cut in salary. A teen-age son was in trouble with the law. He was finding it hard to pay his bills. "One thing after another," he said, and added, "isn't it strange how troubles seem to come in bunches all at one time?"

I started to outline methods for handling his problems but he stopped me. "Don't be concerned," he said. "I just took this advantage of meeting you to open my heart a bit. But actually I'm on top of things. Nothing can really get me down, and it will all come out okay." Standing on that street I heard them again—the seven magic words—and never did they sound more dramatic, never did they seem more real, than when this hard-hit man said with positive assurance, "I can do all things through Christ. . . ." He had what is required to keep going.

Still another evidence of the power of these tremendous seven words came to me in a speaking tour among American servicemen in Vietnam at a time when that war was at its height. I was at an outpost to speak at a memorial service for a marine division on Hill 44. A number of men had lost their lives and their comrades were gathered for a solemn service in memory of them. It was an unforgettable experience to address some seven hundred men far up in the battlefront on an occasion which deeply moved all of us.

Before the meeting I had a few minutes with a group of chaplains. One of them, a Roman Catholic priest, had to leave to travel some miles to give Communion to men occupying an extremely dangerous forward position. To reach these few men, the chaplain himself would be forced to pick his way through mine fields, always in danger of stumbling upon a land mine that could destroy him.

"Did you volunteer for this kind of duty, Chaplain?" I asked.

"Yes," he replied.

"And why?" I prodded.

"Why?" he echoed. "Why, because I am a servant of our Lord and those men are His children. They are His sheep and I am His shepherd."

I was deeply moved by the simple sincerity of this dedicated man who was willing to put his life on the line for the "sheep," namely, lonely American boys in a deadly danger spot. "Must take a lot of courage," I commented with genuine admiration.

His answer was classic. "Oh, I don't know. I just depend upon the help that will always come to me." He hesitated, then added, "He has never let me down and He never will, no matter what happens." So saying, he walked out in the direction of danger, possibly even death. I was profoundly affected by this man and his faith. He rested everything upon the seven magic words. He had an inspiration and a powerful motivation to help men and serve God. And with it he possessed the power to keep it going. The positive principle was his way of life.

And now a recapitulation of the ideas presented in this chapter:

1. The power of words to change your life reaches maximum helpfulness in the seven magic words: "I can do all things through Christ. . . ."
2. The seven words can help you to overcome any defeat.
3. Never think you "haven't a prayer." You *do* have a prayer to carry you through.
4. Spiritual commitment is not for oddballs but for "with it" people.
5. Confidence and self-trust are by-products of the seven magic words.
6. Let self-confidence knock out your inferiority complex.
7. In crisis let the seven words take over. They will carry you through anything, everything.
8. You are always watched over in danger.
9. Live by the faith that will never let you down.

SEVENTH WAY TO KEEP THE POSITIVE PRINCIPLE GOING

You Can Do Wonders If You Keep Trying

If you really try, you can—! That is right, the things that you now think have you defeated, licked, beaten—those things can be handled, dealt with, overcome. And how? Just simply by *trying*. Only a minuscule few of those who accomplish things in this world are in any sense super-intellects. However, they have one super quality that keeps them going: They just plain try. You'll never know what you can do until you try—just try. Indeed, that is the name of the game.

The attitude taken toward problems and difficulties is far and away the most important factor in controlling and mastering them. The motivational writer Kermit W. Lueck* reports on a university research program which was set up to determine the factors in the formula for success. They are listed as four in number: I.Q., knowledge, skills and attitude. And according to Lueck, attitude accounts for an astonishing 93 percent of success. Of primary importance is the I-will-keep-trying attitude, the

* *This Is Your Life*
One Small Step, One Giant Leap-Goals, distributed by Self Image Products, Inc.

never-give-up, the stick-with-it, the hang-in-there, the keep-it-going attitude.

MY MOTHER MADE US TRY

My mother was a sweet and gentle lady. But she could be a very strict disciplinarian, for there was one thing she would never permit her children to do and that was to quit. I can still hear her strong voice, firm and clear, saying, "Remember this and never forget it—the Peales never quit." She deliberately tried to build tenacity and dogged perseverance, undeviating persistence, into the fabric of her children's minds.

Of all the subjects in school, the most difficult for me was mathematics. I liked English and history, studied them faithfully and enthusiastically, but must admit I tried to goof off, shall I say, on math. But would my mother let me get away with that? Hardly! "You can get it if you will just try and try again, and keep on trying," she insisted, and added, "You might as well get busy and master it because I personally am going to make you keep trying until you do." Well, my mother's wise discipline paid off, for while, of course, I have never been offered a professorship in mathematics, I did learn one vital lesson to the effect that if you simply try, you have learned one of the greatest of all success secrets.

Actually, those who perfect the "try" technique may not be endowed with brilliant talent, but they go places in life, sometimes even to the attainment of stellar achievement, because they become indomitable and undefeatable competitors. It becomes utterly impossible for them to accept the mediocre or to cease from striving for seemingly elusive perfection.

TY COBB—ALWAYS THE COMPETITOR

The late Branch Rickey's fine documentary on our longtime national game* is a classic of its kind, especially in its appraisal of the great athletes in baseball history and the qualities that make a top baseball player.

Rickey's choice for the two greatest players of all time, at least up to his day, were Honus Wagner, famous shortstop of the Pittsburgh baseball

* *The American Diamond*, Simon and Schuster: New York, N.Y. 1965.

club, and Ty Cobb, the immortal Georgia Peach of the Detroit club. He calls Cobb, "the choice of that *one* player for that *one* game that *had* to be won." Rickey says that Cobb did not have a great arm; so to compensate, he practiced almost by the clock in throwing from the outfield. His object was to have the ball skip when it hit the ground on its first contact and not to bounce with retarded speed. That meant definite control of the spin and the proper trajectory. "Did anyone," asked Rickey, "ever hear of a baseball player who voluntarily and alone would impose upon himself such arduous practice? As a result, he developed an accuracy, elevation of the throw and right rotation which made him the greatest of all fielders."

Cobb never took a double step on his throw from the outfield. He threw right where he caught the ball. He had figured that "the runner is moving at full speed and will run fifteen feet while I am stepping five." He became the terror of base runners because he always tried to make himself as near-perfect a baseball machine as possible. Rickcy calls him "baseball's most earnest and assiduous learner—the greatest perfectionist both on offense and defense." He had a lifetime batting average of .367 and the almost incredible record of 892 stolen bases.

Zig Ziglar is a popular motivational speaker at sales meetings. In his fascinating book *See You at the Top,** he tells a story about Ty Cobb that further illustrates the "always try" principle which went into the making of this immortal figure of baseball. When Cobb got on first base he had an apparently nervous habit of kicking the bag. It wasn't until he retired from the game that the secret came out. By kicking the bag hard enough Cobb could move it a full two inches closer to second base. He figured that this improved his chances for a steal or for reaching second base safely on a hit. Compete, compete, compete—this is the keep-it-going spirit by which the person who tries will ultimately make records.

Trying, of course, cannot be for a time only but, rather, must be a continuous process constantly sustained at high level. When this is done, then in due course the goal will be achieved, the objective attained. Continue, continue, continue, is a three-point formula for success. The pity of it is, however, that all too many individuals do not continue long enough but instead become tired or discouraged or overcome by a sense of futility.

So they simply chuck the effort and cease trying. "It's no use, I'm going

* We Believe, Inc., Dallas, Tex. 75251.

to skip it." So saying, they embrace the ultimate failure. They simply quit. But often, had they continued the effort just a bit longer, the thing for which they had given so much effort would have been attained. How pathetic, just to up and quit when, unbeknownst, the objective was about to be accomplished. Dr. V. Raymond Edman quotes William J. Cameron as saying, "The last dejected effort often becomes the winning stroke."*

Somewhere I heard a story of a prospector for gold in the old days out West. For days he had driven his pick into the earth looking for a vein of gold which he was sure was there. Day after day he swung his pick and sweated in the process. But finally the virus of discouragement got to him. With one angry and futile gesture he drove the pick into the ground, gathered up his gear and went away. Many years later the pick, now rusted, the handle rotted away, was found just six feet from a rich vein of gold. Persist, hang in there, keep it going—that is the answer. That is the positive principle that gets results, reaches objectives, gains goals.

BUT HOW DO YOU KEEP IT GOING?

To manage the problem of long and arduous sustained effort, it is important to harness the power of imagination, the technique of imaging. Form a mental picture or image of the goal you wish to attain and another picture of that goal as now in the process of being achieved, and you have put wings under the hard toil of trying.

For example, you want a beautiful home. How will you go about getting it? By saving and by hard work, of course. But that can become a long and hard process that may take the enthusiasm out of your effort. Therefore, form a picture in your thoughts of that house as already built. There it stands, with lawns, trees and flowers surrounding it. You can almost hear the key turn in the lock as you make ready to enter. Always realizable objectives are formed mentally before they are actualized in fact.

There was the man in New York City who was motivated by one of my talks to go ahead with a business he had long wanted to undertake but had delayed in starting because of the hesitant feeling that he couldn't make it go. Once encouraged to start, he found the going slow and difficult. He

* From V. Raymond Edman, Ph.D., "The Disciplines of Life."

was a persistent character and he worked long and hard, but that he was beginning to tire and run out of enthusiasm became increasingly evident. Then we had a talk in which I outlined what Maxwell Maltz used to call "the imagineering principle." I suggested that he begin at once to activate imagination and to image successful outcomes, to see his business as turning in one success after another and achieving good results. He proved to be an excellent student of scientific truth principles, for he began affirming the best, visualizing the best and soon was having one best after another occurring in his business enterprise.

PRAYERIZE, VISUALIZE, ENERGIZE, ACTUALIZE

It was more than interesting, actually even inspiring, to observe this man as he employed dynamic visualization techniques which, when coupled with assiduous attention to the business and long hours of work, plus concentration, began to produce definitive results. He moved steadily onward toward the creation of a successful enterprise out of humble beginnings. When he had brought the business out into the clear as a proven achievement, he explained that a four-point formula was responsible for his success. And that formula was (1) Prayerize, (2) Visualize, (3) Energize, (4) Actualize. By that curious explanation he meant, of course, that he received guidance and strength through prayer. Then he developed a mental picture or image of his undertaking as already demonstrating success. Then he gave it sustained energetic activity. And finally, his experience once again proved that images strongly held in consciousness, when supported by the trying principle vigorously applied, will indeed actualize into solid results. He was able not only to develop dynamic motivation but also to keep that motivation going through the varied difficulties which confronted him.

The *prayerize*, *visualize*, *energize* and *actualize* procedure exerts a profound power force in the experience of the individual who has the wit to employ it. Roy Burkhart lived by this creative principle and it was responsible for seemingly incredible success outcomes for him. One experience may serve as an example of the astounding thought system which characterized his outstandingly successful life. On one occasion he put on a campaign in his home city of Columbus, Ohio, for an organization called World Neighbors, of which my friend John Peters is now the head. The function of this organization is to develop a caring concern for the less fortunate. Roy Burkhart staged a huge meeting in the old

Memorial Hall in Columbus and invited me to be the speaker. He exultantly declared he was imaging a remarkable outpouring of neighborliness at this meeting.

THE HALL IS FULL

I arrived in Columbus at about two o'clock on the day of the meeting in a driving downpour of rain. The meeting was scheduled to begin at 8 P.M. Sodden skies overhead promised continuous rain and it was coming down in sheets as I dashed from the airplane into the airport building. There I met Roy, who had a most enthusiastic shine on his face. "Great to see you!" he declared, grabbing my hand. "Sure is good to have you in Columbus. The hall is full, the hall is full."

"What do you mean, 'The hall is full'?" I asked, bewildered. "Do you mean to tell me that a three-thousand seat auditorium is full at 2 P.M. on a soaking rainy day for a meeting scheduled to begin six hours from now?"

"The hall is full," he repeated, "full up to the top balcony, and everything is all set for a terrific meeting." Then I understood. The hall was full in his mind. He had a mental picture of a full house and of an enthusiastic capacity crowd.

At 7:45 P.M. I arrived at the hall on Broad Street in a wild, wind-driven rainstorm. About half soaked, I walked onstage and what did I see? A capacity crowd, every seat taken and people standing. I looked at Roy's beaming countenance. Was he surprised? Not at all. He had imaged it, pictured it, seen it in advance. Then I realized that before the actual hall was full it had been full in the mind of a man who had prayerized, visualized, energized, and by working his head off it was actualized into a fact. And so impressed was I that never to this day have I ceased to be amazed by the strange and marvelous power of "imagineering" that puts wings, powerful uplifting wings, under the try-and-keep-on-trying principle. Ever afterward when any difficulty arose, I would remember Roy and "The hall is full," and so I became better able to keep the positive principle going.

The visualization technique depends for its validity upon careful and thorough study, upon the application of diligent activity and effort. But always there must be involved a mental attitude of intelligent and positive faith if the forces of success are to be activated into a process of achievement. Of all such forces, the most basic and the most powerful is that of imagination, or the exercise of the viable and effective image.

VISUALIZES HIMSELF AS WINNER

It happened in the Bellerive Country Club in St. Louis, scene of the 1965 United States Open Golf Championship competition. Posted on the large leader board were the names of the greats in golf, all winners of previous U.S. Opens.

A man stood looking up at that board with its list of distinguished winners. The last name was Ken Venturi, who had won the coveted prize the year before. There was a blank space reserved for the as-yet-unknown champion for 1965. But the man gazing at that leader board, a golfer from South Africa, saw a name in that blank space. And the name he saw was his own—Gary Player.

He had already won the British Open in 1959, the prestigious Masters in 1961, and the coveted PGA cup in 1962. But until now the U.S. Open had been elusive. When Gary Player took that stellar competition, he would become the third man to win the "Grand Slam" of golf, the two others being Gene Sarazen and Ben Hogan, immortal figures in the realm of golf.

In his thrilling book,* the first chapter of which is called "Visualize Winning," Gary says, "I saw something no one else could see." He writes:

> All week long I had been reading and studying *The Power of Positive Thinking* by Norman Vincent Peale, and what he had to say made a lot of sense to me. His words "visualize winning" were etched deeply in my mind. This had been my pattern for many years, but now the techniques for visualizing a goal emerged in concrete form.
>
> In spite of the intense heat I played very well. After fifteen holes my lead over Kel Nagle had lengthened to three strokes. I recall walking down the 15th fairway with Mr. Hardin of the United States Golf Association and that he said, "Well, you've got it all locked up." And I remember replying, "No, you can never say that until the last putt has been holed." I was so right!
>
> On 16 my 4-wood off the tee nosed right into a bunker. Somehow this seemed to trigger disaster, and before finishing the hole I'd taken a double bogey. And to make matters worse, just as I walked off the green, the news squawked through the walkie-talkie that Nagle had birdied 17. My three-stroke lead had dissolved, and now we were even. The heat was on and I knew it.

* *Gary Player; World Golfer* Word Books: Waco, Texas.

But as I concentrated, the positive side of my mind began to take over. I had to have a par on 18 to stay even with Kel, but a birdie would give me the one-stroke lead needed to win. Why not try for it?

The 18th at Bellerive is a tough par-4—trees on the left, out of bounds on the right. My drive landed in excellent position on the right side of the fairway, and a 5-iron second shot came to rest on the green just fifteen feet from the hole. Then came that big moment of truth. After studying the greens, I sighted the putt carefully, and then . . . it moved right along a line directly toward the cup but faltered to a stop just a fraction short. It's true golf is a game of inches, but this was unreal.

. . . My easy tap-in insured a tie with Nagle at 282—two strokes over par—and we were headed for an 18-hole playoff the next day. *Visualize winning?* I still was, but it would have to wait.

I went into the next day's round feeling good and hitting well. After four holes I was leading Nagle by one stroke. The pressure he felt as he teed up for number 5 must have been tremendous, for disaster struck. Kel's drive arced badly and bopped a woman spectator right on the head. Blood poured from her scalp as she toppled over unconscious. I tried to reassure Kel: "Don't let it get you." But obviously shaken and unnerved, he moved up to the ball again and this time blasted a grass-cutter that ricocheted off another woman's ankle. The remaining thirteen holes slipped by without much excitement, at least when compared to number 5.

The results after eighteen holes: Player, 71; Nagle, 74. The United States Open, America's biggest golf championship, was mine . . . all mine. It had not been won by a foreign player since Ted Ray captured the title in 1920—forty-five years before.

With this win I had joined ranks with Gene Sarazen and Ben Hogan. Now there were three members of the gilt-edged Grand Slam Club . . . and I was one of them. This had to be one of the happiest moments of my life.

So at last the name of Gary Player went up on that leader board where the champion had visualized it. That which he visualized had actualized. But naturally all of this tremendous achievement was not limited to mental practice. Player works. He has always worked, constantly struggling to perfect his stroke, his stance, his entire performance. A few years ago while in his country I wanted to reach Gary Player, who was at home at the time, but missed him on my telephone call. Next morning very early, perhaps at 7:30, from the airport I called again, only to find that he had gone out about an hour earlier, and for what reason? Why, to practice, of course. Always working to improve, always striving to do better, the great Grand Slam golfer had the realistic background upon which to perform the amazing power of visualization.

Also operating in the experience of this great athlete is a power that has worked wonders in his long and outstanding career. "Faith," he says, "is the most dynamic and energizing force in my life . . . faith in God, faith in other people, faith in myself. For me, at least, the three are inseparable." In all the struggles and vicissitudes of intense competition, Gary Player has never lost the inspiration nor the motivation nor the ability—always to keep the positive principle going.

THE RELAXED EFFORT METHOD

The type of trying that works wonders must also involve the relaxed attitude toward effort when that is indicated. All too many sincere and conscientious people expend every energy in trying hard and even harder to accomplish their goals but finally push their energies to a breaking point without attaining the goals for which they have put forth every ounce of strength. They become victims of the overpress and thus the overstress. The problem under such circumstances is to employ the relaxed trying method; the "easy does it" approach.

This consists of deliberately breaking the strain of constant and undeviating effort, the dogged force of will, the driving persistence, by a letting up; a relaxing of strain. There is a danger in rigid overpressure or insistence upon trying too hard; the creative flow, which is vital to doing anything well and competently, may be subordinated. As a result you just do not work or accomplish efficiently.

I recall one beautiful winter day in the country at our farm on Quaker Hill when I was laboring hard on an article, the deadline for which was looming up in demanding immediacy. Up at the crack of dawn, starting work long before breakfast, I went at this job with the determined attitude that I was going to finish the thing by noontime and get it in the afternoon mail. That was the hard-driving schedule. No deviation from it would be tolerated by me!

"You can do anything if you work and keep on working; if you try and never let up on trying," is what I said to myself as I went to work. All went well for a time and definite progress was being made. The words seemed to march along like soldiers in orderly fashion. There was a rhythmic flow to the ideas, and all in all it seemed to be shaping up as a pretty good piece. "Boy," I exulted, "I'll knock this off in no time flat." But as is often the case, pride goeth before a fall. The inspiration suddenly ran out and to keep it going required redoubled effort. I pumped up my flagging energies but finally had to admit I'd gone stale. The ideas no longer flowed, the words got all messed up. Sentences were laborious and involved and really awkward as well.

Finally I slammed down my pencil, got up, walked around the room, firmly sat down again. "I'll stick this out and see it through. I'll keep at it all day if necessary, but I'm going to finish this job—period," I growled. But it was no go. The inspiration had up and fled, and that which had started out so terrifically had now ground to a stop—an uninspired, dismal stop.

Looking out the window to the snowy landscape, I saw the whited hills silhouetted against a clear blue sky. Tufts of snow clung to the pine trees like cotton balls. Everywhere the snow glistened like myriads of diamonds flung all around by some gigantic hand. It was one of those cold, crystal-clear, perfect winter days. "What," I asked myself sympathetically, "am I doing here cooped up in this house, slaving my life away, when I could be outside there enjoying myself?"

I FALL INTO THE RIVER

Pushing the papers aside with a masterful "to heck with it," I put on a windbreaker, a fur hat, some warm gloves and went for the kitchen door. There patiently waiting was my huge dog Tonka, all ready for a hike. Tonka and I headed across the lawn on which the snow lay a foot deep; down through a valley and across a meadow, working up a sweat even in 15 degree cold due to the struggle of pushing through deep snow. In the woods dark tree trunks stood stark against the glistening white. Tonka and I stopped to listen to the singing of the wind, which strangely did not seem to interfere with the deep quietness. Tongue hanging out, the dog looked and listened. I, with tongue almost hanging out, did likewise.

Then on we went past the huge old red barn, one of the oldest and largest in Dutchess County, until finally we stood by the little river that splashes down our four-stage waterfall from its source high in the Connecticut hills. Perhaps it was more a creek than a river, actually a "crick," as we called it when I was a boy in Ohio. Anyway, it was full up to the banks and coated over with ice. I watched as Tonka stepped easily across the ice to a place on the far shore where there was a cold spot of cold water from which he drank with obvious pleasure. I envied him, for the water looked fresh and good, but having read numerous news stories about polluted water, I suffered my thirst.

Tonka, who must weigh close to 15 pounds, seemed to negotiate the ice so well that I decided to follow him across. But I found that there must be a difference between four feet and two, for halfway over the ice broke, depositing me into perhaps three feet of ice-cold water. Struggling back to the bank, I floundered a mile and a half through that heavy snow and uphill all the way, followed by the sympathetic and loyal Tonka. Though the exertion warmed me up, I took the precaution of wrapping myself in a bathrobe before the blazing fireplace, meanwhile swallowing a copious drink of boiling-hot lemonade. "You'll catch your death of cold," warned Ruth, and I had visions of pneumonia putting an end to my "literary" career.

But suddenly like a flash it popped into my head—the idea for which I had been so futilely struggling. Thoughts began to flow out of my mind like that stream into which I had fallen. Rushing back to my study, I put words down on paper so rapidly that the article was finished before lunch, and by four o'clock it was typed, in the post office and on its way.

I do not mean to imply that one can do better, when hard trying doesn't work, by going out and falling into the river, especially when it runs icy cold. But it is a fact that wisdom dictates a backup from overpressure, a detour from excessive effort. Relaxed trying, a combination of effort and tension-breaking, restores an even thought balance and thus allows concepts and expression to flow freely again. In fact, it may have the effect of restoring a person to mental-physical correlation and thereby a recapturing of the effectiveness which intense strain may have stymied.

DRAMA IN A WORLD SERIES

An old friend was a famous star pitcher a few years back when the Dodgers were in Brooklyn. Carl Erskine made a record for the most strikeouts in World Series play, a record that stood up for a good many years. I often talked with Carl about the relationship of hard trying and the danger of overpressing, as one tended to tense up under pressure. He pointed out the importance of the mental ability to "go away in thought" momentarily into an atmosphere of calm, even while in the midst of a hard-fought game.

He told of one occasion, an extremely hot day when the pressure mounted and he became very tired. While he walked about the pitcher's mound picking up dirt and wiping his hands on his pants, he returned in memory to a misty morning when he and another pitcher were fishing and from across the water came the sound of singing at a morning prayer meeting. The song was an old hymn of peace and quiet. In the few seconds of this "memory trip," Carl recovered strength and poise and performed effectively, with energy to spare.

At another time it was the fifth inning of the fifth game of the World Series and Carl Erskine was on the mound for the Brooklyn Dodgers. That day also happened to be Carl and Betty's fifth wedding anniversary. Carl was going well and had amassed a four-run lead, the score standing at 4–0 in favor of the Dodgers. Perhaps the pitcher was trying too hard and overpressing, the result of which is often to throw him off his rhythm. Whatever the cause, suddenly the opposing team began connecting with the ball and two runs were in with two men on base. Tensed up, Carl threw a fast ball straight over the plate to the next batter, who promptly sent it sailing for a home run. This put the Yankees ahead, 5–4.

In the ensuing bedlam the Brooklyn manager, Charlie Dressen, one of the great managers and a student of human nature, walked slowly from the dugout to the pitcher's mound where Carl waited rather despondently. Dressen took the ball from Carl, tossed it up a couple of times, kicked the dust, then said, surprisingly, "Carl, isn't this your fifth wedding anniversary?" Astonished, Carl replied, "Yes, Mr. Dressen, this is our fifth wedding anniversary."

"Well, continued Dressen, "aren't you going to take Betty out to dinner tonight?"

I think all of us have wondered what is said in those dramatic conferences between pitcher and manager in crisis moments of a baseball game. Carl himself was amazed. He looked around at the great stadium packed with seventy thousand excited fans and here was his manager calmly talking about Carl taking his wife out for a wedding anniversary dinner that night. "Yes, Mr. Dressen, I am taking Betty out for dinner this evening to celebrate five years of marriage."

Dressen handed the ball back to Erskine. "You're my man, Carl. Finish this game before dark." In the six innings that followed of that World Series game, nineteen opposing players came to bat but not one got to first base. The Dodgers drove in two more runs and the game ended in a victory for Erskine by a score of 6–5.

Dressen knew what he was doing. With consummate understanding, faith and psychology, he steadied a pitcher who was trying too hard and therefore pressured. This able manger knew that his pitcher had the ability and the control to win the game if he could relax him. This he did by a simple, human, but extraordinarily adroit method. He employed the simplicities and nostalgia of a loving relationship in such a way as to draw off tension and restore a relaxed and powerful control. He renewed in Carl the power to keep it going under pressure.

LET GOD HELP YOU TRY

I received from one of my readers, Dorothy Sheckels, a beautiful wall hanging done in needlepoint. It is an exquisite piece of work by a woman who had passed through many troubles, including ill health. She was trying always for a better and more useful way of life. After a long period of frustrating circumstances she turned herself over to God saying, "Well, God, if You cannot change me, then just use me as I am."

The idea came to begin doing embroidery for family and friends, and in the process she became quite expert. Then she was asked by someone to do a piece of needlepoint, but her first reaction was that she could not do anything so demanding. But she studied and she tried and tried some more. She had learned to let God help her and accordingly she improved amazingly in this craft. And with it her whole life-style and way of living improved.

I cite this incident, for the piece of needlepoint sent to me expresses a compelling thought of subtle wisdom—don't try to do it all yourself, but let God do it through you. The piece says in needlepoint (and it is beautifully done):

Trust in the Lord with all
thine heart and lean not
unto thine own understanding.
In all thy ways acknowledge
Him, and He shall direct thy
paths. Prov. 3:5–6

This woman, in circumstances less dramatic than the sports figures previously described and in a setting of ordinary living where most of us are situated, learned a top secret, namely: Don't try too hard; let God help you. When this practice is followed, the result inevitably is unexpected guidance in the form of fresh insights. Edison had a sign on his laboratory wall which read, "There's a better way to do it—find it." That better way is often blocked off by tense and uptight attitudes. The required insights cannot come through. Always in consciousness are ideas that can change your life and greatly improve your performance. The best way I have ever found to start these better ideas flowing is through faith; by letting God who made you now remake you by normalizing your entire personality. Then creative things really start happening.

As one man put it, "I found that I couldn't do it very well, but when I took God into partnership He and I did it very well indeed."

You can do wonders if you will only try and believe and always keep it going.

This chapter has emphasized the following important points:

1. You will never know what great things you can do until you try—really try.
2. Hang in there—stick with it—hammer at it—keep it going.
3. Trying as a continuous process sustained at high level is a viable goal-achiever.
4. Use the amazing power of imagination, the creative technique of imaging, to make the trying more effective.
5. Prayerize, visualize, energize, actualize.
6. Picture your goal; "see" it clearly as now in process of formation, already becoming fact.
7. Practice until you achieve the relaxed trying principle.
8. When trying makes you stale, divert the mind, break the strain. Ideas will start flowing again.
9. Let God help you try. Experts are made by this procedure.
10. Always keep the positive principle going.

EIGHTH WAY TO KEEP THE POSITIVE PRINCIPLE GOING

How to React Creatively to Upsetting Situations

"Everyone has inside himself—what shall I call it—a piece of good news."* I noted this striking and thoughtful statement framed and on the wall of a beautiful home in Bermuda. With Commander Geoffrey Kitson, whose home it was, I discussed the meaning of these provocative words. We agreed that each of us does have a big piece of good news deep within ourselves. Such good news is the fact that with God's help we have what it takes to meet all upsetting situations and to react creatively to them.

So, as you read this book, if you are faced with an upsetting situation, the message for you, loud and clear, is that you can handle it, and effectively. And if that upsetting situation has worn you down and perhaps depleted your supply of faith, draw on the positive principle again and this time keep it going. A resupplying of belief in yourself and in God will get you going with increased courage. New insights and a strong grasp of the situation will come, however complex and difficult the sit-

* Sister Mary Corida.

uation may appear to be. We use the phrase "may appear," for generally the outcome of any problem, good or otherwise, depends upon how it appears to us. Most outcomes are first determined in mental outlook. So take a strong, positive look at your hitherto upsetting situation and apply the positive principle in reacting to it creatively.

First, let us consider a situation which seems to arise periodically, one in which many persons during economic recession or business adjustments may find themselves out of gainful employment. This is a situation which can of course be terribly upsetting. Hardly anyone expressed this problem with more poignancy in the last period of recession than a father of nine children, when he wrote the following newspaper piece:*

OUT OF WORK AND SCARED

> Let me tell you what it's like for one guy to be 52 years old and jobless.
>
> As a recently fired middle-management executive of a division of one of America's top 500 companies, I have sent out over 150 resumes. Less than 10% have drawn a response of any kind. Five percent drew requests for additional information, while less than four percent resulted in a personal interview. None resulted in a job.
>
> As an infantry veteran of World War II in the South Pacific, I've had some experience with fear, and how men deal with it. I like to feel that I don't scare any easier than the next guy, but to be 52 years old and jobless is to be frightened—frightened to the marrow of your bones. Your days start with it, and end with it. It's all-pervasive. It's numbing. It's mind-boggling.
>
> Things you've always taken for granted fall apart. You can no longer maintain your hospitalization insurance, and for the first time in 28 years you and your family are unprotected against a medical emergency. You are unable to meet the payments on your life insurance. The bank holding your mortgage warns that foreclosure is being considered. Bills to the utilities are overdue and you're keeping vital services only through partial payments, aware of the fact that time is running out.
>
> It's to tell a fine 14-year-old son that you haven't got the five bucks you owe him for the great report card he brought home.
>
> It's to pass local merchants on the street and feel embarrassment, wondering when you'll be able to pay them what you owe them.
>
> It's to feel the disintegration of your confidence as a man and your ability to protect your family from economic disaster.
>
> It's to envy just about everybody who has a job, any job.

* Edward B. Furey, Poughkeepsie (N.Y.) *Journal*. Reprinted from *Moneysworth*.

It's to see the doubt on the faces of your children about what's going on in their house, when so many of their friends are unaffected.

It's to add a crushing dimension to the natural self-doubts that are part of the process of growing older.

It's to stand silently on unemployment lines with other surplus members of America's work force, waiting to sign for your unemployment check.

It's to see what the neighborhood looks like at 10:30 on a Tuesday morning.

It's to feel embarrassed to answer the ring of the telephone at the same hour.

And in the late evening, when your household is quiet and you switch off the bedroom light, it's to be alone, alone like you've never been before. To lie there looking at the darkness and wonder if you're going to lose the home that you've worked all your life for, the home that represents the only equity you've been able to accumulate in 30 years of working hard and raising a family.

And finally, it's to lie sleepless in bed waiting for the dawn of a new day.

Quite apart from the question of economic conditions that permit such tragedies to occur in our society, our discussion here is limited to the problem of how a person may react creatively in dealing with such an unsettling situation. Perhaps the first step is to remind the individual that he still possesses within himself the "piece of good news," and therefore that there is an answer, that a solution can be found. Accordingly, a basic procedure is to begin and resolutely continue an affirmation that the situation is in no sense hopeless. The affirmation must contain a positive assertion, constantly repeated. Perhaps the following formula may be a guide: "With God's help and guidance I can achieve a creative outcome to this situation, and I am now getting such a solution."

Repeat this affirmation until by a process of intellectual osmosis the idea passes into the unconscious and is accepted as fact. Immediately, then, positive forces will go into operation and produce the actualization of the affirmation. Remember that a negative affirmation is also extremely powerful, and if you should affirm and continue to affirm failure outcomes, the mind will function in a similar manner to actualize a failure pattern.

Therefore the first step is to develop an awareness of your own inherent or built-in creative power; and the second is to affirm positively that successful outcomes not only are possible but are also now operating powerfully and creatively in consciousness, and that they are currently materializing.

COOL IT; DON'T PANIC

A third step in dealing with an upsetting situation is to draw off heat from it and to cool it, calm it and resist panic in any form. So important is this procedure that it might properly rate as step number one. But whether it be point one, two or three, it is absolutely vital never, never, *never* to panic when facing an upsetting situation. I am quite well aware that the avoidance of panic is not easy—far from it. Always the tendency in times of difficulty and crisis is to react emotionally, and the mental cooling process requires strong discipline which is not easily applied when the mind is agitated or alarmed or bitter or angry or in any other way conditioned emotionally.

However, we need at all times to be sensitively aware that the human mind cannot function at its maximum best when it is hot, as overcharged emotion tends to make it. Only when the mind is cool—better still, cold—will it correlate in smooth, well-organized functioning. Only then will it produce those dispassionate, rational and objective insights that lead to solutions. When facing an upsetting situation the objective is to be as collected mentally as possible, for in order to deal with such a situation one must really think, and thinking can be accomplished most effectively only when the emotions are under strict control.

One man who passed through a difficult unemployment experience (and I was reminded of him when I read the newspaper piece printed earlier) told me of a successful formula he used for cooling the mind, for curbing emotion; one that helped immeasurably in maximizing the ability to think and therefore to act constructively. His formula or method was to "pass through the mind" such statements as the following: "Thou wilt keep him in perfect peace, whose mind is stayed on thee."* And again: "Come unto me . . . and I will give you rest."† And still another: "In quietness and in confidence shall be your strength."‡

* Isaiah 26:3.

† Matthew 11:28.

‡ Isaiah 30:15.

He was quite an ingenious fellow from the standpoint of mental culture in that he could also mentally reconstruct or recall the most quiet and peaceful scenes he had ever experienced. Examples were a covered bridge in Vermont on a colorful autumn day; another, a remote sea beach on the Maine coast where he spent summers in camp as a boy. This practice of "memorized peacefulness," as he described it, seemed to exercise a salutary effect in drawing off heat from his thinking and therefore made him better able to consider pertinent matters objectively and dispassionately. When we are able to think in such balanced manner, we have a much improved chance of capturing creative insights and ideas to help us out of our troubles.

A person who is in panic due to what he regards as a desperate situation is perhaps likely to be impatient with such scientific anti-panic methodology as here described. "You just don't know my situation; you can't really understand," he might declare heatedly. And this reaction is understandable and deserving of sympathy. However, making every allowance, such an attitude can hardly be valid, for many people who have developed the positive principle to support them in upsetting situations do not panic but, on the contrary, act intelligently and in a controlled manner.

PILOT'S ARM CUT OFF

The horrifying experience of Brian Steed comes to mind.* If anyone faced an upsetting situation, it was this Canadian bush pilot who operated a light pontoon plane in isolated areas. A company had sent him to scout a wilderness lake as a possible supply base. He had landed on the lake with no difficulty, but when he headed into the wind for takeoff his cap was blown into the water. It was a favorite hat and he did not want to lose it, so he turned the plane near to the floating cap and throttled to low speed. Climbing down to the pontoon to grab the cap, which was bobbing in the water, a slight pitch caught him off balance. His feet slipped and he plunged forward toward the propeller.

Brian Steed felt a whack on the shoulder and then found himself thrashing in the water. He did not feel hurt particularly and concluded that probably he had hit a strut. But his right arm did not feel quite right,

* Retold from a story in *Guideposts*.

and he swam with his left. Then in attempting to climb back into the plane he discovered to his horror that the right arm had been completely severed by the turning propeller and that he was bleeding profusely at the shoulder. At once he knew that unless something could be done quickly he would certainly bleed to death. Then came the thought that perhaps death was to be desired, for how could he live without a right arm? But this thought passed quickly as he remembered his wife and small children. He was definitely growing fainter, blood streaming from the shoulder stump. Here was, indeed, a setup for panic—right arm cut off, severe bleeding, alone in a wilderness and far from help.

Why was there no panic in this crisis? The answer! This bush pilot was a man of powerful faith—the real thing. He knew where a better-than-human help was to be found. He found strength to climb into the cockpit. This Helper showed him how to apply, with one hand, a makeshift tourniquet to stanch the flow of blood from the shoulder. He gunned the plane to take off, flying without any tendency toward fainting to a base camp where he received help from two friends who flew him to a hospital for treatment.

Says pilot Brian Steed of his incredible experience, which could have been completely shattering, "Many people have told me that most bush pilots would have panicked had they found themselves in my predicament. Perhaps I would have, too, had I not known that there is truth in those words, 'God is our refuge and strength, a very present help in trouble.' "* Obviously that Help was very much present when his trouble struck. Anyone can panic, but people with the quality of faith which this bush pilot possessed are able to handle panic and therefore deal creatively with upsetting situations, no matter how terrifying they may be.

HE SOLVED AN UNEMPLOYMENT PROBLEM

In thinking of the fifty-two-year-old man whose heart-moving article is included earlier in this chapter, I recall a similar case from years ago. This chapter is being written at the Mountain View House in the White Mountains, a beautiful hotel where our longtime friend Schuyler Dodge is the owner and to which our family has been coming for many years. It looks out on the spectacular Presidential Range in New Hampshire.

* Psalm 46:1.

Here, some twenty years ago, I received a long-distance telephone call from a very distracted man. It was shortly after *The Power of Positive Thinking* was published, and this man, having just read the book, was strongly impelled to talk with me. I had never met him and so, of course, knew nothing about him.

As I listened to the story of a lost job and futile efforts to find a new position with no result, it occurred to me that perhaps by allowing him to talk out the problem he might possibly develop his own solution, as often happens. This man had the greatly-to-be-desired ability to state a problem in organized fashion, which of course indicated an exact quality of mind. He was not in any sense negative or complaining or bitter, though understandably he seemed disturbed that he had been unable to make a business connection, particularly since his savings were practically exhausted. The sense of anxiety came through in his conversation, but it was controlled, though obviously not without effort.

Finally I said, "Look, you don't know the answer to your problem and neither do I. So I suggest that we bring in a Consultant, One whose know-how is of top quality, and put the matter directly to Him. Then let's leave it to Him to point the way."

He at once grasped the meaning of this suggestion and said, "Okay, you talk to Him for both of us."

So then and there over the telephone, separated from my caller by a thousand miles or more, I sent out a request asking for the needed guidance. On the supposition that somewhere there was a job for this man, I asked that the man and the job be brought together. "Let me know what happens," I said, and was rather surprised at the reply: "I've got a strange but strong feeling that something is going to happen, and soon. Thanks a lot."

Then the positive principle went to work to produce an intelligent result.

Perhaps three weeks later I received a phone call from this man at my New York office. It seems that he had secured a position with a restaurant, a totally different type of occupation from any he had contemplated. This job did not pay nearly so much as his former connection, but enough to get by on. And he must have done all right in this new business, for later on he acquired two restaurants of his own which he operated successfully until his death some seventeen years later.

When asked how the job opportunity had come about, he replied, "Funny thing. It was really weird. You see, I was eating in this restaurant and idly got to thinking that it seemed a well-managed place. It was on the inexpensive side but everything was neat and clean and obviously it was operated by someone with imagination. Suddenly I had a strong feeling that I would like to work for these people." He hesitated. "It was almost like being home, as if, you might say, I was meant to be there. So while paying my check I asked if I might speak with the manager.

"He was a friendly fellow and I became aware that he was sizing me up. It was more than a perfunctory conversation. Finally he said, 'Well, it's sort of funny, but maybe you have happened along at the right time. You see, I've just lost my right-hand man, who died ten days ago. Been trying since to handle everything myself. But I'm lost without Ralph, as he seemed to know just what to do all the time, always on top of things. Know anything about this business?' he asked.

"I just had to level with him. 'Not a thing except general business principles,' I said. 'But your restaurant seems to have—what shall I call it—a spirit. It's different and imaginative. I suppose the way to run a restaurant is to give people good food in a pleasant atmosphere at reasonable prices and make a reasonable profit on your investment.'

"The owner grinned at that. 'Not bad, not bad at all.' Then he continued, 'I have been expecting the right man to come along. [Much later when they had become friends he confessed he had prayed for that "right man."] Well, give me some references. Are you willing to take the long hours this business requires?'

"I'll stick with you all the way," my man replied, and added, "I sort of feel that this job was meant to be." And indeed so it proved, for later he became a partner, then, on the other man's retirement, bought him out and ultimately added a second restaurant. His explanation of the entire experience was succinct and to him represented the facts. "Someone," he said, "was on my side." And we may add Someone is always on your side, too. Never doubt it.

THE IN-AND-WITH-IT PEOPLE

These persons who react creatively to upsetting experiences invariably demonstrate certain impressive qualities. They do not panic; they do not emotionalize. They think coolly, dispassionately, objectively. This type of person takes a positive viewpoint, rejecting the negatives no matter how unpropitious the situation may appear to be. And without exception they have a sustaining faith that helps to keep them going as they keep the positive principle activated.

This is the twenty-fourth book I have written, and in each book I have strongly stressed spiritual faith as a necessary factor in successful living. But now and then someone will write or say something to the effect that "I take your practical suggestions, but skip the religious stuff." Such objections are a minuscule minority in this better-educated era, but there are still a few who seem to have the notion that spiritual techniques are somehow a kind of aberration to be differentiated from practicality.

In their old-fashioned view, the practitioners of religious truth principles have a sort of "oddball" streak. On the contrary, the in-and-with-it people regard spiritual concepts as a truly scientific way of life. Science, of course, is a thought pattern based on demonstrable techniques. Science in the field of thought is no less valid than science in a laboratory, for in both instances it is based on workable and proven formulas.

Indeed, the prophecy made years ago by one of America's greatest geniuses of science is currently being verified to such an extent that knowledgeable persons now recognize the validity of spiritual principles as verifiable scientific procedure. These principles work when worked. Faith produces results. Power operates through the mind as surely as through wires. Communication comes directly into consciousness no less surely than television pictures are transmitted via satellite.

The above-mentioned scientist was the famed Dr. Charles Steinmetz, who, when asked what line of research would have the greatest development during the next fifty years, said:

> I think the greatest discoveries will be made along spiritual lines. Some day people will learn that material things do not bring happiness and are of little use in making men and women creative and powerful. Then the scientists of the world will turn their laboratories over to the study of God and prayer and the spiritual forces which, as yet, have been hardly scratched. When that day comes, the world will see more advancement in one generation than it has seen in the last four.*

I HAVE HAD UPSETTING SITUATIONS, TOO

In discussing reaction to upsetting situations and how to keep going under difficult and trying circumstances, I am not here dealing with a theoretical matter, for I also have had my share of such problems. One arose after *The Power of Positive Thinking* became what in the book trade they

* Reader's Digest.

call, rather exaggeratedly I always thought, a "runaway best-seller." The book did have and has continued to have an enormous sale. For some reason this roused the ire of some of the left-wingish and far-out liberal clergy. Indeed, their violently hostile attitude was described by one magazine as "the rage of the intellectuals." At any rate, they had it in for me and berated me behind and before, even to the extent of preaching sermons against what they angrily called "Pealism."

Prior to this experience I had always believed that all ministers were uniformly gentlemanly persons who, while they might disagree with one's ideas and strongly express divergent opinion, still did not attack an individual as a person or use harsh and intemperate language in castigating him. And I hasten to add that the vast majority of the clergy are kindly and considerate people who, if they take a different viewpoint, do so with courtesy. But in the violent and bitter-tongued few I found what literally amounted to an appalling hate psychosis which seemed shocking indeed.

WHY WERE THEY SO HET UP?

The rationale for this violent anti reaction was, one supposes, that the book was written in a direct and simple style using language and thought forms readily understandable by the average man on the street. Indeed, the book was intended for him and not for supersophisticated scholars, although perhaps any person might have used its principles to advantage.

Since the point of view of the book was that through positive attitudes one could achieve better things in life and do a more constructive job on oneself, the critics, who sometimes seem constitutionally negative, bristled at the mere mention of the word "success," even when it was not intended to mean making a pile of money or getting one's name in the paper. Since, if things should go better both for individuals and for society there would be less to carp about, the negativist tends to take a jaundiced view of the concept of positive thinking. And finally, the book being highly successful from a publishing viewpoint in terms of the number of copies sold, that pesky jealous element when a colleague is fortunate enough to have a project turn out well can sometimes affect attitudes, rationalize it as we will.

Well, whatever the reasons, and perhaps some criticism was well-founded, the barrage of opposition let loose on me was formidable. I was be-labored hot and heavy by my vocal and vindictive detractors. The situation was potentially upsetting indeed. As a matter of fact, I was bewildered and somewhat hurt and hard put to it to understand this mistreatment, for my simple book was intended only to help people. Of course, thousands of kindly persons came to my support and I felt upheld and strengthened by their confidence. But still, nobody can be attacked, often viciously, as I was, especially by men in one's own line or profession, and not tend to be upset.

I FOUND THE WAY TO OVERCOME THE SITUATION

The natural tendency in such a situation is to fight back, to give as good as received. Some friends suggested, "Tell them off in words they cannot fail to understand." But this did not seem advisable, and besides, it would constitute a denial of the truth principles I believed and taught. Accordingly, not without some personal struggle, I decided upon the policy of putting into active practice the principles of scientific truth which I had suggested as viable to others in upsetting situations.

1. I decided not to answer criticism or to make any explanation, nor to defend myself, but to take it in silence.
2. I decided to examine every criticism to ascertain whether it was valid, and if so, to try to correct my own position. For example, once in Chicago I was met by reporters who showed me a violent attack on me by the then Dean of the Yale School of Theology. One reporter read it to me and asked for a comment. I said, "The Dean is a distinguished man, and if he feels about me as he stated, then it is my duty to re-examine myself and my teachings." Being all set for fuel to keep the fire burning, they were obviously disappointed. No story in that, from their reportorial point of view.
3. I went out of my way to be nice to my enemies. From time to time I issued a list of recommended books and gave highest marks to a book by one of my chief detractors. This was done only because I considered it an excellent piece of work. The book was considered on an objective and not an emotional basis.
4. I continued quietly to teach that Christianity is a scientific, practical, workable way of life; a philosophy of thought and action that can help anyone in whatever circumstance. Everyday people by the thousands accepted that teaching to their great benefit, as reported in a mass of letters of appreciation.

Well, either I outlived my enemies or they came to see things in a different light or the viewpoints I expressed gained wider acceptance. Whatever happened, the opposition finally subsided. And many who once opposed me violently wrote that they had changed their minds, not only about my ideas but about me personally. I did not necessarily want or even expect people to admit that they were wrong and that I was right. What I really wanted was to demonstrate to myself and perhaps to others that spiritual truth principles are viable and will work when truly worked. It was my desire to prove conclusively, to my own satisfaction primarily, that I could react creatively to an upsetting situation. And I found that indeed I could, with God's help, keep the positive principle operative. Enthusiasm for the message I was dedicated to communicate was not one whit diminished.

WHEN GRIEF COMES

It so happens that, because my writings deal primarily with people-centered problems of a very personal nature, thousands of letters are received from individuals everywhere telling of upsetting situations which they face. To sit down with, say, a hundred such letters is profoundly moving and can be even a heart-rending experience, for such letters reveal the wide panorama of human suffering. Every Good Friday, for example, our Peale Center for Christian Living conducts a twenty-four-hour Prayer Vigil dealing with from 25,000 to 40,000 requests for prayers which come in for that day. If you wished to know what is disturbing or upsetting people, a sampling of these communications would awe you by the extent and depth of suffering and anxiety which are daily prevalent everywhere. Looking at a crowd of people in a church or music hall or theater or at an athletic event, one observes no evidence of such problems. It is the mark of a sophisticated person to dissemble, not to reveal outwardly, the inner fears and troubles which afflict him. But to one whose work it is to deal with such matters in a sympathetic manner, the full extent of burdens is poured out without reserve.*

One of the most acute of all upsetting situations is that of grief occasioned by the death of someone dearly loved. Scarcely any form of mental

* If I can be helpful to any reader, please write me c/o Peale Center for Christian Living, 66 East Main Street, Pawling, N.Y. 12564.

pain quite equals this poignant human experience. It is a blow, a shock, a devastation that cuts deeply and acutely into the bereaved person's mind. This experience, inevitable in due course to everyone, must be faced, when it comes, with dignity, strength and understanding. But this of course is not easy to do. Indeed, it is an upsetting situation from which recovery and healing of mind can be an extraordinarily difficult process.

To be supportive of a person suffering from the shock of grief, a genuine transference of love is no doubt a most effective form of helpfulness. But many persons admit feeling inadequate to expressing the concern and sympathy really felt under such painful circumstances. Actually, words are not vitally important; the conveyance by attitude of the felt affection performs its own healing.

As a very young man I was called upon to conduct the funeral of a little girl in Brooklyn, New York. It was only the second funeral of my then brief career as a minister, and the first for a child. The body of the sweet little girl lay in a white casket. I remember that she was dressed in white and had pink ribbons in her golden hair. It really broke me up. I stood hesitantly, trying to say something to comfort the crushed young parents, but the words would not come. Finally I went across the room to the parents, the mother only twenty-one and the father twenty-three, impulsively put my arms around them and said brokenly, "Listen, Jim and Helen—listen and never forget it—God loves you." That was all I could say. Some forty years later the father told me, "When you put your arms around us that terrible day, we knew that you loved us and," he added, "you made us know, really know, that the love of God is real. And I've loved Him—and you—ever since." The love that passed between us that day taught these sad and crushed parents how to keep going in the traumatic pain of grief.

LOVE, THE GREAT HEALER

Fine words, facility of speech, sound argument, even convincing expressions of faith—none of these has the power to convey warmth as does the outgoing of genuine and loving friendship. Indeed, I have often felt that the power of the words of Scripture to comfort the sorrowing is largely due to the fact that they give assurance of God's love. For that reason they never fail to provide comfort and serenity. How many countless thousands, in the upsetting situation of sorrow and loneliness, have found peace and solace in such grief-healing words as "I am the resurrection, and the life: he that believeth in me, though he were dead, yet shall he live: And whosoever liveth and believeth in me shall never die."* Or, again: "In my Father's house are many mansions: . . . I go to prepare a place for you. . . . that where I am, there ye may be also."† And the incomparable picture of a loving Father: "They shall hunger no more, neither thirst any more; neither shall the sun light on them, nor any heat. For the Lamb which is in the midst of the throne shall feed them, and shall lead them unto living fountains of waters: and God shall wipe away all tears from their eyes."‡

A leader of industry, onetime president of General Motors Corporation, lost his wife after more than fifty years of marriage. Shortly thereafter mutual friends indicated that Alfred P. Sloan wished to talk with me, as he was inconsolable. He fixed his penetrating eyes on me and with characteristic directness said, "I want to ask a straight question and want a straight answer. No vague generalization or weasel speculation."

"Okay," I said, "you ask the question and you'll get a straight answer."

"What I want to know is this: Will I ever be with my wife again or is she forever lost to me?"

"If you live in faith as she did, you will meet her in the afterlife where there is no separation. And meanwhile you will sense her nearness even on this earth."

He looked searchingly into my eyes. "How sure are you?" he insisted.

"Absolutely sure," I replied. He was too big a mentality to demand philosophical proofs. All that he wanted was a positive principle on which to rest his own momentarily shaky faith. He then went on to tell me how much he depended upon his wife; how, even in business decisions, he trusted her judgment. Touchingly, one became aware how even a strong man, seemingly self-sufficient, had a sense of dependence upon his companion of the years. As I sat looking at this big, intelligent but wounded and lonely man, I felt a surge of love for him. But you can hardly tell a tough man like this that you loved him, so without thinking I walked over and gently laid my hand on his head. He looked up like a child with tears in his eyes. As he showed me to the door and bade me good-bye with a crushing handclasp, all he said was, "Thanks. I'm okay now. I can keep going."

* John 11:25–26.

† John 14:2–3.

‡ Revelation 7:16–17.

I'LL NEVER FORGET MYRON ROBINSON

I have personal reason to know how love without words can help overcome the upsetting feelings caused by grief because I knew Colonel Myron Robinson. He was a big, rough kind of man, a prominent New Jersey politician in his day. He had a heart as big as all outdoors. And he was a member of my church in New York.

One Friday night some years ago after a memorable evening with my mother and the entire family, I took a night train from upstate New York to New York City, as I had a speaking engagement in a church at Elberon on the Jersey coast on the coming Sunday morning.

But early Saturday morning, shortly after arrival in the city, I had a telephone call from my wife, Ruth, that my mother had just died of a thrombosis. Shocked and grieved, I told Ruth that I would return immediately to Canisteo, New York, the family home, but in talking it over we decided that Mother would want me to carry on and keep my engagement to preach the Gospel, in which she believed so deeply. But I was sad and sorrowful and under shock. It was so unbelievable. My mother, whom I adored, was dead.

On Sunday morning early I boarded a train at Penn Station and sat disconsolately looking out the window when along came Myron Robinson walking through the coach. He took the seat beside me. "Where are you going, Myron?" I asked.

"To a big Republican clambake down at Ocean City. Big time today. Everyone will be there. Wouldn't miss it."

"Well, I hope you have a good time," I remarked.

Suddenly he looked at me. "What's the trouble, Norman? You're not your usual self. Something bothering you?"

So I told him what had happened in not too many words, as it sort of broke me up to talk about it. All Myron did was to pat me on the knee with his big hand.

When we came to my station of Elberon, to my surprise Myron left the train also. "Why are you getting off here? You have to stay on for Ocean City."

"Oh, I've decided I want to go to church with you instead of that clambake. Don't really like 'em, anyway," he said evasively. He accompanied me to church, sat right in front of me in the first pew, and took me to lunch following. We returned to the station and boarded the train back to New York with hardly any conversation between us. Arriving in Penn Station, where he was going uptown and I downtown, he stopped a moment and a look, really a beautiful look, came upon his face. He punched me in the chest. "I understand, boy, I understand. You've helped me through some hard ones; hope I've been a little help today." Whereupon to hide tears he turned with a wave of the hand and was gone.

Well, Myron Robinson has now himself gone over to the other side, but I will never forget this kindly man who had a heart full of love, a lot of which spilled over to me on that sad day long ago. He helped me to react creatively to one of my most upsetting situations and to keep going on the basis of the positive principle.

In this chapter on the important matter of reacting creatively to upsetting situations, the following points have been made:

1. Everyone has inside himself a piece of good news.
2. Affirm daily, "With God's help and guidance I am now getting creative outcomes to upsetting situations."
3. In tough situations, never panic, always cool it.
4. Remember, there is always Someone on your side.
5. Never make judgments emotionally. Think dispassionately and objectively.
6. Never react emotionally to criticism to the extent of allowing it to affect sound judgment. Analyze yourself to determine whether it is justified. If it is, correct yourself. Otherwise, go on about your business.
7. Always affirm there is an answer and solution to any problem and that you can find it; indeed, that you are now finding that answer.
8. When grief comes, remember and never forget that God loves you. He will see you through, always and surely.

NINTH WAY TO KEEP THE POSITIVE PRINCIPLE GOING

You Can Cope With Anything; You Really Can

You can cope with anything; you really can. And one thing is sure—the only way to handle this life successfully is to learn to cope. *Cope* means to handle, to confront, to stand up to, to deal with.

TWO LITTLE GIRLS

And finding out that one must cope is often encountered early in life. It is only as one develops this skill that ultimate and final personal victory comes. I happened to be on a Florida-bound train one day, but my destination was the Thirtieth Street station in Philadelphia. At North Philadelphia two little girls boarded the train. They were about ten and twelve years of age, I judged. I saw them first outside the window saying a tearful goodbye to two middle-aged people.

There was an empty seat alongside of me and the older girl sat there; the other little girl took the seat across the aisle. They were very sweet, demure, well dressed; indeed, very ladylike. They were wearing little immaculate white gloves. The girl sitting next to me was quite solemn;

and then I saw a tear, like a pearl, on her cheek. In her little hands she clutched a camera. So I asked, "Are you going to take some pictures?"

She replied in a tone so low that I could hardly hear. "We love them so, and we have to leave them. We love them so very much."

"Whom are you leaving, your parents?"

"No, our grandparents."

"And where are you going?" I asked.

"To St. Petersburg, to see our father, to live with him. We haven't seen him for three years. We hardly know him. [Apparently a broken family situation.] But our grandparents—we don't want to leave them. We love them so much."

"Oh," I said, "you'll like St. Petersburg, with its blue sparkling water, its golden sunlight, its white beaches, its fine people. And your father will be so glad to have his little girls. Just go down there and love him."

She was silent. Finally she said, as though speaking to herself, "But God will take care of us." By this time we had arrived at Thirtieth Street station in Philadelphia and I arose to leave. She stood up. Very politely and gravely she extended her hand to me, a stranger.

"Yes, honey," I said, "never forget it; God will take care of you." As the long sleek train pulled out of the station heading south, I reflected on the little human drama just experienced. Two frightened, lonely little girls, going out into the unknown, were learning early in life that it is necessary to cope. But they had also learned a basic philosophy: With God's help you can cope with anything—you can, for sure.

Of course, when we say that you can cope with anything, it is making an almost incredible claim. But, you see, we have an incredible God to support us. He is more than equal to any crisis, any difficulty in this world. We are told: "With God nothing shall be impossible."* It doesn't say that with God some things are not impossible. It says that "nothing" shall be impossible. Again in the Scriptures: "Eye hath not seen, nor ear heard, neither have entered into the heart of man, the things which God hath prepared for them that love Him."† And one of those tremendous things is the ability to cope with whatever difficulty, frustration or fear may assail us. Another statement gives assurance: "I can do all things through Christ which strengtheneth me.‡

* Luke 1:37.

† I Corinthians 2:9.

‡ Philippians 4:13.

It is never smart to disclaim the possibility of a great, even incredible attainment. Theodore N. Vail, a prominent industrialist, said, "Real difficulties can be overcome; it is only the imaginary ones that are unconquerable." Right, mostly; but even the imaginary ones can be overcome by right thinking. No difficulty, real or imaginary, is impregnable. But in asserting the claim that you can cope with anything, I remind you of a subtle and sound comment by the writer William Feather: "Success is seldom achieved by people who contemplate the possibility of failure." So hold the thought, hold it tenaciously, that you can cope with anything, especially when you allow God to help you.

GRAB A THISTLE

And how is this incredible feat accomplished? First of all, never vaguely and indecisively fool around with a difficulty; take hold of it and handle it. Do not be afraid, timorous or doubtful. Simply grab hold of the problem and deal with it masterfully.

In the office of John Bowles, a businessman, I learned of a number of difficulties he had overcome. I thought he seemed very relaxed and unhurt. So I said, "John, how come you were able to handle all you have been telling me about? These troubles would be sufficient to overwhelm many people."

He pointed to a vase in which was a big thistle. "Why a thistle?" I asked. "Couldn't you get a more exotic flower?"

"Oh," he replied, "since I experienced all those difficulties the thistle represents qualities most people do not recognize."

"There must be something behind that remark," I vouchsafed.

"There certainly is. Tell you what, take hold of that thistle," he directed.

"I don't like the looks of it; it's spiny; it will sting and hurt."

"Go ahead," he urged, "take hold of it."

Hesitatingly I reached out and gingerly touched it. "It pricks," I complained.

"You must be more of a philosopher than that," he said. "You see, the thistle represents the difficulties of life. And if you know how to handle a thistle, you have learned a primary step in handling difficulties. So grab that whole thistle; grab it hard." I did and, believe it or not, it didn't hurt a bit. It crushed in my hand.

Of course, this incident does not mean that difficulties, when you stand up to them, won't hurt. But they will hurt far less if you handle them forthrightly. When you have a difficulty with which you must cope, don't hold off; grab it, deal with it.

SHE TAKES LIFE IN HER TWO HANDS

It's like the lady I met in a radio broadcasting studio. She was interviewing several of us, and the conversation turned to some rather deep subjects. I had noticed, as she walked into the broadcasting room, that she was crippled, with one leg shorter than the other. And she was no glamour girl either, being along in years. But she had a beautiful face; actually there was a kind of light on it.

On the show we got to talking about human difficulty, and she said, "Really, there is only one way to handle difficulty. Simply trust God and believe He is with you and helping you all the time. Using that principle, I simply take hold of life with my two hands and handle whatever comes."

I glanced at her hands, noting that they were very small, even delicate, and I thought. "There is not much strength in those hands, but there is a lot of power in the woman." Aloud I said, "Your hands are little, but you tell me that you take hold of life with those two hands."

"Oh," she said, "I also have a secret. I know that my hands are small, but if I put my little hands in the two great big hands of God, that makes four hands. And with God, remember, nothing is impossible."

So, when something very tough comes along with which you must cope, the best procedure is simply to deal with it forthrightly and at once. Handle your difficulty by visualizing your two hands as being placed in the hands of God. This "four hand" concept means that nothing is impossible. Remember this dynamic radio personality. She made a lasting impression on me because of her keen insight into the problem of coping. She underscored the fact that you can cope with anything if you simply grab hold of the matter strongly and intelligently and keep the positive principle going.

So, when you have a big difficulty, the number-one technique is to say to yourself: "With God nothing is impossible." Say that affirmatively and always with faith. Continue that affirmation. Then relax, get quiet physically and mentally, cool it, and believe that the necessary power is coming through to help you handle the situation. In this manner you will learn to keep the power to cope always operative. At all times be philosophical, be relaxed and quietly thoughtful. Do this and the coping process will become easier and surer.

I FIND AN OLD DIARY

At our farmhouse in the country my wife recently got on a housecleaning "binge." She insisted that we needed to discard some things, and she started with a closet. It is astonishing how much stuff can accumulate in a closet, and this was a big one. Away back in that closet I found a box in which was a diary written by my father. It began in the spring of the year 1888.

Father went to school when they taught real penmanship, and his handwriting was beautiful. The ink was good, too, for it was very clear after all these years. It was a moving experience to read this diary of my father, who meant so much to me. It stated that he was valedictorian of his high school class. In fact, the diary began with commencement night, which, strangely enough, was in the middle of April 1888. They had to get through school before spring planting, presumably. There were six students in the class, four boys and two girls. He named them, and I remembered every one from my own youth. The diary told quite a lot about the young boy who later became my father. Let me record a few of his entries:

> Thursday, May 31, 1888
> I shovelled gravel today. I get $1.25 per day.
> Went to Young Folks prayer meeting tonight.
> Wednesday, June 6, 1888
> At the Democrat Convention in St. Louis
> Grover Cleveland was renominated for
> President of the United States
> I went to Young Folks prayer meeting tonight.
> I went swimming for the first time this year.
> Thursday, June 7, 1888
> Allen G. Thurman was nominated for Vice
> President of the United States.
> I went to missionary meeting at Dr. Garner's tonight.
> Went swimming.
> Wednesday, June 25, 1888
> Gen. Benjamin Harrison was nominated for President by the Republican Party today. Also Morton of New York for Vice President. I took my last chew of tobacco today. I also smoked my last cigar. I mean by this that I quit.

I never knew that he chewed or even smoked. But it indicates that away back there he was coping with a habit that bothered him. But he learned how to cope; he went to the young people's prayer meeting and the missionary meeting, and so was developing a coping faith.

That fall he entered the Medical College of Ohio, as it was called at that time. He studied hard and became a physician. Later he became a preacher, for he could not resist the "call." But he was always a physician type of preacher, dealing with health of body, mind and soul.

The diary goes on to enumerate something else with which he had to cope—he didn't have much money. His father, Samuel Peale, ran a general store in the little town of Lynchburg, Ohio, where they lived, and from him he learned to be careful with the little money he had. He kept an accurate account of all he spent. Note the price structure of that time:

September 10, 1888 (At College)

Board one week	$2.00
Room rent one week	1.25
Shave	.10
Oyster stew	.20
1 dozen bananas	.05
Dinner	.15
Supper	.10
Postage stamp	.02
Candy for brother	.05
One load of coal	2.00
Church collection	.05
Gave to a poor woman	.10

Those figures indicate how matters stood financially in this country in those days. The average person was not affluent; but there is every indication that he was strong and sturdy, with a deep faith that helped in everyday living.

Toward the end of the diary my father expressed the coping wisdom he had learned, the positive principle he had mastered:

> As a young boy and in my later experiences I discovered a great truth, and it is this: If you stay close to Jesus and have faith in Him, He will see you through anything. He always has and He always will.

My dear father wrote those words on September 10, 1888, when he was eighteen years old. He never knew that one of his sons would be quoting them in a book a long lifetime later. But the principles that my father found workable so many years ago helped him to cope in his day.

They are still workable currently. So, as my father put it, "Stay close to Jesus." Always believe that with God, nothing is impossible. By these sound principles you can cope with anything, you really can.

One thing is sure: We are all going to face difficulties in this life. Indeed, there will be lots of them, and some are bound to be severe and acute, even painful. What we do about these difficulties will determine whether circumstances master us or whether we master circumstances. Marcus Aurelius, the great Roman philosopher, is credited with a picturesque statement, one that is surely packed with truth: "Man must be arched and buttressed from within, else the temple wavers to the dust."

In coping with your difficulties, it is of vital importance to develop a philosophical attitude. Do not become tense; never get worked up; always remain unperturbed. Remember, easy does it. Never let yourself be disturbed. Be philosophical. Always maintain emotional balance. Keep the mind operating and in constant control of the emotions.

VISIT TO A SHINTO SHRINE

Once in Tokyo I was visiting a Shinto shrine. It is approached down a long avenue of small shops or stalls. In the center of the plaza fronting the temple stands a huge Japanese-style urn from which steaming incense emanates. Tradition has it that if you have an illness or any bodily weakness and you direct the incense over the affected part, you will be healed. I noticed that people were using a circular motion with hands and arms to direct the incense toward various portions of the body. One man, whom I immediately took to be an American, was waving the incense in the direction of his heart. A look of unquestioning faith showed on his face.

"Do you think this incense will heal you?" I asked.

"Why not?" he replied. "They say it will."

"Continue to believe it," I answered. "But how come you are directing the incense toward your heart?"

"Because that is the weakest place in my body."

So after he stepped aside, I waved the steam onto my head.

Believe me, the head *is* most important; for when you face a difficulty it is so terribly necessary always to keep the mind calm and quiet in order that it may be controlled and thereby function efficiently. Of course, that will not always be easy to accomplish. But in order to cope with your difficulties it is important to cultivate the qualities of a philosopher. Be quiet and thoughtful, take things as they come. And always depend upon the calm knowledge that you can be master of anything that may happen to you.

PHILOSOPHICAL BASEBALL PLAYER

When the Brooklyn Dodgers National League baseball club was in Brooklyn playing in the old Ebbets Field, I knew almost every man on the Dodger roster. One player was a powerful hitter, averaging regularly over .300, which is good and then some.

One night he was coming to our house for dinner with some of his teammates. It had not been possible for me to go to the game that day in early April, but I did listen to part of the game on the radio as I drove in my car to and from engagements.

This mighty hitter came to bat in the second inning and ignominiously struck out—one, two three. I turned off the radio.

That night when the players came to the house this hitter, to my surprise, was in a happy and relaxed mood. "I was sorry to hear that you struck out in the second inning today," I said.

"Oh," he replied, "that isn't all of it. I struck out again in the fourth inning."

Astonished, I asked, "Do you mean to tell me that you can be so unconcerned about striking out twice in one of the early games of the season?"

"Why not?" he replied. "You see, on the basis of my batting average I will strike out about ninety times in the season, and I'm always comforted by the law of averages." I thought that was quite a mouthful for a baseball player. "Yes," he continued, "that law of averages is a great comfort. So today when the game was over and I went into the clubhouse, I said to the boys, 'What do you know! Isn't it great? I only have eighty-eight more times to strike out this season!' "

That is what you can reasonably call a relaxed, philosophical attitude toward a difficulty.

Most difficulties are handled effectively in proportion to the degree to which we untense ourselves. Though this fact was pointed out in the previous chapter, I must underscore it here, for calmness of mind is vital to coping with problems. An uptight, nervous individual is not likely to get into the easy flow of personality in which the thinking process can grapple with difficulty efficiently; when troubled with panic and apprehension feelings, such a mind cannot function with the cool, philosophical attitude of the batter who took comfort in the law of averages.

NINE GUIDELINES FOR COPING

Some years ago I worked out nine effective guidelines for coping with difficulties which have been personally helpful, and these include the positive principle we have been discussing:

1. Don't panic. Keep calm. Use your head. Think.
2. Never be overwhelmed. Never dramatize the difficulty. Affirm confidently, "God and I can handle it."
3. Practice "de-confusion." To do so, write on paper every element of the difficulty, mentally clarifying each part.
4. Skip the postmortems. Take the problem from where you are at this instant.
5. Look for an answer, not for the whole problem, but for the next step.
6. Practice creative listening. Get quiet so that insights can come through your mind.
7. Always ask what is the right thing to do, for nothing wrong ever turns out right.
8. Keep thinking, keep believing, keep working, keep praying.
9. Keep on actively employing the positive principle.

Those are nine workable guidelines. Practice them diligently and you can develop the ability to cope with your difficulties in an effective and certain manner. I suggest that they be written on a card small enough to fit into your pocket. Read them every day until they become a definite part of your mental equipment.

HELP OTHERS COPE AND YOU HELP YOURSELF

Another workable and effective way to meet and overcome difficulties is to take on someone else's problems. It is a strange fact, but you can often handle two difficulties—your own and somebody else's—better than you can handle your own alone. That truth is based on a subtle law of self-giving or outgoingness whereby you develop a self-strengthening in the process. If you have a tough difficulty, look around until you find somebody who has a worse difficulty than yours, then start helping that individual. You will find in so doing that your own problem, when finally you have helped the other person with his, will be much simpler, much clearer, much easier to handle.

I often think of a story told by Arthur Gordon about the editor of a small-town weekly newspaper, a man who was having some difficult problems. One day the editor's neighbor, a man named Bill, took his wife and little son out on the river in a canoe. Suddenly the canoe overturned. Both wife and husband were good swimmers. They tried desperately to save their boy, but tragically he was swept way and drowned. The father was inconsolable. "Why did I do this?" he berated himself. "Why didn't I do that?" So he argued in futility and desperation. Ceaselessly he walked the streets. People would see him on county roads, walking, walking, always walking.

One night Jack, the newspaper editor, was working late in his office. About midnight came a rap on his door and there, disconsolate, stood his neighbor, Bill. "You're out late tonight, Bill. What are you doing?"

"I'm just walking, Jack, just walking. You see, I can't forget. Why did that have to happen? Why did I take the boy out in the canoe? Why couldn't I rescue him? I can't understand it, Jack."

"Come in, Bill. Sit down and let's talk." Bill slumped in the chair. "I can't talk. I just don't feel like talking."

"Okay," the editor said, "that's all right. Just sit there and I'll go on with my work. Whenever you're ready to talk, let me know." After a while he asked, "Bill, how about a cup of coffee? It will warm you up."

Bill said, "Yes, I'd be glad to have one. But I'm still not ready to talk."

It got to be on toward two o'clock in the morning. Then Bill said, "Now, Jack, I'm ready to talk." For an hour he reasoned it all out, lived it all over again. Jack listened. There are times when one of the most helpful things a person can do for another is simply to listen and let that individual know that you care. This was one of those times. Finally, completely spent, Bill slowed to a stop. "I guess that's all I've got to say tonight, Jack." He got up to go.

Jack put his hand on the broken man's shoulder. "We all love you," he said kindly. "I wish I could help."

"But," said Bill, "You have helped me—more than I can ever tell you. You're helped me because you've listened and you didn't argue. I know that you like me, that you're my friend. You've helped me a lot. I will never forget. Goodnight, Jack." He walked out into the night.

Jack sat lost in thought. All of a sudden his mind went back to his own problems. To his astonishment, that which had been unclear was now clearer; that which before he could not see his way through he now saw objectively; that which had seemed to overwhelm him now seemed easier to cope with. He felt that he had more power to handle his own problems.

When you become detached mentally from yourself and concentrate on helping people with *their* difficulties, it is a fact that you will be able to cope with your own more effectively. Somehow, the act of self-giving is a personal power-releasing factor.

HE FOUND THAT HE COULD COPE WITH ANYTHING

A great human story of coping with, perhaps, the ultimate in human problems is that of Orville E. Kelly, a newspaperman from Burlington, Iowa. He will always rank as one of my unforgettable characters. Orville Kelly has profoundly demonstrated that a person can, indeed, cope with anything, and successfully.

I first heard of Kelly in a newspaper story telling how, as a terminal case, he developed the philosophy that "death is part of life." He originated the now well-known M.T.C. (Make Today Count) program. Impressed by his sound pattern of thinking, I wrote to Mr. Kelly expressing admiration for his courageous and rational attitude. Subsequently he visited our Foundation for Christian Living where, in his sincere way of speaking, he deeply moved and inspired everyone. When he finished his talk, each of us felt that, with the same spiritual power demonstrated by Orville, we, too, could cope with anything we might have to face.

MAKE TODAY COUNT

Because of the widespread effects of cancer, touching as it does not only the thousands who have the disease but other thousands of loved ones who are affected, I am reprinting part of Orville Kelly's story as he wrote it for our publication, "Creative Help for Daily Living."* Read this human drama carefully and I'm quite sure you will think twice before again questioning the ability of a person, with God's help, to cope with anything. Here is a man who lives and deals with life on the basis of the positive principle and does it gloriously and victoriously.

"Terminal cancer," the doctors said.

My first reaction to this death sentence was disbelief. Such a thing could not happen to *me*, I told myself. The doctors had made a terrible mistake. But I knew they hadn't. It was true, I was going to die before my time.

My next reaction was deep depression, a state that engulfed me for days. Thoughts of suicide even crossed my mind. And I dragged my wife and children down into a state of gloom with me. How could God have let this happen to me when everything was going well for me and my family? I was only 42 years old. I had a good job as a newspaperman and a bright future before me. We had a nice home. All of us were active and busy, and we were good churchgoing Christians. Why me?

I would still be plunged in this kind of despair if I had not finally seen the light, accepted the Lord's way and taken positive action not only to help myself but to also help others whose path is taking them into the valley of death before their time.

My inner reaction was fear. Living with cancer was a frightening experience, not only for me as a victim but for my family, relatives and friends. My wife, Wanda, and I had not discussed it openly because I did not want to worry her, and she had remained silent out of fear that she would upset me. People stopped dropping in to see us because it was too depressing for them.

I began to understand that it was the prospect of death that frightened me, not the thought of having cancer. That is when depression—despair—took hold of my life. Wanda was under a physician's care for a severe case of nerves. The situation reached its low point as we were driving home one day from Iowa City after a session of chemotherapy. It was a beautiful fall day, but as I glanced toward my wife, I saw a look of complete dejection on her face. We drove silently across the prairie.

HE TAKES POSITIVE ACTION

Finally I decided something had to be done, and fast, to help Wanda accept my fate. It was then I found myself looking again to God for guidance, I asked for His help. Then I turned to Wanda.

* For a reprint of Orville Kelly's story, "Make Today Count," write to Peale Center for Christian Living, 66 East Main Street, Pawling, N.Y. 12564.

"Let's talk about it," I said. "I'm going to die from cancer unless something else kills me, but I'm not dead yet. So let's start enjoying life again." I told her that we should explain the situation to the children since they already knew something was wrong, and that we should face my terminal illness as a family in a positive way. We went home and told the children. It wasn't easy, but I did tell them.

There are those who might wonder about this approach to death. I felt I had nothing to lose and everything to gain by trying the simple thought of making each day count. After all, none of us *really* know when we are going to die. We are all "terminal" in a sense.

Family life gradually returned to normal; not perfect, but normal. All of us realized that things would never be completely all right again, but we learned that it is possible to live with cancer instead of just giving up. My new philosophy could be summed up simply: "Each day I will accept not as another day closer to death, but as another day of life. I accept each day as a gift from God to be appreciated, enjoyed and lived to its fullest."

This new attitude gave me a renewed interest in life, and I began writing again. I started by doing an article for our local newspaper in which I advocated the formation of an organization of terminally ill patients who could meet informally to help one another cope with their problems in a positive way.

The telephone began ringing as soon as the article appeared. People called to tell me that they had gone through the same emotional crisis I had faced. So many called that I invited them to what became the first meeting of the organization we called "Make Today Count." Eighteen people attended, among them cancer victims, relatives of terminal patients, ministers, nurses and nursing students. I made it clear that no one was to cry on anyone's shoulder or try to gain sympathy for his suffering. We were there to seek positive ways to make the rest of our lives more meaningful.

Nearly 50 attended our third meeting. Make Today Count was described in news-agency feature articles and on radio and television. This brought letters pouring in from people who wanted to start chapters in their home towns. Some who wrote were not physically ill, just depressed; they saw in Make Today Count the possibility of improving their lives. Chapters have been established in many states and abroad.

Meetings are informal, unstructured, and there are no chapter officers. Just bringing people together to talk and share their problems over coffee can accomplish a great deal. Through our conversations we are learning to accept the idea that death is part of life.

LIVE FOR TODAY

During the period when I was severely depressed, I was being treated efficiently and with kindness and sympathy by the physicians who had pronounced the death sentence. Ministers discussed life after death. But no one seemed to mention living for today!

I'll have to admit that though I may be helping others through Make Today Count, I am also helping myself. I have stopped measuring time in months and years. Seconds are the framework in which I operate. The trace of a smile on my wife's face, the laughter of my children, a flash of sunlight. They are of the moment, and of a lifetime.

Of course my wife and I dreamed of growing old together, but we have learned that life is fragile and unpredictable for everyone. Of course I didn't want to have cancer, but I didn't have any choice. So I say to myself, "What do I have to lose by trying to be happy?"

Some people have achieved immortality through their art or through acts of heroism or nobility. Since I am neither especially talented nor heroic, facing death has been especially difficult. The fear and uncertainty that confronted me when I learned I had terminal cancer were worse than the idea of death itself. Looking back to those first days of shock, I know now that my family and I grieved about a death that had not yet occurred. But by discussing death and being open about cancer and its problems, I have found myself more concerned with life than with death.

In other words, until we realize that death is a part of life, I don't think we can truly enjoy life. Because I feel that way, when a man recently said to me, "We have something in common; we are both dying of cancer," I was able to reply, "No, we have in common the fact that we are both still alive."

The other day a little girl at school remarked to my nine-year-old daughter, "I saw your daddy on TV and he is dying of cancer, isn't he?"

"Yes," my daughter replied, "but he's not dead yet!"

Not by a long shot. Today is where I am and today I am alive. I am not especially concerned about yesterday or tomorrow. I am concerned about *today* . . . right now! I am trying to make time count.

NEW AWARENESS OF LIFE

Looking back, I find it difficult to believe today that I am the same person who blamed God for my cancer and who doubted His existence. Perhaps, in my case, death made me aware of life.

One night when I found it difficult to sleep, I wrote a prayer. It goes like this:

Our Heavenly Father . . .
Give me the strength to face each night
Before the dawn.
Give me the courage to watch my children at
play,
And my wife at my side,
Without a trace of sorrow in my smile;
Let me count each passing moment,
As I once marked the fleeting days and nights,
And give me hope for each tomorrow.
Let my dreams be dreams of the future.
But when life on earth is over,
Let there be no sadness,
But only joy, for the golden days I've had.
Amen.

You have read the profound philosophy and faith of a man who is demonstrating in a practical way that one can cope with anything. You have read a sound, in-depth description of life at a top level of victory. This is the vibrant positive principle in action.

My wife, Ruth, and I had lunch with Orville and Wanda and other friends one golden autumn day when the maple- and oak-covered hills of Dutchess County were at their height of glorious coloring. We sat in a restaurant by the side of a highway with heavy traffic going by. But beyond the highway was a meadow and beyond that the hills, and in the meadow cows were grazing.

Orville looked beyond the traffic to the cattle and the meadow and the hills in their dress of red and gold, and with misty eyes said, "What is so beautiful as cows grazing peacefully in an autumn landscape?" He was silent for a moment, then said musingly, "This morning coming down from Connecticut I saw a red bird sitting on a fence post. It looked so bright and happy. I think I shall always remember that bird on a fence post one bright morning in Connecticut.

His were not the eyes that were misty as he spoke. All of us around the table in that busy restaurant became keenly aware of the triumphant life of our friend. Actually, we became conscious of God at that moment, who can make a human being into a victorious spirit. So please believe it, for it is true. You can cope with anything—you really can.

What suggestions have been made in this chapter to help you cope?

1. Take life and its problems with your two hands.
2. Then put your hands in God's hands.
3. Remember that God will see you through anything, so stay close to Him.
4. Keep unperturbed—never panic. Be a philosopher. Think, always think. Do not react emotionally. Use your head; think. You will find that you can cope.
5. Always believe that you can, and you will find that you can.
6. Help other people to cope with their problems and your own will be easier to cope with.
7. Always—Make Today Count.

TENTH WAY TO KEEP THE POSITIVE PRINCIPLE GOING

The Fabulous Secret of Energy and Vitality Thinking

"If we did all the things we are capable of doing we would literally astonish ourselves." So said the great inventive genius and thinker Thomas A. Edison.

Did you ever astonish yourself? Did I? Embarrassing but provocative question, isn't it? But if we potentially possess all that capacity—and it must be so if as great an authority as Edison says so—then the question is: How may it be released? I have discovered that one way to release the potential of an individual is to activate the fabulous secret of energy and vitality. Add to that an underscoring of the positive principle, and any person can become altogether different; indeed, very different.

A physician asked me to see a man whom he rather inelegantly described as "rolling in money" but who was completely out of energy and vitality. "I can continue to pamper him and feed him pills, but that kind of treatment doesn't jibe with my idea of ethical medicine. He isn't really ill, but his thinking sure is diseased. He is a person of real ability, but it is far from operative. How about taking a crack at this guy? Maybe your kind of medicine will do him some good." So ended the breezy case history by a doctor who nevertheless had pretty keen insights not only into human disability but also into psychological reactions.

I SEE THE DE-ENERGIZED PATIENT

When I arrived at his sumptuous apartment, the man went into a long and detailed account of his ill feelings of mind and body and how weak, depleted and absolutely down he felt. "I used to have lots of drive and go," he declared feebly, "but now I have no more energy than a cat." Which I thought an inaccurate comparison inasmuch as all the cats I know, while they may act lazy, can leap up and spring like a bullet out of a gun.

As he talked I recalled the wise advice of my good doctor friend, Dr. Z. T. Bercovitz, to the effect that "to get in tone it is necessary to get in tune." So I said, "Look, I'm not a medical doctor, as you know, but I try to serve as a kind of doctor of the mind, and perhaps the soul, too. And a good many medical men believe that not a few feelings of physical illness and depletion take their rise in diseased mental and spiritual attitudes."

He rather blinked at that one and went off on a lengthy description of his mother and father, "always poor in this world's goods, but great Christians. Yes, sir, real Christians. In church every Sunday," et cetera, et cetera.

"Well," I responded, "what they were may have no bearing on what you are, but, incidentally, have you any evidence that their piety rubbed off on you?"

He began to get the point, for in replying to that question he said, "Guess you've got me there. Got to admit I'm pretty much of a heel; been through every sin in the book. You wrote a book on positive thinking, but you're looking at the biggest negative thinker in this town. Tell me what you are going to do about that."

"It isn't what I'm going to do, but what are *you* are going to do? Mope around here thinking negative thoughts and being pseudo-sick the rest of your life? How old are you, by the way?"

"I'm fifty-two years of age and I've had it."

By this time I was liking this man more by the minute, for underneath it all he was basically honest and forthright. And he had brainpower, too; that was not to be denied. Indeed, he had the makings of a real, honest-to-goodness, healthy man.

"Look," I said, "what do you say we drain off all that mental and spiritual infection that is sapping your energy and leaving your whole system tired and devitalized?"

Perhaps unconsciously he had wanted this kind of treatment, for he began to open up and come clean. It was hard for him at first to discuss intimate matters with a stranger, but I guess he trusted me as a pastor, for he began to pour out a mass of sick thinking and unhealthy action that went back to his youth. He had an enormous sense of guilt, and despite his bombastic demeanor he was, surprisingly, filled with quite a lot of inadequacy and inferiority attitudes.

Finally he asked, rather piteously, if I thought God would forgive him. "Why not ask Him?" I suggested.

"You mean now: I never prayed in public before."

"Oh, I'm not the public, just your friend. So go on, ask Him to forgive you."

That he did in slow and hesitant words, but with great sincerity. "What did you feel the Lord say to you?" I asked.

With a sense of wonder and a very relieved kind of look, he said, "I'm forgiven, I really feel I'm forgiven. I remember He promised that all you have to do is to ask and He hears and forgives. But still I don't feel as peaceful as I expected."

"You've got one thing more to do, or maybe two things. The first is to forgive yourself. You see," I continued, "we all have a built-in censor which tells us we must be punished for evils we have done. And that censor is pretty difficult to call off. But you have had your share of self-inflicted punishment, so now say aloud, 'I hereby forgive myself even as God has forgiven me.' "

"That," he declared upon repeating the statement, "makes sense—a great big lot of sense."

"Okay," I said, "the second thing is to believe that in the name of the Lord and of yourself [I remembered the doctor's diagnosis] you are a well man. Really believe that. Now get up and get out of here and get going." He took me to the door, gave me a crushing handclasp that was vastly different from the flabby hand he had extended earlier. "Keep that good old positive principle going," I admonished.

"Sure will," he declared. "Just watch me and see."

I did watch him and I did see. A week later I called on the telephone to inquire about him and found that he was back on the job and going strong. And he kept going with continuous vitality and enthusiasm.

I do not want it to be inferred from this rapid get-well story that I am any healer or that such cases always work out so immediately. Actually, in a sense, the man healed himself through complete surrender to God. And he continued re-energized and revitalized for some twenty years, for I often saw him in our congregation at the Marble Collegiate Church. As he told me, "I'm on the mental and spiritual beam and will never get off it again." He kept that promise until he died in an accident at age seventy-three.

The incident was enlightening and educational for me, too, for it showed the powerful effect on bodily reactions of an unhealthy pattern of thought. Many times since that experience I have done a rehabilitation job on my own thoughts when I found myself tired or run-down or in any sense de-energized. Unconsciously we can have a mental buildup of sick thinking which may result in debilitating or even serious illness. Certainly it can reduce efficiency. The fabulous secret of energy and vitality thinking should be used in activating the positive principle. And invariably the result is renewable personality force.

CONTACT THE LIFE FORCE

It was in the writing of Myrtle Fillmore, who with her husband founded the Unity School of Christianity, that I first became aware of the important life force concept. This is based on the principle that we were not created and endowed with vital life only to have it at once start to decline. The truth is that we can constantly be in a re-creative process through which the powerful life force is ever renewing vitality. I have observed that those who practice the fabulous secret of energy and vitality thinking keep vibrant power going amazingly despite all of those enemies of well-being which tend to deplete strength.

Over the years of an extremely active schedule of writing, speaking, editing, publishing and administering, I have kept my own energy and vitality going by constant affirmation of the life force, visualizing it as continuously flowing through mind and body. This practice has steadily renewed strength and kept an unimpeded flow of energy operating without diminution. Certainly I become tired, but it is never a tiredness that a good night's sleep will not cure. My particular job requires keeping a number of balls in the air at the same time, so to speak, and being called upon daily to make decisions in a variety of fields. And always there is the necessity to keep producing. Since without energy and vitality no active person can sustain a vigorous program, it is a matter of utmost importance to learn how to keep it going.

THE WAY A DOCTOR KEPT IT GOING

In my early years in New York when I was constantly gearing up to an ever increasing schedule and experiencing the tension that often accompanies such driving activity, I became a friend of the late Dr. William Seaman Bainbridge, who practiced medicine on Gramercy Park in Manhattan. He was an extraordinarily busy man, not only in his own profession but in many societies and organizations, in which he was inevitably a leader.

One day I gave a vigorous talk to the New York Rotary Club, of which he was president and I a member. These meetings are scheduled to close promptly at 1:45 P.M., for the Rotarians are all business and professional men who have schedules to keep. Dr. Bainbridge, who always had an office full of patients waiting for him, scheduled his first afternoon appointment for two o'clock. "Come on, Norman," he said hurriedly, "let's grab a cab and go downtown together. I want you to stop by my office for five minutes on the way to your office." At 1:50 we arrived at his old brownstone on Gramercy Park and went into his private office. Outside in the waiting room was a formidable lineup of patients.

"That was a great talk you gave at Rotary," he said. "You sure did pour it on. You are bound to be on a high tension level and so am I, and we've got to cool it. Let's relax and get the old energy and vitality going to compensate for the big expenditure of energy we have been making." So saying, he flopped into a big chair, his legs straight out, arms hanging limply over the sides of the chair and head back against the headrest. "Do the same," he directed, and I flopped down similarly.

After a minute of silence he said, "Peace and quietness are filling our minds. Renewal is now taking place in our physical bodies. We are now being re-created in every part of our beings. We are being given energy control sufficient for our needs." Another moment of silence followed this impressive affirmation. Then, "Okay, now we're ready to begin a busy afternoon. That's a prescription for you, my friend," he concluded in his kindly fashion. Whereupon he called for his first patient and I went out into the hectic city of New York "raring to go." I have faithfully followed the doctor's method for re-energizing oneself since he taught it to me over thirty years ago.

THE WAY AN AMBASSADOR KEPT IT GOING

Lawrence Townsend, once Ambassador to Austria and other countries, was a tall, lithe, vigorous man up into his nineties. His erect carriage bespoke military training as a young man. He had all the graciousness and savior faire associated with traditional ambassadors and was a close friend of the late King George V and Queen Mary. I knew him quite well in his later years and visited him one day in his Florida home.

I found him in his "place of meditation" in his spacious garden. This was an enclosure done in stained wood somewhat like a log cabin, with no top, being entirely open to the sun. He was in bathing trunks and I noticed that his skin was tight, his body muscular, fat-free and tanned. His eyes were bright and his face was wreathed in smiles as he greeted me. "Excuse this informal welcome, but I'm performing my daily vitality and energy ritual. It's this practice that has kept me going strong over the long pull," he explained. "Excuse me a moment while I get dressed and then we will visit and have lunch."

"No, Lawrence, don't stop. I could use a good vitality and energy ritual myself. Please let me watch your procedure." Thus encouraged, and being an avid believer in affirmative processes, Mr. Townsend said, "Okay, here it is." He then stood straight up, "reaching for the sky with the crown of my head," as he put it. By such reaching he drew every organ into place and counteracted the sag that mars the physical form of so many of us. He then raised his arms high and reached for the sky with his fingers. Then followed a rather usual type of exercising and I could see the strong muscles rippling under the skin.

"So much for the physical part of it," he said, breathing easily, with no puffing or other sign of exertion. "Now for the more important mental and spiritual exercise." Still standing erect and tall, he said something like the following, which I copied word for word at the time and practiced so often that, while the written formula has long since disappeared, it remains in memory. "Lord God Almighty, my Creator and Heavenly Father, as the sun from heaven shines upon and renews my body, so does the sunshine of Your great Spirit warm my mind and my soul, renewing me by the power of Your wondrous grace." He used the old stately terms most impressively. "I am now emptying from my mind every thought, idea and memory that is not in harmony with Your goodness. I hereby drop from consciousness every selfish, evil and unworthy thought. I let go all uncharitable attitudes, every fear and every vestige of ill will and resentment. As my mind is now emptied and clean of every unhealthy thought, You are now filling it with thoughts of goodness, love and faith. Thank You, dear Lord, for I can feel at this moment Your freshening and renewing power. And it feels so wonderfully good! Thank You, thank You."

FORMULA OF THANKSGIVING

To this he added what he called "the formula of thanksgiving." Still standing tall, he said, "Thank You, O Creator, for my wonderful body which only You can make; for my strong heart, my good stomach, my healthy liver; for my keen eyes, my sensitive ears and my brain; all parts of my body are now serving me as well as when I was a youth. Then, Heavenly Father, thank You for that immortal part of me, my soul, which I place once again in Your keeping. I affirm my desire to serve You all the days of my life until evening falls and I enter into rest and on into eternal life, still with You whom I have loved always. Thank You for Your gracious forgiveness and for the peace of mind You are giving me every day all the way."

I stood entranced, admiring this unusual man. Some might regard what I have just described as an oddball kind of thing, but I assure you this man was as sharp as they make them; a highly innovative and effective personality. He lived as a strong, healthy man until about age ninety-five, then one night he lay down to sleep and did not awaken in this mortal world.

But I have little doubt that on the next morning in some brighter and more beautiful place of meditation he was still practicing his ritual of energy and vitality thinking. Many to whom I have suggested this procedure have testified to its efficacy. I often do it myself, and it works wonders in the energy renewal process. You can perform it right in your own home even without sunshine. That can be mentally induced. Every organ in the body will respond and you will feel good. Try this aspect of the positive principle and keep it going, for it will keep you going.

DON'T DRAG THROUGH LIFE

It is a pathetic fact that multitudes of people actually drag through life in a dreary sort of way, having little or none of the zest and enthusiasm which should normally characterize a human being. And the big majority of such people probably have nothing really wrong physically. But they handle the duties and responsibilities of life in a half-hearted and desultory manner, just getting by. When a person is only getting by, it is a fact that he is not really getting with it. Under such circumstances life can, of necessity, be only partial; the good-better-best that it should be just does not come through.

But when a person of this type has a real energizing and vitalizing experience, he is astounded by the powerful new quality of life which changes everything for him. Thomas A. Edison's statement previously mentioned spectacularly applies: "If we did all the things we are capable of doing we would literally astonish ourselves." So it pays to find and practice the fabulous secret of energy and vitality thinking. Those old, tired, desultory feelings will be eliminated by a surging infusion of new interest, zest and enthusiasm.

RUN-DOWN CAREER WOMAN

An incident of personal energy renewal I very much like to recount concerns a brilliant and hard-driving New York City career woman, a great friend of Mrs. Peale's and mine. This superenergetic person finally cracked under the unreasonable and uncontrolled pace and suffered a nervous breakdown which took the form of complete drainage of energy and vitality. Formerly dynamic, she was now listless and weary. She would sit staring ahead, uncaring and disinterested, sadly deteriorated in spirit; indeed, completely changed from the excited and competent person she had been.

Her doctor suggested a change of scene and she went off to a seaside resort where she wandered about disconsolately or sat drained and apathetic. Then she took to going to the beach, not to swim but to sit or lie indolently on the sand. It was during the off season and the beach was practically her own. She welcomed the loneliness, for this formerly gregarious person now avoided people; it was too tiring to try to talk with anyone.

Even though the weather was growing colder, she spent many days on the beach. She liked the stimulating crispness. One day she suddenly began to pray, and in depth. She was a religious person with a leaning toward scientific spiritual truth, and she believed in the reality of Divine healing as not being inconsistent with medical treatment. She began to pray specifically for the healing of her condition. Presently she had a strangely certain feeling that her prayer was being granted.

And it came about in a curious manner. One day as she lay on the beach amid some tall beach grass, she found herself listening to the sound of the surf; and as she listened intently she noticed a regularity of rhythm in the surging of the sea on the shore. Then her eye caught a single blade of beach grass moving gracefully in the gentle breeze. As she watched she began to note that it, too, moved in rhythm, and the wind that moved the beach grass was also rhythmical. It occurred to her to take her own pulse and, astonishingly, it also possessed rhythm not unlike that of the sea and the beach grass and the wind.

Impressed by this phenomenon, she meditated on the fascinating reality upon which she had stumbled. Was it true that all nature is in rhythm, including her own being? Could this be the answer to her intense prayer for healing? She caught herself thinking those familiar words, "God moves in a mysterious way His wonders to perform."* Suddenly a healing thought flashed up in consciousness. Her trouble was that she had got out of rhythm in her thinking. As a result she could no longer work easily; there was too much overtense drive and not enough controlled emotional relaxation. "What I need is that wonderful thing called 'the peace of God, which passeth all understanding.' "† Now she was on the way to recovery, intuitively realizing that renewal of body would follow renewal of mind and spirit. Gradually, with consistent practice of the rhythmic principle, she discovered the secret of energy and vitality thinking and experienced a full return of health and vigor.

Because it illustrates the positive principle and a truth technique of wholeness and orderly personality organization, I like this true story and had often told it to people in similar condition. It carries with it a profound and practical truth principle: Get into rhythm with nature, with yourself, with your job, with other people and with God, and you will truly know the joyous fullness of life. Nor is it necessary to go to some lonely beach and lie on the sand to achieve a result. This process of renewal of energy and vitality can be employed where you are and at any time, for it is an exercise in mental therapy.

Never let yourself be driven or agitated to such an extent that the rhythmic flow of personality gets off center. An important procedure for

* Olney Hymns (1779), No. 35, by William Cowper.

† Philippians 4:7.

you and for me and for all of us in this modern, high-strung world of tensed-up people is to keep working in rhythmic harmony with the fabulous secret of energy and vitality thinking. Every day spend some unhurried moments in thinking energy, thinking vitality, actually "seeing" the life force at work in you. By thus emphasizing and underscoring such a creative operational experience, your energy and vitality will continue on and on and still on. You will keep the positive principle ever working for you.

I KNOW THESE ENERGY PRINCIPLES WORK

It is with complete assurance that I advocate these principles of energy and vitality thinking to my readers, for I have applied them successfully in my own personal experience. Indeed, nothing in this book is theoretically presented, for all of its principles have been tested both by me personally and by persons in whose integrity and honest judgment I have the greatest confidence.

Over a six-month period I carried out a weight-reduction program, taking off substantial poundage in the process. All went well until I began to experience periods of weakness and a startling diminution of energy, with a corresponding reduction of vitality. Inasmuch as I had always enjoyed a seemingly boundless supply of energy and vitality, this new feeling of weakness was disturbing, even bewildering. I was advised to change my diet to include some items in moderation which had been eliminated to effect the weight loss. But, having worked assiduously to take off the pounds, I was not about to take the chance of putting some back on again.

Medication to upgrade energy was prescribed. I took an energy-producing pill for a few mornings and it did have some effect. But then I decided that I did not want to get increased energy by the use of drugs, however innocuous. Accordingly, on the assumption that my problem was basically mental in nature, I began a regular routine of visualizing or imaging myself as having my old-time energy in full measure. Daily I practiced energy affirmations, declaring that the life force was revitalizing my mind and my body. I affirmed the value, in health terms, of the reduced weight and that my entire system was responding with new vigor. The effect of this procedure became increasingly noticeable with each passing day. The dramatically reduced diet was continued, weight was reduced to a new low level, but the weak feeling passed off and my usual energetic vitality pattern returned in full measure.

There are, of course, cases of energy loss in which the cause is basically physical in nature, in which event medical treatment employing medication is indicated. When loss of energy occurs, one should consult a physician and faithfully carry out prescribed treatment. But even in such cases it would seem that mental treatment would serve as an aid in the recuperative process. And along with the medical and mental approach, the application of spiritual therapy can hardly fail to have a salutary effect. Indeed, I know of one doctor who, in cases of energy loss, adds to his regular prescription a verbal "spiritual prescription." He advises his patient to pass daily through the mind the following words, which he says he has known to effect recuperation: "They that wait upon the Lord shall renew their strength; they shall mount up with wings as eagles; they shall run, and not be weary; and they shall walk, and not faint."* That affirming of the positive principle is a viable energy-producing agent.

MOTIVATION ENDED INERTIA

At a national trade association meeting where I addressed the delegates at their annual convention banquet, I spoke on the subject of why positive thinkers get positive results. Following my talk, a man asked if he could speak to me about a matter that seemed to be bothering him considerably. He appeared to be about forty-five years old, but, to my surprise, said he was thirty-five, or ten years younger than I had guessed. The older aspect was conveyed by a drawn look on his face and a pronounced slump of the shoulders. He rather gave the impression of a person slowly recovering from an illness, and he appeared to be low in spirit.

As we sat in the hotel lobby he explained that he just wasn't getting anywhere and that he didn't enjoy his job anymore. His job, it appeared, was an executive type position, neither at the bottom nor at the top, and he remarked glumly, "One thing is sure—I never expect to go any further in the business. I've hit my top."

"Why not?" I asked. "And what is your 'top'?"

"Oh," he replied in a weary and depressed tone, "nobody thinks very much of me. They know I haven't much on the ball. I've been written off. It's a wonder they don't fire me. Wouldn't blame them if they did."

* Isaiah 40:31.

"Ever come up with any new ideas, any fresh, innovative suggestions? Are you really on the company team? Do you show an interest in what goes on? Are you pulling full strength on your oar?"

"Oh, no, I never have any ideas, and so how can I be innovative? And besides, I'm a slow starter in the morning and never get going very strong at any time."

Suspecting the possibility of a physical problem, I asked if he had a medical checkup and it seemed that he had come through such examination successfully except that the doctor had commented on a general sluggishness. But beyond that his health seemed passable.

Then he rather took me aback. "I hate to tell you," he said rather diffidently, "but I read your book, *Enthusiasm Makes the Difference*, and it really teed me off, got me all steamed up, and for a while I went places. I did, for a fact. But then that enthusiasm began to leak, and just look at me now!"

When I asked what happened to cause the leak, he began to tell me of a few blows and setbacks. "They really threw me," he admitted.

"But you see, my friend," I explained, "it just isn't a real, bona fide enthusiasm if it can't stand up to a few blows or even to a lot of shock. Enthusiasm isn't only for fair weather and easy going. Almost anyone can keep it going when all is fortuitous. It is when the setbacks come—and it is the nature of setbacks not to come singly but in bunches—that enthusiasm needs to go to work. It is designed to give you the lift you need when things are tough. Guess you didn't read the book all that perceptively, or perhaps I didn't convey this idea to you with clarity. You must have another go at that enthusiasm. You know what the word means, do you not? It is derived from *entheos*—Greek for 'God in you.' So may I suggest that you need more of God in you."

"But how is that done? Frankly, I do not understand. I'm a now-and-then kind of churchgoing man. A believer, but I guess I never got with it, at least in the terms you are using."

I tried to explain that there exists a powerful energizing force in the spiritual life principle. All energy began with the Creator, who infused it not only in all natural processes, but also into that higher form of nature called human nature. The more closely, then, that a person identifies with the Creator, the more surely he will experience within his own nature the process of re-creation which operates in all creation. The individual who has permitted himself to run down in spirit can be renewed by returning in mind to the Creator, whose function it is to re-create as well as to create. I quoted a Bible passage which bears on this type of reasoning: "In Him we live, and move, and have our being."* That is to say, in the Creator and Re-creator we live (have vitality) and move (have energy) and have our being (function as a well-organized person).

That was all the time I had to talk. We shook hands and parted. He kept in touch, however. He went home and happened to tell one of his friends about our conversation and was surprised to hear that he, too, had been down the same road but had found the answer that changed his attitudes and so changed him. He took our man to a businessmen's weekly breakfast, a spiritually oriented meeting, where he was warmly welcomed. As he told me later, "Those men, all of them leaders in our town, had a quality of life I'd never seen before. Through their kindly understanding, after some weeks of attending these meetings, I finally did as you suggested and in my own way I'm sure that I have found the Power. That old enthusiasm is really coming back. It's surprising how this new motivation is ridding me of that inertia that was taking me down the failure road."

This man changed his depressed thought pattern by using the fabulous secret of energy and vitality thinking. He found the positive principle, and now has learned how to keep it going.

HE GOT HIS MENTAL ATTITUDE HEALED

I watched Gary Nolan, a star pitcher for the Cincinnati Reds National League baseball team, as he pitched brilliantly in the deciding play-off game of the 1975 season with the Pittsburgh Pirates. But before Gary Nolan could clinch this victory over a powerful challenging team, he had first to achieve a personal victory over negative thinking. The following newspaper story, given here verbatim, very well describes the process of mind control which preceded the arm control of this great pitcher. He discovered the secret of energy and vitality through application of the positive principle. But read the news account† for yourself:

> Fireballing pitcher Gary Nolan credits Dr. Norman Vincent Peale and his "Power of Positive Thinking" philosophy with salvaging his baseball career.

* Acts 17:28.

† By Marty Gunther, from *The National Tattler*.

Nolan admits he was ready to give up the game at 26 before Dr. Peale's words inspired him to make a dramatic comeback.

Nolan was a star righthander for the Cincinnati Reds before the All-Star Game in 1972, compiling a sensational 12–3 record.

But he soon developed shoulder problems that have plagued him ever since.

He developed an unusually large bone spur. It rubbed painfully against his finely conditioned muscles. Things got so bad that Nolan announced his retirement midway through the 1974 season.

But surgery during the winter and help from a book written by Dr. Peale have returned him to the starting rotation.

"I was lower than a snake's belly," Nolan said.

"But that was until I was reminded of the guy who felt sorry for himself because he had no shoes and then met up with a guy who had no legs."

At the depths of despair but still hoping to regain the form that earned him recognition as one of the top pitchers in the National League, he submitted to the surgeon's scalpel.

It was a reluctant choice.

"I didn't want to have it," Nolan said. "It was purely psychological. Mention surgery around any pitcher, and everyone hushes up."

But the operation was a success. Doctors removed the spur, but not the impression of two years of pitching failure that it had left on Nolan's mind.

It was then that he came in contact with the book by Peale, one of the leading exponents of man's ability to overcome even the greatest odds with the right frame of mind.

"I borrowed it from Tony Cloninger, a former teammate," Nolan said. "He got it when he went to Peale for help. He gave it to me at a point when all of my confidence was gone.

"It stressed the power of positive thinking and inner strength."

Nolan read the words carefully and captured the full impact of Peale's message. His self-confidence returned. It has shown in his game.

With one-third of the season behind him, the 27-year-old hurler is among the top 15 in the league in allowing fewest runs per innings pitched.

And the Reds are leading the Los Angeles Dodgers, their arch rivals and 1974 pennant winners, by a comfortable margin.

Cincinnati Manager Sparky Anderson has received unseen pitching help at the hands of Norman Vincent Peale.

Summing up the tenth way to keep the positive principle going:

1. Learn the fabulous secret of energy and vitality thinking.
2. Empty the mind of all unhealthy thoughts, replacing them with wholesome, creative concepts.

3. Visualize the life force continuously at work within you, refreshing body, mind and spirit.
4. Affirm daily—more than once—that you are now renewing energy and vitality.
5. Get into harmony with the basic rhythm of life which the Creator set in motion.
6. Remember Edison's remark: "If we did all the things we are capable of doing we would literally astonish ourselves."
7. Astonish yourself!
8. Always keep your mental attitudes healthy.
9. Relate all activity to the positive principle and keep going strong every day all the way.

ELEVENTH WAY TO KEEP THE POSITIVE PRINCIPLE GOING

In-Depth Faith Always Wins Over Difficulties

As the roller coaster car reached the summit of its steep climb and began the downward swoop with rapidly increasing speed, the young boy became terrified. Wildly he envisioned the careening car flying off the track, killing everyone aboard. In acute fear he gripped the bar in front of him. The father, sensing his son's reaction, put a strong arm around him, hugging him close. Assured by this evidence of protection, the boy's terror came under control.

VICTORY OVER FEAR

Many years after this incident in a midwestern amusement park, the boy, now a man of twenty-five, was exposed to a much more intense fear experience. This time he found an in-depth faith that not only sustained him but actually gave him freedom from fear forever. Jerry Adams told his exciting and moving story as we drove to the airport one morning after I had addressed a meeting in his city. We had been discussing the important place of faith in successful living, and the subject of destructive fear came up. He quietly made the statement that he was no longer affected by fear, that he felt certain he would never be afraid again, either in life or in death. This was said with calm assurance and with a complete lack of bravado. It was evident that Jerry Adams had attained that in-depth quality of faith which eliminates all fear. He had achieved the faith that wins over difficulties.

Being deeply interested in any human victory over fear, that greatest of all adversaries, I asked the reason for his sturdily expressed conviction. It developed from an incident that happened on the U.S.S. *Oriskany*, an aircraft carrier, off the coast of Vietnam.

As a bombardier/navigator Jerry was flying two missions daily over enemy territory. Twice every day his plane was catapulted into the air. This is not exactly the most calming experience, as I know personally, having myself been catapulted from the deck of the U.S.S. *Kitty Hawk*. Over North Vietnam Jerry and his comrades faced the danger of antiaircraft fire. And on each return the men had to find that little speck of landing deck in the wide expanse of sea. All of this provided plenty of opportunity for fear to take over. But Jerry's chief dread was that of being shot down and captured by a reputedly ruthless enemy.

MOST TERRIFYING EXPERIENCE

Then came the most terrifying experience of all, but one in which he found the boon of complete deliverance from fear. Jerry's bomber crew was made up of Lieutenant Commander Richard Walls and Lieutenant (j.g.) Ignatius Signorelli, plus an ensign going along as a passenger to Saigon. A bomber blast-off is always an awesome experience, the object being to hurl thirty-five tons of aircraft into the air from a standstill position to a speed of two hundred miles an hour on only 150 feet of deck.

The crew was checked out and ready to go. Heads back against headrests, the men were waiting for the powerful thrust of the catapult. The noise increased to terrific volume, pressure swelled, the aircraft screamed against the restraining cables. The boy who had been afraid on that midwestern roller coaster so long ago sat awaiting the thrust of the catapult that would send them off on another mission. But instead of the routine takeoff came a sharp jolt and a crash, metal crunching and ripping all around. The wreck of the aircraft slid down the deck and over the edge, plunging wildly one hundred feet, or the equivalent of ten stories, down into the sea, with the men trapped inside.

On this tragic fall into the ocean, the certainty of death flashed into Jerry's mind. But then also came the overwhelming conviction that he was not alone. He had an awareness of the presence of Jesus, feeling that presence keenly and without any doubt. He knew instantly that whether it was to be life or death, he would be taken care of. He seemed to feel around him the strong arm of a Heavenly Father, and there was no panic. There was no fear.

Plunging from the great height of the carrier deck, he and his companions were driven perhaps fifty feet deep into the water. It grew darker and darker the farther down he sank. Struggling to locate the escape hatch, he found there was no cockpit; there was nothing left. He was still strapped in his seat, and something, doubtless a part of the wrecked aircraft, dragged at his feet. This made him wonder whether he would ever reach the surface of the water again, since there was no real feeling in either leg. Then the realization came that both legs had been broken. Responding automatically to his survival training, he freed himself of his lap and shoulder harness, inflated his Mae West and, lungs screaming for air, shot up to the surface. He saw the massive bulk of the *Oriskany* only a few feet away. It swept by so closely that he was under the overhang of the great ship. The captain had swung the carrier around, thus protecting the men in the sea from the ship's gigantic screws. All of them were rescued. Jerry, hoisted by helicopter, passed out from incredible pain. After twelve months in the hospital and several operations, he was able to walk again. But as he finished his dramatic story, he repeated, "I know now that the Lord is always near and I shall never fear again. And when death finally does come, I shall not be afraid, for He will be there to take care of me."

This man had come upon one of the greatest of all facts in this life. Perhaps it is the supreme fact; that we are not alone. In his near-death experience he discovered that ultimate value called in-depth faith, the kind of faith that wins over all difficulties. Before this experience he had been a regular churchgoer and as a boy had been trained in Sunday School. But this was different—this was a new faith in depth. It brought to him a profound and unshakable assurance and absolute certainty, without any doubt whatsoever, that, in this world or the next, there is nothing to be afraid of, for always the Father's protecting arm is around you.

BIGGER THAN YOUR DIFFICULTIES

This experience of the positive principle leads to the realization that you are bigger than your difficulties. No matter how menacing, how formidable, how terribly awesome they may be, you possess the potential power to stand up to difficulties and overcome them, all of them. And the potential to which we refer is in-depth faith, the greatest power available to a human being, the force by which you can move mountains of difficulty. Remember what the Bible says on this subject? "If ye have faith, and doubt not, . . . ye shall say unto this mountain, Be thou removed, and be thou cast into the sea; it shall be done."*

But the kind of faith able to accomplish such extraordinary feats is an extra-real type of belief, a down-deep attitude that never accepts defeat. It is an intensity of belief, an intensity of positive attitude, an intensity of faith in God, of faith in life and of faith in yourself. It is a powerful concept embedded in consciousness, really embedded in the inner essence of the mind, that, when needed, will marshal powerful creative forces to your aid. And so strong is this belief that it will admit of no doubt, no doubt whatsoever. Indeed, doubt has no effect upon intense faith, upon faith of in-depth quality.

Of course this is not to say that no doubt ever intrudes. There are times when doubt comes to everyone, and it can be grim indeed, darkening the mind with discouraging negatives. But the difference between having no faith or a bland, formal-like faith and an in-depth faith is that doubts bombard the latter futilely. Such faith is impervious to doubt and so presently the attack of doubt ends and the practitioner of intense faith proceeds to handle his difficulties victoriously. He exerts his power to keep the positive principle going.

Doubtless the question at once arises as to how the average individual can cultivate a faith of this in-depth quality. And of course the answer is to develop God-conditioned attitudes or, to put it another way, to grow in God-consciousness to such an extent that mentally, at all times and under whatever conditions, any frightening difficulties simply do not frighten you or have any power over you. But this again may seem incredible until one undertakes to develop intensity of belief through practice and through a mental buildup of faith attitudes.

Once in Alberta, Canada, I gave a talk at a Chamber of Commerce

* Matthew 21:21.

annual dinner. It was a large and enthusiastic crowd and in the speech I developed my concepts of positive thinking. Afterward, while shaking hands with the people, a man breezed up; no other expression can quite convey his demeanor and attitude of joy, enthusiasm and obvious aliveness. In a few sentences, delivered rapidly and with force, he gave me one of the most valuable mental-overcoming formulas I have ever heard. Other people in line were pressing forward, and he spoke so succinctly and swiftly that he was gone before I could get his name. But that bright and glowing countenance and those potent words shall ever linger in memory.

DENY THE ADVERSE

"Everything once got me down," he asserted. "I was licked by practically every difficulty that came along, and believe me, they were at me constantly. Always I was expecting new and bigger difficulties and I wasn't disappointed, for they seemed to grow bigger all the time. Then," he continued, "I happened to read an article in a little magazine someone had left on a seat in a bus. It was about denying the adverse. I thought, 'How crazy can you get, that if you deny the adverse it will go away, just like that?' But the article contained a statement that made a powerful impression on me. It was this: 'If God be for us, who can be against us?'* As I thought about it, I personalized it: 'If God be for me, who or what can be against me?'

"Well, anyway I started denying the adverse things that were crowding me, and at the same time I practiced affirming that God was for me and what could therefore be against me? You ought to try it," he asserted triumphantly. "It will put you on the victory road like it did me." So saying, he crushed my hand in a viselike grip and was off into the crowd.

Well, I was so impressed that I took his advice, I did start denying the adverse and affirming spiritual support and was amazed to find that the difficulties seemed fewer in number and certainly less formidable. They did not all go away, of course. In fact, I still periodically have some to deal with, and always will. But their power has lessened and my dominance over them has increased. This is a fact, a very wonderful fact.

I quoted elsewhere the statement attributed to Sigmund Freud to the

* Romans 8:31.

effect that the chief duty of a human being is to endure life. That we must endure certain things, learn to live with some factors that are unpleasant and from which there seems to be no alternative, is, of course, true, at least in our present state of unenlightenment. But if that were the entire story, existence would be pretty grim. I prefer to think that the chief duty of a human being is to get on top of life and its difficulties. This chapter, therefore, is about the power of in-depth faith to help us win over those difficulties. The man in Canada, in our brief but unforgettable encounter, transmitted the fact of an intense belief as the source of his remarkable ability to deny the adverse. It proved to be a dynamic new expression of the positive principle.

ORGANIZE YOUR DIFFICULTIES

The famous research scientist Charles F. Kettering once indicated that a good statement of a problem is half the solution. One important step in handling difficulties is to organize them in orderly fashion so that you are able to see them as they actually are and each in relation to the other. Themistocles, a famed soldier-statesman of antiquity, called attention to the value of talking a problem out rather than thinking of it subjectively: "The speech of man is like embroidered tapestries, since like them this too has to be extended in order to display its patterns, but when it is rolled up it conceals and distorts them."* Similarly, the elements of a problem, when fear or panic are involved, tend to assume a degree of formidability not warranted by the facts. Well-organized facts are what we must have if any problem is to be successfully solved.

Another reason a practical faith is of utmost importance and value is that one of its by-products is a nonemotionalized reaction to any problem. A believer of this stature, having had the fear element reduced if not entirely eliminated, is thereby able to think clearly and with objectivity. He sees facts as they are and not as colored by emotionally tinctured supposition. He is able to face up to a situation that, if viewed emotionally, could seem extremely difficult if not impossible, and proceed to get a good outcome.

Faith too often has been made to appear as a kind of vague, churchy point of view, a sort of nice attitude, but really out of touch with hard

* From Plutarch, *Lives*, *Themistocles*, Sec. 29.

reality. Fortunately, people today are now aware that faith is much more than that; indeed, it is a dynamic process of mind conditioned by practical and scientific formulas. Increasing numbers of persons are learning that spiritual teachings contain scientific and practical techniques which work when worked. A simple example in everyday living is that if you dislike people you are bound to get back dislike in return, and this tends to take the joy out of life. But if you love people, as spiritual law dictates, you inevitably get back love in return and thereby experience a joy that makes you a happy person. So, don't be one of the so-called practical persons who wants to insist that faith is theoretical and impractical. How out-of-it can you get?

One of the chief marks of in-depth faith is common sense. A very astute businessman in a certain area was also an outstanding spiritual leader. He had that all-too-rare combination of spirituality and practicality that proves these two qualities as having natural affinity. I can still recall his whimsical version of St. Paul's words: "And now abideth faith, hope and love, these three; but the greatest of these is common sense."*

"AS A GRAIN OF MUSTARD SEED"

In-depth faith and its practical system of organizing the mind when dealing with difficulties were pointed up by the experience of a television interviewer when I was a guest on his popular show in a city in the Southwest. He wanted to discuss what he called my ideas of positive thinking and their relation to spiritual concepts. In the interview I outlined my positive spiritual techniques of thought and action and insisted that they were practical, viable and highly workable. I remember saying that the spiritual mind is an organized mind which has the power to handle problems with extra effectiveness because it can marshal all factors for a scientific approach to the problem.

This concept rather threw my host, as he had the traditional notion that the spiritual is some sort of idealized and dreamy attitude quite unrelated to the practical affairs of the world. "You mean to say that by this thing which you call in-depth faith I can solve a personal problem that happens to be worrying me at the present time?"

"Certainly," I responded.

* I Corinthians 13:13 (paraphrased).

"But," he continued, "my faith cannot, even by stretching, be called in-depth. In fact, while I do believe, still and all my faith is, you might say, rather cursory and indefinite."

I told him that he did not need to have all that much faith and quoted the words "If ye have faith as a grain of mustard seed [small but real] . . . nothing shall be impossible unto you,"* adding that the question isn't the extent of one's faith but the reality and in-depth quality of that which he does have. Even the essence, when it is honest and real, has the power.

HOW HE SOLD HIS HOUSE

Our TV conversation went on before a big crowd in the studio and of course a large listening audience over the air, and I was careful, as always, to make no claims that could not be factually substantiated. Indeed, I have never knowingly, in public talks, in books or articles, or in a one-to-one conversation made any statement that I did not believe to be absolute truth or one that could not be attested to by the experience of myself or others whose veracity I trusted. So therefore when he outlined his personal problem I assured him that by the application of scientific spiritual principles he could get a practical answer that would be right and proper for all concerned.

This man explained that he had nearly all his savings tied up in a house in a Michigan city from which he had some months previously been transferred to his present location. He had tried every possible way to sell this house, but with no result. Meanwhile, nothing was coming in from the property and he was hard hit with taxes. Finally he had tried prayer "as a last resort," but even this extreme expediency had not worked. He was "still stuck with the house." "Now," he said, "here you come along with this idea of in-depth faith as a practical system of procedure. Now get me straight; I really don't doubt what you say and I know you sincerely believe it to be true, but I sure would like to know how to apply these common sense precepts to my practical problem."

"Okay," I replied, "let's take a look at what you have been doing. Let us organize this problem. From the way you tell it, I get the reaction that you are pretty uptight about the matter. That must first of all be corrected, for sound, practical thinking never comes through an uptight

* Matthew 17:20.

thought system. Secondly, I get the notion that you want to make a killing on this sale. I don't blame you for wanting a fair profit, but greediness is self-defeating as a usual thing."

"You've got me on both counts," he confessed. "Maybe I have priced it higher than a fair consideration warrants."

"Now you say you have desperately turned to prayer. Desperate prayer," I pointed out, "is much less effective than affirmative prayer, in which you confidently affirm that forces are now in motion on a spiritual basis that will culminate in a satisfactory sale of the house. Relax mentally and get your mind into the unhurried tempo at which spiritual things happen," I said.

Finally I asked him about whom he was thinking in this hoped-for transaction. Surprised, he answered, "Myself. Who else?" I then went on to another principle which I felt was important. I asked him to visualize the type of people for whom the house would be ideal. He replied, "I've never thought of that. It really is just made for a young couple with three children."

"Well, then, what do you say we form a mental image of such a family, one that is searching for just that sort of house, and 'see' them as finding yours? Now, when they come to see the house, since you know that it is intended for them, work out terms that will help them to buy it and by which you can come out all right on your investment." He gave me a strange sort of look. "Do you know something? That makes sense. It really does. I'll work at it."

With astonishment but also with enthusiasm, he telephoned me a few weeks later. "They did come—just the family we visualized. And they are wonderful people. We made a deal, one that is fair to each. And, boy, am I sold on that practical and scientific in-depth faith principle!"

"Glad things worked out so splendidly," I replied, equally pleased, and then added, "Keep it going." and why not, for it is a fact, a true fact, that in-depth faith wins over all difficulties. So why be defeated by difficulties when defeat is not at all necessary, especially since you have the spiritual formula that turns defeat into success?

POWER OF MENTAL CONDITIONING

The human mind is an amazing instrument and the thoughts that activate it can determine what happens to a person and how well he handles the problems which come up daily. In a true sense we are what we think over a long period of time. At this moment you are what your dominant thought pattern has been, shall we say, over the past ten years or so. If you and I want to know what we will be ten years from this date, the answer can very well be in terms of what you and I think over the coming decade. The positive principle is a scientific thought process designed to make things better, ever better.

Fear thoughts can destroy creative capacity, and what is of even more sinister effect, they can bring to pass things that are constantly feared. One of the most arresting statements in that book of truth called the Bible is this terrible line: "The thing which I greatly feared is come upon me. . . ."* By persistently fearing some trouble or illness or accident or failure, and by keeping that fear vital and active over a length of time, forces are encouraged, perhaps even created, that actualize those things so long feared.

Likewise, things that have long been believed, things like good outcomes and health and achievement and success, can also come upon us. While fear and negativism can destroy, faith and positivism can create and develop. It is therefore of extraordinary importance to practice persistently, doggedly, and assiduously dynamic faith attitudes. There is power in them. In more ways than one.

BASEBALL TEAM TURNED INTO CHAMPIONS

One of the most readable of the old sportswriters was a man named Hugh Fullerton, who wrote a yarn in some newspaper years ago. I have forgotten the name of the paper but recall the story very well indeed. It was about a manager of a Texas team whose name was Josh O'Reilly. Mr. O'Reilly's team was not doing well that season despite the fact that he had seven .300 hitters on his squad. It seemed that every team in the league was regularly beating his men, who definitely had championship quality. But the team was in a deep and protracted slump, and no amount of criticism or threatening or cajoling could get them out of it.

It so happened that an evangelist named Reverend Schlater was holding meetings in the neighborhood. Reverend Schlater was reputed to be a spiritual healer, and, far and wide, people had great faith in him as almost a miracle worker.

* Job 3:25.

One day, unable longer to endure his team's horrendous performance, Josh O'Reilly demanded of each player his two favorite bats. He put them in a wheelbarrow and went off with them. Later, just before that afternoon's game, the manager returned with the bats and explained that he had taken them to Reverend Schlater, who had blessed them. The players were astounded. They looked at their bats with reverential awe. And they became different men. That afternoon nothing could stop them as they drove in twenty-one runs. For the rest of the summer they hammered their way to a league championship. It was said that for years ballplayers would pay large sums of money for a Schlater bat.

Now with all due respect to Reverend Schlater, we must believe that no change was wrought in those wooden weapons called baseball bats. But a strange magic had been done to the minds of those believing men who wielded the bats. A reconditioning of their minds had taken place by which they were no longer wallowing in a defeatist slump but had instead become invincible and victorious.

The average person who supinely accepts and goes along with negative assumptions that lead him to defeat can radically change such a state of affairs by becoming a person of real faith, in-depth and powerful, the kind that wins over all difficulties. A reconditioning of the mind, intense enough to change attitudes, will enable any person to become powerfully inspired, and what is more, to keep that positive principle going whatever or however harsh a situation may be.

ALWAYS THE "BREAK RECORDS" PRINCIPLE

The people who really go for in-depth faith are those who have a deep inner drive to do more, and then even more, with themselves. They are the extra-motivated individuals who are never content with present performance. They are inevitably driven by an inner and ceaseless urge to scale new heights, reach dizzier levels, break old records and set new achievement standards. In-depth faith, the positive principle and the climbing instinct are of the same piece.

I am writing this chapter while seated on a balcony of the Mont Cervin Hotel in Zermatt, Switzerland, of which my good friend, Theodore E. Seiler, is the owner. It is a sun-kissed afternoon, and from my balcony the great Matterhorn stands out sharp and clear, with its almost always present white cloud scarf trailing out against the blue sky. There is perhaps no mountain in the world equal in stern beauty and historical romance to this vast finger of stone standing solitary and aloof from the huge mountains in the Alpine range of which it is a part. Indeed, the Matterhorn has been described as more than a mountain; it is a presence, a brooding and ever-fascinating presence.

Men who have it in them to respond to high places have always wanted to climb the Matterhorn. In early years they feared to invade the home of the evil spirits who were presumed to dwell amid its crags and eminences, ready to hurl down ice and stone upon any intruder. Regardless of these ancient superstitions, efforts were made to find a way to the top; but for long years no climber succeeded in reaching the mysterious summit.

Then the famed Zermatt mountain guide Peter Taugwalder made known his belief that the vast, inscrutable mountain could, for a fact, be climbed from the Zermatt side. So the British mountain climber Edward Whymper, then twenty-five years old, and a companion, Lord Francis Douglas, started out for this then isolated mountain hamlet of Zermatt. There they found the Reverend Charles Hudson, perhaps the best known of all mountaineers of the day, who had made the first ascent of the mighty Monte Rosa ten years earlier on August 1, 1855.

They organized a party of seven to make an assault on the hitherto impregnable Matterhorn. The imperious Whymper took charge, and the group included Lord Douglas, the Reverend Mr. Hudson, the guide Michel Croz, of Chamonix, Robert Hadow, a nineteen-year-old student and a rather inexperienced climber, and the two best Zermatt guides, Peter Taugwalder and his son. Together they made their courageous and audacious decision to try to scale The Mountain. Whymper describes the thrilling epic in his *Rambles in the Alps*. But it was scarcely a ramble, for while they did reach the top—the first men ever to stand on that elusive height—at 1:40 on the afternoon of July 14, 1865, their elation was short-lived. For on the descent Hadow, tired by the climb, slipped, knocking over Croz and dragging Hudson and Douglas down. The weak hemp rope connecting the two parties broke. Despite the superhuman efforts of Whymper and the two Taugwalders, the four men plunged down the four-thousand-foot terrible north wall to their deaths. For over one hundred years their skeletons have reposed somewhere in the mountain vastness. That pathetic broken rope may be seen today in the Alpine Museum in Zermatt.

Studying the Matterhorn this day, I'm impressed by a curious fact about firsts or record-breakings. Almost as soon as some person becomes the first to achieve a long-frustrated goal and breaks a record, along comes another to perform the same feat or even go beyond it. In the case of the

Matterhorn's first climbing by Whymper and his companions, three days later a famed mountaineer, J. A. Carrel, and his party reached the summit on the perilous Italian side from Breuil. The glory of the first climbers was not all theirs for long, which brings to mind some thoughtful words ascribed to Goethe: "The deed is all, the glory naught."

Since those heroic men led the way, many persons have climbed the great Matterhorn. Once it was demonstrated that it could be done, others proceeded to do it also, for they were persuaded, by the example of the pioneers, to have the belief that they, too, could climb, achieve, surmount. So indeed it is the deed that is important and not the glory.

PEOPLE STILL WANT TO CLIMB

Times change, but do people change all that much? The motivating upthrust to get to the top is still built into people. One hundred years to the day after the first ascent of the Matterhorn, my wife and I were sitting on the terrace at Schwarzsee looking up at the little hut situated high on the flank of the mountain, from which ascents are begun at daybreak. A young man dressed for climbing came along and sat down near us. Recognizing us, he began to talk somewhat self-consciously about himself. He took a rather dim view of himself as a failure who just couldn't seem to make it. "I want to do things, accomplish something. I want to make a success in life, but at each try I seem to get knocked down," he said glumly. He told us he had been in Switzerland since early springtime, climbing hills at first, then small mountains, then bigger ones, and now he was going to take a shot at the biggest of all—the Matterhorn.

The boy seemed loath to leave, though the afternoon was waning and he was scheduled to meet his guide at the hut at sunset to be ready for the start upward at dawn. "I really believe I can do it," he mused. "I've got to do it. I've just got to climb, for if I can do this ascent I know I can move up in other things, too!" He stood up, shook hands with us and waved acknowledgment of our "Good luck—God bless you." He proceeded perhaps a hundred yards or so, then turned and came back to where we sat. With some embarrassment he asked, "Will you do me a favor?"

"Sure will; anything you ask."

"Okay, then pray for me, will you? If I can get some of that positive faith you write about, I know I can do things." So saying, he moved off up the long trek to the mountain. We watched until he disappeared around a shoulder. He did climb the Matterhorn, and has been successfully climbing other kinds of mountains ever since.

People still want to climb and break records and they are doing that regularly. Everywhere one sees the results of the in-depth faith that makes achievement possible. Everywhere are those inspired, enthusiastic and highly motivated individuals who have the spirit, the indomitable spirit, to keep the positive principle going.

The phenomenon of firsts and record-breaking as a demonstration of the extra-real faith that wins over difficulties is today occupying not a little space in newspapers. For instance, there is the story of John Walker, the New Zealand mile runner, who ran the mile in 3 minutes 49.4 seconds, slicing 1.6 seconds off the previous record of 3:51 set by Filbert Bayi of Tanzania. Walker was the first runner ever to go the mile distance in less than 3 minutes 51 seconds.

All this brings back memories of the era when sports writers were of the unanimous opinion that it was impossible for anyone to run the mile in four minutes flat, and that it would never be done. Well, "never" is a long time and he is foolish indeed who believes that it can "never" be done by anyone. Mile runners' sights continued to be fixed on that "impossible" four-minute mark. Sweden's famous Gunder Haegg and Arne Andersson both got near to it, but the man who made track history was Britain's Roger Bannister, who achieved this proclaimed "impossible" in 1954 at Oxford by clocking the mile at 3:59.4.

To the objection that big-time mountain climbing and mile running have no bearing on the average individual, the fact is that the principle of climbing and breaking past records is applicable to all activity. To be more than you are, to do more than you are doing, to achieve higher standards and greater results are definitely inherent in each of us. And constantly persons like the readers of this book are aiming for and achieving higher and ever higher marks in whatever their goals may be. The principle of in-depth faith is of powerful help in keeping the motivation going, even in the presence of setbacks.

My longtime friend Frank Wangeman, vice-president and general manager of the Waldorf-Astoria Hotel in New York City, in commenting upon setbacks, made a wise and pertinent remark: "Maturity of experience," he declared, "proves that no setback is final." With in-depth faith one can just keep going, regardless of resistance, until finally all difficulties are overcome. And then with whetted anticipation of more victories, you are ready to take on a new flock of setbacks and so break ever new records, continuing in this valiant manner throughout life on the basis of the positive principle.

Perhaps one of the chief and most desirable qualities of all is to have the ability to persevere doggedly against adverse conditions. In a review of a book called *Nothing Venture, Nothing Win,* by Sir Edmund Hillary, famous climber of Mount Everest, the reviewer, John Rupp, pictures Hillary as "a formidable man." "When he and his party were attempting to move up-river through appalling rapids, Hillary says, 'at any moment we felt we must come to easier water and we became so engrossed in the struggle that the dangers were forgotten.' " What a stimulating thought! Engrossed in the struggle, Hillary was able to overcome his fears. So, the prime secret is to hang in there and always keep going.

The late, great, big-league baseball manager Casey Stengel had it right. It was said of him, "Defeat did not awe Casey, for he was on good terms with hope. In the midst of defeat he was always looking for victory." Which, of course, was one reason his victory average was very high indeed.

HE REPROGRAMMED HIS THINKING

In the title of this chapter we have made a rather all-inclusive claim in the statement that in-depth faith wins over all difficulties. This might be modified by the semi-doubting person to an acknowledgment that one can win over some, perhaps even over many, difficulties, but to be all-inclusive is a strain on credulity. But having observed the amazing power of in-depth belief, I long since came to the conclusion that the power of down-deep and all-out faith is infinitely greater than the average person estimates. In my experience, both personally and from observation of others who live out a wholly committed faith in God, it is definitely possible to live with, adjust to, or win over all difficulties, without qualification.

I was scheduled to speak to a public meeting of business people in an eastern city and upon arrival at the hall entered by the stage door and took a seat backstage while waiting for the program to begin. Soon a rather stocky, well-built man of above-average height came back to where I waited and introduced himself as the master of ceremonies for the meeting. He was an animated person, obviously charged with vigor and enthusiasm, and I was impressed by his positive spirit and attitude.

He told me that he had been a helicopter pilot in the war in Southeast Asia. He was shot down, and in such serious physical condition that it was expected he would die. Due to suspected brain damage, doctors came to a projected diagnosis that if he did live he would, as he expressed it, "be a vegetable." Indeed, he did undergo a brain operation, and parted his hair to indicate a plate in the top of the head. Removed to a military hospital in the United States, he was unable to move his legs or arms. But speech was not affected, nor was his ability to think.

One day he said to his wife, "I want you to bring me a book I once read by Norman Vincent Peale and read it to me." Day after day his wife read about the powerful creative and re-creative principles of faith and positive thinking until this desperately wounded man developed an intensity of faith in God's healing power, as well as in his own power of self re-creation. Then came the conviction that he, too, could be healed despite the disheartening prognosis.

He told his wife that, beginning then, he was going to reprogram his mind. He would work with the power of the mind to take charge of his broken body through an in-depth faith in God and in himself. Accordingly, he entered upon an intensive and persistent routine of belief and faith plus spiritual affirmation, thus infusing his mind with a powerful directive force. The healing did not come in a miraculous manner nor all that easily, but it did come, as was evidenced by the physically strong and mentally alert person who told me this story. It is an example of what a motivated human being can do with himself when his faith is strong and deep enough in content and force. Later as I watched this remarkable man emcee the meeting with humor and spirit that set a tone positive and enthusiastic in nature, I once again reaffirmed my own certain belief that in-depth faith does, for a great, big, glorious fact, win over all difficulties. So keep the positive principle going—always keep it going.

Finally, let us recapitulate in brief the ideas and principles put forward in this chapter:

1. Seek until you get a certainty of The Presence. Then, like Jerry Adams, you will be afraid no more.
2. Know for a fact that you are never alone. A great Someone is with you always.
3. Believe that you are bigger than your difficulties, for you are, indeed.
4. Through study and practice, develop intensity of belief, in-depth faith, as contrasted with the nominal variety.

5. Become expert in denying the adverse.
6. Organize your difficulties and problems. Then you will have half the solution, and the rest will come more surely and easily.
7. Learn the relationship between in-depth faith and common sense.
8. Practice until you develop expertise in the power of mental conditioning.
9. Always keep going the "break records" principle.
10. Retain the vital "want to climb" instinct that has been built into you.
11. Reprogram your thinking and become an in-depth practitioner of the positive principle. Then miracles will start happening.

TWELFTH WAY TO KEEP THE POSITIVE PRINCIPLE GOING

Keep Going Strong with the Excitement Principle

The night was bitter cold—30 degrees below zero. Some 18,000 United States Marines in Korea were facing nearly 100,000 Communist troops. And both sides expected battle in the morning. Now, at midnight, a huge marine was standing by a tank, its metal sides so intensely cold that fingers actually stuck to it. Blue with cold, covered with caked and frozen mud, tiny icicles hanging from his heavy beard, the marine was eating cold beans out of a can with a penknife.

A newspaper correspondent watched the big marine as he ate his unappetizing meal, leaning against the tank in a bleak climate and facing an uncertain future. Evidently the newsman was impelled to some philosophical thinking, for suddenly he put to the marine a profound question: "If I were God," he asked, "and were able to give you anything, what would you ask for?"

The marine, continuing to eat his cold beans, reflected long before answering; but when he did speak, his statement was equal in philosophical content to the question. The simple reply was "I would ask for tomorrow."

This man, in a dismal and critical situation, ready to do whatever circumstances might demand of him, had one desire; and that desire was for continuing life, a tomorrow with home and family and a future.

Since the desire for vital life is basic in the consciousness of every person, it is natural to respond to motivation, to inspiration, to enthusiasm, to dynamic stimuli, all of which give reality and meaning to the experience of living.

Having written a number of books and given many speeches on inspirational subjects, I have had some experience in judging human response to the power of motivational thinking. People generally want to be inspired and they respond to enthusiasm when they relinquish desultory and negative attitudes. When so released, most men and women eagerly go for a vital quality of positive thought and action like the excitement principle. As a result, many become genuinely inspired and enthusiastic and thereby move to an upper level of living, one that is superior to anything previously experienced.

TO KEEP THE POSITIVE PRINCIPLE GOING REQUIRES SKILL

But to maintain a high level of enthusiasm and inspiration and to keep it going constantly over a long period of time is not all that easy. It requires consistent reinspiration, renewed motivation, together with education in the skills of controlling and directing mental processes. Motivational attitudes are subjected daily to a terrific bombardment of depressed, gloomy and negative ideas. It seems that there is, in effect at least, though probably not in any sense planned, what amounts to an effort to undermine positive and hopeful attitudes about the country, about the future, indeed about just everything. Some years ago there was a radio news commentator in the New York area who came on the air many a night with the gloomy words "There's bad news tonight, folks." While current news commentators do not perhaps use that particular trademark, to some extent they are professional purveyors of bad news, professional underminers of positive thinking.

Of course there is bad news, indeed quite a lot of it, but of late years it has been so constantly underscored that the casual listener or reader comes to assume that there is no good news at all, that the country and the world and even life itself are just one gigantic flop. One wonders why, along with the bad news, there cannot be some such creative emphasis as, for example, "There's bad news tonight, folks, but so what? We've got what it takes to improve things." That might go far toward changing the bad news into good news.

Actually, I do not intend to be critical. My purpose is constructive in simply raising the question as to why we cannot be equally concerned with positive solutions as with negatives. As a onetime newspaper reporter, I am aware that news is a departure from the normal state of affairs. As the old saying had it, "When a dog bites a boy, that is not news, because it happens so often. But if a boy bites a dog, that is news."* If the time should ever arrive when it becomes news to report decent, law-abiding people, instead of chronicling the actions of thieves and criminals, we would indeed be in a sorry mess. The good is still the norm, and departure from the good is still news.

But the individual who desires to move to an upper level of motivation and enthusiasm must maintain a discriminating thought skill: namely, the ability to deal with the negative creatively but at the same time to reject the assumption that he must become a negative thinker to be an "in" person.

Enthusiasm and positive attitudes being under constant bombardment from negative and depressive sources, the individual who wants to be an upbeat type of person is hard put to it to sustain enthusiasm. This fact, added to the ordinary run of difficulty, adversity, hardship, sickness, sorrow and trouble, can take an extraordinary toll of one's inspirational vigor. It is to counteract this siphoning off of inspiration that I have written this book, *The Positive Principle Today*. The purpose throughout the book has been to suggest ways and means, workable procedures for keeping inspiration, motivation and enthusiasm going in the face of the attacks upon this positive pattern of thought and action by the adverse, the difficult, the negative.

MAINTAIN BUILDUP OF SPIRIT

To keep it going requires a vigorous counterattack against the erosion of inspirational attitudes, and this consists, we believe, of a buildup of spirit. The word "inspiration" actually means an enspiriting or renewable infusion of fresh and powerful new spirit-vitality. Since spirit under constant blows tends to run down, we must become so organized mentally

* John B. Boger, city editor, New York *Sun*, 1873–90.

that almost automatically, instead of running down, spirit runs up again. The creative factor involved in this process is a constant repowering of the thought pattern, undeviating emphasis upon the excitement principle.

I am reminded of an old lady whom my wife and I recently encountered on a fairly rugged mountain trail at Riffealp near the Gornergrat in Switzerland. On these trails devotees of high-altitude hiking have a sort of camaraderie and, it being the German-speaking part of Switzerland, the usual greeting is "*Gruss Gott*," or "Greeting in God's name." This elderly lady was hunched over and walking with the aid of a sturdy cane in a kind of dogged determination. She was accompanied by a man, obviously a guide. As we met she looked up at us with bright eyes from under an old-fashioned hat. Instead of the previously mentioned usual greeting, she said, "*Bonjour, madame, bonjour, monsieur.*"

"*Bonjour, madame,*" we replied. Whereupon she went into a rapid flurry of French, to which finally I said, "*Ah, madame, non parle français.*" At which she veered into Italian and then into German, and while I can struggle through a simple conversation in the latter language, she saw that she was not communicating too well.

"You look like an American; perhaps you can speak English," she laughed merrily.

"Yes, madam, I talk some English, American style."

"Oh, I like American style," she said, "it's so picturesque."

She then informed us that she was eighty-nine years old. "You are a wonderful woman," I commented admiringly. "You speak four languages fluently, your mind is sharp, you wear no glasses and you climb mountain trails at age eighty-nine. Just how do you keep going so strongly?"

"Oh," she replied, "you see, I'm so excited about everything. The world is such a wonderful place; people are so interesting. In fact, I awaken every morning with as much excitement as when I was a girl."

"Well," I said, "if you were as excited then as you are now at eighty-nine, you must have been a ball of fire when you were young."

"But you see, monsieur, I am still young. Oh, yes, this body is a bit warped in the back, but I'm quite strong and healthy. But it is the spirit that makes the difference. I'm excited because my spirit lives in a perpetual state of excitement."

"You mean that you keep it going with the excitement principle?"

With a bright smile she answered, "Oui, oui, monsieur, that is it precisely. I keep it going with—what do you call it?—the excitement principle. That is good—really good—the excitement principle." So saying, she moved away on up the trail, pushing resolutely ahead with her cane against a backdrop of mighty peaks. We watched her, marveling at how tremendous a human being can be when the spirit remains strong, even invulnerable. No matter the onslaughts of depressives and adversities, such a person can always keep going and going strong with that precious secret of spirit buildup, the excitement principle.

PRACTICE BEING EXCITED

The acquiring of skill in mental attitudes, as in all aspects of perfection, requires practice. One can hardly expect to keep excitement going unless one practices being excited. And a viable method of practice is deliberately to think in terms of how exciting life is, how exciting your job, how fascinating your opportunities. I once knew an actress in the movies, a brilliant artist, a woman named Hattie McDaniel. She was a rare and radiant personality. She told me that it was her custom to step outside every morning and no matter what the weather conditions, rain or sunshine, she would say aloud, "Hello there, good morning! You're so wonderful; I'm so terribly excited to be alive. Thanks, dear God—thanks a lot!" Hattie McDaniel practiced the excitement principle and so became an exciting and unforgettable person.

Everywhere I meet these exciting people who are practicing the excitement principle. I was breakfasting one morning with a man in a Los Angeles hotel. The coffee shop had a beautiful canary-color motif. Our waitress wore a nice outfit of similar hue. But it was the girl's spirit that captivated us. "Good morning, gentlemen. Now for a delicious breakfast that will set you up for a wonderful day. Everything we have is good. Let me bring you something nice." Actually she didn't even take an order, and we were so impressed that we thought the food she set before us was perfect. As we left the restaurant she said, "Think a good day and have a good day."

"Where did you get that terrific thought?" I asked.

"Why, from you," she answered brightly. "One of your 'Pocket' cards—'Think a good day, plan a good day, pray a good day.' "

"Well," I commented, "you certainly have improved on my writing."

"Oh, you see, I find that if you practice being excited, that is the way it is."

The practice of excitement can bring anyone out of the doldrums of downbeat thinking. For example, I received a telephone call from a jeweler in a southern city who was very depressed and discouraged. He said he was a reader of my books and, while he at times thought he had got the hang of the positive principle, still he could not stick with it. How could he keep it going, especially when he was in such a dull business as selling jewelry, a business bequeathed by his father?

I expressed astonishment that he could possibly appraise a jewelry business as a dull occupation, pointing out the romance inherent in diamonds and other gems and that jewelry is related to the instinct for beauty and is symbolic of love and affection. Indeed, I argued, any commodity for the welfare of people, even bread and sugar and vegetables, could not be construed as dull, for they are of the essence of life. And jewelry, relating as it does to the expression of thoughts too deep for words, should be perpetually exciting.

"But," he complained, "economic conditions in our area are not very good and people are not buying luxury items under these circumstances."

I even questioned the rationale of writing off his merchandise as a luxury item to be marketable only in affluent times. "Beauty," I countered, "is a necessity of the human spirit, especially when it speaks of romance and abiding affection. And that is even more important when times are hard."

I asked him to read me samples of his local advertising. One ad read, "Buy Jewelry at X's, Oldest Quality Merchants in the Country." And another: "Finest Jewelry at X's, Founded 1893." "Well," I said, "I am no expert in advertising copywriting, but I think you are only stating the obvious—that you have been in business a long while and are dealers in quality merchandise. That is true, of course, but hardly likely to motivate the buyer. He or she must be reached emotionally if desirable action is to be stimulated."

"Okay," he responded, "what would you suggest?"

Hardly taking his request seriously, I said, "Well, how about this? 'Put a sparkle on her finger like the sparkle in her eye.' That is for the young and in love. Another might be, 'A wedding ring from X's will be just as beautiful when there are silver threads among the gold.' And how about this for an aged woman on an anniversary: 'Add the beauty of her toil-worn hands to the loveliness of a ring from X's famous jewelry shop.' " And so on.

"Boy," he said, "come down here and I will give you a job. You almost make me want to buy my own things."

"I want to bring some excitement into you about the wonderful opportunity you have of putting lights in people's eyes and smiles on their faces by your articles of beauty. Tell you what. Every morning when you awaken, say aloud, 'How exciting to be a dealer in jewelry! All day long I'm going to bring that extra touch of joy to young and old.' Practice enthusiasm and excitement and, as you do, inspiration will come flooding back into your mind. Then keep it going."

This is the procedure that really keeps it going. Think excitement, talk excitement, act out excitement, and you are bound to become an excited person. Life will take on new zest, deeper interest and greater meaning. You can think, talk and act yourself into dullness or into monotony or into unhappiness. By the same process you can build up inspiration, excitement and a surging depth of joy. For a fact, we tend to become precisely what we practice, whether gloominess or excitement. And, since the latter is so much more to be desired, the part of wisdom is to keep it going by the daily practice of the excitement principle.

SUPER-SALESMAN FROM SORRENTO

I have great admiration and pride in the career of a positive and energetic young man, John Milano, whom I first met nearly twenty years ago in Sorrento, Italy. While visiting that beautiful town Mrs. Peale and I went into a shop where we were greeted by an attractive, friendly and, I must say, persuasive young man who spoke excellent English.

He proceeded to show Mrs. Peale his merchandise and, because I recognize a master salesman when I see one in operation, I at once became aware of the impending danger to my pocketbook. And indeed he did sell my wife a rather large order. Watching the young man operate, I admired the force and charm of his personality, recognizing at once the outstanding ability which he so obviously possessed.

I asked John about his aspirations and goals and he replied that he wanted to go to America and be an American businessman working in the opportunity afforded by the American system of free enterprise. He waxed quite enthusiastic as he outlined his clearly defined objectives. But then he added that it was difficult to get to America, having little money and no one to help him.

Becoming more interested in this dynamic individual, I outlined the principles of visualization, explaining that a specific goal held tenaciously in mind will develop in consciousness into actuality. I suggested that he study and practice the power of positive thinking, meanwhile affirming and reaffirming that he would achieve his specified ambition of becoming an American businessman. Then I added, because I became enthusiastic, that when he came to New York he was to look me up and I would help him secure a job. This was, you might say, going out on a limb, but my enthusiasm was unbounded.

Sure enough, in a few months John showed up in my New York office to get the promised job. It was getting along toward Christmas and I wrote to presidents of a half dozen of the leading men's shops in the city somewhat as follows and listing on each letter the various store executives to whom the same letter was going:

> Dear Sir:
> In Sorrento, Italy, I met the greatest natural-born salesman I have ever encountered, and my acquaintance with super-salesmen is considerable. This man is now in New York and is available for a position. The first one of you who responds to this letter gets him.
>
> Sincerely yours,

The response was immediate, and John was assigned to the men's hat department of a Fifth Avenue haberdashery. When the Christmas business season ended, special help was let go; but not John, whose selling ability was recognized. And so the years passed until only recently I received a letter from John Milano, now president of possibly the largest hat manufacturing company in the country. And when I dress up, whose hat do you think I am wearing? Why, of course, it is a beautiful hat of which I'm very proud, a gift from my old friend, the super-salesman of Sorrento, now one of America's successful businessmen.

In the light of such a human story who can say that America is no longer the land of opportunity? It is, and always will be for the positive-thinking, motivated and excited John Milanos. They are the men who live by the positive principle and know how to keep it going. In so doing they keep America going.

GET INTERESTED, INTENSELY INTERESTED

Interested people are excited people. In such persons the zest for living does not run down. They keep the fun of work and responsibility and the fascination of involvement always going, and that in turn keeps them going. Others may run down in spirit and grow into the "I've had it" type, but this never happens to the intensely interested.

On a speaking trip I encountered Senator Everett Dirksen in one of the long walkways of O'Hare Airport in Chicago. I had met him before and, indeed, had once spoken with him on the same platform at a trade association convention, but that had been several years previously and I was not at all sure he would remember me. So I started to introduce myself. "My name is—"

"Now, hold it," he said, taking my hand in both of his. "Norman Vincent Peale. Do you recall that night when we spoke together? And here is what you said in your speech." To my utter astonishment, he repeated my remarks almost word for word. Indeed, with his remarkable gift for speech he enhanced them considerably.

"How," I asked, "can you, with all your activity, remember so accurately an occasion several years past and so amazingly repeat a talk made by a fellow speaker?"

"The reason, Norman," he replied, "is that I was interested. I'm always interested. Every experience becomes vivid for me and indelibly imprinted on my mind because I am interested." Then he went on in his inimitable way to talk about the fascination, the excitement of public speaking on subjects of importance to human well-being. The senator has now gone on, but never shall I forget those moments when I listened to him in that busy airport as he poured out the zest and unalloyed excitement of his facile mind. Everett Dirksen surely ranks among the few greatest public speakers in American history, an exciting, dynamic speaker, and the secret was his eager and profound interest in people and in affairs.

Once, in the old Cleveland railroad station, early one morning, I ran into my longtime friend, former Congressman Walter Judd, and we had breakfast together at the lunch counter. He told me of the number of speeches he was making that week all over the country, and I commented on how tired he must be and didn't such a program take it out of him? "Not at all, not at all," he replied energetically. "You see, I believe in everything I say and am intensely interested, so how can I run down?" Here was a great and perpetually excited man. Both of these men practiced the excitement principle and so they knew how to keep going in high gear.

EXCITING CHANGE OF LIFE-STYLE

Some years ago, an attractive and very chic young woman made an appointment to see me at my office in Marble Collegiate Church. Her name was Mary Brinig and she had, it appeared, two objects in mind. One was to tell about how her life had been changed spiritually. She spoke in a sincere, charming and most affecting manner. She explained that she and her husband, Harold, a paper manufacturer's representative, had both found an exciting new life pattern which had brought amazing joy and meaning to them and had a powerful compulsion to share it with other people who were perhaps still going down dead-end roads.

Mary Brinig's other purpose in calling on me was to offer their services in establishing creative spiritual relationships with people who were not so fortunate as themselves in finding answers to the problems of modern living. I soon became impressed with the outgoing and profound interest of Harold and Mary in the younger people with whom New York City is filled who, for one reason or another, had missed the secret of satisfying and constructive living. I soon saw that they had a rare skill in getting to know such people and in establishing a communicable relationship with them. Having found their own answers by committing their lives to God, the manner in which they transmitted this experience to the most diverse and unexpected types of individuals marked them as two of the most effective people I have ever known or known about.

The secret of this couple is a combination of profound commitment, a love of people and a consuming interest in helping them. They brought to an exciting life-style some of the most desperately defeated. Always excited, always loving, as well as being down-to-earth and intelligent, they attracted to themselves and, through them, to God hundreds of people over the years who also found new and exciting life.

Finally Harold and Mary left New York to live in a small village in New Hampshire. There they found the same modern people-problems as in New York. Recently Ruth and I visited them and sat with a group of attractive moderns who had also found that effervescent excitement which, of all motivational forces, possesses the power to keep life going strong. The Brinigs, from a depth of spiritual reality, became practitioners of the excitement principle. And the outgoing quality of their interest in people helped them to find true happiness and kept them perpetually charged with excitement and youthfulness.

Excited and interested people are to be found in all lines of activity. And such people never have a dull job, because they are not themselves dull. At long last, life is inevitably what you are. If you are prosaic and apathetic, your job and indeed your life will reveal those same characteristics. But when you experience a spiritual awakening and come alive in the mind and in the spirit, then that old dull job becomes invested with excitement . . . even, you might say, with glory.

"ALL HEAVEN BROKE LOOSE"

On the highway when I see a lot of trucks parked at an eating place I always stop for a meal, for these men know where the good food is. One night I sat at a counter beside a long-haul truck driver and soon we were having a sprightly conversation; couldn't help it, for this man was full of fun and laughter. And when I introduced myself, this big jovial fellow seemed to know me.

He told me, "Over many years I have seen about as much concrete as any man alive. Day after day, night after night, it was always the same, rolling down interminable miles of concrete or blacktop. The monotony of it, the absence from home, the lousy motels, the go, go, go of it, made me hate it. What a dull, drab, no-account life. I detested it.

"Then," he continued, "our boss subscribed for your magazine, *Guideposts*, for all of his employees. And I got to taking it with me to read on trips. Those stories of how people found happiness and excited living through getting close to God finally began getting to me. I had never prayed much, except when in trouble. God was just a name, actually, I'm ashamed to say, more of a swearword than anything.

"But one night I was rolling down the Ohio Turnpike and for no reason at all I began talking to God just like He was riding with me in the cab. I opened my heart and told Him everything. And I had the feeling He was right there listening, I really did, for a fact.

"Then suddenly 'all heaven broke loose'—I was happier than ever in my life. I began to cry and then to sing. I bellowed out hymns I'd learned long ago in Sunday School but thought I had forgotten. Don't know whatever in the world happened to me, but suddenly I was an altogether different man. And I've been happy ever since, and I mean happy. I love this job now, for God rolls with me every mile, every night, every day, all the way."

Talk about being excited! This man gave me a terrific lift, one that has stayed with me ever since. He was the living embodiment of the excitement principle. I stood watching in admiration as his huge truck roared off into the night. And I kept repeating that vibrant phrase of his: "all heaven broke loose." As I drove down the road in the opposite direction, I recalled some delightful lines by a good friend, J. Sig Paulson, who said:

Sometimes I throb with laughter
and tingle with glee
As I ponder
the delightful, inevitable
project of being me!

That is the excitement principle in action, and the positive principle too!

THE FASCINATION AND THE THRILL

In Chapter 4, I spoke about the importance of maintaining enthusiasm in old age. Certainly practicing the excitement principle is equally vital no matter what one's age. You can keep your life going with vitality as long as the mind and the spirit are alive and zestful. There is no logical reason why the life force should be inhibited or permitted to decline unless, of course, some devastating physical disability occurs. But even in such cases many persons have been able to keep the positive principle operative by a strong dominance of the mind and the spirit over the physical.

How pathetic is the unhealthy preoccupation of Americans with age. At the very outset of hiring, at perhaps age twenty, retirement and pensions and the end of the road are built into the work psychology. Then it is "ten years until retirement"; "only five years to go, then I'm on the shelf." So goes the mournful tune. To anyone who has added up a few years comes the warning-tinctured advice: "You would do well to ease it off. Better slow down. Remember, you're not as young as you once were." How many times have well-meaning friends come up with these cautionary and negatively tinged remarks.

Personally, this author has never entertained any thought of retiring or of slowing down. Of course, I may reshuffle the several different types of work which have consumed my time for years; but as for quitting, that is inconceivable. I have never found work to be a hardship or a chore; certainly never a bore. It is truly enjoyable, even exciting. I intend to keep on being interested, active, excited and, as they say "with it"—always with it. No ease-up, no slowdown; but, rather, to give it all I've got every day all the way.

When one job ends for any reason, find another, even in a different area or field of endeavor. Some of the happiest years for many have been those spent in activity unrelated to their life work pattern. Only this will satisfy creative desire and keep happiness going at top level. Why quit? The total life span seems almost too short as it is.

HOUSE PACKED; MOSTLY YOUNG PEOPLE

There are many great human beings who have the same viewpoint of forgetting age and continuously living on the positive vitality principle. Recently in London Ruth and I attended a performance by Dame Edith Evans at the Haymarket Theatre. She was appearing in *An Evening of Entertainment*. The program notes showed that Dame Edith's career began about 1912.

The house was packed to the third balcony and, surprisingly, the audience had a high percentage of young people. The curtain went up on an empty stage. Movie clips of Dame Edith's long career appeared on a screen. Then came on this white-haired woman who had to be well over eighty years of age. Her hands, I noted, though graceful, had a parchment-like look. Dressed in a white gown, she came forward with an ever-so-slight totter.

She proceeded to give readings ranging all the way from Amy Lowell of New England to William Shakespeare of Stratford-on-Avon. And they were read, too, every word of them. At times she would fumble her glasses down toward the end of her nose, perhaps to see her manuscript a little better; and there was a bit of quaver in her voice.

Alone on a vast stage! I, myself, not in the same league with her, have had to walk out before big audiences on a stage all by myself and, believe me, that is not an easy thing to do. But Dame Edith was perfectly poised and, in a charming though not strong voice, performed masterfully. I sat marveling. What did she have that enabled her to grip these people so powerfully? And the young people were shouting "Bravo!" to a woman old enough to be great-grandmother to some. She was calm; she was self-assured, because she knew from years of experience how to draw an audience to herself. Her secret was, in part at least, that she simply forgot her age and lived her life. She was just going on being the great person she had always been. She was perpetually interested, perennially excited, constantly thrilled.

Sometimes the tendency of older people (to say nothing of younger ones) is to get into the habit of thinking negatively about so many things that living loses its flavor. Life gets dull because the individual gets dull. I once advised such a man to try a simple formula designed to put the zest back into living. Every morning, first thing, he was to say aloud three times, "What do you know—life is terrific!"—the first part of the sentence an affirmation of surprise, the second an affirmation of its quality.

Sure—that practice could be written off as superficial. But what do you know—it worked! That man took on new interest. He came alive.

A friend, an insurance executive, was coming up to retirement due to age. His spirit was aging, too, for he could think of nothing else. Then he had a vital spiritual experience and astonished everyone, including himself, by the amazing manner in which he rebounded right back into the marked excitement that had characterized him in earlier years.

When he retired he moved to a small upstate village and got into all sorts of activity. He found two cronies, retired men like himself—one an engineer, the other an accountant. All three were handy with tools and could do anything with their hands that they put their minds to. When one found a job to be done, the other two pitched in to help do the work. All three were active in church and community affairs. Together, in one project, they transformed an old barn on the church property into an educational and recreational building, utilizing the horse stalls as classrooms. The low haymow was made into a stage for dramatics. When my friend stopped by my house recently, I invited him to stay the night. "Thanks," he said, "I'd love to, but I can't. Got to get home for a project we are starting tomorrow morning." And with that he was off, radiating vigor, happiness, interest. According to his reports, "Everything is terrific. My only complaint is that I run out of time." He is certainly keeping it going with the excitement principle.

THINK FUTURE

The positive principle never thinks in past terms but always thinks future. "The best is yet to be" is its poetic expression. Such a positive-principle thinker is an older man who wrote to say that he had read a book of mine with good results. In fact, he was very excited about it. He explained that he had endured an inferiority complex from childhood and was now ninety-three years of age. This was by all counts the longest inferiority complex I had ever known about. "I read your book on positive thinking. I studied it. I believed it. I practiced it and am now writing to give you the good news that after ninety-three years I am at last free of my inferiority complex." But the payoff was in the P.S.: "The future looks great!"

Everywhere today one hears a dismal phrase from old and young alike: "I've had it." This variously expresses boredom or weariness. It also means, "I'm a 'through' person. My future is behind me. There's nothing ahead." But the future thinker has never "had it." Always out there ahead is the great excitement, the big thrill, the wonderful goal.

I well recall the day when the famed baseball executive Branch Rickey had been fifty years a leader in big-league baseball. Rickey, whom many authorities consider one of the greatest men the sport ever produced, was a strong, vigorous, dynamic person until almost the moment of his death at age eighty-three. He was invariably excited and enthusiastic. On his fiftieth anniversary he was asked, "What was your greatest experience in fifty years of baseball?"

Rickey drew down his bushy eyebrows and barked, "Don't know. Haven't had it yet!" Even then he was deep in plans for the formation of another big league. Branch Rickey was never an old man because he was an enthusiastic, excited, future thinker. He invariably kept the positive principle going.

Dr. Harry George Thomas, father of my friend and neighbor Lowell Thomas, possessed the same dynamic qualities which were so well demonstrated by his world-famous and adventurous son. At eighty-two Dr. Thomas enrolled as a student in a university. He did so well in his studies that he was asked to be an instructor, a faculty member, and served in this capacity until university authorities discovered that Dr. (of medicine) Thomas was eighty-four years old, nineteen years beyond retirement age! Dr. Thomas was, of course, a future thinker, practicing the power of the positive principle in so-called retirement. And his son, Lowell, continued as America's oldest newscaster until 1976 when he signed off after 46 years of nightly broadcasting. He remained involved in many projects until his death in 1981 at 89 years of age. The Thomases, it seems were future thinkers.

LIVE YOUR LIFE AND FORGET YOUR AGE

This type of person bases his activity on the vital principle of "Live your life and forget your age." He does not get hung up on age thoughts. Indeed, he does not think age, he does not act age, he does not talk age. As far as his mental attitude is concerned, he is ageless. His mental equipment functions in the now; always he is a "now" person. He takes himself as he is and goes on participating, doing what he has always done or something different; but still doing what he wants to do, with no concern at all about the date on his birth certificate. Or any other negative factor.

Frank Bering was still running three big hotels in Chicago—the Sherman, the Ambassador East and the Ambassador West—when well over eighty. I had known Mr. Bering since childhood. He and my mother were high school classmates in Lynchburg, Ohio.

I always stayed with Frank at the Sherman when in Chicago. One day I was speaking there at a trade association convention in the huge ballroom of the hotel. Frank was on top of everything, calm, efficient, authoritative—complete master of all the complex functioning of a 2,200-room hotel and a large convention besides.

Admiringly I said, "Frank, you sure are a great manager and executive," then asked, "How old are you?"

"What's the matter," he said, "don't you like your room? Isn't the service in this hotel okay?"

"Oh, certainly," I replied, "it's all perfect; but to think—at your age. Anyway, I know how old you are, for you were in school with my mother."

"Well, then," he said factually, "why bring it up? What has it got to do with anything as long as we are doing the job as well as or better than any half-baked forty-year-old could do it?" Then he leveled his finger at me. "Young man," he said, "I'll give you a valid principle to live by—live your life and forget your age." This man always operated on the positive principle.

Please do not get the impression that I am not fully aware of the pain and sorrow of human existence, nor that the resistances to excitement and positive attitudes are many and often severe. I have not been dealing intimately with people for a good many years without knowing that life is indeed no bed of roses. But still it is my belief that by the exercise of the positive principle we can rise above, live with and overcome the trials and problems we must face.

When recently the wife of a friend died he was, of course, devastated, but I was impressed by the depth and quality of his mental victory over his great loss and sorrow. He told me that shortly after his wife's passing he "felt" her presence most definitely and "by an inner ear" heard her speak to him. He thanked her for coming to comfort him and plaintively said, "Please come to me soon again." To which she answered, "Why, I am always near to you." Asked how he felt about the reality of this experience, he answered simply, "I'm excited to realize that she lives. She is not dead but alive. Isn't that wonderful?"

Faith of such quality is possible to those who practice the positive principle—and keep it going.

Now to add up the ideas in this chapter:

1. Keep wide open and acute your response capacity to inspiration, motivation and enthusiasm.
2. Maintain sensitivity at high level—sharp and keen.
3. Follow a steady program of renewing and revitalizing your positive attitudes. Never allow your reactions to become dull or insipid. Keep them new, fresh, vital.
4. Develop strong mental shields to ward off the bombardment of negatives.
5. Maintain a constant spirit buildup by a counterattack against the erosion of inspiration.
6. Become intensely interested. Fan your interest daily. Keep it vitalized.
7. Get the spiritual experience that really changes things; the in-depth type that brings you alive and keeps you alive every day all the way.
8. Live your life and forget your age.
9. Keep contact with spiritual re-creative power and you will always and forever keep the positive principle going.

ENTHUSIASM MAKES THE DIFFERENCE

Contents

This book is dedicated
to our grandchildren

LAURA STAFFORD PEALE
CHARLES CLIFFORD PEALE
SARAH LACY PEALE
JENNIFER RUTH EVERETT
and to
JOHN, CYNTHIA, *and* JENNIFER ALLEN

in the hope they will learn that
enthusiasm makes the difference.

Introduction

Enthusiasm—the priceless quality that makes everything different!—that is the message of this book.

Life is not all sweetness and light, not by a great deal; certainly not with its manifold difficulty, pain, and frustration. This book faces life exactly as it is. But, a creative solution is offered—a solution that works. This is an in-spite-of type of book. In spite of all the negatives you can bring forth the positives.

Interest, excitement, aliveness—that is what this book is about.

It shows that you need not have a dull, routinized, desultory existence—not at all! Never settle for such a thing. And regardless of harsh, painful, and discouraging situations you can be alive, vital, and on top of things.

You can put new spirit, new creative skill into your job. Indeed, you can do better with everything. Enthusiastic, zest-packed living is yours if you want it. And who doesn't want it?

Personally, I believe one hundred percent in the message of the book. I have seen the tremendous things enthusiasm has done for so many. Believe me it works!

NORMAN VINCENT PEALE

1

WHAT ENTHUSIASM CAN DO FOR YOU

Like an enormous map, the city of New York lay sharp and clear on that bright April day. From the window of a towering downtown office building, Sandy Hook could be seen far to the south and the George Washington Bridge to the north. To the west the low hills of New Jersey retreated in mystic blue haze. The deep-throated whistle of an outward bound ocean liner came faintly from the harbor. The vast network of the world's greatest city spread out below us.

The man behind the desk was obviously worried and the concerned look on his face underscored his feelings. "Sometimes I wish I might escape my responsibility for the people in this organization," he said. "Being the executive dealing with personnel can be a headache, believe me. Often I am compelled to do things that I dislike very much. To have the future destiny of people in my hands is something I do not enjoy at all."

"But their destiny is not really in your hands," I countered. "In the final analysis every man's destiny is in his own hands. But I sympathize with your problem, for you do indeed have to make decisions concerning people that can vitally affect their future."

"And that," he replied, "is exactly why I have asked you to come here today. It's about our mutual friend, Fred Hill. This is one of the most painful decisions I have ever had to make about the future of a man, and I need your help." I assured him that my help was available but that it was not quite clear to me how I, who knew nothing of the business problems involved, could give any practical assistance.

"But you see, it's not entirely a business problem; primarily it's a human problem. As a matter of fact, this conference may well determine what happens to a dear friend; to his wife and three sons. How effective Fred can be henceforth, not only in business but in other capacities such as the church and community, gives me great concern. You see," he continued, "there will be an opening in this organization within the next six months and from the business structural point of view, Fred is the logical choice for the job. I've wrestled with my conscience, and in all fairness to the company, I cannot recommend him. So I'm hoping you and I might figure out some way to help revamp Fred and, incidentally, I realize this is a mighty big order."

"What needs to be done?" I asked. "He seems a top-notch man. I can't imagine anything wrong with him, except perhaps that at times he seems apathetic."

"That's just it," the executive exclaimed. "Fred is well trained; he's had good experience; he has an attractive personality. He's a good husband and a fine father. But he lacks drive and vitality. Fred hasn't an ounce of enthusiasm. If we could help him acquire enthusiasm, he'd be the right man for the right job."

"In six months' time?" I asked.

"Six months," he repeated.

I was lost in thought, for this was a real problem. At last I said, "You know, it's possible that Fred has never been awakened."

My friend quickly picked up that suggestion. "You may be right. If it's so, he's not the only one. In personnel work, I see it all the time—capable people who've never been awakened. If only we could motivate them—starting with Fred. You know, I want to see him realize his potential."

As I rode home in the subway, I studied the faces of the passengers—worried faces, dull faces, unhappy faces. I counted only a few people whose countenances reflected vitality and a positive attitude toward life. Many of us too often accept the humdrum life without making a fight for a better one. We think in a downbeat way that maybe we don't deserve more.

Just then it occurred to me that one of the greatest human needs of our time is a weapon to fight mediocrity, one that will teach us how to make use of zest and vitality and the creative forces buried deep within us. What we so desperately need is the capacity for exercising enthusiasm. Then and there, I determined to write this book, *Enthusiasm Makes the Difference*. For I truly believe that enthusiasm makes the difference between success and failure.

As regards Fred Hill—in Chapter Five we will take up in detail what happened to him.

But now I want to talk about enthusiasm and its significance to you. Having carefully observed people over many years, I am convinced that the fortunate individuals who achieve the most in life are invariably activated by enthusiasm. The men who do the most with their lives are those who approach human existence, its opportunities and its problems—even its rough moments—with a confident attitude and an enthusiastic point of view. Therefore, it seems timely to stress the vital power of enthusiasm and to suggest procedures to develop and maintain this powerful and precious motivating force.

Enthusiasm can truly make a difference—the difference in how your life will turn out. Consider, for example, the vast disparity between two current types. One group consists of the optimistic, the cheerful, the hopeful. Since they believe in something, they are the dynamic individuals who set events in motion, always working for the betterment of society, building new enterprises, restructuring old society and creating, hopefully, new worlds.

MODERN YOUTH IN REBELLION

Contrast these energetic optimists with those purveyors of gloom, the rebels who defy not only their parents and teachers but their barbers. Lacking the vision and strength to help humanity by righting great wrongs, they play childish games and their rebellion shows itself in rude manners, an aversion to the bathtub, muddled thinking and a cult devoted to nothingness. Enthusiasm has never been a part of a negative cult.

So we must learn how to utilize enthusiasm in order to move into the exciting and creative segment of the human race, the achievers. You will find among them total agreement that enthusiasm is the priceless ingredient of personality that helps to achieve happiness and self-fulfillment.

Sir Edward V. Appleton, the Scottish physicist whose scientific discoveries made possible worldwide broadcasting and won him a Nobel prize, was asked for the secret of his amazing achievements. "It was enthusiasm," he said. "I rate enthusiasm even above professional skill." For without enthusiasm, one would scarcely be willing to endure the self-discipline and endless toil so necessary in developing professional skill. Enthusiasm is the dynamic motivator that keeps one persistently working toward his goal.

Voltaire once described a man as being like a warming oven, always heating but never cooking anything. Commenting on this viewpoint, Harold Blake Walker points out that many people live without zest, dragging themselves through their jobs without vitality; in a word, heating just enough to get by but never really cooking.

But amazing things do happen, he points out, when a person really catches fire and starts the cooking process. Walt Whitman said of himself, "I was simmering, really simmering; Emerson brought me to a boil." What an apt description of a personality, gifted but lacking in power until the fire of enthusiasm brought it to the boiling point. As a result, Whitman created immortal poetry. Isn't it perhaps time to stop "simmering, really simmering," and become fired by a new and vital enthusiasm? The mental and spiritual heat created by enthusiasm can burn off the apathy-failure elements in any personality and release hitherto unused, even unsuspected powerhouse qualities. Walker puts it another way: "Go beyond simmering, even to boiling, and you will discover talents and powers you never dreamed were yours."

Years ago I came across a quotation from Charles M. Schwab, one of the dynamic men who built the American industrial structure. "A man," said Schwab, "can succeed at almost anything for which he has unlimited enthusiasm." And that is an important fact, as we shall show in this book.

It is, of course, true that most outstanding achievements are accomplished over great odds. At the start of every enterprise there are invariably the negativists who darkly opine, "It just cannot be done," as they eagerly marshal all the arguments against success. The pessimist is so eager to be able to say, "I told you so." Of course such people seldom if ever are constructive, which could be the reason they hope you won't be either.

Recently, I had the pleasure of conferring an Horatio Alger Award of the American Schools and Colleges Association upon John H. Johnson, Editor and Publisher of the highly successful publication *Ebony* and other periodicals. He had an idea for a great magazine to serve the black community but was, as is often the case, short on money. So he was advised to "forget it."

It is some years later, and those so-called friends still cannot forget that they might have owned stock in what is now an immensely profitable enterprise. Mr. Johnson and his wife own all the stock today because he was the only one who had enthusiasm for the project. His enthusiasm bred faith, and faith stimulated action. John H. Johnson is a living example of Charles M. Schwab's declaration that "a man can succeed at almost anything for which he has unlimited enthusiasm." George Matthew Adams expresses the matter equally well: "Enthusiasm is a kind of faith that has been set afire."

But I urge you to understand that enthusiasm is related to fire in a special way. It is fire under control, which is the only kind of fire that counts. Fire must be harnessed to produce power. The world belongs to the enthusiast who can keep cool. Thinking in depth and sound action always require coolness. So the process may be described as follows: enthusiasm builds a fire within a person, but he must control his enthusiasm for an idea or a project rather than be controlled by it. He must never allow uncontrolled anticipation to run away with judgment or reason. Like any powerful force, uncontrolled enthusiasm can destroy, as controlled enthusiasm can create.

LITTLE GOALS ADD UP

As Mr. Johnson developed *Ebony* magazine, he decided not to attempt immediately the larger goals for which enthusiasm for his project inspired him. Instead, he wisely chose to set and accomplish what he called "little goals," one after the other. The attainment of one small goal gave him the feel of success and taught him technique. Then he proceeded with growing experience to tackle the next "little goal," and presently those small goals added up to an immense goal. The "little goal" philosophy is sagacious advice, especially for overheated enthusiasts who, tricked into believing the world is their oyster, attempt too much too fast, only to end up in defeat and frustration.

While warning against overheating, we must with equal emphasis also warn against becoming too cool. A high degree of combustion in the mind is required to keep enthusiasm hitting strongly on all cylinders. The super-sophisticated, who unfortunately control much of the thought-affecting media of our time, superciliously play enthusiasm down. Indeed, any emotion to them, except perhaps existential sadness, seems to be looked at askance as being corny.

My friend, Raymond Thornburg, himself an irrepressible enthusiast, in commenting upon the downgraders of enthusiasm, quoted Anatole France's wise insight: "I prefer the folly of enthusiasm to the indifference of wisdom." Or shall we call it tired-out cynicism?

Indeed, one should never hesitate to be on the warm side. Even though enthusiastic commitment may carry with it the risk of being wrong, still only those who take the chance will ever attain complete creativity. The committed person, win or lose, is the one who finds the real excitement in living.

Betty Friedan, author of *The Feminine Mystique*, makes a statement which registers. "A good woman," she says, "is one who loves passionately, has guts, seriousness and passionate convictions, takes responsibility and shapes society. I'm horrified by the word 'cool.' Coolness is an evasion of life. Being cool isn't at all. . . . I'd rather be hot and wrong. I'd rather be committed than detached." Amen. So would I. So would any do-something-about-it-person. And this is precisely why enthusiasm makes the difference. It lifts living out of the depths and makes it mean something. Play it cool and you may freeze. Play it hot and even if you get burned, at least you will shed warmth over a discouraged and bewildered world.

There are, of course, quite a few people in the "couldn't care less" category, who are neither hot nor cold. This emotionally empty crowd apparently has always been around and has never rated very high either. As a matter of fact, in Biblical times they were referred to as ". . . lukewarm, and neither cold nor hot, I will spue thee out of my mouth." That is a pretty rough evaluation and forthright treatment, but it describes a pretty innocuous lot. If we can help reduce the number of lethargic people and bring even a few of them into the creative enthusiastic class, not only will they get more out of life personally, but the world itself will be improved.

HE COULDN'T CARE LESS—HE SAID—BUT HE DID

There are many people today who pride themselves on indifference to the normal way of life. They are jaded and bored, and conceal their destructive thinking under the guise of "I couldn't care less." Perhaps it is their defense against living, because life demands total commitment and commitment is apt to bring pain as well as challenge.

Harry Simpson fell into this category. He was the most apathetic man I have ever known. He said he'd been everywhere and had seen everything, including some of the human race which didn't inspire his esteem. He announced he was fed up with the young rebels and the middle-aged stuffed shirts. As for politics, what difference did it make who was elected? In his opinion, politicians were all crooked, and no matter which party won, the people always lost. He attended baseball games, without even rooting for a team. Even in the World Series, he remained apathetic. He was a cynic and like most cynics, totally selfish and self-indulgent. He felt no obligation to participate in church or civic affairs. As for charities, his was a token gift, simply, as he put it, "to shut them up." He couldn't care less about the needy. Finally his negative attitude won him the nickname of "Les," obviously borrowed from his well-known couldn't-care-less philosophy. In spite of this he was a convivial person; a good golfer, bridge player and club member. He and his wife did considerable entertaining. He had more than average success in his professional career.

Then enthusiasm slipped into the picture and what a difference it made in Harry Simpson. It happened this way. He and his wife decided they needed a change of pace. They came to New York and went the usual round of shows, restaurants and night clubs. Mrs. Simpson enjoyed it, but Harry was unimpressed. "I couldn't care less for this junk," he growled. "Let's clear out of here."

But they had promised a business associate back home to look up a friend in New York and reluctantly Harry telephoned the man. Surprisingly a cordial invitation to dinner was extended, and more surprisingly Harry accepted. "I never knew why," he explained, ". . . until later."

There were several other couples present and it proved to be the gayest and happiest evening the Harry Simpsons had spent in years. "I can't figure those people," Harry said when they were back at the hotel. "Nobody had a drop to drink, at least as far as I could see. But how come they were all so high? And they actually made politics and world affairs interesting. Did you notice they referred to religion as though it really mattered to them? What have they got that we haven't?"

"I don't know," replied Mrs. Simpson, although she thought she did but wanted him to find out for himself. "Why don't you see our host again and ask him?"

So Harry invited his host to lunch and asked, "How come a group of metropolitan people, supposedly sophisticated, showed such effervescence and excitement?"

"Well," explained the other, "there is a history to the things you noticed. That group is pretty modern and every one of them in varying degree had gotten generally fed up. For myself, I'd about decided that life was just more of the same and I got no real interest out of living. Oh, business was going pretty well but Betty and I were on edge much of the time. The parties we went to were all dull, the same people, the same inane conversation—you know how it is."

"Yeah, I sure do," said Harry. "That description fits me like a glove. Go on."

"Well, anyway," the other man continued, "quite accidentally I ran into the minister of a New York church. In fact, he came to my place of business to make a purchase. I had never met him but had read one of his books. I asked him to step into my office. He never said a word about religion, but I found myself opening up and telling him all about my frustrations and boredom. He listened quietly until I ran down. I thought sure he would start selling me on going to church or pull out a Bible and read to me. But he didn't. He sat thoughtfully, then asked me 'What's next?'

"It seemed a queer question, but of a sudden I actually said, 'What's next? What's next?—I know what it's all about. I need God.' I was shocked to hear myself saying that—it just didn't sound like me at all.

"The minister said, 'Could be. Guess that's what we all need. We human beings do have unsatisfied hungers and the principal one is for God.' The minister rose to go, 'If you want to pursue this further give me a ring.' Before I knew it he was on his way and I sat back and smiled, saying to myself, 'Boy, what a salesman! He leaves me reaching for his merchandise. He knows I am going to buy.'

"Well, I finally went to see this minister and he introduced me to a man, saying, 'Get to know this fellow. He's got what you're looking for.' This man asked me to join him and a few others for breakfast, of all things. I looked around at the group and they certainly were a regular crowd of good guys yet I never knew men to be so enthusiastic. The atmosphere they created began to get to me. Breakfast over, they started sharing 'spiritual experiences' with each other. They told how they applied 'practical Christian strategy' to business and personal relations and I could see that these fellows were *released*. I knew then this same release was what I needed. And staying with that crowd I found it, too. That's the story. Wouldn't have told you if you hadn't asked."

"So that's it," Harry said, after a moment's silence, "just plain old Christianity in new language. But you should see the church I belong to. I seldom attend because it's dull and the minister is a kind of half-baked socialist, if you ask me. I can't abide him. Not many others can either, it seems, for only a handful show up on Sunday for services. Our minister needs what you're talking about, that's for sure."

"Well," said the other, "why don't you get it and then pass it along to your minister? Maybe he is looking for the same thing, but won't admit it. He certainly can't be happy about a dead religion."

"Don't dump that on me," Harry grumbled. "I'm not about to be a missionary to a God-is-Dead minister. I've got myself to think of." But later, he mused, "Maybe God *is* my answer. Isn't it something? I came to New York to get away from it all, but instead I've got myself into something—really into it."

Harry, puzzled though he was, made a spiritual commitment in his own way. "From now on, I'm putting God at the center of my life," he said. Naturally, he had to think and study to "get the hang of it." But the strange and reassuring phenomenon in such matters is that whenever a person consciously or unconsciously desires spiritual rejuvenation and begins working toward it on a simple and genuine basis, amazing things do begin happening. The change in Harry did not come about at once or even quickly. But a definite change did begin and it continued, and gradually people became aware of a new Harry Simpson.

"You ask me to name our local ball of fire," said one of his golfing partners some months later, "and who do you think I'll name? You've gucsscd it. Harry Simpson."

"And what made the difference?" I asked.

"Enthusiasm, a new and terrific enthusiasm that *made* the difference. He is no nut—far from it. In my book he is the sharpest businessman in town. But ever since he got this enthusiasm he exudes a strange sense of power and contentment. He was never like that before," he concluded pensively.

I cite Harry's case because when enthusiasm develops in depth, usually a religious factor is involved. But for that matter, any upsurge of spirit, religious or otherwise, that introduces into the personality a verve, an excitement, an outgoingness, and which raises slow simmering to a boil, will bring about the quality of enthusiasm that makes the difference. Once enthusiasm took over, Harry lost his "couldn't-care-less" attitude. The new virtue and the old fault were not compatible.

ENTHUSIASM—THE SPICE OF LIFE

I have no idea whether Mr. John Kieran, the well-known writer, is religiously inclined, but that he has avoided apathy is evidenced by some potent expressions of his on the subject of enthusiasm. "William Cowper, the English poet, is the man who handed down the opinion that 'variety is the very spice of life' but I disagree and I point in passing to the fact that Cowper was three times locked up for insanity, which only shows what too much variety can do to you," writes Kieran.

"As for me, I believe that enthusiasm is the spice of life. Emerson wrote: 'Nothing great was ever achieved without enthusiasm.' When I was a college student I heard David Starr Jordan, then president of Stanford University, tell of a man who said that the only way to make good coffee was to 'put some in.' And that was also Dr. Jordan's advice about life, given to us as students and future citizens. I can still hear him thumping on the desk and saying: 'Put some in. Whatever you attempt, go at it with spirit. Put some in!'

"I'm prejudiced in this matter," continued Mr. Kieran, "because I'm full of enthusiasm for and against persons, places and conditions. It's more fun that way. An enthusiast may bore others—but he has never a dull moment himself."

Mr. Kieran's comments are reminiscent of a statement by the historian, Arnold Toynbee, who said, "Apathy can only be overcome by enthusiasm, and enthusiasm can only be aroused by two things: first, an ideal which takes the imagination by storm, and second, a definite intelligible plan for carrying that ideal into practice." Here again are the basic elements of enthusiasm, namely, heat and intelligence and some profound motivation which drives off apathy and cynicism.

Jack London, whose books charmed many of us years ago, summed up the matter thus: "I would rather be ashes than dust. I would rather that my spark would burn out in a brilliant blaze than be stifled by dry-rot. I would rather be a superb meteor, every atom of me in magnificent glow, than a sleepy and permanent planet. The proper function of man is to live, not to exist."

That, of course, is precisely why I undertook to write this book. So very many people are not really living; so many are apathetic and unhappy; so many are failing in life rather than succeeding as they should, so many lacking dynamic motivation. The reason, and it is often a primary reason: they are short on enthusiasm.

My friend, Alfred Krebs, proprietor of the beautiful Grand Hotel Regina in Grindelwald, Switzerland, once told me: "There can be no success without enthusiasm. The secret of a full life is lots of enthusiasm, the kind that keeps you fighting and winning over all obstacles—and enjoying every minute of it."

Of course Alfred Krebs is right, for being enthusiastic is being fully alive. It is a strange, sad fact that many individuals exist, yet are not really alive. And when one is not alive, days come and go in an unending march of mediocrity. Henry Thoreau, one of the half-dozen great thinkers who set the intellectual tone of our country in its beginning, said, "Only that day dawns to which we are awake."

ENTHUSIASM REBUILDS A COLLAPSED PERSONALITY

In a city where I was scheduled to speak at a dinner meeting I was seated beside a local judge, an alert man of thirty-five. He said, "I think you might be interested to hear about the reawakening of a collapsed personality in this city."

"Please say that again, Judge," I requested.

"Yes, that's what I mean; the reawakening of a collapsed personality," he repeated.

"This man George is a police officer assigned to my court," the judge continued. "He stands six feet two inches tall and physically is strong and impressive. At first he did a good job for us. Then I began to notice a change in him. It seemed as though all interest leaked out of his mind. He just sagged; lost vitality and dragged himself through the day's work. We sent him to the doctor who, after careful examination, reported 'There is nothing wrong physically except that his whole energy and bodily function levels are down, and that goes for his mental outlook too. When the body is run down, often the mind is involved, since mind and body function together.'

" 'This man must have something troubling him mentally or emotionally,' the doctor continued. 'Maybe you had better have a psychiatrist run a check on him.'

"Instead of doing that," said the Judge, "I decided to work on George myself. 'Just how do you feel?' I asked him, and he replied, 'Well, Judge, I've got some personal worries, but they shouldn't make me collapse. Seems like I just haven't got any strength left. Living has become too much for me, I guess. I'm ashamed of being such a weak character.'

" 'Look, George,' I said, 'here is a book. I'll admit that it's a religiously slanted book, but it's written in simple style—no preachy stuff in it—and I think you will be interested in what it has to say. I want you to take it home tonight. Read the first chapter and study it carefully. Then come to my office tomorrow and I will quiz you on it.' "

Every day the Judge put George through an examination on each succeeding chapter until, after two weeks, the officer had read and studied and had been examined on the total book. "I doubt that George had ever read a book in his life before." Then he asked, " 'George, give me in a few words what this book has said to you.'

"George didn't hesitate a moment. 'Judge, this book says that if a person puts his life in God's hands he can overcome his weaknesses. That's what I make out of it, although there is a lot about thinking right.'

" 'That is exactly what I have been trying to get across to you, George. Maybe you should start putting the principles of the book into operation. It could work for you as it has for others, you know. Many people have really been helped by this book.' "

"And what happened?" I asked.

"Well, George got the message. He started studying creative spiritual principles. I supplied him with other books and pamphlets which might help him. I'm glad to tell you that he has pretty well worked out of his trouble. He is certainly no longer a collapsed personality. He has a new enthusiasm that has made all the difference in the world in him, though he still has much to learn about spiritual power as a source of real living. But he is learning. The main thing is he wants to learn, and so I am confident George is on the way."

Next morning while having breakfast in my hotel room, I turned on the television and happened to tune in to a panel on which three policemen were discussing "Safety Week." One officer was a big, vital man who talked about how wonderful life is and how important safety precautions are. The way he spoke, with great enthusiasm, telling the viewers how exciting life can be, convinced me that this was the officer of whom the judge had spoken. This was the former collapsed personality come alive. It was a thrilling and conclusive demonstration of how enthusiasm had made a difference in one man once he really went all out for it.

And there will be a great deal more about enthusiasm making a difference in people. So read on if you want your life improved, for enthusiasm can make a vast difference in every area of your life, in your work, your relationship with family and friends, in your entire outlook.

2

ENTHUSIASM THAT NEVER RUNS DOWN

I shall never forget the night I met Miss Nobody. After making a speech in a West Coast city, I was shaking hands with people who came up to greet me, when along came a young woman who gave me a limp handshake and said in a small timid voice, "I thought I'd like to shake hands with you, but I really shouldn't be bothering you. There are so many important people here and I'm just a nobody. Forgive me for taking your time."

I took a look at her and said, "Will you do me a favor? Please remain a few minutes. I'd like to talk with you."

In some surprise she did as I suggested. When I had finished greeting the others, I said, "Now, Miss Nobody, let's sit down and have a visit."

"What did you call me?" she asked in surprise.

"I called you by the only name you gave. You told me you were a Nobody. Have you another name?"

"Of course."

"I thought you must have," I said. "One reason I wanted to talk with you is to find out how anybody can get the idea she's a nobody. Another reason is that referring to yourself this way is in my opinion an affront to God."

"Oh, Dr. Peale!" she exclaimed, "you can't be serious. An affront to God?"

"You are a child of God, created in His image. So it really bothers me, it hurts me, to hear you say you're a nobody." And I asked, "Tell me a little about yourself."

She proceeded to describe her circumstances and problems. She talked haltingly, but with evident relief at being able to confide in someone. "So you see," she concluded, "I've quite an inferiority complex and sometimes I get terribly discouraged. I came to hear you tonight hoping you might say something that would help me."

"Well," I answered, "I'm saying it to you now: You are a child of God." And I advised her to draw herself up tall each day and say to herself, "I am a child of God."

She looked at me with a lovely smile and promised to follow that advice. And she added, "Pray for me."

And I did, I prayed that the Lord would help her to acquire real enthusiasm about herself and some proper self-confidence as well.

Recently I was speaking in the same area and an attractive young woman approached me asking, "Do you remember me?"

"Have me met before?" I asked.

"Yes, we have. I'm the former Miss Nobody."

Then I remembered. And I knew that she had fared extremely well since our first meeting. I could tell it from her manner and the sparkle in her eyes even before she had time to report anything in words. She had discovered her extension powers as a child of God.

This incident underscores an important fact. You can change! Anybody can change! And even from a dull nobody to an enthusiastic somebody.

In addition to "Miss Nobody," I have seen many people change and change greatly. They cease to be defeated and unhappy people and become altogether different in nature, so they are hardly the same individuals. Less attractive qualities have given way to better ones and their personalities have been dramatically brought out and enchanced. As a result they enter upon a life so full of happiness and success and creativity that people around them marvel. And they themselves marvel. And why not? For it is a marvel.

In the years that we have taught creative living through spiritual practice, I have seen people who were literally packed full of hate changed into people equally full of love. I have watched defeated individuals shed anxiety as they absorb the amazing secret of victory. I have observed people who suffer from fear transformed into courageous, worry-free persons.

ENTHUSIASM WILL IMPROVE YOUR PERSONALITY

There is another important form of change, one perhaps more complicated, related as it is to complex moods, to the cyclic rise and fall of emotional reaction. It is the change from apathy to enthusiasm, from indifference to exciting participation; it is an astonishing personality change which sensitizes the spirit, erases dullness and infuses the individual with a powerful motivation that activates enthusiasm and never allows it to run down.

Most people acknowledge the possibility of personality change in connection with hate, fear and other common forms of conflict, but seem to doubt that they can be made over into enthusiastic persons. They argue, "Sure I would like to have enthusiasm, but what if you just haven't got it? You cannot make yourself enthusiastic can you?" This is always said in anticipation of an of-course-you-can't agreement. But I do not agree at all. For you can make yourself an optimist. You can develop enthusiasm, and of a type that is continuous and joyous in nature.

The important fact is that you can deliberately make yourself enthusiastic. Actually you can go further and develop a quality of enthusiasm so meaningful and in such depth that it will not decline or run dry no matter what strain it is put to. It has been established by repeated demonstration that a person can make of himself just about what he wants to, provided he wants to badly enough and correctly goes about doing it. A method for deliberately transforming yourself into whatever type of person you wish to be is first to decide specifically what particular characteristic you desire to possess and then to hold that image firmly in your consciousness. Second, proceed to develop it by acting as if you actually possessed the desired characteristic. And third, believe and repeatedly affirm that you are in the process of self-creating the quality you have undertaken to develop.

MAKE USE OF THE "AS IF" PRINCIPLE

Many years ago the noted psychologist William James, announced his famous "As if" principle. He said, "If you want a quality, act as if you already had it." Try the "As if" technique. It is packed with power and it works.

For example, let us suppose you are a shy and diffident individual with a miserable inferiority complex. The procedure for change into normal extrovertism is to start visualizing yourself not as you think you are, but rather as you'd like to be, a person confident and assured, able to meet people and to deal with situations. Once the thought or image of what you desire to be is deeply imbedded in your consciousness, then deliberately start acting in a confident manner, as if you are competent to handle situations and personal encounters. It is a proven law of human nature that as you imagine yourself to be and as you act on the assumption that you are what you see yourself as being, you will in time strongly tend to become, *provided* you persevere in the process.

This law of self-assumed personal change has been demonstrated by many and diverse people. For example, the famous religious leader John Wesley was terrified in a violent storm on the Atlantic as he sailed to America in the seventeenth century. But some people aboard the wildly tossing ship were calm and confident during the storm. Wesley was so impressed by their imperturbability that he asked their secret. It proved to be simply a serene faith in God's providential care. When Wesley sadly confessed that he did not have such faith, one of them said, "It is a simple secret. Act as if you do have such faith and in time faith of that character will take hold of you." Wesley followed the advice and ultimately developed such powerful faith that he was able to overcome the most difficult situations. So therefore if you are afraid, discipline yourself to act as if you had courage. If you are tense, deliberately act as if calm and assured. Shakespeare, whose insights into human nature have scarcely ever been equalled, supports this method. "Assume a virtue if you have it not," he tells us in Act III of *Hamlet*.

Another outstanding illustration of the law of acting "As if" and as you desire to be is that of Frank Bettger, a top insurance man. In his book *How I Raised Myself from Failure to Success in Selling** Mr. Bettger tells of his early experience as a professional baseball player on a minor league

* Copyright 1958, Prentice-Hall, Inc., Englewood Cliffs, N.J.

team from which he was summarily discharged. The manager regretted letting him go since Frank possessed the basic qualifications of a good player. But though competent, he was dropped for one reason only—lack of enthusiasm.

Bettger, signed by another team at a lower salary, continued to play the same desultory kind of game. Then one day he encountered a famous oldtime professional who asked, "Frank, don't you really like baseball? You have real ability, but you are totally lacking in enthusiasm, and until you get that you will never go ahead in this sport, or for that matter, in anything else in life. You must have enthusiasm. It's a primary requisite for success."

"But," complained Bettger, "what can I go? I haven't got enthusiasm. You just can't go out and buy it in a store. You either have it or you don't. I haven't, so that's it, I guess."

"You're wrong, Frank," said the older man urgently. "Make yourself act enthusiastic. It's as simple as that. Act with enthusiasm, play ball with enthusiasm, and pretty soon you will have enthusiasm. Once you're fired with conviction your natural talents will take you to the top in this sport."

Finally Frank Bettger's chance came. He was taken on by the New Haven ball club, and when he went out to play that first day he resolved to take his old friend's advice and act as though he was charged with enthusiasm. He ran like a man electrified. He threw the ball so hard it seared the gloves of other players. He swung like mad at the ball and actually made some hits. He literally burned up baselines; all this, while the temperature was over ninety in the shade.

The New Haven newspapers the next day asked where this terrific new player Bettger came from. He was a human dynamo, they reported. Soon they were calling him "Pop" Bettger. As he continued to play with such vigor he found himself feeling like a new man. And why not, for he was just that. He became such an enthusiastic player, that a scout for the St. Louis Cardinals spotted him and before long he was playing in the National League.

Later, having taken up a career in insurance, Bettger was once again plagued by apathy and he was once more courting failure. Then he recalled how he had deliberately cultivated enthusiasm, and applied the same "As if" principle to his insurance work. The result was that he rose to the top in his selling field as he had in baseball. Mr. Bettger's experiences demonstrate that enthusiasm can be cultivated and developed by deliberately thinking and acting with enthusiasm. You too can activate yourself into enthusiasm by use of the "As if" principle. What you are comes to you. This remarkable principle is thus stated by Emerson, "A man is a method, a progressive arrangement; a selecting principle, gathering his like unto him wherever he goes." So act as you want to be and you will be as you act.

MENTAL VENTILATION LETS IN ENTHUSIASM

Another practice important to the development of optimistic attitudes is that of mental ventilation. A mind full of gloomy foreboding thoughts makes difficult the cheerful and spirited quality of thinking that stimulates enthusiasm. This is true also of such dark closed thoughts as hate, prejudice, resentment and general dissatisfaction with people and world conditions. Discouragement and frustration form a heavy cloud-blanket over the mind and condition mental attitudes accordingly. Mental ventilation, then, is a highly important step in reconditioning the mind to accept the creative thought climate in which enthusiasm may develop and finally become the dominant factor.

This concept of mental ventilation was first suggested to me some years ago by Mr. A. E. Russ, an old friend who operated a drugstore on lower Fifth Avenue near Twelfth Street in New York. Mr. Russ, a member of my church, had a remarkable gift of native wisdom and insight. He was a natural philosopher, a keen and discerning thinker, a voracious reader, and a successful businessman. His spiritual life had depth, the kind which results when personal suffering emerges into understanding and victory. He knew how to help people and communicate to them a sense of meaning in life, as is evidenced by my personal experience with him.

Discouragement was once somewhat of a problem for me and it would occasionally plunge me into pretty low feelings. Though enthusiastic and optimistic by nature, I was sometimes given to depressions. During such low periods, it seemed that nothing went right. In those days I preached at Marble Collegiate Church on Sunday nights as well as Sunday mornings. (Later the morning congregations grew to such proportions that it became necessary to give the same sermon twice on Sunday morning; the evening service was handled by associates.) But at the time of which I write, I felt I had done particularly badly in my sermon one Sunday evening. Avoiding as many people as possible I plunged out into the dark misty night and walked glumly down Fifth Avenue toward my home.

Passing Mr. Russ's drugstore, I decided on an impulse to go in to see him. He was making sodas at the fountain, so I sat at the counter and watched him. "How come you are making sodas?" I asked. "Where is your regular counterman?"

"He left me, so I'm shorthanded," he replied.

"Tell you what," I said. "I preached a terrible sermon tonight. Can't imagine why I ever took up preaching in the first place. I'm a flop. How about giving me that soda jerk job?"

"Sure, why not?" replied Mr. Russ without a change of expression. "Come around the counter and make a soda for me. I want to see how good you are before taking you on." So Mr. Russ sat at the counter while I donned an apron and proceeded to put together a chocolate ice cream soda. It had a fairly good head on it, I thought. I laid a straw against it as I'd seen the experts do and put it in front of him. He took a long draw while I waited for the verdict. Removing the straw from his mouth he said, "Better stick to preaching."

Climbing down off the stool he locked the front door. "Closing time," he explained and then added, "Come into my back room and let's talk." He led me into those mysterious recesses behind the drug area to which druggists retire to compound prescriptions. There, I must say, he made up a "thought prescription" for me for which I have been grateful through the many years that have passed since that gloomy night.

Mr. Russ began to tell of his personal battles with discouragement. As I listen to his story of difficulties, reverses and sorrows, my depression seemed trifling indeed. "But I can tell you honestly," he declared, "that since I began a certain mental and spiritual practice I have never had any lasting discouragement. And I'm sure you will agree I'm on the enthusiastic side."

"I don't know a man of more genuine enthusiasm than yourself. What is this mental and spiritual practice which helped you?"

"Daily mental ventilation," he replied. "That's what did it and, I may add, still does it. Keeping the mind free of darkness is a day to day job."

He went on to emphasize the importance of the process of daily mind-emptying. "If you allow dark thoughts, regrets, resentments and the like to accumulate, your whole psychology can in time be so adversely affected that a major effort may be required to bring it back to a normal state of balance." I knew he was right, for our religio-psychiatric counseling service at the church was even then working with the pathetic problem of a man who had, as he himself put it, "accumulated a putrifying mass of old unhappiness in the mind." Weeks were required for our ministers and psychiatrists to cleanse and restore his psychological equipment to proper working order.

Since then I have used the mental ventilation system employed daily by Mr. Russ, both personally and in other cases, and with such effective results in stimulating new enthusiasm that I set it down here for the benefit of all who may read this book. He "emptied" his mind at the end of every day to prevent unhealthy thoughts from lodging in consciousness overnight, for he knew such thoughts can take root quickly if allowed to accumulate even for as long as twenty-four hours.

This mental emptying took the form of a recapitulation of unpleasant incidents that had occurred during the day; a sharp word, an insinuating remark, a hostile act by some other person. Also a review of his own mistakes, errors or stupidities. To these he added disappointments, frustrations and every form of unhappiness that had clouded the preceding hours. He held all these in a strong mental view, deliberately drawing from them all the experience and understanding they had to give. Then he "lumped" them together and mentally "dropped" them out of consciousness, saying as he did so these therapeutic words: "Forgetting those things which are behind, and reaching forth unto those things which are before . . ." (Philippians 3:13)

Mr. Russ stated that when he first began to use his "lumping" and "dropping" practice, the mental accumulation, as he put it, readily "lumped" but just did not "drop." However, the continued application of a determined and disciplined mental effort resulted in due time in a remarkable ability to forget the useless and unhealthy material that had previously cluttered his mind, siphoning off zest and enthusiasm. In these procedures, Mr. Russ made use of the law that one can do practically anything he wants with his thoughts, provided he consistently continues the effort.

"You cannot possibly realize until you try it for yourself what a powerful upthrust of joy surges through your being when you find that you can actually 'lump' and 'drop' those pesky enemies of a happy mind," he declared. "Ventilate—that's the answer. Ventilate. Let them go; throw them out, 'lump' and 'drop'—ventilate the mind.

"Now take yourself," he exclaimed, "you say you've had a bad evening; that you preached a disappointing sermon. All right then; analyze it carefully. Determine what you did that may have been wrong. Learn something from your analysis. Then 'lump' and 'drop'—ventilate. The old enthusiasm will bounce back."

He punched me affectionately on the chest as we said goodbye. I went home and at once started practicing Mr. Russ's mental ventilation system. It took some time and some doing over many days, but finally I got the hang of making my mind obey me. Then it was easy. Believe me, this method is a sure-fire secret of having boundless enthusiasm.

TELL YOURSELF ALL THE GOOD NEWS YOU KNOW

A vital element in developing enthusiasm is the manner in which you start the day. You can pretty well condition a day in the first five minutes after you wake up. Of course,, some people are naturally slow starters and for them it takes time to become fully awake and adjusted to a new day. But even so, careful attention to the matter of setting the tone of a day in the early hours is likely to have a determinative effect.

Henry Thoreau, the American philosopher, used to lie abed for awhile in the morning telling himself all the good news he could think of; that he had a healthy body, that his mind was alert, that his work was interesting, that the future looked bright, that a lot of people trusted him. Presently he arose to meet the day in a world filled for him with good things, good people, good opportunities.

This good news technique each morning can help make your day, despite the fact that there may be disappointing news that must be faced. Still, the more good news you tell yourself, the more such there is likely to be. The practice will also help you take bad news in your stride. At any rate, that which the mind receives upon awakening tends to influence and to a considerable degree determine what your day will be.

One man whose enthusiasm is always in evidence, even when the going is rough, has his own method for beginning a day. He takes a few minutes before breakfast for what he calls a "quiet time." This consists of reading a brief spiritual or inspirational piece and is followed by three or four minutes of quiet during which he affirms and practices a quiet state of mind. Regardless of how busy his program for the day, in those few minutes no hurry or haste is permitted, even in thought.

He then pictures every person he expects to contact during that day and prays for each one. "Then I commit the day to God and get going," he says. And he really does get going. Everyone he touches is revitalized by this man whose boundless enthusiasm seems never to diminish. And a principal reason for its vitality is that his practice of spiritual motivation at the start of each day infuses him with new zest.

EVERY MORNING A NEW SET OF FACTS

Apprehension about the day ahead is characteristic of some people, particularly if they find difficult and trying problems looming ahead. They view the prospect with distaste, perhaps even fear, so they have little enthusiasm for the exciting challenge that problems present. But I do admire the attitude of a friend toward each day. He has experienced some tragic trials and reverses in his lifetime, enough in fact to completely destroy many men. But he says, "A reversal is not a disaster, merely an incident in a total business career." He approaches each day on the principle that you get a new set of facts each morning. Then you convince yourself that you are going to take this new set of facts, be happy with it and do something constructive with it.

This man, whose enthusiasm and ability are considerable, declares, "There are only two kinds of days for me: Some days I'm happy. Other days I'm hysterically happy." The policy of taking hold of a new set of facts each morning and being happy about it seems to be a real factor in sustaining high-level enthusiasm. It has been said that every tomorrow has two handles. You can take hold of either the handle of anxiety or the handle of enthusiasm. The continued choice of handle determines the character of your multiplying days. Choose enthusiasm daily and you are likely to have it permanently.

HOW TO HAVE CONTINUING ENTHUSIASM

The problem of sustaining enthusiasm is often difficult, especially for older persons. The natural enthusiasm of youth may take a fearful battering as the years add up. Disappointments, frustrated hopes and ambitions, the drain-off of natural energy all conspire to dull excitement and enthusiastic response.

But such deterioration of your life force need not occur. In fact, it will happen only if allowed to happen. You can arrest the decline of spirit; you can be perpetually motivated by enthusiasm despite age, pain, sickness, disappointment and frustration.

I have known people who have remained enthusiastic until the end of their lives and then seemed to go out of this world with flags flying, the light of enthusiasm for life still in their eyes. Nothing could ever happen to destroy the precious gift of enthusiasm.

In thinking of such energetic and enterprising people, Huxley's insight comes to mind—that the true genius of living is to carry the spirit of the child into old age. And what is the spirit of the child, but that of wide-eyed open wonder, excitement and zest; the optimistic attitude that nothing is too good to be true, that the world is literally a wonderful place?

In Montreux, Switzerland, I met Mr. and Mrs. William P. Daggett, schoolteachers from Long Beach, California, and their children, Lucy, Cathy and Larry. Mrs. Daggett mentioned a quotation from Thoreau which hangs on her kitchen wall at home. "None are so old as those who have outlived enthusiasm." Well, believe me, that is an auspicious saying that could well be engraved on the wall of the mind. It is a fact that the oldest, saddest people are those who have outlived the enthusiasm of their youth.

That quotation from Thoreau set me thinking. I am writing these lines on a balcony of the famous Montreux Palace Hotel of which my friend Paul Rossier is general manager. My balcony looks out on an incomparable vista across the blue waters of Lac Leman (Lake Geneva) to the misty heights of the Alps towering above. Nearby and downlake at the water's edge stand the grim gray walls of the ancient Castle of Chillon, immortalized by Lord Byron.

I well recall my first visit to this old-world city and hotel forty years ago. I was very young and enthusiastic and wanted to travel to Europe and see the places I had read about in history books. Having scarcely two nickels to rub together I organized a tour party for which I earned the cost of the trip and a couple of hundred dollars besides. It was the experience of a lifetime. My mind was full of the romantic future, and I lived in perpetual excitement. Like "The Youth, who daily farther from the east must travel, and by the vision splendid is on his way attended," so I was fascinated by sights and sounds. The Montreux Palace Hotel, to my wondering eyes, was the most elegant hostelry imaginable. And I was actually looking for the first time at the Alps and Lac Leman. I just could not believe it. It was all so incredible and wonderful.

Well, four decades have passed since that first enthralling visit. The question now is: How about those youthful dreams? What has happened to that glorious excitement? What is the state of that ardent enthusiasm?

What would be your own honest answer to such reflections? Ponder well those words from Thoreau: "None are so old as those who have outlived enthusiasm." And just what have we got, you or I, if we have outlived enthusiasm? The Bible had a graphic picture of such persons. "When they shall be afraid of that which is high, and fears shall be in the way . . ." On that basis, one can be old at twenty, and some are. It is the rejuvenation of the mind that keeps enthusiasm alive and, as a matter of fact, restrains aging in spirit and mind, perhaps even in body too.

Well, what is your answer? Want to know mine? I can honestly report that the excitement and enthusiasm of forty years ago are still very much alive, only deeper and more satisfying. So I know from personal experience that enthusiasm can be perpetual; that it need never run down. And that is a fact too, a great big wonderful fact.

KEEP THE FIRES OF ENTHUSIASM BURNING UNDER YOUR GOALS

What an ingredient it is, this vital thing called enthusiasm! And a factor that keeps it perking is an irresistible goal, a fascinating objective, a consuming purpose that dominates, motivates and will not let go of you. Set yourself a goal that you've just got to reach. Then build under it the fire of anticipation and keep it burning—you will acquire enthusiasm and never lose it. That goal will keep beckoning, saying: "Come on after me." And when you reach your goal still new goals will succeed one another as each is attained. New goals, fresh objectives—these are the self-perpetuating motivators of enthusiasm.

Take my friend Paul Chow as an example. I first met Paul in Hong Kong. He had literally walked out of Red China with his family. His astonishing enthusiasm is reflected in a glorious smile and a radiant face. Paul had a dream, a goal, to come to America to raise his family. He was very poor and one of the thousands of refugees crowding into Hong Kong. But Paul had something of much more value than money. He had faith, purpose, enthusiasm.

It is a long story, but one Sunday I looked from my pulpit in New York City, halfway around the world from Hong Kong, and there amidst that huge congregation, right in the front pew, sat Paul Chow and his family. And he was smiling up at me as if to say, "We made it to New York."

Mrs. Peale and I visited his new home in a section of New York where crowding, noise and filth brought back memories of their ordeal in Hong Kong. "Not another day shall they live in this hell-hole," we agreed. We helped them move to Pawling, New York, where Paul has become a valued worker in our publishing plant at the Foundation for Christian Living, and where his family has made a real place for themselves in the community life.

Stephen Chow has become a top honor student in high school, and

Ruth and Martha Chow are leaders in their classes. The family has made a second move to a better house. They work hard; indeed they work like Americans worked in the old days. Stephen cannot understand why some young people fail to realize the tremendous privilege and opportunity they have in schools in America.

One vivid picture I carry in mind. Mrs. Peale and I were leaving our farm at Pawling on a beautiful July Saturday afternoon for a vacation in Europe. Paul and Stephen were painting a long white fence. They are always working. They have a goal, so they work. The road runs below a high bank atop which Paul, spattered with paint, was making that fence white and beautiful as his sense of perfection dictated. As we drove away he stood there paint brush in hand, etched against a blue sky and a field of waist-high corn, his face alive with a happy smile, waving farewell to us.

As we drove down the road to the airport I marveled at how far that Chinese refugee family had come from such unpropitious beginnings with so many obstacles ahead. What can possibly explain it? That's easy. It was a goal, an objective, a purpose. It was aspiration for a better way of life. It was enthusiasm that never weakened because it was subject to constant renewal.

Dwayne Orton expressed a solid truth when he said: "Every business organization should have a vice-president in charge of constant renewal." If it is good for an industry constantly to renew itself, then surely it is important for the individual to have an automatic self-motivator that keeps him alive and vibrant, always alert to the dynamic present in which he lives. In the absence of constant renewal he may fail to keep pace with changing times. Then life races ahead of him. He becomes not a living, vital man, but a relic who fades each day further into the dead past. Possessed of enthusiasm one is a citizen of the present regardless of how many years he has dwelt upon earth. Such a vitalized person cannot possibly become a *has-been*. He is perpetually the *is-now* type.

Happy expectations make the ultimate difference in any person. "Every man is enthusiastic at times. One man has enthusiasm for thirty minutes—another has it for thirty days—but it is the man who has it for thirty years who makes a success in life." So says *The Catholic Layman*.

ENTHUSIASM AND FINGER LICKIN' GOOD

Colonel Harland Sanders was sitting on his porch in Shelbyville, Kentucky, on his sixty-fifth birthday when the mailman came up the walk and handed him an envelope. It contained his first social security check. While grateful to the government for this tangible expression of concern for its older citizens, Colonel Sanders had no mind to settle down to a nonparticipation status in business. With boundless confidence despite his limited financial position, he turned his thoughts toward using that modest check to begin a new career. What an exciting experience it would be to launch a new career at an age when one is expected to start playing shuffleboard.

Sitting on his porch that day, do you know what he did? He started thinking—and ideas came to his mind. Ideas change things. He remembered the delicious fried chicken his mother used to make, crispy brown and tender. The very aroma seemed to be wafted across the years, filling him with nostalgia. The recipe for that fried chicken was imprinted indelibly in his taste buds and on his memory.

Then came the creative idea that was to change his life. Why not sell the recipe for his mother's fried chicken on a royalty basis to restaurant owners? Immediately he took action on the thought. Getting into his battered car he set out calling on restaurant owners, everywhere, enthusiastically telling them of his out-of-this world fried chicken. But no one would go for his idea. Across the country from Kentucky to Utah restaurant men maintained that their own recipes for fried chicken were good enough for them and their patrons. In Salt Lake City a restaurant owner who doubted that his northern clientele would respond to Kentucky-type fried chicken was swayed by the Colonel's enthusiasm, and finally agreed to give it a trial.

The result—people crowded his restaurant clamoring for those golden brown chicken pieces for which the positive-thinking colonel had coined the graphic selling phrase: "It's finger lickin' good."

Colonel Sanders, a striking figure in immaculate white suit and black string tie, finally sold out his interests for two million dollars, and then was hired by the new owners as goodwill ambassador at an annual salary of $40,000. His ruddy face is full of humor and intelligence; he is now over eighty years old but he still reaches out enthusiastically toward a future that calls for fresh thinking. And what is the motivation of this man and others like him? It's enthusiasm, the kind of enthusiasm that believes there is always something new and better ahead. It is creative conviction that never runs down.

Finally there is a prime factor in the maintenance of continuing enthusiasm, one that brings all other ingredients together into powerful focus. And that is a profound spiritual feeling, a faith in God, that activates a sharp awareness of life and a consuming interest in living. Age does not dull it. Pain and problems do not take the edge off of it. The blows of time and circumstance do not affect it. With this faith, a sense of confidence in life itself continues, unaffected by all the difficulties of human existence. A deep personal and vitalized faith in God is the basic factor in developing enthusiasm that never weakens. And it is vividly expressed in a statement from the Bible: "Be renewed in the spirit of your mind." (Ephesians 4:23)

I tried making a list of the most enthusiastic men I have ever known and discovered that this fundamental statement explained the enthusiasm of them all. One man on my list is an old friend, Bryson F. Kalt. One of New York's top salesmen with a phenomenal selling record, Bryson has the ability to maintain enthusiasm (without which no man can succeed as a salesman) with the help of the principle stated in those words "be renewed in the spirit of your mind."

Asked the secret of his continuing and undiminished vitality over many years, Bryson replied, "Well, it's like this. You taught me to love God and people and life and to keep my mind and spirit renewed and at a high level. I followed your positive teaching and the result has been happiness and enthusiasm that never runs down."

There you have, I believe, the basic answer to the problem of undiminished enthusiasm. Simply "be renewed in the spirit of your mind." Keep the mind perpetually renewed and you're in.

3

ENTHUSIASTIC PERSUASION

There is a magic formula for success.

No enterprise can succeed without it; any enterprise can succeed with it. Indeed, it can lead to success in life itself. The formula is stated in six powerful words—short words, only three of them containing as many as four letters. They are these—and mark them well: *find a need and fill it*.

Every business enterprise that has achieved success and demonstrated outstanding performance has been predicated on that formula. The managers of such enterprises discovered a need for some service or commodity that was generally required by people. They went about filling that need, they filled it well, and so their efforts were rewarded by corresponding response.

The great men of history were those who saw a need, who became aware of some timely requirement. They proceeded to fill the need, they met the requirement, and so were leaders and benefactors of mankind. They became outstanding and successful personalities, being possessed of the great quality of timely participation. These men were need-watchers, situation-handlers, condition-rectifiers, requirement-fillers.

Success is not based on smug cleverness, sharp practice, shady promotion, or super high pressure. These may carry one along for a while, but they have no substance, they don't hold up, and so presently they show through, they wear thin. Loud-talking, simulated enthusiasm that is usually coupled with high pressure is another false procedure that doesn't have what it takes to persuade and communicate and produce long-lasting results. It washes out inevitably.

But a salesman's enthusiasm based on a sincere belief that his goods or services are needed, and that such goods and services will meet people's needs with validity, is the kind of enthusiasm that does succeed, and it is entitled to do so. It will succeed if it isn't overpressed. An overpressing salesman creates resistance. But sincere enthusiasm attracts confidence.

So if you are a salesman and have something to sell, something that people really need, which when purchased will honestly fill that need, you have the makings of a successful career. But you must be certain that what you are trying to do or be is right. If it isn't right, it's wrong—not half-right, not half-wrong. It is either right or wrong and nothing wrong can ever turn out right. Unless it's good, it's bad, and nothing that is bad can be good. So get with the right—get with the good.

When you have something you really believe in, then you can put the amazing power of conviction behind your efforts. Then it is that enthusiasm is activated, develops and starts working. And when enthusiasm—real burning enthusiasm for something, for a product or a service—gets involved, then persuasion becomes a factor. Enthusiasm that persuades is perhaps the most powerful communicator on earth. It puts you in a position to reach people, to make them aware of their need and it also conveys to them that you can supply their need. You then become a vital necessary factor in their lives—and why not? You have what they need. You are essential to their happiness and welfare, and they know it.

But the strange fact about human nature is that people are not always aware of their needs. So they often resist buying that which they really need for their own best interests. This is the point at which communication and persuasion are so profoundly required. The art, skill or science of communication is the process by which you persuade another person or many persons to walk the road of agreement with you. Communication and persuasion—these are the two absolutely essential qualities that every human being *must* have if he desires to affect the lives of other people; to get them to buy a product, accept an idea, share a conviction or walk with him toward a goal.

HOW TO BE A REAL SALESMAN

This chapter largely has to do with salesmanship. And I feel entitled to write on this subject, having spoken before many sales meetings and been closely associated with the selling profession even to the extent of making a motion picture entitled *How to Be a Real Salesman*.

How do you become a real salesman? Well, this chapter will outline and illustrate some suggested methods. I want to list here an eleven-point salesmanship technique which I believe gives important elements in effective selling.

1. Find a need and fill it. It's pretty hard to sell something no one needs. Believe that you are selling what people really need.
2. Since you must sell yourself even before selling your goods, it's important to sell yourself on yourself. So believe in yourself.
3. Want to sell. Get the thrill of selling desirable goods or services.
4. Get full of enthusiasm, the kind that keeps you excited about your job and about people.
5. Don't ride enthusiasm so hard that you become offensively high pressure. All that will get you is resistance and no sale.
6. Develop the powerful motivation that comes from deep inner enthusiasm that never runs down.
7. Don't be a half-a-minder. Be an all-out, not a half-out. Give your whole mind, your whole self. That will provide the impact that achieves results—real results.
8. Concentrate—think—concentrate—think. Keep your mind working and keep your mind on your selling. Thinking produces ideas and ideas sell.
9. Learn to communicate. Develop rapport with people. Know people and like them. They will like you and buy what you have to sell.
10. Ask God to guide you in your planning. Then plan your work and work your plan.
11. Believe that being a salesman is the greatest, most important job in the American economy. Believe that you are a trustee of free enterprise and freedom. Be proud you are a salesman.

ENTHUSIASM PERSUADES AND PERSUASION SELLS

From boyhood I have personally been fascinated by salesmanship. Always I wanted to sell—to sell something to somebody—to offer people some value. I clerked in a candy store after school and sold candy, at least that which I didn't eat. I worked in a grocery shop and got a big charge out of *selling* groceries, not merely filling orders. I sold the Cincinnati *Enquirer* and worked early and late getting new subscribers and did so in large numbers.

My selling career as a boy included selling men's clothing for my dear old friend, Emil Geiger. Years ago he operated one of the best haberdashery shops I ever knew back in Bellefontaine, Ohio. Emil was one of the most effective communicators and practicers of the art of persuasion I have ever watched in operation. He offered good quality merchandise. Actually he loved his goods. To him, they were the best; there was nothing better.

He was patient, wanting the customer to have that which was the best for him. Rather than allow a man to go out of his store with a suit that wasn't just right, Emil would tell him to look elsewhere. I have even known him to phone a competitor to supply a customer when he felt honestly he could not do it himself. People always came back to him, for they trusted him. He knew how to sell and what is perhaps more important, how to keep on selling. Honesty and integrity were the hallmark of this man who remains in my memory one of the greatest salesmen I ever knew.

He was like the late Amos Sulka, famous New York City haberdasher, who was also a friend of mine. Sulka told me that the late William Randolph Hearst, publisher of the Hearst chain of newspapers, once came to his shop to lay in a new supply of collars. Sulka felt that the style of collar worn by Mr. Hearst was entirely unsuited to him and as a matter of fact not even in good style. He suggested in his best persuasive manner another type collar. Hearst bristled, "I know what I want. Do you want to sell me that or not?"

Sulka, unruffled, pleasant and polite, still was firm. But he knew how to communicate. "Mr. Hearst," he said to the big, stern, beetle-browed publisher, "you are the greatest seller of newspapers in the world. You know what people need and you sell them what they need. I, Sulka, am the greatest haberdasher in the world. I know what people need in the way of clothing. I'm the world's expert in suiting the proper item to the man, especially the great men."

The eyes of the two strong personalities, the two supersalesmen, met. Sulka's never wavered, "I want Mr. Hearst to look Sulka's best, and that is the best."

Hearst grinned. "All right, you old egotist, put the collar on me that you think is right."

Sulka believed in his goods. He knew what was right. He couldn't compromise. And he wasn't afraid of a world-famous customer. He was no sycophant. He communicated with the other's strong mind and will. His enthusiasm, his honesty and integrity, plus undisputed preeminence in his field, made him a salesman extraordinary.

Well, to get back to Emil Geiger—he said to me one day, "You're always going to be a salesman, Norman, but it will be a system of ideas you will be selling. You will sell Christianity, for I know that you are going to be a minister. So let me give you some advice. Give people a religion that will work, one that will help people the way they need helping. And believe in it yourself. Be sincere. Then be enthusiastic about it. Be persuasive. Learn to communicate and they will buy."

Emil was of the Jewish religion, but now and then in later years he used to come to my church in New York and he would clap me affectionately on the back. "Give them the real thing, for that's what they need," he would say. "Be enthusiastic, communicate, persuade—that will sell them." And, of course, Emil was right, for the preaching and teaching of Christianity as a way of thinking and living is a form of salesmanship. By these approaches, one tries to get people to accept the message and persuade them to walk a road of agreement with him.

I SELL ALUMINUM POTS AND PANS

I learned through a selling experience years ago how enthusiasm and persuasion add up to successful communication, and bring about creative results. In those days everyone got himself a summer job, and one year I became a salesman of aluminum-ware kitchen utensils. It was a house-to-house canvassing job, with now and then a staged cooking demonstration to show the advantages of aluminum pots and pans. The idea was to persuade some popular housewife, well-known for her cooking, to invite several neighborhood women to a luncheon at which time you would give them a sales talk on the advantages of the cooking utensils.

An avid devotee of Ohio-Indiana cooking, which was strong on fried chicken, mashed potatoes and gravy, I naturally exuded enthusiasm and persuasiveness. I exclaimed over the delicious food! My zeal communicated itself to the women so compellingly that my order book bulged with sales.

But that cold house-to-house selling! Believe me, that called for extra courage, perseverance and super-enthusiastic persuasion. At that time, I lived in Greenville, Ohio, and was so nervous and self-conscious that I decided to "work" Union City, Indiana, just across the state line. Hesitantly that first day I started up what appeared to be a promising street, having already passed by several on untenable excuses.

The first house was a bit run down. I said, "Those people are not progressive enough to buy aluminum ware," and passed it up. The next house was trim and neat. I reasoned, "These people are progressive and probably already have aluminum ware." By this time I was conscious of my own fear-conditioned rationalization. So taking myself in hand I mounted the steps, rehearsing the sales talk that had been given me along with my kit of merchandise. Then praying that no one would be at home, I timidly pressed the bell. The door was flung open and to my nervous gaze the biggest woman (or so she seemed) I had ever seen filled the doorway. "What do you want?" she barked, glaring at me.

"You don't want any aluminum ware, do you?" I said in a weak voice.

"Of course not," she snapped and banged the door shut.

Abjectly I dragged myself and my case of aluminum ware back home. But not liking to take a licking, I went to see a friend named Harry. "Have you ever sold aluminum ware?" I asked. When he replied in the negative, I shouted, "What? You've never sold aluminum ware? Why, that's the greatest business in the world." My enthusiasm swept him off his feet and in no time at all I had sold him a half interest in the business. I gave him the sales talk to study and told him that we would get started early the next morning for a day of selling to Union City.

Next day we got off the streetcar at the scene of my ignominious failure of the previous afternoon. "Shall we sell on this street?" asked Harry.

"No," I replied, "let's skip this one. I worked it yesterday."

Approaching the next street I felt a strange new sense of enthusiasm and confidence, inspired no doubt by the presence of my friend. "You take that side. I'll work this one," I directed, "and listen—don't take *no* for an answer. Be enthusiastic—persuasive. She needs this merchandise, so make her realize it."

I walked up to the door, full of the joy of salesmanship. I was going to persuade a woman to buy something she needed which would be of lasting satisfaction to her. It was positively thrilling. As I pressed the bell Harry gave me a wave of the hand. "Sell her, old boy," he shouted.

The door opened and a little wisp of a woman appeared (at least she looked little to my confident gaze). Soon I was in her kitchen, actually drying dishes for her, extolling the virtues of my aluminum ware. I positively raved about it. "My, my, but you are an enthusiastic young man. Just how can you get so worked up about cooking utensils?" This opened a flood gate of scientific information about cooking that had the lady's mouth open wide in astonishment. She signed the order and thanked me all the way to the door.

This woman was my friend until she passed away, and once years later when she came to hear me preach she said, "You sell the Gospel with the same enthusiasm and persuasion that you sold me those pots and pans. And," she added, "I'm still using a couple of them. They were as necessary to me as you said."

"Yes," I replied, "and so is the Gospel that I'm now advocating."

"Oh, I bought that long ago," she smiled.

Enthusiasm and persuasion—formula extraordinary—add up to successful communication.

ENTHUSIASM AND THE GOOD LIFE

Everyone can make use of enthusiastic persuasion in making a better and more successful life for himself and his loved ones. My mother has been gone for over twenty-five years, but I am very conscious that whatever I am doing today of a creative nature has its roots in her enthusiastic persuasion during my boyhood. And the same can be said by the children of every good and alert parent.

Actually my mother was a saleswoman and she had something to convey. She was thrilled by people and their personalities and potential abilities. She was always selling young people on what they would become. She was one of the greatest experts I ever knew in building fires in people's minds, fires that got them moving. And of course the effect of her vibrant spirit on her own children was profound. A meal at our house was always an exciting experience. Mother talked about all the wonderful things not only in our town, but all over the world.

She was in charge of women's missionary activities for a big denomination and she received letters from missionaries everywhere. She was in touch with events and movements in many countries. And she traveled the world over, her adventures even taking her through bandit-infested territory of China and into war-ravaged areas. All this she brought to the dinner table and used it in trying to persuade her three boys to make something of themselves and to contribute something worthwhile to the world. She could sell anyone on an idea because her ideas were good and she put behind them the motivational power of enthusiasm.

Mothers and fathers are salespeople, their job being to sell vibrant, creative life to their children. If they do not sell it to them, then some long-haired, sad misfit may sell their children the big lie: that the United States and life itself are flops and turn them to the LSD route or some other dead-end failure pattern.

The wife of Ramsay MacDonald, one-time Prime Minster of Great Britain, on her deathbed said to her husband, "Whatever you do, put romance and enthusiasm into the lives of our children. With those qualities their lives will be good."

Enthusiastic persuasion is a real happiness producer. It has the power to invest the prosaic, if not with romance, perhaps at least with exciting interest and meaning. We are living in a time when many of those who have been favored with education and opportunity, beneficiaries of the wealth and culture produced by centuries of sacrifice and toil, have now concluded that life is meaningless and devoid of value. And as for enthusiasm, the mere mention of the world would cause bewilderment to flit across their uncomprehending faces. So we must admit that this isn't the most propitious era in which to advocate enthusiasm. Or maybe because of the circumstances it *is* the most propitious. At any rate, enthusiasm is not the most widely used commodity of our time. In fact, any reference to enthusiasm would be considered in some circles as unsophisticated, if not actually downright corny.

James Dillet Freeman, who writes potently, says: "We live in a time of revolt against reason. Revolt against beauty. Revolt against joy. Artists dribble paint out of paint cans onto canvas. Sculptors weld together pieces of old iron and concrete they have scavenged from a junkyard. Musicians blow klaxons and bang tire irons for symphonies. Poets babble trivial obfuscations. Philosophers prove by reason that reason can prove nothing."

And he continues, with not so much gentility as one might expect of a philosopher, "Life stinks, people say. Especially the intellectual people say this. Sophisticated people. Educated people. The people who read books—even more the people who write them—the artist and scientists and teachers and scholars. For them," says Mr. Freeman, "life stinks." Well, now, isn't this inspiring? We have come to a day and age when seemingly to be erudite you must take a dim view of enthusiasm and settle for life that is putrid.

TAKES GUTS TO PRACTICE ENTHUSIASM

Recently at luncheon I was seated by a distinguished woman, Judge Mary Kohler, who has done notable work among the underprivileged, especially children, in the ghettos of New York City. Though white of hair, she is an eternally youthful type; her face has an indefinably attractive radiance. She laughs out of sheer exuberance of spirit. She is a respected scholar too. Pleasantly she asked what extra thing I was doing now. "Writing a book," I said.

"Oh, isn't that interesting! And what is the title?"

"*Enthusiasm Makes the Difference.*"

"What do you know about that," she exclaimed. "Why, I think you are wonderful! I congratulate you on your audacity and courage, that you would actually write a book on enthusiasm in a day like this."

Well I was surprised to know that this required courage and audacity. Since then I've concluded that it does rather run contrary to the mainstream or present-day so-called American intellectual thought. But I'm not writing to the intellectuals, I'm writing to the mass of American people whose simple faith is that life can be good.

ENTHUSIASM EQUALS LOVE

And how does one have enthusiasm in life? Actually, it is as simple as this: Cultivate the ability to love living. Love people, love the sky under which you live, love beauty, love God. The person who loves becomes enthusiastic, filled with the sparkle and the joy of life. And then he goes on to fill it full of meaning. If you're not enthusiastic, begin today to cultivate the love of living. Like Fred, for example.

It happened in Detroit one cold winter night. It was about nine-thirty when I checked in at my hotel and since I hadn't had dinner I asked a bellboy, "Is there a restaurant in this hotel where I can get a sandwich and cup of coffee at his hour?"

"There's room service," he suggested, and handed me a menu.

Now I'm a frugal soul, and when I saw that the cheapest sandwich on the menu was two dollars and fifty cents and coffee thirty-five cents I asked, "Isn't there a lunch counter around here?"

"Yes, up the street there's a place called Fred's," he said. "It doesn't look like much, but the food is very good."

So I walked several blocks to Fred's. And the bellboy was right; it wasn't much on the outside, nor even on the inside. Seated at the counter were some seedy-looking old men (and when I sat down that made one more!). The man behind the counter was a big fellow, with sleeves rolled up revealing great hairy arms. He had a big apron tied around him. There was no style to this place whatsoever, but I liked it at once.

Resting a big hand on the counter, the man in the apron asked me, "Okay, brother, what'll you have?"

"Are you Fred?"

"Yep."

"Over at the hotel they told me you have good hamburgers."

"Brother, you never ate such hamburgers."

"Okay, let me have one."

Along the counter was an old man who looked extremely miserable. He was sitting there with his fingers shaking. Whether it was a nervous condition or delirium tremens, I wouldn't know, but after big Fred had put my hamburger in front of me he went over and put his hand on that of this old fellow. "That's all right, Bill," he said. "That's all right. I'm going to fix you a bowl of that nice hot soup that you like. How'll that be?" Bill nodded gratefully.

Then a minute or two later another old man got up and shuffled over to pay his check. Fred said to him, "Mr. Brown, watch out for the cars out there on the avenue. They come pretty fast at night. And have a look at the moonlight on the river. It's mighty pretty tonight."

I looked at the man in admiration—his love, roughly given, which is sometimes the greatest kind of big-hearted love, was sort of tender. It was really touching. And he was a salesman, too. He said to me, "You oughtn't to end up without a piece of this marvelous pie, brother. Just look at it; isn't that beautiful? Mary baked it right here on the premises."

"That is surely beautiful, but I have what's known as will-power."

"That's the trouble with some of you people. How do you expect us to stay in business?" But he gave me a big smile as he said it.

When I paid my check I couldn't help remarking, "You know something, my friend? I like the way you spoke to those old men. You make them feel that life is good."

"Why not?" he asked. "I love living myself. And they're pretty sad old guys and our place is sort of like home to them. Anyway, I kind of like 'em."

As I walked back to my hotel that night I had a new spring in my step. I felt happy—because in a rough place I had met a marvelous thing, the spirit of a man who loved life—a genius in enthusiastic persuasion, making people feel that life is good.

So don't depreciate life by enumerating all the things that are wrong with it. Things *are* wrong, and something has to be done with them. But focus mentally upon all that is right about life; life is mighty good, a lot better than not having it, I should think. A lifetime on this wonderful earth doesn't last very long, either. It is here today and gone tomorrow. So love it while you can, and be full of enthusiasm.

HE HAD PSYCHOSCLEROSIS!!

One day with two other men I took a taxi in New York City and had a most enlightening experience. As we got into the cab we greeted the driver affably commenting on the weather (which we thought was good) and asked him how he felt and how business was. To each of these genial inquiries he responded with a glum and depressing grunt. I had noticed that this youngish-looking man had a dark, dismal look on his face. He was obviously in a depressed and pessimistic frame of mind.

In our conversation the two men repeatedly called me "Doctor." This seemed to interest the driver. He looked around several times. Apparently he concluded that he had in his cab a doctor of medicine and saw a chance to get a little free medical advice. During the lull in our conversation he said, "Doc, I wonder if you'd give me a little advice."

"What advice do you want?" I asked.

"Well," he said, "I've got a pain in my back and I've got another pain in my side and I don't sleep well and I'm tired and I just don't feel good. What do you suppose is the matter with me? Can you give me something to help me feel better?"

"Well," I replied, falling in with the physician myth, "I must tell you, my friend, that I seldom practice in taxicabs or give prescriptions in this manner, but since we're here, I'll be glad to advise you as best I can.

While I don't like to give an off-the-cuff diagnosis, it does seem that you have the symptoms of psychosclerosis."

Whereupon he nearly ran up onto the sidewalk. I guess it sounded like an extraordinarily formidable disease. "What is this psychosclerosis?" he wanted to know with some apprehension.

I wasn't too sure myself, but I continued, "You've heard of arteriosclerosis, haven't you?"

"Well," doubtfully, "I guess so. What's that?"

"Arteriosclerosis is hardening of the arteries. Any kind of sclerosis is a hardening—either of arteries or of tissues. Now what you seem to have is psychosclerosis, hardening of your thoughts, of your attitudes. It is a loss of the flexibility of spirit. And," I said, "that is a terrible disease and is no doubt one reason you have those aches and pains. How old are you?" And he told me he was thirty-five. "Nobody should have such aches and pains at thirty-five," I said. "Yours undoubtedly come largely from your psychosclerosis."

Psychosclerosis—I coined the word myself—aptly describes the condition of a great many people who have lost their interest and whose thinking has become hard and fixed. And one of the greatest antidotes to this disease of the spirit is enthusiasm.

When a child is born Almighty God builds enthusiasm into him. As he emerges from infancy into childhood, he is filled with excitement; with the wonder and the glory of life. To him everything is fresh, new and fascinating. But as he grows older, if he becomes sophisticated and cynical and his viewpoint hardens, he loses one of the finest elements of human nature—enthusiasm. Huxley said that the secret of genius is to carry the spirit of childhood into maturity. That is, it's important to preserve natural, God-given enthusiasm. A physician told me, "I have actually seen people die for lack of enthusiasm. Of course, I can't write that on the death certificate, but the person without enthusiasm can lose the will to live."

Lots of people fail in selling, in management, indeed, in any kind of leadership because they are victims of psychosclerosis, hardening of the thoughts. New methods, progressive ideas, adjustment to changing times and situations just cannot break through rigid old patterns.

Of course I informed the taxi driver that I was not a medical doctor but rather one who specializes in state of mind and condition of spirit. But I assured him that many medical doctors find important health connections between mind, spirit and body.

I sent this man a copy of my book *The Power of Positive Thinking.** He faithfully practiced the mental and spiritual procedures presented in it. He came one day with a grin to give me the good news that his "psychosclerosis" was a lot better. "When I got my thinking straightened out, it's surprising how different I felt." He actually showed some signs of enthusiasm, which I am sure had to do with his obviously improved condition.

Enthusiastic persuasion, to be effective, must have direction; it must be slanted toward definite purposes and objectives. Just to be enthusiastic in a vague general way may possibly produce a bright and attractive personality, but still not result in that communication in depth which makes desired things happen.

John Bowles, Vice-President of Beckman Instruments, told me of a salesman who called on a customer regularly every Tuesday morning for six months. Homer would come in, sit around, project his enthusiastic personality, talk excitedly about sailing and golf and finally wind up by saying, "Guess you don't want anything, do you?"

Sam, the proprietor, became quite fond of salesman Homer. The two became golfing companions on Saturday afternoons and occasionally Sam went out in Homer's small sailboat. Always Homer exuded enthusiasm about everything and was real good company.

One day, relaxing in the clubhouse after a round of golf, Homer said, "You know, Sam, I don't get it. I've called on you very week for six months and we have become good friends, but—doggone it—you've never bought anything of me."

"That's not hard to figure," replied Sam. "You've never told me what you're selling. You never really asked me to buy."

Think of all that enthusiasm, all that persuasion gone to waste. "You don't want anything, do you?" never told the customer what he sold. Seems incredible but it is representative of so much desultory, no-objective effort that can only result in futility. One thing is for sure; nobody ever raised money, sold goods, helped anyone to a better life or got a wife, who did not ask. The Bible says, "Ask, and ye shall receive." Even enthusiastic persuasion will never persuade unless and until the objective is definitely sought. Direction-purpose-objective—these are the qualities that measure success. And you've got to be all-out, too.

* © 1956, Prentice-Hall, Inc., Englewood Cliffs, N.J.

DON'T BE A HALF-A-MINDER

I had a curious encounter a couple of years ago in the Hotel Sherman in Chicago. After speaking to a convention I was in my room when a woman called on the phone and forthwith announced that she was bringing her husband to see me. Her tone was so firm I had no alternative but to agree. When they arrived, the woman's look was firm, too. Addressing her husband as Charley, she told him to sit down—and Charley sat. And Mabel was half his size.

"Now," she said to me, "I want you to do something for Charley." As if to say that as far as she was concerned she had worked with Charley for years and had given it up.

Charley seemed a nice, easy-going, likeable fellow, but as I later discovered, he was undisciplined, undirected, actually pretty much a failure in his sales job. His firm had been unusually patient with him. I met with him at intervals over some months and got to know him very well. He rather baffled me. Finally I noticed that he had one stock phrase that he used continuously. It was so repetitive that it gave the same impression as a phonograph needle stuck in a groove. Charley would be talking about something and he would say, "You know, I have half a mind to do something about that." Or, "I've half a mind to investigate that." And once when I was urging him to think positive, he said, "You know, I've half a mind to do that."

Finally I said, "I know what's wrong with you, Charley. You're a half-a-minder. Everything you think of doing you have half a mind to do. But you had better realize no one in this world ever got anywhere with only half a mind. Most of us need more than we've got. We certainly need all we do have. A half a mind just isn't enough."

It wasn't until Charley began to employ all his mind that he really began to get results in life. When he did, his ability to achieve developed amazingly. When he started giving his job all he had, his natural talents eventually put him into the top-producer category.

To be a success requires the giving of your whole self, your whole mind. In so many instances men who do give their whole mind to the job demonstrate not only the enthusiasm that makes the difference, but extra efficiency as well. A friend of mine, John Imre, is superintendent of our farm on Quaker Hill in Dutchess County, New York. He has made it a place of beauty, and keeps it running well because it receives his complete interest and concern. He studies every problem carefully and so his ratio of right conclusions is very high.

Refugees from Hungary, John and his wife Maria recently became citizens and have gained the respect of the community. He is successful in his work because he is a whole-minder, not a half-a-minder. As a well-known athletic coach remarked, "It's the all-out, not the half-outs, who become top performers."

There is another point at which enthusiastic persuasion is very much needed. To approach it another way, just about the greatest selling job you will ever have is to sell yourself on yourself. To bring yourself to an enthusiastic acceptance of yourself is one of the biggest feats of all. How to make yourself believe, really believe, in yourself, in your abilities, talents, capabilities, requires the most enthusiastic persuasion.

It is tragic how many people are conditioned not by a normal, realistic and objective appraisal of themselves which brings the facts about their abilities into focus, but by an inferiority concept that distorts the proper self-image. True, there are some blatant egotistical self-worshipers, but they are infinitesimal in number by comparison with the many who struggle always against self-doubt and feelings of inadequacy. The market for selling people on themselves, believe me, is very great indeed. But when you get a person to apply enthusiastic persuasion to himself, it is remarkable how he can be sold on a proper realization of his own worth.

AIRPLANE WASHROOM EPISODE

This is perhaps the strangest experience in personal counseling of my entire career. I was on a jet airplane between New York and Chicago and every seat was occupied, including those in the lounge. I went forward to the washroom and as I was entering I felt someone behind me also trying to get into the room. I stepped back to let this man go ahead, but to my surprise he said, "I want to talk with you privately, and since the plane is crowded maybe we could talk in the washroom."

Well, I was a bit suspicious that I might have some kind of oddball on my hands and I left the door ajar in case a getaway seemed indicated. "What's on your mind?" I asked, half perched on the sink.

"Oh, I'm miserable and low. I just don't feel adequate to my job. I have no faith in myself. I feel like crawling into a hole and pulling it in after me. I've got a great big whopping inferiority complex." So ran his gloomy self-appraisal.

Trying to get a further line on my strange visitor, I asked, "What business are you in?"

"Oh, I'm just a peddler, a plain ordinary peddler," was his self-deprecatory reply.

"And in what form of salesmanship are you engaged?"

His answer rocked me. "Well, you see, my bosses send me around the country to make inspirational speeches at sales meetings."

"Well, your bosses must be pretty stupid to send out a gloom artist to try to inspire other fellows to believe in themselves and their products."

"My bosses aren't stupid. They're the smartest men in the business!" he declared with the first show of spirit.

"If that is the case, and I do not doubt it, they must see some qualities in you that you do not see yourself. That is to say, your bosses believe in a man who does not believe in himself. In the few minutes we've been talking you have depreciated your profession and yourself."

"My profession?" he asked in surprise.

"Yes, your profession. You wrote yourself off as 'only a peddler,' downgrading one of the greatest professions in this country, that of salesmanship—the process by which a vital product or service is made available to people who need it to enjoy better living for themselves and their families. What do you mean 'a peddler'? You are a salesman and more than that, a teacher and inspirer of salesmen.

"And moreover, you are a self-downgrader. Do you know who made you? Who gave you those extraordinary abilities of leadership that your keen-eyed bosses see in you? Come on, tell me, who created it all?"

"Well, I suppose you mean God," he mumbled doubtfully.

"Precisely. I do mean God. And here you are running God down by casting aspersions on His workmanship. Boy, you sure do have your thinking messed up."

"Gosh, I never saw it in that light before. Sounds different the way you work it out." He grinned slightly for the first time.

"Now look, another thing I noticed about you—you slump. You have a good height of about six feet."

"Six foot two," he corrected.

"Well, you're using only about five foot ten of it. So stand up straight. Try to touch that wall with as much of your body as possible. Carry your head high. Reach for the ceiling with it."

"This is a strange procedure," he commented.

"That's nothing. The whole setting of this conversation is strange. But let's not allow that to interfere with doing a job on you.

"Now hold that straight-up position and repeat after me the following—'I am a salesman, the greatest profession in the world. I am a vital part of the American free-enterprise system. I help make available goods and services to people who need them. Without men like me the economy would wither on the vine. I am an important trustee of free civilization."

"You actually want me to say that?"

"I sure do, so let's get going." Hesitantly he repeated the words, but as he got into it he began to show some evidence of feeling. "O.K.," I said, "that's good. Now let's pray." A dead silence fell. "Well go on," I prompted.

"Me pray? I was waiting for you to offer a prayer. I never prayed in public in my life."

"This is hardly in public," I commented, "so go on and pray."

That was some prayer of his, memorable and unforgettable. Of course, I did not record it and have to repeat it from memory, but as best I can recall it went something like this: "Lord, I need reorganizing. Please reorganize me. Help me to get outside myself. Yeah, Lord, that's it—help me to get outside my tied-up self. Help me to be a real salesman and amount to something. Amen."

"That was a real prayer," I said, "because you meant it. And I'm sure that God heard it too, for he rides the airways."

Later we shook hands at the airport and he went his way, but I hear about him from time to time, and from all I gather he is going strong with a new emphasis on enthusiastic persuasion. For this man enthusiasm made the difference, a huge creative difference. He sold himself on himself, which is an important thing for anyone to do. For when an individual does that, provided he keeps some humility, he is on his way.

CHAMPION GOLFERS AND POSITIVE THINKING

Many of our great athletes use self-persuasion in their preparations for an athletic event. Here, too, enthusiasm plays a vital role. For instance, Gay Brewer called upon positive thinking and enthusiasm to help him in the 1967 Masters' Tournament and his skillful performance brought him victory. The gallery, watching enthralled, had no idea that Gay Brewer had played through tournaments without indication of potential greatness. Yet he always felt the inner resources were there. But they seemed to be shut up inside of him. So he took inventory and found on the debit side a lack of faith and enthusiasm. How could he perform like a champion when inwardly he felt like a loser? His very attitude was conspiring against him.

Then by good fortune—and because he'd begun a real search for self-help—Gay found the writings of men who had fought and won over their feelings of inadequacy; men who out of their own experiences had devised practical rules for constructive, enthusiastic living. Gay Brewer tried these suggestions and to his amazement they worked for him. The results showed not only in his golf game but in his entire way of life. As a result, he was calm yet aggressive in the Masters' Tournament. He played an offensive game with a positive attitude. He wanted to win, he concentrated, he believed in himself and he thought positively. He played champion golf because he had equipped himself mentally as well as physically to become a champion.

Gary Player, the great South African golfer, one of only four men who have won the "grand slam" of golf, the U.S. Open, British Open, the Masters' and the U.S.P.G.A. title, recently told me of his experiences.

"As you know, we golfers live under continual strain. Now this can get under your skin and make you tense. I'd like to tell you how I overcame it when I played Arnold Palmer and Jack Nicklaus in the World Match Championship in London.

"This golf course happened to be particularly suited to the talents of my opponents. Most people doubted that I could win over these great players. But I didn't allow the pessimistic opinion of press and public to influence me. Nor would I let myself grow tense. I remembered one of the quotations from *The Power of Positive Thinking* and I knew that 'in quiet and confidence would be strength.' I knew also, Dr. Peale, that I would do my best 'through Jesus Christ Who strengthens me.'

"Then when I played in the U.S. Open, I again called on the suggestions from the same book. I visualized, I prayerized, I actualized—and won the U.S. Open.

"Since the Bible is our greatest source of inspiration and energy, and since your writings, Dr. Peale, have brought the Bible closer to our everyday lives, I always recommend your books, particularly to young people, for constant reading. As a result of your influence, I base my own life on these Big Three: Faith, education and physical fitness."

FOUR STEPS TO ACHIEVEMENT

And here is another great formula for successful living. It is by William A. Ward. He calls it Four Steps to Achievement. It might be called the Eight P Plan: Plan purposefully. Prepare prayerfully. Proceed positively. Pursue persistently.

So do believe in yourself. Practice the principles of enthusiastic persuasion. Make yourself believe that you can be better than you think you are. And remember—if you think you can, you can! Bring bona fide enthusiasm to your life style—for enthusiasm always makes the difference.

4

HOW ENTHUSIASM CANCELS FEAR AND WORRY

"Killed by thirty years of thought!"

So a London newspaper headlined its report of the strange death of a woman tennis star. This woman, as a small girl thirty years before, had watched in terror as her mother had died suddenly of a heart attack while being treated by a dentist. The traumatic experience so profoundly affected the child that in the thirty years that followed, she absolutely refused any dental treatment. The mere suggestion of going to a dentist terrified her. And this, despite the realization that the dentist to whom her mother had gone had no responsibility for her mother's death. It was merely a coincidence that the heart attack which caused her death occurred in a dentist's office.

Finally dental work became so necessary that the woman was compelled to have it done in spite of her terror. She insisted, however, that her physician accompany her to the dentist's office. But it was to no avail. As she sat in the dentist's chair, just like her mother had thirty years before, she was suddenly seized with a heart attack and died.

Thirty years of thought had indeed killed her—thirty years of a killing fear thought. Consider how thirty years of faith thoughts, thirty years of enthusiastic thoughts, might have changed the life of this woman.

But let me tell a human story of another sort, one with a much happier outcome. It concerns a man who suffered from fear until he was around fifty years of age. Then he got fed up with his state of mind, did something about it and got over it; in fact, he got so completely over it that he was never bothered by fear again. How was this remarkable deliverance accomplished? By enthusiasm. He hit upon the wonderful fact that enthusiasm powered in depth can cancel fear and worry. And just how does enthusiasm accomplish this astonishing feat? That question I intend to answer in this chapter.

The fears and anxieties of this man seemed to have begun in childhood and took many forms. Whenever he had a pain, which occurred frequently, he was sure it was cancer or some other fatal malady. When any of his children were out late at night he feared a phone call would bring news of an accident. Shyness activated by fear made him timorous with other people. Accordingly he did not show up well in personal relationships.

But despite his fear problems, and this is often a curious phenomenon in such cases, he was efficient in business. He had worked up to a position of top leadership. His associates who respected him highly would have been astonished had they known the full extent of his inner struggle and misery. They would not have believed or understood his deep inner conflict. But the fact that his trouble did not show on the surface indicated a basic strength, which suggested that if ever he made up his mind to do something about his fear he could get release and relief.

That is precisely what he did. It came about in this way: I chanced to be speaking one noonday to some two thousand men in the ballroom of the Conrad Hilton Hotel in Chicago. During the talk I dealt with the terrible effect of fear and worry on the human mind and described how through the efforts of our American Foundation of Religion and Psychiatry, people had been healed of anxiety. Following the luncheon, a man whom I had met earlier at a reception given by the officers of this outstanding business association, made some sort of pleasant reference to my speech, but instead of passing on he hesitated—"I don't suppose you might have a moment to speak with me?" He rather shyly added, "Something you said in your talk is pretty important to me."

Something about the man, some intensity, almost desperation, communicated itself and we went to my room for a talk. No sooner had the door closed than he began talking. It was highly nervous talk as though he was driven by some inner compulsion. Presently he stopped. "I'm embarrassed. I've never gone on like this before or told anyone of the hell I've lived in all my life. But your speech about fear has started me off, I guess."

"Go on and talk it out," I said. "Say everything. You must completely open your mind if you expect to exorcise the mass of fear imbedded in your consciousness. If you close up now and it freezes in, you may never again have opportunity to empty it out. So let's deal with this problem now, right down to bedrock. Keep talking."

He talked for an hour recounting one fear experience after another, many of them going back to his boyhood. It amounted to a complete mental housekeeping. Finally almost spent, he sighed with relief. "I sure do feel better. Thanks for letting me ramble on like this. I know it will do me a lot of good." I reminded him that while such mind-emptying does make one feel better, to leave the matter there would mean that the basic cause of his fear psychosis had been only temporarily eased up. The mind would in time fill up again with anxiety and worry.

I suggested that he come to New York for some intensive counseling at our American Foundation of Religion and Psychiatry. I explained that while an initial process in the cure of fear might well be such mind-emptying and relief as he had experienced, the next step was to gain insight into the basic cause of fear. Finally, constructive steps would be taken to teach him how to recast his thinking to eliminate such attitudes as were causing these irrational anxiety reactions.

He came for counseling with our psychiatric-pastoral team and proved so cooperative that his anxiety began to lose its dominant hold on him. The roots of fear, running back to childhood, were clipped. I do not have space here to deal with the psychiatric counseling process conducted by our professionally trained staff, except to say that it was extremely thorough and scientific, and fortunately proved effective.

The clinic staff reported that while a longer counseling program was recommended, the prognosis was such that he seemed ready for another step, the spiritual healing procedure. So I informed our patient that on Sunday mornings at Marble Collegiate Church it is our custom to have a period we call "creative spiritual silence," and I suggested that he come to church and participate. Actually this is a form of group therapy, though hundreds of people are involved.

THE POWER OF CREATIVE SPIRITUAL SILENCE

On Sunday morning I explained as usual to the congregation the healing power of creative silence, stating that any person who consciously let go his problem, dropping it into the "pool" of spiritual silence created when hundreds focus in prayer and spirit, would be relieved and through their faith be healed.

An amazing thing happened. Some might perhaps call it a miracle, but not I. For over many years I have seen so many astonishing personal changes take place as a result of creative spiritual silence, that to me it is not at all a miracle, but rather the scientific operation of spiritual law at work in personality. I had previously outlined to this man the amazing principle of "Let go and let God," urging him consciously and volitionally to "let go of his fear and let God take it." This seemed "a queer sort of thing he had never heard of before," but I reminded him that undoubtedly there were many vital things in spiritual practice that he had never heard of before. And to the extent that he took hold of fresh techniques hitherto unknown to him he could achieve the new personal qualities he so desired.

In the silent period with spiritual mood and atmosphere deepening, the man experienced, so he declared, "an overwhelming sense of the presence of God." His fear "seemed small in that tremendous Presence." Then, for the first time, the unbelievable thought flashed up that he could throw off fear, not in the future but now, immediately, and for good and all. Accordingly, in the silent period he said, speaking directly to the Lord, "I *now* let my fear go; I now give it to You. Please take it now and take me too. I'm Yours forever. Thank you, Lord, for healing me *now*," and he understood the now.

A powerful new motivation following his sense of release so excited him that he came literally charging into my private office. "He heard me! He really heard me! The fear was lifted from me. I gave it to Him. It's all gone. I've never been happier in my life."

He stopped, flushed with embarrassment. "Don't be embarrassed," I said. "It's wonderful, isn't it? That is how God sometimes works. Usually, release from a long-held fear comes more gradually, but sometimes it does eventuate dramatically as in your case, and both experiences of renewal are equally valid." At any rate, this man was delivered from the old fear he had suffered so long. He became full of enthusiasm about his business, his church, his Rotary Club, his community. He developed an intense interest in all aspects of life. Such is the quality and vitality of his spiritual and intellectual enthusiasm that every residue of his old fear seems to have been eliminated. It has not returned with passing of time. This case proved what can happen when one deeply *wants* something to happen and when enthusiasm is given a chance to *make* it happen.

FEAR IS REMOVABLE

A primary fact to know about fear is that it is removable. Do you, for example, have the tendency to become angry? Anger is removable. You can get over it. Do you tend to become depressed? Depression is removable. Anything disruptive to human happiness and well-being, anything that fastens itself adversely onto the human spirit, is removable. Not without difficulty, but still removable. And fear, one of the worst of all enemies of human personality, is removable. Fix that fact firmly in mind. Hold it tenaciously. No matter how many worries and anxieties harass you, remember always that they are removable. Enthusiasm with its immense mental and spiritual power can cancel out all fear.

Do not give in to the notion that you must live with fear all your life. You need not. It is removable. Do not assume that because your father or your mother or your grandparents had fears and anxieties that you must have them also. You need only have what you are willing to have. If you are willing to live with fear, you probably will. And once a person knows fear is removable and decides, with God's help, to remove it, then comes the process of removal. This involves the steps outlined above and also another factor which perhaps is not popular with this generation of Americans, namely, self-discipline. Don't overlook this fact, that you can do positively anything with yourself that you deeply desire *if* you have what it takes to discipline yourself accordingly. And deep within you the power of self-discipline exists, waiting only to be used.

In former days this powerful capacity, widely known as willpower, was highly regarded in the United States. Depreciation of will power threatens now to produce a generation of Americans in which incidence of neurotic states will likely reach a new high. Apparently Americans were formerly more normal psychologically. One primary reason may be that they were taught to practice self-discipline. They believed that any enemy of personality is removable, and so with God's help they simply proceeded in disciplinary fashion to remove it. This is not to say that they had no worries. Of course they did.

Therefore, a good method of canceling out worry is the deliberate assiduous use of enthusiasm plus self-discipline. As I pointed out earlier, in order to have enthusiasm, simply act enthusiastic. Similarly, substitute enthusiasm for worry, eliminating the destructive emotion in favor of a constructive one. A direct frontal attack on a personality weakness such as worry may be effective, especially if faith is emphasized. But in most cases an oblique attack in the form of a substitute procedure or a psychological bypassing, is likely to get surer results.

Let us illustrate this anti-worry method with the history of a man who consulted me regarding an anxiety problem. His anxiety, judging from his dramatized description of himself, while seemingly extreme to him, appeared to me as something less than deep. For one thing he had developed a kind of rabbit's foot approach designed to assure opposite outcomes. He was like the avid baseball fan who always bet against his favorite team, believing that in so doing he would cause them to win. I got the impression that this man's anxiety had within it a considerable dash of self-manufactured hysteria. But even so his suffering was real and he was entitled to relief.

He was extraordinarily negative in comment and seemed to expect the worst to happen. Yet even this negativism seemed to have a false ring, for there was evidence that he did not really expect things to turn out badly. Here again was that curious quirk of thinking, that if one talks negatively, the opposite is more likely to occur. So in this man's mind was a strange, conflicting mixture of anxiety tinged ideas, which he feared yet didn't believe in. But he did believe in them enough to be dominated by them. The result not only caused unhappiness, but also an enormous leakage of mental energy that might have been employed for constructive purposes.

I decided to prescribe the oblique method for attacking worry. Rather than encouraging him to stand up to his anxiety, hitting it straight on as he bravely talked about doing, I said, "No, no, let's not do that. Let us outsmart your worry by coming at it from its blind side. If your fear is really strong the straight-arm approach may send you reeling back in defeat, and that could discourage you. So rather let us be like the prize-fighter who dances away from his opponent, keeping out of range, but hitting unexpectedly when the other's guard is down."

I outlined a daily regimen, assuring him that if used as directed he could change from a consummate worrier into a practicing enthusiast. "And then," I promised him, "you will become happier than you ever thought of being. Your job will become child's play. You will do it so easily."

FIVE-POINT PROGRAM FOR ATTACKING WORRY

Specifically the method outlined was thus: *First* he was to carefully practice listening to himself. He was to note and study with meticulous attention every comment he made, so that he might become fully conscious of the amazing number of doleful and negative remarks he was constantly uttering.

"Never talk without listening, appraising, dissecting your remarks," I suggested. "You are not going to enjoy this for it will be a ruthless self-revelation and not a pleasant one, but it will be a primary step. Listen with your ears and your whole mind to the depressing stuff you are articulating all day."

Second, he was to start being absolutely honest so that when he heard himself making a negative statement he was to ask himself: "Now look, do I honestly believe what I am saying or am I actually mouthing negativisms that I do not really believe at all? If I want the Mets to win, why don't I start believing they are going to win and say so? And skip the infantile practice of betting against them on the stupid assumption that it can help them to win by an absurd reverse procedure."

Third, he was to adopt the practice of saying exactly the opposite of what he usually said, and he was to note how much better the new utterances sounded. He might regard himself as a hypocrite in so doing, but hypocrisy would be nothing new. Actually had he not been saying what he did not mean for a long time?

As he continued in this new procedure, it would grow ever more exciting to hear words and ideas full of life and hope and expectancy coming from his mouth instead of the old defeatist remarks. He would soon discover that something really exciting was happening to him, namely an upsurge of dynamic enthusiasm. As he worked on this advice he would realize the value of the honest, analytical listening, new-style talking element in his process of personal change.

Fourth, he was to keep track of everything that happened as he worked in his new procedure, carefully noting and computing even the smallest results. If he had been, for example, in the habit of saying glumly: "Things aren't going to go well today," now (since he was no longer mouthing negativisms) he was to note that things were much better, as they usually are. He was to admit honestly that he had in fact expected them to go well, but now he was no longer lying to himself concerning his expectations. He wasn't afraid any longer to expect the best.

Fifth, he was to practice putting the best connotation on every person and every action each day. This is one of the most exciting of all personal development practices. I first came upon it through the late Harry Bullis, a leading figure in the flour-milling industry in Minneapolis. Harry was a genuinely enthusiastic man, so much so, that being impressed I asked for an explanation of his happy nature. "I decided long ago," he said, "to put the best possible connotation on the words and actions of every person and every situation. Naturally I was not blind to the realities, but I always tried to emphasize the best connotation, for I believe that such practice actually helps stimulate a good outcome. This best connotation resulted in enthusiasm for people, for business, for church and other interests, and greatly added to the joy of life, and it certainly helped oust worry from my mind. In fact, I have not worried since I began practicing this enthusiasm-producing technique."

I ALMOST WALK OUT OF A CHURCH

I have myself often had occasion to put this principle of Harry Bullis's into operation. Only recently I attended a Church of England Sunday morning service in Europe. The clergyman conducting the service was a regular man who gave a solid rugged message, and I liked him immensely. It is a custom upon occasion for a layman to read the lesson. The congregation was composed mostly of English people, and I had been observing the many vigorous young men present. Then to my astonishment a young man who resembled a beatnik rose to read the lesson. Not only did his hair hang in long ringlets, but a thick beard circled his face.

I could hardly take it, to listen to this character read publicly out of the greatest Book in the world! For once in my life, I actually thought of walking out of church and could easily have done so, being in the last row of seats near the door. But Harry Bullis's principle came to my mind, and I decided that the Scripture read by anyone, even by one who seemed an offbeat character, might just possibly do me good. And I had to admit that overcoming an antipathy would be spiritually therapeutic. It was then I noticed that this fellow had a pleasing masculine voice and grudgingly I had to admit that he read the immortal words impressively, with feeling and reverence. Seeking further to put the best connotation on the matter I decided that maybe that rector had a better strategy going than I did; that if we could get young rebels involved in the Church, perhaps they might be made into real men after all. Anyway, this exercise of the best connotation principle left me in a better state of mind, and helped to escalate my feelings of enthusiasm for people in general.

Let us return to the man for whom I outlined a five-point procedure for attacking his worry problem. He did succeed because he was sold on the plan and conscientiously put the suggested principles into operation. However, this did not come easily, representing as it did an almost complete reversal of old mental habits. He related later that his struggle to achieve a normal worry-free state of mind was "really painful. But the more I tried, the more clearly I saw the possibility, at long last, of getting worry off my neck. And each time I achieved one small victory over myself, I got such a kick out of it that I went eagerly after another victory—until finally, I did begin to change."

Some months later, I happened to go to his city to make a speech and he met me at the airport. It was a dark overcast day, but the clouds seemed to dissipate in the presence of this revitalized man. He insisted on taking me out to his house to meet his wife, whom he evidently adored. She seemed to adore him, too, for they greeted each other with an enthusiastic embrace. By this time, he had inspired me with such enthusiasm that instead of shaking hands, I kissed her, too.

Before we left for my hotel—where I had not yet had the opportunity to check in—his wife asked gently, "Might the three of us have a prayer to thank God for the wonderful change in my husband? He is a new man and life is so different." So we joined hands in prayer, giving thanks to God for this man whose fears and anxieties had been canceled. It was a most moving experience. Later, as we drove downtown, he said, "The thing that really gets me is the miracle of change."

DON'T BE AFRAID OF OTHER PEOPLE

If you keep enthusiasm up, especially enthusiasm for human beings, another weakness that will cease to bother you is the fear of people, and this is a big worry to many, though maybe few will admit it.

When I was a young reporter on the old Detroit *Journal* my editor, Grove Patterson, took a kindly interest in me, a young man fresh out of college and working on a metropolitan newspaper.

He was a man of keen, perceptive insights. One day he called me to his office. He could always make one feel at ease, even though he was top man on the paper and his visitor in this case was the lowliest.

"Norman," he said, "I sort of get the feeling that you have a lot of fear and anxiety in your system. You must get rid of it. Just what in the world is there to be afraid of anyway? Why should you or I or anybody go skulking through life like a scared rabbit? The good Lord told us that He will be with us and help us. So why not just take that at face value, hold up your head, look the world in the face and hit it real hard? And for heaven's sake, don't be afraid of anything or anybody!"

I remember the scene in the old Detroit *Journal* office on Jefferson Avenue as though it were yesterday.

"But," I said, "that's a pretty big order. How can anyone possibly go through life afraid of nothing or of nobody?"

He sat, feet on his desk, and leveled a long, inky finger at me. There always seemed to be ink on Grove's finger, and when he pointed that finger and looked at you with those piercing eyes, you listened.

"Listen," he said, "I'll tell you how. 'Be strong and of a good courage; be not afraid . . . for the Lord thy God is with you whithersoever [you go].' Just hang onto that promise," he added, "and don't forget that it's made by Someone who never lets anybody down."

That was sound advice and I needed it, for since early boyhood I had been afraid of people. In fact, I was absolutely awestruck by some.

My father was a minister, and in his denomination ministers frequently changed churches. In fact, every fall, along in September, the church voted whether or not to invite the minister to remain for another year. It was customary for a pastor to be appointed by a bishop for only a one-year term. This one-year system put the minister's security at the whim of the congregation whose support might easily turn to hostility, especially if it was engineered by someone who wanted to manipulate things. And occasionally, in fact more than occasionally, that was the case.

As a result of this climate of insecurity, I was awestruck by some of the leading members of the church, watching them apprehensively for any sign of approval or disapproval of my father's leadership. I remember sitting in the pew on Sunday mornings studying certain faces to see whether they liked his sermon. My father, an urbane sort of man, did not worry about these local big shots, but I did. And for years this anxious concern about the attitude of other people had a strong effect on me. But, I got over it in due course. As a boy, however, I was afraid of Mr. So-and-so or Mrs. So-and-so. Therefore I built up quite a fear of people.

My father had a habit, too, that certainly did not help me in overcoming my fear of people. When we moved to a new community, he would, in introducing me to prominent church members, say, "He's a big banker," or "He's a big lawyer," or "He's a big grocer in this town." That gave me the pathetic idea that I must tremble in the presence of these "big" characters. So my hypersensitive fear of people was always being accentuated.

In school, also, I was awed by overbright, cocky, loud-mouthed students who seemingly could talk glibly on any subject. As for myself, I was shy and reticent and rather inarticulate for the most part. I knew the subject matter but expressed it poorly. If any other student laughed or smiled as I spoke, I froze immediately. So I gave way in my own thoughts before these smug fellow-students who cockily acted as if they had all the answers. I believed they were all far ahead of me in ability, and so I was afraid of them. From the vantage points of later years I wonder where these students are now. Actually I have even forgotten their names. For the most part none of them have ever been heard of since. Apparently they shot their little bolts in school.

But this fear was indeed difficult for me to overcome; that awestruck fear of the prominent or well-known or those with money or position. I felt inferior and inadequate in the presence of anyone who threw his weight around. So when Grove Patterson confronted me with the undeniable fact that I must rid myself of inordinate fear of people, he was hitting on a very sore nerve. Our conversation in the newspaper office really made me resolve to reorganize myself so that no longer would I tremble before any human being.

Even while I have been writing this book, however, I had a personal experience which shows that I need to practice more faithfully the fear-of-nobody principle. My wife Ruth and I drove one day from our farm in Pawling, New York, up to Syracuse, New York, where I was to speak to the Mutual Agents Association Convention. It is a trip of about two hundred and fifty miles up the Taconic Parkway and the New York Thruway.

On the Thruway we stopped at a gasoline station and were waited on by a very authoritative young man. Even in his comments about the weather he somewhat flattened me by asserting that I was entirely wrong in my weather prognostication. I didn't think it was worth arguing about and I didn't continue the discussion. While he was filling the gasoline tank, he put up our car hood to check the oil, water and battery. "Oh brother," he exclaimed, "something has to be done about that fanbelt and two other belts in there."

Now one thing I know absolutely nothing about is what is under a car hood. "What is the matter with them?" I asked, alarmed.

"Why," he said, "look at that frayed place on that belt. I have seen cars come in here off the Thruway with these belts wrapped around them so tight that it took us a couple of hours to get them off. Those belts of yours have got to come off immediately."

I looked at the belts. For the life of me I couldn't see anything wrong with them, but he was so authoritative that I began to feel awestruck and tongue-tied. Assuming that he seemed to know what he was talking about, I gave in. He pulled the car over to the side and started taking all belts out. I noticed another car alongside and the belts were being removed from that one also. I was hesitant and doubtful; abjectly I asked the man inside the station, "Does this young man know what he is doing?"

"Oh, yes," he said, "he knows exactly what he is doing."

"Well," I said, "the belts look all right to me."

"If he says the belts aren't right, then the belts aren't right," he replied. At which I completely folded.

Then my wife came over and inquired what was going on, and I told her. She asked, womanlike, "What's wrong with the belts?" Now, my wife is a very clear-minded thinker and she does not let people overawe her.

I said feebly, "This young man knows all about belts and these belts, he says, have to come off. He says cars come in here off the Thruway with belts wrapped all around the engine. We have to have new belts put on."

She saw that he had two of the belts off already. She examined them, and she said, "There is nothing wrong with these belts. This is a racket. Please put the belts right back on."

Well, I was embarrassed by this plain talk and walked away to buy a newspaper. By this time my wife had three of the four gas-station men around her and she proceeded to inform them in a very polite but firm tone that it was a racket. Well, the old belts in our car have been running just beautifully ever since; in fact, ten thousand miles since. This assertive, cocky and, shall we say, "shady" young man actually did almost succeed in selling me the unneeded belts because of the belligerent, superior manner in which he exercised his authority. Awed by him and his know-it-all attitude, my old fear of people reappeared. But my wife was not impressed in the slightest by his manner; only by facts. That is why when one keeps his thinking rational and is impressed only by facts, his fear of people vanishes.

So never be afraid of anyone; of your husband, or your wife, or (heaven help you) your children; or the boss, or the loud so-called big shot. And, of course, the best procedure for doing this is to love people and always see the best in them. Enthusiasm for them will grow in you and as it does, it will cancel out your shyness, your fear of others and your worry about what they think of you. And then, as you forget about yourself, your heartening relationship with people will add to your enthusiasm for life itself.

Careful study of worry-free sickness will reveal in many cases an abnormal preoccupation with self. Worry presupposes an acutely sensitive self-reference in which apprehension exists concerning one's self and those close to him. The more ingrown one is, the sharper the worry is likely to be. Therefore any cancellation of the worry habit must of necessity involve getting outside of one's self.

It is this fact that makes enthusiasm so terribly important, for it is one of the most effective mechanisms for developing an outgoing personality. The ingrown individual has little concern for the world around him. Nervously he scans the daily paper and is invariably sure that everything is going wrong. But his interest in matters of social significance is only passing, tenuous and vague. His principal concern is how things may affect him personally. So he gives only fragmentary attention to outside conditions and continues to stew and fret in a self-conditioned worry mess which agitates his mind. And given enough of such worry the result can be actual strangulation of personality.

WORRY, AND YOU CHOKE AND STRANGLE

The word worry derives from an old Anglo-Saxon verb *wyrgan* meaning to choke or strangle. If someone were to grasp you around the neck with two hands, pressing as hard as possible, and thereby cutting off your air supply, he would be doing to you dramatically what you gradually do to yourself as a confirmed worrier. Through worry you are actually strangling your creative powers. In an early Anglo-Saxon illustration, worry is graphically depicted as a huge angry wolf with teeth in a man's neck.

Relief from worry is what this book is endeavoring to provide. Even more than relief, it offers a positive cure in the form of vital enthusiasm which can actually cancel worry.

The power of enthusiasm to perform so is illustrated in the case of a widow whose worry habits tended to remain minor during her husband's lifetime. After he died, however, anxiety took over. Soon she was in the grip of a severe fear reaction. Her husband had left her moderately provided for, enough to care for her comfortably if she was prudent. She was frightened of making decisions since hitherto they had been almost altogether made by her husband. She had been dependent on him for everything involving judgment. She told me she was sick with worry. I believed her, for worry can indeed make one sick.

I counseled with her in an attempt to shift her mind from the dependence she had always had on a strong husband to dependence upon a strong God. But while she was a believer of sorts, she did not seem able to muster a faith realistic enough to overcome her fears. Therefore she sank deeper into a pervasive worry state.

One noonday, passing through the lobby of the Commodore Hotel in New York City, en route to the weekly meeting of the Rotary Club, I noticed her sitting near the entrance of the Rotary dining room. She was staring moodily ahead. In answer to my inquiry she said she came every Rotary day because, "Bill never missed a meeting and I just sit here in the lobby outside the Rotary meeting room and think about him. But, oh, Dr. Peale, whatever will I do? I am so worried. Nothing matters any more. Life is all over." And again the dull complaint, "I'm sick with anxiety."

"Look, Mary," I said, "we're going to do something about you, so just sit here until this meeting is over. Then you and I are going to have a talk. I am not going to stand by and let a strong, intelligent woman like you continue being panicky with worry. Also, I am going to tell you exactly what Bill would say to you. I know you pretty well and I knew Bill even better. So just wait for me."

All through the Rotary meeting I turned the problem over in my mind. This woman had energy and not a little capacity for enthusiasm. I decided to try a treatment of enthusiasm to heal her fear, feeling that it might stimulate her capacity to have faith, which had become stultified since her husband's death.

At Rotary I happened to notice a man, head of one of the great sociological service agencies dealing with the poor and infirm. I asked him, "Jerry, do you need more staff in your work?"

"We surely do; we are very shorthanded. But we've already used up our budget and I cannot take anyone else on."

"Well, could you use a capable, intelligent, though untrained woman of about fifty, who will work for free?"

"Yeah, I know the kind: a couple of hours per week between bridge games to give herself a sanctimonious feeling. No thanks."

But I assured him that this woman would give a full half-day, five days a week from nine to one o'clock. Rather grudgingly he said, "Well, O.K., send her along. But if she won't work regular hours I won't keep her. I want people who are on the job, not the bleeding hearts who get their kicks out of thinking they are doing good."

Returning to the lobby where Mary waited, I said, "Now, please come to my office at Marble Collegiate Church. I will see you there in an hour. But I want you to walk to the Church. No taxi or bus. And see if you can figure a pace of about four miles an hour, which means you will have to walk vigorously. This is the rate Dr. Paul White advocates for those who walk to avoid heart attacks."

"But I'm not used to walking," she exclaimed in surprise. "And whatever difference does it make how I get to your office?" I assured her that there was a very good reason in my request and extracted a promise that she would walk.

An hour later she arrived and for the first time there was good color in her cheeks. "Why, I actually feel good, better than in months," she said. "This crisply cool day and the blue sky overhead and the colorful shop windows are really wonderful."

"You didn't stop to look in those shop windows, did you? I wanted you to keep that vigorous four-miles-an-hour pace," I said. She resolutely claimed she had done so.

WALK YOUR WORRIES AWAY AND BUILD ENTHUSIASM

"Why did you insist on my walking?" she asked. I told her of an old friend of mine, the late Dr. Henry C. Link, a practicing psychologist. When a worry-ridden patient came to him, before beginning the interview Dr. Link often asked that person to walk vigorously around the block three times. Three times around the block was about half a mile. Dr. Link explained that the brain has an upper and lower section and that we worry with the upper brain while the lower controls motor reaction. "So," he said with a grin, "if I can get the patient to practice walking, he uses the lower brain which works the legs and thus relieves the upper from the strain of worry thoughts." He felt that it was easier in this way to "float the worries off."

My friend Ernest Zingg of Berne, Switzerland, with whom I have often walked in the high Swiss Alps, gave me a paper entitled *Walking—as a Cure* by Dr. Felix Oesch, medical commissioner of the city of

Berne. It says in part: "Walking not only activates circulation of the blood, it also speeds up and intensifies respiration and enables greater absorption of oxygen . . . The body of the walker is absolutely free, the feet only are put periodically on the earth and rolled off. In no other position . . . will blood circulation be nearly as free . . . Walking, in addition, brings a whole orchestra of large and small muscles into action and to an accord . . . Their 'eurythmic' . . . sends the blood towards the heart as the valves of the heart only allow this direction . . . Walking has a healing influence and balances large and small psychical troubles and conflicts . . . With the distance from home one also gains distance more easily from the miseries of the world. Perspectives, the 'blue horizons' enable personal grievances to be put in a better proportion to the sorrow rucksack of the world . . . a walk taken in harmony with nature very often replaces the psychiatrist."

"So, Mary," I said, "one recommendation for you is more physical activity and I suggest walking. But when you walk do not stroll; really walk. And make it a daily practice, rain or shine."

I suggested a further technique which many have found extremely helpful, one that I often use personally. It is to punctuate vigorous walking with the saying of certain Bible texts. Breathing deeply, say, for example, "Bless the Lord O my soul; and all that is within me, bless His holy name."

Or, "I will lift up mine eyes unto the hills, from whence cometh my help." The effect of articulating these passages in rhythm with walking is to activate blood circulation, toning up of the system and the mind. This practice, I assured her, would activate enthusiasm, shake down her worries and increase her capacity to exercise faith.

And I stressed that it would be through rejuvenated faith that the real cure of her worry would occur. "The whole effort is to open, enlarge and build up your shattered faith capacity. Then you will enter upon a normal, creative and even happy life."

I then told her of the "job" I had secured for her at the agency, and further informed her that I had promised she would go to work on the agreed schedule next day. This was rather a shock. She was a slow starter mornings, and to report to an office by nine o'clock would be a startling new departure. I gave her no comfort in this objection, merely remarking that a "startling new departure" was an integral part of the cure of a worry problem. Whether it was the stimulation of the vigorous walk or the prospect that a new life might open, or both, she did agree to undertake the agency work on the specified condition. She reported the next day on the stroke of nine.

The man in charge phoned me a couple of weeks later to say, "This lady is a rare find. She is mastering our system of work and entering into it enthusiastically. She has a warm, human sympathy for the unfortunate people we deal with. Her eagerness to help them as persons is of a kind we rarely see in professional social work."

I think I need not belabor this case further except to say that a strong and vital enthusiasm took over in this woman's mind. As this occurred prayer became meaningful and presently she said, "I'm on the way to getting that dependence upon God you spoke of."

FORMULA FOR HANDLING A WORRY PROBLEM

To sum up the suggested therapy for a worry problem:

1. Practice vigorous walking.
2. Engage in disciplined regular human service.
3. Develop an awakened concern, even love, for the unfortunate.
4. Find new meaning in prayer and the actual reality of God's presence.

These factors produced a curative enthusiasm that canceled out the festering worry which threatened this woman's future, and it has been effective in other cases as well.

ENTHUSIASM MAKES HARD DAYS GOOD DAYS

I was a guest in the home of my friend, Dr. Georg Heberlein, head of the great Heberlein textile company of Watwill, Switzerland. At dinner Georg asked the title of my new book. When I told him it was *Enthusiasm Makes the Difference*, he expressed approval of the theme as being extremely important to anyone who really wants to do something with himself. As a successful industrialist he knows that enthusiasm plays a vital role in success and failure. His son-in-law Mark Cappis, a dynamic young man whose enthusiastic participation in business and civic affairs marks him as a coming leader, at once affirmed that worry can have no control over an enthusiasm-conditioned person.

Mark told how he and his young wife Bridgett came to New York to make their way in a foreign country, to learn English, make friends and thus prepare themselves for their important international business. Day after day, during a down period in the economy, Mark tramped the streets of New York looking for a job which he insisted on getting on his own, without pull or influence. There are, thank God, still young men like him in the world. The couple lived in a tiny two-room apartment and used a packing box, covered with travel posters, as their dining table.

"Didn't you get discouraged during those hard says?" I asked.

"They were not hard days," Mark and Bridgett exclaimed together. "We had fun. It was exciting to be together with the future entrancingly before us. How could we worry?" Mark added. "You see, we were excited about life and about the United States. We loved the people there. We were overflowing with enthusiasm about everything, and so naturally worry just didn't have a chance with us."

And that is just about the truth of the matter. Keep enthusiastic and worry will never have a chance to get its grip on you.

I was driving one night with John Robison, from Columbus to Findlay, Ohio, where I was scheduled to make a speech. I noticed soft, yet efficient lights on poles near many of the farmhouses we passed. John, who is connected with the Columbus and Southern Ohio Electric Company, explained these were mercury-vapor lamps. They light up automatically at twilight, being triggered by the dark, and go off automatically at sunrise. The protecting light relieves the farmer from worry about possible night intruders.

It seemed a kind of parable. It is a fact that anyone who keeps the light of enthusiasm burning in his mind at all times dissipates that darkness of the mind in which worry grows. Remember, worry and enthusiasm simply cannot occupy the same mind at the same time. They are utterly incompatible.

It was summed up by the Honorable Dan Liu, Chief of Police of Honolulu, recently voted the most popular man in the Hawaiian Islands. The Chief said simply, "Due to Christ I never buckled under any anxiety and have always been sustained in the dangers of my profession." Spiritual enthusiasm does indeed cancel worry.

I have always liked that familiar and reassuring statement by Victor Hugo, "When you have accomplished all that you can, lie down and go to sleep. God is awake."

And a physician has a good idea. He tells his patients to say their prayers and then to say further, "Good night worries. See you in the morning."

And I may add, as you develop some real enthusiasm, worries won't be there to trouble you in the morning. Or if they are, you will be able to handle them. And never forget those tremendous words of Isaiah (35:4): "Say to them that are of a fearful heart, be strong, fear not."

5

TRY ENTHUSIASM ON YOUR JOB

One of the most exciting races in American sports history took place in the Dwyer Stakes at Aqueduct in July 1920 between two famous horses, Man o' War and John P. Grier. Man o' War was the outstanding racehorse in America, undisputed champion of his time, and one of the most notable of all time. There have been few horses to equal him. What a magnificent animal he was!

I saw him run only once but the race lives in my memory. The jockey and the horse seemed as one. Watching that magnificent animal in action was one of the greatest sports experiences of my life; an exalted, unique and unforgettable moment—comparable to the occasion when I saw Jackie Robinson at Ebbets Field steal three bases, including home plate, in one game. Man o' War had been the champion for a long time. Then another horse began seriously to challenge him. But that horse, as it later proved, did not have the heart of a real champion.

I am indebted for an account of this memorable race to my friend, W. Clement Stone, who with Napoleon Hill co-authored the inspiring book

*Success Through a Positive Mental Attitude** in which this story appears. The challenger, John P. Grier, looked real good and many people actually thought he might be the one to beat Man o' War who, the sports writers suggested, was slipping while John P. Grier was in his ascendancy. The coming runoff was the talk of the hour. Could the upstart put the old champion in the discard?

Finally the great day came and the two horses were poised and ready. At the starting bell they got away cleanly. They were even at the first quarter post; neck and neck at the second. Then the immense crowd leaped to its feet electrified. John P. Grier was edging ahead. Man o' War was facing the challenge of his career.

The experienced little jockey riding Man o' War did some quick thinking. He knew his horse to the depths of the great animal's being, knew the immense reserves of strength and spirit which it possessed. He had never touched Man o' War with a whip. The magnificent horse had always delivered sufficient power without its use. But evidently this time Man o' War was not coming through with enough power to win. As the jockey watched John P. Grier's nose edge slowly ahead, he knew the moment for summary action had come. Down went the whip against the flanks that had never before felt its prodding.

The whip worked instant results. The response to the stinging lash was immediate. From somewhere deep within Man o' War came an enormous surge of power, a new and tremendous motivation. The charging legs beat like pistons as every ounce of muscle, wind and spirit were drawn upon; and the new spirit carried him like a ball of fire past John P. Grier. To the roar of the crowd Man o' War crossed the finish line several lengths ahead. He was still champion. Men pounded each other's backs, shouted themselves hoarse; tears were in the eyes of many. It was the race of a lifetime.

This fascinating story from the history of American track has a significant point to be considered with profit. The question is what happened to John P. Grier? The race in which momentarily he passed the old champion was, it seems, his chief moment of glory, his one great opportunity. Apparently his defeat with victory so close had a devastating effect on the animal. I am no authority on the psychology of a horse but it would appear that deep down inside himself John P. Grier was too soft.

* © 1960, Prentice-Hall, Inc., Englewood Cliffs, N.J.

He was no real competitor, for at a moment of crisis the spirit went out of him.

Had a horse the power to think, he might have reasoned: "O.K., I almost beat that old Man o' War. A little more practice and next time I will take him over for sure." He evidently did not have within him the true makings of a champion. But Man o' War was of a different breed. He possessed those qualities that keep horses and men, also, on top of life's competition. He almost lost that race but at the crucial moment he drew on the extra power which he possessed. Man o' War had a deep enthusiasm for victory. His job was to run and to win. And he won gloriously when in a crisis his basic enthusiasm for competition was reactivated.

There is, I believe, a profound relationship between sports competitions and the problems of life itself. You and I too have that extra built-in power. The Creator put it into men as well as horses; into men infinitely more than in horses, I am sure. Deeply built into human beings is the desire to excel. It is in the essence of nature for men to compete, if not with others, at least with themselves. And perhaps competing with oneself, ever trying to improve over present performance, is the highest form of competition. But unhappily many men live and die without ever drawing upon that extra power from which comes greater excellence and higher achievement. As a result some fall behind when actually they need not. The cure for such failure is to probe deeper into the spirit and to find new enthusiasm for the job one has to perform.

THE BOY WHO USED ENTHUSIASM AS A STEPPING STONE

It has been demonstrated that enthusiasm makes a considerable difference in any person's work performance. Expose your daily occupation to apathy, as many individuals tend to do, and your job can scarcely be anything but difficult and tiresome. It is hardly possible that a job will go well for the person who considers it just another dull chore that has to be done, that provides neither satisfaction nor interest. Let's face it, you may say, my job is dull. But could it be that you have a dull attitude toward it? Try enthusiasm on your work, whatever it may be, and watch it change. And, incidentally, see how you change with it. Enthusiasm changes the quality of a job because it changes people.

Never let the excuse that yours is a tedious job keep you from applying enthusiasm in an effort to enliven it. Many enthusiasts have had tremendous results with jobs that originally appeared devoid of interest. Take, for example, a job that very well might be considered dreary, that of a busboy in a big hotel. This work consists of picking up used dishes in the dining room and carrying them to the kitchen. In the rigid hierarchy of European restaurants, it is about the lowest job in the echelon of white coats at the bottom and white ties and tails at the top. Most busboys consider the job so lowly that they treat it with contempt and perform it in a perfunctory, even surly manner. As a result it becomes a dull, boring job performed by a dull uninterested person. It becomes self-defeating.

But I know one young man who used enthusiasm on that job with astonishing results. He gave it that extra-touch technique and what exciting creative results came about! His name was Hans and I met him one summer when we were staying for a month in a European hotel. I soon noticed this pleasant-faced, good-natured German boy in the dining room. He had an outgoing manner and was so interested and enthusiastic that he stood out among the other service personnel. He was alert to everyone's needs and eager to be helpful, not only to the guests, but to his fellow-workers as well.

He assisted the waiters with their work, doing whatever needed doing—unlike the men who refused to perform the slightest function outside their own specific jobs. One came to realize that this busboy was a distinctly different type. He liked responsibility and it showed in his manner. Enthusiasm was what he had in extraordinary measure and with it he was upgrading his job so it eventually became an opportunity.

"You seem to be enjoying yourself, Hans," I commented.

"Oh, yes, this is a wonderful hotel. I love the excitement of mealtime in a dining room where the service is the best and is done just right. This is dining at its best. And the guests—they are the finest in all Europe. And our chef—he is the greatest artist in the business." So ran his enthusiastic conversation. That he was the lowest on the totem pole in that dining room did not bother him in the least. Talk about enthusiasm on a job! It was evident in his every move.

From our talks, I learned that Hans had a goal, a specific goal—not a fuzzy, hope-to-get-somewhere-someday one. His objective was precise and sharply defined. He wanted to become the director or general manager of a great European hotel. And being the best possible busboy was, his keen mind knew, the start of reaching his objective. He also knew that giving the best possible service in the most pleasant manner played a big part in achieving his goal. But he was not simulating happiness and enthusiasm for an ulterior purpose. He just happened to be cheerful and enthusiastic.

To reach his goal he knew it was necessary to go to London for essential training in the international restaurants there. "But," he added, "London seems a long way off and my pockets are empty."

"Empty pockets never held anyone back," I said. "It's only empty heads and empty hearts that do it. You are on the right track. You know exactly where you want to go. Meanwhile you are giving this job all you've got. Begin now believing that you are going to reach your goal. Hold this picture in your conscious mind until, by a process of mental and spiritual osmosis, the image of your goal sinks into your subconscious. At that point you will have it; for it will have you, all of you. Meanwhile, study and observe carefully the people who do every job the best. Continue to make friends. Practice loving people. Remember that some of the people in this dining room are unhappy, bearing heavy burdens of sorrow and discouragement and trouble. Just keep on loving them personally and they will love you in return. People who love people go far in this world, believe me."

I gave him a copy of the German edition of my book *The Power of Positive Thinking*. "You are already a positive thinker if I ever saw one," I told him, "but I want you to read this book and learn the principle of putting your life in God's hands, of being divinely guided, of thinking right and eliminating negatives." During his off hours I saw him poring over the book and he would occasionally come to our table to discuss certain points.

Well, we left the hotel at the end of our vacation period and gradually I forgot about Hans. Several years passed. One day we were in London having dinner in a well-known restaurant that was crowded to the doors. The headwaiter, immaculate in dark coat and striped trousers, came to our table. He described the various items on the menu in a manner that made everything sound so delicious. His whole attitude was exceptionally friendly and he made us feel very much at home.

Some of his German-English expressions made us take a closer look at him. Then with a smile he said, "I'm still practicing positive thinking, Dr. Peale."

"Hans!" I exclaimed. "It's Hans, our old busboy!"

"The same," he agreed.

"You're the same, yet not the same. You've grown. You've developed. So you made it to London! And you're still on your way."

"*Ja, ja,*" he replied, "I'm still going for that Director's job."

"And you're still helping people in the same kindly way, aren't you?"

"*Ja*, I'll always be doing that, I promise."

Will Hans attain his goal? How can he miss? In the story of Hans, who began as a busboy, there is vivid proof that dullness is not inherent in a job, but rather in the individual who does the job. When a person applies enthusiasm to his job, the job will itself become alive with exciting new possibilities. So if you long for a new job, try instead to apply enthusiasm on your present one. See what amazing things happen to it and to you.

HOW FRED HILL WENT ENTHUSIASTIC

Well, how does one go about applying enthusiasm to his present job? For answers to that question, let us return to the case of Fred Hill mentioned earlier in this book. This man was in line for an opening soon to occur, but the personnel executive felt he could not recommend advancement, despite Fred's recognized abilities, the main reason being that he lacked enthusiasm.

The company official stated, however, he might justifiably recommend Fred Hill for the promotion if within six months we could instill some enthusiasm in him. Could it be accomplished within the allotted time, and how? That was the problem.

I gave considerable thought to the matter since the future of Fred Hill and his family was definitely at stake. The executive gave me permission to discuss the problem freely with Fred, even to the extent of warning him that his future in the company was in jeopardy. A natural opening came when I ran into Fred at a luncheon.

After the amenities, I led into the situation by remarking, "Fred, you must have an exciting job down at your place."

"What makes you think it's exciting?" asked Fred a bit sourly. "It's pretty dull if you ask me."

"Why," I countered, "I should think that you, as one of the executives, would get a big kick out of making decisions and seeing your thinking turn into creative action."

Whereupon Fred proceeded to set me straight on how unimportant, to his mind, an executive actually was. "Don't think that a guy is necessarily a big shot because he is labeled an executive," he grumbled. He followed with a dissertation on the power structure in a big organization and how no one man makes decisions, not even the corporate president. Fred described the latter as a "highly paid errand boy who has to consult this or that committee before authorizing the purchase of a box of pencils." It was quite a bitter analysis of big business where, according to him, "the individual is an infinitesimal frog in a huge puddle packed full of other little frogs.

"I work," he continued, "in a building with nine thousand people who jostle one another in commuter trains, subways and elevators. No matter how important you are, or think you are, when you get pushed around in that daily mob you know you are nobody! So what do you mean 'exciting'?"

It was evident from these remarks that Fred's problem was not only apathy but also resentment, perhaps even the sort of contempt for his job that many humdrum employees experience. So I put it to him straight. I asked him what his reaction would be if he failed to go any further up the ladder in his organization. "I don't believe I would care too much," he said, to my surprise. "From what I observe, the higher you go, the duller it gets; and the more of a stuffed shirt you have to become." Subsequently though, I found that Fred did care, and very much.

Meanwhile, I realized at once that we had to be honest with Fred, and he agreed to an appointment for a talk. When we met, I proceeded to describe the situation in regard to himself in his business. He turned pale. "You mean they are going to hold me back just because I'm not the typical eager beaver? Why, those dirty double-crossers!" His anger came out in the open. Then getting quieter and more reasonable he asked what he could do "to improve his image." Now, having emptied himself of his spleen, his sincerity shone through and it was clear that he *did* care. He really wanted to correct his failure. He grew terribly concerned as the import of his problem sank in.

"What we must do," I suggested, "is to work on building up that required enthusiasm. But first, may I point out that griping does not go with an enthusiastic attitude. So let's get rid of all gripes and resentments you came out with in our luncheon talk." He disclaimed these on the grounds that the day of our previous talk happened to be one of his bad days, but I persisted in asking him to empty himself of all anger and frustrations. He had managed to keep these feelings well out of sight of most people.

Under urging, he finally emptied himself of hatred for people and for the modern way of life in which he was trapped and for which he felt such contempt. This cleansing process was not accomplished easily. A number of interviews were required before he could rid himself of an accumulation of resentments and hatreds. In the organization he was regarded as a calm and quiet man—too quiet, perhaps. No one had any idea of the tempests that seethed behind his quiet exterior. I had the distinct feeling that the churning angers of this man included a deep dissatisfaction with himself. To this he presently admitted. So we were ready for the next step.

VITAL CENTER FOR CREATIVE LIVING

In dealing with personality problems it has frequently been my practice to get the people involved, whenever possible, to come to our own Marble Collegiate Church in New York. We have attempted over the years to make this church a vital center for creative living. An atmosphere of concerned understanding, victorious living, genuine joy, and personality healing is felt, I believe, by nearly all who enter its doors. It is a church composed of several thousand people, most of whom have worked through difficult problems by utilizing spiritual techniques, the kind that change attitudes and so change life itself. We believe, and long experience has validated this belief, that anyone who opens himself to the atmosphere of this church will in time acquire the power of faith, the kind of faith in depth that awakens enthusiasm and makes the difference in one's life.

Fred was a spiritual believer in an apathetic sort of way. But for the most part, he was a non-churchgoer. When I prescribed regular exposure to the dynamic atmosphere of Marble Church, Fred groaned, "You mean I've got to travel fifty miles every Sunday morning to go to church?"

"Yes, you said it. It is not merely your going to church that I am interested in, but rather that you expose yourself to a personality revamping. If we can accomplish this for you, it will be worth the fifty-mile trip and then some."

By now Fred realized that his future depended upon carrying out the mental and spiritual treatment recommended and he agreed to follow all directions. After a month of exposure to a dynamic spiritual atmosphere, he admitted it was taking hold. "Something is getting to me," he said. That it was indeed doing so was evident by his voluntarily expressed determination to stop hating people and to start loving them. The churchgoing had stimulated valid insight. He saw his irritation and hate as a definite impediment to the creative enthusiasm we were working to develop.

To implement further change, I suggested to Fred that he start practicing a constructive principle that I had known to work in similar cases.

He was deliberately to send out kindly thoughts to people on commuter trains, subways and in elevators. He was to see them not as exasperating mobs but as individuals, each of whom was trying to live meaningfully. This practice at first struck him as rather absurd. But he did try it and actually got so he enjoyed it. As the irritations were siphoned off, he began to change, so much so, that he actually arrived at work feeling, as he put it, "Pretty good, in fact *very* good." He began to act really happy.

As a result he started conducting himself with a new vitality which amazed everyone. It was real too, not assumed. In fact, he changed to such an extent that the difference was evident to all who had known him before. Enthusiasm was generating within him.

I must point out that this change did not come easily. As a matter of fact, in a weaker man it would have been much longer in coming. But Fred basically was top-quality, the type for whom there is no weakening once the decision to change is made. He meant business. Of course, change in depth cannot be expected to happen overnight. But neither does the process have to be interminable.

Now, to conclude the case of Fred Hill, as an example of how one develops the capacity of trying enthusiasm creatively on the job, let us recapitulate.

(1) He had to learn enthusiasm or go no further in his work.

(2) He had to see himself objectively as he was—well-equipped but lacking in motivational power.

(3) He had to rid himself of an accumulated mass of well-concealed but ill-controlled complaints, hate and resentment. These had been effectively blocking the enthusiasm he so greatly required.

(4) He needed to be exposed to a scientific and stimulating spiritual treatment.

COME ALIVE WITH ENTHUSIASM

As a result Fred's personality now began fully to come alive. His personality took on the characteristics defined by Dr. Rollo May, educational psychologist, who in an address to the New York Academy of Medicine said: "Your personality means the aspect of yourself which makes you effective in life. It is evident that there are two aspects of effectiveness of individuality. First, how do you affect or stimulate others? This is your stimulation value. Second, how do others affect you? How do you respond to others? That is your response aspect of value. Put these together, your effect upon others and others' effect upon you, and that is virtually your personality."

Well, Fred did exactly that. He put these two aspects of personality together and his rapport with people improved tremendously. Consequently, his personality took on remarkable new vitality and enthusiasm. The job situation, so my executive friend reported not without awe, was immeasurably upgraded. Fred could now have the promotion. But then there was an ironic switch. Fred did not want the promotion. Inspired by new-found enthusiasm, he decided to go into business for himself. The new enterprise was based on his recently achieved confidence. "This proposition is out of this world," he said, with elation, "and I know I'm going to put it over big. I am having the time of my life with it!" Fred did succeed, as anyone will, who really puts enthusiasm into his work.

Among other effective techniques for applying enthusiasm on your job which have been successfully used is one suggested by the late Dale Carnegie, a good friend of mine. Dale wrote one of the great best sellers of all time, *How to Win Friends and Influence People.* He also developed the Dale Carnegie speech courses. Through his books and programs he probably helped more men and women release personal talents and abilities than any man of our time. He came from a background of poverty and adversity. The hardships suffered in youth developed in him a positive obsession to help others move up, always up, to better lives. Thousands owe their success to the inspiration and guidance of this great man.

Like all men of accomplishment Dale Carnegie had a highly organized but sensitive nature and suffered moments of deep discouragement and depression. "But," he said brightly, "I figured out a mental trick for reinstating my usual enthusiasm for life and the job. I would deliberately imagine that I had lost everything: job, property, reputation, family, everything I valued. I would sit in the deepest possible gloom. Then I would start adding up what I had not lost, which included that entire list in reverse; and presto the old enthusiasm for the job was back and at a new high. Try that sometime. It really works," he said. I was impressed and did try it. He was right. It does work.

WHAT WOULD AN IMAGINATIVE PERSON DO WITH YOUR JOB?

Another effective technique may be tried on the job for which you have little enthusiasm, which you may even regard as obnoxious and deadly dull. Try asking yourself what someone else might see in this job. Let your imagination consider what he would do with it. Perhaps he is an individual who is doing exceedingly well in his own work. Try to imagine what such a man would do if suddenly he took over your job. How do you think he would react toward it? What fresh and imaginative action would he take to put new life and achievement into what you consider a dull job? Jot down on paper what you think that person might do if he had your position.

Then apply to your work those skills you think that man would use if he were in your shoes. Because you've had experience in the job, there are within you hidden qualities, both of knowledge and experience, which he lacks. There is always something new and imaginative that you can bring even to a familiar job. This fresh approach will inspire you with unexpected strength and enthusiasm for the task.

The sales manager for a wholesale grocery house once told me a story that illustrates our point—what a man with imagination can do with a job that has been branded as hopeless. This company sold its merchandise in four key cities. In City B, a section of the town had been designated by the salesman as an area where nothing could be sold. He had a fixed idea about it. He had accepted this notion from his predecessor, who wasn't a particularly competent salesman either, and it didn't add incentive to his already pessimistic frame of mind. So he dismissed this section as worthless, convinced that no selling could be done there.

In time, management transferred this pessimist elsewhere. They brought into City B a new man who had no idea there were designated arid spots in his territory. Since he was by nature friendly and energetic he approached customers with the idea of sales and service. Since he had no foreknowledge that "no one could sell in that particular section," he was not paralyzed by negative thinking. He began to call on potential customers in that neglected area and soon he was making impressive sales. He reported enthusiastically to the home office that there was virgin territory here and he was moving in on it. He couldn't understand why previous salesmen had neglected it.

There may be a lesson for all of us here. Is it perhaps possible that there is virgin territory in your job that can be turned similarly into a veritable gold mine? Enthusiasm for possibilities increases those possibilities and so in turn increases enthusiasm itself.

This kind of thinking is essential even to a calling like mine. At Marble Collegiate Church in New York City, where I have been minister for thirty-five years, we are constantly reexamining and requestioning our methods in order to develop more imaginative and creative means of reaching the greatest possible number of people.

An important factor in any job is timing. This is the art of doing the right thing at the right time in the right way. Those who approach a job in a negative way sacrifice the delicate sense of timing. No matter how well a task has been done previously, it can be improved by the application of imagination and enthusiasm and timing.

Unending search and the subsequent satisfaction of discovery put excitement into the structure of a job and compound its interest. No work need be dull or unproductive if you make up your mind to find the potentials in the job and develop them. You may fear there are no possibilities for those who are stuck at the lowest end of the job scale. But before you turn to the government for help, assert your sense of independence for the final attempt at improving your condition. Pray, think, work with enthusiasm, no matter how inconsequential the job. Often enthusiasm is the bridge between poverty and prosperity.

WHAT ENTHUSIASM DID FOR A PORTER

"I wrote you some time ago," a man wrote me recently, "about being laid off from a job I'd held seventeen years and the difficulty I had finding other work as an unskilled laborer. But I continued to have faith and confidence as you said, and finally I took a job as a porter. Months went by and I kept asking God, 'Is this the abundance Dr. Peale was talking about, above all that I could ask or think? God, I have two boys ready for college and a girl going into high school. How am I going to take care of their needs as a porter?' "

His faith sometimes slipped a bit. But he stuck doggedly to his dream and he ended each prayer with, "I believe everything is going to be all right, abundance more than I could ask for or think of." Finally after six months, there was an opening for a handyman. He took it and his pay went up to $78.00 a week. He said in his prayers to God, "It is a little better. At least we are moving."

Then he went to the library and borrowed books on boilers. Think of it, a porter studying about boilers. He asked God for guidance; he worked hard; he believed that hard work and cooperation were necessary. He finally took the test for No. 6 Oil Burner License and passed. Two weeks later, his boss asked him if he would run a school that needed a superintendent. He prayed for God's guidance.

"Well, God and I took the job," he continued in his letter. "Since He had put all the material down here so they could build the school, I knew that we together would not have too much trouble running it, so God and I are making $145.00 a week and I love my job.

"This is not the end because God and I will someday manage a whole group of buildings and manage them well. My son has a bank loan to go to college. My other son has a $4,000 scholarship to college and my daughter won an appointment to high school which carries a scholarship. You are wrong, Dr. Peale, when you say God gives in abundance. You should say God gives in super-abundance."

Here is a man, humble, poor, struggling, with little education. Yet he has learned one of the greatest truths in life, that a man who believes, who thinks confidently, who is full of faith in God, and who will work and study can accomplish amazing results.

The enthusiasm of the writer of that letter is as boundless as his faith. The result is that he reactivated remarkable blessings in the lives of his family and himself. He gives the lie to those dreary prophets of gloom, who usually blame the American way of life for their own personal failure.

It has been my experience that those who are fired with an enthusiastic idea and who allow it to take hold and dominate their thoughts find that new worlds open for them. As long as enthusiasm holds out, so will new opportunities.

HOW A PIECE OF PIE ACTIVATED ENTHUSIASM

I spoke one night in Indiana to a large crowd at dinner. Sitting beside me at the head table was the president of the organization that had staged the affair. He was a most interesting and enthusiastic man. We had a stimulating conversation about various matters and I was impressed by his lively manner and alert attention. This was a man who seemed to be enjoying life immensely. He told me he was in what he considered "the greatest business in the world." This statement interested me and I asked, "Just what is the greatest business in the world?"

"I make pies," he said with a smile, "and what this country needs is good pies, the kind I make."

I drew him out and discovered that formerly he had been a salesman. He did pretty well on his job but the results were scarcely spectacular. Then one day something happened that was to determine a new career for him. He ate a piece of pie. This epoch-making piece of pie was served to him in a plain little restaurant in a small town where he had stopped for lunch. Never had he tasted pie like this! It was a delicious work of art. On his rounds the following week, he stopped in again. The pie was just as delicious. This routine went on for some weeks. Then one day the pie turned out to be just another piece of pie: tasteless and commonplace. So he asked the restaurant owner what had happened. The man explained that the woman who baked the pies was taken ill and could no longer deliver.

To my dinner companion, this news came as a major disaster. No more of those delicious pies! On his way home, still shaken by the news, he remembered that his wife had culinary skills. As a matter of fact, she used to bake superbly, but recently she had fallen back on the bakeshops for desserts.

Whereupon, my enterprising friend persuaded his wife to bake a half-dozen assorted pies. He sampled one and it was great. He took them to a local restaurant and invited the proprietor to sample them. The restaurateur bought all six and ordered more. Pies in bakeshops were then selling for 39¢ but my friend thought his were worth 75¢ and asked for that sum. The restaurateur said the price was high, but not "if it kept customers coming back." The home baked pies were an instant success and the man's wife went into the venture full time. Business grew so rapidly that additional helpers soon were required. Ultimately the couple had a large pie plant that delivered fresh baked goods each morning to all the restaurants.

The man beamed. His voice vibrant with conviction, he assured me that the original homemade quality and the personal touch still distinguished his product. Being a born pie lover myself, to the distress of my waistline, I shared his enthusiasm. That night when I reached my room and made ready for bed, a knock came. There was a bellboy holding two hot pies that my friend had thoughtfully sent; one apple, the other cherry and every bit as delicious as I expected them to be.

Here was a man who really tried enthusiasm in his job and with an amazing result. I gathered from others that his enthusiasm, triggered by the excellent pies, extended to the community at large in which he took considerable leadership. He found that enthusiasm makes the difference, a real difference, whether for pies or whatever your commodity happens to be.

ENTHUSIASM BRINGS GOOD DAYS

Religion is designed to provide strength and enthusiasm for living in a difficult world. Not all so-called religious people are enthusiastic, indeed far from it. Some appear to have the curious notion that gloom and pessimism are the hallmark of Christianity. This is a distortion of the message of Jesus Christ who said, "These things have I spoken unto you, that my joy might remain in you, and that your joy might be full," and who also said, "Rejoice in the Lord always: and again I say, Rejoice." Christianity can put joy and enthusiasm into people's minds for the purpose of helping them to live creatively and victoriously in this trying world.

One man who holds to this faith happens to be one of the most efficient salesmen in American industry. He has marketed some of the most widely used items in the economy today. He is a keen-minded, brilliant activist whose service to church and community is outstanding. From humble beginnings he rose to influential leadership and his benefactions to all kinds of human service are notable. I asked what he thought about the future. He replied that he thought it would be very good. When pressed for his reasons for optimism and enthusiasm, he declared that "good days are ahead for the very good reason that we will make them good days."

He stated his belief that "God Himself gave us power and authority over every day to make it either good or bad. Every morning," he said, "we have the choice whether it shall be a good or bad day. As for me I decide every morning that with God's help I will make it a good day. I can tell you that as a result, my days while not always easy are still good." This man believed that a day called bad by some people could be transformed into a good day by taking charge of it to make it good.

He said he had a "foolproof" formula for making good days—a six-point technique that I've found will indeed help anyone who wants to use enthusiasm on his job.

FORMULA FOR MAKING ANY DAY GOOD

1. *Think a good day.* To make a day good, first see it good in consciousness. Do not allow any mental reservation that it will not be good. Events are largely governed by creative thought, so a positive concept of the day will strongly tend to condition it to be as imaged.

2. *Thank a good day.* Give thanks in advance for the good day ahead. Thank and affirm a good day. This helps make it so.

3. *Plan a good day.* Specifically and definitely know what you propose to do with the day. Plan your work and work your plan.

4. *Put good into the day.* Put bad thoughts, bad attitudes, bad actions into a day and it will take on bad characteristics. Put good thoughts, good attitudes, good actions into a day and they will make the day good.

5. *Pray a good day.* Begin each day with that powerful affirmation from Psalm 118:24: "This is the day which the Lord hath made; we will rejoice and be glad in it." Start the day with prayer and finish it the same way. Then it is bound to be good even if it brings tough experiences.

6. *Fill the day with enthusiasm.* Give the day all you've got and it will give you all it's got, which will be plenty. Enthusiasm will make a big difference in any day and in any job.

The top sales producer who gave me these rules said, with a chuckle: "Here's a quotation I picked up somewhere; a fellow named H. W. Arnold said it. I believe it's on the beam. 'The fellow who is fired with enthusiasm for the boss (that is to say the job) is seldom fired by the boss.' "

This reminded me of an employer who told me he was going to fire a man out of the business. I asked, "Why not fire him into the business? Get him to try enthusiasm on the job." He did, and the employee became presently a very important man in the concern. He was fired all right but it was not out. Enthusiasm fired him to new participation in his job. He became a new personality: successful, happy, creative. Try enthusiasm on your job. The result can be amazing.

6

TENSE? NERVOUS? LET ENTHUSIASM COME TO YOUR AID

We sat together at the speaker's table looking out on a crowd of some fifteen hundred people that filled the large hotel ballroom. This man, master of ceremonies for a big dinner event, was the most nervous of toastmasters. He picked at his food and constantly moistened dry lips. His hand shook like an aspen leaf, and once when inadvertently it touched mine, it felt cold as an icicle.

"You seem a bit nervous," I commented sympathetically.

"Well, if you think I am nervous now, you should have seen me six months ago," was the surprising reply.

"Were you more nervous six months ago than you are now?" I asked.

"Sure was," he said, "and when I introduce you, you'll hear how I started improving."

Presently the toastmaster arose, knees shaking, voice trembling, and came out with the following: "Friends and fellow citizens, tonight I want to introduce our speaker, a man who has done me no end of good. Some time ago, tense and full of stress, I was on the edge of a nervous breakdown. I couldn't sleep nights and everything was upsetting to me. But just at that time a friend sent me a book by our speaker. I took the book to bed with me and believe it or not, I hadn't read three pages before I was sound asleep."

This well-intentioned remark rocked the crowd with laughter, a reaction that did not appreciably reduce the toastmaster's tension. Later he asked if we might talk privately. When we were alone I said, "Let's face the fact that you are by no means out of the woods on this tension problem, though you are making progress." I reminded him that there are two kinds of tension: (1) the good type, which puts directed drive into a person, and (2) the bad type, which shakes a man to pieces. To overcome the latter and gain the former, I urged him to become a practicer of enthusiasm. For enthusiasm has the power to take one out of himself and change his thinking from that acute state of self-reference and ultrasensitivity in which tension thrives. The less conscious one is of himself, the weaker the hold of tension upon him is likely to be.

Whenever enthusiasm for any reason declines, tension seems to increase. That is the time for action. Personally when I feel a diminution of enthusiasm I carefully appraise my state of tension and if possible, even for a brief period, I try to get away to a place which has tension-reducing qualities. Usually this is my farm in Dutchess County, New York.

But after one particularly busy season, I needed to get far away, so I boarded a jet and seven hours later landed in Switzerland. I drove at once to a serene and peaceful place, the high Alpine Valley of the Engadine, often called the roof of Europe. Here three great mountain passes, the Julier, the Maloja and the Bernina shield the traveler from the outside world. Such a retreat from the tension of the job enables one to cope with problems upon return to the familiar routine. To find relief from tension does not require a trip abroad, of course. Often a walk down the street under the stars will do the trick, and much more cheaply.

St. Moritz is a lovely Alpine spa nestling in a magnificent mountain-encircled valley six thousand feet above sea level. The air is tonic, always fresh and crisp-cool. Golden sunshine warms you by day. Bright stars that seem very near indeed light the evening sky when the incredible afterglow has faded. Nights are cold and one snuggles contentedly under huge puffs that produce a gentle warmth in which deep slumber comes.

My friend Andrea Badrutt, one of Europe's delightful hosts, whose Palace Hotel is where I stay, says the air, sun and water of the upper Engadine have worked wonders in the lives of some of the world's busiest people. "Tension cannot remain in you," he declares, "in the soothing, relaxing atmosphere of a valley where people have come since ancient times to be healed."

With so much tension in modern life one must occasionally retreat *from* the world, in order to live effectively *in* the world. The governor of an American state told me that he joins a group of men in a yearly retreat where, in a religious atmosphere, strict silence is imposed for forty-eight hours.

"How," I asked, "can a politician keep quiet for two days? It seems incredible."

"That is part of the cure," he replied with a grin. "The tension-healing value of discipline is helpful, and in silence you may rediscover yourself and God. Deeper insights come as the fitful fever of life is eased."

He quoted Thomas Carlyle's wise remark, "Silence is the element in which great things fashion themselves." And I thought of Isaiah 30:15: "In quietness and in confidence shall be your strength." This text incidentally expresses an interesting progression. Silence leads to confidence, and confidence to strength. And silence, confidence and strength pay off by making you a more competent and certainly a happier, more enthusiastic person.

Well, the tension subsided for me on that visit to the wide sunbathed valley framed by massive peaks. Dark forests gird broad mountain flanks, and above, a deep blue sky suggests Italy just beyond the Bernina peaks. Here the air is lighter than in lowlands, and possesses a tonic quality which, with the powerful sunlight, seems actually to produce a kind of gentle massaging effect. Mineral waters and Alpine peat baths contribute to a sense of well-being.

Yet something more basic than sun, air and water is required, for the control of tension may be psychological and spiritual. The secret of overcoming tension is a controlled mental attitude and this often depends upon spiritual factors.

At St. Moritz a wealthy, balding playboy told me he had "nothing but time and money." He had taken the cure in every spa in Europe, but complained that still he "itched" constantly. "Must this miserable itching go on forever?" he asked pathetically.

I told him of a woman who had "itched" for several years. Her medical doctor sent her to me, explaining that for some reason she was "scratching herself on the inside." She was extremely tense. Our talk uncovered an old bitter anger for a sister over their father's will. This hatred, according to the physician, had no doubt caused the physical manifestation of itching. We persuaded her to give up the hate and gradually, as tension abated the itching ceased.

It is not necessary to settle for being tense, even in an age of anxiety.

You can live without tension, and one way to do so is through the development of enthusiastic attitudes and techniques.

Your tension problem may be in part or entirely medical, in which case treatment will be handled by a physician. On the other hand, it may be a result of psychological or spiritual factors. If so, read on, for this chapter is intended for you. It may creatively aid you.

BUSINESSMAN HEALED OF TENSION

I was able to help bring about healing of tension through enthusiasm in the case of a well-known business leader, a longtime acquaintance. He was seriously troubled by tension and desperately wanted help. He was able to get help because he humbly followed a workable program. Any person can be helped if he really wants to be, and if he will study, believe in and practice techniques that have proved beneficial to others with similar problems.

This man, Joe K______, started coming to hear my sermons in the hope that he might get relief from an acute tension condition. Shortly thereafter he made an appointment to see me and described his highly nervous state, one manifestation of which was an inability to make decisions. Whenever called upon to make a decision he would "get into a cold sweat" and feel like he was "going to collapse." This state of mind was a serious problem for in his business he had to make important decisions each day.

Formerly, decision-making had not bothered him at all. Indeed he had been very intelligently decisive. Otherwise, he could not have arrived at his present executive position. Doctors had diagnosed his trouble as acute hypertension, a decision phenomenon, so they explained, resulting from an old subconscious anxiety. Medication had been prescribed. When an important decision faced him, one that "had a lot of implications riding on it," he would take the medication and it would pull him through. "But," he said plaintively, "I can't grab a pill the rest of my life every time I have to make a decision. My only hope lies in some permanent easing of tension, else I guess I'll have to retire and then die."

He sat silently for a long moment, then in a most affecting manner he said, "I believe God can heal me. Yes, I believe He will heal me."

"Since you believe that, sincerely and in depth," I said, "healing is already taking place." I referred to the immense power inherent in faith and reminded him that the New Testament is filled with instances of healings—and how very important in each circumstance was the power of simple belief. For example, the sick woman who reached out timidly through the crowd and touched the hem of Jesus' garment. She did not even speak to the Lord, but simply believed that she would get well if she could just touch His garment. And she was right, for she was healed.

"Though you are an important man, Joe," I said, "you seem also to have the rare genius of childlike faith, and as a result I believe you can be healed of your tension." I quoted the words: " 'If ye have faith as a grain of mustard seed . . . nothing shall be impossible unto you.' "

"I believe that. I do for a fact," he exclaimed. "Now, what do I do?"

"Nothing at all," I said, "except to keep on believing, deeply and confidently. Just continue thanking God for His healing grace, and for giving it to you now. Don't ask for it as something to be granted later, but give thanks for it as a current fact. That is to say, affirm it with gratitude as having been received. Also underscore every statement in the New Testament about faith and commit as many to memory as you can, so that your mind may become deeply saturated with faith. Fifteen minutes a day devoted to this will work wonders. The chief purpose of this treatment is to deepen faith, for primarily it is faith, rather than any activity, that will heal you."

THE HEALING POWER OF ENTHUSIASTIC FAITH

The patient almost at once began to develop release and with release came enthusiasm—indeed in such a torrent that he would telephone me saying, "Listen to this. Isn't this terrific?" And he would quote a statement from the Bible about faith or healing or peace. "Sorry to bother you," he would then apologize, "but boy, isn't that one a honey? Goodbye, see you soon."

He was a rare breed; the all-out type. People of this sort enthusiastically take faith and go all-out with it. They are true believers—and this kind of believer always sweeps everything before him, including tension and nervousness, or whatever the problem may be.

Joe had been a go-getter all his life. So he was conditioned to the psychology of belief and, as pointed out, he also had the quality of humility. All-outness together with humility is a tremendous combination in personal power build-up. He had the quality of mind that was big enough to be simple and he possessed that superior faculty, the capacity to believe.

Perhaps Jesus Christ had big-minded men like Joe in mind when He said, ". . . whosoever shall not receive the kingdom of God as a little child, he shall not enter therein." If you have what it takes to become simple, humble and unaffected, with a childlike belief that nothing is too good to be true, it is possible for you to enter into the greatest blessings of this life. At any rate, Joe was able to develop an enthusiasm that really made a difference in him.

Another thing we taught Joe was to practice God's presence. It is said that "Jesus Christ [is] the same yesterday, and today, and forever." So we may assume that healings similar to those He performed in His physical lifetime are occurring today in His continuing spiritual lifetime. When the sense of Presence becomes strong, the individual who practices it finds himself in the flow of the same healing power as were those persons whose healings are recorded in the Scriptures, and with similar results.

Therefore the process of relieving tension in this man showed progress when he started strongly affirming belief. Since he accepted the idea that healing was in process, curative enthusiasm was stimulated to start coming through. As he continued to saturate his mind with faith and to practice "the Presence," the tension began to lessen; enthusiasm took hold. The procedure was so successful that in time Joe developed a boundless excitement and vitality, of which there has since been no lessening.

An associate of this man who confidentially knew the treatment being given commented, "I wouldn't have believed possible the amazing change in Joe." And he added feelingly, "Only God could have done it."

And that is a fact. Only God could have done it. And God did do it. Why not, for "in him was life; and the life was the light of men," meaning that you really live when God puts new life in you. Tolstoy expressed it conclusively, "To know God is to live."

This healing of tension was brought about by thinking, believing, practicing—the magic threesome. Since tension existed in the mind, it was ousted by mental displacement in which a more powerful thought pattern, built around the concept of God, was substituted. This powerful concept was strengthened by daily practice. We suggested that upon awakening Joe should "talk" to God, giving thanks for a good night's sleep, and adding all of his reasons for being grateful and joyous. Then, mentally he was to place the day in God's hands, believing that guidance regarding all his activity would be given to him. He was to say, "Lord, I have some important decisions to make today. Since You are going to guide me in every one, how can I possibly go wrong?"

Then he was to do some vigorous physical exercises, affirming meanwhile: " 'This is the day which the Lord hath made; we will rejoice and be glad in it.' "

At the office before starting work he was to say, "Lord, I must go to work now. Stay with me and help me." I told him of a framed statement that my friend the late Fulton Oursler, the famous writer, had by his door, where he could always see it upon leaving the house: "Lord, I shall be very busy today. I may forget thee but do not thou forget me." I never was aware of Fulton forgetting God, and he was assuredly one of the most enthusiastic of men.

Joe was also urged to repeat fragmentary prayers throughout the day. For example, he might have a telephone call of importance. He was to pray, "Lord, guide me in this conversation. Thanks." When about to dictate a letter, a quick similar prayer might be said. Such fragmentary "flash" prayers were designed to drive into consciousness the fact of God's presence, not as a dim figure off in the sky somewhere, but as a guiding friend. As he followed these procedures, which he did in a sincere and believing manner, decision-making gradually became easier for him, until one day he told me excitedly, "I've finally relearned how to make a decision and then having made it, to forget it. I'm no longer making myself tense through nervous post-mortems." His new-found enthusiasm lifted him above tension. As a result of this he found revitalized mental power and gained a firm grasp of each situation.

Finally, at night he was to say, "Thanks, Lord, for being with me all day long. We had a good day together. Now bless me with restful sleep. Goodnight, Lord." As the sense of Presence grew in this man's mind, the upthrust of enthusiasm drove tense and nervous thoughts from consciousness and he became finally a well man. Enthusiasm had once again worked its healing power.

I knew he was truly well when, forgetting himself, he began to say, "Lord, what can I do for You?" This latter emphasis is important too, for the cure of tension is never complete until the individual becomes enthusiastic enough to get outside himself. Seneca said, "The mind is never right except when it is at peace with itself." And the mind cannot be at peace when abnormally concerned with self. Indeed the more tied up one is, the more likely that tension will develop. Actually tension is not so much the problem of the busy person as of the acutely self-centered. Those disorganized, hectic and even frantic individuals—the mentally undisciplined—are tense, and naturally so. But people with organized outgoing minds, the mentally well-controlled, are able to live in an urbane manner and without tension.

FORGET YOURSELF AND TENSION FORGETS YOU

A man consulted me who complained desperately that "tension was driving him crazy." Indeed he was not far from a state of hysteria. It seemed that living in New York had all but driven him "nuts," and he just couldn't take the noise, stress and confusion much longer. If only he could get to the country, among hills, meadows and babbling brooks. . . .

"John, a move to the country wouldn't help you any," I said, breaking into his halcyon dream of peace. "You would find the same tension there. Your trouble isn't in the city: it's in your mind." I told him of the man I once met on a street in New York, who in answer to my routine inquiry regarding his health, began a long high-strung dissertation on how tense he was. He waved his hand as though to take in the entire city and exclaimed, "The very air of this town is filled with tension." I had to disabuse him, by replying, "If you took a sampling of this air into the laboratory for scientific analysis, no doubt there would be plenty of dirt. But not one speck of tension. Tension is not in the air but in the minds of people who breathe the air."

Having told him this story, I urged the troubled man to try putting enthusiasm in his thoughts in order to counteract the mass of self-concern which was building up nervous tension. "Enthusiasm," he snorted, "that's the last thing I've got."

"Maybe that is what is wrong," I replied. "So let's try getting some for you."

"All right," he growled, "you're the doctor. But just how?"

"If I'm the doctor, I'm going to prescribe something that will get healing enthusiasm to work in your seething mind."

Now be assured that I knew my man quite well. I was completely aware of his abnormal self-interest and his excessive concern for his own well-being and physical comfort. I knew that seldom, if ever, did he give money either to his church or social enterprises, and he never gave time either. He was inbound, ingrown—a tied-up person, although he did have many amiable and attractive qualities. His tension was actually a sickness brought on by self-emphasis as well as by pressure. To reduce it would require rather extreme measures; that is, extreme for him.

"John," I asked, "can you spare an hour to do something for me?" He was a bit surprised, but agreed that maybe he could. "All right then, I want you to call on a friend of mine who is having a lot of trouble. His son got mixed up with a hairy crowd. The boy considers himself a liberal and therefore is in rebellion against everything, from his father to the United States government. He got smart with his employer whom he called a fat capitalist and was fired. Since then he has steadily deteriorated. He is so obnoxious that nobody will have him around. He sponges off his father, who can ill afford it, since his business is not too prosperous.

"But recently an even harder blow struck the father. The doctor broke the news that his wife is desperately ill. No hope is given for her recovery. I've been trying to be supportive but the poor man is in real trouble."

"Boy, I feel sorry for the poor guy," John said, "but hasn't the man any faith? Faith is what he needs." Such a comment was the last reaction I expected to get from John.

He protested that he had nothing to give the stricken man, and reminded me that he himself was in trouble, that he had come for help. "And what could I possibly say or do to help this man?" he asked.

I told him that often I myself had the same problem, but that I simply sent up a little prayer asking for direction, then tried to say and do what seemed best. "Just try that method," I suggested. "Go and see this man for me, and let me know how it goes."

He went doubtfully and hesitantly. I did not hear from him for several days, and was beginning to think he had failed me. Then he telephoned to give the most amazing report. "I've really got this old boy on solid ground," he reported excitedly. "I told him that there was no trouble that faith can't handle. Believe it or not, I prayed with him. First time I ever prayed with anybody. And I had him out to dinner last night. You know that beatnik son? Well listen, that kid isn't too bad. He is just mixed up. Could be that some of his gripes about society have some basis in fact. Anyway, believe it or not, he is going to dinner tonight with me. But I insisted that he put on a jacket and a clean shirt. And do you know, he said he was fed up with looking like a bum. He actually seems glad that a friend told him to dress up a bit."

"You seem to be enjoying yourself with this case, John. How's that tension of yours?"

"My tension? Well, don't think I haven't still got it. But Dick's problems make mine look like kindergarten stuff. See you later." He did see me later, much later. Indeed he became so preoccupied with Dick and the son that he had no time for his personal problems.

I conducted Dick's wife's funeral some months later. And there was John, sitting by the husband and son. It was evident that he was the rock upon which they depended in that sad hour of bereavement. John has been back to see me, but not about his tension. His enthusiasm for people wiped it out. He has moved out of town now to a midwest city, and the last I heard he was creatively doing some real human service in a new kind of tension, racial tension. In an effort to heal that larger social problem, his own personal problem has eased up. Enthusiasm helped in his healing.

Medical men emphasize the danger of stress in physical illness. Any procedure that can cut down tension adds to well-being. And, sound, well-directed enthusiasm helps in many cases. Dr. Hans Seelye has for some years been saying that stress is a root cause of all disease, due to its imbalancing effect upon the function of the human organism. A prominent heart specialist showed me X-rays of the hearts of three people taken when each was sixty-five years of age. He pointed out certain evidences in the X-rays and said, "Actually, they should be dead. But as a matter of fact, they are now about seventy years old and living satisfactory lives." Asked the reason, he replied that each had mastered tension and stress. They had thrown off gloom and developed healthy enthusiasm. As a result, the prognosis in each case looked very good indeed.

ENTHUSIASM IS GOOD MEDICINE

Dr. Paul Tournier, a celebrated European psychiatrist, in his book *The Healing of Persons** develops the thesis that wrong thinking can have physically devastating effects. He says, "Most illnesses do not, as is generally thought, come like a bolt out of the blue. The ground is prepared for years, through faulty diet, intemperance, overwork, and moral conflicts, slowly eroding the subject's vitality. When at last the illness suddenly shows itself, it would be a most superficial medicine which treated it without going back to its remote causes." Quoting a fellow doctor, Dr. Tournier adds: "Man does not die. He kills himself."

A patient was sent to our clinic at Marble Collegiate Church by an upstate physician, who said, "This man is actually killing himself by

* *The Healing of Persons* by Paul Tournier, Harper & Row, New York, N.Y.

abnormal depression. I know of no medication that can heal him. Give him some fresh enthusiasm for living or he may die." Fortunately we were able to help the man to take the "medicine" of enthusiasm, and he not only lived but overcame his depression.

Dr. Tournier points out that "every act of physical, psychological or moral disobedience of God's purpose is an act of wrong living and has its inevitable consequences." Many doctors whose technique is that of treating the patient, rather than the disease, and who are perhaps not so religiously oriented as is Dr. Tournier, nevertheless subscribe to this doctor's conclusions as to the effect of hate, evil, gloom, and depression on mankind.

One doctor, for example, who states that he never attends church services or uses any religious terms, told of one patient who died of "grudgitis." He defined this as "a deep sickening hatred so virulent in nature that toward the end his breath became unbelievably foul, the body organs seeming to deteriorate at once." Then hc added, using a quotation with which I was surprised to know he was familiar, " 'The wages of sin is death.' "

Wrong thinking does not always result in illnesses as dramatic as the foregoing. But it is an authenticated fact that any procedure that upgrades and freshens the mind as do hope, optimism and enthusiasm is on the side of health and well-being. Therefore, if you are tense and nervous, enthusiasm can help you as it has helped so many others.

WORRY BEADS, FIDGET STONES AND TWISTED PAPER CLIPS

This age of tension seemingly has affected people everywhere. Having made many journeys to the Middle East, an area far removed from the materialistic climate of Western civilization, I have observed even there a tendency toward nervousness. Devout Moslems usually carry a string of beads behind their backs as they walk, fingers restlessly moving from one to another of the thirty beads, each bead representing the name of some deity. Used as "worry beads," they are supposed to be efficacious in reducing tensions and anxiety.

If you are inclined to write off this practice as "superstition," may I tell you about my visit to a Fifth Avenue shop where the owner showed me his outstanding inventory of jade? Among other objects, he exhibited a flat piece of jade, perhaps two or three inches long and a couple of inches wide, with an indentation to fit the contour of the thumb. This he called a "Fidget stone." He generously presented one to me and said he was selling them in large numbers to New York City and Westchester residents.

The stone came in a chamois cover with a small folder conveying the following message to the purchaser: "Relaxation is at your finger tips. Pressure and tensions vanish as your fingers move over the soothing surface of the Fidget stone. It is of jade, beautifully handcarved as though fitted to your personality and you will be proud to show it. For centuries orientals have attributed their tranquility and impassiveness to the effect of fingering pieces of jade. Everything good was attributed to jade and everything evil was prevented by it."

So now it appears that sophisticated Americans, like the supposedly "superstitious," are clinging to the hope that fingering jade has some mysterious, magical soothing effect. Possibly a restless fidgeting and doodling may momentarily arrest anxiety. Thousands of paper clips are twisted daily into all kinds of shapes by tense businessmen. Thus it seems that worry beads, Fidget stones and twisted paper clips are symptoms of an unconscious desire for release from tension. But the futility of such procedures is obvious, for the real cure is not in agitated use of the fingers, but in controlled, cultivatable mental attitudes. Only in deeper levels of the mind can peacefulness be found.

TO STOP BEING TENSE, STOP

The current style in dealing with emotional problems is usually analysis in depth with supportive psychiatric assistance. This is both proper and valid. But it is also a fact that much tension can be conquered once a patient makes a commitment deep within his consciousness that he is resolved to overcome tension. Of course, insight is required into its causes, and insight can be achieved by counseling. But there must come a moment when one actually decides to substitute controlled emotional reactions for those of an undisciplined nature. Perhaps not everyone is strong enough to employ this disciplinary method, but some are, perhaps more than they realize. No matter how much psychiatric counseling one receives, and regardless of the quality of such guidance, the ultimate fact is that every person, on his own, by himself, with God's help, must take that final decisive step that activates the cure of unhealthy mental patterns.

For example, a few years ago I dined with friends one evening in the open-air terrace restaurant of the Royal Danielli Hotel in Venice. The night was balmy. A full moon was overhead and the romantic songs of the gondoliers came across the silvery waters of the Grand Canal. The conversation turned on the beauty and peacefulness of the evening and how beneficial such environment was for tense and hard-driving people such as those gathered about the table—a New York business executive, a Hollywood producer, a metropolitan stock broker, and their wives.

The movie producer aired his opinion that current ways of dealing with emotional problems should attach more curative value to what he called "disciplined decisiveness." He emphasized his point by a story concerning his father. "My father," he said, "was the most controlled man I ever knew. He was completely in control of every emotional reaction. However, he was not a cold personality as might be expected from this description. On the contrary, he was a man of vast enthusiasm and warm deep feeling. But emotional control was his middle name."

He told how his father, before age forty, had had a wild and ungovernable temper. He would fly into fearful rage, then fall into deep black depression. "This fiery and undisciplined conduct was repeated often in my youth. But about the time my father was forty years old he suddenly took hold of himself. He changed, absolutely, and I never again knew him to go into a rage or a depression. Instead, he became a controlled person of tremendous enthusiasm and happiness. Emotionally he was completely normal—all abnormalities disappeared.

"Years later," continued the Hollywood producer, "I asked my father how he managed to effect so dramatic and complete a change. His answer was classic: 'Son, I simply got tired of being the way I was. I believed in prayer and in God. So I told God I was fed up with the kind of person I was and asked Him to change me. I believed God would do that and, of course, He did. My prayer was answered; that's all there is to it. I asked God to change me and He did.' My father apparently never doubted his prayer would be answered.

"I asked Dad if he ever felt the old anger coming up again. He replied, 'When I do, son, instead of flying into a great rage, I fly into a great calm.'

"My father always said that God, decision, guts and enthusiasm saved him from a crack-up. That may be a crudely expressed formula, but if you ask me, it proved a pretty effective combination."

Whenever I encounter people who insist hysterically that they cannot overcome tension, my mind goes back to that conversation in Venice.

The important fact is that you can do more in a disciplinary way with yourself than you think possible. There is a certain sardonic humor in the story of the New York business executive who had a nervous breakdown. Turning the business over to a staff of young subordinates, he went off to a famous spa for treatment. This executive believed he had overworked himself into a nervous breakdown, but it would be more accurate to say he had wished himself into it. But having plenty of money, he could afford the nervous breakdown.

While he was having his breakdown, his young staff got into trouble. He was implored to return to the firm to "get it out of a hole." He became keenly interested in the problems which had accumulated, and as a result began to feel much better. Knowing that his stay in his office was only temporary until the situation improved, he did not feel as much pressure as formerly. Indeed, he had quite the time of his life for six months until the problems were straightened out. Then, there being nothing further for him to do, he said, "I'm no longer needed here, so I will return to the hospital and resume my nervous breakdown."

This case reminds me of the poor woman who had experienced one trouble after another, but still preserved her quiet composure. Asked the secret of her imperturbability, she replied, "Well, I just handle each trouble as it comes, and if two troubles come I handle both of them. I have to, you see. There is no other way. Of course, if I were a rich woman I would just have me a nervous breakdown."

I do not mean to minimize the actuality and misery of tension. I know full well its dangers. Nor do I present enthusiasm as merely a buoyant spirit, a rosy glow, and ebullient effervescence. In its deeper meaning, enthusiasm is a calm and practiced attitude of mind that exercises quiet control.

For years I have known a man with an impressive ability to maintain calm in the midst of commotion and stress. Always in full control of himself, he is a particularly enthusiastic person. Formerly he had been very tense, but he had "practiced his way out of that miserable condition." This emphasis makes sense, for practice is indeed important in the cure of tension. This man made use of a four-word program described as follows: 1. Enthusiastically. 2. Gratefully. 3. Phlegmatically. 4. Philosophically.

He said, "I live enthusiastically. I receive gratefully. I face failures phlegmatically and I take whatever comes philosophically." That four-word formula must have value. It worked for him. Tension ceased to be a problem; enthusiasm and quiet control took over.

DAILY ANTI-TENSION TECHNIQUE

There is another helpful technique which I once wrote out as a "prescription" for a man who had long suffered from tension, and it proved to be effective in his eventual healing. It consists of "healing" statements to voice and to meditate upon daily throughout the week.

MONDAY—

Peace I give unto you . . . Let not your heart be troubled.

TUESDAY—

Thou wilt keep him in perfect peace, whose mind is stayed on thee.

WEDNESDAY—

My presence shall go with thee, and I will give thee rest.

THURSDAY—

Rest in the Lord, and wait patiently for him: fret not thyself.

FRIDAY—

Come unto me, all ye that labour and are heavy laden, and I will give you rest.

SATURDAY—

Let the peace of God rule in your heart.

SUNDAY—

He maketh me to lie down in green pastures: he leadeth me beside the still waters. He restoreth my soul.

The man to whom I gave this suggestion carried the quotations in his wallet until, by repeated use, the Bible verses became imbedded in his consciousness. Presently they induced a peace so satisfying that tension gradually gave way and a fresh zest for life developed. Faith and enthusiasm in depth revamped his thinking and brought about quiet control that changed his life.

JUST A FINAL WORD

I do not mean to imply that tension is altogether undesirable. It has a proper use as a motivating force. Tension is also designed to key you up to a creative level which is vital to above-average accomplishment. Steel without tension is lacking in quality. Similarly a person without tension is innocuous and flabby. The most important thing is to make tension work for you rather than against you.

Batten and Hudson in their book *Dare to Live Passionately** quote Dr. James G. Bilkey as saying, "You will never be the person you can be if pressure, tension and discipline are taken out of your life."

Still one can have plenty of relaxed drive without abnormal tension. To attain relaxed power is an important secret of successful living. One man who learned this skill is my old friend John M. Fox, president of the United Fruit Company. Years ago I heard Mr. Fox, who was then merchandising frozen orange juice, tell of his struggle with tension. In a speech before the Rotary Club of New York, John Fox said that enthusiasm had made a great difference in life though he, like many, had to conquer tension to attain it.

"I should like to tell you of an experience I had during the early days of the company," he said. "It happened in the winter of 1947. Our problems were seemingly insurmountable. The new 'mousetrap' we had brought to the world had laid a giant egg—nobody was beating a path to our doorstep. Working capital had fallen to a zero level, sales were nonexistent, the frozen food industry generally was on the verge of going broke. As the saying goes, 'When the tide goes out, the rocks begin to show.' Everywhere I looked there were rocks!

"At this point I decided to attend the canners' convention in Atlantic City," John Fox continued. "This was a mistake. My gloom was merely an echo of the gloom I found on all sides. Misery loves company and I found a crowd that year on the boardwalk.

"My stomach began to ache. I worried about the stock we had sold to the public. I worried about the employees we had wheedled away from secure, well-paying jobs. I went to sleep—eventually—at night worrying. I even worried about the sleep I was losing.

"My family lived in Atlantic City so I was staying with them. Besides, it saved hotel expense we could ill afford. One day near the end of the convention, my father asked me if I would like to accompany him to a Rotary Club lunch. I had little stomach for it but I knew he'd feel hurt if I refused.

"My unhappiness deepened when I learned that the guest speaker was a minister of the gospel. I was in no mood for a sermon. The minister was

* *Dare to Live Passionately* by J. Batten and L. Hudson, Parker Publishing Co., Inc., 1967.

Dr. Norman Vincent Peale. He announced that his subject would be, 'Tension—The Disease That Is Destroying the American Businessman.'

"From the first words he uttered I felt as though he were talking only to me. I knew I was the tensest man in the audience. It was a great speech, one that he has given again and again all over this country. His formula for relaxing and putting aside worry I would like to repeat:

"First, you relax physically. This is done by stretching out in bed or in a comfortable chair. Then you methodically and carefully concentrate on relaxing each part of your body. Start with your scalp, then your face, your neck, your shoulders and so on down until you are as loose as a pan of ashes.

"Second, you relax your mind. You recall a pleasant incident in your life—a vacation, your honeymoon, a play, a book, anything that brings back into your mind's eye a pleasant scene.

"Finally, you relax your soul. This for most of us businessmen is a little tougher. But it can be done by renewing your faith in the Lord. You get right with God. You check your fears and worries with Him. He can handle them much better than you can. You do this in prayer. If you know no other prayer, the age-old children's one will do quite well. 'Now I lay me down to sleep. I pray the Lord my soul to keep.'

"The first thing you know you'll be fast asleep. I know because in desperation I tried it out that very night after hearing Dr. Peale tell about it. It worked, for I awoke the next morning refreshed and renewed and convinced we would get out of our jam some way. We did."

Such is the testimony of a very successful businessman who tried my suggested techniques and found that they work.

7

ENTHUSIASM WORKS MIRACLES IN PROBLEMS

Eleven words can make an amazing difference in your life. Here they are: *Every problem contains within itself the seeds of its own solution.*

This eleven-word formula, a masterpiece of insight and fact, is by Stanley Arnold who is considered by the many business leaders who have employed his problem-solving talents as America's idea man number one.

In fact, Stanley Arnold has built the business of problem-solving into a million-dollar enterprise. Where others see nothing but discouragement and defeat, he finds amazing opportunity that leads to achievement. He discovered and utilizes the fact, unrealized by so many, that every problem has buried within itself an inherent good. But his own classic phrase says it best. *Every problem contains within itself the seeds of its own solution.*

Stanley Arnold has dedicated his entire life to solving problems, his own and others. He does his job by thinking and reflecting. And he learned this skill early in life. In the book *The Executive Breakthrough** Auren Uris describes Arnold's early beginnings.

* *The Executive Breakthrough* by Auren Uris, Doubleday & Co., Inc., New York, N.Y., 1967.

"Stanley Arnold, thirteen years old, leaned against a backyard tree and brooded about the fact that he was probably the worst broad jumper in the entire Cleveland school system. 'If I'm so bad at jumping forward,' he thought, 'maybe I could learn to jump backward.' Stanley stood up, hopped back, and tumbled down on the lawn. He tried it again, and this time, didn't stumble. Before long, he was able to jump backward several feet, with even a measure of grace.

"When he told the gym teacher about it, and suggested that the class might have a backward-jumping contest, the man looked at his spindly pupil and said, 'Perhaps; it might be fun.' At the next gym class, the coach announced, 'Now we'll try a standing back jump.' The teacher explained that it was like a regular broad jump, except that the contestants would be measured on the basis of how far back they could go.

"One by one, the class's top athletes took their positions, flung themselves backward, and landed a few inches away, flat on their rumps. When Stan's turn came, the others leaned forward, expecting the usual clownish performance. He bent low, and then unwinding like a coiled spring, flew gracefully in reverse, landing neatly on his feet. Unquestionably, the school had not only a new and exciting event, but the world's first champion backward broad jumper.

"Since that time, Stanley Arnold has jumped on to considerably greater things, invariably creating the same sort of excitement for his clients that he created as a youngster for his schoolmates. Today, he is president of Stanley Arnold & Associates, Inc., an organization whose sole function is to contrive novel ways for companies to increase the sales of their products."

So, always remember Stanley Arnold's great statement: "Every problem contains within itself the seeds of its own solution." And you will have the enthusiasm that works miracles in your problems.

ENTHUSIASM EQUAL TO THE TOUGHEST PROBLEMS

Enthusiasm is no Pollyannish, sweetness and light, bright and fortuitous concept. It is a strong, rugged mental attitude that is hard to achieve, difficult to maintain but powerful—so powerful!

The word enthusiasm from the Greek *entheos* means God in you, or full of God. So when we claim for enthusiasm the power to work miracles in solving problems we are actually saying that God Himself in you supplies the wisdom, courage, strategy and faith necessary to deal successfully with all difficulties. We need only to discover how to apply efficiency, enthusiasm and right thinking to our problems. And let's start with a really tough one.

I have dealt with several cases, all somewhat similar in nature, of which that of a West Coast woman is an example. While I was on a speaking engagement in that area, a woman telephoned me; she was sorely distressed, for her husband had left her for a twenty-three-year-old woman who ran an expensive cosmetic shop. It seems he had told his wife he was infatuated with this female. As I delved into the problem, it seemed to me that the predatory young woman, who obviously was not uninterested in his money, knew how to get around the fellow. She had asked sweetly for his advice about her affairs. It seemed that the cosmetic business wasn't going too well. The fatherly advisor status had taken on a more romantic nature. So the husband had advised his wife that although he loved her, he just had to follow the insistent call of romance and take himself off with the young beauty. And the wife, like an indulgent mamma, had allowed him to go, telling him tearfully that she would be patiently waiting for his return. "But now what shall I do?" she asked me poignantly. "That sacrificing spirit doesn't seem to work, and I just don't like it at all."

Despite her rather naïve attitude, I became aware that I was dealing with a woman of potential strength and insight, who, for all her efforts to be "modern," was profoundly shaken. "Well, now," I said, "let's apply the technique of creative enthusiasm to this problem."

"Enthusiasm!" she echoed unbelievingly. "How in the world can this possibly be a time and place for enthusiasm?"

"Enthusiasm can release powerful forces and get them working for you. They can rehabilitate your shattered marriage," I replied.

I described the curious wife-mother-lover relationship sometimes existing between a husband and wife; how a man can for a fact actually love his wife and at the same time fall into an infatuation. That he had told her the situation so frankly indicated also that he regarded her less as a wife than as an indulgent mamma who would give him anything he cried for. And when he did not want it any more he could come home to mamma (the wife-mamma) whom he loved. Home to him was understanding affection plus a nice, indulgent forgiveness. In this manner would he find peace of mind and freedom from guilt. But this curious mental mechanism does not take into account the fact that the wife-mamma may also turn out to be a real woman, who wants not a child, but a man. The fact that he could desert his true love for a physical infatuation was considered by her a violation of herself as woman-wife.

"Let's understand the situation," I said to her, "men your husband's age often become infatuated with younger women. It has to do with their fear of getting old. And it is just possible that you are not as aware and as understanding of the physical factors in your own relationship with your husband as you ought to be."

Then I advised the wife to change her attitude. Her husband felt too secure about her. This old security should be shattered. "Give him a big surprise," I advised. "Go off some place where he cannot possibly find you. If he cannot locate his always present, loving mamma, he may become desperate. Stop being the tender forgiving wife, waiting for the wanderer to return. Disappear. Become a wife dropout. Let him find you if he can."

She was loathe to follow this suggestion but finally agreed to the strategy. In fact she said she would hie herself to Japan. "Well," I said, "Japan is a super-way of carrying out this prescription. But if absence makes the heart grow fonder, maybe distance will do the same. And distance often produces perspective. Besides Japan is about the last place he would look for you, isn't it?"

"Maybe," she replied shrewdly. "We have always said if our romance ever declined, we would go back to Japan in cherry blossom time. You see, that is where we met. Our parents were missionaries over there."

Smart girl, I thought. I warned her that we were taking a gamble, but I had a sneaking feeling that it might just work. So I said, "Get going to Japan and settle down there. It may be quite some time before bad little boy wants his mamma."

I urged her meanwhile to reflect upon her own responsibility for her wandering husband's romantic proclivities. Had she grown indifferent after that basic biological function of marriage—the production of children? Was she disinterested in the art of lovemaking? Did she think it silly for two middle-aged people still to be interested in sex? Did she feel their relationship now should be just a lovely companionship? Had she in any sense driven him away?

She admitted this was not the first time he had strayed. "But even though he does these things, he just cannot seem to leave me," she said in bewilderment.

"And you made it tough for him when he did return?" I asked.

"I sure did. I gave him a terrible going over."

"And then," I continued, "in sex relations, he was rather, if not completely, impotent—was he not?"

"Why, yes. But how do you know that?"

"That's easy. In his deep unconscious he was attempting sex relations with a berating, punishing mother figure."

"But," she demanded, "do you mean that I should let him come home from some other girl, and just gush over him in a honey sort of way?"

"Not at all. But for goodness sake, use what God gave you: your femininity. Get yourself up so attractively that you can outsmart any other female. Really pretty yourself up. Get a hair-do at the swankiest shop in town. Deck yourself out in the smartest clothes you can buy. Charge them to him."

OUTSMARTING A GOLD DIGGER

"Look what is on your side," I continued: "love in youth, ties of family, honest-to-goodness marriage and devotion to God. Balance that with what is on the girl's side: clandestine practice, danger of disease perhaps, the fear of disgrace. You've a powerful lot going for you; a lot more than the other woman.

"So take a trip. Do some soul-searching and some real changing. Try to restore the qualities he first fell in love with. You've got what it takes to outsmart that character he has momentarily fallen for. I believe he will come running home to mamma wiser, though certainly poorer. But on his return, don't let him find mamma whom he doesn't need, but a fascinating woman whom he *does* want. Then bring some spiritual know-how into your lives. Put some dynamic positive enthusiasm into this project, and I'll wager that you'll be in."

So off to Japan she went. Several months passed. Spring had come round when a man called me on the telephone from California. "Dr. Peale, do you possibly know where my wife has gone? I've just got to find her. I've thought of putting the Missing Persons Bureau on her trail but I found a note saying she is O.K. but is gone for good—that as I left her, so she was leaving me. Someone told me she talked with you. Do you have any idea where she is?" He was truly upset.

"How are you doing with the sweet young thing?"

"Oh, I'm so fed up with her that I've told her to go to hell."

"That's what it always comes back to, isn't it—hell?" I mused.

"It sure does," he said contritely.

"Do you really want a wife or do you want a mamma?" I asked.

"I only want my wife." He really sobbed this time.

"O.K.," I said. "Cherry blossoms is the answer."

"Cherry blossoms?" he repeated mystified. "Oh, cherry blossoms! I believe I get you."

"I advised her to meditate in the Stone Garden of Kyoto, that ancient peaceful Shinto shrine and to try to figure how to become a better wife."

"Good bye," he shouted, "and thanks. Oh, thanks a lot!"

HE GOT HIMSELF A NEW WIFE

Much later I had a long distance call from San Francisco. "A lot you know about women," a man's voice said. "You don't think I found her meditating in the Stone Garden of Kyoto, do you? Do you know where I found her? Well, I'll tell you. I found her, looking ten years younger—a dream of a gal, dancing with some Englishman at the Miyako Hotel. She didn't seem what you call thrilled to see me, but I convinced her that there is nobody in the world for me but her."

"Great," I replied. "You sure know women."

I never did tell him that I cabled her that he was on his way to Japan. There is more than one way to solve a problem. But one day I "remarried" them at the altar of the church in a symbolic renewal of vows. There was now genuine dedication and love between those two.

Enthusiasm, prayer, strategy will solve any problem, however tough. In fact, they just don't make problems tough enough for that powerful combination. Enthusiasm can work miracles in problems.

THE PHILOSOPHY OF ENTHUSIASM

Enthusiasm to perform such miracles presupposes a sound and workable philosophy. It is a fact, I believe, that a problem is widely considered rather a bad thing, something to be avoided if at all possible. It would seem that most persons take a dim view of a problem. But actually is a problem a bad thing, or on the contrary, might it not be a very good thing?

Let me answer that question by telling of an incident. On Fifth Avenue in New York City I saw approaching me a friend by the name of

George. From George's disconsolate and melancholy demeanor it was evident to me that he was not filled to overflowing with the ecstasy and exuberance of human existence. His obvious depression aroused my sympathy and so I asked, "How are you, George?"

This was only a routine inquiry but it represented an error on my part. George took it seriously. For fifteen minutes he enlightened me in detail on how badly he felt. And the more he talked, the worse I felt. "But, George," I finally asked, "what seems to be the trouble? I would like to help you if I can."

"Oh," he replied, "it's problems. Life is nothing but problems. I've had it. I'm fed up with problems." George became so exercised about the matter that he quite forgot to whom he was talking and began to castigate his problems, using in the vitriolic process a great many theological terms. I knew what he meant. He had the power to communicate.

"What is it that I can do for you, George?" I asked.

"Get me free of these problems, that's what I want. Tell you what. Get me free and I will give you a thousand dollar donation for your work."

Well, I am never one to turn down such an offer. I meditated and cogitated and came up with a solution which I thought possessed merit. But apparently George did not go for it. I have yet to receive the aforementioned one thousand dollars.

"So, you want to be completely free of problems, do you, George?" I asked.

"You said it!" he fervently replied.

"All right, here is how it can be done. The other day I was in a certain place on professional business, if I may thus characterize it, and was told that there were in that place over one hundred thousand people, and not a single one had a problem."

The first indication of enthusiasm lighted up his eyes and suffused his countenance. "Boy, that's for me. Lead me to this place."

"O.K., you asked for it," I replied, "but I doubt you will like it. It's Woodlawn Cemetery."

And of course no one in that or any other cemetery has a problem. For them "life's fitful fever" is over; "they rest from their labors." They have no problems.

Problems constitute a sign of life. Perhaps the more problems you have, the more alive you are. The man who, let us say, has ten good man-sized problems is twice as alive as the apathetic character who has only five problems. And if you have no problems at all, I warn you, you are in great jeopardy. You are on the way out. The best procedure might be to pray to the Lord saying, "Don't you trust me any more, Lord? Please give me some problems."

A new in-depth philosophy of the good values inherent in problems should be accentuated. Problems are treated these days as inherently evil. In the social services, a genial idea has gained currency that human well-being can be served only by relieving people of problems. Overcoming injustice, relieving poverty, the promoting of better housing—these are extremely valid and important, but so also is the basic American concept that people grow strong and create better conditions by facing problems and solving them.

I was walking on Nob Hill in San Francisco when I met an intellectual. Now how did I know he was an intellectual? He told me so. Had he not done so, I would not have suspected. For the valid intellectual I have the profoundest respect, but the fake intellectual is something else again. This character was definitely in the latter category.

One clearly evident characteristic of the pseudo-intellectual was his so-called "profoundly concerned" look. But, being a simple soul, I appraised it as a sour look. Nowadays this sour look is an inevitable concomitant of a sobersides type upon whom there seems to rest a heavily weighted "concern" for the whole world. One is not really "in" unless he goes about mouthing traditional sociological jargon and wearing upon his face the concerned-sour look.

What a switch from the old days! Formerly this sour look was on the visages of those who wished to give the impression of piety. They, like their modern intellectual counterparts, were the pretentious pious of those earlier times.

How well I recall as a boy sitting in church beside my mother. Nearby sat old "Brother Jones," a leading deacon and ostensibly a pillar of the church. this character always had a sad expression on his face. I used to whisper to my mother, "Why does Brother Jones have that sour look?"

"That is not sour. It's a pious look," my mother replied. My mother seemed to equate a pious look with saintliness. This did not impress me, for I and the kids around town knew a few things about Brother Jones that my mother did not. We boys had him realistically sized up.

But nowadays the genuine exponent of bona fide Christianity wears a happy look. And why not? He has been released from conflicts and misery. He has experienced victories. Having discovered that they possess within themselves the power to handle problems, creative Christians long ago abandoned the sour look which has become currently the hallmark of the modern pretentious intellectual.

A second characteristic of this curious fellow on Nob Hill was the outlandish manner in which he was dressed. It is odd that not a few beatniks seem to equate individuality with alienation from the bathtub.

In Geneva, Switzerland, my wife and I were sitting in the lobby of a hotel when a young crowd arrived for a fashion show. Personally I couldn't care less for such a show, but my wife insisted on watching. However, it didn't take long for her to be as revolted as I by the utterly unattractive dresses worn by the models and by the crowd in attendance. I could have endured it, however, had there been just one pretty girl. But all had successfully eliminated every whit of charm and beauty so as to equate with the ugliness of the costumes. And the boys were even less attractive. "I've had it," I said to my wife. "Let's get out and breathe some fresh air." And this, dear friends, was in the most luxurious hotel of an international city in Europe.

NOT A HAIR ON HIS CHEST AND NOT A POSITIVE THOUGHT IN HIS HEAD

Well, to return to our friend on the street in San Francisco, he wore a black shirt of good quality, obviously costly. His shirt was open to the third button—no jacket or necktie, naturally, and no undershirt, the effect intending to reveal a manly chest. But the chest looked rather peaked to me; there wasn't a hair on it. The slacks revealed no familiarity with a pressing iron, and the white shoes, also of good quality, had been deliberately beat up, from which I concluded he was a beatnik who probably lived in a garage and spouted existentialist glumness, taking a dim view of the world in general.

Well this fellow fixed his sour-concerned look on me and said, "I'm glad to meet you." I asked the Lord to forgive me and told him I too was glad to meet him. He said, "You're that bright, happy Pollyannish individual who runs around the country prattling about Positive Thinking, aren't you?"

"Well," I replied, "since you have propounded this inquiry in your urbane, academic and scholarly manner, let us carefully consider the implications you have so meticulously raised." I can throw the jargon around also when necessary. Continuing, I said, "I do run around the country, and I do talk about Positive Thinking, which is not bright-happy nor Pollyannish, as you indicate. Perhaps a definition of a positive thinker might provide you with some enlightenment. A positive thinker is a tough, rugged person who sees every difficulty and faces all facts realistically. But he is not licked by what he sees. He practices the philosophy of optimism which holds that the good in life outbalances the evil thereof, and he believes that in every difficulty there is inherent good which he intends to find." I added, perhaps more maliciously than proper, "A person must be somewhat of a man to be a positive thinker, which makes it difficult for some people I might mention."

But then, thinking he really had me, he asked, "But don't you know that the world is full of trouble and problems?"

"You don't say so!" I exclaimed. "Do you think I was born yesterday? Why, son, in my business we know more about troubles and problems in five minutes than you will know in five years. And there is a further basic difference between us. Despite all the difficulty of this world, we aren't licked by it—as you are. For we know that difficulty contains all kinds of creative possibilities."

I came up with a comeback. Most of my comebacks come to my mind long after they are needed. But this one emerged right out of the subconscious, and I said, "Certainly the world is full of trouble and problems, but the world is also full of the overcoming of trouble and the solving of problems." This baffled him; he went down the street shaking his head. I could hear it rattle all the way down the block.

STRUGGLE IS PART OF NATURE

Of course the world is full of trouble, deep, dark, grievous trouble. The world is full of problems, too, hard knotty problems. It always will be so. If any politician or preacher tells you that all problems are going to be eliminated from this world through some panacea, do not fall for it. The constitution of the universe does not support it. The world is made on the basis of struggle; and struggle is inevitably attended by difficulty, often by pain plus hardship.

The Bible, the writers of which had seen a lot of life and evolved an in-depth philosophy of human existence, says, "Man is born unto trouble, as the sparks fly upward." (Job 5:7) And again, "In the world ye shall have tribulation." (St. John 16:33) But the Bible also says, "Be of good cheer; I have overcome the world" (St. John 16:33), meaning through faith in Christ we, too, can overcome all that the world throws at us. Religion does not blithely promise some sort of no-trouble, no-problem, no-poverty world; but rather a spirit, a power, an enthusiasm that endows everyone with the ability to overcome any and all of it. Out of struggle we produce better conditions. But as to trouble and problems you can count on them all your life.

A psychiatrist has said, "The chief duty of a human being is to endure life." That is a fact. There are certain things in life that must be endured. There are inevitabilities from which there is no escape and for which there are no alternatives. But if the psychiatrist's appraisal was the whole story, life would be grim and bleak indeed. A better statement of the matter is, I believe, that the chief duty of a human being is not merely to endure life, but to master it. So, a sound philosophy is important in order to deal effectively with problems.

Enthusiasm helps to work miracles in problems by helping us master them in thought and practice. Enthusiasm is an attitude of mind, and mental attitude in a difficult situation is the important factor in its solution. In a public speech, I made the statement that attitudes are more important than facts. A man who heard this remark had it made up on a laminated board suitable for hanging on an office wall. He sent one to me. This man said it had made him aware that he was being defeated not by hard facts, but by taking a defeated and negative attitude toward those facts. Enthusiasm changes the mental outlook of fearing facts to the solid belief that there is an answer.

One man looking at a tough problem says glumly, "There are the facts. There is nothing I can do but accept them." So the facts have him defeated. Another man, blessed with enthusiasm, looks at the same facts. "Sure, those are the facts all right, and they are indeed tough. But I never yet saw a set of facts to which there was not a solution. Perhaps some facts cannot be changed, but maybe I can by-pass or weave them into a new pattern or readjust my strategy. If necessary I can live with them and ultimately use them to advantage." That man's attitude brings the magic of creative believing into play. That in turn stimulates hitherto unused and unsuspected ingenuity.

If you question the practicality of this principle, let me tell you of a man I met at a convention at which I was a speaker. He remarked, "Wish I could get hold of that magic of believing you were talking about at the convention session this morning."

"Figure out a method of your own for practicing the magic of believing," I suggested. "You will find that it works."

He really did figure out a method, one that worked very well indeed.

THE MAGIC OF BELIEVING

Like many executives, he had on his desk a receptacle for incoming mail and other papers, and a second container for outgoing mail and papers. Here is what he did. He added a third receptacle labeled, "With God All Things Are Possible." (Matthew 19:26) In it he placed and let rest all matters for which he did not yet have answers; and problems for which no solution had been determined. To use his own phrase, he held these matters in "prayerful thinking. I surround the matters in that box with the magic of believing and the results are amazing." So reported a highly respected executive who tested out in actual practice the principle that faith and enthusiasm work miracles.

This man's experience demonstrates still another principle, one that first came to my attention in a book by a friend, the late Albert E. Cliffe, an outstanding Canadian food chemist. His book called *Let Go and Let God** is a simple, direct-style chemist's formula type of book, one which makes sense and is full of workable ideas. "As a chemist," Cliffe writes, "I have faith in science and I can prove it every day. I am no theologian and have no desire to study theology in any university. I simply believe that God is my Father, and I am His son, and that my mind is part of His divine mind—and by this magic of believing I can be in tune with that tremendous mind of His at any time I choose, and by so doing and by so believing I can gain the answer to any problem which I have to face."

Dr. Cliffe early in his career faced an acute health problem, indeed was given up to die. In his hospital bed he read the Bible text, "All things are possible to him that believeth." (Mark 9:23) Sick as he was, he felt this was his message of hope. So he reached out mentally for healing, believing implicitly in this promise. "I let go and let God; and God healed me," he said simply. This he believed to be the explanation of his restoration to health. He said further, "What you get out of religion is entirely up to you. You can make your faith a super-atomic dynamo, or a routine affair without progress. You can be healed and your healing can

* *Let Go and Let God* by Albert E. Cliffe, Prentice-Hall, Inc., Englewood Cliffs, N.J., 1951.

start at any time, regardless of how serious your condition may appear to be, if you will let go your fears and give God His rightful place in your life."

Al Cliffe had an enormous and undiluted enthusiasm for faith and to my personal knowledge stimulated many healings. He told me that in his moment of deepest sickness when the life force was at lowest ebb, he felt a warm glow of assurance and with it a steady inflow of healing power.

As a result, this scientist spent his subsequent life enthusiastically urging people to let go and let God. Actually, the Bible—textbook for believing—is a book of power techniques and power formulas. Jesus said, "Ye shall receive power . . . ." (Acts 1:8) It is a power promise and a power delivery to those who believe and practice, who let go and let God. Such believers discover to their amazement that enthusiasm can indeed work miracles in problems.

I have observed that, generally speaking, men who enjoy problems do better in solving them. I gave a talk at the twenty-fifth anniversary of a prominent industrialist. About two thousand people attended the dinner honoring him on a quarter-century of leadership during which his company achieved remarkable growth. Seated together on the dais, I asked him, "What has been your greatest satisfaction in your quarter-century as head of this organization?" I was certain that he would refer to the company's growth and development. Instead he answered, "It's the fun I've had with problems. And believe me, some have been plenty tough. When you have no more problems, that is the time to watch out, for enthusiasm will go next and then you will go. That's why I'm suspicious of a big dinner like this. It could give the impression we've licked all our problems, and when that happens I'll be through. And I don't want to be through. Not me. I like working with problems too well."

SELF-MOTIVATORS AS PROBLEM SOLVERS

My friend, W. Clement Stone, president of the Combined Insurance Company of America, with whom I am proud to be associated at the American Foundation of Religion and Psychiatry, has more real, genuine enthusiasm than any man I know. Furthermore, it is of the kind that never takes defeat for an answer. I once asked him: "What is the secret of your enthusiasm, as it applies to problems, either business or personal?" And this is what he told me:

"As you know, the emotions are not always immediately subject to reason, but they are always immediately subject to action (mental or physical). Furthermore, repetition of the same thought or physical action develops into a habit which, repeated frequently enough, becomes an automatic reflex.

"And that's why I use self-motivators. A self-motivator is an affirmation . . . self-command . . . platitude . . . or any symbol that you deliberately use as self-suggestion to move yourself to desirable action. You merely repeat a verbal self-motivator fifty times in the morning . . . fifty times at night . . . for a week or ten days, to imprint the words indelibly in your memory. But you do so with the *deliberate purpose of getting into action* when the self-motivator flashes from your subconscious to your conscious in time of need.

"When I have a problem, because I have prepared myself, one or more self-motivators will automatically flash from my subconscious to my conscious mind, as such:

> (Serious personal problem) *God is always a good God!*
> (Business problem) *You have a problem . . . that's good!*
> *Within every adversity there is a seed of an equivalent or greater benefit.*
> *What the mind can conceive and believe, the mind can achieve.*
> *Find one good idea that will work and . . . work that one good idea!*
> *Do it now!*
> *To be enthusiastic . . . ACT . . . enthusiastically!*

"There is very little difference in how I meet business or personal problems. But, there *is* a difference. If a personal problem involves deep emotions, I always use man's greatest power *immediately* . . . thc power of prayer. In solving business problems, I will also pray for guidance, but not necessarily immediately."

HE COULD TAKE ANY PROBLEM APART AND PUT IT TOGETHER RIGHT

As a young man, I had close association with a remarkable human being. His name was Harlowe B. Andrews of Syracuse, New York. Andrews Brothers, wholesale grocers, was a famous upstate concern. Harlowe Andrews is credited with operating the first "supermarket" in the United States, bringing in perishable goods from California by fast, refrigerated express and having them on sale in his Salina Street store within four days. Some say he invented the first dishwasher, perfecting a workable machine that was later sold to a big company. He was very religious, and having made a fortune, retired to go into full-time religious work—leaving the conduct of the business to a brother who promptly lost the fortune. Brother Andrews, as he was called, returned to the business, made another fortune, this time retiring the brother and keeping that fortune.

A Syracuse banker told me he had never known any man with such a remarkable faculty for making money. To use the banker's graphic description, "All Brother Andrews needs do is to extend his fingers and by some special magnetism money springs to him." I was impressed. I hung around with Brother Andrews for a long time, but never acquired the gift.

Despite his religious characteristics, Brother Andrews had sporty tendencies. Long before the advent of motor cars, he raced a team of horses down James Street in summer and over frozen Onondaga Lake in winter. When motor cars came in, he was rated a local speed demon.

He had a remarkable sense of humor coupled with sharp, keen insight. Before Ruth and I announced our engagement—indeed, before we were quite aware of the possibility—I took her to visit Brother Andrews at his farm. Walking in his garden he picked a pea pod, opened it and pointing at two peas snuggled inside, remarked not too subtly. "You see, everything is designed in pairs." Whereupon he chuckled to his great enjoyment, my embarrassment, and Ruth's amusement.

The old man had so much downright native wisdom, penetrating insight and sharp intuition, plus the ability to think creatively, that he became a constant source of guidance for me. And I never knew a man who enjoyed problems as he did. He actually became excited by them; the knottier the problem, the more it interested him. He even thought that the big social problems were positively wonderful. His explanation of enthusiasm for problems troubling the world was a stimulating one. "Always be glad when there is trouble on the earth," Brother Andrews explained, "for it means there is movement in heaven; and this indicates great things are about to happen." Taken literally, that could mean things are really looking up for mankind.

Well, I had a problem that had me stumped. It seemed overwhelming and I wrestled with it for days. Finally I took it to Brother Andrews. "I've really got a problem, a terribly tough one," I announced glumly.

"Congratulations," he cried. "That's great. Always be glad when you've got a big, tough problem. That means things are happening, that you're on the move." This reaction astonished me, for I'm frank to say that I had not even thought of viewing the matter in the manner he indicated.

"Don't you know," he said with a chuckle, "that God has a sense of humor? God likes to play hiding games. When He wants to give you some big wonderful value, do you know what He does? He hides it in a big tough problem. Then He hands you that problem and says, 'Let me see you find that value I've hidden there.' And He watches with interest, pulling for you all the time. When finally you find that wonderful value, is He happy? He sure is.

"Tell me about it, son," he said. "Let's get this problem of yours right out here on the table and take a good look at it."

Thus urged, I really poured it out, enumerating one tough, hard situation after other, followed by a marshaling of negatives such as you never heard. Finally I ran down. "Well, that's about it, I guess. Some problem, isn't it?"

He got up from his chair and walked around the table making motions with his hands like heaping up an imaginary pile. "I'm heaping up this big problem of yours, and boy, it's a beauty." His eyes shone.

"Now, look, son," (he was always calling me son, and that suited me all right for he was like a father) "the first thing is to pray about it. What do our little minds know about it anyway? So let's ask God's guidance." After a few minutes, he said, "Thanks, Lord, Amen."

"Now, son," he said, "God is working with us, so let's start thinking. Get that sad look off your face. Get enthusiastic, for something big and wonderful is about to happen."

Once again he started walking around the table, poking his right forefinger at that heaped up problem. Brother Andrews had arthritis in his fingers, and a knob on the first joint made his index finger crooked. But he could point straighter with that crooked finger than anybody I've known with a perfectly straight finger.

He stopped and acted as if he had his finger in a hole in the problem. He worried it like a dog with a bone. He started to chuckle, "Ha, ha, son, come around here. What did I tell you? Every problem has a soft spot." Then he began to take the problem apart and reconstruct it with a skill and an understanding the like of which I never saw before or since. "Boy, what an opportunity you've got. The only question is whether you can handle it. But you can, because God will help you. And I will too if you need me."

With God and Brother Andrews, how could I miss?

I drove home through a starlit, moon-drenched night thrilled to my fingertips, having learned one of the greatest lessons of life, that enthusiasm works miracles with problems. Try eight sure-fire guidelines and see for yourself:

First: Don't panic. Keep calm. Use your head. You'll need all your wits.

Second: Don't be overwhelmed by your problem. Don't get dramatic about it. Just tell yourself confidently, "God and I can handle it."

Third: Practice de-confusion. A problem generally becomes surrounded by confusion. So de-confuse it. Take a paper and pencil and write down every element of the problem.

Fourth: Skip the post-mortems. Don't say, "Why did I do that? Why didn't I do this?" Take the problem from where you now are.

Fifth: Look for a solution, not for the whole problem but for the next step. One step leads to another and so on to the complete solution. So be content with tackling the next step.

Sixth: Practice creative listening.

A friend of mine, the president of a big company, when faced with a tough problem would call his dog and go into the woods. He said his dog had more understanding than a lot of people. He would sit on a stump, the dog at his feet looking up at him. Then he would describe the problem out loud to the dog. Of a sudden he would hear—not by the outer ear but by the deep inner ear—the answer. He and the dog would then go home. You don't have to have a dog or go into the woods to practice creative listening.

Seventh: Always ask yourself what is the right thing to do in a given situation. If what you do isn't the right thing, then it is the wrong thing. Nothing wrong ever turned out right. So do the right thing and you'll come out right.

Eighth: Keep praying. Keep thinking. Keep believing. And keep enthusiasm going, for it works miracles in problems.

8

ENTHUSIASM—POWERFUL MOTIVATION THAT MAKES THINGS HAPPEN

This chapter is filled with exciting human stories about people whose dynamic enthusiasm acted with such powerful thrusts that the most amazing events happened to them. The more I meet such individuals or am told of them, the more excited I become. For there is an amazing potential in human beings to grow taller and bigger than they are and to do much more with life than they ever believed possible. It was this tremendous realization that activated me to write *Enthusiasm Makes the Difference* for enthusiasm has made such an astonishing difference in the lives of so many people that I simply had to tell about as many of them as could be crammed into a book of reasonable size.

To begin with, here is one of the great human stories that I have encountered in a lifetime of collecting narratives of people who have done tremendous jobs with their lives. This is another thrilling American story, one of those deeply human episodes that warms your heart and fires your mind with wonder at life's limitless possibilities.

Mary B. Crowe was one of nine children. Her father worked in a steel mill in Ohio and never earned more than fifty dollars a week. But on this meager income he raised a large family.

It was Mary's job to wash her father's grimy overalls every day, and were they dirty! In those days, there were none of those magic detergents you see demonstrated on television. She really had to toil to get them clean. Then an amazing thing happened, and it took place in her thoughts, the place where all great things originate. Something that she had never heard of got to working in her mind. It was positive thinking and the motivation of the positive follow-through. It was the magic of the inspired mental image. As she sloshed overalls in that sudsy water, a breathtaking image flashed up in her mind. College! She saw herself in a cap and gown coming to the platform before a large crowd of people to accept her diploma, together with a handshake from the college president. Mary Crowe with a college degree? But how silly can you get? No money, no help, no pull, no chance at all. No member of her family had ever gone to college. It was inconceivable. Forget it! But she couldn't forget, for a creative image had come; enthusiasm had been born, and with it the kind of motivation that makes things happen.

So she kept on washing overalls, and meanwhile, she went to high school. Came commencement day and Mary graduated with honors. The parish priest called her into his office and pulled out an envelope from his desk, one which he had held there for four years. It contained a scholarship to St. Mary's of the Springs College. He had been waiting for someone to earn this coveted scholarship. He had been watching Mary's progress. The image was working—a scholarship for a girl who had never heard of St. Mary's of the Springs College, but who had imaged, dreamed, worked, and practiced positive thinking and studied diligently, while washing the inevitable overalls.

Enthusiastically she went to college; she worked as a waitress in the country club, as a housemaid, as a cook, anything to get the funds to prepare for the life to which her faith and enthusiasm were motivating her. But things got very rough. In her senior year, it seemed as though she would have to quit college. But a member of the country club was so impressed by the spirit and ability of this girl that he lent her $300 on a $1,000 policy with a cash value of $20, and that pulled her through to graduation, again with honors.

That loan did something more; it interested Mary Crowe in life insurance. Her career had been saved by life insurance. Could it not do miracles for others also? She took a course in insurance. She went to an insurance office and asked for work as an agent. But the manager snorted, "What do you know about life insurance, or about selling? You don't know anyone. Besides," and this was the clincher, "you're a woman. The answer is no!" This man turned her down time after time as she continued to ask for a chance. But she sat in his office daily until finally in desperation and to rid himself of her, he snapped, "O.K., here's a rate book and a desk, but no drawing account and no help. Starve yourself to death if you want to." She failed to oblige, and a few days later came in with her first policy sale. As the years passed she made the Million Dollar Round Table. Twenty-five years after she was grudgingly hired, her associates gathered at a dinner honoring her as a distinguished insurance saleswoman. Her formula of success? Well, it was a process of imaging, praying, having faith and positive thinking, plus enthusiasm and motivation. Taken together, the power-packed formula made things happen. Mary Crowe demonstrated that enthusiasm is a powerful force, backed by prayer and faith, that motivates top job performance, overcomes every potential defeat and makes big things happen. Since it was not in her plan to take defeat, she became a winner.

"You *can* change your thinking and thereby change your life," says Mary Crowe. "You can do this by deliberately imaging into your subconscious good ideas, positive images, instead of negative ones. You are constantly in a state of *becoming*. And *you do become what you think!* This philosophy does not mean, of course," says Mary, "that your life will be without problems. What it means is that feeling the presence of God within you and about you, you will be able to meet any problem that life presents, full of confidence that God will give you the courage and the strength to face it, and that He is standing ready to help you solve it. You need only ask—and believe!"

Mary Crowe's stimulating story proves once again that enthusiasm is the powerful motivation that makes things happen. And, of course, if this can happen to one person, it can happen to others; it can even happen to you.

GOOD LOSERS BECOME STEADY LOSERS

The process of creative imaging is also part of the successful philosophy of one of our great athletes.

"How do you become a successful quarterback in professional football?" was asked of Fran Tarkenton, star quarterback of the New York Giants.

"Carry the image of victory in your heart," Fran quickly replied. "In our society of today," the famous football star says, "we seem to go to extremes. For a while there was an overwhelming emphasis on the importance of winning. It went all the way down to the kiddie leagues. Then a reaction set in. 'We're not being realistic,' intelligent parents would say. 'Our children must learn how to lose, for isn't defeat a part of life?' Quite true," says Fran Tarkenton. "Winning can be overstressed. We need to know how to lose gracefully. But then the extreme comes. Kids who think too much about being good losers forget that the purpose of sports, and life too, is to succeed at what they are doing. You show me a good loser, and I will show you a steady loser."

The famous quarterback tells how he went into a playing slump, one so discouraging that he considered quitting the game altogether. But "still down in the deep reaches of my heart I carried the image of the first big victory I'd had. And I did not give up on the idea that I could recapture that success. Many games later I did. But without this image of victory to sustain me over so many defeats, I could well have quit on myself."

This demonstration of steady, deep-rooted enthusiasm as a powerful motivation that makes things happen, and happen well, brings to mind a significant point by Bernard Haldane, the success motivation teacher. "Learn from your successes, rather than from your failures," he counsels. This is, of course, a switch from the usual advice. A failure can show how not to do something. But who wants to know how not to do it, when it is more important to know how to do it right and good? So when you do it right, and succeed at what you are doing, it is smart to success-educate yourself. Ask yourself, "Now just how did I do that so well?" Then try to repeat the next time. Let us say you make a terrific golf shot. Don't blithely move on, thinking, "Boy, what a shot!" Ask yourself meticulously just how you executed that shot. Then deliberately try to repeat it.

You can learn from your failures. Edison is said to have remarked after many failures to make an incandescent bulb, "well, that adds up to over five thousand ways how not to do it." But finally when he succeeded, he made other bulbs on the basis of what he learned from that success. So be a good loser, but not so good that you work losing into a virtue. Get enthusiasm for winning so deeply imbedded in your consciousness that it becomes a powerful urge for making things happen right.

In his fascinating book, *The American Diamond*, a classic on the great American game, Branch Rickey selects his own list of baseball immortals, the two outstanding being Ty Cobb and Honus Wagner. Rickey calls Cobb "the choice of that one player for the one game that had to be won," meaning, of course, that Ty Cobb was first, last and always a competitor. He had only one object—to win. "He had an uncontrollable urge to excel. His genius removed him from all courtesies of sportsmanship when in strife or contest. In physical struggle, he was a competitive paranoiac. In rivalry on or off the field his genius was a do-or-die personal effort to beat someone or something. Cobb would have been the only Greek necessary at Thermopylae."

Rickey declares that Cobb's competitive spirit, his unbounded enthusiasm for winning made him one of the most scientific players the game ever produced. "Cobb did not have a great arm, but accuracy and elevation of the throw and right rotation of the ball were his habitual possessions. He never took a double step on his throw from the outfield. He threw now, right now, when he caught the ball. 'The runner is moving at full speed and will run fifteen feet while I am stepping five feet.' He was precisely scientific in every move. No one ever heard of a base runner taking chances on Cobb's arm—no one.

"He practiced almost by the clock," continued Rickey. "In throwing from the outfield, his objective was to have the ball skip when it hit the ground on its first contact—not bounce with retarded speed. That meant definite control of the spin and proper trajectory. Did anyone ever hear of a baseball player who voluntarily and alone would impose upon himself arduous practice of this sort? I never did."

Of course, Cobb had vast enthusiasm and a restless, ceaseless motivation to make the greatest possible things happen in baseball, which was his life. That attitude made him the one and only Ty Cobb, the "Georgia peach," the greatest of them all.

Rickey himself said, "The game of baseball has given me a life of joy. I would not have exchanged it for any other." But Branch Rickey did not become the greatest baseball man of all time without a burning enthusiasm. This was his motivation that made great things occur in his life.

I once asked, "Branch, what is the greatest experience you have had in your fifty years of baseball?"

He pulled down those big beetle brows. "I don't know," he snapped. "I haven't had it yet." Enthusiasm—that's what makes great men who make great things happen.

PUT UP A REAL FIGHT— ENTHUSIASM WILL GO FOR YOU

Get the good old tough competitive spirit going. Rugged enthusiasm will motivate you to put up a real fight in life. Human beings have in them by nature the creative instinct, the desire to excel. To deny that is actually suicide of personality. One of the basic statements made in American history, one that will forever hold a high spot in Americana, was made by the sweet but tough-minded mother of Abraham Lincoln. In the poverty and hardship of the western wilderness, she said to the gangling boy in whom she instinctively sensed a strange greatness, "Abe, be somebody."

But how times have changed. "Be nobody" seems to be the concept of the far-out-left-wing of our time. But the be-nobody concept won't last since it is a false notion running counter to human nature. Even as a seed put in the ground naturally grows up toward the sun, so does a human being in the essence of his nature want to move up—always up. So this book is definitely, deliberately, unashamedly designed to cater to people who want to get somewhere, and to stimulate and motivate people to be winners, not losers; in other words, to be somebody and stop deluding themselves that it's so nice to be nothing.

Life is a struggle, a fight, no matter how much emphasis is put on reducing the harsh, hard elements. To lift burdens off the backs of humans, or at least to ease them; to improve the lot of all mankind; to wipe out ghettos and slums; to overcome injustice; and to improve race relations—these are important objectives. But even when all these are accomplished, life will still not be one grand, sweet song, one continual happy party.

Therefore, whoever wants to be somebody and have good things happen had better figure on the element of struggle in his life program. And if he has enthusiasm, he will possess the powerful motivation that will help him "fight the good fight" in order to make those things happen.

It would be highly unfortunate if the youth of our affluent society were ever to forget the plain downright courage that went into the making of this country. This nation was created by a breed of people who practiced what I call the five Gs—grit, gumption, guts, grace and God. It can be maintained only by the same kind of people.

Donna Reed, writing in *Guideposts*, gives a heart-moving vignette of people whose enthusiasm and fight against every difficulty helped to shape the prosperous land we have today.

"Sitting in the comfort of our lovely Beverly Hills home, I began to talk about how I was one of four children and how we lived on a farm near Denison, Iowa.

"My family on both sides had pioneered in that state before I was born. As children all of us had chores to perform. I could and did milk the cows and drive the tractor, bring in water from the pump and coal and wood for the stove; to this day I can bake my own bread. The most obvious difference between my childhood and our children's is not that I lived on a farm, but that back in Iowa during the terrible pressure of the Depression years we were quite poor.

"I doubt that any people in America suffered more than some of the Midwestern farmers of the early 30's. These people, our friends and neighbors, were struck with a series of Job-like afflictions. Times were bad everywhere, of course, and there was little money, but on top of this came the drought that withered crops and parched the earth only to be followed by the wind that swept the dry topsoil into great, dark choking dust storms. Family after family loaded their belongings into rickety automobiles and left. . . .

"Poverty, need, these are awful things to have happen to you, but worse, I think, to watch in others. I remember the sounds of our animals crying for food and water. I remember how a little girl from a nearby farm came to say that she would not be playing with me any more because her family was going away. She didn't know where they were going; they were simply leaving, giving up.

"When I think back to those harsh days, I think mainly in terms of my parents, and the anguish I felt inside as I saw them up early and late to bed, day after day, laboring hard with no returns. As children we had few toys and I always yearned for a bicycle which I never got, but I can't recall these things as having been very important to me when I knew so well the inescapable realities of our situation. We might have left the farm, too, if it had not been for Dad.

"His name is William Mullenger and he is a stubborn man. He would not give up. One by one we had to sell our livestock. One by one our neighbors deserted their farms and each time my father would say to us calmly but with undeniable vigor shored up by his faith:

" 'It will not always be this way.'

"I used to wonder how Dad could be so sure when so many others were not. And then, on Sundays, I'd get a glimpse of the answer. On Sundays, Dad would pile Mom and the four kids into that old car we drove for 15 years and we'd rattle to the Methodist Church in Denison. You could get strength just from sitting next to Dad in church. When the minister would read from the Bible, Dad would lean forward a little, as though this especially he had to hear. Watching his face, we children could see that the ancient words were food to his spirit, strength to get him through one more week.

"Our minister used to read a lot from those books of the Bible that rang with hope. Only recently, I searched through the Bible to see if I couldn't find some of the familiar passages and there, in Isaiah, I came across some verses which brought back the whole experience of parched farms and poverty as clearly as though I were there again, sitting in the pew next to Dad. Just listen to these words:

" 'When the poor and needy seek water, and there is none, and their tongue faileth for thirst, I the Lord will hear them . . . I will make the wilderness a pool of water, and the dry land springs of water.' (Isaiah 41:17–18)

"Dad was a family man, a real family man. 'If there is family strength,' he used to say, 'that old Depression's not going to get us.' And the Depression did pass and it did not get us."

This father had the faith and determination that made things happen. He made good things happen because he had in-depth enthusiasm for something basic, and he possessed motivation, incentive to action, and perseverance. And moreover, he had those good old five Gs going for him—grit, gumption, guts, grace, and God. It's pretty hard to turn out a loser if you stay with that combination.

What a tremendous theme, the dynamic fact that enthusiasm, when lodged deeply in the human mind, becomes a powerful activating factor that makes great events take place, causes amazing things to happen. Believers, positive thinkers, enthusiasts—these people do big things.

ONE OF THE WORLD'S GREATEST POSITIVE THINKERS

Let us take, for example, one of the world's greatest positive thinkers and practitioners of enthusiasm. It was not in America, traditional home of positive thinkers and enthusiasts, that I met this man, but rather in the wilderness of Judea, where long ago John the Baptist preached. His name was Musa Alami, and he made the desert to blossom as the rose—a desert which in all the history of the world had never blossomed heretofore. He succeeded because he believed that he could, and kept at it until he did, which, of course, is the way you succeed at anything.

Musa, a young Arab, was educated at Cambridge and came back to Palestine where he became a well-to-do man; that is, by Middle Eastern standards. Then in the political turmoil he lost everything, including his home.

He went beyond Jordan to the edge of Jericho. Stretching away on either side was the great, bleak, arid desert of the Jordan Valley, the lowest spot on earth—1,290 feet below sea level. In the far distance to the left, shimmering in the hot haze, loomed the mountains of Judea, and to the right, the Mountains of Moab.

With the exception of a few oases, nothing had ever been cultivated in this hot and weary land and all the experts said that no crop could be raised, for how could you bring in water? To dam the Jordan River for irrigation was too expensive and besides, there was no friendly power to finance such a project.

"What about underground water?" asked Musa Alami. Long and loud they laughed. Who ever heard of such a thing? There was no water under that hot, dry desert. That sandy waste of parched earth had lain there since the beginning of time. And having been covered ages ago by Dead Sea water, the sand was full of salt, which further added to its aridity.

Musa, meditating, saw the shimmering surface of the Dead Sea nearby and agreed that the saltiness of the earth was indeed a problem. But what were problems for but to be solved? God, so he reasoned, had made it a good earth even here and all that was necessary was to bring life-giving water to it.

He had heard of the amazing rehabilitation of the California desert through subsurface water. He decided that he could find water here also. So sure was he that he went ahead and mapped out roads for a ranch where he intended to establish a school for refugee boys. All the old-time Bedouin sheiks said it couldn't be done, government officials agreed, and so did solemn scientists from abroad. There was absolutely no water there.

But Musa was unimpressed. He thought there was. A few poverty-stricken refugees from the nearby Jericho Refugee Camp helped him as he started to dig. With well-drilling equipment? Not on your life. With plain old picks and shovels. Everybody laughed as this dauntless man and his ragged friends dug away day after day, week after week, month after month. Slowly they went down deep into the sand where no man since creation had plumbed for water.

For six months they dug. Then one day the sand became moist, and finally water gushed forth. Life-giving water had been found in the ancient desert! And they who had known the burning sands for centuries could not speak, so great was their wonder and gratitude. They did not laugh or cheer. They wept.

A very old man, sheik of a nearby village, heard the amazing news. He came to see for himself. "Musa," he asked, "have you really found water? Let me see it and feel it and taste it."

The old man put his hand in the stream, splashed it over his face, put it on his tongue. "It is sweet and cool," he said. "It is good water." Then placing his aged hands on the shoulder of Musa Alami he said, "Thank God. Now, Musa, you can die." This was the simple tribute of a desert man to a positive thinker who did what everyone said could not be done.

Now, several years later, Musa Alami has many wells supplying a ranch three miles long and two miles wide. He raises vegetables, bananas, figs, citrus fruit and boys. In his school, he is cultivating citizens of the future, farmers and technicians, experts in the trades. Produce is flown to Kuwait, Bahrein, Beirut, as well as to nearby Jerusalem. Imitating Musa, others have also dug until now many thousands of acres are under cultivation and green growth is spreading over the ancient sands of the onetime desert.

I asked this amazing man what kept him going, kept him believing when everyone said it couldn't be done. "There was no alternative. It had to be done," he said and added, "God helped me."

As twilight turned the Mountain of Moab and the Judean Hills to red and gold, I sat watching a huge stream of water gush from the heart of the desert. And as it splashed into a deep, wide pool, it seemed to say, "It can be done, it can be done." So don't let your difficulties get you down and do not believe those malcontents who say you cannot do it. Remember Musa Alami, positive thinker of the wilderness of Judea. And remember that enthusiasm is the powerful drive that makes things happen. Enthusiasm makes a difference in the wilderness of Judea, just as it can make a difference in the wilderness of many people's lives.

The thrilling fact is that there are people who have a sound, solid, irrepressible enthusiasm for real values and are willing to give all of themselves to attain the goal they're enthusiastic about.

ENTHUSIASM AND THE FIRST MOTOR

Henry Ford had a burning enthusiasm for the motor car. People said he was "touched." He was; he was touched by enthusiasm and the object of his enthusiasm took shape. Edison was enthusiastic about electric light and the talking machine and a lot of other inventions, and due to his insatiable motivation they all happened. The Wright brothers were enthusiastic about a machine that would fly. It flew. Kettering was enthusiastic about a self-starter and about paint that could be sprayed on automobiles, which of course "they" said could not be done—but both were done. Continue with the list right up to the present day, for the principle still withstands the acid test—what you are enthusiastic about can happen.

But invariably someone comes up with the pious reproof that it is wrong to encourage people to hope for something they cannot attain, that only the gifted, the well-favored can attain the goals. But such individuals are wrong, as usual, the plain fact being that any person, however seemingly impossible his circumstances, who develops enthusiasm for something and the fortitude to carry it out can make the most utterly astonishing things happen.

NOBODY COULD DO IT, BUT HE DID

For example, if you entertain the foolish notion there is something you cannot accomplish because of vast odds and obstacles, consider the following story by an African boy, Legson Kayira, from our magazine *Guideposts*. His amazing story is called *Barefoot to America*.

"My mother did not know where America was. I said to her, 'Mother, I want to go to America to go to college. Will you give me your permission?'

" 'Very well,' she said. 'You may go. When will you leave?'

"I did not want to give her time to discover from others in our village how far away America was, for fear that she would change her mind.

" 'Tomorrow,' I said.

" 'Very well,' she said, 'I will prepare some maize for you to eat along the way.'

"Next day, October 14, 1958, I left my home in the village of Mpale, in northern Nyasaland, East Africa. I had only the clothes I wore, a khaki shirt and shorts. I carried the two treasures I owned: a Bible and a copy of *Pilgrim's Progress*. I carried, too, the maize my mother had given me, wrapped in banana leaves, and a small ax for protection.

"My goal was a continent and an ocean away, but I did not doubt that I would reach it.

"I had no idea how old I was. Such things mean little in a land where time is always the same. I suppose I was 16 or 18.

"My father died when I was very young. In 1952 my mother listened to the words of the missionaries of the Church of Scotland (Presbyterian), with the results that our family became Christian. From the missionaries, I learned not only to love God, but also that if I was ever to be of value to my village, my people, my country, it would be necessary for me to have an education.

"At Wenya, eight miles away, was a mission primary school. One day when I felt I was ready to study, I walked there.

"I learned many things. I learned I was not, as most Africans believed, the victim of my circumstances but the master of them. I learned that, as a Christian, I had an obligation to use the talents God had given me to make life better for others.

"Later, in high school, I learned about America. I read the life of Abraham Lincoln and grew to love this man who suffered so much to help the enslaved Africans in his country. I read, too, the autobiography of Booker T. Washington, himself born in slavery in America, who had risen in dignity and honor to become a benefactor of his people and his country.

"I gradually realized that it would be only in America that I would receive the training and opportunities to prepare myself to emulate these men in my own land, to be, like them, a leader, perhaps even the president of my country.

"My intention was to make my way to Cairo, where I hoped to get passage on a ship to America. Cairo was over 3,000 miles away, a distance I could not comprehend, and I foolishly thought I could walk it in four or five days. In four or five days, I was about 25 miles from home, my food was gone, I had no money, and I did not know what to do, except that I must keep going.

"I developed a pattern of travel that became my life for more than a year. Villages were usually five or six miles apart, on forest paths. I would arrive at one in the afternoon and ask if I could work to earn food, water and a place to sleep. When this was possible, I would spend the night there, then move on to the next village in the morning.

"It was not always possible. Tribal languages change every few miles in Africa; often I was among people with whom I could not communicate. This clearly made me a stranger to them, perhaps an enemy; they would not let me into the villages, and I had to sleep in the forests, eating herbs and wild fruit.

"I soon discovered that my ax sometimes gave people the impression I had come to fight or to steal, so I bartered the ax for a knife I could carry unseen. I was actually defenseless against the forest animals I dreaded, but although I heard them at night none of them approached me. Malaria mosquitos, however, were constant companions, and I often was sick.

"But two comforts sustained me: my Bible and my *Pilgrim's Progress.* Over and over again I read my Bible, particularly finding confidence in the promise 'Trust in the Lord with all thine heart, and lean not unto thine own understanding. . . . Then shalt thou walk in thy way." (Proverbs 3:5, 23)

"By the end of 1959, I had walked 1,000 miles to Uganda, where a family took me in and I found a job making bricks for government buildings. I remained there six months and I sent most of my earnings to my mother.

"In *Pilgrim's Progress,* I read many times of the tribulations of the Christian who wandered through the wilderness seeking God, and I compared this to my own wanderings toward the goal I believed God had put into my heart. I could not give up, any more than the Christian had given up.

"One afternoon at the USIS library in Kampala, I unexpectedly came upon a directory of American colleges. Opening it at random, I saw the name of Skagit Valley College, Mount Vernon, Washington. I had heard that American colleges sometimes gave scholarships to deserving Africans, so I wrote Dean George Hodson and applied for one. I realized that I might be refused but I was not discouraged. I would write to one school after another in the directory until I found one that would help me.

"Three weeks later, Dean Hodson replied: I was granted a scholarship and the school would help me find a job. Overjoyed, I went to the American authorities, only to be told that this was not enough. I would need a passport and the round-trip fare in order to obtain a visa.

"I wrote to the Nyasaland government for a passport but it was refused because I could not tell them when I was born. I then wrote to the missionaries who had taught me in my childhood, and it was through their efforts that I was granted a passport. But I still could not get the visa at Kampala because I did not have the fare.

"Still determined, I left Kampala and resumed my trip northward. So strong was my faith that I used my last money to buy my first pair of shoes. I knew I could not walk into Skagit Valley College in my bare feet. I carried the shoes to save them.

"Across Uganda and into the Sudan, the villages were farther apart and the people were less friendly to me. Sometimes I had to walk 20 or 30 miles in a day to find a place to sleep or to work to earn some food. At last I reached Khartoum, where I learned that there was an American consulate and I went there to try my luck.

"Once again I heard about the entrance requirements, this time from Vice-Consul Emmett M. Coxson, but Mr. Coxson wrote the college about my plight. Back came a cable.

"The students hearing about me and my problems, had raised the fare of $1,700 through benefit parties.

"I was thrilled and deeply grateful; overjoyed that I had judged Americans correctly for their friendship and brotherhood. I was thankful to God for His guidance and I pledged my future to His service.

"News that I had walked for over two years and 2,500 miles circulated in Khartoum. The Communists came to me and offered to send me to school in Yugoslavia, all expenses paid, including travel, and a subsistence during my studies.

" 'I am a Christian,' I told them, 'and I could not be educated into the kind of man I want to be in your godless schools.'

"They warned me that, as an African, I would have racial difficulties in the United States, but I had read enough in American newspapers to feel this was a diminishing factor. My religion had taught me that men are not perfect, but as long as they strive to be they will be pleasing to God. The American effort, I felt, was why the land was so blessed.

"In December, 1960, carrying my two books and wearing my first suit, I arrived at Skagit Valley College.

"In my speech of gratitude to the student body, I disclosed my desire to become prime minister or president of my country, and I noticed some smiles. I wondered if I had said something naïve. I do not think so.

"When God has put an impossible dream in your heart, He means to help you fulfill it. I believed this to be true when, as an African bush boy, I felt compelled to become an American college graduate. This became true when I graduated from the University of Washington. And if God has given me the dream of becoming president of Nyasaland, this too, will become true.

"It is when we resist God that we remain nothing. When we submit to Him, whatever the sacrifice or hardship, we can become far more than we dare dream."

This remarkable story, this "utterly impossible" experience, demonstrates how enthusiasm acted as the powerful motivation to make something tremendous take place. I wonder why everyone does not realize and predicate his actions on the fact that enthusiasm does activate the greatest possible achievements. So many could be spared the dullness of mediocrity, the frustration of failure, the loss of hope, if only they would cultivate the amazing power of enthusiasm.

Some people not in the know regard the job of a minister as lacking in color, romance and dramatic achievement, but believe me, the principle of enthusiasm as the motivating factor that makes things happen operates in this field as elsewhere.

Take, for example, the case of Dr. Robert H. Schuller, who was sent by the Reformed Church in America, the oldest Protestant denomination in the United States, the religious body to which I myself belong, into Orange County, California, to establish a church. In this county, said to be the fastest-growing in the nation, our denomination had not one single member. Schuller was given a modest salary and $500 for promotion and told to start a church. But Dr. Schuller was as long on enthusiasm as he was short on money, and he had a powerful motivation. He wanted to build a great, modern church in the midst of a teeming population explosion.

So he leased a drive-in movie theater for Sunday morning services and by attractive advertising began to build a congregation out of the people that were flocking into Southern California. He gave them friendship and the inspiration of the Gospel. A year after he began from scratch, I spoke at his invitation to thousands of people seated in their cars. He told with conviction about the "great" church that was to be. I knew then it would be in fact, for it already existed in his mind, and he had the energy, ingenuity and the faith to bring it to pass.

Ten years later, Dr. Schuller invited me to return to speak, this time in a shining modern structure of steel and glass set on twenty acres which were planted with grass and flowers and dotted with splashing fountains falling musically into pools of water. Now he had over 3,000 members, an average attendance Sunday mornings of more than 4,000 persons who packed the church and adjoining gardens, still other hundreds listening in cars that overflowed the huge parking area. I helped turn the earth for the "Tower of Hope," a graceful soaring ten-story structure where trained counselors will help the troubled find peace and a constructive way of life.

As I looked at the vast congregation both inside and outside the glorious church and its lovely gardens, I realized once again the tremendous fact that enthusiasm is indeed the powerful motivation to make things happen.

9

ENTHUSIASM BUILDS POWER UNDER YOUR DIFFICULTIES

Suppose you must face extra hard difficulties and problems. Are you then expected to practice enthusiasm? If so, how can you? Well, that is just the kind of situation in which enthusiasm comes into its own, when it really goes to work and produces big results. For enthusiasm builds power under difficulties—under all difficulties.

Let's get down to cases. Let me tell you about a friend who had enough enthusiasm and faith and courage to lick two extra-sized difficulties—alcoholism and cancer.

His name is J. Arch Avary, Jr., and he is one of the best known and most highly regarded citizens of a large southern city. His story, for sheer courage, faith in the Lord and enthusiasm, can scarcely be matched. His difficulties were overcome by the power of enthusiasm, and it was an enthusiasm for something specific, namely, his faith in Jesus Christ and God. He is an example of the astonishing power that can be built under any difficulty.

Incidentally, I wrote to one of those professors who teach the "God is dead" theory and asked how he would explain the rehabilitation of Arch Avary on the basis of God being dead. He replied to the effect that God had nothing to do with this amazing comeback: Avary was rehabilitated by what this theological babe in the woods called "the caring community." This was a grim joke. The community couldn't have cared less. In fact, the "caring community" kicked the poor fellow in the teeth.

Mr. Avary granted me permission to use his dramatic personal story, saying: "Your other books helped me, and I should certainly want my experience to help others."

Arch Avary, at twenty, was elected secretary of the Central Florida Institute of Banking and at twenty-one became its president—which I believe is still a record in United States banking circles. From then on his rise in banking was meteoric. At twenty-seven, he became an officer of the First National Bank of his city. In the Air Force during World War II, he rose quickly to rank of colonel. Back at First National again, regardless of his knowledge of banking and wide acquaintance in the industry, he was fired in 1956 for excessive drinking.

HE HIT BOTTOM WITH A BANG

His decline was as rapid as his rise had been. He really hit bottom. His wife filed for divorce. He was broke. Each job, poorer than the last, had the same result. He was fired for being a drunk.

Arch describes his skid to the bottom thus: "Drawing blanks brought on my greatest fear. Spending much of my time at two social clubs and at their bars, I saw many influential people each day. When they would see me in the bank the day following a big night, and would mention a subject we had discussed, and about which I could not recall one thing, I would suffer a cold chill along with a great wave of fear. I didn't know what I had said and what might result from it.

"As this experience repeated itself, and my nerves began to show strain, I required more liquor in order to calm down, and that produced more dire results. This went on for nearly ten years when I was in a senior position, very close personally and officially to the president of the then largest bank in the Southeast. The president was 'retired' early and in about a year he put a pistol in his mouth and ended his life. This should have sobered me, but it didn't. About two years later I was 'retired' for the same reason."

Those who knew the facts tell me that Avary, but for this weakness, would have become president of one of the greatest banks in the country. Instead, he was forced to walk the streets panhandling from friends and former associates; anyone who could spare a handout.

He knew he had to take himself in hand so he committed himself to a state institution for alcoholics and soon was wearing the uniform of an inmate. He was set to washing dishes, but apparently he was a failure at this too. After he had finished the first dishwashing chore, the woman in charge told him that her father was a trackworker on the same railroad of which he had been a director. She said, "Arch Avary, you have been a big banker, and a railroad director who went to West Point on the front of a locomotive with a special train. Fire sirens blew and flags were waving to celebrate the centennial of the Atlanta and West Point Railroad. But today you are a plain inmate of this institution and an ordinary drunkard like the rest. So get your hands back into that dishwater and get those dishes clean that you left in such awful condition."

A HOBO WHO KNEW HIS STUFF

Arch was rocked by this experience, which had a therapeutic effect upon him. A few days later while the ex-banker and ex-railroad director was raking leaves on the institution grounds (another job which made him do some more basic thinking), he began talking with a fellow inmate, a hobo who confessed he had often "ridden the rods" on Avary's railroad without benefit of ticket. The hobo, a thoughtful fellow, commented on Arch's membership on the official board of the First Methodist Church. "Avary," he said, "I like you a lot but I have been wondering. I have no religion. Don't want any, and know very little about it. But I would like to know what kind of religion you have that would let you wind up in a place like this, same as I?"

"I didn't sleep that night," Avary declares, "and it dawned on me that if a professional tramp in a state institution for alcoholics believed my religion needed to be reexamined, it was high time I was doing the same thing. I saw that my so-called religion was only part of a pattern—like belonging to the Piedmont Driving Club, the Capital City and Breakfast Club, like wearing the gray flannel suit, the mark of a successful banker. Mine was no religion at all; it was a sham and it broke down, so I landed in a state institution for alcoholics."

Avary resolved to find some real religion and he went all out to get it. "As I walked through those iron gates at Briarcliff, something walked out of there with me, stronger than man, because I have never since had the slightest desire to touch a drop of alcohol. And for a man who consumed over a fifth a day for over ten years, I submit that I do have a faith that has been made real and rewarding.

"When I walked under that iron arch over those massive gates," Arch continues his story, "I stopped and looked back and asked the good Lord to give me strength and courage to straighten out my life. If he would do that, I would do my part in working at it and begin to pay off my debt by constructive service in the vineyard of the Master. I have been at it ever since. I asked the Lord for an opportunity to get my chaotic life straightened out. I had to take over the running of my life like I knew it should be run.

"When I left Briarcliff," he continues, "I returned to my old hometown. I was broke, and had very few friends, and didn't deserve any. My wife was suing me for divorce. For the next six months, I stayed with my father and mother. I didn't go anyplace except to church which was located next door to my home. I had a circuit that I walked every day which was about twelve miles. I would stop at the foot of Pine Mountain and sit in the old spring house from which I drank as a boy. I got me some cedar and white pine that I would whittle. As I sat there in the spring house whittling, I could hear the train whistles blow and I would think about that old hobo back at Briarcliff when he asked: 'What sort of religion do you have?' "

HE STOPPED RUNNING FROM HIMSELF

"For the past twenty-five years I had been running from something, mostly from myself. You can't run from anything, particularly yourself. As I sat there the first two or three days I was nervous and jittery, until all of a sudden a Bible verse came to my mind, 'Be still and know that I am God.' My nervousness left me and I haven't had it since. During those days of whittling at Pine Mountain, I made the greatest discovery of my life. I discovered a man named Arch Avary from whom I had been running for many years. When I really got to know him, I found out that basically he was a fairly decent person who had been on the wrong track for a long time.

"I did a lot of thinking and walking in those six months. Every day at Pine Mountain I conferred with myself for at least an hour. While I was wrestling with my chances to make a comeback and reestablish myself, I was indulging in a lot of soul-searching. I didn't have much courage, but one day this verse from the Bible came to my mind, 'If God be for us, who can be against us?' This gave me a lot of encouragement. The more

I thought about it, the more I thought that with the help of the good Lord I could do anything I made up my mind to do. Another verse came to me, 'Commit thy way unto the Lord; trust also in Him; and He shall bring it to pass,' and this gave me a lot of encouragement.

"About ten years before this, my mother had given me two of Dr. Norman Vincent Peale's books hoping these might bring me to my senses. I had never cracked them. But now I began to read *Faith Is the Answer** and *The Power of Positive Thinking*. One day the thought occurred to me that if I really believe faith is the answer, I could take this philosophy and combine it with the power of positive thinking and make a package deal out of it. I tried it. It won!"

Well, one thing is sure, Arch Avary found faith; not a vague faith but a powerful life-changing faith in Jesus Christ. As he himself eloquently expresses it: "First and foremost my soul has been saved. I am blissfully happy." I have known many enthusiastic Christians in my experience but no one more so than this man.

But this new-found faith, this happiness and life change which came to Mr. Avary were in for a formidable test. He moved back up the business ladder and in due course was once again one of the leading bankers of his city. Quite a feat when he had been told that the chances of his returning to the business life of his community was in the ratio of ten thousand to one, so badly had he wrecked his career. But now he was sober, keen, competent, once again outstanding in business and religious influence. He was asked to speak before all kinds of groups, telling them how God can change lives and free men from any defeat. His enthusiasm was boundless.

FIRST ALCOHOLISM THEN CANCER

And then the blow came. He had cancer of the colon. Years before a friend of his had had a colostomy. Arch was so moved that he vowed if ever he came to this state, he would end his misery with a pistol. So this tragic news was expected to unnerve him; would he reach for the bottle again? That was an erroneous assumption, for now he had faith and spiritual power to hold him steady. He had a new enthusiasm that made

* *Faith Is the Answer* by Norman Vincent Peale and Smiley Blanton, Prentice-Hall, Inc., 1950.

a big difference. In fact, after being told of his cancer, he went to Sea Island to speak to a group of a thousand women bankers. At the convention, he attended several cocktail parties and was urged by some unthinking people to take something to "steady the shock" but he did not need anything beyond the new power within him.

"The fact that I had no desire for a drink under these circumstances convinced me that I was pretty well cured," he observed. Indeed the astonishing thing is that he had so licked his problem, the problem being himself, that not only was he without fear, but he was also in firm control of his new tragedy as well. In fact, he turned his colostomy, which he defines as a "hole in the stomach" into an asset. He uses the daily irrigation time of an hour and a half for reading, study, prayer and meditation.

"When they removed the bandage from my stomach and put a plastic receptacle on it, I couldn't look at it," he said. "My doctor suggested that I change this receptacle instead of letting the nurses do it, because the sooner I got used to doing so the better off I would be. I balked for four or five days, but finally made up my mind that I had to live with this thing.

"When I made the decision to face my problem and look at that hole in my side and not let it scare me, I won one of the greatest victories of my life. Changing that receptacle one time changed me, and gave me confidence that opened a new vista of sunshine to an otherwise dark outlook—the courage to face unpleasant things.

"I decided I was going to live with this hole in my stomach and make it a blessing instead of a curse. I recalled preachers talking about Paul and his infirmities. I figured if the greatest man in Christendom next to Jesus Christ could use his infirmities and do what he did, that I could make mine an inspiration also and try to use it to the best advantage. I never had any idea that I was a Paul, but I did agree with what he wrote to the Philippians, 'I can do all things through Christ which strengtheneth me.'

"I had read many times Norman Vincent Peale's book *The Power of Positive Thinking*. It was so helpful in my troubles with alcohol, I read it again and renewed my inspiration and determination to face again and master a difficult problem."

Well, for several years now Arch Avary, ex-alcoholic, ex-panhandler, ex-cancer victim—now cancer victor—has been president of the state cancer society. He is an enthusiastic and compelling speaker and has saved hundreds of lives by persuading people to have examinations.

THE WORST TROUBLE COMES TO THE BEST MEN

Eugene Patterson, editor of the *Atlanta Constitution*, says of Mr. Avary: "A man like that just might defeat anything. Maybe the worst trouble comes to the best men because they can handle it."

What is your difficulty or problem? Whatever it is, you can handle it. Do as Avary did and get yourself some real faith. Go far beyond formal belief in God; really go into faith in depth. Out of it will come dynamic enthusiasm and you will have the same kind of strength, and gain the same fabulous victory. Never settle for any defeat. Stand up to your difficulty courageously with lots of faith, and let enthusiasm put power under it. With God's help you can lick your difficulties and problems.

Put this one great fact in mind: God himself is on the side of the enthusiastic believer. That being true, how can you lose?

Consider, for example, the case of a man named Ed Furgol who became one of the greatest golfers in the history of this popular sport. When Ed was ten years old, he fell from a swing onto a concrete pavement, landing hard on his left elbow, which was driven up through the skin, projecting out of the arm. He was rushed to the hospital, where everything was done that could have been for the little boy. But he found himself with a left arm nearly ten inches shorter than the other. The traumatic effects of such an accident on a normal, vigorous ten-year-old boy might have been great indeed. But these were overcome by a vital power that had captured his mind: enthusiasm. His enthusiasm was for golf. He actually had a burning and consuming ambition to become U.S. Open Champion. But how pathetic, how utterly unrealistic can one get? Someone must gently remove such ideas from the mind of this poor kid with a hopelessly withered shortened arm. Thus people must have talked sadly. And, of course, the average, negative person would have folded completely in the presence of such a handicap.

But Ed Furgol was of a different breed. He had some immense assets working for him. When he added them up, they outbalanced in his mind that withered arm. And what were those assets? One was a goal, not a fuzzy vague sort of goal, which of course is not a goal at all; but a specific, clearly defined objective, to be a golf champion. Crippled arm or not, that was what he wanted, what he expected for sure. He believed in himself. He was convinced that with God's help and his own efforts, painful though they surely would be, he could manage to put the golf ball where it was supposed to go. And he knew that anyone who could do that could become champion. Difficulties or no difficulties, he intended to be champion.

DON'T BE AN IF THINKER—BE A HOW THINKER

Ed had another asset, an important one. He was not an *if* thinker. He was a *how* thinker. The *if* thinker says: "If I hadn't done that . . . If it had not happened to me . . . If only I'd had a better break"—one hopeless *if* after another. Well, this so-called handicapped boy bypassed all the *ifs* and emphasized the *hows*. He asked himself, *How* do I compensate for this short arm? *How* do I get my whole body into the shot? Yes, *how* do I become champion? All of which underscores the fact that Ed Furgol had the quality of enthusiasm which generates power under difficulty. Difficulty was what he had for fair, but his enthusiasm canceled out difficulty.

He had to compensate for his short arm by using his whole body in a golf shot. He had a kind of hacking motion as he went at the ball. But he brought the whole body into a flow so that its full weight hit the ball. Observers say that until one got used to it, Ed did look a bit pathetic playing alongside some of the most magnificent physical specimens in the United States. Here was this boy with a ten-inch differential in one arm trying to play big-time golf.

Before the big competition, he was awakened in the night, he tells us, by a voice which seemed to whisper in his ear, "Ed, tomorrow you will be the Open Golf champion." The next day the *how* thinker, the handicapped lad with the enthusiasm that makes the difference, did become champion.

Reporters asked Ed to predict future champions, suggesting names. "No, he'll never make it," Ed said of the first person they suggested.

"Why will he never make it?"

"Because he hasn't suffered enough."

A second name was mentioned. Again, he shook his head, "No, he'll never make it either."

"Why not?" they asked.

"Because he's never been hungry enough."

Of a third, he said, "He won't be champion ever, because he has never been defeated enough."

It seemed that none of these golfers had enough trouble or experience or the enthusiasm that makes the difference. It takes struggle, a goal, and enthusiasm to make a champion.

Well what is *your* ten-inch-short arm? Maybe it is not a physical handicap but a weakness of mental attitude or a defect in your arm of faith. Most of us do not appreciate the power of faith in helping people be what God meant them to be, and what they want to be. By the power of God, anybody can be free from any weakness; anyone can be released to creative living, no matter what obstacle stands in his way.

To believe this is an essential qualification of the person who desires to move forward in this life. It is a fact that difficulty does help to make strong people, and happy ones, because in the long run no one can be either strong or happy or efficient who has not had rough spots knocked off by the refining process of living.

ENTHUSIASM AND THE TUMBLING BARREL

Ever hear of a tumbling barrel? Well, I had not either, until Andrew van der Lyn, a friend in the manufacturing business, told me about it. Some ideas he got from tumbling barrels helped him to overcome difficulties so successfully that I became interested in his philosophy of relating difficulty to enthusiasm. A tumbling barrel is an industrial device for smoothing newly made pieces of metal. It is a cask or drum equipped to revolve at a predetermined speed. In it are put steel castings or manufactured metal pieces. An abrasive such as powdered alumina or Carborundum, is put into the barrel; or maybe sand, rubber pellets or steel balls, depending upon the character and hardness of the metal parts. In some cases water is added.

The tumbling barrel is then rotated. With each revolution the metal pieces are carried part way up the side of the drum; then they fall free and drop back down. As they tumble and spill against each other and are rubbed by the abrasive, the burrs disappear and the rough edges are smoothed. They are then in shape to function properly.

This ingenious process strongly suggests the way men are tumbled about in life. We come into the world with burrs and edges characteristic of raw newness. But as we go along, we tumble against each other and also rub against hardships and difficulties. This affects us much as the abrasives in tumbling barrels affect new pieces of metal. Such friction and attrition make for a rounding and maturing of personalities.

There are well-meaning people who believe that life is too harsh. They are the ones who would like to plan and arrange the world so that no one need suffer. But without struggle, how could the end product of personality be achieved? How could a person become rounded and mature and strong?

When you realize that not only are trouble and suffering inevitable, but serve a definite creative purpose as well, you are upgrading your philosophy of human existence. You no longer waste time complaining or pitying yourself, getting resentful or giving in to discouragement. You gradually learn to take difficulties as part of the maturing process. So when the going gets tough, take the attitude that rough spots are being knocked off, that you are being shaped for the real purpose of your life.

This shaping process makes men. As tough and unpleasant as difficulty may be, it is the source of potential development. Surround every difficulty with prayer, with faith and with straight thinking. Then let enthusiasm build power under it. On this basis, you can handle any situation that can ever develop.

AIRLINE HOSTESS FACES DEATH—BUT—

Let me tell you about a young woman who certainly did get shaken about in the tumbling barrel. But a long acquaintance with God developed such a sense of inner victory in her mind that even a terrifying experience could not overwhelm her.

Jackie Myers, airline hostess, did not foresee on that beautiful morning when she walked out to a huge jet on the runway that within moments she would face the greatest crisis of her life. For shortly after takeoff, Jackie suddenly found herself face-to-face with death. At what seemed certain to be her last moment a remarkable realization came to her; that she had such faith and enthusiasm for God that she could even meet death without fear.

"Eleven minutes after takeoff," Miss Myers says, "our beautiful, huge, shiny jet went into a nosedive. We were 249,000 pounds of weight hurtling through space. We went into a dive at 19,000 feet and it wasn't until 40 seconds later that the captain pulled us out of it at 5,000 feet—just 8 seconds before we would have crashed!

"As we pulled out of the dive, the No. 3 engine tore out of the wing and dropped to earth. No. 4 was hanging by a few bolts. We lost most of our hydraulic fluid and a lot of electrical power. Several other mechanical failures developed.

"But our captain landed that powerful plane at an Air Force field as gently as one would handle a newborn baby. Had eggs lined the runway, they would hardly have been damaged. It was truly the greatest miracle I shall ever experience."

Jackie Myers tells of her feelings and thoughts in those agonizing forty seconds during which the plane was in a nosedive. It is said that a person can relive a large part of his life in a few seconds. Here is an instance of it.

"When we started to encounter turbulence, I ran to my jump seat in the tail of the plane. I was thrown off balance and grabbed onto a shelf when we nosed over. At first I just couldn't believe it was happening. I knew our pilots were superbly skillful. I felt certain they would be able to pull us out of it.

"But the fact was unmistakable—we were smoothly and quietly plunging through space. I became very close to God when I accepted this. I felt no fear. I thought of a beloved aunt who always says a little prayer for me every night. I thought how happy I was to have been a small part of our church. I thought how strongly I had endorsed the power of positive thinking and the Golden Rule. At no time did I experience fear. I was so happy about my life including religion. I did tell God there were so many things I wanted to do yet. I wanted to stay just a little while longer. I said, 'Lord, I never got my happy marriage and my happy family.'

"But we were still hurtling downward and I reluctantly terminated my conversation with God. I accepted the fact that we would be blown to bits upon impact. I added a little P.S. to God: 'If this is the way You want it, Lord, I guess this is the way it's going to be.' Then suddenly the plane righted! I could hardly believe my senses but it was real. We were flying merrily along on a level."

Later she said, "I found in this terrible experience that by positive thinking and right thinking from day to day, you can develop an inner condition that will sustain you through life's worst ordeals and roughest moments."

And that inner condition needed by everyone is a spiritually dynamic faith, and with it enthusiasm that builds power under difficulties. These change people so much that changed people change situations.

A businessman was having a hard time of it, and, in a dark mood, he told a friend that he was thinking of blowing his brains out.

"Why not blow your brains *up* rather than out?"

Startled, the depressed man asked, "What do you mean?"

"Get your brains blown up, full of enthusiasm," the other replied.

He got the discouraged fellow to attend Marble Collegiate Church where he became reactivated spiritually. Result: this man now has power, the kind that comes from spiritualized enthusiasm. When he started blowing his brains *up* rather than out, he made the amazing discovery that there was real potential in his brain. With so many new constructive ideas, he has gone on to become an executive in his company. When in his case spiritualized enthusiasm took over, it drove out the depression that had nearly taken his life. But instead of losing his life, he found it. Difficulties no longer bothered him for he had the enthusiasm that built power under them.

The real secret of dealing with difficulties is a proper conditioning of the mind. Anyone can make his mind perform as desired by conditioning it to thoughts of faith, courage, enthusiasm and joy. I do not minimize the harsh, cruel, and extremely difficult experiences that people have. But if while depending on the help of God you really try to build a dynamic spirit of victory under your problems, you will gain a new power over them. Let me tell you of two people whose lives demonstrated this truth.

A woman, a brilliant individual, suffered a sudden stroke. She recovered about fifty percent of the use of her members. She was deeply depressed. But ultimately she returned to her job as school principal. During her illness, she asked, "Give me a few words to say that will help me to have courage." I told her about Dr. Paul DuBois, the great Viennese psychotherapist who taught the therapy of words. He himself used to repeat the word *indomitable.* I also told her about the famous doctor who used the word *acquiescence.* I said that the word I like is *imperturbable* and that I repeat it often to myself. She wrote me, "I have a better word than any of those. It is the word *rugged.*" She said, "I say it over to myself, rugged, rugged. Nothing can defeat me."

But the greatest words of all to put into your mind are those of the Scriptures such as (1) "Who shall separate us from the love of Christ?" (2) "I can do all things through Christ who strengtheneth me." (3) "If God be for us, who can be against us." (4) "In all these things we are more than conquerors through Him that loved us."

Next time you are faced with a difficulty, open the Great Book, pick out words like these, commit them to memory, repeat them until they take possession of your mind. Your mind will give you back exactly what you put into it. If over a long period, you put defeat into your mind, your mind will give you back defeat. If over a long period you put into your mind great words of faith, your mind will give them back to you.

A friend was in a hospital. He had had one leg amputated some years ago and recently the second leg was taken off. This man told me that he had the phantom foot. Though his foot was off he could still feel it and still wanted to move his toes. This could have produced a nervous and tense reaction. But this man was so happy, so enthusiastic that nothing defeated him. He was the life of the hospital.

I said to him, "Everyone tells me you are the happiest person in this hospital. You are not putting it on, are you?"

"No, no, I am as happy as can be."

"Let me in on your secret," I asked.

"Do you see that little book lying over there on the table?"

It was the Bible. He said, "There is where I get my medicine. When I feel a little low, I just read the Book and after I have read some of these great words I am happy again."

A drunken man came into the hospital looking for a friend and staggered around the ward with a bunch of flowers. Finally he said, "I cannot find my friend, but if I find a happy man in this hospital, I am going to give him my flowers."

The nurses were anxious to be rid of this unwelcome visitor, but they were afraid of him. They allowed him to go around peering into every room. He looked at each patient with a searching scrutiny and said, "I never saw such a gloomy bunch of people." Then he came to this man with no legs, and he put his face up close to his and looked at him for a long while. Then his brain seemed to grow sober and he said, "You have sure got something my friend. You have got what I am looking for. You are a happy man and I am going to give you my flowers."

10

THE CONTAGION OF ENTHUSIASM

"Enthusiasm, like measles, mumps and the common cold, is highly contagious," says Emory Ward.

But unlike measles and mumps and colds, enthusiasm is good for you. Hope you catch it, and good.

Recently, while writing this book, I happened to encounter Henry S., an old friend. He was favorably taken with the title. "Boy, do I go for that one," he exclaimed in his usual ebullient manner, "and you know why?" Of course I did know why, for in a small way I had a part in the change that saved Henry's life. "But don't water down what should really be said," he warned me. "It's not just enthusiasm in general that is important, but enthusiasm in particular—enthusiasm for God, for life, for people. So tell your readers for me that you're not kidding when you say that enthusiasm makes the difference. I believe there is a terrific contagion in enthusiasm."

There was reason for Henry's positive emphasis, for he had nearly become a victim to the American disease of overpressing, a malady which may be defined as anxiety-tension raised to the nth degree. The first result of his trouble was a decline in efficiency. For people work well only when there is harmony in the flow of power mentally, spiritually and physically.

To illustrate, take the case of a famous baseball pitcher who some years ago went into a lengthy slump. Normally a pitcher of excellent control, he started walking batters and was "hit all over the lot" freely. Slow-motion movies had been made of him at the peak of his performance. Now similar pictures were taken of him in the slump. They revealed that when he pitched, his right foot was about three inches advanced, and his delivery was less smooth, even jerky and tense. Psychiatric and pastoral counseling brought to light family problems of a serious nature which were worrying him, one being the necessity for more income, for greater financial resources. The pitcher's mind developed such nervous anxiety about his performance that he wasn't functioning effectively. He was tied up in the effort to make good and to justify an increase in pay which he so desperately needed. The results backfired. He was pressing too hard and he went into a slump. Pastoral and psychiatric counseling helped to reduce the problem and a satisfactory solution was brought about. The anxiety tension relaxed. The foot was drawn back, the delivery became normal, and pitching efficiency returned.

In similar manner, Henry S. had been overpressing for a good while. He had grown tense and unhappy. His natural buoyant enthusiasm had given way to a grim, hard driving, punishing pace, though he continued to mouth the jaunty jargon of the old happy, successful days that had made him a leader in the real-estate business.

Then something happened, the end result of which justified his forceful admonition to me to "lay enthusiasm on the line."

Henry S. was one of the most successful realtors in the rapidly developing section where he was "making a killing," which incidentally nearly killed him. In fact, he had a mild heart attack, a "warning," so he was told. That shook him up, but he was "a big strong guy and that stuff wasn't for him." So he passed it off as trivial and proceeded at the same fast pace, the hard sell by day and entertaining customers by night.

Result: another heart attack. This one laid him flat on his back in a darkened hospital room for several weeks. There he had opportunity to think. "I'm a damned fool," was the straightforward result of his cogitations, "and I've got to get on the common-sense beam, or the only real estate I'll be concerned with is six feet in a local cemetery."

But he wasn't as big a fool as he declaimed. He knew the score, and furthermore had a lot of basic faith, though he had not been exercising it. This parenthetically brings to mind a sign my brother, Leonard Peale, saw in a railroad station, "God isn't dead—only unemployed." So Henry came around to see me when a speaking tour brought me to his city. "What shall I do?" he asked. "I don't want to die or quit work. I want to live, and I mean live. That is to say, I don't want to be an invalid. How can I really live? Give it to me straight and I'll love you for it."

I liked his forthright spirit, and I knew God loved him too. God always loves real men like him, for He is a real God—a man-sized one, not a nicey-nice, as He is sometimes made out to be.

"O.K.," I said. "I'll give it to you straight. You better get right with God. Cut out the rough stuff in your life. Clean it up. You are better than you've been living. Surrender your life to Christ, or is that too pious for you?"

"I said I wanted it straight, and if you didn't give it to me that way, boy, would I be disappointed in you! So don't mince any words. I've asked for a real Christian treatment, and that's what I expect you to hand out," he declared resolutely.

So he opened up and spilled out all the dirt and then he asked the Lord to forgive him and "clean him up and help him go straight. I'm full of fear and tension and rot," was his plain statement to God in a simple, honest sort of prayer.

SPIRITUAL HEART TREATMENT

"But what about that old heart of mine?" he asked plaintively.

"Look, Henry," I said. "Do you recall those words of Jesus? 'Let not your heart be troubled; ye believe in God, believe also in me.' " He nodded. "Well, then," I continued, "here is what I suggest that you do. Every morning and every night, and maybe other times in between, put your hand on your heart and imagine it's the healing hand of Jesus, and say, personalizing the Scripture, 'Let not *my* heart be troubled, neither let *my* heart be afraid.' Do that and live this faith straight and joyfully, and I'll bank you for the long pull."

He looked at me wistfully and blew his nose. He didn't fool me, for I saw the tears. Anyway, he followed the suggested treatment. His tensions subsided along with his fears. His prayer was answered and peace came to him, and with it healing. It must have been a proper treatment, for it has been seven years and he is still going strong. He appears to be a healthy man, and very much alive. He has become master of the relaxed drive. He no longer overpresses. He is in that harmonious flow of body, mind and soul that was created in us, but which all too often we lose. And is he enthusiastic? Why shouldn't he be?

The contagion of his enthusiasm acts as a tonic on everyone who comes in contact with him. Few are aware of the cause, but they realize that obviously it comes from the deeper levels of spirit. This remarkable thing called the contagion of enthusiasm, this enormous fullness of joy, shows up in people who have undergone basic changes as Henry did.

CONTAGION OF ENTHUSIASM MAKES GREAT SALESMEN

For example, there is Charles Kennard, whose story of release from alcoholism many years ago I described in one of my books, though not by name. Charles Kennard is one of the most successful salesmen I have ever known, and I have spoken to scores of sales gatherings and know a host of sales people. Enthusiasm has made an enormous difference in his work and life.

Charles has sold an inspirational, interfaith magazine called *Guideposts* to a list of industrial organizations that could well be the envy of salesmen of any product or service. He has persuaded scores of hard-headed businessmen, who have a sense of responsibility and regard for people, to subscribe in enormous quantities to this inspirational publication for their employees. Charles Kennard believes that the deeply moving human interest and personal stories which *Guideposts* brings each month into some two million American homes will make better people, who will make better products, hence better business and a better country, and more important than all, a better life for everyone.

Because of his dedication, he is deeply convincing and the contagion of his enthusiasm transmits itself not merely into sales, but into the stimulation of a similar dedication in hundreds of people. As a result of his enthusiasm he has played a large part in one of the most dramatic successes in American publishing history, the development of *Guideposts*, from a small beginning to one of the most widely read and influential periodicals in the United States today. The story of Charles Kennard is an example of what the contagion of enthusiasm can do.

One of the most enthusiastic men I have ever known is Elmer G. Leterman, author of two fine books. *The Sale Begins When the Customer Says No* and *How Showmanship Sells*. Elmer is one of the great salesmen in America, and one of the most interesting personalities as well. He has boundless zest and self-reliance and a powerful lot of common sense. His contagious spirit is expressed in the following statement from his book, *How Showmanship Sells:*

"I can't fathom clock-watchers, people who regard their jobs only as a means of getting money for the things they want to do. Each working day must become a Chinese torture to them, a steady drip, drip, drip of monotony which, over the years, dehumanizes them.

"What a shame that these people do not learn that business is fun, that it combines the ingredients of all the better games and sports. And the ground rules change too often for it to become boring . . .

"When I look back over my career, I consider it one grand lark. I still go to work each day with relish. I enjoy setting new sales records—more in a day, more in a month, more in a year. I welcome the challenge of new men who appeared on the scene, threatening my old records and keeping me from becoming complacent. To me, material success without enjoyment would be no success at all."

Newspapers recently carried an account of the continuing heavy program of public service of former Governor Averell Harriman of New York. Now over seventy-five years of age, he covers the world on assignments for the President, and seems constantly imbued with zest and energy. In reply to an interviewer's question, Governor Harriman said that the secret of an active and enthusiastic life at his age was to "pick your ancestors wisely, then keep up your enthusiasm." Well, there is little we can do about our ancestors, but there is much we can do to cultivate the contagion of enthusiasm. There is no doubt it will help to keep you going strong, for in my experience the people who, like Mr. Harriman, continue to be effective despite increasing years, are those who have indeed kept up their enthusiasm.

BRANCH RICKEY'S ENTHUSIASM LEADS TO HALL OF FAME

When I get to thinking of such people, one man always comes to mind, Branch Rickey, who died at the age of eighty-three and who was recently voted into Baseball's Hall of Fame, possessed such heartening enthusiasm as few people I have ever known. Branch Rickey, onetime head of the St. Louis Cardinals, the old Brooklyn Dodgers, and the Pittsburgh Pirates, was a big, rugged, lovable man. His last words, spoken to a large audience gathered to honor him and to hear one of his marvelously unique speeches, were these: "Now I am going to tell you a story about spiritual courage . . ." Then he slumped into unconsciousness from which he did not recover.

Those final words were entirely characteristic of Branch Rickey. Spiritual conviction was what he himself had to a high degree. He was just as enthusiastic about his religion as he was about baseball, which is saying a great deal. He had his share of courage, too. For example, once when he was head of the Brooklyn Dodgers, he was at a meeting negotiating a contract for pro football at Ebbetts Field. The deal involved many thousands of dollars. But suddenly Rickey threw down his pencil, pushed back his chair and growled, "The deal's off."

Surprised, the other men asked, "But why? We are coming along well in our negotiations. There's real money for all of us in this. How come this sudden break-off?"

"Because," said Branch Rickey, staring hard under his beetle brows at one of the football men, "you've been talking about a friend of mine, and I don't like it."

"But what friend do you mean? I haven't been talking about anyone, let alone a friend of yours."

"Oh, yes, you have," replied Rickey, "you've mentioned him in almost every sentence." Thus he referred to the other's constant profane use of the name of Jesus Christ.

"I get you," said the other man slowly, "I get you. I won't do it again. You can depend upon it." To have broken off this negotiation would have cost Rickey a lot of money, but his contagious enthusiasm was not for money, but for conviction.

Later, when Branch was ill, I called on him, and the same man happened to be present also. I said a prayer. Then Branch asked his wife, this man and myself to join hands. "Now let me pray," he said. I shall never forget that prayer by the old master of baseball. It brought us all close to God. The football executive whom Rickey had rebuked could not hide the tears in his eyes. "He is the greatest human being I've ever known," he said to me afterward. He knew a man, this fellow did, when he saw one. That's the kind of spiritual courage Branch Rickey had, which helped to make him a beloved leader of men. Perhaps even more than courage made an indelible impression; it was also the contagion of spiritual enthusiasm.

I often sat in with him at the old Ebbetts Field in Brooklyn. To be Branch Rickey's guest at a game was a rare experience. His knowledge of every player was encyclopedic. He knew their characters, their families, their histories; indeed, everything about them. His conversation was an exciting blend of baseball, psychology, philosophy and religion. And Rickey was a profoundly religious man, a sturdy Christian, truly dedicated. He deserves to be one of the immortals in Baseball's Hall of Fame.

BALL PLAYER LEARNS SOME SPIRITUAL KNOW-HOW

Rickey often told me that his greatest purpose in sports was not to win games, tough competitor though he was, but to make men. He had boundless interest in his young men and was always concerned about them. Once he had a player who after every inning would rush in and telephone his wife to make sure she was at home. Rickey said to me, "Maybe he should see one of the psychiatrists at your clinic."

I asked what kind of girl the wife was. "The very best," Branch replied. "Sweet, clean, good in every sense. Completely trustworthy and loyal." If she weren't, you could be sure Branch would have known, for he knew people.

I suggested maybe the player himself was off the reservation, two-timing his wife and projecting his own disloyalty upon her. So I suggested calling the player in and delicately sounding him out. Well, Rickey did call him in, but he wasn't what could be called delicate. He said bluntly, "O.K., son, let's level. Who you running around with?"

The player had his back to the wall and knew it. "Well, Mr. Rickey, you see, it's this way. You know how it is when you're on the road with the boys. There is a lot of pressure on you. . . ."

"Sure," said Rickey, "but where are your inner braces? If you had some, they would make a man of you instead of a cheat on that fine girl you married. Well, here's the way it is. I won't tolerate that kind of character on my team, so you'd better straighten out. Or else."

But Branch Rickey also had a creative answer for the wretched young man. He said, "Now look, son, if you really want to go straight, there's someone who can help you, and you know who he is, as you were brought up a good Christian boy by godly parents." And Branch actually prayed for that player.

I had heard Mr. Rickey pray in times of personal crisis, and I never knew any man who communicated with the Lord better than he. He was a two-fisted man and his spiritual enthusiasm was a contagious thing. He brought something real into that young player's life and saved a marriage and a player too. The boy stayed on the reservation thereafter and played good ball.

I used to get many a sermon illustration from Branch, and he knew it, for he often came to my church. Once, in a game in Brooklyn a batter was thrown out at first. Rickey exploded, "The boy could have made it if he'd really tried. But," he added, "there's a sermon illustration in that for you."

"What's the illustration?" I asked.

"Why, it's obvious," said Branch. "That runner just didn't try hard enough; he didn't run that baseline with all he had. And I can give you a Bible passage to go with it, too; 'This one thing I do.' You see, that player was chewing tobacco, and enroute to first he actually expectorated."

"Yes, but what's the illustration?" I persisted.

"This one thing I do: get to first base, then spit!" grinned Branch.

Here was a rare and unforgettable man who loved life, baseball, his country and God. The contagion of his enthusiasm inspired not a few of our greatest athletes and others over the years, and the fire he ignited is still burning in many men, including the writer of this book.

The attitude of a person toward himself, that is to say, his self-image, is vitally important in the quality of performance, and in the outcome of his whole life. It is a fact, at least so I have observed, that many people hold an unreasonably low opinion of themselves. They tend to underrate themselves and to minimize their abilities. Of course, there are some who seem to have an exalted and often unwarranted high appraisal of themselves. But these are in the minority, and actually in not a few such cases, it has been my experience that what appeared to be unjustifiable egotism was, in fact, bravado to cover up an inward conviction of inferiority.

In all such cases a proper infusion of enthusiasm can make a great difference. To gain a sense of enthusiasm for one's job and a good wholesome and healthy knowledge of one's self has often made a profound change in a defeated and self-minimizing person. Expose such an individual to true self-knowledge and the contagion of enthusiasm will take hold.

THE IMPORTANCE OF ENTHUSIASM TO THE SELF-IMAGE

A rather classic example which shows the importance of a positive self-image is told by John Murphy in his book *The Secrets of Successful Selling*.

"Elmer Wheeler had been called in as a sales consultant to a certain firm . . . A certain salesman always managed to make almost exactly $5,000 per year, regardless of the territory they assigned to him or the commission he was paid.

"Because this salesman had done well in a rather small territory, he had been given a larger and much better one. But the next year his commission amounted to almost the same amount as that he had made in the smaller one—$5,000. The following year the company increased the commission paid to all salesmen, but this salesman still managed to make only $5,000. He was then assigned one of the company's poorest territories—and again made the usual $5,000.

"Wheeler had a talk with this salesman and found that the trouble was not in the territory, but in the salesman's own valuation of himself. He thought of himself as a $5,000 per year man, and as long as he held that concept of himself, outside conditions didn't seem to matter much.

"When he was assigned a poor territory, he worked hard to make that $5,000. When he was assigned a good territory, he found all sorts of excuses to coast when the $5,000 was in sight. Once, when the goal had been reached, he got sick and was unable to work any more that year, although doctors could find nothing wrong with him, and he miraculously recovered by the first of the next year."

When the salesman faced up to the fact that it was his attitude, not his salesmanship, which was holding him back, he quickly improved his record. It wasn't too long before he had doubled his yearly earnings.

Many of us are subtly bound by the same chains that held this man back. Often our low status in life is not because our abilities are inferior, but because our opinion of ourselves is inferior. Reevaluate yourself. Maybe you're a superior type who has settled for being a lesser personality. If so, make up your mind today, right now, to *re-gear* your thinking, *revise* your strategy and *rebound* from where you are to where you should be. Let the contagion of enthusiasm grip your mind. It can make all the difference.

ELEVENTH COMMANDMENT SUGGESTED

I am reminded of a stimulating observation by Amos Parrish, one of America's leaders in the merchandising field, who is a philosophical thinker as well. He says there should perhaps be eleven instead of ten commandments and suggests as the eleventh, "Thou shalt use all thy talents to the uttermost." It certainly fits the teachings of Jesus Christ, Who said He came to "preach deliverance to the captives." What captives? People behind bars in prisons? Well, maybe, but definitely, He wants to set free those who are incarcerated within their own fears, their inferiority feelings and self-doubts, who are imprisoned in their own depreciative states of mind.

And when contagious enthusiastic faith in God and in yourself releases you from the self-built prison of your mind, then you begin to change, and as you change, your whole life changes also. Buddha said, "The mind is everything. What you think you become."

Harold Robles, a successful businessman, found this to be true. "Approximately ten years ago," he said, "I was building skyscraper-sized obstacles in my mind. Nervous tension had me confused. Then a fortunate turn of events occurred which was to change my life. I will never forget the day I came to Marble Collegiate Church. It thrilled and stimulated my negative and dormant mind. I returned home exalted and free of all depressing and unhealthy thinking. My mind became alert; healthily composed, strongly directed. In time a positive concept developed within me." Harold Robles became a dynamic, spiritually reenergized man with a powerful source of enthusiasm motivating him.

The power of contagious conviction in making men, or in remaking men who have failed in their goals, is another reason that enthusiasm makes the difference. Defeat in due course comes in one way or another to everyone. So the question isn't whether or not you experience defeat, but how you handle it.

What are you going to do with defeat? Let it destroy you, or turn it into a positive, creative experience from which you can extract much know-how and wisdom; and thus gain strength to stage a comeback? The individual who has at the center of his thinking the affirmation "I can do all things through Christ" can recover from any defeat and creditably handle any situation.

At a convention in St. Louis, I got into conversation with a man who had been awarded an honor that year as the leading producer in his industry. This man was a complete extrovert. He said, "I want to tell you something. I'm really on the ball if I say so myself. I've read all those books about how to get ahead. And, believe me, I've gotten ahead. How about that? I'm now the biggest producer in the industry. And I'm on my way to realizing my big ambition."

"What is your big ambition?" I asked.

"To make ten million. Yes, sir, that is what my life is set up to accomplish. Ten million bucks."

"Fred," I ventured to remark, "it's all right to make money, even lots of it, but don't set that up as the big ambition of your life."

"Now don't give me any of that religious stuff," he retorted. "I'm going places. I'm for the money."

It didn't seem to me that he was making the most of Amos Parrish's idea.

But there was something engaging about this man, even though his ideas and values were mixed up. After that day, we became good friends and I would hear from him from time to time. And in grandiose manner he would write me, "I've done this or that. I've sold this. I've accomplished that." Then I noticed that the effervescence was missing in his letters. Finally he wrote me, "I don't know what's wrong with me. I've messed everything up. I've made one mistake after another. I've lost a lot of money. I'm a long way from that ten million." And in an excess of self-pity and self-blame he went on, "I'm no-account. I don't amount to anything. I'm stupid. I'm a fool."

I decided this called for strong talk on my part, so I got him on the telephone. "Fred, when you let disappointment and setbacks get you down, you're just making it much worse for yourself. Let's start a creative comeback program. What do you say?" I suggested a series of steps for him to follow.

SEVEN STEPS TO A COMEBACK

1. Stop running yourself down. There's a lot that's right in you. You have the same capacity you had before. Empty your mind of your failures and mistake and start respecting yourself.

2. Eliminate self-pity. Start thinking of what you have left instead of dwelling on what you have lost. List your assets on a piece of paper.

3. Quit thinking of yourself. Think of helping others. Actually go out and find someone who needs the kind of help you can give and give it. For you will never have a continuing flow of abundance if your thought is only for yourself.

4. Remember Goethe: "He who has a firm will molds the world to himself." Almighty God put a tough thing into human beings called the will. Use it.

5. Have a goal and put a timetable on it.

6. Stop wasting your mental energy on gripes and postmortems, and start thinking about what you do now. Think, think, think, as my friend, W. Clement Stone, says so impressively, "Think, think, think. Amazing things will happen when you think constructively."

7. Last, but not least: Every morning and every night of your life articulate these words: "I can do all things through Christ which strengtheneth me."

Quite a while later, Fred telephoned me, "I want to tell you that something really special has happened to me," he said. "I now realize that I never really lived until I started going with those ideas you gave me. New insights have shown me how to turn defeats into victories. I've turned the corner."

Well, Fred got the message. And once he did, the contagion of enthusiasm began to take hold. Now to get ten million dollars and quickly was not his big goal. He still wanted to do well financially; but he had a bigger goal; to upgrade his life into a creative category that involved doing something for his church, his city and for people having a hard time making a go of life. And he developed an amazing outgoing enthusiasm for Jesus Christ. In fact, the Lord's program for this world became his consuming interest. "I'm on His team with all I've got, money included, but principally myself."

You can figure it as you will but Fred started moving in life and is still going with the power of enthusiasm. And it is opening for him a vision of life he never dreamed possible.

Let me conclude this chapter with another tremendous illustration of the contagious quality of enthusiasm. This is again one of those thrilling success stories that has made the American dream the wonder of the world.

GUIDANCE THROUGH ENTHUSIASTIC FAITH

One Sunday, Mrs. Peale and I were invited by our friends and church members, Mr. and Mrs. Frank L. Small, to a luncheon at one of the big hotels in New York. Their cosmetic company salesmen, about a thousand, were assembled, representatives of one of the most prosperous black controlled businesses in the country.

A large group of our church members are among the dynamic individuals who make up this great sales organization. I was given the honor of extending greetings and then had the privilege of listening to one of the greatest platform speakers I have heard since as a boy I was thrilled by the incomparable William Jennings Bryan. And indeed, this marvelous speaker, S. B. Fuller, had many of the qualities of Bryan's—eloquence, humor, down-to-earth salty wisdom, religious emphasis and inspiration of an unusually high order. Mr. Fuller's speech and the manner of his delivery, were a memorable experience. I was tremendously moved by this remarkable man, a great business leader and vital Christian.

His story is told in part in a fascinating book entitled *Success Through A Positive Mental Attitude* by W. Clement Stone and Napoleon Hill. The contagion of enthusiasm transmitted by Mr. Fuller at the luncheon in New York; how he used it to build a successful business enterprise is explained in the story of his life.

S. B. Fuller's parents were black tenant farmers in Louisiana—the family was poverty-stricken. The boy went to work at the age of five. By the time he was nine he had become a mule driver. That was about as far as anybody would have expected him to go.

But S. B. Fuller had one great blessing, an intelligent, wonderful mother. Everybody in the community maintained that poverty is an act of God; people were poor because God wanted them to be poor. But young Fuller's mother said to him, "Don't you ever believe that poverty is of God. If that is true, then why did the Lord fill this beautiful world so full to overflowing of plenty and joy? God meant us to feast upon plenty. I'll tell you why we're poor; because your father always thought he was meant to be poor. Your father is a wonderful, kind man. But he has the idea that we are God's poor." And she tried to get her son to realize what great possibilities he had in him.

Can't you just see this intelligent little boy listening with wide-open eyes and a wide-open mind and a wide-open heart? And he came to believe in the potential greatness of himself under God. He decided to get better work and started selling soap in Chicago. He sold soap for twelve years, earned good money—and saved it. Then he heard that the company which supplied him was going on the auction block and that the price for the company was one hundred and fifty thousand dollars. He had saved out of his earnings twenty-five thousand dollars. So he went and put down all he had saved as a deposit. That left him a hundred and twenty-five thousand to pay and they gave him ten days to raise it. The contract also specified that if he didn't produce this money he would forfeit the twenty-five thousand dollars he had paid down—all his savings.

He had built up his opinion of himself to the point where he had that glorious quality called courage which comes through faith. He also had made many friends. He went to see them. By the night before the final deadline, he had raised a hundred and fifteen thousand dollars. But after exhausting every resource, he was still lacking ten thousand dollars. So on his knees he prayed, "Lord, You came to me when I was a little boy and through my saintly mother You told me that I could do something in the world. And now, Lord, I'm in a difficulty. I can lose everything and this big opportunity unless You guide me now."

Do you believe in guidance? I do. And perhaps if you believed in it more intensely, you would have miracles taking place in your life.

For this is how it happened to S. B. Fuller. Within his being, he heard words of guidance and he truly believes they were directed by the Lord. "You drive down Sixty-first Street in Chicago until you see a light in a building." It was then about midnight. "And you go in there and talk to a man."

Now S. B. Fuller had such an uncomplicated, childlike faith that he went out, got in his car and started down Sixty-first Street. And after he'd gone a few blocks he saw a light in a building. He went in. He recognized a contractor whom he knew slightly and he said to him, "Would you like to make a thousand dollars?"

The contractor, who was worn out from trying to solve his own business problems, said, "I sure would."

S. B. Fuller said, "If you will loan me ten thousand dollars, I will bring you back eleven thousand dollars." And he explained the entire venture. The contractor looked at him and saw something in him, and loaned him the ten thousand dollars. The next day S. B. Fuller bought the company. He now owns that company and six other companies. Yet he might have lived all his life as a mule driver, if not for an upthrust in him, put there by God and released by God. And he became a victorious child of God.

What is your trouble, what is your problem, what is your weakness, what is your difficulty? Bring up against these obstacles the glorious fact that the Kingdom of God is within you. Submit yourself to the higher power, for the only power is of God. God can release you so that you can go on to whatever heights in life you believe you can attain. Keep yourself always humbly obedient to His guidance and will, and you can release the God-power that is within you. You really can. Get aboard with the contagion of enthusiasm and you can make your life whatever you hope for, dream of and work toward.

11

ENTHUSIASM AND OUR FUTURE

Some young people seem to have no real happiness in living today. To them, enthusiasm is puerile and outdated. In their search for new values, they experiment in drugs, drinking, sex. But such excesses don't bring about new healthy values; instead, they send the searchers deeper into the vacuum of nothingness. "Let's live it up," they cry, but it sounds like a deathwatch and there is nothing more tragic than spiritual death in the young.

Some who are aware of the deep trouble in the young are shocked and worried. Others condemn them. But all too few look for a creative solution. This is odd, considering that there is a solution both creative and high in potential. That solution is simply the application of spiritual enthusiasm that puts genuine honest-to-God excitement back into life. I use the name of God advisedly, for as previously pointed out, *entheos*, God within, is a source of enthusiasm not only in semantics but in fact.

So I feel it is important to talk abut the problem of youth, of youth in relation to the older generation, and certainly in relation to the new confusing problems that beset our country.

People began to lose faith in our country's future as they watched on

TV or read in the newspapers about the riots on the campus at Berkeley, the crudities and insulting behavior of rebellious youth and the cynical exploitation of sex in moneymaking books and films.

But those sordid disheartening days, it would seem, are on the way out. Perhaps American youth is finally disillusioned, for droves of them have started once again going for God, country and ideals.

It could just be that the playboy stuff and the pretentious cynicism are on the way out. For the new knowledgeable generation finds it hard to accept such infantile nonsense. All of which demonstrates that young Americans are not as dumb as the New Left presumes them to be. Sure, Americans are big for fads. They may be taken in for a while. But presently they grow wise and give cults and dubious characters their walking papers. So maintain your enthusiasm and faith in the young of our country.

America is due for a terrific rejuvenation. Actually, it has already started rolling. Those who have long been awed or cowed by the cynical weird ones, who were shamed out of their happy, enthusiastic idealism, are getting started on their own counter-rebellion. And it is gaining momentum fast. The trend is getting into reverse and maybe it won't be long before the oddballs will have struck out. They just didn't come up with what young Americans really wanted. Already lots of the young are making the turn and discovering that spiritual enthusiasm adds up to real vitality in living.

An important reason for the new excitement sweeping the nation is that we are getting into a real revolution; one that is bound to bring vast benefits of freedom, hope and well-being to millions who unhappily thought the best they would ever know is the disappointing world to which they have been accustomed for so long. This revolution is likely to be the biggest setback in history to the New Left, the new immorality, the sex exploiters, and to a shabby, depleted communism.

NEW DYNAMIC LEADERSHIP ON THE WAY

This world is longing for new dynamic leadership based on the ideal of the greatest revolutionary of all time. His revolutionary principles of love, integrity, honesty and brotherhood are ripe for the takeover. One reason the time is ripe may be that Communist world leadership seems tired, old and possibly all but passé. Look at its chief exponent today: Ho Chi Minh, a dried-up old man, dreaming the weary dreams of the aged.

Cannot communism come up with something better, some alert, modern leader drawn from youth, or is the movement itself so worn out and sick that it can no longer spawn vital, young leadership? And the same may be said for that creaking, old man, Mao Tse-tung, who seemingly is having a tough time trying to hold his decaying communism together. It is possible that communism has reached its peak and is on the way down. The wave of the future didn't have what it takes to wave. It just couldn't deliver and so it could be starting down the long road to oblivion that is littered with so many other highly touted ideologies.

So currently we do have a vacuum in leadership. The New Left with its new impudent morality seemingly cannot make it; which is not unnatural, since it is constructed only on protest and cynicism. Without a constructive program, it is doomed to extinction. Leadership in this great crisis in history demands healthy and vigorous action. That is why the new spiritual freedom movement may be the answer. It is vital, alive and youthful.

One of the creative spiritual leaders of our time was an Englishman, Peter Howard, a cynic, wielder of a bitter pen, a brilliant writer for the Beaverbrook press in England. Moral Re-Armament was becoming popular. This movement was based on the premise that we must develop a modern man equal to modern times: We must have not only scientific giants, but moral giants as well. It began to attract a lot of attention, so Beaverbrook told Howard to see what it was all about and expose it.

Howard went to scoff, but remained to pray. For the first time he saw that the real Jesus Christ is not at all the kind of Jesus Christ that he had thought Him to be. He saw that Jesus is the greatest brain with the best blueprint for human beings in the history of mankind.

Howard became in many ways the greatest spiritual leader of his time. A friend of Aldous Huxley, he said, "In my day the apostle of the new morality was Aldous Huxley. Later in life Huxley got honest."

In his great book *Ends and Means*, Huxley said, "I had motives for not wanting the world to have a meaning, consequently I assumed that it had none, and was able without any difficulty to find satisfactory reasons for this assumption—for myself, as no doubt, for most of my contemporaries, the philosophy of meaninglessness was essentially an instrument of liberation. The liberation we desired was simultaneously liberation from a certain political and economic system and liberation from a certain system of morality. We objected to the morality because it interfered with our sexual freedom."

What about that? To satisfy their own lust without sense of guilt these men actually led thousands of mixed-up youth down the path to emotional and moral destruction. And since it is a fact that a nation deteriorates in its thinking before it deteriorates in its institutions, this negative leadership laid the ax to the tree of Western civilization, but it is likely that we will recover from the blow.

Professor J. D. Unwin of the University of Cambridge in his book, *Sex and Culture,* a work of highest importance according to Huxley, says (in discussing the trends of society and the tides of civilization through centuries of time): "Sometimes a man has been heard to declare that he wishes both to enjoy the advantages of high culture and to abolish continence. Any human society is free to choose either to display great energy or to enjoy sexual freedom; the evidence is that no nation can do both for more than one generation."

So the great question is—shall this country deteriorate due to weakening from within; through sexual license as advocated by the New Left, New Morality? Or shall it be strengthened once again through the takeover by stronger, wiser men?

New, fresh, dynamic leadership is required. And we have that leader awaiting the signal to go if we are smart enough to follow Him. But youth has got to make the decision, for half of the population of the world is under 25 years of age. In Japan, it is under 20 years of age. In Russia, fifty percent are under 26 years of age. In Red China, there are more children under 12 years of age than the entire population of the United States, that is to say, there are over 190 million human beings in China younger than 12. Leadership must come from youth, for the world is composed of youth. That is the problem. Will they go for Jesus? Mounting evidence is that they will.

I know what you will say in bewilderment, that we have the greatest universities, the highest-paid faculties in history, and the most complete laboratories ever devised. We have the greatest store of knowledge and know-how in the history of the world. Yet how come these universities turn out weird youth who growl about no meaning in life, who snarl that civilization is a flop, uncritical sycophants of the loud-mouthed minority, most of whom are not students at all, but professional exploiters on college campuses.

Vermont Royster writing in the *Wall Street Journal* said: "One way to revive your faith in the future of the species is to spend a few days among some of the young who do not conform to the sterotype. Even at Berkeley there are thousands of students who do not think they have lost their souls if they bathe their bodies, and who are quietly preparing themselves to better the world instead of just lamenting it."

ALL YOUNG PEOPLE NEED IS SOMETHING REAL TO GO FOR

I certainly don't mean to depreciate young people as a group. I think they are generally great. I went to Boston recently to make a speech and intended to fly back, but a blizzard grounded all planes, so I came back by railroad; five hours in a coach packed to capacity. People were standing in the aisle. Some were sitting in the aisle. Most were young boys coming from schools for Easter vacations. Of course, many of them wore the badges of the New Left—New Morality—ragged coats, unpressed trousers, dirty shoes. But do you know something? Five hours spent with them was enlightening. Some of the boys had swarthy faces, others light complexions, dark eyes, blue eyes, but all had lustrous eyes and wonderful faces. All that remained was to put a dream in those eyes, a light on those faces, to get them to follow a real leader.

DON'T BE DISCOURAGED—THE PAYOFF IS IN SIGHT

Will they pass up sex-conditioned cynicism for something beyond satisfying the biological urge? Well, let's see. Take Vietnam for example. I am told that a dozen students came to Premier Ky and said, "Turn over a province to us, let us administer it." He was startled at their audacity, but found they had dreams and practical plans to go with it. Whether they realized it or not, they were talking the language of the real leader, Jesus Christ.

"All right, boys," he said, "I'll give you a province."

So Ky gave them a province. University students in the Far East are never supposed to dirty their hands. They are in a class above that. Ky saw them digging in the mud and operating bulldozers. He saw a law student helping farmers with livestock. He saw a medical student with red mud oozing into his sandals. They drained the swamps. They cleaned up inadequate sewer systems. They built 600 homes. They erected a hospital and 17 health centers. This was a depraved section of 30,000 population, a hotbed for running communist information in and out of Saigon. Inside of a year, they had closed up that leak altogether. They had cleaned up the entire surroundings; they had made it a place of health—so much so that Ky said, "I would that I could do with the whole country what you young people have done with one province."

Think what youth with a sense of meaning and purpose and who know the score can do for this world, following the most practical, has-what-it-takes leader of all time. Jesus Christ is no mystic figure in a stained-glass window. He is alive—fully alive, a tough man mentally and spiritually. And he has the answers that really answer. Will youth go for this? They will indeed. In fact, they are going for it in ever-increasing numbers, as will be pointed out later in this chapter.

And those who are going for it are not the oddballs, but the cream of the crop. Into this movement for an invigorating, revitalized world come strong, attractive, intelligent youth, best product of a land that is perpetually young and dynamic.

The dedicated, tough breed of real American men has not run out. Their enthusiasms for a renewed, reborn country will make the difference between a faded worn-out civilization and a healthy one with a promise of hope and opportunity for all.

HUNDREDS NOW LIVING NEVER HAD A THRILL

There are hundreds of thousands of young people living today who have never known a genuine thrill. Lacking it, they fall back on synthetic substitutes—narcotics and violence.

But they are entitled to know in their time what former generations knew in theirs: what it is to be part of something truly great—something that endows living with fascination and excitement. They simply cannot understand how spiritual commitment can supply this quality but when they really find it, they do go for it.

Now we come to the vital news of our time which promises real hope for the future. It is the amazing story of Christianity on the beaches—the surging power of the sing-out, up-with-people Youth Movement. This is the modern upbeat message to the youth of the world; indeed to everyone.

That the belief in spiritual enthusiasm can dent the cynicism of the so-called beat generation is demonstrated in the following story written for *Guideposts* by Van Varner. It shows that a new conviction is on the move, something thousands never heard of before. It's a new enthusiasm that will make a substantial difference in out country's way of life, and much for the better.

"Every spring vacation a modern phenomenon occurs," writes Van Varner. "College students pour out of dormitories and fraternities and by plane, train, car, or thumb they head for beach resorts in Florida and California.

"These are the places 'where the boys are' and 'where the action is' and each year tens of thousands of students are drawn together for a week of frenzied communion with nature and with each other.

"They bring with them only the barest necessities; surfboard, guitar and the inevitable six-pack. They preen themselves in the sun, shout their way through thronged thoroughfares, dance the latest fad-gyration into the night. Sleep is a minor concern—finding a *place* to sleep is often major—but nothing matters so long as one has fun, fun, FUN.

"The search for fun, however, often ends in either boredom or trouble.

"In the past few years a new trend has started. Into these same resorts move thousands of students with a different objective. Picture, for instance, an encounter like this one:

"A tow-headed sophomore from Pomona College is sitting alone on the beach. He is bored. Along comes a strapping football player from Redlands U; and the two start talking.

" 'Having much fun?' asks the Redlands man.

" 'No. Not really. Actually I'm a bit hung over.'

" 'What are you looking for?'

"The boy from Pomona laughs.

" 'Are you kidding? What is everyone looking for?'

" 'Not the same things. I'm quite sure of that.'

" 'What do you mean?'

"The boy from Redlands sifts sand through his toes, reflecting: 'Two years ago I came down here looking for some kind of blast and ended up finding something quite different and wonderful.'

" 'Like what?'

" 'Jesus Christ.'

"Ordinarily the Pomona boy would have been startled and pulled away. But there is something so natural in the way this stranger speaks that he isn't repelled. In fact, he's intrigued that there could be any compatibility between Christ and a beach blast.

"And so the Redlands football player tells how two years ago he met several young people from an organization called Campus Crusade for Christ. They were full of fun and joy, but it obviously did not come from a bottle. Their questions to him had been on target: 'Where was real happiness and fulfillment? What was the main point of life?' Soon he is shown that the answers lie in Jesus Christ.

"The students from Redlands and Pomona talk at length. Before his vacation ends, the Pomona boy has a new direction to his life.

"A skylarking convention of vacation youth on the prowl hardly seems the place for a serious approach to religion. Yet two years ago on the beaches of Balboa, a thousand college students made personal decisions for Christ. Last year 2,000 made the same choice.

"These beach conversions don't just happen out of thin air. They are all part of a carefully planned campaign involving hundreds of rigidly trained Campus Crusaders. The remarkable thing about these Crusaders is that they are all such good-looking, tanned, athletic, joyous young people that anybody would stop and listen to anything they had to say anytime. Not only are they regular Joes and Janes, but they are campus leaders, too, student council presidents and football captains.

"The actual idea for reaching out to the beaches started with Dick Day, who hopped into his MG one day in 1962 and drove down to Newport Beach. Newport is a yachting center of the West and Balboa Island—or 'Bal'—is part of it. During normal times, it has a population of 35,000, but during The Madness it crawls with some 150,000.

"Dick had no specific reason for going there that day, but it didn't take him long to find one. 'Do you know what I found out?' he said recently. 'Those kids thought they were having fun, but most of them were just bored. I knew immediately that they'd welcome the chance to hear what we had to tell them.'

"Forty Crusaders were in prayer. One of the things they were praying about was a banner, the one outside their window saying 'Jesus Is the Answer.' No sooner had it gone up than 15 guys in an apartment across the way put out a banner of their own. It read: 'BOOZE is The Answer.'

"The Crusaders accepted the joke, but they were ready to do battle for the last laugh. For days they prayed for those 15 guys. At last there was a breakthrough. A young man by the name of Steve came across the way, knocked on the door and said: 'How about it? Any of you in there want to live it up a bit?'

ENTHUSIASTIC SPIRITUAL STRATEGY GETS THEM

"Steve was welcomed in—with the eventual result that seven of the fifteen boozers switched sides to learn more about Christ. Steven today calls himself a 'Gung-Ho Christian.'

"Each year Campus Crusade's beach army has grown. Last year over 400 Crusaders enlisted for 'Bal Week.' Weeks ahead of time they organized sign-in stations, a communications system and a network of meeting places. They had the cooperation of residents who offered their homes and the blessings of the Police Department and such local clubs as Kiwanis and Rotary.

"During Bal Week the Crusaders went to the beaches, conducted seminars. They took over a night club and every evening presented a big, splashy show called 'College Life Classic' with music, campus leaders and a dazzling young magician named Andre Kole. The theme of the evening's entertainment: God and Youth.

"The beach operation is but one aspect of the Campus Crusade's total thrust. For a movement only fifteen years old, it has made spectacular strides, reaching now to campuses throughout the world. The Crusaders believe that the reason so many students protest these days is that they have nothing to proclaim. The Crusaders are tired of college classrooms where Christianity can be openly knocked but no one is permitted to promote it, where there is freedom *from* religion but not *for* it. And so they are urging students to speak out."

And they are increasingly doing just that with intelligence and enthusiasm and effectiveness.

BIG NEWS—SPIRITUAL EXCITEMENT IS HERE

From this and other phenomena, it is clear that the rising tide of spiritual conviction is beginning to show, one that promises the makings of a new day. Everything in life has its cycle and then it runs down and plays out. People get tired of it. A college senior said, "Where do they come with this childish 'beat' stuff? Like a dope I fell for it once, and it nearly threw me. But I've had enough of it. And whether they like it or not, I believe in God, and I'm now really looking into Christ's way of life. Already I've seen enough to know that He has something those fellows never heard of."

Rather plain talk, but that Jesus Christ goes for it I have no doubt at all. He is a pretty tough man Himself and takes life as it comes, dirt and all. And moreover, He knows what to do about it, and does it. The heartening news of our time is that an immense number of young people are going for Him, and with Him. So perhaps it's time to cease condemning the behavior of some young people and start understanding that it's a rebellion against an older generation which has lost its way. It's a flamboyant attempt to find the meaning that was never given them by their parents, their teachers, even the church. Some attack the problem with eccentric dress and long hair. They think an unbathed body is a badge of rebellion. But they will go for a more creative type of rebellion, raised against meaninglessness by those who have found meaning and are terribly excited abut their discovery. Their motivation is spiritual enthusiasm that has come of age.

For example, not long ago Dodge City, Kansas, was getting ready to start the day the same way it started days in Dodge City for years when a special train pulled into the Santa Fe Railroad station, with a big sign on it reading *Sing-Out '65 Express!** The train doors opened and out poured two hundred and seventy-five good-looking, terrifically alive young men and women. Only a short time before they had been idling on the streets of Harlem, on the mountainsides of Appalachia or along the lush beaches of California, but they had come together and found a "new direction."

As they surged out of the train, some were carrying loudspeakers which they set up, others came running with long cords to hook up to electric power, a band assembled and soon the whole group began to play and sing. Several thousand citizens of Dodge City converged upon the railroad station.

They listened astonished as these young people sang. And what singing it was—full of life and power, songs about American freedom, about the future of America, and America under God. And they announced joyously that a new breed of American youth was taking over from the sad sacks who'd had so much free publicity. Then the whistle tooted, the whole joyous company got back aboard, and the long, sleek train pulled out, leaving the citizens of Dodge City with their mouths open and a new light in their eyes. For they had heard something they hardly expected to hear again, songs of faith in the great old American tradition, being sung once again by the nation's youth.

On across the West rode the young people of the *Sing-Out '65 Express*. Some of them took planes to Japan, where seven thousand Japanese students, who had hated the United States, received them and were soon saying that if these are the Americans of the future then they were all for

* Clarence W. Hall, "Sing-Out, America!" *The Reader's Digest*, May 1967.

America. They have conviction. They have commitment. Will they take over? What do you think? They are making their lives mean something.

The future belongs always to the believers, who are *for* something, never to those who are only against something.

Who are these for-something new breed of young people, and how did they get that way?

SING-OUTS ARE PUSHING OUT THE FAR OUTS

Clarence W. Hall answers that question. He researched this amazing new phenomenon among America's youth and wrote the exciting story in *The Reader's Digest* under the title "Sing-Out, America!"

"On an early summer's day back in 1965," writes Mr. Hall, "the proceedings of the youth conference at Mackinac Island, Michigan, were going as planned. Sponsored by the Moral Re-Armament movement, the conference aim—'to give youth a goal and purpose for their lives'—was right on the beam.

"Then, suddenly, an interruption. A young college coed stood up. 'It seems to me that some youth leadership is needed right now. I for one am fed up to here with the image of American youth being created by beatniks, Vietniks, draft-card burners, campus rioters and protest marchers.'

"The conference came awake with a rush. From all over the auditorium came cries of 'Yeh! Yeh!'

"The young delegate went on: 'You and I know that such scruffy types don't represent the great majority of us. But does the public? Do the peoples of other countries? We need to do something spectacular to change this image.'

"The response was electric. Said John Everson, a track star from Iowa State University: 'The loud-mouthed, pacifist minority scream about what they're against. Why don't we stage a demonstration of what we're for?' "

Mr. Hall quotes Richard (Rusty) Wailes, an Olympic gold medalist and one of the conference's directors, who said: "If we're going to debunk the myth of a soft, indulgent and arrogant America and show the world we care about tomorrow, we've got to *sing-out* our convictions, loud and strong."

"That was it—a 'sing-out!' A musical show that would travel across the land, appear on college campuses and military bases or wherever else they were invited, and express in song their commitment to God and country.

"To whip the cast into shape, Henry Cass, famed British producer of 'Old Vic,' was flown over from London. Brought in were the Colwell Brothers, a trio who had lifted folk singing to a fine art, written more than 300 original songs, sung them in 48 languages and dialects around the world. Invited to create 'Sing Out America,' they passed up a fat Hollywood contract to accept, saying, 'We're not interested in orchestrating the moans and groans of a sick society. But if we can help set a generation on the move to build a better world, count us in.'

"From the thousands of young people eager to be in 'Sing Out' a first cast of 130 singers and instrumentalists was selected. It represented 68 colleges and high schools in 41 states, was made up of Whites, Negroes, and American Indians. These, together with a crew of young technicians skilled in staging, sound and light engineering, gave up scholarships, turned down attractive job offers, sold cars, emptied savings accounts to help finance the venture.

"For weeks, Cass and the Colwells drilled both cast and crew, honing their performance into a fast-paced production that the late Walt Disney called the happiest, most hard-hitting way of saying what America is all about that he had ever seen or heard.

"In fourteen months 'Sing Out America' (in some places presented under the title 'Up With People' the name of one of its hit songs) had spread its unabashed patriotism over 300 college campuses, at the four U.S. service academies and 81 military bases in the United States and Canada; had traveled, at the invitation of governments and national leaders, through Japan, Korea, Germany, Austria, Spain, Puerto Rico, Panama, Jamaica and Venezuela; had produced a one-hour TV spectacular seen by 100 million in the U.S., and another seen by 25 million in West Germany and the Eastern Zone. Also, it had grown from one to three full-time traveling casts in the U.S. with 150 exuberant youths in each; had inspired and trained more than 130 regional Sing-Outs, involving 10,000 college and high school youths; had launched an international magazine called *Pace*, with a monthly circulation of 400,000, and inspired the founding of a four-year liberal arts college, Mackinac College, to train young men and women for national leadership in politics, business and the professions.

"From the moment it first hit the road, 'Sing-Out '65' was a smash hit. In Watts, they sang before thousands of Negro teen-agers.

"An example of how deep was the change wrought at Watts was seen in one young Negro who had taken part in the riots. He testified later: 'I measured my life against what these kids represented, and was ashamed.

I went to stores I'd looted and offered to pay for the things I'd taken during the riots. Now I want to help show a new image of my community to the world.' He joined with other area students to create their own Sing-Out Los Angeles, a unit still going strong.

"Observers trying to analyze Sing-Out's almost electric appeal ascribe it to two factors: the character and content of its songs, and the enormous gusto of these young people.

"All songs in a Sing-Out repertoire have catchy tunes set to a lively beat, highly singable, with choruses that invite audience sing-alongs. Zestiest favorites with most audiences are two: 'Up With People,' an action song plugging brotherhood and praising the power of ordinary citizens, and the rousing 'Freedom Isn't Free!' with its toe-tapping, memorable chorus: 'You've got to pay a price, you've got to sacrifice for your liberty.'

"Every song makes a tuneful pitch to worthier living or higher national goals. There are songs debunking racial prejudice ('What Color Is God's Skin?'); skit songs satirizing some of modern youth's kookier aspects; a rollicking call to high moral standards ('You Can't Live Crooked and Think Straight').

"At show-time, Sing-Outers don't emerge onto the stage; they explode onto it, race to their places like a football team taking the field, are assembled in ten seconds or less. The sparkling program, like the kids themselves, moves at a fast clip. It shifts so smoothly from one to another of the 30 or more numbers that the audience is scarcely aware of any break. Lights dim, microphones are shifted, a new singing group or combo moves to center stage, spotlights click on—and the scene is changed, all in a matter of seconds. For the show's entire two hours the stage is a scene of constant movement, exemplifying one of its songs, 'Don't Stand Still' the chorus of which affirms, 'We are moving and we don't stand still; we've got a mighty fine job to fill; the world's awaiting to be remade by every gal and gay young blade! . . .' "

Incidentally, further evidence of the powerful impact these young people are having on the world was demonstrated by a vicious effort against them at Harvard. But before this group of committed young people had finished their thrilling program, even the pickets started joining them. It seems that youth, when shown the truth, goes for the spirit and purpose of the Up-With-People Sing-Out group, even though they had been coached against it by the cynical new-left-new-morality professionals. An account of the attack at Harvard proves it.

"Harvard* was the scene of the most powerful presentation of Up-With-People ever made.

"Prior to the show a crowd of pickets stood outside in the icy weather carrying signs and singing songs protesting against the show. Those who wanted to get into the theater had to fight their way through a line of booing, hissing students.

"Filled with excitement, the cast roared onto the stage as if this was the only show they would ever give. The entire production burst with dynamism, enthusiasm and determination. The applause of the majority of the audience drowned out the smears and hissing of the group of 50 hecklers. Every reference made to God, faith, sacrifice, hard work and the military was hissed by the minority. In many cases, the majority group demonstrated back thunderous applause in support of the cast on stage. The louder the protesters got, the more determined the cast became. Smiles expanded, gestures sharpened and eyes sparkled.

"Olympic gold medalist John Sayre and William Storey of Indio, California, spoke on behalf of the cast, outlining the challenge presented to college America in the modernization of man.

" 'We do respect the great universities of today, including Harvard, for what they have given to humanity,' they said. 'But if brain power alone were enough to solve the world's problems, it would have been done years ago. We do need economic and social programs but unless university America learns to live the quality of life that grips and captures the wills and hearts of men, we will have failed miserably. College America, equipped with Moral Re-Armament, would be the most revolutionary men and women on earth, able to win both the Communist and non-Communist world.'

"Following the performance the students rushed towards the members of the cast, firing questions at them concerning burning issues of the day and the how and why behind Up-With-People. Many stayed for hours testing the cast to see if they were actually living the quality of life they were demonstrating on stage. Many Harvard and Radcliffe students asked to get application forms to join the show immediately.

A number of the pickets who had protested against the show beforehand, after seeing the demonstration and meeting the cast, said, 'We want to work with you.' "

* *Tomorrow's American*, Vol. III, No. 29, March 29, 1967. A Pace Publication.

Clarence W. Hall continues, "Nowhere has Sing-Out been more vociferously received than among the U.S. armed forces. The morale boost imparted was obvious and overwhelming. Said Lt. Gen. Bruce Palmer, Jr., commanding general at Fort Bragg: 'In these days of draft-card burners and Vietniks, sit-ins and teach-ins, how refreshing to discover that the patriotic spirit still burns bright in these United States!'

"At West Point, 2,200 cadets gave the cast a 27-minute standing ovation. At the U.S. Naval Academy at Annapolis, the midshipmen gave Sing-Out a 'hats in the air' salute and a 31-minute salvo of applause. Said one: 'In my four years here I've never seen any response like it. You show the thing in America worth defending.'

"But if Sing-Out '65 set Americans cheering, it caused a sensation when it went abroad. To show Asians what young Americans live for, they proved that a large segment of youth everywhere has the same hunger for positive purpose as those in the United States.

"In Japan, Sing-Out performed before standing-room-only crowds of Japanese youth at universities, in the famous Kabuki theater, at the Tokyo Olympic Gymnasium (with Prime Minister Eisaku Sato, U.S. and Soviet ambassadors present), and at Japanese and American Army posts.

"In Korea, their platform, a flag-bedecked railway car was only a few miles from the Communist lines. 'Thank God you came,' said a U.S. Army colonel. 'You've totally erased a very bad impression of American youth we were getting over here.'

"In West Germany, acclaim was even warmer. Wrote the mass-circulation daily *Bild Zeitung*: 'A musical tornado has gone through the city of Hamburg with gold and dynamite in their voices. Their singing is like an explosion, and the idea behind it shakes you up.' In Munster, the *Westphalischer Nachrichten* reported: 'Citizens of this town, normally known as sober and reserved, rose from their places in a public demonstration and sang and danced.' In the opinion of *Die Welt*, West Germany's national daily, ' "Freedom Isn't Free" could well become the theme song of our Western World.'

"The spread of the 'Sing-Out explosion,' at home and abroad, has been little short of phenomenal. In almost every place where the traveling casts have appeared, local and regional Sing-Outs have formed. Nation-ranging casts sprang up in Japan, Korea, Germany, East Africa, Australia, Latin America. Patterned carefully after the American format, national versions travel full-time through their countries, sparking, as in the U.S., the proliferation of innumerable local Sing-Outs. Following the visit of the U.S. group to Caracas, for example, casts totaling 400 sprang up in Venezuela; in Puerto Rico, 'Sing-Out San Juan' recruited more than 1,000.

"Notably zooming is Japan's own Sing-Out called 'Let's Go '67.' Having recruited more than 500 members, 'Let's Go '67' early this year sent a traveling cast to the Philippines and Indonesia, inspired the formation of similar groups in Taipei and Seoul, announced plans to take the program 'to every corner of Southeast Asia.'

"Another observer got close to Sing-Out's secret when he declared: 'This is vastly more than a show. It dramatizes a philosophy and a way of life once familiar to this nation's pioneers, but which has somehow been lost in our affluent society. Call it a revolt against the cynicism and moral relativism which have diluted the country's traditions, and in favor of bold new standards and purposes for us all.'

"Sing-Outers speak with disarming frankness about their acceptance of these new standards and purposes. A good example is Esther Diaz Lanz, an attractive young refugee from Castro's Cuba who, when Sing-Out came to Florida, had just graduated from a Miami high school. Impelled to join the group as a singer, she first went to her school principal to say: 'I don't deserve my diploma. I cheated on the final exam'—and insisted upon being given a new test, which she passed with better grades than before. Another is William Storey, a handsome young man who before joining Sing-Out was the leader of one of the toughest youth gangs on Chicago's West Side. Says Storey: 'The kids in Sing-Out seemed to have an answer to the hate and violence in the world. I decided to do something to help spread that answer. Now I find it takes more guts to stand up for what is right than it did to take part in the gang fights.'

"One father declared, 'I can't recognize my son since he joined this Sing-Out thing. Formerly he was wild and shiftless, with no purpose or goal. Now he's got more of both than I can comprehend!'

"Sing-Outers themselves find their aims not at all incomprehensible. As one of them wrote recently in their publication *Pace*: 'Our generation is looking for ideas we can believe in, fight for, demonstrate. We want peace, but not at the price of freedom. We'd rather be challenged by hard work and sacrifice than mothered by society. Ours is a generation on the move, ready to be disciplined and to dare. It wants to cure poverty, immorality and division—and do it with a revolution of character far more effective than hate-propelled violence.'

"Witness, for example, what Indonesia's youth did to save their country recently—and what China's Red Guards are doing to wreck theirs.

Don't knock what these kids are doing with their Sing-Out. And above all, don't underestimate it!" So concludes Clarence W. Hall's appraisal of American youth who know the score, the very different new generation.

We are still a young country. Our original basic strength came from the principles we believed in, not only religious and political freedom, but a sense of compassion toward each other which was foreign to the old countries. We wanted to treat our neighbor as we would have him treat us. Having belief and faith and the marvelous enthusiasm that is the birthright of the young, we established a nation unique in the history of our civilization. It is heart-warming to find a resurgence of those basic strengths in a vast group of our young people. Their extraordinary action reminds us that enthusiasm is a *young* trait. It belongs to those young in heart and spirit and need not be hampered by chronological age.

I've known men of eighty who were young—among them my dear late friend, Dr. Smiley Blanton—and I have known boys of eighteen who were old. If youth is a state of mind, then enthusiasm is a part of it. And if you have enthusiasm, you'll have no need of hormones, face lifts, hair dyes and other artificial rejuvenators. Enthusiasm brings sparkle to the eyes, color to the cheeks and a joyous life to the heart.

So make enthusiasm your contribution not only to your own well-being but to this exciting pro-American counter-revolution that is being born in our country. If there is one trait the young will accept from their elders, it is enthusiasm. They long for dynamic action. They want a positive platform. We can make it possible by our mature wisdom and positive help, to aid the new crusaders. Fill your heart with faith, your spirit with enthusiasm and join the youth, the middle-aged and the senior citizens in a rich rewarding spiritual crusade. God will be with you.

12

ENTHUSIASM MAKES THE DIFFERENCE

S. S. Kresge, founder of the immense empire of nearly a thousand retail stores bearing his name, had the cool quiet enthusiasm that smashes barriers and achieves spectacular results. This remarkable man lived for ninety-nine and one-half years and his philanthropic gifts have benefited thousands.

The Kresge story is in the tradition of the American saga; up from poverty to achievement, fostered by the proud Pennsylvania Dutch virtues of hard work, thrift, scrupulous honesty, faith and enthusiasm. S. S. Kresge was a devout Christian, a down-to-earth person and a keen thinker. He had a dry sense of humor. When Harvard bestowed an honorary degree upon him and he was to respond with a speech, he stood up and said, "I never made a dime talking." And sat down. It was probably the shortest speech ever delivered at the university, maybe one of the most sensible. He made some $200,000,000 in his lifetime, but gave most of it away. He never lost sight of God or the dignity of people. To use his own words, "I tried to leave the world a better place than I found it."

I once asked him the secret of his amazing life. "I have a simple philosophy," he said, "go early to bed; get up early; don't eat too much; work hard; help people; don't let anything get your goat; tend to your own business; be enthusiastic; and always keep God in mind." With this simple philosophy, he went through life building, always building, with enthusiasm and faith.

"When one begins at the bottom and learns to scrape, everything becomes easy," Mr. Kresge declared. Certainly it does if you have the character and courage, the faith and enthusiasm to keep scraping. Such ability is greatly aided and abetted by built-in enthusiasm, the kind that overcomes barriers. What barriers? Why, of course, everything that gets in the way of a better life, of real success, of your God-given motivation to do the best possible with the capacities you possess.

A woman came up to me recently after I had made a speech. She turned out to be a high-school classmate of mine whom I had not seen since graduation. "Norman," she said, "I've been studying you as I listened to you. You've really done quite a lot with the little you had to start with." At first I felt let down. Then I realized that her remark was really a compliment. If you have only a little to start with but you do the best you can with that little, it is astonishing how much it may become.

HAVE A MADE-UP MIND AND MOVE ON UP

Enthusiasm develops and maintains the quality of determination which is vitally important in overcoming barriers to a better life. I have been tremendously moved by the story of Mahalia Jackson, one of the most outstanding singers of gospel songs this country has ever known. Barriers she had aplenty, but she also had "a made-up mind," enthusiasm, and faith in God. So she had what was required to "move on up."

Mahalia Jackson, up from poverty, has sung to vast and enthusiastic crowds in Berlin's Sportspalast, in London's Albert Hall and in many other great concert halls of the world. She was reared in New Orleans where her father worked on the river docks during the week and was a preacher on Sunday. Her people were very poor. She had little schooling, not even a formal musical education. But she heard the showboat music along the lower Mississippi. She listened fascinated to the great jazz bands. She felt something expanding in her and came to realize that she had been given a truly great voice. From the early thrill of singing in the choir in her father's little church, where she would lift her magnificent voice in moving gospel songs like *How Wonderful That Jesus Lifted Me,* she went on step by step to great success. One of her recordings, *Move On Up a Little Higher*, sold eight million copies.

"What do you want to be?" she asks. "Where do you want to go? God will lift you up." But there is a condition: "You've got to have a made-up mind."

She says that if God could lift her out of the washtubs on the levee in Louisiana, if He could take her knees off the floors she used to scrub, if He could lift her above the sorrow which her race suffers, then, says Mahalia Jackson, "He can lift you up too." And this is a fact. There isn't anybody whom God cannot lift far above any goal he ever hoped for or even imagined. But you must have a "made-up mind." You've got to want it and you've got to let Jesus Christ lift you up. Then you achieve victory over weakness, over troubles, over yourself. So be wise; be one of those who takes hold of life which is life indeed. Mahalia Jackson's story is another demonstration of an inspiring fact. You can have what you want from life provided you've got the enthusiasm that pushes barriers aside. You can indeed "move on up" with faith.

TIRED SICK COUPLE FIND REJUVENATING ENTHUSIASM

I saw a run-down, middle-aged couple develop enthusiasm for life, an enthusiasm of such power and vitality that they literally smashed the barriers of sickness and dullness that had been blocking their way to a happy and creative life.

This exciting human experience occurred one memorable May morning at our farm in Dutchess County, New York. In a meadow on our property is an old, weather-beaten, uninhabited house, which we use for storage. Hard by this house is an enormous stand of lilac bushes. The grass was deep and in the mist of the morning there was mystery and beauty around that old weather-beaten house. The lilacs themselves were heavy with great globules of dew. When you put your face into them the water was cool and fresh, the fragrance was lovely, and it felt very clean. Two Black Angus steers came up and looked at me through the fence. And I looked at them. There seemed an interesting, friendly expression on their big placid faces. I liked them, so I said, "Hi, boys. How are you?" But all they did was to blow long streamers of steam out of their nostrils.

Then the morning mist began to roll away. Long shafts of sunlight fell upon the lavender of the lilacs. The morning became dazzling bright.

There came to mind from across the years something my father used to say of a happy and enthusiastic person. "He's as bright as a May morning." I stood in the deep grass thinking how many May mornings I'd lived, and I was happy because it still excited me the same as when I was a boy. I offered a prayer there by the lilac bushes that my up-beat spirit would never become eroded, that always, every day, life would be full of wonder, mystery and glory, full of tremendous excitement and enthusiasm

The Bible offers intriguing advice, "Take hold of the life which is life indeed." We are told that Jesus came that we might have life "more abundantly." For it isn't the natural world, charming as it is, that gives the greatest excitement or joy or makes life most deeply meaningful and satisfying; rather it is the experience of the enhanced spirit, of revitalized sensitivity and boundless enthusiasm that gives it meaning.

So many people become jaded, old and tired before their time. They grow cynical and take on a condition of mind they call sophistication. But actually it isn't sophistication at all, for the real meaning of the term is "to be smart or wise in the ways of the world." And it is hardly smart to grow dull and to lose excitement. But it is a part of wisdom to come alive so that emptiness and deadness fall away.

Well, on this particular May morning, a couple drove to my farm to see me. I knew them as typical, bored sophisticates from the city. They were nice people, but they'd had it. Life had run down. The man said, "Helen isn't well and I'm terribly worried about her. And," he added, "I'm not well either."

"You look pretty husky to me," I remarked.

"Maybe so, but I'm not well in my thoughts, and I've lost the creative ability I had." This man is a music writer and an editor of distinction. "Something has left me," he said. "I've lost enthusiasm and the sense of being thrilled that I have always had. I want to know how to get it back again. Life is no good without it."

"Now look, Bill, you've come to the wrong person," I said, "I am a minister of the Gospel and you are one of our super-modern sophisticates. How come you're asking me how to get the thrill of life back again? You've made a mistake in coming to me about this problem, because I will give you a simple answer, one that is on the spiritual side. I'm not hopeful because you probably aren't simple enough to accept a simple answer. You are too complex, or shall we say too advanced for that—or at least you make out that you are. But if you will come down off that complicated, sophisticated perch of yours and show some humility, I can give you a real answer that will really answer."

"Boy," he said, "you're being a little rough on me, aren't you?"

"Maybe that will do you good," I replied, grinning. But we understood each other.

"You name it, I'll take it," he said. And I got the distinct feeling he was really reaching for something this time.

"Okay, come inside." I took Bill and Helen into the house and went into the library. "Now," I said. "See that rug? It is a good Chinese rug that my wife is still paying for. It's thick and will cushion your knees, which doubtless haven't been on the floor in prayer in years. So get yourself down by this chair on your knees."

They both knelt, and we prayed. I found that I had misjudged these people. He really poured his heart out, and she did, too. They didn't mince words, but came right out and asked the Lord Jesus Christ to re-create them. And, believe it or not, right there in my library on that May morning, I witnessed that tremendous phenomenon where a man is re-created. And a woman, too. Presently they walked out with a spring in their step and a new light in their eyes.

A year later, Bill wrote me a letter, and evidently the enthusiasm still held. It was poetically expressed, for Bill tends to be poetic, and it says: "The skies were never more blue; the grass was never more green; the fragrance of the flowers has never equalled that of this year; the song of birds has been positively ecstatic. We never knew that life could be so wonderful. Helen is better, and I've been released." They kept the revitalized enthusiasm they found on that picture postcard May morning; it has never dimmed. They discovered the enthusiasm that smashes all barriers to a worthwhile and joyful life.

ENTHUSIASM KNOCKS OUT BARRIERS TO BETTER LIFE

Barriers to better life are many and varied. There is, of course, fear. That is a big barrier, indeed. And along with fear goes caution. Proper caution is wise and prudent, but don't be too cautious. The fearful, the timorous, the extra-cautious never surmount the barriers beyond which lie the really wonderful values of this world. Too much caution is actually bad for you.

At our farm one day, an oil truck came to make a delivery. But presently I noticed that the driver did not get out of the cab. I walked over and asked, "What's the matter?"

Nervously the man answered, "Look at that dog." Now, we have a big dog of no recognizable breed, just a plain dog, who has an enormous bark and mean look to go with it. But actually he is a fake. Mean look and bark are all he's got. "Why, that dog wouldn't hurt a fly," I said.

"I'm not interested in flies," the man retorted. "I'm interested only in not being bitten."

"Look," I said, "if you will just get out of that cab and walk right at this dog, he will fade."

But he was taking no chances. "Look at his eyes," he said. "No thanks." And he sat right where he was.

I turned to the dog. "Go away, Petey!" I commanded. "Go away!" But to my surprise and embarrassment he came at me instead with a mouthful of barks. I almost jumped aboard the truck myself!

Petey knew he had this delivery man buffaloed and he was going to see if he could scare me too. "As long as you're afraid of this dog," I told the man, "he knows it and is determined to keep you sitting in that cab."

Finally my assurances prevailed. The cautious fellow climbed out. Together we walked straight toward the dog. When Petey saw he was not scaring anybody he retreated, and fast. After that he just hung around the edges growling while the man went about his business.

Well, it's no news that an animal, sensing your fear, will often do its best to intimidate you all the more. The longer you permit yourself to be cowed by anything, the more scared of it you become.

A person who has been in an automobile accident is likely to feel shaky the next time he rides in a car. But the sooner he does so, the better. If he puts it off, he may develop a fear of cars that can develop into a phobia against all modes of travel. Fear sometimes increases with the passage of time and also undergoes "generalization"—that is, it spreads from the original threat to other areas.

So it is plain that too much caution is bad for you. By avoiding things you fear, you may let yourself in for unhappy consequences. It is usually wiser to stand up to a frightening experience, meet it head-on, risking bruises or hard knocks. You are likely to find that it is not as tough as you had anticipated. Or maybe you will find it plenty tough, but also discover that you have what it takes to handle it—and thereby become a stronger person.

John Ruskin in his early twenties became painfully aware of being extremely timid. During a stay at Chamonix in the French Alps this tendency caused him acute distress. Having watched other young men climbing the mountains, he tried a few of the lesser peaks himself; but fear made him physically ill and he almost gave up mountain climbing.

In the stress of this difficulty he wrote: "The question of the moral effect of danger is a very curious one; but if you come to a dangerous place and turn back from it, though it may have been perfectly right and wise to do so, still your character has suffered some slight deterioration; you are to that extent weaker, more lifeless . . . whereas if you go through the danger, though it may have been apparently wrong and foolish to encounter it, you come out of the encounter a stronger and better man, fitter for every sort of work and trial."

The essence of the matter is summed up in advice which Henry J. Taylor, well-known news correspondent, received years ago from his father: "Don't worry too much about yourself and about getting hurt. People who go through life being cautious miss a great deal. Take your chances wherever you have to. It's better luck, you'll see more, and you'll probably live as long anyway."

Then another barrier that needs smashing is resentment. Have you ever realized that the term resentment is derived from a word which means to re-hurt? This may explain the mental soreness and pain felt when you resent, for you are actually re-hurting yourself, keeping the old wound open. The expression "sorehead" rather graphically pictures the pain in the mind caused by resentment, for mental soreness is continually activated. Resentment is indeed a big barrier to real life, but enthusiasm can get you over that hurdle too.

Still another barrier is self-isolation that avoids concern about other people. It could be that much of today's unhappiness and lack of enthusiasm may be attributed to an acute self-interest that refuses to become involved in any human need. It was estimated that at least thirty-nine people heard the screams of a woman being stabbed to death in New York City, and incredibly, these people shrugged it off as no business of theirs.

"Why should I get mixed up in this?" they tried to reason. "It isn't my funeral." But it was their funeral. The poor woman lost her physical life. They lost life in their souls. How can they ever forget those agonizing cries to which in their dull selfishness they failed to respond? Their non-involvement will forever haunt them. This desire not to be involved in the sorrow, pain and tragedy of other people is a huge barrier to top-quality life. But real enthusiasm for human beings smashes such indifference and produces a quality of happiness that can hardly be found in any other way. As Arthur Gordon puts it, "Enthusiasm is the state of caring—really caring."

DRAMA IN THE SUBWAY

Take, for example, the way Sal Lazzarotti, Art Director of *Guideposts* magazine, rose to the challenge of a potential tragedy in which he allowed himself to become involved one morning in a New York City subway on his way to work. A few feet from where he was sitting stood a nice, clean-cut looking boy of about eighteen holding onto one of the center posts in the swaying train. And seated across from Sal was a well-dressed young woman of perhaps twenty-five years of age, reading a paperback. As the train stopped at a station, this girl arose and walked past the boy toward the door. Then suddenly she screamed, "You fresh punk! Don't look so innocent! I know you touched me!" And she flew at him, scratching at him like a tigress. The boy, astonished, threw up his hands to protect himself and in so doing apparently touched her face, for suddenly there was a speck of blood on her lip. Then, breaking free, he ran from the car down the platform—she after him, high heels clicking, crying, "Police! Police!" The train doors closed. The startled passengers shrugged their shoulders and went back to their newspapers. To them, it was just one of those things.

Now from where Sal sat he had seen quite clearly that there had been no contact between the boy and the girl before she screamed. The boy was completely innocent. Sal wondered what would happen to the boy and whether some witness—himself—ought to get in touch with the police. He tried to persuade himself that it was none of his business, that the boy had probably got away anyway, and that he had better stay out of it. He was too busy to get involved in somebody's trouble. But he couldn't get the boy out of his mind.

What he did then completely ruined his day's work. To begin with, it took four telephone calls to locate the police precinct to which the boy would have been taken had he been caught. The desk sergeant told him yes, the boy had been brought in and had been sent from there to Juvenile Court. Sal called Juvenile Court and got the boy's name—Steve Larsen—and his parents' name and address; got Steve's mother on the phone; learned that the family had no money for legal help; took upon himself the job of finding the boy a lawyer; and along with the lawyer and mother, Sal went to the courtroom as a witness.

When questioned by the judge, the girl gave an impressive story of how she had been attacked. Sal listened in amazement, knowing that nothing she was saying had occurred. At one point the judge interrupted to tell the girl, "There is a witness to the incident present, so be sure of what you say." The girl looked around the room, saw Sal, recognized him, stared at him incredulously and went completely to pieces. She fumbled her words, contradicted herself, made a spectacle of herself. The judge called the girl's lawyer and Steve's into a huddle, decided the girl was in need of psychiatric help, and dismissed the case.

If Sal Lazzarotti had decided that the incident was none of his business and had avoided getting involved, the boy would undoubtedly have been convicted; he would have gone to jail, a blot on his record, he might consequently have become a criminal. He was saved from catastrophe by the presence in that subway car of a man who felt a responsibility toward a human being he didn't even know.

But Sal had a burning enthusiasm for people—he really cared, and his enthusiasm smashed the barrier of non-involvement which stands across the path to happy life.

HARD HITTING SURPRISE FOR GANG OF HOODLUMS

Still another enthusiastic barrier smasher of the paralyzing attitude of non-involvement was Naval Reserve Airman James R. George, age 23, from Georgia, on leave in Philadelphia and intent on seeing the historical sights of that city. In the subway station at the corner of Race and Vine, he was confronted with a sight he hadn't expected to see in Philadelphia, cradle of human liberty. Fifteen or twenty young hoodlums had cornered a young girl and were about to rape her. Six men were just watching, making no move to intervene. George called to them, "Come on! You're not going to let them get away with this, are you?"

But they shrugged their shoulders. "None of our business," was their attitude. "Don't want to get mixed up in it. Not our fight."

But this boy was made of sturdier stuff. It was his fight. He threw off his jacket and sailed all by himself into that vicious gang of punks. He threw them right and left, sent them sprawling all over the platform. They came back at him, beating him up, but he finally drove them off and saved the girl. The six men, meanwhile, just stood idly by.

The Mayor of Philadelphia held a public ceremony in George's honor, cited him for his courage and sense of responsibility and made him an honorary citizen of the city. When it came time for George to respond with a few words before the microphone, the first thing he said was, "I have enjoyed my stay in Philadelphia . . ." Of course, he had, not withstanding his bruised face and other marks of violence. Why had he enjoyed himself? Because his conscience was clear. Because when decency demanded, he had given himself for one of God's defenseless children. He had what it took to get involved. He had enthusiasm for people, especially for the helpless and defenseless.

Still another barrier to happiness that spiritual enthusiasm overcomes in a victorious way is the fear of illness, the fear of losing a loved one. This is a matter of deep and anguished concern, one of the profoundest anxieties of life, but the person who has found spiritual answers develops a positive, powerful and enthusiastic faith that carries him over this, one of the greatest of all human problems.

BOY SAVED BY LETTING GO AND LETTING GOD

One noonday while speaking at a luncheon meeting in a Chicago hotel, I noticed at the back of the hall a number of waitresses standing and listening. Afterward, hurrying through the lobby to catch a plane, I heard my name called. There was a young woman perhaps thirty years of age, in a waitress's uniform, her face all alight. She rushed up to me and, taking both of my hands in hers, surprised me by saying, "Doctor Peale, I just love you!"

"Well, don't announce it so loudly!"

"Oh," she repeated. "I just love you."

Touched by her candor and sense of joy, I said, "Do you know something? I love you too. But please enlighten me. Why do we love each other?"

"I'll tell you," she answered. "I have a little boy. His father deserted us, but I thanked God all the more that He'd given me this wonderful child. Then when my boy was five years old he became sick. The doctor told me it was very serious. And one day he said, 'Mary, you've got to be strong. I don't know whether we can save your boy or not.' He was preparing me for the worst. I was so terribly distraught, I felt my whole world would go to pieces if I lost my boy. I loved him so much. He was my entire life.

"Then a neighbor gave me one of your sermons in which you said 'If you have a loved one who is ill or about whom you are worried, don't hold this loved one too closely. Give the loved one to God. God gave him to you. He isn't yours, really; he is God's. So give him to God, for God is good, He is loving, He is a great kind Father who holds each child in His love. Let go and let God care for him. No harm, only good can come to him when he is in God's hands.'

"Well," she continued, "I'd never heard anything like that before. It seemed awfully hard to do. But something inside my heart told me that it was right. So I prayed like you said and I put my boy in God's hands." And she put her hands out as though handing a child up into the great hands of God.

"Yes, and what happened?" I asked gently.

Smiling through tears of joy, she said, "Isn't God good? He let me keep my boy. And now God and I are raising him together."

Several other witnesses, Mary's friends, had come and stood listening. There were tears in everyone's eyes, including mine. And I said, "Mary, I want to tell you something. You're really a great mother, that is what you are. And you're one of the strongest and wisest human beings I ever met."

The other waitresses agreed, "She's everything you say!" So we separated. And I went my way refreshed by yet another wonderful human drama. That young woman really had the power of enthusiastic faith, and with it she had overcome one of the toughest of all human problems.

A familiar barrier to going ahead is the tendency to exaggerate obstacles. How many years I have listened to people trying to explain why they can't! If they would utilize half of the time consumed in telling why "they can't," to doing what they could, they would find that they can after all!

My old fifth-grade teacher George Reeves, a huge man physically, and even bigger in faith, left a lasting impression on his students. He had the curious habit of suddenly writing the word CAN'T in big letters on the blackboard. Then, eraser poised, he would ask, "What can we do about that word?" And the well-trained class would chant, "Knock the T off the CAN'T!"—which he would do with a wide sweeping stroke of the eraser. "See that you go through life knocking the Ts off the CAN'Ts," he would admonish, adding, "You can if you think you can!"

NEVER BUILD A CASE AGAINST YOURSELF

I first heard that statement of power-packed truth in a conversation with my old friend, Robert Rowbottom, up in Berkeley, Rhode Island, where

I had my first church; and it hit me, "like a ton of bricks." For you see, that was exactly what I had been doing—building a case against myself. But with Rob's positive concept working in my mind, I began to realize I was going at life with an entirely wrong attitude, one that could only end in a negative result. Therefore, I decided to do a mental about-face. I asked God to change me and give me a more positive attitude, and I meant it with all the strength I could summon.

Fortunately, God heard my desperate prayer, for believe me, it is miserable to live with that painful state of mind called an inferiority complex. Being freed from it was one of the greatest things ever to happen to me. So I began to experiment with this powerful technique. With insight came new concepts that made a terrific difference in my life—the power of positive thinking and of enthusiasm. But these two tremendous mental and spiritual qualities must be learned and mastered, a discipline that does not come easily. But once they do take over fully, then you can smash barriers which otherwise would surely defeat you and could result in the ruin of your life plan.

Of course, it might not be that drastic a result for you. But I knew that it would be for me. In my case, it was a matter of survive or perish, so deeply rooted were my insecurity and inferiority feelings. Therefore, I grasped for the mastery of positive thinking and enthusiasm, and relying upon the help and guidance of our Lord Jesus Christ, went to work to build my life on that foundation.

Positive thinking is how you think about a problem. Enthusiasm is how you feel about a problem. And the two together determine what you do about a problem.

TURN TYPHOONS INTO TAIL WINDS

I was sitting at one time in the copilot's seat of a DC-6 airplane in the Far East, in the area where typhoons, a big blow with a sinister name, roam violently over land and sea. I asked the pilot about the problem of flying in typhoon territory. "Well," he drawled, "they're not exactly anything to fool with. They may cover an area of three to five hundred miles and consist of circular high winds rotating counterclockwise."

"Well, what do you do when you encounter a typhoon?" I asked.

"Oh," he replied, "one thing is sure. I don't try to buck it. I just get on its edge and go the way it's going. In that way I turn typhoons into tail winds."

Positive thinking and enthusiasm do just that. They turn problems and difficulties into tail winds, so that you can ride them to successful outcomes.

There is, of course, always a danger, in advocating the development and use of enthusiasm, that it may result in overtension. Even enthusiasts need to practice the easy-does-it principle, lest they fall victim to the tendency to overpress or become unduly excited. Enthusiasm is not necessarily a flashy or heated phenomenon, but rather a strong, controlled motivation, and may be present in the quiet and restrained person, as well as in the vigorous extroverted individual. The world belongs to the enthusiast who can keep cool.

Of the people whom I have observed who fit this description, the late Calvin Coolidge comes to mind. He was such a quiet man that he was referred to as "Silent Cal." But he had a personality in which enthusiasm operated under cool control. He was one of the few politicians to use words sparingly. His speeches were short and succinct. He said what he wanted to say and no more. He won the liking of a great many people simply by not talking too much.

A college student and I were received at the noonday reception the President had in his office at the White House for members of Congress who wanted to introduce their constituents to the Chief Executive. Brashly, I gave him the Phi Gamma Delta fraternity grip. He returned the grip and said, "I belong to the Amherst chapter."

"I know that, Mr. President," I replied. That was the end of the conversation.

Before his career as a public servant, Coolidge was a lawyer in Northampton, Massachusetts. He had a downtown office and his home was up the street. Coolidge never drove to his office; that would have been expensive. He believed in being economical. He used to walk from home to office every morning at precisely the same time. This route took him past a house where lived a friend by the name of Hiram. Every morning when Coolidge came along, Hiram would be leaning over the fence. And for twenty years the daily conversation ran something like this.

"Hi, Cal," said Hiram.

"Hi, Hiram," said Cal.

"Nice morning," Hiram added.

"Nice morning," agreed Cal.

That was the way it went for twenty years. Then Coolidge was elected Lieutenant Governor, then Governor, then Vice-President of the United States. And then he became President. He was gone from Northampton for quite a few years. His Presidency ended, Coolidge returned to Northampton and to law practice. He dusted off the furniture, got his office ready, and one morning not long afterwards, he walked once again from his house to his law office. And sure enough, there leaning on the fence was his old friend, Hiram.

"Hi, Cal," said Hiram.

"Hi, Hiram," said Cal.

Hiram said, "Nice morning."

Cal said, "Nice morning."

Just like it had always been. But then the heavens fell. Hiram, this taciturn New Englander, added, "Ain't seen you around lately, Cal."

"Nope, been away a spell," Cal replied. All the business of being Governor and President was over. Life was what it was now. Calvin Coolidge took it as it came. He had enthusiasms of the quiet kind and they ran deep. He was enthusiastic about the United States, and to him it stood for something. But as to himself, he did not take Cal Coolidge too seriously. He was a quiet, relaxed enthusiast. The drive was there, but it was controlled.

The purpose in writing this book is to point out the incalculable value of enthusiasm, especially to the individual who has the urge to accomplish something worth accomplishing in life. I agree with the publisher, B. C. Forbes, who said, "Enthusiasm is the all-essential human jet propeller. It is the driving force which elevates men to miracle workers. It begets boldness, courage; kindles confidence; overcomes doubts. It creates endless energy, the source of all accomplishment."

I have sought to show by various examples how enthusiasm has made an immense difference in the lives of many people. By now you are aware that in my opinion the chief importance is spiritual enthusiasm, for it makes you a new person with new spirit, new energy and new know-how. Now you have guidance. As a result, you develop the enthusiasm that smashes barriers, those you have erected in your mind, as well as barriers on the outside.

LISTLESS CARL REACTIVATED BY ENTHUSIASM

I was scheduled to speak to a sales convention of a certain industry, and before the meeting, a businessman approached me and said, "Dr. Peale, I have one salesman who wouldn't have the initiative to come to this convention on his own, so I invested two hundred dollars to bring him.

Having read your *Power of Positive Thinking*, I expect you to get him activated so I get my money back through his increased sales. I have gotten him a front seat. I recall reading in one of your books how you built a fire under another sleepy guy in similar circumstances."

"The fire was built in him, not under him," I replied. "I'll do what I can for your man."

He pointed the man out to me. As I was talking, I looked at this salesman now and then. He had a kind of blank, aimless expression on his face; showed no sign of reacting to anything.

However, after the meeting, he came up to me. "My name is Carl," he said. "I'm the dull salesman Mr. . . . invested money in to bring here to this convention and to get me motivated."

"You know about it then?"

"Sure, how could it be otherwise? He has been telling everyone about me." He said this without bitterness; in fact, he did not seem to care.

I asked him to my room that we might talk. "What's the matter with you, Carl?" I asked.

"I don't know. I just don't know."

I tried a few exploratory questions to get acquainted.

"Did you go to college? Did you do all right there?"

"Well, I got by."

"And how have you been doing in business?"

"Oh," he answered, "I get by."

"Boy, you're not getting by very far, if you ask me," I said. "Your boss is really upset about you. He says you're not producing, yet he thinks you've got what it takes to be a real salesman if only you get motivated."

"But I haven't any energy. I'm clean out of enthusiasm. In this competitive work, you've got to be alert, you've got to be on the ball, you've got to get out and after them. Drive is what you must have, and lots of it."

"Where did you hear all that sort of thing?" I asked.

"In the sales meetings. And," he added, "it wears me out to hear them talk that way. It all seems stupid, but I just have no interest in anything."

"Do you go to church?" I asked, trying a new tack.

"Oh, once in a while. But it leaves me cold."

"Do you belong to any clubs or associations?"

"No, nothing. What the heck—I have no interest in that stuff."

He seemed completely apathetic and listless. Yet he was gifted with a rather nice personality, or it could be if he had some force.

"Carl, I want to ask you something. Do you believe in God?"

He said of course he did.

"What are we to learn from Jesus?" I asked.

"Well, He teaches us to be good," Carl replied uncertainly.

"That's true," I agreed, "but did it ever occur to you that Jesus Christ is also energy, that He is vitality, that He is life, and that if you get Him in your mind you will come alive? Fill your mind with thoughts of God and Christ and you will have boundless enthusiasm and energy."

The man looked at me with interest, the first I had seen in him. "You really believe that, don't you?" he asked. "Well, that makes sense. I'll try it if you will help me."

"Let's pray about you," I suggested. "What do you say?"

He said, "I'd like that. Maybe that's what I need." So I offered a prayer, then asked, "Now, Carl, how about you saying a few words?"

I cannot remember Carl's short prayer word for word. I wish I could for it was one of the best I ever heard. It was most affecting. It went something like this: "Lord, I'm a dull, sleepy, no-account guy. But I really don't want to be that way. Honestly, I don't. I'm sick of being the way I am. I just don't amount to anything, and I'm asking, please revitalize me, Lord. Amen." Then he looked at me, and after a long silence said, "You know something? I think the Lord is going to answer that prayer."

"I think so, too," I replied, for I felt sure of it.

Before we parted, I told Carl something I had heard when I was a very young man which gripped me and had meant much to me all across these years. I heard a man say, "You can become strongest in your weakest place." He was referring to weakness of character or personality. I recalled how this man used as an illustration the process of welding, in which two pieces of metal are fused under intense heat. He asserted that if an effort should be made later to break the joined metal, it would probably not break at the welded place since, due to molecular fusion under heat, that had become the strongest part.

"That is for me," said Carl, "for apathy is sure my weakest place. I promise you I will follow your advice and try to get spiritually welded." But I did not leave it to him altogether. I contacted a minister in his city whom I knew to be a vital, enthusiastic man of faith. He took Carl on and got him related to a group of business men, all of whom had experienced changes in their personal life. In the positive atmosphere of that fellowship, Carl's apathy began to give way. The intense heat of real faith and prayer and joyous release fused his conflicted personality until he did become strongest at his weakest place. In fact, he became positively dynamic and alive in the fullest sense.

He became active in his church; he joined one of the service clubs in town and really got into its work. Within three years, he was president of the local chamber of commerce. It seems eventually, according to many, that he did more for his town to build it up than any man in a decade. People used to come and tell me, "Carl is a ball of fire." And that was an understatement. At Carl's request I went to his town to make a speech. He met my plane.

I said, "Carl, I've been on the go steadily. I want to go to my hotel room and lie down and rest before my speech."

"Rest?" he echoed. "Why should you rest? Where's that energy and enthusiasm you're always talking about?"

I gave in sheepishly. "All right, let's forget the hotel. Where do we go next?" He really showed me around, and his enthusiasm so rubbed off on me that I forgot all about being tired.

Carl is only one of the hundreds of people across the years in whom I have seen the marvelous process of spiritual change take place, whereby the dead (the alive dead) learn to live again. Listless, de-energized, even cynical, those men have in one way or another got into proximity with the dynamic Person who said, "I am come that they might have life, and that they might have it more abundantly."

And then something happened in each case, some emanation of stepped-up vitality and energy passed into them, so that no longer were they the same men. They became completely different from what they had been. The new spirit showed in their eyes, in their step, indeed, in their entire demeanor. And it showed also in the amazing results that came to them in the form of up-graded creativity. The New Testament says, "All things are become new." These men had their lives changed. Bursting now with eagerness and aliveness, with a grip on their lives and their jobs, they know for a fact—for a wonderful fact—that enthusiasm makes the difference.